CORPORATIONS

CORPORATIONS

Third Edition

By

ROBERT W. HAMILTON

Minerva House Drysdale Regents Chair in Law
University of Texas School of Law

BLACK LETTER SERIES®

WEST PUBLISHING CO.
ST. PAUL, MINN.
1992

610 Opperman Drive
P.O. Box 64526
St. Paul, MN 55164–0526

Printed in the United States of America

Library of Congress Cataloging-in-Publication Data

Hamilton, Robert W., 1931–
Corporations / Robert W. Hamilton. — 3rd ed.
p. cm. — (Black letter series)
Includes index.
ISBN 0-314-00741-5
1. Corporation law—United States—Outlines, syllabi, etc.
I. Title. II. Series.
KF1414.3.H348 1992
346.73'066—dc20
[347.30666] 92-10938
CIP

ISBN 0-314-00741-5

Hamilton — Corps. 3rd Ed. BLS

PUBLISHER'S PREFACE

This "Black Letter" is designed to help a law student recognize and understand the basic principles and issues of law covered in a law school course. It can be used both as a study aid when preparing for classes and as a review of the subject matter when studying for an examination.

Each "Black Letter" is written by experienced law school teachers who are recognized national authorities in the subject covered.

The law is succinctly stated by the author of this "Black Letter." In addition, the exceptions to the rules are stated in the text. The rules and exceptions have purposely been condensed to facilitate quick review and easy recollection. In addition, a **Text Correlation Chart** provides a convenient means of relating material contained in the Black Letter to appropriate sections of the major casebooks on corporation law.

If the subject covered by this text is a code or code-related course, the code section or rule is set forth and discussed wherever applicable.

FORMAT

The format of this "Black Letter" is specially designed for review. (1) **Text**. First, it is recommended that the entire text be studied. (2) **Capsule Summary**. The Capsule Summary is an abbreviated review of the subject matter which can be used both before and after studying the main body of the text. The headings in the Capsule Summary follow the main text of the "Black Letter." (3) **Table of Contents**. The Table of Contents is in outline form to help you organize the details of the subject and the Summary of Contents gives you a final overview of the materials. (4) **Practice Examination**. The Practice Examination in Appendix B gives you the opportunity of testing yourself with the type of question asked on an exam.

In addition, a number of other features are included to help you understand the subject matter and prepare for examinations:

Short Questions and Answers: This feature is designed to help you spot and recognize issues in the examination. We feel that issue recognition is a major ingredient in successfully writing an examination.

Perspective: In this feature, the authors discuss their approach to the topic, the approach used in preparing the materials, and any tips on studying for and writing examinations.

Analysis: This feature, at the beginning of each section, is designed to give a quick summary of a particular section to help you recall the subject matter and to help you determine which areas need the most extensive review.

Examples: This feature is designed to illustrate, through fact situations, the law stated. This, we believe, should help you analytically approach a question on the examination.

Glossary: This feature is designed to refamiliarize you with the meaning of a particular legal term. We believe that the recognition of words of art used in an examination helps you to better analyze the question. In addition, when writing an examination you should know the precise definition of a word of art you intend to use.

We believe that the materials in this "Black Letter" will facilitate your study of a law school course and assure success in writing examinations not only for the course but for the bar examination. We will you success.

THE PUBLISHER

SUMMARY OF CONTENTS

APPENDICES

*

TABLE OF CONTENTS

APPENDICES

CAPSULE SUMMARY

I. CORPORATION LAW IN GENERAL

A. "CORPORATION" DEFINED

A corporation is a type of legal institution or concept that defines relationships among people. Several different theories have been proposed to describe these relationships.

1. Entity Theory

A corporation can be most readily envisioned as an artificial, fictitious entity created for the purpose of conducting a business. In this view, the basic elements of a corporation are:

a. The artificial entity has the power to conduct its business entirely in its own name.

b. The artificial entity is formed by a grant of authority by a government agency.

c. The artificial entity must be generally recognized as such by the creating state, the Federal Government, and private citizens who deal with the corporation.

d. The artificial entity in a fundamental sense is a fiction. Courts may refuse to follow the artificial entity analysis to its logical conclusions, if it leads to fraudulent or significantly unfair consequences, frustration of clearly defined statutory policies, or other undesirable results.

2. Concession Theory

A second theory of corporateness is that a corporation is a "grant" or "concession" from the state. The theory is based on the role of the state in the formation of the corporation.

3. Contract Theory

A third theory of corporateness is that the charter of a corporation represents a contract (a) between the state and the corporation, or (b) between the corporation and its shareholders, or (c) among the shareholders themselves. This theory is likely to surface in the current context in disputes between different classes of shareholders, or in disputes in which one class of shareholders claims that the class is being discriminated against in some way.

4. "Nexus of Contracts"

A fourth theory of corporateness is a "nexus of contracts." This theory, utilized by economists for analytic purposes, rejects the notion that the shareholders are the ultimate owners of the corporation and treats them instead as contractual providers of capital in anticipation of receiving a desired return. A corporation can therefore be analyzed as a "nexus of contracts."

a. Under this theory, state corporation statutes are viewed as providing standard rules suitable for the average corporation but which may be modified by provisions in the articles of incorporation.

b. A few scholars have argued that this theory should protect corporations from amendments to state corporation statutes on the ground that such amendments violate the federal constitutional provision that prohibits states from impairing the obligation of contract.

B. CONSTITUTIONAL INCIDENTS OF THE CORPORATE "PERSONALITY"

A corporation is entitled to some but not all of the constitutional protections available to individual persons. For example, a corporation is not a citizen of a state or of the United States for purposes of the privileges and immunities clause, but a corporation has rights of free speech which may not be restricted as such by state statute. A corporation also does not have a privilege against self incrimination, but is protected against deprivations of property without due process of law and is entitled to the constitutional right of equal protection of the law.

C. SOURCES OF LAW

The law of corporations is derived from several sources.

1. State Incorporation Statutes

Every state has a general incorporation statute. Two sources of statutes have been particularly influential in modernizing and liberalizing the state statutes.

a. The Model Business Corporation Act (1984) prepared and maintained by the Committee on Corporate Laws of the Section on Corporation Banking, and Business Law of the American Bar Association; and

b. The Delaware General Corporation Law (GCL).

2. State Common Law Principles

Most common law principles are interstitial in nature in the law of corporations. They supply supplementary principles when the statutes are silent or they construe statutory provisions.

3. Federal Statutes

A significant portion of the law applicable to publicly held corporations is federal in origin, based on the Securities Exchange Act of 1934 and the Securities Act of 1933, and rules promulgated thereunder.

4. Federal Common Law

A general federal jurisprudence of corporations does not exist, and federal law applied to corporations is more or less firmly grounded in the securities acts and regulations.

D. FUNCTIONAL CLASSIFICATION OF CORPORATIONS

The basic distinction underlying much of the law of corporations is between the closely held corporation and the publicly held corporation.

1. Definition of a Closely Held Corporation

A closely held corporation is a corporation with most of the following attributes:

a. It has a few shareholders, all or most of whom are usually active in the management of the business;

b. There is no public market for its shares;

c. Its shares are subject to one or more restrictions on transfer; and

d. It has never registered a public distribution of shares under the federal or state securities acts.

2. Definition of a Publicly Held Corporation

A publicly held corporation is a corporation with most of the following attributes:

a. Some of its shares are held by members of the general public and the overall number of shareholders is usually large;

b. There is a public market for its shares which may be on a securities exchange or among brokers "over the counter;"

c. The corporation is subject to reporting and disclosure requirements under the securities acts;

d. It has made a distribution of shares to members of the general public that has been registered under the Securities Act of 1933.

3. Theoretical Significance of the Distinction Between Closely Held and Publicly Held Corporations

The most important distinctions between closely held and publicly held corporations are the number of shareholders and the marketability of their shares.

a. The presence or absence of a public market for the corporation's shares is a most important difference between the two types of corporations. Because of the nonexistence of a market for shares in the closely held corporation, a minority shareholder may be "locked in" to an unsalable asset. In contrast, in a publicly held corporation a dissatisfied shareholder can always sell his or her shares on the public market.

b. A second major difference is that in a closely held corporation, most of the shareholders are likely to be employed by or earn their livelihood through the corporation's business, while in a publicly held corporation most of the shareholders are not connected with management and have only a limited say in the policies adopted by the corporation.

c. A third difference is that the presence of public shareholders unconnected with the business of a publicly held corporation is thought to present a strong case for governmental regulation of internal aspects of a public corporation's affairs.

E. "EFFICIENT" SECURITIES MARKETS

Virtually all modern economic analysis of publicly held corporations rests on the hypothesis that securities markets are "efficient." This hypothesis is usually called the "efficient capital market hypothesis" or "ECMH."

1. The Concept of an Efficient Market

In an efficient market, there are many purchasers and sellers all seeking to make a profit in the market. Prices move rapidly—indeed almost instantaneously—to reflect all public information that is available about securities traded in that market.

a. While the empirical evidence in favor of the ECMH as applied to securities markets is generally viewed as persuasive, some anomalies exist that are not explained by that hypothesis. Alternative theories to the ECMH may be developed in the future.

b. The evidence supporting the ECMH is largely based on studies of securities traded on the New York Stock Exchange and other major markets. Some publicly traded securities are traded in thin markets and the ECMH may not be an accurate description of such markets.

2. Inferences That May Be Drawn From the ECMH

A number of inferences may be drawn from the ECMH:

a. Price movements in any one stock are random. It is not possible to predict from the previous transaction whether the next transaction will be higher or lower.

b. Persons who rely on historical changes in prices, often called chartists, are engaging in futile and irrelevant analysis, because the market price already incorporates that information.

c. It is not possible for a person to develop and apply a trading strategy that consistently outperforms the market.

d. Large institutional investors cannot hope in the long run to have portfolios that perform better than the broad-based market indexes.

3. Persons With Nonpublic Information

Persons trading on the basis of undisclosed nonpublic information about a specific security may consistently outperform the market.

4. Judicial Recognition of the ECMH

The ECMH has been partially accepted by the United States Supreme Court. It has also been cited and relied upon by the Securities & Exchange Commission, and lower federal courts.

F. STATE COMPETITION FOR CORPORATIONS

Beginning in the late Nineteenth Century, states have competed to attract businesses to incorporate under their state statutes. Today, the uncrowned winner of this competition is the state of Delaware.

1. Advantages of Incorporation Business

The incorporation business provides tax revenues for the state, fees for members of the local bar, filing fees, and the like.

2. Success of Delaware

Over one-third of all the corporations listed on the New York Stock Exchange are incorporated in Delaware. The Delaware Legislatures and the Delaware Supreme Court are therefore the principal sources of modern corporation law today in terms of the number of corporations directly affected.

3. Reasons for Success of Delaware

The reason for the popularity and primacy of the state of Delaware may be explained partially by history, partially by the continued efforts by the bar of that state to provide an effective, flexible, and modern body of corporate law, and partially by the familiarity of corporate lawyers around the country with the Delaware GCL. Major contributors to Delaware's primacy is the existence of a sophisticated judiciary and sophisticated filing office that assures reasonable and knowledgeable decision making.

a. The Delaware GCL is flexible and simplifies the problems faced by the corporation in conducting its routine internal business under that statute.

b. There is "more" corporation law in Delaware today than in any other state. As a result, there are fewer areas of uncertainty in Delaware corporation law than in the law of any other state, and corporation lawyers may plan transactions with a relatively high degree of certainty.

c. The sophisticated judiciary, corporate bar, and filing authorities in Delaware are familiar with corporation problems arising in the modern context, particularly in the areas of contests for corporate control and derivative litigation.

d. Procedures exist in Delaware whereby unsuspected problems may be expeditiously dealt with by amendments to the Delaware GCL.

e. Delaware case law generally permits corporations to adopt defensive tactics to combat unwanted takeovers.

4. Economic Analysis of the Reasons for Delaware's Success

The earliest explanations of Delaware's success was that the Delaware GCL was unduly permissive and permitted management the maximum freedom to operate without constraint. In this view, Delaware had won "the race for the bottom."

a. Economists pointed out that if this explanation were accurate, corporations that reincorporate in Delaware should suffer a loss in the value of their publicly traded shares as a result of the efficient capital market hypothesis. Empirical investigations did not reveal such a loss.

b. An alternative explanation is that state statutes provide an array of incorporation alternatives ranging from "weak" (as in Delaware) to "strong" (as in California), and that corporations decide where to incorporate based on the most useful statutory provision to them. In this view, the competition in state corporation statutes encourages efficiency.

c. Yet another theory is to view the Delaware statute as a result of the interplay of a variety of interest groups involved with corporations.

II. FORMATION OF CORPORATIONS

A. SELECTION OF STATE OF INCORPORATION

The first question that must be resolved in forming a corporation is what state should be the state of incorporation.

1. Local or Closely Held Businesses

For small enterprises planning to transact business primarily in one state, the choice of the state of incorporation usually comes down to the state in which business is principally conducted or Delaware.

2. Interstate or National Businesses

For larger enterprises transacting business in many or all states, incorporation in any one of several states is usually feasible. Most large publicly held corporations are interstate or national in character and may incorporate in any one of the 50 states. Many such businesses incorporate in Delaware.

B. VARIATIONS IN STATUTORY REQUIREMENTS AND NOMENCLATURE

1. Statutory Requirements

To form a corporation, it is essential to comply with the specific statutory requirements of the state chosen for the state of incorporation.

a. There is a surprising degree of uniformity and consistency in most modern statutes.

b. Most states only require a single filing with a state official. The state official is usually the secretary of state but some states have differently named filing offices.

c. Some states, such as Delaware, also require a local filing in the county in which the registered office is located. Other states, such as Arizona, also require a public advertisement in a newspaper of general circulation of the fact of incorporation.

d. Variations among the states also exist with respect to filing fees, franchise taxes, stock issuance or transfer taxes, and similar items.

2. Nomenclature

The Model Business Corporation Act nomenclature is followed in most states. The document filed with the secretary of state is called the "articles of incorporation." Many states require the secretary of state also to issue a formal document called a "certificate of incorporation" to evidence the acceptance of the filing.

In Delaware, the basic document filed to create a corporation is called the "certificate of incorporation."

C. DOCUMENTS FILED IN THE OFFICE OF THE SECRETARY OF STATE

The basic filing requirement is that articles of incorporation which conform to statutory requirements be filed with the secretary of state and be accompanied by the appropriate filing fee.

1. Procedure Under Older Statutes

Under most older state statutes, duplicate originals or an original and a copy of the articles of incorporation, must be filed.

a. The articles of incorporation must be verified or acknowledged under oath before a notary public.

b. If the articles of incorporation conform to the statute, the secretary of state attaches the certificate of incorporation to the copy or duplicate original and returns both documents to the incorporators or their representative.

c. A receipt for the filing fee is also usually attached.

2. Procedure Under Newer Statutes

To reduce the problems of handling many pieces of paper, some states authorize the filing of only a single original executed copy of the articles; the incorporators receive only a receipt for the filing fee as the sole evidence of incorporation.

3. Procedure Under the Model Business Corporation Act (1984)

The MBCA (1984) eliminates requirements that documents be verified or acknowledged; the person executing a document must simply designate the capacity in which he or she signs. One exact or conformed copy of the executed document must be filed with the document; the secretary of state attaches the fee receipt or acknowledgement of receipt to the copy and returns it to the filing party.

D. INCORPORATORS

Articles of incorporation are executed by one or more persons called "incorporators."

1. Formal Requirements

In most states, incorporators have no significant responsibilities, duties, or liabilities.

a. Only a single incorporator is required. There are usually no age or residency requirements. Corporations, trusts, and other entities may serve as incorporators in many states.

b. Earlier requirements of oaths, verifications and seals have been eliminated in the MBCA (1984) and the statutes of many states.

c. Incorporators execute the articles of incorporation and receive back the certificate of incorporation or receipt for the filing fee. They generally serve no other function.

d. In some states, the incorporators meet to complete the formation of the corporation. Under the MBCA (1984) the meeting of incorporators is an optional method of completing the formation of the corporation.

2. Dummy Incorporators

The practice is widespread of using one or more "dummy" incorporators, i.e. persons or entities unconnected with the future business who are willing to allow their names to be used as incorporators.

E. CONTENT OF THE ARTICLES OF INCORPORATION

1. Mandatory Requirements

a. State statutes traditionally require the following *minimum* information to appear in articles of incorporation:

1) The name of the corporation;

2) Its duration;

3) Its purpose or purposes;

4) The securities it is authorized to issue;

5) The name of its registered agent and the address of its registered office;

6) The names and addresses of its initial board of directors;

7) The name and address of the incorporator or incorporators.

b. Virtually all corporations elect the duration to be "perpetual" and their purpose to be "the conduct of any lawful business."

c. The MBCA (1984) provides that every corporation automatically has a "perpetual" duration and a purpose to "conduct any lawful business" unless a narrower duration or purposes clause is inserted.

2. Discretionary Provisions

State statutes provide that additional provisions may be included in the articles of incorporation at the election of the corporation.

a. State statutes provide that corporations may elect to eliminate or modify specified rules of fundamental corporate governance by specific provision in the articles of incorporation.

b. Many other discretionary provisions may be placed either in the articles of incorporation or the bylaws.

c. State statutes generally make it unnecessary for corporations to include any provisions relating to corporate powers. References to specific powers may be helpful where the state statute is silent or unclear on whether corporations generally possess the specific power.

F. THE CORPORATE NAME

A corporate name under most statutes must (i) contain a reference to the corporate nature of the entity, (ii) not be the same or deceptively similar to a name already in use or reserved for use, and (iii) not imply that a corporation is engaged in a business in which corporations may not lawfully engage. The Delaware General Corporation Law and the MBCA (1984) substitute the test of "distinguishable upon the records of the Secretary of State" for the "same or deceptively similar" test.

1. Name Uniqueness

The requirement that each corporation have a unique name is primarily to avoid confusion in such matters as sending tax notices and naming defendants in law suits. Statutes prohibiting the use of "deceptively similar" names may involve an unfair competition standard as well as name confusion.

2. Reservation of Name

An available name may be "reserved" for a limited period of time (usually 120 days) for a small fee. The reservation of a name permits the preparation of corporate documents, ordering of stationery, etc., with the assurance that the proposed name will be available if the articles are filed within the period the name is reserved.

3. Registration of Name

Many states allow a foreign corporation not transacting business in the state to register its name with the Secretary of State to assure that no local business obtains the right to use its name. Registration of a name thus protects the foreign corporation's good will reflected in its name and preserves its option to later expand its operations into the state under its current name.

4. Use of Assumed Name

Corporations generally may adopt and do business under assumed names.

A foreign corporation that has not previously registered its name may discover that its own name is not available when it seeks to qualify to transact business in a new state. In this situation, the statutes of many states require the foreign corporation to qualify to transact business under an assumed name in the new state and file an assumed name certificate with the Secretary of State.

G. PERIOD OF DURATION

Statutes authorize the corporation to have "perpetual" existence. It is almost never desirable to create a corporation with a shorter period of existence because to do so creates the risk that the corporate existence may expire without renewal with uncertain rights and liabilities of participants thereafter.

H. PURPOSES

Modern statutes authorize very general purposes clauses, e.g. "The purpose of the corporation is to engage in any lawful business."

1. History of Purposes Clauses

The nature of purposes clauses has evolved over a long period of time, reflecting varying attitudes of mistrust toward the corporation. They were formerly of much greater importance than they are today.

a. In the earliest period all corporations were formed by special legislative enactment. In effect, each purposes clause was separately negotiated.

b. In the nineteenth and early twentieth centuries, under the earliest general incorporation statutes, corporations could only be formed for a single specific purpose.

c. State statutes were modernized to permit corporations to include a number of specific purposes clauses. Many persons forming corporations adopted the practice of including tens or even hundreds of specific purposes clauses routinely in every articles of incorporation. This practice quickly eliminated any significance the purposes clauses might have.

d. The modern practice of allowing corporations to have the general purpose of engaging in any lawful business is a logical simplification of the practice of using multiple purposes clauses.

e. Today, there is little or no reason to have a purposes clause at all, and doctrines based on limited purposes clauses, such as ultra vires or implied purposes, have little modern relevance.

f. The MBCA (1984) provides that every corporation automatically has an "any lawful business" purpose unless a narrower clause is set forth in the articles.

2. Limited Purposes Clause as a Planning Device

A limited purposes clause may be used today as a planning device or as a protection for investors. The effectiveness of such a clause is problematic at best.

I. SECURITIES

The securities a corporation is authorized to issue must be described in the articles of incorporation.

J. MINIMUM INITIAL CAPITALIZATION REQUIREMENTS

Fifty years ago virtually all states required that a corporation have a minimum amount of capitalization before it could commence business. One thousand dollars was the most common amount.

1. Current Trend

The modern trend is to eliminate such requirements because they are arbitrary and do not provide any meaningful protection to creditors. Less than half of all states have such requirements today.

2. Failure to Meet Minimum Initial Capital Requirements

Directors are usually made personally liable if business is commenced without the required minimum capital.

a. This liability is usually limited to the difference between the minimum required capitalization and the amount of capital actually contributed.

b. A few state statutes have been construed to impose unlimited liability on directors for all debts incurred before the minimum capitalization was paid in.

c. There is no requirement that a corporation maintain any specified surplus of assets over liabilities after incorporations.

3. Share Subscriptions

Share subscriptions are agreements to purchase shares in advance of incorporation. Persons subscribing for shares have financial obligations to the corporation and possibly to other subscribers.

K. REGISTERED OFFICE AND REGISTERED AGENT

The registered office and registered agent at that office must be specified in the articles of incorporation. They serve the purposes of providing a location where the corporation may be found and a person on whom process may be served.

L. CORPORATE POWERS

Every state statute lists general powers that every corporation possesses. It is unnecessary and undesirable to list some or all of these powers in the articles of incorporation. The MBCA (1984) provides that every corporation "has the same powers as an individual to do all things necessary or convenient to carry out its business and affairs as well as a list of general powers."

1. General Powers

The general powers possessed by corporations under modern statutes include the power:

a. To sue and be sued;

b. To have a corporate seal;

c. To purchase, receive, lend, sell, invest, convey and mortgage personal and real property;

d. To make contracts, borrow and lend money, and guarantee the indebtedness of third persons;

e. To conduct its business within or without the state;

f. To elect or appoint officers or agents, define their duties, fix their compensation, and provide pension, profit sharing, and stock option plans;

g. To purchase shares or interests, in or obligations of, itself or any other entity;

h. To make charitable, scientific or education contributions or donations for the public welfare;

i. To be a partner or manager of a partnership or other venture;

j. To make and alter bylaws for the administration and regulation of its internal affairs.

k. To indemnify directors and officers against liabilities imposed on them while acting on behalf of the corporation, and to provide liability insurance for them.

MBCA (1984) also permits a corporation to make political donations or contributions to influence election to the extent permitted by state law.

2. Acts in Excess of Powers

If a corporation does an act which it does not have power to do, it is acting ultra vires.

3. Partial Enumeration of Powers

The danger of a partial enumeration of statutory powers in an articles of incorporation is that a negative inference may be drawn that the inclusion of some enumerated powers implies the exclusion of unenumerated ones.

M. ULTRA VIRES

"Ultra vires" means beyond the scope of the powers of a corporation. It is used to describe acts that exceed either the stated purposes or powers of the corporation.

1. The Common Law Ultra Vires Doctrine

The early common law view was that an ultra vires transaction was void since the corporation lacked the power to enter into the transaction. Over time this view softened, since the common law doctrine often led to unfair or unpredictable consequences.

2. Modern Trends

Four factors have greatly reduced the importance of the ultra vires doctrine in the modern era:

a. The use of multiple purposes clauses and "any lawful business" purposes clauses.

b. The broadening of the statutory powers of corporations.

c. Recognition that a corporation may amend its articles of incorporation in order to broaden its purposes clause after an ultra vires issue is raised.

d. Statutes treating the subject of ultra vires.

3. Statutory Treatment of the Ultra Vires Doctrine

Modern statutes sharply limit the ultra vires principle. Under these statutes, the claim that an action is ultra vires may be raised only:

a. In a suit by a shareholder against the corporation to enjoin an ultra vires act, if all affected parties are present in the litigation and the court finds that it is equitable to enjoin the ultra vires act;

b. In a proceeding by the corporation against incumbent or former officers or directors of the corporation; or

c. In a proceeding by the state attorney general to dissolve the corporation or enjoin the ultra vires act.

4. Modern Areas of Ultra Vires Concern

Ultra vires issues may continue to arise in some states on the question whether or not the corporation has power to enter into the following acts:

a. Making political contributions or engaging in lobbying to influence legislation;

b. Granting unusual employee fringe benefits;

c. Entering into partnerships;

d. Making large charitable donations that appear to provide no benefit to the corporation;

e. Guaranteeing indebtedness of others that provides only incidental benefit to the corporation; and

f. Making loans to officers or directors.

State statutes grant every corporation the express power to enter into some or all of these acts.

N. COMPLETION OF THE FORMATION OF THE CORPORATION

The filing of articles of incorporation is only the first step in forming a corporation.

1. Additional Steps

Lawyers are expected to complete the formation of the corporation. Steps include:

a. Prepare bylaws;

b. Prepare minutes of the various organizational meetings, including waivers of notice or consents to action without formal meetings where appropriate;

c. Obtain blank share certificates and make sure they are properly prepared and issued;

d. Prepare shareholders' agreement, if any;

e. Generally oversee the preparation and execution of the various forms, certificates and other documents;

f. Obtain taxpayer identification numbers;

g. Open a bank account for the corporation;

h. Determine whether the S corporation tax election should be made, and, if so, make that election;

i. Make sure the directors and officers understand the nature of their duties and responsibilities.

2. Consequences of Failure to Complete Formation

The consequences of a partial formation of a corporation usually arise in the context of a suit against officers, directors, or shareholders seeking to hold them liable for an obligation incurred in the name of the corporation. A number of cases hold that no personal liability is created so long as articles of incorporation have been properly filed. If personal liability is imposed despite the filing of articles of incorporation, the result is likely to be analyzed as a case involving:

a. Promoters' liability;

b. Piercing the corporate veil; or

c. The failure to comply with a mandatory condition subsequent.

Personal liability is usually (but not invariably) imposed if business is commenced before articles of incorporation are filed.

3. The Need for Organizational Meetings

Organizational documents may consist of "minutes" of meetings prepared by an attorney before the corporation is formed. The question may arise whether it is necessary to actually hold meetings to reflect what the minutes describe. If the corporation is closely held, and there is no disagreement about what is to be done, actual meetings in the physical sense are not usually held.

a. In most states, unanimous written consents may be used instead of minutes to avoid any meeting requirement.

b. If the consent procedure is unavailable, and minutes of meeting must be used, lawyers may insist that an informal meeting actually be held.

O. BYLAWS

The bylaws of a corporation are a set of rules for governing the internal affairs of the corporation. They are typically adopted as part of the formation of a new corporation.

III. PREINCORPORATION TRANSACTIONS

A. PROMOTERS

"Promoters" are persons who assist in putting together a new business. These individuals serve important social and economic functions.

1. Basic Function of Promoters

In promoting a new venture, promoters:

a. Arrange for the necessary business assets and personnel so that the new business may function effectively.

b. Obtain the necessary capital to finance the venture.

c. Complete the formation of the corporation.

2. Location of Discussion of Promoters in this Capsule Summary

Part III, B of the Capsule Summary deals exclusively with problems of contracts entered into by promoters in arranging for the necessary business assets and personnel so that the business may function. Parts III E & V discuss the problems of raising capital. Part III, C discusses the fiduciary duties of promoters when carrying out these activities. Part II, N describes the steps necessary to complete the formation of a corporation.

B. PROMOTERS CONTRACTS

Promoters may enter into contracts on behalf of the venture being promoted either before or after articles of incorporation have been filed. Most problems are created by preincorporation contracts. The legal consequences of these contracts vary depending in part on the form of the contract itself.

1. Contracts Entered in the Name of a Corporation "To Be Formed"

A contract of this type shows on its face that the corporation has not yet been formed. A typical form of execution is "ABC Corporation, a corporation to be formed." Such a contract may be analyzed in several different ways.

a. The most traditional analysis is that the promoter is personally liable on the contract and will remain severally liable along with the corporation if it is subsequently formed and adopts the contract. Under certain circumstances the promoter may be entitled to indemnification from the corporation.

b. A related analysis is that the promoter is personally liable until the corporation is formed and adopts the contract. Thereafter the promoter is discharged from liability. This is an example of a "novation."

c. A third possible analysis is that the promoter is not personally liable on the contract but has promised the other party to use her best efforts to cause the corporation to be formed and to adopt the contract. The promoter may be liable on her promise if no steps are taken to form the corporation even though she is not liable on the contract itself.

d. A final possible analysis is that no one is liable on the contract until the corporation is formed and adopts it.

e. The test of which of these alternatives is the appropriate one in a specific case depends on the "intention" of the parties. Most cases find the promoter personally liable on one theory or another.

2. Contracts Entered Into in the Corporate Name

These cases differ from the preceding ones in that the contract is entered into in the name of a corporation that has not been formed and one or both parties erroneously believe the corporation has been formed.

a. Under general agency principles, if a promoter represents that she is acting on behalf of a corporation when she knows no steps have been taken to form a corporation, she is personally liable on the contract. This result may be justified on two grounds:

   1) A person who purports to act as an agent for a nonexistent principal is personally liable on the contract;

   2) A person who purports to act as an agent for a principal warrants his or her authority.

b. The common law developed concepts of corporations *de facto* and corporations *de jure.* The finding of the existence of either a *de jure* or a *de facto* corporation absolves the promoter of liability. However, the state may attack a *de facto* corporation.

c. A corporation *de jure* has sufficiently complied with the incorporation requirements so that a corporation is legally in existence for all purposes. Compliance with all *mandatory* statutory requirements gives rise to a *de jure* corporation; failure to comply with less important *directory* requirements do not affect the *de jure* status.

d. A corporation *de facto* is a corporation that is partially but defectively or incompletely formed. These corporations are immune from attack by everyone but the State. The traditional test of *de facto* existence is threefold:

   1) There must be a valid statute under which the corporation might incorporate;

   2) There must be a "good faith" or "colorable" attempt to comply with the statute; and

   3) There must be an actual use of the corporate privilege.

e. Modern statutes substitute a more objective test for the common law *de facto/ de jure* distinction. Under these statutes the issuance of a certificate of incorporation (or acceptance of the articles of incorporation for filing) is conclusive evidence that the corporate existence has begun.

1) Statutes in about half of the states add that individuals "who assume to act as a corporation" without authority so to do are liable to creditors. This language is taken from MBCA (1969) § 139.

2) The MBCA (1984) § 2.04 provides that "all persons purporting to act as or on behalf of a corporation knowing there was no incorporation under this act" are jointly and severally liable for liabilities incurred. The results reached under these modern statutes are nearly as varied as the results reached under the common law *de facto/de jure* distinction.

3) One court has applied the *de facto* concept to a corporation that had filed articles of incorporation prior to commencing business.

4) With respect to transactions before the articles of incorporation are filed, most courts accept the statutory language at face value and conclude that the filing of articles of incorporation is a "bright line" test, leading to personal liability on all transactions taking place before that filing.

f. Some courts have held passive investors not personally liable on transactions occurring before the articles of incorporation are filed either on the theory of *de facto* corporation or on the theory that statutes referring to persons "assuming to act" on behalf of a corporation have no application to purely passive investors.

g. Filing of the articles of incorporation should avoid all claims based on defective incorporation; claims, however, may be asserted thereafter under the piercing the corporate veil or other doctrines.

h. Some cases apply a concept of "corporation by estoppel" that appears to be independent of modern statutes and the common law *de facto* corporation concept. Under this concept, a third party who relies on an innocent representation that the corporation is formed is "estopped" from denying the existence of the corporation.

1) The concept of "corporation by estoppel" is actually "reverse estoppel" because the person erroneously representing the existence of a corporation is permitted to escape liability while the person who relied on the representation is estopped from disputing the representation.

2) Only persons who honestly but erroneously believe that articles of incorporation have been filed are able to take advantage of the corporation by estoppel concept since the concept, if carried to its logical conclusion, would permit anyone to obtain the benefits of limited liability simply by consistently representing that a corporation existed when in fact it did not.

3) The doctrine of corporation by estoppel is also applied when a defendant seeks to avoid liability on the ground that the plaintiff may not sue because it is not a lawful corporate entity.

i. Unpredictability of result and irreconcilable precedents abound in this area.

1) Under a common sense approach it may be argued that there should be unlimited personal liability for all obligations entered into in the corporate name before the corporation was formed.

2) It may also be argued that where third persons deal on a corporate basis with an apparent corporation, they receive a "windfall" if they may subsequently hold individual investors or promoters liable. This is particularly clear when the failure to complete the formation of the corporation is discovered only after the litigation is commenced. Some courts therefore have refused to impose personal liability even in circumstances where no steps toward incorporation have been taken.

These two approaches are fundamentally irreconcilable.

3. Liability of Corporation on Promoter's Contracts

A corporation is not automatically liable on its promoters' contracts; the newly formed corporation may accept or reject all preincorporation contracts.

a. An acceptance of a preincorporation contract by a corporation is an "adoption" of that contract.

b. This rule allows subsequent investors to some extent to review promoters' contracts and reject those that seem improvident.

c. Adoption may be express or implied but presupposes knowledge of the contract. A recovery in quasi contract is normally available where benefits are received even though the contract is not adopted.

d. Mere existence of the corporation does not constitute an "adoption" of a contract for legal services leading to the formation of the corporation. An attorney providing legal services may therefore be unable to enforce a fee agreement made with a promoter against a newly formed corporation.

4. Relationship Between Promoter's Liability and Corporate Adoption

Corporate adoption of a contract generally releases the promoter from further liability only if the parties agree that a novation is to occur.

a. Williston argued that a novation is almost always contemplated.

b. Under a "complete novation" theory, promoters may form "shell corporations" solely to escape personal liability after it is clear that the promotion will fail.

C. PROMOTER'S FIDUCIARY DUTIES

Co-promoters of a venture owe fiduciary duties to each other, to the corporation, and to subsequent financial interests in the venture.

1. The Corporation as the Beneficiary

After the corporation is formed it may obtain from the promoter any benefits or rights the promoter obtained on its behalf.

2. Co-promoters as the Beneficiary

Any benefits or rights one promoter obtained must be shared with the co-promoters much as though they were partners.

3. Subsequent Investors as the Beneficiary

A major issue relating to promoters' fiduciary duties is the extent to which subsequent shareholders or investors are protected by fiduciary duties.

a. Two rules have been established. The "Massachusetts rule" allows the corporation to attack an earlier transaction if the subsequent sale to public investors was contemplated when the earlier transaction was entered into. The "federal rule" does not allow the corporation to attack the earlier transaction if all the shareholders at the time of the transaction consented to it.

b. The "Massachusetts rule" has been more popular than the "federal rule."

c. The real issue in this type of case is the lack of full disclosure about the promoters' transaction.

d. Many cases of this nature arise in the modern era as "disclosure" or "securities fraud" cases rather than as "promoters fraud" cases.

4. Creditors as the Beneficiary

Some cases have applied fiduciary concepts to protect creditors against unfair or fraudulent transactions by promoters.

D. AGREEMENTS TO FORM CORPORATIONS

A preincorporation agreement to create a corporation is enforceable in the same way as any other contract. However, the preincorporation agreement or contract may not survive the formation of the corporation unless specific and precise provisions to that effect are included in the agreement or the corporation thereafter adopts the agreement.

E. PREINCORPORATION SUBSCRIPTIONS

A preincorporation subscription is a promise by a person to purchase a specific number of shares of a corporation at a specific price after the corporation is formed. Under modern statutes these promises are irrevocable for a stated period even if they are not supported by consideration. Statutes also require subscribers to be uniformly treated after the corporation is formed.

IV. PIERCING THE CORPORATE VEIL

The phrase "piercing the corporate veil" (PCV) is a metaphor to describe the cases in which a court refuses to recognize the separate existence of a corporation despite its proper formation.

A. TRADITIONAL TESTS

The traditional tests for PCV are to "prevent fraud" or to "achieve equity." Courts have also applied concepts of "instrumentality" or "alter ego" as the basis for PCV. Courts state that the general rule is that each corporation is independent of its shareholders and that PCV liability should be imposed "reluctantly" and only in "extreme" circumstances.

1. One Person Corporations

One or two person corporations are treated no differently than other corporations in PCV cases.

2. Motive

The separate corporate existence may be recognized even though the corporation was formed solely to avoid unlimited liability.

3. Brother-Sister Corporations

The separate existence of related corporations, i. e., corporations with common shareholders, may be ignored so that the two corporations are treated as a single entity.

4. Inactive Shareholders

Active shareholders may be held liable for corporate debts on a PCV theory while inactive shareholders may be found not to be liable.

5. Estoppel Against Shareholders

PCV is generally only available against the corporation itself or its shareholders and may not be used affirmatively by them. A few cases, however, have permitted "reverse piercing" of the corporate veil at the request of a shareholder.

6. Publicly Held Corporation

PCV is almost exclusively a doctrine applicable to closely held corporations and not to publicly held corporations.

B. INDIVIDUAL SHAREHOLDER LIABILITY FOR CORPORATE DEBTS

1. Consensual Transactions

In most cases involving transactions in which a third person dealt voluntarily with the corporation (usually contract claims) the third person should not be able to PCV and hold the shareholders personally liable because he has voluntarily dealt with the corporation and "assumed the risk." PCV may apply in consensual cases, however, in unusual circumstances or where the corporation is being used in an inequitable way. Many but not all cases accept this approach.

2. Nonconsensual Transactions

In most cases involving nonconsensual transactions (usually torts) courts should be more willing to accept PCV arguments because there is no element of voluntary dealing. To recognize the separate existence of a nominally capitalized corporation in such a case may result in an unacceptable shift of the risk of loss to members of the general public.

a. The number of such cases, however, is much smaller than cases involving consensual dealing and the percentage of cases in this class in which the court permitted PCV is lower than in contract cases.

3. Failure to Follow Corporate Formalities

The failure to follow corporate formalities is often a significant factor in PCV cases and may result in the imposition of individual liability in both contract and tort cases.

4. Artificial Division of a Single Business Entity

An important factor in many PCV cases is whether a single business is artificially divided into several different corporations to reduce exposure of assets to liability. Usually the entire entity is held responsible for the debts of such a business.

5. Inadequate Capitalization

Inadequate or nominal capitalization should normally not be a major factor in contract cases but should be important in tort cases. Liability insurance should be viewed as capital for this purpose.

6. Transactions Between Related Corporations That Affect Third Parties

Cases sometimes arise in which transactions between related corporations affect interests of third persons. Since the terms of the transaction between the related corporations are not negotiated at arms length, there is a possibility that the transaction may be structured in a way detrimental to third persons. The test for transactions of this character is good faith and whether the terms of the transaction approximate the terms that might be negotiated at arms length if the corporations were unrelated.

C. PARENT CORPORATION'S LIABILITY FOR OBLIGATIONS OF SUBSIDIARY CORPORATIONS

Courts often PCV when the shareholder is itself a corporation. Data indicates, however, that cases of PCV when the shareholder is a corporation are not more common than cases where the shareholder is an individual.

1. Types of Issues That May Arise

PCV in parent/subsidiary context may arise in several ways in addition to the question whether the parent corporation is liable for the debts of a subsidiary:

a. The issue may be whether transactions between parent and subsidiary or between two subsidiaries must be recognized by third persons who are affected by the transaction.

b. The issue may be whether a parent may conspire with its subsidiary, or whether two subsidiaries may conspire together, to violate law or the rights of third parties.

c. The issue may involve a question of statutory construction: e.g., do statutes that refer generally to "corporation," "owner," or "operator" apply to both parent corporations and affiliated or subsidiary corporations.

2. Confusion of Affairs

Parent liability for the subsidiary's debts usually arises from a failure to maintain a clear separation between parent and subsidiary affairs. Conduct such as mixing assets; mixing business affairs; referring to the subsidiary as a "department" or "division" of the parent, etc., may lead to parental liability.

3. Permissible Activities

If practices similar to those described in the previous paragraph are avoided, a PCV argument should be rejected even though one corporation owns all the shares of the corporation; the corporations have common officers, directors, or employees; the corporations share common offices; the corporations file a consolidated tax return or report their earnings to their shareholders on a consolidated basis; and the corporations utilize a centralized cash management program.

4. Conclusion

Most courts appear to apply the same PCV principles to parent/subsidiary relationships as are applied to shareholders who are individuals. With the continued growth of corporate groups in the future, and the increased number of regulatory and environmental laws, it is possible that a unique set of principles for PCV in corporate groups will evolve.

D. USE OF THE SEPARATE CORPORATE EXISTENCE TO DEFEAT PUBLIC POLICY

The flexibility of the corporate fiction often permits it to be used in a way that arguably tends to defeat or undercut public or statutory policy.

1. General Principle

The issue in such cases generally revolves more around the strength and purpose of the public policy than the degree or extent of formation or method of operation of the corporation.

2. Qualification of Shareholder for Employee Benefits

A corporation may be used to qualify a person for public benefits available to employees which that person would not be entitled to if she conducted business in her own name. The validity of this practice depends on an evaluation of the policies underlying the grant of benefits.

3. Other Policy Issues

A PCV analysis may be used to determine other issues, such as whether a parent corporation is bound by a subsidiary's union contract or whether a parent is an "owner" or "operator" of hazardous waste disposal sites managed or owned by a subsidiary under CERCLA.

E. CHOICE OF LAW IN PIERCING THE CORPORATE VEIL

Some states today are more liberal than others in permitting PCV. Until about 1980 no attention was paid to the choice of law issue thereby created, since there did not seem to be significant variations in the law of PCV from state to state. The few cases in which the choice of law issue was raised generally concluded that the law in each possible state was the same and it was unnecessary to determine which law was applicable. In many cases arising during this period, the court simply applied the law of the forum without discussing the choice of law issue.

1. General Principles

The rule generally followed in the few cases that have addressed the issue is that the liability of a shareholder for the debts of the corporation is a matter of the internal affairs of a corporation, to be governed by the law of the state of incorporation. This rule is likely to be followed where the corporation has significant economic ties to the state of incorporation, particularly if the shareholders are themselves residents of the state of incorporation.

2. Possible Exception for Tort Claims

Under general conflict of laws principles applicable to torts, a court sitting in the state where the accident or event occurred may determine to apply local law to the PCV issue if the contacts of the corporation with the state of incorporation are minimal, and all significant contacts are with the forum state.

F. THE FEDERAL LAW OF PIERCING THE CORPORATE VEIL

Federal courts hold that where the enforcement of a federal statute is involved, and a uniform federal policy of PCV will further the federal policies, the federal courts should establish a federal law of PCV. In determining what this federal rule should be, the court may consider not only the federal policy involved, but also the federal decisions applying state PCV principles in diversity cases.

1. CERCLA

The Comprehensive Environmental Response, Compensation and Liability Act imposes responsibility for clean-up and response costs on all "owners" and "operators" of hazardous waste disposal sites. Much of the current litigation involving the federal law of PCV arises under this statute.

G. PIERCING THE CORPORATE VEIL IN TAXATION CASES

The Government has broad power to ignore or restructure fictional transactions which have as their sole purpose the avoidance or minimization of taxes.

1. Recognition of Corporation in General

The separate corporate existence of a corporation is generally recognized for tax purposes if it is carrying on a bona fide business and is not merely a device to avoid taxes.

2. Estoppel Against Taxpayer

The taxpayer is generally bound by her selection of the corporate form of business and cannot argue that the separate existence of the corporation should be ignored for tax purposes.

H. PIERCING THE CORPORATE VEIL IN BANKRUPTCY

Courts have considerable flexibility in dealing with corporations and shareholders for the purpose of preserving the rights of creditors when the corporation is unable to meet its debts as they become due.

1. Complete Piercing the Corporate Veil

The court may ignore the separate corporate existence and hold the shareholders individually liable for all corporate obligations.

2. Reclassification of Transaction

The court may refuse to recognize or may reclassify or change the form of transactions between shareholder and corporation where it is equitable or reasonable to do so.

3. Subordination

The court may subordinate claims of shareholders to claims of other creditors where the claim of the shareholder is in some sense inequitable. This power, called the Deep Rock doctrine, is viewed as inherent in the bankruptcy jurisdiction of federal courts and is now codified in the bankruptcy statute.

I. OTHER USES OF THE PIERCING DOCTRINE

While PCV is usually limited to the liability of a shareholder for corporate obligations, the same doctrine is sometimes referred to in other contexts. For example, a plaintiff may seek to obtain jurisdiction and service of process over a corporation by serving a subsidiary of the corporation and arguing PCV. The principles applied in these other contexts appear to be the same as those applied in traditional PCV cases, but the nature of the issue involved dictates whether the doctrine is narrowly or broadly applied. In the case of service of process on a subsidiary, for example, the test appears to be whether the controls exercised over the subsidiary are such that day-to-day decisions are in fact made by the parent rather than the subsidiary. While this test may be referred to as PCV, it is in fact more stringent than the test usually applied in shareholder liability cases.

V. FINANCING THE CORPORATION

A. IN GENERAL

There are four likely sources of capital for a corporation.

1. Equity Capital

Capital contributed by investors in exchange for shares of stock is called "equity capital."

2. Loans From Shareholders

Capital loaned by the shareholders to the corporation may be substituted for equity capital in whole or in part.

3. Loans From Third Persons

Capital loaned by third persons to the corporation is usually referred to as "debt financing" and should be distinguished from loans by shareholders because of the significantly different economic and legal consequences of such loans.

4. Internally Generated Funds

Capital internally generated from the corporation's business through the retention of earnings, creation of reserves, sales of appreciated assets and the like is a final source of funds needed by a corporation.

B. THE ISSUANCE OF COMMON SHARES

Under the MBCA (1984) the articles of incorporation must set forth the number of shares the corporation is authorized to issue. If the corporation is authorized to issue more than one class of shares, the number of shares of each class, and a distinguishing designation for each class, must also be set forth.

1. Common Shares Defined

The rights of common shares need not be described in the articles of incorporation. The two basic rights of common shares are: (1) entitlement to vote, and (2) entitlement to the net assets of the corporation when distributions are made or upon dissolution.

2. Par Value

In about 30 states, the articles of incorporation must also state the par value of the shares of each class (or state that the shares are issued "with no par value" or "without par value"). The remaining states, like the MBCA (1984), have eliminated the concept of par value, and the current trend is toward the elimination of this concept in additional states as an historical anomaly.

a. "Par value" is an arbitrary value associated with shares of stock. The par value of shares is set forth in the articles of incorporation and appears on the face of certificates for shares. The complex legal operation of this concept is described in parts 4 and 5 below.

b. Even in states that have eliminated par value, it may be used on an optional basis at the election of the corporation.

3. Authorized and Issued Shares

It is customary to authorize additional shares over what is planned to be issued at the outset in the event additional capital is needed at a later date.

4. The Price at Which Shares are Issued

a. Under modern statutes such as the MBCA (1984), there is no minimum issue price for shares. The price at which shares are issued is set by the board of directors, and so long as all shares being issued at the same time are issued at the same price, any price may be set by the board.

b. In states with par value statutes, the board of directors may set the price at which shares are issued, but shares should never be issued for less than par value.

c. The consequence of issuing par value shares for less than par is the creation of "watered shares" and a resulting liability on the part of the recipient to pay to the corporation the difference between par value and what the shareholder actually paid.

d. It is customary in modern practice to use "low par" or "nominal par" value shares rather than "high par" value shares.

e. There appears to be no benefit or advantage to the corporation in using a high par value for shares since lenders do not put weight on this factor in deciding whether or not to extend credit.

5. Par Value and the Capital Accounts

Corporation statutes that retain the concept of par value provide that the aggregate of the par values of issued shares constitutes the "stated capital" of the corporation and any excess received for the issuance of shares over stated capital is "capital surplus."

a. A major advantage of reflecting the bulk of the capital contributions as capital surplus is that under most state statutes stated capital is "locked in" the corporation for the benefit of creditors while capital surplus may be distributed to the shareholders or used to reacquire outstanding shares merely with the approval of shareholders.

b. The stated capital of a corporation is determined by the aggregate amount of the par values of all issued shares. Stated capital in turn determines the legality of dividends and distributions as described below.

   1) In some states, stated capital may be called simply "capital" or "capital stock" or "common stock."

   2) The board of directors may increase the stated capital of a corporation by directing that amounts from surplus accounts be transferred to stated capital.

   3) The corporation may reduce its stated capital by amending articles of incorporation to reduce the par value of shares.

c. Shares may be issued for a consideration in excess of par value. The excess consideration in most states is allocated to capital surplus rather than stated capital. The general practice in states with par value statutes is to issue shares for nominal consideration, e.g. $1 per share for shares to be sold at $10 or $50 per share. As a result in most corporations there is a lot of capital surplus and relatively little stated capital.

d. In most states that have mandatory par value statutes, "no par" shares are a permitted alternative. These shares may also be designated as "without par value." The rules with respect to such shares are tied into the rules with respect to par value shares.

   1) The consideration for no par shares issued in par value states is allocated to stated capital, but the board of directors may determine that some part of that consideration may be allocated to capital surplus rather than stated capital.

   2) There is no minimum price at which no par shares must be issued. The price is simply set by the board of directors or shareholders. However, watered stock liability may be created if the no par shares are actually issued at a price below that set for their issuance by the board of directors or shareholders.

e. Many states prohibit shares from being issued for promissory notes or promises of future services. This prohibition is technically not part of the par value structure but it appears most commonly in states that have retained the concept of par value.

1) Shares issued for prohibited consideration may be viewed as watered shares.

2) Such shares may also not be validly issued and may be subject to cancellation.

3) The MBCA (1984) does not contain this prohibition.

4) State statutes provide in effect that "in the absence of fraud in the transaction, the judgment of the board of directors * * * as to the value of the consideration received for shares shall be conclusive." Provisions of this type are absolutely essential to assure that shares are validly issued, fully paid, and nonassessable.

f. Watered stock is a generic term used to describe the issuance of shares below par value or, in some situations, shares issued for a price below the price set by the board of directors, or shares issued in whole or in part for ineligible consideration.

g. "Treasury shares" are shares of the corporation that were once lawfully issued but have been reacquired by the corporation and held in its "treasury." Under traditional statutes, treasury shares have an intermediate status between being issued and unissued. They are not outstanding for purposes of voting, quorum determinations or dividend payments. They are viewed as "issued" for other purposes.

h. Treasury shares are widely used by corporations formed under par value statutes to avoid the rules set forth in this part of the Capsule Summary.

1) Treasury shares, having once been issued for more than par value, may be resold by the corporation without regard to the relationship between the sales price and par value.

2) Treasury shares, having once been issued for an eligible consideration, may be resold by the corporation in exchange for future services, promissory notes, or other consideration that is not eligible consideration for the issue of new shares.

i. Stated capital is not reduced by the par value of treasury shares; such shares are reflected on the financial statements by a special entry showing that they are held as treasury shares and restrictions are placed on the earned surplus and/or capital surplus accounts to reflect that the purchase price for the treasury shares has been charged to those accounts.

C. ISSUANCE OF MORE THAN A SINGLE CLASS OF SHARES

Common shares are the residual ownership interests in the corporation. Other classes of shares with limited or preferred rights may also be created. The MBCA (1984) does not use the terms "common shares" and "preferred shares" but these terms are widely used in practice and in many state statutes.

1. Preferred Shares

"Preferred" means that shares have preference over common shares either as to dividends or on liquidation or both. A "preference" simply means that the preferred shares are entitled to a payment of a specified amount before the common shares are entitled to anything. Most preferred shares have both dividend and liquidation preferences.

a. Preferential rights are defined in the articles of incorporation, and the attributes of preferred shares may include some rights normally associated with common shares.

b. A dividend preference may be noncumulative, cumulative, or cumulative-to-the-extent-earned.

c. Preferred shares may be redeemable and convertible into common shares. They may be voting or nonvoting.

2. Preferred Issued in Series

Many state statutes authorize the creation by the board of directors of one or more "series" of preferred shares, the financial or other terms of which may vary from series to series.

3. Classified Common Stock

Common stock may be issued in classes with variations in rights from class to class. Classes of common shares are often used as planning devices in closely held corporations.

4. Equivalence of Shares Within a Class or Series

All shares of a class or series must have identical preference, limitations and relative rights with those of other shares of the same series or class. This requirement is a matter of controversy in some defensive tactics against takeovers where the corporation may distinguish between holders of the same class of shares on the basis of outside events.

D. DEBT SECURITIES

Typical debt securities are bonds, debentures, and notes.

1. Bonds and Debentures Described

Bonds and debentures are usually long-term negotiable unconditional written obligations to pay a specific amount at a future date. A bond is a secured debt while a debenture is unsecured. A promissory note is a short-term negotiable instrument payable to the order of a specific person representing an unconditional promise to pay that may be secured or unsecured.

a. Bonds and debentures traditionally were payable to bearer and the interest obligation was reflected by coupons to be detached and submitted for payment to the issuer. The modern practice, however, is to issue bonds and debentures in registered form, in the name of a specific person. Interest payments are made automatically to the registered owner. Many bonds and debentures are held in book entry form.

b. The 1980s saw the creation of novel types of debt instruments.

2. Debt Instruments Compared With Preferred Stock

Bonds or debentures are debt securities that differ significantly from preferred stock, which is an equity security:

a. Bonds or debentures pay interest that is legally required whereas preferred stock pays dividends that are usually discretionary with the board of directors.

b. Bonds or debentures usually have a fixed maturity date whereas preferred stock is outstanding indefinitely or permanently.

c. Bonds theoretically have a right of foreclosure upon the property that is their security whereas preferred stock does not.

d. Bonds or debentures are created pursuant to indentures that usually appoint a trustee to handle the rights of security holders whereas preferred stock is created by provision in the articles of incorporation of the corporation.

3. Advantages of Providing a Portion of the Initial Capital in the Form of Debt

a. There are tax advantages for shareholders in a C corporation to lend a portion of the initial capital to the corporation. Interest on a debt is deductible by the corporation while dividends are not. A repayment of debt may be a tax-free return of capital rather than a taxable dividend.

b. There are also nontax advantages of using shareholder debt to balance out capital contributions and to provide advantages in bankruptcy.

4. Third Party Debt

Loans from third persons to the corporation do not provide the tax or planning benefits of loans from the original investors; however, such loans may provide the advantage of leverage.

5. Debt/Equity Ratio

The ratio between a corporation's equity capital and its long term debt is the corporation's debt/equity ratio.

E. APPLICATION OF THE FEDERAL AND STATE SECURITIES ACTS

The possible impact of federal and state securities acts must always be considered when raising capital. The federal statute is the Securities Act of 1933 and state statutes dealing with this subject are called "blue sky laws."

1. General Description of Purpose

These statutes are designed to protect the public investor from fraudulent or misrepresented promotions or sales of securities. The goal is usually full disclosure of all relevant facts about the securities being sold.

2. Cost of Registration

The registration process, particularly at the federal level, is so expensive as to be impractical for most small and medium-sized public offerings.

3. Exemptions From Registration

Attention must be focused on the availability of exemptions for a particular offer. The principal exemptions under the Securities Act of 1933 are the following: Regulation D, Rules 504, 505 and 506; Section 4(2); Section 4(6); Section 3(b); and Section 3(a)(11).

4. Restrictions on Transfer of Unregistered Securities

Since the availability of several exemptions is dependent on the ultimate investors having certain knowledge or sophistication, or being residents of specific states, SEC regulations and accepted corporate practice require restrictions on transfer to be imposed on securities sold pursuant to an exemption.

5. Control Persons and Secondary Distributions

A secondary distribution is a public distribution of unregistered shares by a person other than the issuer—either an acquirer of unregistered shares or a "control person." Secondary distributions must be registered unless an exemption is available.

6. What is a Security?

Securities acts define "security" broadly. A "security" is judicially defined as any contract, transaction, or scheme whereby a person invests money in a common enterprise and is led to expect profits solely or primarily from the efforts of others.

7. State Blue Sky Laws

The provisions of most state "blue sky" statutes roughly parallel the federal securities act. Some state statutes do not adopt the "full disclosure" philosophy of the federal act but permit distributions to be registered and sold in the state only if their terms are "fair, just, and equitable." The private offering and other exemptions in state statutes are often more numerical and objective than the corresponding exemptions in the federal act. Generally, the registration requirements of the state statutes are in addition to the requirements of the federal securities act, though a considerable degree of coordination exists in many states.

8. Coordination With Disclosure Requirements of Securities Exchange Act of 1934

Publicly held corporations that file regular reports with the SEC under the Securities Exchange Act of 1934 may usually utilize the information previously filed in such reports in registering new issues of securities under the Securities Act of 1933. Regulations authorizing this use of previously filed material are called the Integrated Disclosure Program.

F. ISSUANCE OF SHARES BY A GOING CONCERN

Shares issued by a going concern create unique problems because the issuance affects the interests of existing shareholders.

1. Preemptive Rights

The principal common law protection for existing shareholders is the doctrine of "preemptive rights," which gives existing shareholders the right to subscribe and pay for their proportionate part of any new issue of securities by the corporation at the price established by the board of directors. Under modern statutes preemptive rights are discretionary and may be eliminated by provision in the articles of incorporation. Some statutes provide that preemptive rights exist in a corporation only if specific provision is made for them.

2. Fiduciary Restrictions on the Oppressive Issuance of Shares

Where preemptive rights are inapplicable or have been eliminated, the power of controlling shareholders to issue new shares may be limited by the fiduciary duties they owe to minority shareholders.

3. Securities Acts Applicable

The federal and state securities acts are applicable to shares issued by going concerns.

G. DIVIDENDS AND DISTRIBUTIONS

A "dividend" is a payment out of current or past earnings; other distributions, to the extent permitted, may be called "capital distributions," "distributions in partial liquidation," or by other names that indicate that they are distributions of capital, not distributions of earnings. Dividends or distributions are typically discretionary with the board of directors.

1. Dividend Policies in Publicly Held Corporations

Publicly held corporations generally adopt stable dividend policies that permit regular periodic distributions even though corporate income fluctuates.

2. **Dividend Policies in a Closely Held Corporation**
   In closely held corporations, dividend policy generally is income tax driven.

   a. If the corporation is not an S corporation, the dividend policy generally adopted is "no dividends." The payment of a dividend carries a higher tax cost than the payment of the same amount in the form of salaries, rents or other payments that are deductible by the corporation.

   b. If the corporation is an S corporation, corporate income is taxed directly to the shareholders whether or not distributions are made. Distributions therefore have no tax effect. A common pattern is the distribution of amounts at least sufficient to pay the income tax due on the corporate income allocated to each individual shareholder under the S corporation election.

   c. The distribution of corporate income in the form of salaries, rent, etc. may give rise to internal disputes since some shareholders may receive larger payments than others, and the payments may bear no relationship to relative shareholdings.

   d. Suits to compel the payment of dividends succeed only rarely and require a showing of bad faith.

3. **Legal Requirements for Dividends and Distributions**
   The tests for the legality of dividends and distributions depend on whether the state retains traditional par value concepts or whether it has eliminated those concepts as contemplated by the MBCA (1984). Some par value states have unique tests for the legality of dividends and distributions.

   a. MBCA (1984) imposes two tests to determine whether a distribution may be lawfully made:

      1) An "equity insolvency" test that requires a determination that after the distribution the corporation is able to meet its obligations as they mature; and

      2) A "balance sheet" test that requires that, after the distribution, assets must exceed liabilities plus the preferential amounts due any class or classes of preferred shares upon dissolution.

   b. State statutes that retain par value concepts usually permit dividends to be paid only out of "earned surplus, but they also usually permit distributions out of capital surplus or other surplus accounts with the consent of the shareholders.

   c. Dividends or distributions made in violation of these rules may lead to the imposition of statutory liability on directors who authorize them. Generally, shareholders receiving illegal dividends or distributions are liable to restore them only if they knew they were illegal.

4. Contractual Restrictions on Dividends and Distributions

Because state statutes provide few restrictions on distributions and therefore little or no protection for creditors, major creditors usually impose contractual restrictions on dividends and distributions in loan agreements.

H. REDEMPTIONS AND REPURCHASES OF OUTSTANDING SHARES

A redemption or repurchase by a corporation of some of its outstanding shares has the same economic effect as a dividend or distribution to the shareholders whose shares are redeemed or purchased. Similar legal tests are applied to redemptions or repurchases as are applied to dividends or distributions.

1. Reasons for Repurchases in Publicly Held Corporation

Share repurchases may occur in publicly held corporations for several reasons: e.g., to provide shares that are available for employee share purchase plans or for the acquisition of other businesses.

2. Reasons for Repurchases in Closely Held Corporations

Repurchases in closely held corporations are usually designed to permit a shareholder to withdraw from the corporation and liquidate his or her investment.

3. Status of Reacquired Shares

Reacquired shares under early statutes are classed as "treasury shares." The MBCA (1984) eliminates the concept of treasury shares. Reacquired shares under this Act have the status of authorized but unissued shares.

4. Redemptions at Option of Corporation

Corporations may issue preferred shares that are redeemable at the option of the corporation. In many states common shares may not be made redeemable at all or may be redeemable only if there exists another class of common shares that is not redeemable.

5. Redemptions at Option of Shareholder

In most states shares may be made redeemable at the option of the shareholder. Such shares have some of the characteristics of a demand promissory note.

I. SHARE DIVIDENDS AND SHARE SPLITS

Unlike cash or property dividends, a share dividend or share split does not dissipate corporate assets.

1. Definitions

Share dividends differ from share splits in degree rather than in kind. They differ in accounting treatment in par value states. In a share split, the par value of each old share is divided among the new shares while in a share dividend the par value of each share is unchanged and the stated capital of the corporation is increased by the number of shares issued as a dividend. The MBCA (1984) refers only to "share dividends" since it eliminates the concept of par value.

2. Effect on Market Prices

The market price of new shares after a split is often somewhat greater than the price of the old shares. A share dividend rarely has a noticeable effect on market prices.

3. Treatment of Share Dividends and Splits

Litigation has arisen over the proper classification of share distributions as principal or as income for trust or fiduciary administration purposes. In most of these situations, the intention of the creator of the interest, if clearly expressed, controls.

VI. THE STATUTORY SCHEME OF MANAGEMENT AND CONTROL

A. THE STATUTORY SCHEME IN GENERAL

1. Shareholders

Shareholders are the ultimate owners of the corporation. Because of the separation of ownership and control, they have only limited power of management and control. Their power is exercised indirectly through the election or removal of directors.

2. Directors

Directors have general powers of management and control. In large, publicly held corporations, they oversee the management rather than actually managing.

3. Officers

In theory, officers carry out directors' decisions rather than make policy decisions though officers may be delegated decision-making authority and have some inherent power.

a. In publicly held corporations, officers in fact exercise virtually complete control over day-to-day matters.

b. In closely held corporations, the shareholders and directors are also usually the principal officers of the corporation.

B. ATTEMPTS TO VARY THE STATUTORY SCHEME

Attempts to reallocate the corporate powers in ways significantly different from the statutory scheme historically have been viewed with suspicion and many have been held to be against public policy and unenforceable.

1. Common Law Approach

The strict common law approach was that agreements between shareholders that attempted to resolve questions that are the responsibility of the board of directors were against public policy as expressed in the corporation statute and therefore were unenforceable and may be ignored by the other parties to the agreement.

2. Relaxation of Common Law Rule by Courts

Courts early relaxed the strict common law rule where only "slight impingements" were involved that injured no one. Courts are more willing to uphold arrangements that interfere with the discretion of directors where all the shareholders have agreed, but at common law not even unanimous agreement could validate a major impingement on the statutory schemes.

3. Orders and Directions of Majority Shareholders

Directors are not agents of the shareholders and need not follow orders or directions of majority shareholders. The shareholders' only recourse is to elect more compliant directors.

a. At common law directors could be removed only for cause. Under modern statutes directors may be removed without cause, thereby simplifying the problem faced by majority shareholders if directors refuse to follow their wishes.

b. The justification for providing a large degree of directoral independence is that directors have fiduciary duties to the corporation and should have freedom to act to meet their duties.

c. Even though the shareholders may not order the directors to approve a transaction, they may recommend a transaction and urge its approval by the board.

4. Delegation of Duties

Directors may not delegate their entire duties of management to third parties. However, reasonable delegation, which includes a power to review the performance of the manager, has been upheld.

5. Directors' Voting Agreements

Directors may not commit themselves in advance to vote by consensus or in the way a shareholder or other person directs.

6. Testamentary Directions

Directions in wills or trusts that shares owned by the estate or trust shall be voted so as to cause the election of specific persons as officers of the corporation at specified salaries have been held to be unenforceable. Even a direction to testamentary trustees that they elect themselves as directors may give rise to potentially serious conflicts of interest.

C. THE STATUTORY SCHEME AS AN IDEALIZED MODEL

The statutory scheme does not reflect the reality of management in either the large publicly held nor the small closely held corporation. It may, however, approximate reality in "in between" corporations.

1. In the Publicly Held Corporation

In large, publicly held corporations, the professional management establishes business policy; directors may be selected by management or by the incumbent board with their selection ratified by the shareholders. Even the CEO may be selected by management and the outgoing CEO rather than by the board of directors.

2. In the Closely Held Corporation

In the closely held corporation, the owners of the business usually serve as shareholders, directors, and officers. The business may be run completely informally.

D. STATUTORY MODIFICATION OF TRADITIONAL RULES

Many states have adopted statutes that modify to some degree the common law rules set forth above. These statutes fall into two broad categories:

1. Statutes Generally Permitting Modification of the Role of the Board of Directors

The statutes of many states permit any corporation to modify the traditional role of its board of directors by appropriate provision in its articles of incorporation. The provision may permit a corporation to dispense entirely with the board of directors and have the business and affairs managed directly by its shareholders or place restrictions on the discretion of directors.

2. Statutes Applicable Only to Specially Defined Close Corporations

The statutes of about twelve states contain special provisions applicable only to electing close corporations. These statutes permit an electing close corporation, among other things, to dispense entirely with the board of directors, to restrict the discretion of directors, and to permit the business and affairs of the corporation to be conducted as though it were a partnership.

a. A "close corporation" is defined in these statutes, usually as a corporation with less than 35 shareholders.

b. A close corporation elects to become subject to these special statutes by including a provision stating to the effect that "This corporation is an electing close corporation" in its articles of incorporation.

c. One court upheld an agreement under these statutes between the two shareholders in a corporation that the corporation would not enter into transactions or new business without the consent of both shareholders despite the fact that no reference to the agreement appeared in the articles of incorporation and the corporation had not elected close corporation status. The court viewed these omissions as technical and subject to the power of the court to order the articles of incorporation reformed. If this approach is followed, these statutes validate most shareholder agreements in nonelecting corporations.

3. Section 7.32 of the Model Business Corporation Act (1984)

In 1991, the Committee on Corporate Laws broadened the provisions in the MBCA (1984) that appeared to permit limited flexibility in the statutory scheme, and replaced them with a new section 7.32, entitled "Shareholder Agreements."

a. Section 7.32 rejects "the older line of cases" relating to statutory norms and adds an "element of predictability currently absent" from the MBCA (1984).

b. Section 7.32 validates virtually all shareholders' agreements relating to corporate governance and the business arrangement, including:

   1) Governance of the entity;

   2) Allocation of the return from the business, and

   3) Other aspects of the relationships among shareholders, directors, and the corporation.

This is a broad but not universal mandate. Agreements that affect third parties and agreements that violate fundamental principles of public policy may not be validated.

c. The agreement must be unanimously approved by the shareholders; it may appear in the articles of incorporation, the bylaws, or a shareholders' agreement.

d. An agreement under § 7.32 is valid for ten years unless otherwise provided in the agreement. It automatically terminates if the shares of the corporation become publicly traded on a national securities market.

VII. SHAREHOLDERS' MEETINGS, VOTING AND CONTROL ARRANGEMENTS

A. SHAREHOLDERS' MEETINGS

1. Annual Meetings

Annual meetings are required to be held for the purpose of electing directors and conducting other business. The time and place of the annual meeting may be specified in or fixed in accordance with the bylaws. The failure to hold an annual meeting does not affect the validity or continued existence of the corporation. The failure to hold an annual meeting also does not affect the incumbency of sitting directors.

2. **Special Meetings**

All meetings other than the annual meeting are special meetings. Such meetings may be called by the board of directors, and under many state statutes by the President, the holders of a specified number of shares (often 10 per cent), and other persons named in the bylaws.

3. **Notice**

Shareholders who are entitled to vote must be given written notice of annual or special meetings as provided in the statute or in the bylaws. Many statutes require at least ten but not more than fifty days' notice.

a. The purposes of a special meeting must be stated in the notice and the business to be conducted at that meeting is limited to that specified in the notice. No purposes of an annual meeting need be stated and any relevant business may be conducted at such a meeting.

b. Notice may be waived by a written document executed before, at, or after the meeting in question. Notice may also be waived informally, as by attending the meeting.

c. In the absence of statute or SEC regulation, there is no common law requirement that shareholders be permitted to vote on matters not required to be considered by shareholders.

4. **Quorum Requirements**

A quorum is typically a majority of the shares eligible to vote, but many states authorize the quorum to be reduced either without limitation or to a specified fraction. The MBCA (1984) permits the quorum requirement to be reduced without limitation.

a. Shares represented by proxy are deemed present for purposes of a quorum.

b. The majority view is that if a quorum is once present, the meeting may continue even though a faction leaves the meeting in an effort to break the quorum.

5. **Shares Entitled to Vote: Class Voting**

Shares entitled to vote at a meeting include outstanding common shares (except common shares that are expressly made non-voting by the articles of incorporation) and other classes of shares expressly entitled to vote by provision of the articles of incorporation. Classes or series of shares that are generally non-voting may be entitled to vote as separate voting groups on specific matters coming before a meeting.

a. Treasury shares and shares owned by a majority-owned subsidiary of the corporation are not eligible to vote under most state statutes.

b. Classes or series of nonvoting shares may be entitled to vote on specific matters that affect the rights of that class or series in ways specified by statute.

1) Most state statutes define such voting as "class voting." The MBCA (1984) uses the phrase "voting by voting groups" to describe the same concept.

2) Where class voting on a specific matter is required, that matter is approved only if it receives the necessary affirmative votes from shareholders of that class as well as the necessary affirmative votes of all shares entitled to vote generally on matters coming before the meeting.

3) On most matters requiring class voting, the statutes require a supermajority vote.

6. Voting

In most states, the general rule is that a majority of votes at a meeting at which a quorum is present is necessary to adopt a measure. The MBCA (1984) adjusts this requirement so that an action is approved if the affirmative votes exceed the negative votes; this eliminates the negative effect of abstentions. The MBCA (1984) also establishes a plurality vote requirement for the election of directors in order to take into account the possibility of three or more factions competing for directorships.

7. Supermajority Quorum and Voting Requirements

Statutes generally allow the quorum and vote requirements to be increased up to and including unanimity at the election of the corporation. The MBCA (1984) also requires a majority of all outstanding voting shares to approve certain fundamental corporate changes.

8. Action Without a Meeting

Most states permit shareholders to act by unanimous written consent without a meeting. A few states allow a majority of the shareholders to act by written consent, binding the corporation.

9. Multiple or Fractional Votes

The traditional rule is one vote per share but many states now authorize shares with multiple or fractional votes per share. All but a small handful of states authorize nonvoting shares even if they are otherwise one vote per share states.

a. Publicly held corporations with minority interests held by a single family have sometimes created classes of shares with multiple votes per share as an antitakeover device. The family members are the holders of these special voting shares which given them effective voting control over the corporation even though they own a small minority of the outstanding shares. Shares with multiple votes are not themselves transferrable but they may be converted to regular voting shares which may be sold to third persons.

b. The SEC adopted a rule designed to limit the use of such shares in publicly held corporations, but in an important decision the Second Circuit held that this Rule exceeded the powers of the SEC since it did not relate to disclosure matters.

10. Manipulation of Meeting Dates

Directors may be tempted to manipulate the rules with respect to meetings for their own purposes. Early cases hold that such manipulation is permissible, but more recent cases hold that such manipulation may constitute a violation of fiduciary duties.

B. ELIGIBILITY TO VOTE

Eligibility to vote is based on "record ownership" on the "record date."

1. Record Ownership

Corporations traditionally issue certificates representing shares in the name of designated persons and the names and addresses of those persons are recorded in the records of the corporation. That person is called the "record owner."

A person who buys shares from a current shareholder obtains possession of the certificate (along with an executed power of attorney from the old owner) and presents the certificate to the corporation, which cancels the old certificate and issues a new certificate in the name of the purchaser. The purchaser thereby becomes the new record owner.

A person who acquires shares without having them recorded in his name is nevertheless the beneficial owner of those shares. The beneficial owner, as against the record owner, may exercise rights of ownership, is entitled to compel the record owner to vote as the beneficial owner directs, and to turn over dividends, and may compel the record owner to endorse the certificates so that the beneficial owner can become the record owner.

2. Record Date

Eligibility to vote at a meeting is determined by the record ownership on a date set by the board called the "record date." A person acquiring shares after the record date may not vote the shares unless he obtains a proxy appointment in favor of the beneficial owner.

3. Voting List

Many state statutes require a corporate officer to prepare an accurate list of shareholders entitled to vote and have it available for inspection at or for a brief period before the meeting.

4. Miscellaneous Voting Rules

Generally only record owners may vote; exceptions are made in many state statutes for executors, administrators and receivers acting under court appointment. Other fiduciaries, such as trustees, must have shares registered in their names as trustees if they wish to vote.

5. Inspectors of Election

Voting disputes are resolved by inspectors of elections who may have discretionary authority to resolve voting disputes based on the corporate records.

C. CUMULATIVE VOTING

Cumulative voting allows a shareholder to "bunch" all the votes he or she may cast in an election for directors on one or more candidates. Cumulative voting is mandatory in a few states and permissive in other states.

1. Straight Voting

Straight voting allows a shareholder to vote only the number of shares he or she owns for each candidate. In straight voting, a majority of the shares elects all directors and a minority can never elect a single director.

2. Mechanics of Cumulative Voting

In cumulative voting a shareholder with 100 shares and three directors to be elected may give one candidate 300 votes or divide the votes among more than one candidate as the shareholder elects.

3. Advantages and Disadvantages of Cumulative Voting

Cumulative voting allows large minority shareholders to obtain representation on the board of directors. It may also increase factionalism or partisanship on the board.

4. Minimization of Effect of Cumulative Voting

The effect of cumulative voting may be eliminated or minimized by several devices: elimination of the privilege entirely (in most states), reduction of the number of positions to be filled at a single meeting (e.g., reducing the size of the board or dividing it into classes as permitted in most states), removal of a minority director, or "working around" such a director.

D. PROXY VOTING

A proxy appointment is a grant of authority to another (the proxy) to vote shares.

1. Prevalence

Voting by proxy is almost universal in large publicly held corporations and may be used in other corporations where an individual shareholder will not be present in person at a meeting.

2. Formal Requirements

Proxy appointments must be in writing and are usually valid for only 11 months. Under the MBCA (1984) a proxy appointment is valid for whatever period is specified in the appointment form.

3. Revocability

Proxy appointments are usually revocable even if stated to be irrevocable. A revocable appointment is revoked by any inconsistent act by the granter, such as appointing a different person as proxy.

4. Irrevocable Proxy Appointments

A proxy appointment is irrevocable only if it is stated to be irrevocable and is "coupled with an interest" which usually requires a property or financial investment in the shares or in the corporation itself. A purchased vote is generally thought to be against public policy and unenforceable.

E. SHAREHOLDER VOTING AGREEMENTS

1. Scope

Shareholder voting (or "pooling") agreements are valid so long as they deal only with matters within the authority of shareholders.

2. Formal Requirements

No formal requirements are applicable to pooling agreements in most states.

3. Determination of How Pooled Shares Should Be Voted

Voting of pooled shares may be specified in the pooling agreement or may be determined by agreement from time to time with arbitration or similar resolution of dispute provisions applicable in the event of a failure to agree.

4. Enforcement of Pooling Agreements

In many states, pooling agreements are made specifically enforceable or irrevocable proxy provisions in such agreements are themselves made enforceable. In the absence of such provisions, one court simply disqualified noncomplying pooled shares from being voted, a solution that in some situations may defeat the essential purpose of the agreement.

F. VOTING TRUSTS

Voting trusts are a device by which the power to vote may be temporarily but irrevocably severed from the beneficial ownership of shares. Voting trusts are formal arrangements by which shares are registered in the name of one or more voting trustees on the records of the corporation.

1. Common Law Attitude

The common law was hostile to voting trusts, an attitude that has been largely changed by statute and judicial decision.

2. Statutory Requirements

Most statutes require copies of the voting trust agreement to be filed with the corporate records and limit the duration of the voting trust to ten years. Failure to comply with these requirements may make the trust unenforceable in its entirety. An arrangement that has the economic or legal effects of a voting trust must meet these statutory requirements if it is to be enforceable.

3. Uses of Voting Trusts

Voting trusts may be used for a variety of purposes, e.g., preservation of control, assuring stability of management, or protecting interests of corporate creditors.

4. Voting Trusts in Publicly Held Corporations

Voting trusts are often thought to be incompatible with corporate democracy in publicly held corporations, and securities exchanges may refuse to list securities if a voting trust exists with respect to such shares.

5. Powers of Trustees

Some decisions have imposed equitable limitations on the power of trustees to make fundamental changes in the corporation or the rights of the shares without the consent of the beneficial owners.

G. CLASSES OF SHARES AS A VOTING DEVICE

Voting power may be allocated as desired by creating special classes of shares with specified voting rights. Court decisions have broadly validated such devices which are essential planning tools in many closely held corporations.

H. SHARE TRANSFER RESTRICTIONS

Share transfer restrictions are contractual restrictions on the free transferability of shares. The most common kind of restrictions are option or buy/sell agreements that require a shareholder to offer his or her shares to the corporation or to other shareholders at a predetermined price upon the occurrence of specified events. Share transfer restrictions are increasingly the subject of statutory recognition. They serve important functions in several different areas of modern corporate practice.

1. Use in Closely Held Corporations

In the closely held corporation share transfer restrictions typically constitute contractual obligations to offer or sell shares either to the corporation or to other shareholders, or to both successively, on the death or retirement of the shareholder or before she sells or disposes of the shares to other persons.

a. The restriction may take the form of—

1) An option running in favor of the corporation or shareholders to purchase at a designated or computable price shares owned by another shareholder upon the occurrence of a triggering event.

2) A mandatory buy-sell agreement obligating the corporation or shareholders to purchase at a designated or computable price shares owned by another shareholder upon the occurrence of a triggering event.

3) A right of first refusal, giving the corporation or the shareholders an opportunity to meet the best price the shareholder has been able to obtain from third parties before selling to those parties.

b. The choice between these three forms of share transfer restrictions depends on the business needs of the shareholders.

c. Share transfer restrictions enable participants in the venture to decide who may participate in the venture. In effect they achieve the corporate equivalent of the partnership notion of *delectus personae.*

d. Share transfer restrictions ensure a stable management and protect against an unexpected change in the respective proportionate interests of the shareholders which might occur if one shareholder is able to quietly purchase shares of other shareholders.

e. Share transfer restrictions may materially simplify the estate tax problems of a deceased shareholder.

1) If the corporation or other shareholders are obligated to purchase the shares owned by the deceased shareholder (a buy-sell agreement) the estate is assured that a large, illiquid asset will be reduced to cash.

2) Either an option or a buy-sell agreement, if established in good faith, is accepted by the Internal Revenue Service as establishing the value of the shares for Federal estate tax purposes, thereby avoiding disputes with the tax authorities over valuation of closely held shares.

f. Share transfer restrictions may be imposed to ensure the continued availability of the S corporation election, e. g., to ensure that the thirty-five shareholder maximum is not exceeded and that shares are not transferred to an ineligible shareholder which causes the loss of the S corporation election.

g. Share transfer restrictions in the form of buy-sell agreements may be used as a device to resolve deadlocks arising from equal voting power being held by two persons or factions.

2. Use in Publicly Held Corporations

In a publicly held corporation, share transfer restrictions are used to prevent violations of the Federal Securities Act where the corporation has issued unregistered shares pursuant to an exemption which would be lost if the shares are transferred to ineligible persons.

3. Other Uses

Share transfer restrictions may be imposed where there are substantive limitations on who may be a shareholder or where governmental authorities wish to review, and possibly limit, who is participating in the ownership of a business.

4. Strict Construction

Share transfer restrictions are restraints on alienation and many courts have stated that they therefore should be strictly construed. Because share transfer restrictions serve important roles within corporations, a trend toward a more liberal approach appears to be developing.

5. Permissible Restraints

At common law, the validity of a share transfer restraint depends on whether it "unreasonably restrains or prohibits transferability." An "unreasonable" restraint may be apparent on the face of the restraint or it may be found in the circumstances in which the restraint is applied.

a. The common law view about the enforceability of share transfer restrictions has caused several states to adopt legislation broadening the types of restrictions that may be enforced.

b. Delaware GCL § 202(c), for example, expressly validates restrictions that require the prior consent by the corporation or the holders of a class of securities to a proposed transfer, require the approval of the proposed transferee by the corporation, or prohibit a transfer to designated persons or classes of persons, if such designation "is not manifestly unreasonable." A restriction imposed to insure the continued availability of the S corporation election or any other tax advantage to the corporation is "conclusively presumed" to be for a reasonable purpose.

6. Duration of Restraints

There is no outer limitation on the duration of share transfer restrictions. It is probable that a restriction remains enforceable without regard to the rule against perpetuities or similar notions of "reasonableness" of duration. Share transfer restrictions may terminate:

a. by express agreement of the shareholders involved, or

b. by abandonment or disuse.

7. Formalities and Notice

Proper formalities must be followed when creating valid share transfer restrictions if they are to be binding on persons who may be unaware of them.

a. Most restrictions on transfer appear in the bylaws of the corporation; they may also appear in the articles of incorporation or in a contract between the corporation and shareholders, or among the shareholders themselves.

b. Statutes require that a reference to a restriction be placed or "noted" on the face or back of share certificates subject to the restriction. Article Eight of the Uniform Commercial Code adds that the reference or notation on the shares must be "conspicuous" if the restriction is to be enforceable against a person without actual knowledge of the restriction. However, a person who knows of the valid restriction before she buys the shares is bound by the restriction, whether or not the above procedural requirements have been followed.

8. Traditional Share Transfer Restrictions: Option or Buy–Sell Agreements

By far the most common share transfer restriction is an agreement that upon a triggering event, the shareholder will offer his or her shares to the corporation or to other shareholders. In an option agreement, the offer must be made but the corporation or shareholders are not required to purchase the shares. In a buy/sell agreement, the purchasers are contractually committed to make the purchase.

a. The option or obligation to purchase shares usually runs either to the corporation or to some or all of the shareholders. They may run to "the corporation or other persons (separately, consecutively, or simultaneously)".

b. The price provisions of shareholder option or buy/sell agreements raise the most difficult and important problems in drafting option or buy/sell agreements.

1) Closely held shares by definition have no market or quoted price, and one simply cannot refer to a "fair," "reasonable," or "market" price.

2) Since it usually is impossible to know whose shares will be first offered for sale under such an agreement, the basic goal in establishing such a mechanism is to be as fair as possible.

3) The following methods are widely used to establish a purchase price:

(i) A stated price.

(ii) Book value.

(iii) Capitalization of earnings.

(iv) Best offer by an outsider.

(v) Appraisal or arbitration, either by impartial appraisers or arbitrators, or by directors or other shareholders.

(vi) A percentage of net profits to be paid for a specified number of years following the event which triggers the sale.

c. Any price fixed in the agreement or by periodic negotiation is enforceable in the absence of fraud, overreaching, or breach of fiduciary duty.

d. "Book value" is by far the most popular method of valuation.

1) This value may be computed by a simple division of a balance sheet figure by the number of outstanding shares and tends to increase as the profitability of the business increases.

2) Courts may order adjustments in the calculation of this value to reflect reality and avoid a "blind adherence" to whatever figures are set forth in the books of the corporation.

e. Appraisal of the value of closely held stock is designed to determine the price at which a ready willing and able buyer and seller would agree upon as the sale price of the shares. Prior purchases and sales of the shares, if any, may be influential in making this determination. In the absence of reliable prior sales, appraisal usually is based on a capitalization of estimated future earnings.

f. An appraiser or arbitrator will usually take into account all the various possible methods of valuation. He may consider, for example, (i) book value, (ii) capitalized value, (iii) estimated liquidation value if the assets were sold and (iv) sales prices of shares in isolated transactions in the past. He may take an average of these values, or if three closely agree, may base his valuation on only those three.

g. After the value of the overall business is obtained, a tentative per share value is usually obtained by a simple division by the number of outstanding shares. However, the appraiser or arbitrator may find it appropriate to apply one or more discounts from the tentative per share value in order to reflect lack of marketability, the minority status of the shares in question if they have no chance of sharing in control, and a variety of other factors that may affect the value of the shares.

VIII. DIRECTORS

A. NUMBER

Today, most states permit a board of directors to consist of one or more directors. Historically, three directors were required and a few states retain this requirement. Some states allow boards of one or two directors only where there are one or two shareholders.

B. CHANGES IN THE SIZE OF BOARD OF DIRECTORS

The number of directors may be increased or decreased by amendments to the bylaws, but a decrease does not have the effect of eliminating or shortening the term of any sitting director. Since the directors generally have power to amend bylaws, the board of directors in effect has power to determine its own size under most state statutes.

1. MBCA Limitations

MBCA (1984) § 8.03(b) and the statutes of a few states impose limits on the extent to which a board of directors may utilize its power to amend bylaws to increase or decrease its own size without shareholder approval. The MBCA prohibits an increase or decrease of more than 30 per cent except by action of the shareholders.

a. MBCA (1984) § 8.03(c) permits corporations to create a variable-sized board of directors: the shareholders or the bylaws establish a maximum and minimum size and authorize the board of directors to determine the actual size within those limits from time to time.

b. A variable-size board of directors may be useful in a publicly held corporation subject to the MBCA (1984) because it gives the board of directors needed flexibility in deciding to add one or more specific individuals to the board or not fill one or more vacancies as they occur.

2. Informal Changes

Some cases recognize that bylaws setting the number of directors may be amended informally, e.g. by electing four directors when the bylaws provide for only three directors. This is not a desirable practice since it injects future uncertainty as to the number of directors to be elected and reduces the value of the written bylaws.

C. MEETINGS, QUORUMS, NOTICE, AND RELATED MATTERS

Regular meetings of the board occur at the times specified in the bylaws. Special meetings may be called by the persons specified in the bylaws.

1. Notice

Unlike shareholders' meetings, directors' meetings may occur without notice or with only such notice as provided by the bylaws. The MBCA (1984) requires that special meetings be called upon two days' notice unless a longer or shorter notice is required or permitted by the bylaws. A director waives objection to defects in a notice of meeting if he or she participates in the meeting.

2. Quorum

A quorum consists of a majority of the board of directors unless a higher percentage is required by the bylaws. Exception is made to fill vacancies on the board. The MBCA (1984) also permits the quorum requirement to be reduced to one-third of the directors.

3. Voting

Directors vote on a per capita basis. A majority vote of those present at a meeting where a quorum is present is necessary for the board to act. The bylaws may increase the vote necessary for approval of an action up to and including unanimity.

a. Del. GCL permits certificates of incorporation to provide that some directors may have a fractional vote rather than a per capita one. Presumably fractional votes may mirror the relative shareholdings of individual shareholders.

4. Objection to Notice

A director waives objection to the adequacy of notice of a meeting by attending the meeting, unless he or she attends for the sole purpose of objecting to the transaction of any business and does not participate in the business undertaken at the meeting.

D. COMPENSATION

Directors traditionally serve without compensation but, publicly held corporations usually provide substantial compensation for outside directors.

E. RESIGNATION OF DIRECTORS

The MBCA (1984) permits resignation either immediately or at a future date. Most state statutes do not expressly cover the resignation of directors. In the case of a resignation at a future date, the director may participate in decisions before that date, including the selection of his or her successor.

F. REMOVAL OF DIRECTORS

Directors may be removed by shareholders, with or without cause, under the statutes of most states. Articles of incorporation, however, may limit the power of removal to removal for cause. Removal by judicial action is also authorized under the statutes of some states.

1. Removal by Shareholders Without Cause

The power to remove directors without cause tends to assure fealty by the board to the majority shareholder. Many publicly held corporations have eliminated the power of shareholders to remove directors without cause as a defensive measure against unwanted takeovers. This provision is usually coupled with the staggering of the election of directors.

2. Judicial Removal

Under the statutes of some states, a court may remove a director for cause specified in the statute, upon the petition of a specified percentage of the shareholders. Removal for cause by judicial action is appropriate in at least two types of situations:

a. In a publicly held corporation, a judicial proceeding to remove a director for cause, when the director refuses to resign, may be simpler and less expensive than holding a shareholders' meeting to remove the director, an action that must be preceded by a proxy solicitation.

b. Judicial removal may also be used in a closely held corporation where the director charged with misconduct declines to resign and possesses the voting power as shareholder to prevent his removal.

G. FILLING OF VACANCIES

Vacancies may be filled by either the board of directors or the shareholders. A few states distinguish between filling vacancies (which may be done by the board of directors) and filling newly created directorships (which may be done only by the shareholders).

H. HOLDOVER DIRECTORS

Directors hold office until their successors are qualified. As a result, directors in office upon a deadlock of shareholders remain in office indefinitely.

I. DECISIONS MUST BE MADE AT MEETINGS

The common law permits directors to act only at meetings.

1. Rationale

The rationale was to provide, for the protection of minority shareholders, the benefits of mutual interchange and discussion.

2. Implications

The meeting principle leads to rules prohibiting directors voting by proxy, requiring strict adherence to notice and quorum principles, and prohibiting the seriatim approval by individual directors.

3. Modern Status of the Rule

The rigidity of the common law rule has been relaxed by statute in certain areas: action by informal written consent and telephonic meetings, and by application of principles of estoppel and waiver. But the rule retains some force.

J. DIRECTORS' DISSENT TO ACTIONS

Directors are deemed to have assented to action taken at a meeting at which they are present unless their dissent is duly noted in writing.

1. Avoidance of Liability by Filing Dissent

To avoid liability, a dissenting director must make sure that his or her dissent is noted in the corporate records or a written notice of dissent is filed shortly after the meeting.

2. Resignation

A director who resigns because of objection to a transaction must nevertheless file the required written dissent.

K. RELIANCE ON OPINION OF OTHERS

Depending on the language of the specific state statute, a director may be able to avoid liability in some situations by showing that he or she relied on the opinion of others in good faith.

1. Scope of Protected Reliance

Generally, a reliance defense is not available to a director who has actual knowledge about, or expertise with respect to, the issue in question. Statutes permit reliance on one or more of the following:

a. The written opinion of legal counsel for the corporation (though, as a practical matter, reliable and unqualified written opinions may be difficult to obtain on questionable transactions).

b. Financial reports prepared by the corporation or by its auditors or accountants.

c. Statements by officers or employees of the corporation with respect to matters within their authority.

d. Reports by committees of the board other than committees on which the director serves.

L. COMMITTEES OF THE BOARD OF DIRECTORS

Committees of the board of directors that have power to act on behalf of the full board are authorized by state statutes.

1. Committees Under the Model Business Corporation Act (1984)

The MBCA (1984) authorizes the creation of committees of the board of directors to exercise functions of the board of directors subject to certain specific limitations on the matters that may be resolved by a committee.

2. Executive Committee

An executive committee may make routine business decisions between board meetings.

3. Audit Committee

Audit committees are required in publicly held companies. Composed entirely of non-management directors, audit committees provide a variety of audit-related functions to the corporation.

4. Nominating Committees

A nominating committee composed primarily of non-management directors provides criteria for directors' nominees and may review and recommend board candidates.

5. Compensation Committees

A compensation committee composed entirely of non-management directors provides review of management and directoral compensation.

6. Public Policy Committees

A public policy committee considers non-business related activities of the corporation, such as policies with respect to charitable contributions. The newest of the committees of the board, its use is gradually growing in publicly held corporations.

7. Litigation Committees

When derivative litigation is filed by a shareholder on behalf of the corporation, a litigation committee composed of disinterested directors may be created to review the litigation and determine whether its pursuit is in the best interest of the corporation. Within a broad range courts respect the decision of an independent litigation committee and may dismiss derivative litigation based on the decision of such a committee.

8. Relation of Committees' Role to Management Control

The audit, nominating and compensation committees are particularly important when assessing the balance of power between management and the board of directors in a publicly held corporation. CEOs in the past have tended to dominate boards of directors; the extent to which the board of directors has developed independence from the CEO varies widely from corporation to corporation. As the independence of the board increases, the power and importance of these committees also increases.

M. OTHER COMMITTEES

Boards of directors may also create advisory or strategic planning committees whose function is to render advice or make recommendations to the board of directors. These committees are not covered by the MBCA (1984) statutory provisions relating to committees (since they do not have the power to act on behalf of the board of directors) and may consist of non-director members as well as directors.

IX. OFFICERS

A. STATUTORY DESIGNATIONS OF CORPORATE OFFICERS

State corporation statutes contain only skeletal provisions dealing with corporate officers. The officers of a corporation, and the functions they are to perform, are usually defined in the bylaws or in resolutions adopted by the board of directors rather than by statute.

1. Traditional Statutes

A typical statute of a generation ago merely states that each corporation shall have a president, a treasurer, a secretary, and (usually) one or more vice-presidents.

a. Under these statutes a person may fill two or more offices simultaneously except the offices of president and secretary. This exception apparently was based on the belief that execution of documents required signatures of two officers, one executing the document and the other attesting to the execution.

b. These statutes also grant unlimited authority to the board of directors to create such additional offices as the board deems appropriate.

2. Flexible Modern Statutes

MBCA (1984) and Delaware GCL do not designate any specific officer titles. Each grants the corporation freedom to determine which officers it chooses to have. These statutes are based on the view that little purpose is served by statutorily designated titles and problems of implied or apparent authority may be thereby created.

a. Both statutes recognize that there must be an officer performing the functions usually associated with the office of the corporate secretary under traditional statutes.

b. Both statutes permit any individual to hold two or more offices at the same time without limitation or restriction.

B. NONSTATUTORY OFFICERS

Bylaw provisions, or the board of directors by resolution, may create nonstatutory offices and provide appropriate authority for the holders of such offices.

C. AUTHORITY OF OFFICERS IN GENERAL

Persons dealing with a corporate officer generally must satisfy themselves of the officer's authority.

1. Oral Representations by Officer

As is generally true in agency law, a representation by an agent as to the scope of his or her agency is not binding on the principal.

2. Reliance on Officer's Title

Since corporate officers have only limited inherent authority, reliance on an officer's title is unlikely to provide assurance that a specific act is authorized.

3. Reliance on Certified Resolution

Obtaining a resolution of the board of directors certified by the secretary of the corporation is the traditional method of assurance that the corporation is bound by the officer's action. It makes no difference whether or not the resolution was actually authorized by the board of directors since the corporation is bound by the secretary's certificate unless the third person knows that the resolution is not accurate.

D. INHERENT AUTHORITY OF THE PRESIDENT OR CHIEF EXECUTIVE OFFICER

Laymen often believe that the president of a corporation has wide discretion to enter into not only ordinary business transactions, but extraordinary transactions as well. Most courts have held that this view is erroneous, though most of the cases taking this position are relatively old.

1. Traditional View

The traditional view is that a corporate president has limited authority to bind the corporation only to routine business transactions.

2. Current Trend

The general trend is to broaden the authority of the president or chief executive officer so that it more closely conforms to the general understanding of the public as to the authority of that office. This trend is clearest in cases of publicly held corporations where the board of directors does not itself manage the business and affairs of the corporation.

E. APPARENT AND IMPLIED AUTHORITY OF OFFICERS

Various common law concepts—implied authority, apparent authority, ratification, estoppel and unjust enrichment—may be used to bind the corporation to acts by its officers in specific situations.

F. FIDUCIARY DUTIES OF OFFICERS

Corporate officers and agents owe a fiduciary duty to the corporation of honesty, good faith, and diligence. The scope of an officer's or agent's obligation to the corporation is determined in part by the nature of his employment with the corporation. The duty of subordinate officers or agents is narrower than the analogous duty of a director.

G. OFFICERS' LIABILITY ON CORPORATE OBLIGATIONS

Corporate officers are not liable on corporate obligations in which they participate as agents except in the following circumstances:

1. Express Guarantee

Such a guarantee may have to be in writing under the statute of frauds.

2. Confusion of Roles

An officer may not clearly delineate that he or she is acting as an agent and may therefore become personally liable under agency or estoppel principles.

3. Statutory Liability

A few statutes provide for officer liability for certain types of corporate obligations. The most important is the provision of the Internal Revenue Code that imposes personal liability on officers who are required to collect employee withholding taxes. The Model Business Corporation Act (1984) imposes a duty of care on officers analogous to the duty of care imposed on directors.

4. Personal Participation in Tortious Conduct

A corporate officer is personally liable if he or she personally participates in tortious conduct.

5. Actions in Excess of Authority

A corporate officer may be personally liable on contracts or other obligations entered into in the name of the corporation if the officer exceeds his or her actual authority to bind the corporation. The corporation is bound if the action is within the officer's apparent authority but in that situation may have an action over against the officer for exceeding his or her actual authority.

H. CORPORATE "NOTICE" OR "KNOWLEDGE"

1. General Rule

General principles of agency law determine when the knowledge of an officer is attributed to the corporation.

2. Agent Acting Adversely to Principal

An officers' knowledge may be imputed to the corporation in some circumstances even though he or she is acting adversely to the corporation.

3. Corporate Criminal Responsibility

Generally, a corporation may be held criminally responsible for conduct imputed to it in the same way as any other principal.

I. TENURE OF OFFICERS AND AGENTS

Officers and agents generally serve at the will of the electing or appointing authority.

1. Employment Contracts in General

While election or appointment does not create a contractual right, officers or agents may be given employment contracts. Such a contract gives rise to a claim for breach in the event of a premature termination of the relationship. An employment contract may extend beyond the term of the office.

2. Lifetime Employment Contracts

Lifetime employment contracts are not favored. A claim that such a contract was given to an officer or employee, usually based on parol testimony, is viewed as being inherently improbable.

3. Discharge for Cause

Officers or agents with employment contracts may be discharged for cause. It is generally unnecessary to consider the issue of "cause" if the officer or employee does not have an employment contract.

4. Compensation Patterns

Compensation of officers or agents may be based on earnings or the market performance of the corporation's shares. Officers or agents may also be compensated in shares or in options to purchase shares. They may also receive various kinds of indirect or deferred compensation, some of which may receive favorable income tax treatment.

X. MANAGEMENT OF THE CLOSELY HELD CORPORATION

A. CHARACTERISTICS OF A CLOSELY HELD CORPORATION

A "close corporation" or "closely held corporation" is a corporation with a few shareholders. In such a corporation unique management problems arise because of the relationship that necessarily exists among shareholders.

1. Shareholder Participation in Management

The management of a close corporation is usually associated with the principal shareholders, or with all the shareholders.

a. The majority shareholders may name the board of directors, and through them, the officers and employees.

b. Usually they name themselves to all important (and the highest salary-paying) positions.

c. Normally, minority shareholders also wish to participate in management. A major aspect of close corporation planning is to develop devices that assure minority shareholders of meaningful participation in management.

2. Informality of Management

The controlling shareholders usually operate the business in an informal manner, more as though it were a partnership rather than a corporation.

a. Shareholders' meetings are held infrequently if at all.

b. Formal directors meetings are also held infrequently. In many closely held corporations, meetings consist of informal discussions or simple decision making by the majority shareholder.

c. The attorney for a closely held corporation should assure that minimal records are kept.

d. Closely held corporations are often called "incorporated partnerships."

3. Lack of Market for Minority Shares

Since a close corporation has only a relatively small number of shareholders, there is no public trading in, or public market for, its shares.

a. Potential purchasers of minority blocks of shares usually must be found among the corporation, present shareholders, or rarely, among outsiders willing "to take a gamble."

b. The market for minority blocks of closely held shares is at worst non-existent and at best a buyer's market. There is little or no incentive for buyers to offer reasonable prices for shares, though minority shares may have some value because they constitute a nuisance and may serve as the basis for litigation.

4. Dividend Policy

In a closely held corporation dividend policies may be established that favor controlling shareholders. The controlling shareholders may divert the bulk of the corporate income to themselves by adopting a "no dividend" policy, refusing to employ the minority shareholders in the business, and paying the bulk of the earnings to themselves in the form of salaries, bonuses, pension fund contributions, and fringe benefits (free use of automobiles, country club memberships and the like).

a. In extreme cases these policies permit the minority shareholders no return at all on their investment and interest in the corporation.

b. These policies may be adopted in an effort to "soften up" minority shareholders and persuade them to sell their shares at a low price either to the corporation or to other shareholders.

c. This tactic is referred to as a "freeze out."

d. Freeze out tactics may lead to litigation seeking the payment of a dividend or other relief against the controlling shareholders.

5. Widespread Use of Shareholders' Agreements

In closely held corporations there is widespread use of shareholders' agreements whenever there is more than one shareholder in the corporation.

a. An important function of shareholders' agreements is to assure that minority shareholders may be able to dispose of their shares when they die, retire, or wish to leave the corporation. This is usually effected by the execution of a binding buy/sell agreement.

b. A second important function of shareholders' agreements is to assure minority shareholders that they will have an effective voice in corporate affairs.

c. A third important function of shareholders' agreements is to assure minority shareholders that they will be entitled to a financial return from their investment.

  1) An employment contract with the corporation is the simplest device to assure a financial return.

  2) In the absence of an effective contract, the position of minority shareholder within the corporations is totally dependent on the good will of the controlling shareholders.

d. A final important function of shareholders' agreements is to facilitate estate planning for shareholders.

6. No Compulsory Dissolution

Minority shareholders in a close corporation ordinarily have no power to force a dissolution of the corporation. In this respect a close corporation differs significantly from a partnership, in which each partner possesses an inherent power to dissolve the partnership.

7. Freezeouts

In the absence of a binding shareholders agreement, the foregoing factors may readily result in a freezeout of minority shareholders in which they are on the one hand "locked in" the corporation for a long period of time, and on the other hand excluded from management and deprived of any return on their investment.

a. Over a period of time in which deaths, withdrawals, or fallings out are likely, the possibility that adverse and hostile interests will develop within a closely held corporation is fairly high.

b. Advance planning, usually in the form of a buy/sell agreement, may avoid freezeouts, though no such planning takes place in many corporations.

B. DEVICES THAT PERMIT SHARING OF CONTROL IN CLOSELY HELD CORPORATIONS

In the absence of special statutory treatment of closely held corporations, such corporations must establish control devices through the use of traditional and accepted shareholder control techniques. Such techniques include increased voting and quorum requirements in order to give minority interests effectively a veto power. This veto power may be applicable at the shareholder level, at the board of directors level, or at both levels. Increased quorum and/or voting requirements are usually referred to as supermajority requirements.

C. JUDICIAL RECOGNITION OF THE SPECIAL PROBLEMS OF THE CLOSE CORPORATION

The traditional view was that all corporations should be governed by essentially the rules set forth in the corporation statutes, and that no special rules could or should be developed for the closely held corporation.

1. Legal Problems Created by the Traditional View

In most small closely held corporations, corporate matters are likely to be resolved by unanimous consent with a minimum of formality and no regard for statutory niceties. Meetings may be held infrequently, if at all, corporate records may be kept on an erratic basis, and decisions may be made without any recognition that the corporation theoretically consists of different layers with different rights and responsibilities.

a. The failure to follow corporate formalities creates several possible legal issues:

1) Will the ignoring of corporate formalities result in the corporate veil being "pierced" and the participants being held personally liable on corporate obligations?

2) Will the participants' control arrangement be unenforceable because it violates the "statutory norms"?

3) Will decisions that are made informally and without following the statutory norms be binding on the corporation and third parties?

2. Early Challenges to Traditional Views

Beginning in the 1960s this traditional view was challenged by several individual judicial opinions urging a more relaxed and more realistic treatment of the closely held corporation. These views usually urged:

a. Application of a greatly broadened fiduciary duty between shareholders in a closely held corporation;

b. Relaxation of the traditional statutory norms to permit more flexible control arrangements within the closely held corporation;

c. Recognition that closely held corporations were "incorporated partnerships," and the selective application of partnership principles, including freedom to dissolve, to closely held corporations; and

d. Enactment of statutory provisions designed expressly for the benefit of closely held corporations.

3. Judicial Acceptance in Illinois and Massachusetts

Strong and influential decisions favoring special judicial treatment of closely held corporations are *Galler v. Galler*, and *Donahue v. Rodd Electrotype Co.*. Decisions in a number of other states have accepted the general principles of these two leading cases.

D. STATUTES RELATING TO MANAGEMENT OF CLOSE CORPORATIONS

Many states have adopted statutes relating to management problems within the closely held corporation.

1. General Statutes Permitting the Elimination of the Board of Directors

The statutes of many states permit any corporation to modify the traditional role of its board of directors by appropriate provision in its articles of incorporation. The provision may permit a corporation to dispense entirely with the board of directors and have the business and affairs managed directly by its shareholders or place restrictions on the discretion of directors. As a practical matter, this option is almost solely utilized by closely held corporations.

2. Statutes Applicable Only to Specially Defined and Electing Close Corporations

The statutes of about 12 states contain special statutes applicable only to electing close corporations.

a. These statutes are intended to permit electing close corporations to manage their affairs with essentially the same freedom as if they were partnerships and to simplify problems of dissension, deadlock, and shareholder succession.

b. A definition of an eligible corporation is usually part of the statute.

c. A corporation that meets the statutory qualifications may become a statutory close corporation by including in its articles of incorporation a statement to the effect that "this corporation is a statutory close corporation."

d. Special state statutes relating to close corporations generally provide the following:

1) Agreements that restrict the discretion of directors are specifically validated if they are set forth in the articles of incorporation.

2) The corporation may elect to dispense with the board of directors entirely.

3) The corporation may elect to conduct its affairs "as though it were a partnership."

4) The corporation may eliminate bylaws, broaden the power to create share transfer restrictions, and in some states, permit the creation of mandatory buyouts upon the death of a shareholder.

5) Special provisions to resolve dissension or deadlock are provided, such as the appointment of receivers, custodians or provisional directors.

e. In *Zion v. Kurtz,* the court upheld an agreement between two shareholders that the corporation would not enter into transactions or new business without the consent of both shareholders (an option permitted under the Delaware special close corporation statute) despite the fact that no reference to the agreement appeared in the articles of incorporation and the corporation had not elected close corporation status. The court viewed these omissions as technical and subject to the power of the court to order the articles of incorporation reformed.

f. Even though a number of states have adopted special close corporation statutes and this development has been widely praised, the actual experience in several states, including California, Delaware, Florida and Texas, indicates that this election is not widely used.

3. Section 7.32 of the Model Business Corporation Act (1984)

In 1991, the Committee on Corporate Laws added a new section 7.32, entitled "Shareholder Agreements" which provides significant freedom to closely held corporations to organize in any way they wish.

a. Section 7.32 validates virtually all shareholders' agreements relating to corporate governance and business arrangements, including agreements relating to:

1) Governance of the entity;

2) Allocation of the return from the business; and

3) Other aspects of the relationships among shareholders, directors, and the corporation.

b. Section 7.32 creates a broad but not universal mandate to customize the management of closely held corporations. Agreements that affect third parties and agreements that violate fundamental principles of public policy may not be validated. For example, a provision in a shareholders' agreement that the directors have no duty of care or loyalty is not within the scope of section 7.32.

c. The agreement under § 7.32 must be unanimously approved by the shareholders; it may appear in the articles of incorporation, the bylaws, or a shareholders' agreement. Its existence must appear on the share certificates or information statements reflecting shares.

d. An agreement under § 7.32 is valid for 10 years unless otherwise provided in the agreement. It automatically terminates if the shares of the corporation become publicly traded on a national securities exchange or public market for securities.

e. The existence or performance of an agreement under § 7.32 is not a ground for imposing personal liability on a shareholder for the acts or debts of a corporation.

E. DISSENSION AND DEADLOCK WITHIN THE CLOSE CORPORATION

Many small corporations at one time or another in their history are wracked by dissension or deadlock; advance planning may help to reduce or eliminate such disagreeable incidents.

1. Dissension

"Dissension" refers to internal squabbles, fights, or disagreements typically in a corporation which has a clearly defined controlling shareholder or shareholders.

2. Deadlock

"Deadlock" refers to control arrangements that effectively prevent the corporation from acting or making decisions.

a. Deadlocks typically involve two factions or two shareholders in a control structure that does not permit either faction to have effective working control. It is possible for a corporation with more than two factions to become deadlocked if each individual shareholder and/or director has a veto power but that is much less common.

b. A corporation is potentially subject to deadlock if:

1) Two factions own exactly fifty per cent of the outstanding shares;

2) There are an even number of directors, and two factions each have the power to select the same number; or

3) A minority shareholder has retained a veto power in one of the ways previously described.

c. A deadlock may occur either at the shareholders' level or at the directors' level.

1) If the shareholders are deadlocked, the corporation may continue to operate under the guidance of the board of directors in office when the deadlock arose.

2) A deadlock at the directoral level may prevent the corporation from functioning at all, though more commonly the president or general manager may continue to operate the business, often to the complete exclusion of the other faction.

3. Voluntary Buyouts as a Remedy for Dissension or Deadlock

The most practical solution for a corporation that is deadlocked or wracked with dissension is usually for one faction to buy out the other. It sometimes may be possible for parties to work out a sale after the dissension or deadlock has arisen, but the more logical solution is to address the problem of possible dissension or deadlock when the parties are in amity and to work out an agreement in advance by which one faction buys out the other at a fair price in the event a serious disagreement arises.

4. Fiduciary Duties Among Shareholders as a Remedy for Unfair Treatment of Minority Shareholders

The traditional view is that shareholders have no fiduciary duty as such to each other, and that transactions that are unfair to minority shareholders cannot generally be attacked as a breach of a duty of loyalty or good faith owed by a majority shareholder.

a. Massachusetts has developed a fiduciary duty theory in this context. In *Donahue v. Rodd Electrotype Co.,* the court analogized the close corporation to a partnership and held that a "strict" fiduciary duty existed and that controlling shareholders owed a duty of the "utmost good faith and loyalty" to the minority.

b. The *Donahue* opinion has been widely cited and relied upon by courts in other jurisdictions. To the extent a tort of "freeze out" is recognized, it can be traced to the *Donahue* case.

c. *Donahue* was followed in Massachusetts by *Wilkes v. Springside Nursing Home, Inc.*, in which the court ordered reinstatement of a minority shareholder to the corporate payroll after he had been fired in violation of his expectation. The *Wilkes* court recognized, however, that the controlling faction needed "some room to maneuver" and that that faction's "selfish interest" should be balanced against its fiduciary duty.

d. Massachusetts courts continue to struggle to establish the line between appropriate majority action and breaches of the *Donahue* fiduciary duty.

5. Minority Dissolution Provisions

The Model Close Corporation Supplement, and the statutes of a few states permit corporations to elect special dissolution provisions that permit a minority shareholder to compel the dissolution of a corporation. In the absence of specific statutory authorization, a minority dissolution right may be created through the use of a voting trust or other device that permits the minority shareholder to compel the majority shareholder to vote in favor of dissolution under specified circumstances.

F. THE TRADITIONAL JUDICIAL REMEDY FOR DISSENSION OR DEADLOCK: INVOLUNTARY DISSOLUTION

The traditional remedy for problems of dissension and deadlock when no buyout has been agreed to is involuntary dissolution by judicial decree at the request of a shareholder. In order to obtain dissolution a petitioning shareholder must establish that statutory grounds for dissolution have been met. In addition, the court may withhold this remedy on equitable grounds.

1. Statutory Grounds for Involuntary Dissolution

Generally, dissolution is not available to a shareholder unless he or she can establish that the situation comes within the precise language of the statute.

a. There is no general common law right of involuntary dissolution and statutes authorizing this remedy are strictly construed.

b. Even if statutory grounds for involuntary dissolution are established, courts generally view that remedy as being discretionary with the court rather than automatic.

2. A New Alternative Remedy: Judicially Ordered Buyouts

A significant modern trend is the increased recognition that courts may order a buyout of shares rather than involuntary dissolution in order to resolve problems of dissension or deadlock. Buyout orders are specifically authorized by statute in some states, and may be viewed as part of the inherent judicial power in states where they do not have express statutory sanction.

a. In a substantial number of cases since 1970, courts have ordered a buyout remedy in involuntary dissolution suits even when not expressly authorized by statute.

b. In 1991, MBCA (1984) § 14.34 was added to the Model Act expressly authorizing an involuntary buyout of shares owned by a shareholder who has filed a petition for involuntary dissolution under § 14.30.

G. ALTERNATIVE REMEDIES FOR DISSENSION AND DEADLOCK

A variety of alternative remedies short of dissolution exist. Some are authorized specifically by special close corporation statutes; some may be part of a court's inherent discretion to fashion an appropriate remedy in litigation generally.

1. Receiverships

Some statutes contemplate the appointment of a receiver as an interim measure before dissolution is decreed; courts in some states may appoint receivers for deadlocked corporations by specific statutory authority.

2. Custodians

Some state statutes authorize courts to appoint custodians for corporations that are deadlocked or otherwise threatened with irreparable injury. A custodian differs from a receivership in that the goal is to continue the business of the corporation and not to liquidate it or distribute its assets. If a custodian is appointed and the cause of the deadlock or irreparable injury is not eliminated, a custodianship may be converted into a receivership.

3. Provisional Directors

A provisional director is an impartial person appointed by a court to serve on the board of directors of a corporation if the board itself is so divided that it cannot make decisions "with the consequence that the business and affairs of the corporation can no longer be conducted to the advantage of the shareholders generally."

a. Provisional directors are usually authorized only in the case of corporations that have elected close corporation status.

b. A provisional director may be removed by majority vote of the voting shareholders.

4. Election of Remedies

1. While shareholders may not wish to have outsiders take over the business of the corporation through a receivership or custodian, or participate in management as a provisional director, these remedies generally may not be disclaimed in advance by a corporation.

H. ARBITRATION AS AN ALTERNATIVE TO JUDICIAL INTERVENTION

Mandatory arbitration is sometimes used as a device to remedy a deadlock short of dissolution.

1. What Types of Disputes are Arbitrable?

Modern arbitration statutes contain virtually no restrictions on the types of disputes that may be resolved pursuant to arbitration.

a. In considering the desirability of arbitration, two questions should be considered:

1) What kinds of controversies is the arbitrator likely to face?

2) What kinds of solutions will he or she be permitted to adopt?

b. Many disputes leading to deadlock in a closely held corporation involve personality conflicts or broad differences in policy. An arbitrator may have no criteria for resolving such disputes, and even if he or she does resolve a specific dispute, it is unlikely that the decision will cure the basic disagreement which led to the original deadlock.

c. Ultimately, if deep personal or policy conflicts continue, dissolution appears to be the only suitable remedy because arbitration cannot cure the root cause of the disagreement.

2. The Advantages of Arbitration

The advantages of arbitration are speed, cheapness, informality (as contrasted with a court proceeding), and the prospect of a decision by a person with knowledge and experience in business affairs. Where the reason for deadlock is a question not involving basic personal or policy matters, arbitration may satisfactorily resolve a dispute and permit the corporation to continue.

XI. MANAGEMENT IN THE PUBLICLY HELD CORPORATION

A. CONTROL OF THE PUBLICLY HELD CORPORATION

The large publicly held corporation bears little relationship to the theoretical structure of state business corporation acts.

1. Limited Role of Small Shareholders

a. The number of voting shares in the large publicly held corporation is so large that the votes of any single noninstitutional shareholder are largely irrelevant on any issue.

b. Shareholders who are dissatisfied with management or the performance of the corporation's shares may readily sell the shares on the public market.

2. The Increased Significance of Institutional Investors

For many years the small shareholder was thought to epitomize the public shareholder. However, largely since World War II the institutional investor has grown tremendously in importance.

a. Institutional investors include pension and retirement funds, insurance companies, banks, foundations and university endowments, and investment companies.

b. As of 1991, institutional investors own more than 50 per cent of all shares listed on the New York Stock Exchange. In many listed companies, a relatively small number of institutional investors—under 30—own an absolute majority all outstanding voting shares.

c. Despite the potential voting power of institutional investors, historically they have not been active in the control and management of publicly held corporations. They have viewed their roles to be as passive investors.

d. This passive attitude appears to be changing as some institutional investors have taken increased interest in issues of corporate governance, particularly those that affect financial returns to the investors.

3. Who Selects the Directors

The directors are selected by the determination of who is put on the management's slate of candidates. Shareholders in effect ratify this selection by their vote.

a. Historically, the slate of candidates was prepared or approved by the Chief Executive Officer (CEO). This practice permitted the CEO to "stack" the board of directors with friends.

b. This practice is gradually changing as the use of nominating committees has grown.

4. Who Runs the Business

Professional management, not the board of directors, manages the business. Directors serve a much more limited role of oversight of management's performance.

B. WHAT DOES THE BOARD OF DIRECTORS LOOK LIKE AND WHAT DOES IT DO?

A great deal of attention has been focused on the board of directors of publicly held corporations. Historically, the board was viewed largely as a rubber stamp for management. While that was at least partially true at some earlier time, the modern board of directors is largely composed of persons unaffiliated with incumbent management and may act independently of the management on many matters.

1. **Composition of Boards of Directors in Publicly Held Corporations**
The board of directors consists partly of management representatives ("inside directors") and partly of outsiders who are not officers or employees of the corporation and whose detailed knowledge of corporate affairs must of necessity be limited ("outside directors").

    a. The Chief Executive Officer (CEO) is usually the chairman of the board of directors, though in some corporations these positions may be held by different people.

    b. The modern trend is strongly in the direction of having a majority of the board of directors consist of outside directors who are not affiliated with the corporation.

2. **Why Is the Use of Outside Directors Encouraged?**
Outside directors serve on important committees—auditing, compensation, and nominating. They also provide other important corporate governance roles.

3. **The Role of the Board of Directors in Selecting the CEO**
Selection of the CEO, review of his or her performance, and removal where performance is unsatisfactory are the most important functions of the board of directors.

    a. In many publicly held corporations, the management tends to be a self-perpetuating body. Incumbent management usually recommends the successor to the incumbent CEO, and that recommendation is usually accepted.

    b. The willingness of the board to accept management recommendations depends in part on the success of the retiring CEO and in part the relationship between that person and the members of the board of directors.

    c. Major shareholders may also have an important voice in the selection, review and replacement of the CEO, but the ultimate responsibility rests with the board of directors.

    d. Where there is no single controlling block of shares, there always remains the possibility that a majority of the board of directors may agree to remove the CEO over his or her objection. Such actions occur rarely but are becoming increasingly common during the 1990s.

4. **The Role of the Board of Directors in Overseeing Management**
The basic role of the board of directors is to oversee the managers of the corporation. The board serves as a sounding board, a reviewer of compensation levels, and a monitor of management.

C. THE ROLE OF SHAREHOLDERS IN THE PUBLIC CORPORATION

1. Berle and Means View

a. Berle and Means in 1933 viewed shareholders as a large group of disorganized small holders who tended to vote blindly in favor of management.

b. This view, arguably valid during earlier parts of the Twentieth Century, is now generally viewed as naive and incomplete.

2. Limitations on Management Control: Law and Economics

The law and economics movement argued that the Berle and Means thesis was fundamentally flawed. Management control, was not limitless, it was argued, and the current system works pretty well.

a. The divergence in interest between managers and shareholders is an illustration of the phenomenon that arises naturally whenever one person has the responsibility to manage assets on behalf of other persons.

b. Shareholders may reduce agency costs by monitoring the performance of managers or by devising incentive systems that encourage managers to maximize the wealth of shareholders.

1) The mandatory disclosure requirements of the SEC permit monitoring; the use of independent auditors to report to the shareholders is another type of monitoring.

2) Incentive devices that link managers' natural self interest to shareholder wealth maximization include stock purchase plans, stock option plans, bonuses based on overall profitability, and the like.

c. There are also significant market forces that work in the direction of assuring that management devotes its efforts to maximization of shareholder wealth rather than their personal wealth.

1) These markets include a market for managerial talent, the market for corporate control, and the securities market itself.

3. The Increasing Role of Institutional Investors

a. While institutional investors traditionally support management, the late 1980s and 1990s have seen increased activism on behalf of shareholders' interests by many institutional investors.

b. Many institutional investors owe fiduciary duties to other persons, e.g. to pensioners or policy holders. These duties may require some institutional investors to take short term profits rather than adopt a longer view more traditionally associated with shareholders.

c. The SEC is considering amendments to its proxy regulations to make it easier for institutional investors to communicate with each other and to influence management.

4. Shareholder Wealth Maximization as Exclusive Goal of Corporation

a. The traditional view is that the objective of a corporation is to maximize the wealth of its shareholders.

b. Statutes in approximately thirty states allow the board of directors and management to take into account the interests of "constituencies" other than shareholders in making decisions on behalf of the corporation. Such constituencies may include employees, customers, suppliers, creditors, and communities or states in which the corporation has facilities or plants. These constituencies are sometimes called "stakeholders."

c. These statutes were enacted, usually without extensive consideration, by state legislatures in response to fears of corporations incorporated in those states that they might be subject to unwanted takeover bids.

1) Management of threatened companies believed that these statutes might permit them to turn down and defeat cash tender offers at above-market prices by relying on the interests of other stakeholders.

2) There have been no reported instances of the actual application of these statutes.

d. These statutes have been widely criticized from several different perspectives. They have also had their defenders.

1) Law and economics scholars have criticized these statutes because in their eyes economic efficiency is maximized if the managers are required to maximize the return to the "residual claimants," i.e. the shareholders. They also argue that stakeholders may usually protect themselves by contract.

2) The Committee on Corporate Laws and the Business Roundtable have criticized these statutes because they increase uncertainty and raise the specter of possible lawsuits brought by other stakeholders who are not protected by director or management decisions.

e. Shareholder wealth maximization is itself a difficult goal to apply in light of the diversity of shareholders, the ease with which shares may be traded, the diversification of investors' portfolios, and the development of options and so-called derivative securities.

f. Management may have incentives to further its interests rather than those of shareholders.

 1) To some extent, compensation devices tied to share prices may outweigh these selfish incentives.

 2) Other sources that may counteract management-oriented incentives include the militancy of some institutional investors, the growth in the number of outside directors, the influence of bankers and other sources of lendable funds, the "market for corporate control" and shareholder derivative litigation to test the propriety of management conduct.

D. NOMINEE AND BOOK ENTRY REGISTRATION AND TRADING

a. Most shares today are registered in the names of nominees or intermediaries who are not the beneficial owners of the shares.

b. Institutional investors routinely use nominees as record holders of shares to simplify subsequent transfers of shares. Nominees are usually partnerships with names such as "Abel and Company."

c. Individuals who own shares may become record owners, but increasingly they permit their shares to be held by book entry. The record owner of such shares is a nominee for a clearing house. The shares owned by a brokerage firm and its customers are reflected in the books of the clearing house, and the shares owned by individual customers are reflected in the books of the brokerage firm. The beneficial owner receives only a statement from the brokerage firm showing his or her ownership of shares.

d. Securities transactions are usually executed today simply by book entries through a clearing house rather than through the physical transfer of certificates. The clearing house settles up with each brokerage firm on a daily basis without any change in the registration of the shares. The principal clearing house is Depository Trust Company (DTC).

e. Most shares that are widely traded are held in book entry form today.

f. In the book entry system, dividends or other distributions are wired by the issuer to DTC and in turn wired to member brokerage firms and banks. As a result, dividends on book entry shares appear on the customer's statement as having been credited on the payable date for the dividend or distribution.

g. The book entry system is highly efficient and has permitted the securities industry to handle trading days involving hundreds of millions of shares per day.

1) One potential disadvantage is that it places two intermediaries—DTC and the brokerage firm—between the issuer and the beneficial owner.

2) Book entry also complicates the distribution of proxy statements, annual reports, and other documents by the issuer to beneficial owners, particularly those requiring action in a brief period of time.

XII. SEC DISCLOSURE REQUIREMENTS AND PROXY REGULATION

Publicly held corporations have obligations to disclose information to shareholders and to members of the general public. These disclosure obligations are closely tied in with the regulation of the solicitation of proxies by these corporations. Most modern law in these areas is of federal rather than state origin. Periodic reporting requirements are set forth in the Securities Exchange Act of 1934. The basic provision of federal law relating to proxy solicitation is section 14(a) of the 1934 Act.

A. CORPORATIONS SUBJECT TO FEDERAL DISCLOSURE AND PROXY REGULATION RULES

Corporations that are required to register under section 12 of the Securities Exchange Act of 1934 are subject to the public reporting requirements that constitute the basic disclosure rules for all publicly held corporations. The SEC proxy regulations, and many other detailed provisions of the Securities Act of 1934, are applicable only to corporations that must register under section 12.

1. Registration Under Section 12 of the 1934 Act

Corporations required to register under section 12 of the Securities Exchange Act of 1934 are corporations (1) having securities that are registered on a national securities exchange, or (2) having assets in excess of $5,000,000 and a class of equity securities held of record by 500 persons or more.

2. Termination of Registration

Once registered, a corporation remains subject to the 1934 Act requirements until (1) the number of shareholders of the class is reduced below 300 or (2) assets are reduced below $5,000,000 and the number of shareholders of the class is reduced below 500.

B. PUBLIC DISCLOSURE REQUIREMENTS

Companies subject to the SEC reporting and disclosure requirements are obligated to file periodic reports with the SEC. These reports, which are subject to detailed formal requirements by SEC regulation, are designed to update on a continuing basis the information that is publicly available about the company. The most important of these forms are the 10–K, 10–Q, and 8–K.

C. FEDERAL REGULATION OF PROXIES

1. Constitutional Basis of Regulation

The Securities Exchange Act of 1934 requirements are based on the regulation of interstate commerce and the use of the mails.

2. Proxy Statements and Annual Reports

SEC proxy regulations require annual proxy statements and annual reports containing specified information. These reports are an important channel of communication to shareholders.

3. Form of Proxy Appointments

SEC regulations prevent undated or post-dated proxies, require shareholders to be given voting options on the selection of directors and other issues, and so forth.

4. Presolicitation Review

The SEC reviews proxy documents on a 10–day review process that does not involve in-depth analysis. The SEC does not pass upon the accuracy or adequacy of the disclosure in this review.

5. What is a Solicitation?

The concepts of "proxy" and "solicitation" are broadly construed to favor regulation in close cases.

6. Exempt Proxy Solicitations

SEC has promulgated exemptions for solicitations that do not require the protection of the Act, e.g. those involving less than ten persons.

7. Corporations That Do Not Solicit Proxies

Corporations usually must solicit proxies in order to assure the presence of a quorum. Some corporations do not solicit proxies because owners of a few blocks of shares may constitute a quorum. Section 14(f) of the Securities Exchange Act requires such corporations to distribute the same information they would have to distribute if they did solicit proxies.

8. Problems Created by Book Entry and Nominee Holdings

These registration practices create problems for the disclosure system.

a. Brokers and dealers are obligated to "pass through" the voting decision to the beneficial owners, and give them copies of the disclosure documents.

b. The SEC requires brokers and dealers to provide issuers with the names of beneficial owners (who do not object to the disclosure) to permit direct communication. Beneficial owners who do not object are referred to as NOBOs.

c. These devices apparently work reasonably efficiently.

d. The MBCA (1984) proposes an alternative device that permits the corporations to establish procedures to treat beneficial owners of shares as traditional record holders.

9. Shareholder Proposals

Rule 14a–8 of the SEC regulations requires corporations to include certain shareholder proposals in proxy statements so that the proposals may be voted upon by the shareholders.

a. Prerequisites

A shareholder who beneficially owns one per cent of outstanding shares or shares with a market value of at least $1,000 for 12 months may submit not more than one proposal for any proxy solicitation. Moreover, repetitive proposals in subsequent years are limited, depending on the support obtained from shareholders on the previous solicitation.

b. Proposals That May Be Omitted

Rule 14a–8 contains over a dozen carefully described exclusions. In addition, the SEC has developed a "common law" of shareholders proposals that flesh out and apply these exclusions.

c. Practical Importance of Shareholder Proposal Requirement

While most shareholder proposals are defeated, the device may serve a useful communication link with management. Institutional investors have used shareholder proposals in a number of instances in recent years to good advantage.

D. FALSE AND MISLEADING STATEMENTS IN PROXY SOLICITATIONS

Rule 14a–9 forbids false or misleading statements in proxy solicitations. Both affirmative misstatements and omissions are covered.

1. Private Cause of Action

The United States Supreme Court held in *J. I. Case v. Borak* that private causes of action exist for violations of rule 14a–9.

2. Nature of Post-*Borak* Supreme Court Litigation

Since *Borak,* the Supreme Court has decided three important cases that have shaped rule 14a–9 litigation. Under these cases, successful plaintiffs may have their attorneys fees paid; however, the definition of a "material" misrepresentation has been tightened to make summary judgments on the pleadings less likely. Further, while the plaintiff does not have to show that specific shareholders relied on the misrepresentation in their voting, a misrepresentation is actionable only if the vote of the solicited shares is necessary for the action to be approved.

3. Remedies in Rule 14a–9 Cases

Where a substantial transaction has been approved on the basis of a proxy statement containing material misrepresentations, courts have difficulty devising a reasonable remedy.

XIII. PROXY FIGHTS, TENDER OFFERS AND OTHER STRUGGLES FOR CONTROL

A. PRINCIPAL FORMS OF CONTESTS FOR CONTROL

Contests for control may take a variety of forms: proxy fights, cash tender offers, exchange offers, "bear hug" transactions, unconventional tender offers, going private transactions, and leveraged buyouts.

1. Proxy Fights or Proxy Contests

In a proxy fight a nonmanagement faction (the "insurgents") seek to obtain sufficient proxies from other shareholders to oust incumbent management. Management usually conducts a competing proxy solicitation. (See part XIII B.)

2. Purchase Type Takeovers

In purchase type takeovers, the outside aggressor (sometimes called the "offeror") makes a public offer to purchase shares directly from tendering shareholders, bypassing the board of directors. The ultimate goal of the aggressor is usually to obtain all of the shares of the target corporation, and, if so, a second transaction to acquire the balance of the outstanding shares shortly follows a successful acquisition of control.

3. Exchange Offers

An exchange offer differs from a cash tender offer in that the aggressor offers a package of its own securities—often a combination of cash, debt, and equity securities—for the securities of the target corporation.

4. "Bear Hug" Transactions

A "bear hug" is a forced embrace of the directors of a target corporation to persuade them to accept voluntarily a merger or other amalgamation which permits the takeover to proceed.

5. Unconventional Purchase–Type Offers

Several cases have involved attempts to acquire a majority of the target's shares by unconventional means such as the private negotiated purchases of shares owned by institutional investors or substantial minority shareholders or by a campaign of open market purchases.

B. PROXY CONTESTS

A proxy contest is simply an election campaign to persuade shareholders to vote out incumbent management.

1. Modern Uses of the Proxy Contest

The classic proxy fight was designed to wrest control away from the incumbent management by an insurgent faction. While some modern proxy fights follow this pattern, most modern proxy fights involve different goals.

a. In some tender offers, the offeror has launched a proxy fight in an effort to compel the board of directors of the target to withdraw poison pills or other takeover defenses that prevent the completion of a purchase-type takeover.

b. In the case of attempted takeovers of very large targets, the aggressor may acquire a substantial minority position by tender offer and then launch a proxy contest in an effort to elect a majority of the board of directors or persuade directors to deal directly with the aggressor.

c. A proxy fight may also be launched by an individual or one or more institutional investors in an effort to get management's attention to the fact that institutional investors own a substantial percentage of the corporation's shares and are unhappy with incumbent management's policies.

2. Management Advantages

Management has the advantages of the natural pro-management bias of shareholders plus access to the corporate treasury for reimbursement of expenses.

3. Insurgent Tactics

Insurgents purchase an equity position in the corporation, obtain a shareholders' and NOBO list and mount a campaign for proxies which may involve individual contact with shareholders.

4. Corporations Subject to Proxy Contests

Small or medium size corporations with older management, weak earnings records, and poor shareholder relations are typical proxy fight candidates. However, in recent takeover attempts against very large corporations proxy fights have sometimes been used as part of the aggressor's overall strategy.

5. Regulation of Proxy Contests

Proxy contests are regulated by the SEC which broadly imposes a "truth in campaigning" requirement.

6. Who Pays the Cost of Proxy Contests?

The corporation may be charged with reasonable management expenses in a policy dispute. Successful insurgents may also have the corporation pay their expenses if approved by the shareholders. The corporation thus may end up paying both sides.

7. Defensive Tactics

Modern courts have intervened to prevent management from using its power to set meeting dates or places as weapons to defeat insurgent proxy contests. A reasonable business purpose may have to be demonstrated for such changes.

C. PURCHASE TYPE TAKEOVERS

1. Definitions

A *cash tender offer* is a public offer by an aggressor to purchase all, or a significant block, of the shares of a publicly held target corporation for cash. In order to be successful, the offer price must exceed the current market price of the target's shares. The difference between the offer price and the current market price is called the "premium". During the late 1980s, premiums sometimes exceeded 50 per cent.

An *exchange offer* is a public offer by an aggressor to acquire all, or a significant block, of the shares of a publicly held target corporation for shares of the aggressor.

A *leveraged buyout (LBO)* is the acquisition of a publicly held target corporation through a cash tender offer in which all or most of the purchase price is borrowed, and the intention is that the target corporation will repay the loans used to purchase control of the target if the offer is successful. This transaction usually involves a statutory merger between the target corporation and the entity that borrowed the funds to finance the purchase.

A *management buyout (MBO)* is a leveraged buyout in which management participates in the buyers' group.

An LBO or MBO usually involves a *mop up merger* following the cash tender offer in order to eliminate public shareholders who did not tender their shares for purchase pursuant to the cash tender offer.

An LBO or MBO is sometimes called a *going private* transaction since after the buyout the corporation is no longer publicly owned.

2. Regulation of Takeovers

Regulation of public cash tender offers is provided by a portion of the federal Securities Exchange Act of 1934 called the "Williams Act." In addition, many other aspects of takeovers are subject to regulation under state law.

a. The Williams Act requires public disclosure of accurate information when (i) a shareholder or group of shareholders acquire 5 per cent or more of the stock of a publicly held corporation, or (ii) a person makes a public tender offer for shares. The Act makes unlawful the use of false, misleading or incomplete information, but the Supreme Court held that a defeated contestant for control does not have a private cause of action for damages for violations of this prohibition. The Williams Act also imposes "rules of fair play" in connection with the details of tender offers.

b. In *CTS Corporation v. Dynamics Corp. of America,* the Supreme Court upheld the Indiana Control Share statute, using language that permits extensive state regulation of many aspects of takeovers of corporations incorporated in that state. Prior to CTS, many commentators believed that there was a national market for corporate control that was constitutionally protected from state interference or regulation.

1) Following CTS, most states have enacted statutes designed to regulate takeovers. These statutes take a variety of forms:

(i) Business combination statutes (enacted by Delaware, New York, and other states) prohibit mergers between target corporations and the corporation taking them over for a specified period. The effect of this statute is to prohibit LBO and MBO transactions from being completed during this period.

(ii) Control share statutes require shareholder approval of transactions by which other shareholders increase their holdings above specified levels; the acquired shares lose their right to vote if approval is not obtained.

(iii) Fair price statutes require the price in mop-up transactions to be no lower than the price set in the original tender offer.

(iv) Pennsylvania has adopted the most draconian anti-takeover provisions, including an obligation on the part of any purchaser of 30 per cent of the stock of a publicly held corporation to thereafter offer to purchase the remaining stock at the same price.

3. Role of Arbitragers

When a cash tender offer is made, the open market price for the shares increases dramatically close to or above the tender offer price. Persons owning shares thus have the choice of selling their shares in the open market (usually at a discount from the tender offer price) or tendering their shares. Most shares sold on the open market are ultimately tendered because of the activities of "risk arbitragers."

a. Risk arbitragers are speculators who purchase shares in the open market at prices below the tender offer price in order to tender them and profit by the difference between the two prices.

b. In many tender offers, the volume of transactions effected by risk arbitragers has been very substantial.

4. Defensive Tactics Adopted by Corporations

Most publicly held corporations have adopted an armory of defenses designed to make unwanted takeover bids from outside sources difficult or impossible to complete.

a. Poison pills are special classes of shares that create additional rights in existing shareholders when a cash tender offer is made or there are acquisitions of substantial blocks of the target's shares. The additional rights may consist of a right to receive assets or debt from the target corporation (to make it less attractive to an aggressor), stock in the aggressor corporation in the case of any subsequent statutory merger, or other rights.

b. Supervoting shares are shares that carry more than one vote per share that are "parked" in friendly hands. Supervoting shares may not themselves be traded; if they are sold, the voting power returns to one vote per share. The SEC sought to prohibit the creation of such shares when it adopted its "One Share One Vote" rule (rule 19c–4), but a federal court has held that rule invalid.

c. Employee stock ownership plans may be adopted to "park" large blocks of shares in the presumably friendly hands of a trustee for employees.

d. Porcupine provisions are changes in the manner of election of directors designed to make it as difficult as possible for an aggressor acquiring more than 50 per cent of the shares to take control of the corporation.

e. Corporations faced with an unwanted tender offer may seek to find a white knight, a more attractive suitor.

f. Corporations faced with an unwanted tender offer may acquire additional lines of business that are designed to create antitrust complications for the aggressor, if successful.

g. Corporations faced with an unwanted tender offer may take steps to drive up the price of the stock, as by declaring an extraordinary dividend or by beginning a program of repurchasing of their own shares.

h. Corporations faced with an unwanted tender offer may negotiate with the aggressor to purchase his shares in the target at a premium (greenmail).

i. Corporations fearing an unwanted tender offer may create covenants in debt indentures that make takeovers difficult to complete without triggering a default.

j. Lockups involve entering into transactions with friendly persons on favorable terms to make takeovers difficult or unattractive. Lockups may involve the sale of shares at bargain prices or the grant of options to purchase shares at current market prices or options to purchase assets at attractive prices.

1) Before an unwanted tender offer is made a corporation may find a white knight and sell to that white knight shares at current market prices, or grant it options to purchase shares at current market prices.

2) A corporation facing an unwanted tender offer may sell or grant options to purchase desirable assets or business lines ("crown jewels") to a favored bidder at a bargain price. This type of lockup is designed to discourage the competing bidder by making the target less attractive.

k. A target may make a selective offer to repurchase or redeem its own shares in exchange for debt obligations but limit the offer by excluding shares acquired by or behalf of the offeror. A selective offer of this type may be devastating to the tender offer since the aggressor may end up owning a corporation saddled with immense debts. In *Unocal Corp. v. Mesa Petroleum Co.*, the Delaware Supreme Court upheld this type of transaction on the basis of an expanded business judgment rule, discussed below. Shortly thereafter, the SEC adopted the "all holders rule" (rule 14d–10) that requires equal treatment of all shareholders of the same class.

l. A target may seek to make itself unattractive by engaging in a leveraged recapitalization or "leveraged recap." Where a leveraged buyout is proposed, the target is in effect doing what the aggressor is proposing to do.

5. Legal Principles Relating to Defensive Tactics

A large number of recent cases have considered the validity of defensive tactics in different contexts. No general theory has developed.

a. Early cases took the position that defensive tactics were simply a matter of the exercise of the business judgment of the directors and such decisions were immune from judicial review under the business judgment rule.

b. In *Unocal Corp. v. Mesa Petroleum Co.*, upholding an exchange offer of debt for stock that excluded the aggressor from participation, the Delaware Supreme Court developed a sliding scale business judgment rule: "A further aspect is the element of balance. If a defensive measure is to come within the ambit of the business judgment rule, it must be reasonable in relation to the threat posed. This entails an analysis by the directors of the nature of the takeover bid and its effect on the corporate enterprise."

c. In *Moran v. Household International, Inc.*, upholding the adoption of a "poison pill" as a defensive tactic in advance of a specific takeover attempt, the court reasoned that the poison pill did not prevent all takeover attempts, and that the management's invocation of the poison pill in response to a specific takeover attempt could be considered when the occasion arose.

d. In *Revlon, Inc. v. MacAndrews & Forbes Holdings, Inc.,* the Delaware Supreme Court held that a "lock up" agreement that favored one contestant in a takeover attempt over another was invalid and should be enjoined since the board of directors had resolved to sell the corporation and, upon making that decision, the board had an obligation to get the best possible price for shareholders and could not arbitrarily favor one contestant over another. The board of directors, in other words, has to conduct an auction to insure that shareholders receive the best possible price.

e. In *Paramount Communications, Inc. v. Time, Inc.,* the Delaware Supreme Court held that where the *Revlon* auction requirement was not applicable, the board of directors (if acting in an informed manner) may adopt a strategy that does not maximize shareholder value in the short term.

6. Auctions and the Revlon Principle

Many takeover attempts during the 1970s and 1980s were contested by two or more different aggressors seeking to take over the target. In *Revlon, Inc. v. MacAndrews & Forbes Holdings, Inc.,* the Delaware Supreme Court held that a "lock up" agreement that favored one contestant in a takeover attempt over another was invalid and should be enjoined since the board of directors had resolved to sell the corporation and, upon making the decision, the board must seek to obtain the best possible price for shareholders and may not arbitrarily favor one contestant over another.

a. The Court held that the duty of the board of directors changes when it "becomes apparent" the target is to be sold. Before that time, the board of directors may be a defender of the target. However, when the decision to sell is made, the board of directors becomes auctioneers charged with getting the best price for the shareholders upon the sale of the company.

b. Following *Revlon,* courts in Delaware and elsewhere struggled with additional basic questions: How is a *Revlon* auction to be conducted? When may the board conclude that the auction has ended? If an offer at an attractive price is received, must the board conduct an auction or may it accept the offer subject to a "market check" that assures that the best price has been obtained?

c. The *Revlon* principle seems to establish the primacy of the interests of shareholders in making takeover decisions.

7. The "Just Say No" Defense

The "just say no" defense states that a board of directors may establish a policy that the corporation is not for sale, and may therefore refuse to discuss or negotiate with possible acquirers. If the defensive armament of poison pills and other devices is impregnable, recognition of the "just say no" defense would theoretically permit the board of directors to reject all proposed transactions, no matter how favorable they may be for shareholders. The status of this defense is uncertain even though the decision in *Paramount Communications* may be read as validating this defense.

8. Role of Institutional Investors

With the growth of shareholdings by institutional investors, their decisions with respect to whether or not to tender is often decisive as to the success or failure of the takeover.

9. Miscellaneous Takeover Techniques

As sophisticated defensive tactics have developed, more emphasis has been placed on unconventional takeover techniques, such as limited offers to institutional investors. A street sweep is an informal offer made to a limited number of arbitragers by the aggressor who is compelled by defensive tactics to withdraw its offer seeking to purchase the shares owned by arbitragers without making another tender offer.

D. ECONOMIC ANALYSIS OF CASH TAKEOVER BIDS

There has been extensive consideration of the causes and effects of the takeover movement of the 1970s and 1980s. Much of the analysis favoring takeovers was written during the 1980s when numerous transactions were occurring. In the early 1990s, financing for takeovers dried up and (either concomitantly or as a result), a number of highly leveraged companies created during the takeover boom filed for bankruptcy under chapter 11. Other highly leveraged companies avoided bankruptcy by negotiating with creditors and by infusing substantial amounts of equity into the capital structure of the company. The proper analysis and evaluation of these developments is highly controversial.

XIV. DUTIES OF DIRECTORS, OFFICERS AND SHAREHOLDERS

Duties owed to the corporation (and to other interests within the corporation) are primarily a matter of state law but the federal securities laws also impose some duties on directors, officers, and shareholders.

A. DUTIES IN GENERAL

Duties to the corporation and to other interests within the corporation to some extent depend on the nature of the relationship between the office held by the individual involved and the corporation.

1. Directors

Directors owe broad duties to the corporation. The relationship is *sui generis*. Directors are not trustees but owe both a degree of care and a high degree of fidelity and loyalty. They are also not employees and need not spend their full time on corporate affairs. Directors generally owe duties to the corporation as a whole rather than to individual shareholders or classes of shareholders.

2. Managers, Officers and Agents

Most managers, officers, and agents are full time employees expected to give their full time and attention to corporate affairs. Depending on their responsibilities, they may owe essentially the same fiduciary duties as directors.

3. Shareholders

Shareholders, as such, have no management responsibility and their duties to the corporation are therefore more limited than the duties of directors and officers. Controlling shareholders owe duties to the corporation. Some courts have also held that shareholders in a closely held corporation may owe duties to other shareholders similar to the duties one partner owes to other partners.

B. DUTY OF CARE

1. Duty of Care Defined

Statutes define the duty of care in terms of the care "an ordinarily prudent person" would exercise under similar circumstances. This definition, however, is not the standard that is in fact applied in most cases in which directoral decisions are challenged, which is the business judgment rule.

2. Business Judgment Rule

The standard usually applied in evaluating whether directors made decisions consistent their duties to the corporation is the business judgment rule, which states that a director has met the standard of care if:

a. The director is informed with respect to the subject of his judgment to the extent he reasonably believes to be appropriate under the circumstances;

b. He is not interested in the subject of his business judgment; and

c. He rationally believes that his business judgment is in the best interests of the corporation.

3. Cases Involving a Failure to Make Decisions

The business judgment rule applies only when "decisions" or "judgments" are made. If a director fails to participate in the decisional process, the business judgment rule is inapplicable and the director's conduct is evaluated under the "prudent man" standard.

a. A decision not to take action is a judgment that is protected by the business judgment rule. Failing to take action because no decision was made one way or the other is not.

b. There are only a few cases involving a failure to direct, and in some of these cases no liability was imposed on the theory that the plaintiff had failed to show that the failure to direct caused the injury or loss in question.

c. Failing to direct cases may impose crushing liabilities on persons unaware of the nature or scope of their obligations.

4. Director Liability Statutes

In 1986, in direct response to the *Van Gorkom* decision, the Delaware legislature enacted § 102(b)(7) that authorize certificates of incorporation to contain provisions eliminating or limiting the personal liability of a director to the corporation or its stockholders for monetary damages for breach of fiduciary duties with certain exceptions.

a. Virtually all states have enacted similar statutes since 1986.

b. Hundreds or thousands of corporations incorporated in Delaware, including most publicly held corporations, have taken advantage of § 102(b)(7) and eliminated directoral liability to the maximum extent permitted by that section.

c. This section makes it clear that the directors of a corporation adopting an appropriate provision are not personally liable for damages even in the case of gross negligence.

d. Section 102(b)(7) only applies to suits for "monetary damages." Suits for equitable relief to enjoin a transaction are not precluded by that section. As a result litigation in due care cases continue to arise despite the enactment of § 102(b)(7). A few state statutes apply to suits for equitable relief as well as to suits for monetary damages.

e. MBCA (1984) added a provision similar to Del.G.C.L. § 102(b)(7) in 1989.

5. Knowing Authorization of Wrongful Act

Liability has sometimes been imposed for authorization of wrongful acts, but even here there is a reluctance to impose liability that may be extremely large for decisions that were intended to benefit the corporation.

6. Reliance on Experts and Committees

MBCA (1984) permits directors to rely on information, opinions, reports, or statements, including financial statements and other financial data prepared or presented by responsible corporate officers, employees, legal counsel, public accountants, or committees of the board of directors.

a. Reliance on materials presented by others is absolutely essential, as a practical matter, for outside directors who are remote from the day-to-day affairs of the corporation.

b. A director may also rely on the reports of committees of the board of directors (of which the director is not a member) if the director "reasonably believes" the committee merits competence.

c. Similar provisions have been adopted in many states.

C. APPLICATION OF THE BUSINESS JUDGMENT RULE TO CONFLICT OF INTERESTS IN GENERAL

A modern trend in corporation law is the recognition of a role for the business judgment rule in the resolution of a variety of issues in which one or more directors have a direct and significant financial interest.

1. Disqualification of Interested Directors

A director who is financially interested in a transaction is usually referred to as an "interested director" or a "disqualified director." A decision by such a director on the transaction in which he is interested is not protected by the business judgment rule.

2. Action by Disinterested Directors

Not all directors may be interested in a specific transaction. These directors are usually called "disinterested directors" or "independent directors." The question is whether disinterested directors may make a decision with respect to the transaction in question that is itself entitled to business judgment rule protection, thereby validating the transaction in which the director is interested.

3. The Danger of Structural Bias

The major argument against the uncritical application of the business judgment rule in such cases is concern about "structural bias," the fear that directors by virtue of their close working relationships and mutual trust and confidence will not make truly independent and objective evaluations of such transactions on behalf of the corporation.

D. SELF-DEALING

1. Definition

Self-dealing transactions are direct or indirect transactions between the corporation and director. The MBCA (1984) defines "conflicting interest" as (1) a beneficial financial interest that the director has in a transaction with the corporation of such significance that the interest would reasonably be expected to exert an influence on the director's judgment if he were called to vote on the transaction, or (2) financial interests that closely affiliated persons of the director may have in a transaction with the corporation that are of such significance to the person that it would reasonably be expected to exert an influence on the director's judgment if he were called to vote on the transaction.

2. The Danger of Self-Dealing Transactions

The danger of self-dealing transactions is that the director may favor his personal interests over the corporation's interest.

3. Common Law Tests

The original common law test was that self-dealing transactions were voidable without regard to fairness. Gradually this view changed and it became accepted that self-dealing should be evaluated on the basis of fairness with weight also given to ratification or approval of the transaction by disinterested directors or shareholders. Transactions that involved fraud, overreaching, or waste could not be ratified.

4. Statutory Tests

Most states have adopted statutes dealing with self-dealing transactions. In 1989, the MBCA (1984) was amended by adding Subchapter F, a comprehensive statute dealing with such transactions. This statute protects decisions made by disinterested directors consistently with the business judgment rule from further judicial review.

5. Remedies

Rescission is normally the sole remedy for a corporation setting aside a voidable transaction.

6. Indirect Conflicts of Interest

Transactions between corporations with a common director are usually judged solely on a fairness test, though the active participation of the interested director may make the transaction voidable without regard to fairness. Subchapter F of the MBCA (1984) applies the same standards to both direct and indirect self-dealing including validation by disinterested directors under the business judgment rule.

7. Exoneratory Provisions for Self-Dealing Transactions in Articles of Incorporation

Provisions in articles of incorporation that purport to validate self-dealing transactions are given limited effect; they may permit the interested director to be counted toward a quorum and may free self-dealing transactions from adverse inferences.

8. Loans to Directors or Officers

Most state statutes contain a provision restricting or prohibiting loans to directors or officers. MBCA (1984) § 8.32 contained a liberalized prohibition similar to these state statutes, but that section was withdrawn in 1989 when subchapter F was approved. That subchapter now governs loans to directors or officers.

E. EXECUTIVE COMPENSATION

Establishment of compensation of CEOs and officers involve elements of self-dealing, when the officer involved is also a director. Publicly held corporations create compensation committees composed entirely of outside directors to establish compensation levels and compensation plans for senior executives. The use of compensation committees lessens or eliminates the perception of self dealing.

1. Test for Excessive Compensation

In publicly held corporations, courts review executive compensation on the basis of whether it is so large as to constitute spoliation or waste. In assessing compensation levels, comparison may be made with compensation levels in other corporations.

2. Tests Under Internal Revenue Code

In closely held corporations, compensation to officer/shareholder may be part of tax minimization schemes. Such compensation is reviewed on a simple reasonableness test and unreasonable compensation is considered a dividend.

3. Compensation Based on Stock Performance

Compensation plans involving stock purchase plans, stock option plans, phantom stock plans, and stock appreciation rights all provide for compensation based on stock price performance.

4. Need for Benefit to the Corporation

Some compensation plans have been attacked on the ground they are not supported by consideration. To avoid this argument it is necessary for the plan to involve some benefit to the corporation which can be used to support the compensation plan.

F. CORPORATE OPPORTUNITIES

1. General Test

A director who personally takes advantage of a corporate opportunity may have to account to the corporation for his or her profits. The test for this doctrine is basically one of reasonable business ethics.

2. When is an Opportunity a "Corporate Opportunity?"

Some states have adopted a pure fairness test; others have relied primarily on a "line of business" standard. An earlier test, now largely rejected as too narrow, is that the corporation have an "interest or expectancy" in the opportunity. One case has applied a "line of business" test coupled with basic fairness.

3. Factors Considered in Evaluating Whether an Opportunity is a Corporate Opportunity

The courts consider a variety of factors to determine whether an opportunity is a corporate opportunity. For example, the courts consider whether the opportunity was offered to the corporation or to the director as an agent of the corporation.

4. Rejection of Corporate Opportunity

Directors may take advantage of a corporate opportunity if the corporation determines that it does not want to take advantage of the opportunity. Such a corporate decision is a type of self-dealing transaction and should be made through procedures appropriate for such transactions.

5. Inability of Corporation to Take Advantage of Opportunities

If the corporation lacks the financial ability to take advantage of the opportunity a director may properly do so. This rule, however, must be cautiously applied; while a director need not lend money to the corporation to assist it to take advantage of the opportunity, he or she may not hide behind the financial inability argument and do nothing to assist the corporation. The ALI Corporate Governance Project does not recognize this ground as an independent basis for a director to take personal advantage of an opportunity.

6. Director's Competition With the Corporation

Since directors are not full time employees they may compete with the corporation so long as they do so openly and do not use trade secrets or engage in unfair competition.

7. Policy Arguments

Commentators have suggested that the benefits of free and unfettered competition dictate that the scope of corporate opportunities should be narrowly confined.

G. THE FAIRNESS TEST

Minority shareholders in a corporation may be injured by a variety of transactions authorized by the controlling shareholder or by the board of directors elected by such shareholders. The test usually applied to such transactions is "fairness" or "intrinsic fairness." However, to an increasing extent, courts are willing to accept the decision of disinterested directors as to the reasonableness of such transactions under the business judgment rule.

1. Transactions With a Partially Owned Subsidiary

A clear example of potentially injurious transactions is transactions between a corporation and its partially owned subsidiary. The minority shareholders of the subsidiary are injured by any transaction that in effect transfers assets from the subsidiary to the parent on less than a fair and equivalent exchange.

a. The parent corporation usually has the power to nominate and elect all the directors of the subsidiary and thereby to name all members of the subsidiary's management.

b. If the transaction involves a proportionate distribution of assets by the subsidiary to all of its shareholders, the minority have no basis for complaint on the ground of domination of the management by the parent corporation.

c. The proper standard for evaluating transactions between parent and subsidiary is that it must be "entirely fair" or "intrinsically fair" to the subsidiary.

d. Because of conflict of interest problems, a parent corporation with a partially owned subsidiary may place outside unaffiliated directors on the board of the subsidiary.

1) When a transaction between subsidiary and parent is proposed, the subsidiary may be represented solely by the outside directors. In this way, the transaction may be subject to the business judgment rule rather than the rule of "intrinsic" or "entire" fairness.

2) In some instances, a majority of the subsidiary's board of directors may consist of unaffiliated outside directors.

e. A parent corporation with a partially owned subsidiary may lawfully eliminate the minority shareholders in the subsidiary through a cash out merger, thereby making the subsidiary wholly owned rather than partially owned.

2. Miscellaneous Transactions

The fairness test is applicable to a variety of transactions which defy precise categorization. These situations also generally involve duties of controlling shareholders or of directors named by controlling shareholders.

3. Transactions Discussed Elsewhere

The fairness test is potentially applicable in a number of other contexts discussed elsewhere in this Black Letter. In many of these areas the appropriate use of disinterested directors may permit the transactions to be evaluated under the business judgment rule rather than the "entire fairness" standard. These areas are:

a. Self dealing transactions.

b. Corporate opportunities.

c. Freeze-out transactions.

d. Discontinuance of derivative litigation.

H. STATE STATUTORY LIABILITIES

State statutes impose personal liability on directors for certain transactions.

1. Acts for Which Liability is Imposed

The acts for which personal liability is imposed typically involve failure to comply with the financial provisions of the statute.

2. Directors Who Are Liable

Joint and several liability is usually imposed on all directors present at the meeting at which the transaction is authorized unless a dissent is formally noted in the corporate records.

3. Defenses

State statutes may provide for defenses usually based on good faith reliance on the opinions or reports of corporate officials.

4. Practical Importance of Statutory Liability

There are very few reported cases involving these statutory liabilities.

XV. DUTIES RELATING TO THE PURCHASE OR SALE OF SHARES

Duties relating to the purchase and sale of shares arise either under state law or under the federal Securities Exchange Act of 1934, particularly rule 10b–5 and section 16(b).

A. STATE LAW IN GENERAL

1. Basis of Liability

The common law originally applied only general principles of fraud to transactions in shares by insiders on the basis of inside information that is not publicly known. Either affirmative misrepresentation or failure to make disclosure within a relationship of trust of confidence was necessary for liability to be imposed. State law, however, has developed three theories under which trading by insiders on undisclosed information may be attacked.

a. Disclosure may be required of "special facts."

b. Disclosure may be required because insiders owe a "fiduciary duty" to shareholders and members of the general public not to take advantage of inside information. This position was adopted in Kansas.

c. Profits from inside trading may be recovered by the corporation on the theory that the inside information is a corporate asset. This position was adopted in New York.

2. Purchase at a Discount of Claims Against the Corporation

If the corporation is solvent, claims may be purchased by an officer or director at a discount unless they constitute corporate opportunities. If the corporation is insolvent when the claims are purchased, the purchase is improper since the officers or directors should try to liquidate outstanding claims as inexpensively as possible.

3. Purchase or Sale of Shares in Competition With the Corporation

Purchases or sales of shares in competition with the corporation are usually usurpations of corporate opportunities.

B. RULE 10b–5

Rule 10b–5 is a broad federal antifraud provision applicable to securities transactions involving interstate commerce. Even though it does not expressly create a private cause of action, the existence of such a private cause of action has been recognized by the Supreme Court of the United States. As a result most securities litigation today is brought in federal court rather than state court.

1. History of Rule

Originally adopted for narrow purposes, rule 10b–5 grew without control until a series of narrowing Supreme Court decisions during the 1970s.

2. Advantages of Rule 10b–5

The popularity of rule 10b–5 is in part a result of the preference of plaintiffs for the federal forum if possible. Advantages are both procedural and substantive, since there is "more law" under rule 10b–5 than there is under state law.

3. Limiting Principles on Rule 10b–5

To state a claim under Rule 10b–5 the plaintiff must meet the following requirements imposed by the Supreme Court of the United States. the plaintiff must establish "scienter." *Ernst & Ernst v. Hochfelder.* The plaintiff must also be a purchaser or seller of securities. *Blue Chip Stamps v. Manor Drug Stores.* Rule 10b–5 also only relates to deception not unfairness. Hence a fully disclosed unfair transaction is not a violation of rule 10b–5. *Santa Fe Industries v. Green.*

4. Rule 10b–5 as an Antifraud Provision

Rule 10b–5 prohibits affirmative misrepresentations and failures to make disclosures when there is a duty to do so or the statements actually made would be misleading in the absence of additional affirmative statements. Rule 10b–5 is potentially applicable to virtually all fraud claims involving securities.

a. Rule 10b–5 is applicable to all transactions involving any use of the means of interstate commerce or of the mails. There is no need to establish diversity of citizenship.

b. Rule 10b–5 is applicable to closely held corporations as well as publicly held ones.

c. The defendant may be any person who makes a false or misleading statement with scienter. The issuer of securities may violate rule 10b–5 if it issues a false or misleading press release, proxy statement, or filing required by the securities acts. The defendant need not be a purchaser or seller of securities.

d. In order to recover in an action for damages, the plaintiff must be a purchaser or seller of securities. The plaintiff must establish that the defendants acted with scienter, that there was a misstatement or omission that was "material," and that the plaintiff relied on the material misstatement or omission. A projection or forward looking statement made by the issuer is misleading if it is not made with a reasonable belief that it is accurate.

e. In the case of open and developed securities markets, there is a rebuttable presumption that shareholders rely on the market price as reflecting all publicly available information. This presumption is based on the fraud on the market theory. If the issuer makes a false or incomplete statement there is therefore a presumption that persons trading the market relied on that false or incomplete statement.

f. The test for materiality is whether there is a substantial likelihood that a reasonable shareholder would consider the statement important in deciding how to vote.

g. Information concerning the existence and status of preliminary negotiations with respect to a merger may or may not be material depending upon a balancing of the probability that the merger will occur and the anticipated magnitude of the event in light of the totality of the corporation's activity.

h. A corporation has no obligation to disclose material information except to the extent (i) disclosure is required by SEC regulation, (ii) disclosure is necessary if the undisclosed information renders previous public statements by the corporation misleading, (iii) there are rumors in the investment community that are generally (though inaccurately) being attributed to the issuer or (iv) the corporation has reason to believe that individuals are trading in the securities markets on the basis of the undisclosed information.

5. Rule 10b–5 as a Prohibition Against Insider Trading

Rule 10b–5 is the source of most of the case law prohibiting trading in securities by persons with inside information that is not publicly available. The scope of this liability is largely established by a series of Supreme Court decisions, but the remedies available to the Government and to private plaintiffs are largely determined by two federal statutes: the Insider Trading Sanctions Act of 1984 and the Insider Trading and Securities Fraud Enforcement Act of 1988.

a. The policy of the federal government is that insider trading is a potentially criminal offense that should be prosecuted vigorously. This policy has been adopted despite considerable academic commentary that inside trading is a "victimless crime" and may have positive economic benefits.

b. Rule 10b–5 is violated when a person employed or affiliated with the issuer of securities trades in those securities on the basis of information that is not publicly available.

c. Rule 10b–5 may also be violated when a person obtains information that is not publicly available in violation of a duty owed by that person to someone else and trades on that information. This is known as the "misappropriation" theory and has been used, for example, to hold a columnist for the Wall Street Journal liable for trades in stocks that are favorably reviewed in the column in advance of the publication of the column.

   1) The Supreme Court has neither accepted nor rejected the misappropriation theory.

   2) The Supreme Court has held that similar transactions may be violations of the mail fraud statute.

d. A "tippee" is a person who acquires inside information from another person and trades on it. A tippee generally is liable if he or she has reason to know that the insider providing the information breached his or her fiduciary duty to the issuer when the information was originally provided. This is established by determining whether the insider personally benefitted from the disclosure.

   1) An attorney, accountant or other person in a position of confidence with an issuer is a "temporary insider," not a tippee, and is subject to the rules applicable to insiders.

   2) The "tipper," the person providing the tip, is also liable for unlawful insider trading by a tippee.

e. The 1984 and 1988 insider trading statutes provide significant remedies against inside trading.

   1) The SEC and the United States may impose civil penalties up to an amount equal to three times the trading profit or loss avoided and criminal penalties for willful violations.

   2) A person who is in control of another person that violates the inside trading prohibitions may also be liable for civil penalties.

   3) An informant who provides information leading to the imposition of a statutory penalty is entitled to a bounty.

   4) Contemporaneous traders may bring a private suit for damages against an inside trader (limited to the profit gained or loss avoided by the trader).

5) Persons who engage in transactions in derivative securities—options, puts, calls, etc.—may also bring a private suit for damages against an inside trader.

6. Rule 10b–5 as a Protection Against Deception of the Corporation in Connection With the Acquisition or Disposition of Shares

Rule 10b–5 may be violated when a corporation is deceived in connection with the purchase or sale of shares since a corporation is a "person" within rule 10b–5.

a. If shares are issued or acquired by a corporation as a result of deception or a failure of some persons to disclose material facts to the corporation, the corporation may have a claim under rule 10b–5, and this claim may be asserted derivatively by a minority shareholder.

b. A rule 10b–5 violation also occurs if the corporation is fraudulently induced to issue shares for inadequate compensation even though such conduct also constitutes a violation of state-created fiduciary duties.

7. Rule 10b–5 as a Regulator of Corporate Publicity

A corporation may violate rule 10b–5 if it issues a false or misleading press release and investors rely on this release in securities trading. This is a variation of the "fraud on the market" doctrine.

a. While the *Birnbaum* rule requires that the plaintiff be a purchaser or seller of shares, there is no similar requirement for defendants: a person may violate rule 10b–5 even though he neither purchases nor sells a security.

b. Scienter is required.

c. Disclosure of pending merger negotiations has been a particularly troublesome issue. *Basic Inc. v. Levinson* holds that the existence of preliminary merger discussions may not be denied if they are actually occurring and are "material." According to the Supreme Court, the materiality of preliminary negotiations depends on an assessment of the specific facts involved. Extremely preliminary inquiries presumably would not be material. The practical problems in this area may cause issuers to adopt a "no comment" policy with respect to all inquiries about merger negotiations.

d. Individual shareholders who rely on a corporate press release that is issued in violation of rule 10b–5 may recover damages from the corporation.

C. SECTION 16 OF THE SECURITIES EXCHANGE ACT

Section 16 of the original Securities Exchange Act, enacted in 1934, is designed to prevent in-and-out short term trading in publicly traded securities by officers, directors, or ten per cent shareholders of the issuer.

1. Purpose of Section 16

Section 16's purpose is to prevent the unfair use of information which may have been obtained by a person subject to the section. It also may prevent attempts at market maintenance or market manipulation by persons covered by the section.

2. Disclosure of Transactions

Section 16(a) requires persons subject to section 16 to file reports describing their initial ownership of the issuer's shares and subsequent reports each month reporting each acquisition or disposition of the issuer's shares. These reports are publicly available.

3. Prohibition Against Short Swing Trading in General

Section 16(b) requires that any profit made by a covered person from a purchase and sale, or sale and purchase, of the issuer's stock during any six month period, is automatically recoverable by the corporation. Scienter or the actual use of inside information is not necessary to establish liability; offsetting transactions within any six month period automatically give rise to liability.

A sale on the basis of inside information not accompanied by a purchase within a six month period, or vice versa, is not a violation of section 16(b). Such a transaction may be, and usually is, a violation of rule 10b–5. Offsetting transactions that occur six months and one day apart are not a violation of section 16(b).

Profits on short swing trading are measured by a matching pattern that ensures that all possible profit is squeezed from a sequence of transactions: the highest sale price is matched with the lowest purchase price, the next highest sale price with the next lowest purchase price, and so on until all possible profit is eliminated. Losses are ignored in this calculation and do not offset profits as so calculated.

4. Application to Unusual Transactions

A great deal of the case law arising under section 16(b) deals with the question whether a transaction that is not a typical purchase or sale of securities should be viewed as a "purchase" or "sale" for purposes of section 16(b). The general test applied is to view unusual transactions as a "purchase" or "sale" if they are of a nature that may lend themselves to the improper use of inside information. The actual use of such information is normally not a factor in this evaluation.

5. Enforcement Mechanism

Section 16(b) permits any shareholder to bring suit on behalf of the corporation to recover profits under section 16(b). As a practical matter, some attorneys regularly review section 16(a) filings to locate possible section 16(b) violations, and then arrange for the purchase of one share in order to qualify a plaintiff to bring suit. Attorneys' fees are payable to a successful attorney or one who brings a section

16(b) violation to the attention of the corporation, and such fees are the motivation for most section 16(b) litigation.

6. Importance of SEC Regulations

The SEC has broad power to grant exemptions from the liability imposed by section 16(b). Historically, the SEC exercised this power narrowly and on a case-by-case basis. In 1991, however, the SEC promulgated a comprehensive set of exemptions to the filing requirements of section 16(a) designed to resolve many of the recurring issues under § 16(b). The SEC has also adopted definitive regulations under section 16(b) dealing with employee stock purchase plans, and similar transactions.

7. Application of Section 16(b) in Takeover Situations

The Supreme Court has held that a purchase by tender offer which causes the aggressor's ownership to exceed ten per cent of the target's shares is not a "section 16(b) purchase." *Foremost–McKesson Inc. v. Provident Securities Co.* Another Supreme Court case holds that a person holding more than ten per cent of the shares of a target may sell its shares in two transactions; if the first transaction reduces ownership below ten per cent the second transaction is not subject to section 16(b).

8. Section 16(b) and Trading Partnerships

Generally a partnership that has a partner who is a director of a corporation subject to § 16(b) is not itself considered to be a director. An exception applies if the partnership has "deputized" the partner to serve on the board.

9. Section 16(b) and Trading in Different Classes of Securities

Generally, section 16(b) does not apply to a purchase of preferred and sale of common within six months. An exception applies if the two securities are trading as economic equivalents. The 1991 SEC regulations deal comprehensively with trading in puts and calls and the underlying equity security.

10. Section 16 in Perspective

Section 16(b) is an erratic section that catches a number of innocent people and permits careful planning to avoid liability. On the other hand, it has largely eliminated short term trading by corporate officers, directors, and ten per cent shareholders, since liability is virtually automatic if offsetting transactions occur within any six month period.

D. SALE OF CONTROLLING SHARES

1. Control Premiums

A person having voting control of a corporation may usually sell her shares at a premium representing the control element that accompanies these shares.

2. Tests for Sale of Control

A controlling shareholder may have to account for a control premium in limited situations:

a. A controlling shareholder must make a reasonable investigation of the purchaser if the selling shareholder has reason to believe the purchaser may loot the corporation. If such an investigation would have revealed that the purchaser was likely to loot the corporation, the seller may be liable for losses suffered from such looting.

b. If the court views the favorable sale opportunity as (1) a corporate opportunity belonging to all shareholders rather than to the majority shareholders, or (2) as a sale of a corporate office rather than a sale for the stock, a controlling shareholder may be compelled to share the control premium with minority shareholders. Some cases have imposed liability for the control premium on the basis of the unfairness of the transaction.

c. Some cases permit recovery by minority shareholders when there is not full disclosure to them of the difference in treatment.

3. Seriatim Resignations of Directors

Control of a corporation may also be sold or transferred by the sale of a minority block of shares if the directors are willing to resign seriatim and elect nominees selected by the purchaser of the block of shares.

If the corporation is a registered publicly traded corporation, disclosure of a transaction involving the transfer of control through seriatim resignations of directors must be publicly disclosed.

4. Empirical Studies of Sale of Control Transactions

Limited studies of price movements of shares of publicly traded corporations in which a private sale of control has occurred indicates that minority shareholders do not appear to be harmed by such a sale of control, and may in fact be benefitted.

XVI. INDEMNIFICATION AND LIABILITY INSURANCE

"Indemnification" permits the corporation to a limited extent to assume and pay the litigation expenses of corporate officers and directors. It may also permit the corporation to an even more limited extent to pay judgments, settlements and criminal fines incurred as a result of their actions as a director or officer.

Liability insurance for directors and officers ("D & O" insurance) provides traditional third party liability insurance against some risks.

A. INDEMNIFICATION AND PUBLIC POLICY

1. Policies Favoring Indemnification

Given litigation costs today, indemnification is essential if responsible persons are to be willing to serve as directors.

2. Policy Limitations on Indemnification

A person absolved of charges of negligence or misconduct in connection with their actions on behalf of the corporation is entitled to indemnification by the corporation. A person found guilty of willful misconduct is generally not eligible for indemnification of any kind. Between these two extremes lie the difficult cases.

3. Sources of Power to Indemnify

All state statutes grant corporations power to indemnify corporate directors. Many statutes also expressly permit indemnification of corporate officers. Corporations may also authorize or require broader indemnification, or limit statutorily authorized indemnification, by appropriate provisions in articles of incorporation or bylaws.

a. Many state statutes provide expressly that they are not exclusive, and the corporation may create broader rights of indemnification. In such states, public policy provides the only limitation on indemnification.

b. The MBCA (1984) makes the statutory provisions generally the exclusive test of when indemnification may be authorized, but permits corporations to broaden the rights granted by the statute so long as the rights are consistent with the general limitations set forth in the statute.

4. Voluntary Restriction of the Right or Duty to Indemnify

Corporations may generally "opt out" of the indemnification statutes by restricting or eliminating indemnification in the articles of incorporation or bylaws. A corporation may do this in order to conserve limited resources or to limit the right of former directors or officers to demand indemnification.

B. SCOPE OF INDEMNIFICATION UNDER MODERN STATE STATUTES

The Delaware GCL, the Model Act (1969), and the MBCA (1984) form the basis for most modern indemnification statutes.

1. Indemnification When the Defendant Has Been Successful in the Proceeding

Under modern statutes the defendant is entitled to indemnification as a matter of statutory right if she "is wholly successful on the merits *or otherwise*". A director with a valid procedural defense is therefore entitled to indemnification without regard to the merits. California omits the phrase "or otherwise."

2. Permissive Indemnification

Under modern statutes, indemnification is permitted as a matter of discretion but not as a matter of right where the defendant acts in good faith and in the best interest of the corporation but is not successful on the merits or otherwise in the litigation, for example, by entering into a settlement. Directors cannot compel corporations to grant indemnification for conduct entitled only to permissive indemnification unless the corporation has voluntarily agreed make such indemnification mandatory.

3. **"Authorization" and "Determination" of Indemnification**
A "determination" relates to the eligibility of the officer or director for indemnification while an "authorization" is a corporate judgment that an appropriate use of corporate resources is to pay the director or officer the amount so "determined." Determinations of indemnification are to be made by directors who are not parties to the litigation, by the shareholders or by special legal counsel. Authorization may be made by the board of directors or by the shareholders.

4. **Court-Approved Indemnification**
A person not otherwise eligible for indemnification may petition a court for a determination that he is "fairly and reasonably" entitled to indemnification of reasonable expenses. A corporation may avoid court-ordered indemnification by so providing in its articles of incorporation.

5. **Advances for Expenses**
A corporation may advance expenses of a proceeding as they are incurred without waiting for a final determination of eligibility for indemnification if allowed by statute.

6. **Indemnification of Officers, Employees and Agents**
Under the MBCA (1984), indemnification of an officer, agent or employee who is not a director is not subject to the limiting principles applicable to indemnification of directors. An officer (but not employees or agents) has the same right to mandatory indemnification as a director and may apply for court-ordered indemnification. A director who is also an officer or employee is limited to the indemnification rights of a director.

7. **Modification of Statutory Indemnification Policies**
The MBCA (1984) provides that a contractual or voluntary provision relating to indemnification is valid if consistent with the policies of the Act. Statutes in Delaware and other states provide that statutory indemnification is not exclusive.

8. **Indemnification of Witnesses**
The MBCA (1984) provides that the corporation has power to pay or reimburse the expenses of a director in a proceeding in which she is a witness but not a party.

9. Notification of Indemnification

The MBCA (1984) requires the corporation to notify shareholders of all indemnifications or advances of expenses in connection with suits brought by or in the name of the corporation.

10. Indemnification in Federal Proceedings

The SEC takes the position that it is against public policy for a corporation to indemnify officers or directors against liabilities imposed by the Securities Act of 1933 except upon order of a court.

C. D & O LIABILITY INSURANCE

1. Structure of D & O Policies

D & O policies are complementary to indemnification. Most publicly held corporations provide both indemnification and insurance.

a. D & O insurance is "claims made" insurance. It insures only for claims that are presented to the insurer during the period of insurance.

b. D & O insurance consists of two different parts.

1) The "corporate reimbursement" portion of the policy insures the corporation against payments it is obligated or permitted to make to officers or directors under its indemnification obligations. This portion of the policy does not insure the corporation against direct claims made by shareholders or others.

2) The "directors and officers" portion of the policy insures directors and officers against obligations that are not indemnifiable by the corporation but which are not within the insurance exclusions of the policy.

2. Insurable Risks

D & O policies only cover insurable risks, thereby eliminating wrongful misconduct and self-dealing transactions, among others, from coverage.

3. Policy Exclusions

D & O policies also contain significant exclusions so that these policies do not cover many potential risks.

4. Policy Coverage and Premiums

Policies are generally purchased to cover all officers and directors of the corporation. Premiums are usually shared, with the officers and directors paying a small percentage of the cost.

5. State Statutes

Many state statutes specifically empower corporations to purchase D & O insurance. In the absence of such a statute, a power to acquire such insurance is likely to be implied. Some states expressly authorize corporation to engage in self insurance through the creation of trust funds or captive insurance subsidiaries that are not true insurers because the spreading of risk is limited.

XVII. INSPECTION OF BOOKS AND RECORDS

A. MANDATORY RECORD KEEPING REQUIREMENTS

State statutes require (or assume) that each corporation will maintain permanently certain basic records: e.g. copies of articles of incorporation, bylaws, a record of shareholders, copies of the most recent annual report, and minutes that show action taken by shareholders and directors. The MBCA (1984) spells out these requirements in greater detail than most earlier statutes.

1. Discretionary Records

Most records maintained by corporations, e.g. financial records, tax returns, samples of advertising, are not required to be retained by the corporation statutes, but their retention may be required by other statutes. Depending on their character and the purpose of the shareholder, discretionary records may be subject to inspection by a shareholder.

2. List of Shareholders Eligible to Vote at Meeting

In addition to the record of shareholders generally, state statutes require each corporation to assemble a list of persons eligible to vote at a forthcoming shareholders meeting. This list must be available for inspection at the meeting, and, under the MBCA (1984) and the statutes of many states, available for inspection for a specified period before the meeting.

B. INSPECTION BY THE PUBLIC

Corporations that are not registered under the federal securities acts generally need not make public disclosures or public filings except to the extent required by corporation and state tax statutes.

1. Documents Available at the Secretary of State's Office

Documents available at the Secretary of State's office include articles of incorporation, designations of registered offices and registered agents, assumed name certificates, and articles of mergers.

a. The MBCA (1984) requires every corporation to file an annual report with the Secretary of State containing current information about the corporation's business, directors, and capitalization.

b. Many states have similar requirements.

2. Documents Available at Other State Offices

Some states require annual reports to be filed with a state office that are publicly available. Information may also be publicly available from franchise tax returns and other filings, but in most states relatively little information is available.

3. Information Available About Publicly Traded Corporations

Considerable information is normally obtainable from the SEC about a corporation that is registered under the federal Securities Exchange Act or has filed a registration statement under the federal Securities Act of 1933. Information may also be obtained from state securities ("blue sky") commissions if the corporation has filed a registration statement under the state blue sky laws.

C. INSPECTION BY THE GOVERNMENT

The government of the state of incorporation has broad visitorial powers under state incorporation statutes, but as a practical matter, those powers are seldom exercised. Specific state or federal offices may also have visitorial powers under specific substantive statutes.

D. INSPECTION BY DIRECTORS

As a manager of the corporation, a director has a broad though not completely limitless right to inspect books and records of the corporation.

E. INSPECTION BY SHAREHOLDERS

A shareholder has a more limited inspection right than a director because he or she does not have management responsibilities and has limited fiduciary duties.

1. Sources of the Shareholders' Right of Inspection

Shareholders' inspection rights may be found in (a) common law principles, (b) statute, (c) rights generally of litigants and (d) rights generally of members of the general public.

a. The common law right of inspection required judicial enforcement upon the showing of a proper purpose by the shareholder. The shareholder had the burden of proving a "proper purpose."

b. Statutory rights of inspection also require a showing of "proper purpose" but many statutes provide that if the shareholder has owned shares for a specified period (usually six months) or owns a specified percentage (usually five percent) of the shares, the burden is on the corporation to show lack of a proper purpose. These statutes also often impose a statutory penalty on the corporation or its officers for not granting the statutory right of inspection without cause.

c. The MBCA (1984) retains the "proper purpose" requirement but eliminates arbitrary time period or holding requirements. The shareholder must allege his purpose with particularity and only records relevant to that purpose need be produced. Enforcement is by summary judicial proceeding with the corporation being required to pay the shareholder's expenses if the refusal was without reasonable cause.

d. The statutory right of inspection provided by the MBCA (1984) supplements the common law right of inspection. In many states the relationship between the statutory and common law rights of inspection is not clear.

e. The MBCA (1984) makes clear that shareholders in litigation with the corporation have litigation discovery rights that are not affected by statutory inspection rights.

f. The MBCA (1984) requires every corporation to make certain basic documents—e.g. articles of incorporation, bylaws, minutes of specified meetings, names and addresses of current directors—available for inspection by any shareholder upon five days notice without regard to purpose.

g. The MBCA (1984) requires every corporation to furnish its shareholders with annual financial statements and specifies the minimum requirements for such statements. Corporations that prepare financial statements reported upon a public accountant must supply those statements to each shareholder.

h. The MBCA (1984) also requires disclosure to shareholders of transactions involving issuance of shares for promissory notes or promises of future services was well as indemnification of directors in connection with suits brought by or in the name of the corporation.

2. Scope of Records Subject to Inspection

a. The MBCA (1984) authorizes inspection of "accounting records" of the corporation, the record of shareholders, and minutes of meetings of shareholders and directors. The scope of the inspection right in other state statutes depends on the precise statutory language, which varies widely from state to state.

b. A corporation may not avoid the right of inspection by offering substitute documents or summaries.

3. Scope of Inspection Right

Most statutes recognize the shareholder may be assisted by an accountant and attorney when inspecting books and records. The MBCA (1984) also authorizes machine copies to be made at the shareholder's expense; most state statutes are silent on this matter though courts often authorize such copies where reasonable.

4. Restrictive Orders

Courts may condition or limit the right of inspection in any reasonable way, e.g. by prohibiting the shareholder from giving information to a competitor.

5. What is a "Proper Purpose"?

A "proper purpose" is one that is reasonably related to the shareholder's interest in the corporation. There has been extensive litigation over what a "proper purpose" is, but generally careful phrasing of a purpose should lead into being viewed as "proper."

6. Inspection Rights of a Beneficial Owner

Nonrecord owners usually have many if not all the inspection rights of a record owner.

XVIII. SHAREHOLDER LITIGATION

"Shareholder litigation" refers to litigation brought by a shareholder in the capacity or role of shareholder.

A. "DIRECT," "DERIVATIVE," AND "CLASS" LITIGATION

1. "Direct" Defined

A direct suit involves the enforcement by one or more shareholders of a claim based on injury done to them directly as owners of shares.

2. "Derivative" Defined

A derivative suit is a suit by a shareholder to remedy a wrong to the corporation as such, rather than to the shareholder individually.

3. Relationship With "Class Suits"

Most class suits are direct suits where the number of plaintiffs forming the class is large.

4. Practical Application of Distinctions

Different procedural and substantive rules are applicable to these types of suits. However, the line between them is sometimes hazy and artful pleading may permit a complaint to be framed either as direct or derivative.

B. EVALUATION OF DERIVATIVE LITIGATION

There are two diametrically opposed views as to the social value of modern derivative litigation.

1. A Major Deterrent to Misconduct

One view is that derivative litigation is one of the major bulwarks against overreaching and misconduct by corporate insiders. A number of judges have expressed this view as have many academic writers.

2. A Device for the Enrichment of the Plaintiffs' Bar

The opposing view is that most derivative litigation is without substantive merit and is instituted for the benefit of plaintiffs' attorneys.

a. This view is often stated by attorneys who represent corporations that are involved in derivative litigation. They rely on personal experience, on impressions, and on anecdotal evidence.

b. Lawsuits instituted for the settlement value of cases and for the benefit of the plaintiffs' attorneys are called "strike suits."

c. Empirical studies based on stock price movements following the announcement of the institution or settlement of derivative litigation are not conclusive, but they tend to support the view that most derivative litigation does not have favorable impact on stock prices.

3. Role of Plaintiffs' Attorneys

Most derivative litigation is attorney-fueled litigation. Plaintiffs' attorneys find possible litigation situations and then seek to find a plaintiff in whose name suit may be brought.

a. Plaintiffs' attorneys advance the litigation costs to pursue the litigation and as a result have a financial interest in the litigation that exceeds that of any single plaintiff.

b. The litigation is directed and conducted by the plaintiffs' attorneys who are motivated at least in part by their financial interest in the litigation.

4. Litigation and Settlement

Most derivative litigation is settled and does not go to final judgment.

a. In settlement negotiations, fees to be paid to plaintiffs' attorneys are normally a major element to be resolved. Agreements as to fees must be approved by the court as part of the settlement process.

b. Derivative litigation is often settled without any payment of money by third party defendants to the corporation but by the corporation agreeing to make changes in procedures and practices.

C. PREREQUISITES FOR MAINTAINING DERIVATIVE SUITS

1. Demand on the Corporation and Board of Directors

Procedural statutes traditionally require that a derivative complaint allege either that demand was made on the board of directors or that demand was futile. The substantive consequences of the demand requirement have become extremely controversial and various rules have been proposed or adopted.

a. The basic theory for requiring a demand is that decisions with respect to litigation are business questions that should be resolved by the board of directors. The board of directors should therefore determine whether the claim should be pursued, settled, or the law suit discontinued as not being in the best interests of the corporation. On the other hand, many derivative suits allege misconduct by one or more directors or high level management, and in these cases it is quite possible that the corporation is not interested in vigorously pursuing the claims.

b. Delaware, like most states, requires a demand on directors unless demand is futile. Futility, however, is defined very narrowly. To establish futility, the plaintiff must establish (from particularized facts alleged in the complaint but prior to discovery) that i) a reasonable doubt is created that the directors making the decision were not disinterested or independent, or ii) the decision being questioned was otherwise not the product of a valid exercise of business judgment.

   1) In Delaware cases are described as "demand required" on the one hand, or "demand excused" or "demand futile" on the other.

   2) In Delaware the classification of a case as "demand required" or "demand excused" has direct impact on the deference given by courts to a recommendation or decision by the board of directors or a litigation committee acting on the board's behalf.

c. The MBCA (1984) and the Corporate Governance Project requires demand in virtually all cases and dispenses with the "demand required"/"demand excused" distinction. The deference given by courts to decisions by the board of directors or a litigation committee is not affected by whether demand is required.

d. The United States Supreme Court has held that federal courts acting in derivative suits brought under federal law or as a result of diversity of citizenship should adopt the rule of the state in which the corporation is formed.

e. The Federal Rules of Civil Procedure require a demand on directors or an explanation of why demand was not made. This is a solely a requirement of pleading and does not of itself have substantive effect.

2. Demand on Shareholders

The Federal Rules of Civil Procedure also require an allegation that a demand was made on shareholders or that such a demand was unreasonable. A number of states impose a demand on shareholders requirement. Applied literally and in all cases, a demand on shareholders would require an expensive proxy solicitation. The MBCA (1984) and most state statutes do not require a demand on shareholders.

3. Contemporary Ownership

Most states require that the plaintiff show that he was a shareholder when the cause of action arose or that he later obtained his shares by operation of law. The federal rules impose a similar requirement.

An equitable principle may prevent persons who acquired most of the shares by purchase from bringing a derivative suit based on pre-purchase claims.

4. Security for Expenses

Statutes in many states require plaintiffs to post security for the defendants' expenses and allow defendants to be reimbursed for their expenses out of this security if the court finds suit was brought without just cause. These statutes are designed to discourage derivative suits brought solely for their settlement values.

Many statutes impose this requirement only on plaintiffs with small holdings. The MBCA (1984) does not contain a security-for-expenses statute on the theory that the requirement unreasonably discriminates against small shareholders. Other statutes have been revised to give the court discretion to impose the security requirement only when the litigation appears frivolous or baseless.

D. DEFENSES IN DERIVATIVE SUITS

1. Application of Business Judgment Rule

A controversial issue is the effect to be given to a recommendation or decision by a litigation committee composed of directors that decides that pursuit of the litigation is not in the best interests of the corporation.

a. In Delaware, in a "demand required" case, the decision by a committee of disinterested directors (or the entire board of directors if a majority is disinterested) that meets the requirements of the business judgment rule is given conclusive effect. If the case is a "demand excused" case a recommendation by such a committee is reviewed by a court, which may evaluate the quality of the decision and, in addition, may utilize its own independent business judgment as to whether or not to dismiss the litigation.

b. Under the MBCA (1984), a "good faith" decision to dismiss litigation that meets the requirement of the business judgment rule is given preclusive effect, without regard to whether demand is required.

c. Under the Corporate Governance Project, the court may independently review findings of the board or committee as to lawfulness of conduct and may also reject findings and conclusions if they are "clearly unreasonable."

d. Some states appear not to give preclusive effect to litigation committee decisions.

2. Failure to Meet Procedural Requirements

A plaintiff who fails to meet the security-for-expenses or similar procedural requirements will have his suit dismissed. Such a dismissal is without prejudice to a later refiling by the same or a different plaintiff.

3. Substantive Defenses

Defenses available to third party defendants may result in a dismissal with prejudice. Such defenses usually may not be raised by the corporation.

4. Disqualification of the Plaintiff

A third class of defense relates to the specific plaintiff. A disqualification of the plaintiff normally prevents him from thereafter serving as a plaintiff but does not bar subsequent refiling of the suit by another plaintiff.

E. DERIVATIVE SUITS IN FEDERAL COURTS

1. Classification of Parties for Diversity Purposes

The corporation is usually aligned as a defendant for diversity purposes.

2. Pendent Jurisdiction

In the absence of diversity, suit may often be brought under federal law and state claims may be attached under the concept of pendent jurisdiction.

3. Securities Fraud Cases

Many federal securities fraud cases are brought as direct claims, either individually or as class actions. Derivative suits may also be based on federal securities law if the conduct complained of injures the corporation.

F. MISCELLANEOUS PROCEDURAL PROBLEMS

1. Necessary Party

The corporation is a necessary party to any derivative litigation.

2. Combination of Claims

A plaintiff normally may not combine direct and derivative claims in the same suit; personal counterclaims usually may not be filed against a derivative plaintiff.

3. Multiple Suits

Multiple derivative suits may be brought by different plaintiffs arising out of a single transaction. Courts have broad discretion to determine which one will proceed and which ones will be stayed. Intervention may be permitted.

4. The Role of Corporate Counsel

The interests of the corporation and the other defendants are different and normally separate counsel are required. Other problems involve the scope of the attorney-client privilege and the possible role of the plaintiff's counsel with the corporation.

5. Jury Trials

While derivative suits are equitable in nature, a right to a jury trial may exist for issues that are legal in nature.

6. Merger of Corporate Defendant

The merger of a corporate defendant may require that the new or surviving corporation be added to the litigation. In the case of a cash-out merger in which the plaintiff receives cash for his or her shares, the plaintiff may no longer maintain the suit since he or she is no longer a shareholder.

7. Collateral Estoppel

Principles of collateral estoppel may prevent defendants in a derivative suit from relitigating issues previously resolved against them in an enforcement proceeding.

G. SETTLEMENT OF A DERIVATIVE SUIT

Historically, secret settlements have been a serious problem in derivative litigation.

1. The Nature of Settlement Negotiations

The settlement of a derivative suit generally involves negotiation between the attorneys for the plaintiffs, the corporation, and the individual defendants. Negotiations may involve a number of issues.

a. The amounts, if any, to be paid by the individual defendants to the corporation.

b. Changes in procedures, if any, to be made by the corporation to prevent recurrence of improper conduct;

c. The amount to be paid to the plaintiffs' attorneys, either out of funds to be paid to the corporation by the individual defendants or by the corporation directly from its own assets.

d. Whether the corporation or the individual defendants will affirmatively support the fees to be paid to the plaintiff's attorneys.

2. Judicial Review of Settlements

All settlements of derivative litigation must be approved by the court. The court normally considers not only the reasonableness and fairness of the proposed settlement in the light of the claims asserted but also the fees to be paid to the plaintiffs' attorneys and the benefits to be obtained by the corporation and its shareholders from changes in procedure. A separate hearing may be held on the fee issue.

a. Courts appear to be increasingly willing to inquire closely into the fees being sought by plaintiffs.

3. Notice and Hearing on Settlement
Shareholders are entitled to notice and hearing on proposed settlements.

4. Derivative Pursuit of Secret Settlement
A secret settlement may be itself made the subject of a derivative suit.

5. Settlement of Underlying Claim
A corporation may itself settle a claim that is in litigation without court approval and without the consent of the plaintiffs' attorneys, but that settlement also may be made the basis of a later derivative suit.

H. RECOVERY IN DERIVATIVE SUITS
Generally, recovery goes to the corporation not the plaintiff shareholder.

1. Justification of Rule
The general rule protects all interests in the corporation, including creditors.

2. Exception Where Wrongdoers are Major Shareholders
Some courts have allowed innocent shareholders to recover directly on the theory that wrongdoers should not be permitted to control the use of the proceeds. These cases are the minority view.

3. Other Relief
In appropriate cases, plaintiffs may obtain injunctive or other relief.

I. RES JUDICATA

1. Final Judgment on the Merits
A final judgment on the merits binds not only the plaintiffs but also all other shareholders.

2. Settlements
Court approved settlements are normally binding on all shareholders.

3. Dismissal of Suit
A dismissal may or may not have res judicata effect depending on the grounds of the dismissal.

J. PLAINTIFFS' EXPENSES
Most derivative suits are settled and do not proceed to judgment in which plaintiffs are successful. In settlement cases, the plaintiffs' fees are usually negotiated as part of the settlement. Where they are not, or in cases where there is no settlement, plaintiffs' attorneys are entitled to fees and expenses in the following circumstances.

1. Creation of a Fund

If the suit creates a payment or fund for the benefit of the corporation, the plaintiffs' attorneys are entitled to their fees from that fund.

2. Non-Fund Cases

If the suit does not result in the creation of a fund but the result is favorable to the corporation and creates a "substantial benefit" for the corporation, the plaintiffs' attorneys are entitled to their fees from the corporation.

3. Amount of Plaintiffs' Attorneys' Fees

The amount of the fees to be paid to plaintiffs' attorneys is set by the court, on application of the plaintiffs' attorneys. Attorneys for the corporation and for other shareholders' may participate in the fee hearing.

K. DEFENDANTS' EXPENSES

In limited circumstances, the defendants may be able to recover their expenses from the plaintiffs by judicial award for misconduct, from the corporation in the form of indemnification, or from insurance companies on the basis of their D & O insurance policies.

XIX. ORGANIC CHANGES

Organic changes include a variety of basic changes in the structure of the corporation. Such changes typically require approval of the shareholders. Historically, approval by two-thirds of all shares, voting and nonvoting alike, was required but the MBCA (1984) and the statutes of many states now only require approval by an absolute majority of all outstanding voting shares, whether or not present at the meeting.

A. AMENDMENT OF ARTICLES

Under modern statutes there are no "vested rights" in specific provisions of articles of incorporation. Any provision may be amended by the appropriate statutory procedure.

1. Statutory Limitations

An amendment may only include provisions that permissibly may be included in original articles of incorporation. Amendments that make changes in issued securities must also be accompanied by a description of how the changes are to be effectuated. Under MBCA (1984), the implementing provisions may appear in the articles of amendment.

2. Procedural Requirements

Generally, an amendment need be approved only by the required majority or greater percentage of shareholders set forth in the statute. Under MBCA (1984), a majority of the votes present at a meeting at which a quorum is present is sufficient to approve an amendment unless the amendment creates dissenters' rights with respect to a class in which case the amendment must be approved by a majority of all of the shares of that class. Such a class is entitled to vote as a separate voting group on the amendment. A nonvoting class of shares may be entitled to vote as a separate voting group on a change burdensome to it. Dissenting shareholders may also have a right of dissent and appraisal on amendments that affect a class in specified ways, for certain types of amendments.

3. Protections Against Abusive Amendments

Procedural protections against abusive amendments consist of the supermajority vote requirement, the right of classes or series to vote as separate voting groups, and the right of individual shareholders to exercise their statutory right of dissent and appraisal.

B. STATUTORY MERGERS AND RELATED TRANSACTIONS

Statutes authorize certain transactions which combine two or more corporations upon the basis of specified statutory procedures. These combinations are usually known as "statutory mergers" or "Class A reorganizations." The purchase of all of a corporation's assets or stock for the purchaser's stock, usually followed by the dissolution of the corporation whose stock or assets are purchased, may have the same economic effect as a statutory merger; these transactions are sometimes referred to as nonstatutory transactions or Class B (stock) or Class C (asset) reorganizations.

Modern statutory mergers are extremely flexible devices that permit the restructuring of financial or other interests in the corporations involved, or amendments to the articles of incorporation, by a less than unanimous vote of shareholders. Some shareholders may be compelled to accept debt, cash, or property for their shares while others receive shares in the continuing enterprise. As a result, statutory mergers may be used to freeze or squeeze out minority shareholders on terms set by the corporation over the shareholders' objections.

1. General Definitions

A "merger" is the combination of two or more corporations pursuant to statute that results in one corporation surviving and the others disappearing into the surviving corporation.

A "consolidation" involves the combination of two or more corporations pursuant to statute that results in all existing corporations disappearing and a new corporation being automatically created. The MBCA (1984) does not recognize the concept of a consolidation as a distinct method of combination.

A "short form" merger is a merger of a 90 or 95 per cent subsidiary corporation into its parent. Votes of shareholders of both parent and shareholder are dispensed with in a short form merger.

A "down stream" merger is a merger of a parent corporation into its subsidiary. An "up stream" merger is a merger of a corporate subsidiary into its parent corporation.

A "triangular merger" involves the merger of a corporation into a subsidiary of the acquiring corporation; the shareholders of the disappearing corporation receive shares of the acquiring corporation, not shares of its subsidiary.

A "reverse triangular merger" involves the formation of a new subsidiary of the acquiring corporation followed by a merger of that subsidiary into the corporation to be acquired. Shares of the parent are exchanged for securities of the corporation to be acquired. Ultimately the acquired corporation becomes a wholly owned subsidiary of the acquiring corporation.

A "cash merger" or "cash out merger" is a merger in which some shareholders are compelled to accept cash for their shares.

2. Procedures

A statutory merger must be approved by the board of directors of each corporation and recommended by them to the shareholders for their approval (except in the case of short form mergers). The shareholders must then approve the transaction. The traditional voting requirement was two-thirds of all outstanding shares, voting and nonvoting alike, but the MBCA (1984) and the statutes of many states require only an absolute majority of the outstanding voting shares.

a. A corporation may require a greater shareholder voting requirement by provisions in its articles of incorporation.

b. Shareholders that vote against a merger have the right of dissent and appraisal if the plan of merger contains a provision that would create a right of dissent and appraisal if it were contained in an amendment to the articles of incorporation.

c. Minority shareholders in a subsidiary which is acquired pursuant to a short form merger have a statutory right of dissent and appraisal.

d. In a statutory merger, classes of shareholders may have the right to vote as separate voting groups on the merger.

3. Statutory Share Exchanges

The MBCA (1984) and the statutes of a number of states permit a corporation to make a compulsory exchange of shares for cash or other consideration in a corporate combination even though a minority of the shareholders oppose the transaction. Such a transaction is subject to the same safeguards as a statutory merger and has the same effect as a reverse triangular merger: the acquired corporation becomes a wholly owned subsidiary of the acquiring corporation. Objecting shareholders have a statutory right of dissent and appraisal.

4. Fairness Standards in Cash Mergers

Where minority shareholders are treated differently from the majority shareholders in a statutory merger, Delaware law imposes "entire fairness" and "full disclosure" standards. Alternatively, a controlling corporation may place independent directors on the board of directors of the subsidiary and negotiate at arms length with them. It is also customary to condition the approval of such a transaction on the affirmative vote of a majority of the minority shares. If done in good faith, these procedures may avoid a full scale fairness review.

C. SALES OF SUBSTANTIALLY ALL ASSETS

A sale of all or substantially all the assets of the corporation is usually treated as an organic or fundamental change in the corporation that requires approval by a majority of the voting shares.

1. Sales in Ordinary Course of Business

A sale of all or substantially all of the corporation's assets in the ordinary course of business usually does not require shareholder approval. The MBCA (1984) also provides that a transaction in which assets are distributed to a wholly owned subsidiary does not require shareholder approval. Most sales of all or substantially all of a corporation's assets are not in the ordinary course of business.

2. Meaning of "All or Substantially All"

Most courts have viewed "all or substantially all" to mean "a substantial or meaningful part of." The MBCA (1984) suggests that the phrase should be construed literally to "mean all or nearly all."

3. Right of Dissent and Appraisal

The right of dissent and appraisal usually exist in connection with a sale not in the ordinary course of business that requires a shareholder vote. Some states, however, do not grant a right of dissent and appraisal for such transactions.

D. NONSTATUTORY AMALGAMATIONS

1. Types of Transactions

A stock acquisition or asset acquisition transaction may have the same economic effect as a statutory merger.

A stock acquisition transaction is often called a "Class B reorganization;" an asset acquisition transaction is often called a "Class C reorganization."

2. Selection of Form of Transaction

The selection of the form of the transaction may have substantial legal, economic, and tax consequences. Persons in control of a corporation may establish the form which is most beneficial to them.

A few courts have held that a transaction which has the same economic effect as a statutory merger must be treated as if it were such a merger. This is the de facto merger doctrine.

E. RECAPITALIZATIONS

A recapitalization is a restructuring of the capital structure of the corporation, often involving an elimination of large arrearages on cumulative preferred shares.

1. Economics of Transaction

A recapitalization may be beneficial to all interests in a corporation, even those who are asked to give up some rights.

2. Form of Transactions

A recapitalization typically takes the form of either an amendment to articles of incorporation or a down-stream merger into a wholly owned subsidiary.

3. Validity of Transactions

While arguments based on "vested rights" are not likely to succeed, recapitalizations may be subject to attack on grounds of "fraud" or "manifest unfairness," or lack of adequate disclosure.

F. "GOING PRIVATE"

"Going private" refers to the elimination of public shareholders to avoid reporting and other legal requirements.

1. Economics of Transaction

A corporation may go public when market conditions are favorable for a high price. Years later, the going private transaction occurs when the market is depressed. Most going private transactions during the 1980s, however, involved leveraged buyouts in which funds to purchase the publicly held shares were borrowed, and the acquired corporation assumed the obligation to repay those debts.

2. Form of Transaction

A going private transaction usually takes the form of a cash tender offer followed by a cash-out merger with the remaining public shareholders being compelled to accept cash. A going private transaction may also take the form of a reverse stock split with fractional interests being compelled to accept cash. The split is set at a level at which all public interests become fractional interests.

3. Regulation of Going Private Transactions

The state law applicable to cash mergers is applicable to going private transactions. In addition, the SEC has adopted disclosure regulations relating to going private transactions.

G. LEVERAGED BUYOUTS

A leveraged buyout is a form of going private transaction in which an acquiring corporation purchases all the stock of the acquired corporation primarily with the use of borrowed funds. The acquired corporation assumes the obligation of repaying those loans.

1. Bust Up Transactions

If the acquiring corporation plans to sell off lines of the acquired corporation's business in order to help pay down the indebtedness, the transaction is called a "bust up" acquisition.

2. Consequences of Failing to Meet LBO Obligations

Many LBO transactions have failed when the acquired corporation was unable to meet the debt obligations it assumed and has gone into bankruptcy.

H. RIGHTS OF DISSENT AND APPRAISAL

1. Scope of Right

Shareholders have the statutory right to dissent and to obtain the appraised value of their shares through a judicial proceeding in connection with specific transactions described in the statute. Several state statutes provide that the statutory dissent and appraisal procedure is the exclusive remedy for dissenting shareholders. The MBCA (1984) states that the remedy is exclusive "unless the action is unlawful or fraudulent" with respect to the shareholders.

2. Procedure for Appraisal

Precise statutory procedures must be strictly complied with if the appraisal right is to be obtained. The price is set by judicial proceeding if a negotiated price cannot be established. The MBCA (1984) provides that payment of the undisputed portion of the value of the shares must be made promptly after the transaction. Most states provide for payment only at the termination of the judicial proceeding.

3. Evaluation of Appraisal Remedy

Appraisal is not a preferred remedy from the standpoint of minority shareholders because it requires expensive and time consuming litigation and because the corporation with its extensive assets is an active participant seeking to establish the lowest possible valuation.

I. VOLUNTARY DISSOLUTION

1. Dissolution Before Commencement of Business or Issuance of Shares

A simplified process of dissolution before commencement of business or issuance of shares is usually available.

2. Dissolution by Consent of Shareholders

Dissolution by unanimous consent of shareholders is permitted in many states. Such consent can only be obtained as a practical matter in closely held corporations. The MBCA (1984) does not contain a special provision to this effect;

though shareholders may act by unanimous consent, action by directors is also required.

3. **Regular Dissolution**
Dissolution requires adoption of a resolution to dissolve by the board of directors, followed by approval by the specified percentage of shareholders.

4. **Notice of Intent to Dissolve**
Some state statutes require a corporation planning to dissolve to file a preliminary notice of intent to dissolve.

5. **Dissolution Procedure**
Notice must be given to creditors. Final dissolution is permitted only after all debts and taxes have been paid, and all statutory requirements complied with. Dissolution is evidenced by filing articles of dissolution.

6. **Equitable Limitations on Dissolution**
The power to dissolve a corporation voluntarily has sometimes been used as a device to eliminate minority shareholders. In these cases, courts have sometimes imposed equitable limitations on the otherwise unlimited power to dissolve upon compliance with the mandated statutory procedures.

7. **Continuation of Existence After Dissolution**
State statutes generally provide that a corporation continues in existence for a stated period (usually three years) after dissolution during which it may be sued on claims arising from its pre-dissolution operations.

8. **Product Liability and Other Post-Dissolution Claims**
Some liabilities may arise after a corporation has dissolved, and after the statutory period for filing claims against a dissolved corporation has expired. Many such liabilities involve product liability claims. Cases involving such claims may also be brought against existing corporations that purchased the assets of the dissolved corporation; the cases involving such suits are in fundamental conflict. MBCA (1984) contains a special provision dealing specifically with the liability of dissolved corporations for post-dissolution claims.

XX. FOREIGN CORPORATIONS

Corporations that are formed under the laws of other states are referred to as foreign corporations. While corporations formed under the law of foreign countries may also be referred to as foreign corporations, the discussion below is limited to corporations formed under the laws of other states.

A. RIGHT TO TRANSACT BUSINESS IN FOREIGN STATES

States generally have the power to exclude foreign corporations from transacting local business within that state but may not exclude foreign corporations from entering into transactions with that state's citizens in interstate commerce. As a practical matter, all states have procedures by which foreign corporations may qualify to transact local business in the state.

1. When Is Qualification Required?

The test of when a foreign corporation's contacts with a state are sufficient to require it to qualify to transact business is necessarily subjective. State statutes generally contain a non-exclusive listing of contacts with a state that do not require qualification.

2. Effect of Qualifying to Transact Business

A foreign corporation that qualifies to transact business in a state generally obtains the rights and privileges of domestic corporations formed within that state and becomes subject to regulation and taxation by that state and becomes subject to suit within that state.

a. A corporation that qualifies to transact business is entitled to the same (but no greater) rights and privileges possessed by a domestic corporation.

b. In order to qualify to transact business a foreign corporation must file an application with the secretary of state or other filing office within the state.

c. In order to qualify to transact business, a foreign corporation must establish a registered office and registered agent within that state. If the corporation fails to do so, the secretary of state automatically becomes the corporation's agent to accept service of process.

d. If the name of a foreign corporation is unavailable, the corporation must qualify to transact business under an assumed name. The name under which a foreign corporation qualifies to transact business in a state is protected from use by other domestic or foreign corporations within that state.

3. Effect of Failing to Qualify When Transacting Local Business in the State

A corporation that is transacting local business in the state but fails to formally qualify to transact business in that state may be subject to a variety of sanctions.

a. The corporation may be disqualified from suing in the courts of that state, or from interposing the statute of limitations in any litigation brought within that state.

b. The corporation may be prohibited from enforcing contracts made within that state.

c. The corporation and its officers within the state may be subject to penalty or fine.

B. NONQUALIFIED CORPORATIONS

A foreign corporation that has not qualified to transact business in a state may nevertheless be subject to suit within that state and may be liable for state taxes in that state. The constitutional requirements for when a foreign corporation may be sued within a state or subject to taxation in that state are less onerous than the test for determining when a foreign corporation must qualify to transact business in that state.

1. Amenability to Suit

In general, a foreign corporation may be subject to suit in a state that arises out of contacts with that state even if those contacts are not sufficient to require qualification.

2. Amenability to State Taxation

A foreign corporation may be subject to taxation in a state in which it is not qualified to do business if the tax is commensurate with the corporation's activities in that state. A federal statute limits the application of state income tax laws where the only contact with the state is solicitation of orders in interstate commerce.

C. INTERNAL AFFAIRS RULE

The internal affairs rule states that matters relating to the internal affairs of a corporation are to be governed by the state of incorporation. This rule is embodied in the MBCA (1984) and the statutes of many states.

1. Special Rules in New York and California

New York and California have adopted statutes that purport to apply domestic law to a limited extent to foreign corporations.

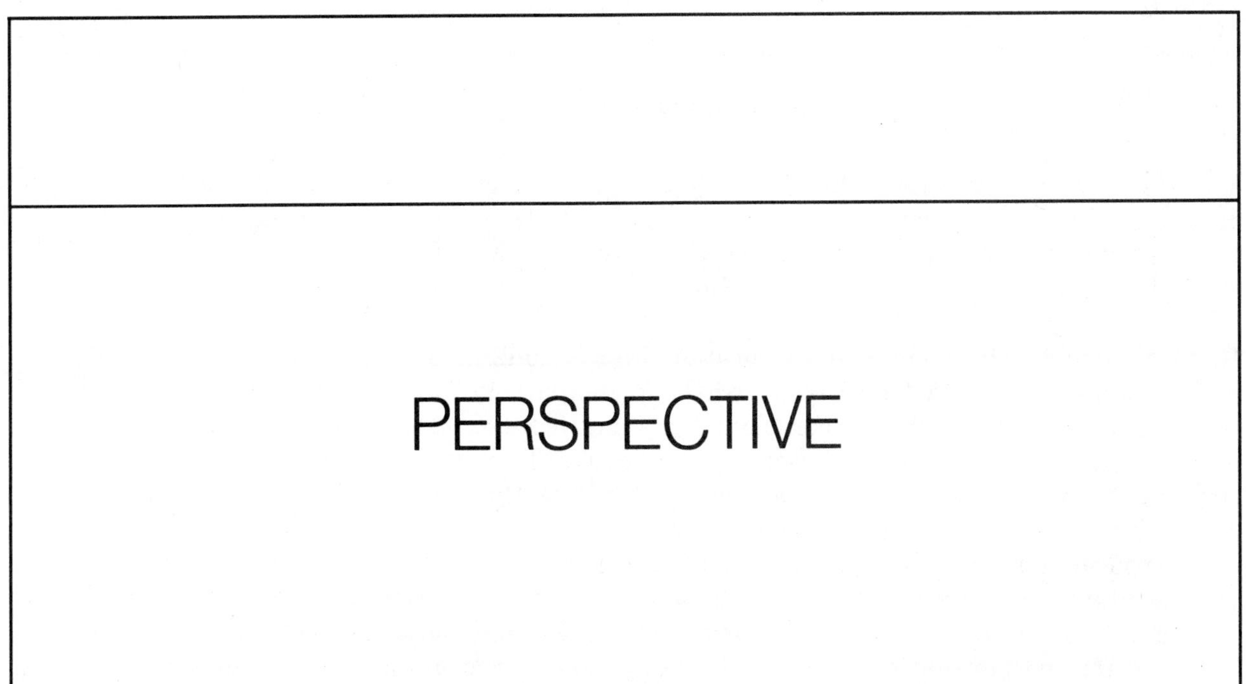

PERSPECTIVE

Analysis

THE SUBJECT IN GENERAL

The great bulk of business that is conducted in modern society is conducted in corporate form. The law of corporations is therefore a central building block in the business law curriculum. It describes the rules relating to both internal governance and the external activities of corporations.

In most schools, the course in corporation law is combined in part with a study of partnerships and limited partnerships, the principal alternative forms of modern business enterprise to the corporation. In many courses, some attention is also paid to novel forms of business enterprise: e.g. professional corporations and limited liability companies, or to older forms of business enterprise that continue to be used: e.g. Massachusetts trusts, joint stock companies, and cooperatives. In a few schools, unincorporated forms of business may be considered in separate courses or combined with a course in agency. In some schools, there are two basic courses dealing with business associations, one covering partnerships, limited partnerships, miscellaneous forms of unincorporated business, and closely held corporation, and the other the publicly held corporation.

Specialized areas of corporation law that are usually the subject of advanced courses are either ignored or are touched on only lightly in traditional corporations courses. The most important of these areas is securities regulation, which considers government regulation of the public raising of capital by business enterprises. Other advanced subjects include corporate reorganization, corporation finance, and the taxation of business enterprises.

With the increase in the number of legal scholars with backgrounds in economics, law school corporation courses increasingly contain reference to economic analysis. Depending on the instructor and the law school, this may range from relatively brief readings in which relevant conclusions derived from economic analysis are presented, to an introduction to basic concepts such as efficient capital markets, or to courses in which economic analysis is the central building block about which the entire course revolves.

This outline discusses corporations, both closely held and publicly held. It does not cover partnerships or limited partnerships, or specialized advanced subjects that are the subject of separate courses in most law schools. It also includes a brief description of inferences drawn from economic analysis that are relevant to the subjects here discussed.

RELATIONSHIP WITH AGENCY

Many problems discussed in the corporations course involve agency principles. Corporation teachers generally assume that students have received a grounding in fundamental agency concepts either in the first year of law school or in separate agency/partnership courses, or in both. Some casebooks contain brief discussions of agency concepts for the benefit of students who feel their grounding in this important area is weak. In general, for the purposes of the corporations course, it is more important that the student understand the fundamental principles of the law of agency, such as the difference between actual and apparent authority, than the technical rules about subjects such as when actual authority is revoked.

RELATIONSHIP WITH FEDERAL INCOME TAXATION

The relationship between the courses in corporations and federal income taxation is somewhat like the relationship between the chicken and the egg. Many areas discussed in the law of corporations are shaped to some degree by federal tax concepts; on the other hand, many issues discussed in tax courses presuppose a working knowledge of corporate concepts. While there is no rigid rule about which course should be taken first, or whether it is desirable to take the two courses simultaneously, the most common pattern is for law students to take corporations without previously having had a course in federal income taxation. As a result, many individual corporation teachers do not emphasize tax concepts (depending to some extent on the casebook that is chosen); even where tax-related concepts are discussed, they can almost always be understood without a broader knowledge of federal income taxation generally. On the other hand, a basic working knowledge of corporations is usually assumed without discussion in federal income taxation courses.

HOW TO PREPARE FOR AND DO WELL ON CORPORATION EXAMINATIONS

The law of corporations is derived partially from state and federal statutory provisions and partly from common law sources. Some teachers use the corporations course as largely an exercise in statutory construction and analysis of the law of a particular state, while others emphasize the broader common law or general issues. In either event, some attention is normally paid to federal law dealing with corporate issues as well as state law. In preparing for an examination a student must recognize the emphasis the instructor has placed on these areas and concentrate his time accordingly. Further, account must be taken of the nature of the examination itself: a short answer or multiple choice examination in a course that has heavily emphasized the statutes and case law of a particular state, should be prepared for quite differently from an essay examination in a course that concentrated on general or federal legal principles without considering as a unit the law of any particular state.

The practice questions included in this outline are designed to give students experience with both short answer and essay questions, though it must be recognized that questions based on state statutory provisions can only be answered correctly by reference to the rules in the specific state in question.

When answering essay questions, a student in corporation law should follow basically the same method of analysis of the question that is applicable to every law school essay exam. However, in considering his or her response, the student must take into account the possibility that the question raises issues of statutory construction or application of federal law as well as traditional common law principles. A student virtually guarantees himself or herself a low grade if he or she answers a question that revolves around the construction of a specific statutory provision on the basis of general equitable principles. The same unfortunate result follows if a student applies principles of federal law to a situation in which no federal jurisdiction exists. The following suggestions may help to avoid these common errors in examination analysis:

1) The first step in any examination is to read the question very carefully and identify the issues and questions raised. While this may seem self-evident, probably more poor answers are the result of inadequate analysis of the question than any other single cause. It may be helpful to ask yourself: Why is the instructor asking me about this factual situation? What areas of the course are involved in this situation?

2) The second step is to isolate the legal principles that are applicable to the issues and questions raised. In corporations, the legal principles may be found (a) in a corporation statute or code (either that of a specific state, of Delaware, or possibly, the Model Business Corporation Act (1984)); (b) in the general case law dealing with corporations that form the bulk of the cases in each of the casebooks; or (c) in the federal law arising under either the federal Securities Act of 1933 or the Securities Exchange Act of 1934. It is possible that a single question may have one or more facets arising under different sources.

3) Having isolated the issues and the sources of legal principles, organize your answer and respond to the issues raised in the same manner as in any other examination. Conclusions should be supported by reasons; if you have rejected an argument that appears to be plausible, it is desirable to refer to both the argument and the reason for its rejection; make sure that your answer responds to all the issues raised by the question, and so forth.

4) Be careful about "just throwing things in" because you know about them. A canned essay on an irrelevant topic almost certainly will not help you, and may well detract from the overall evaluation of your answer. Also, some exam questions in corporations (and in other subjects as well) may be designed to test whether you know that some principle is *not* applicable; for this reason you should concentrate on why the principle is not applicable, not on what would happen if the inapplicable principle were applicable.

I

CORPORATION LAW IN GENERAL

Analysis

E. "Efficient" Securities Markets
   1. The Concept of an Efficient Market
   2. Inferences That May Be Drawn From the ECMH
   3. Persons With Nonpublic Information
   4. Judicial Recognition of the ECMH
F. State Competition for Corporations
   1. Advantages of Encouraging Local Incorporations
   2. Success of Delaware
   3. Reasons for Success of Delaware: Race for the Bottom?
   4. Reasons for Success of Delaware: The Best Product?
   5. Reasons for Success of Delaware: Other Explanations
G. Review Questions

A. "CORPORATION" DEFINED

A corporation is a type of legal institution or concept that defines relationships among people. It is "more nearly a method than a thing." *Farmers' Loan & Trust Co. v. Pierson*, 222 N.Y.S. 532, 543 (1927). Several different theories have been proposed to describe these relationships; each is to some degree a useful picture of what a corporation is.

1. ENTITY THEORY

A corporation may be most readily envisioned as an artificial, fictitious entity created for the purpose of conducting a business. The basic elements of this artificial entity are the following:

a. The artificial entity has the power to conduct its business entirely in its own name, including entering into contracts, buying or selling land, bringing suits or being sued, filing tax returns, paying taxes, and the like.

b. The artificial entity is formed by a grant of authority by a government agency, in most states, the secretary of state. A document, usually entitled "articles of incorporation," must be filed, a filing fee paid, and other formal steps taken to form the entity. The "grant of authority" may be evidenced by a "certificate of incorporation" or other document issued by the government agency.

Caveat: The terminology varies from state to state. In Delaware, for example, the document that is filed is called the "certificate of incorporation."

c. The artificial entity must be generally recognized as a separate entity by the creating state, the federal government, and private citizens who deal with the corporation.

Caveat: The artificial entity in a fundamental sense is a fiction. In the bright eye of reality, real people conduct a business, whether or not it is in corporate form, and real people enjoy the profit or suffer the loss from the business. In some limited situations courts may refuse to follow the artificial entity analysis to its logical conclusions, if it leads to fraudulent or significantly unfair consequences, frustration of clearly defined statutory policies, or other undesirable results. *Farmers' Loan & Trust Co. v. Pierson*, 222 N.Y.S. 532 (1927). These situations are discussed in somewhat greater detail below under the doctrine "piercing the corporate veil." (See part IV A.)

2. CONCESSION THEORY

A second theory of corporateness is that a corporation is a "grant" or "concession" from the state. Cf. *Association for the Preservation of Freedom of Choice, Inc. v.*

Shapiro, 174 N.E.2d 487 (N.Y.1961). This theory is based on the role of the state in the formation of a corporation described above.

a. This theory was more popular at an earlier time when corporate charters were ringed with restrictions or limitations.

b. This theory is sometimes referred to today in the debate over "social responsibility" of corporations. The argument is that because a corporation is a grant or concession by the state, it may be qualified by the state as it sees fit; the state may therefore validly impose restrictions on corporate behavior and withdraw the corporate privilege completely if the restrictions are not complied with.

Caveat: The concept that a corporation is based on a "grant of authority" or "concession" from the state is itself largely a fiction. The process of incorporation today involves only routine or ministerial acts and no significant substantive decision is made in this process either by the state or by the government agency charged with issuing charters to corporations.

3. CONTRACT THEORY

A third theory of corporateness is that the charter of a corporation represents a contract (a) between the state and the corporation, or (b) between the corporation and its shareholders, or (c) among the shareholders themselves.

a. The argument that a corporate charter represents a contract between the state and the corporation has less appeal today than in an earlier day. It was relied upon by the United States Supreme Court in *Trustees of Dartmouth College v. Woodward,* 17 U.S. (4 Wheat) 518 (1819) to prevent the state of New Hampshire from enacting a statute amending the charter of the College. However, the case is primarily of historical interest today because, following a suggestion in the opinion in that case, all modern state statutes specifically reserve the power to subject outstanding charters to subsequent statutory amendments.

Example: MBCA (1984), § 1.02 provides: "The [name of state legislature] has power to amend or repeal, all or part of this Act at any time and all domestic and foreign corporations subject to this Act are governed by the amendment or repeal."

b. The argument that a corporate charter represents a contract between the shareholders or between the corporation and the shareholders often surfaces in the current context in disputes between different classes of shareholders, or in disputes in which one class of shareholders claims that the class is being discriminated against in some way. Rights of senior classes of securities (e. g., preferred shares) are defined and limited by the basic corporate documents;

the provisions in these documents relating to the rights of the senior securities are described as the "contract" between the senior securities holders and the common shareholders.

Example: Articles of incorporation provide that preferred shares are "entitled to receive, when and as declared by the board of directors, dividends equal to but not exceeding two dollars per share per year before any dividend is declared or paid on common shares." The corporation has an exceptional year and the directors are considering paying dividends in excess of $20.00 per share. The preferred shares are nevertheless only entitled to receive two dollars per share; if the directors attempt to declare a discretionary dividend of, say, ten dollars per share on the preferred, that is a "breach of the common shareholders' contract" which entitles them to enjoin any dividend on the preferred in excess of two dollars per share.

4. NEXUS OF CONTRACTS

The economist has evolved his or her own theory of corporateness that permits analysis of the corporation as an economic phenomenon. This theory rejects the notion that the shareholders are the ultimate owners of the enterprise but treats them, along with bondholders and other creditors, as providers of capital in anticipation of receiving a desired return. The "nexus of contract" includes all arrangements by which capital, labor, material, and managerial services are obtained by the corporation.

Caveat: Many arrangements made by corporations are "contractual" in the free will sense. For example, employment contracts are entered into by corporate officers and employees. Many arrangements, however, are not. For example, shareholders who acquire shares of stock on a public market do not enter into "contracts" with the corporation in any meaningful sense. Tort creditors and other persons affected by corporate actions typically also have non-contractual claims. The nexus of contracts theory assumes that all arrangements are contractual; it is argued that arrangements not the subject of actual contracts are "implicit contracts," i.e. contracts that might reasonably have been entered into had there been contracting. In the case of shareholders who acquire shares on a public market, the terms of those implicit contracts basically are the terms economists believe would reasonably be entered into by investors under similar circumstances.

Caveat: So far as shareholders are concerned, the initial subscribers to shares when the corporation is formed do typically enter into contracts with the corporation. However, in the case of large, publicly held corporations, virtually all shares are held by persons who are not initial subscribers.

Caveat: The "nexus of contracts" approach is an economic model of the modern corporation. Economic models are useful because they permit study of economic phenomena in a simplified environment where inferences and conclusions may be drawn in a logical fashion. One must always remember, however, that a model is not necessarily a reflection of the real world, and conclusions drawn from economic models may be applied to real world phenomena with confidence only if one is satisfied that the model itself incorporates the critical variables affecting the real world phenomena.

a. Since the corporation is contractual, according to this theory, it follows that the state should not—and indeed perhaps constitutionally may not—prescribe mandatory rules for corporations by statute that are inconsistent with the express or implicit contracts. The role of corporation statutes, according to this theory, is to provide standardized, "off the rack" principles that most corporations will utilize, thereby providing savings for corporations that do not need to incur the cost of independently drafting such provisions.

   Caveat: Many scholars reject the implication of the nexus of contracts theory that all statutory protections for shareholders should be viewed as permissive and subject to modification by provision in the articles of incorporation. Mandatory minimum voting rules for fundamental changes in the corporate structure and the right of dissent and appraisal are cited as examples of provisions that should not be subject to modification.

b. A small group of scholars have extended the "nexus of contracts" theory to argue that attempts by states to impose restrictions on takeovers constitute a violation of the clause of the United States Constitution that prohibits states from impairing the obligation of contracts. These scholars argue that those attempts impair the terms of express or implicit contracts inherent in the corporation.

   Caveat: This argument has been criticized as an attempted "end run" around United States Supreme Court decisions reserving to the states considerable power to establish rules regulating corporations formed under their laws. See *CTS Corporation v. Dynamics Corp. of America,* 481 U.S. 69, 107 S.Ct. 1637 (1987); *Kamen v. Kemper Financial Services, Inc.,* ___ U.S. ___, 111 S.Ct. 1711 (1991). There is no modern legal authority that supports the argument that the clause of the federal constitution prohibiting states from impairing the obligation of contracts limits or prohibits amendments to state corporation statutes in states that have retained the express power to amend those statutes. All state corporation statutes retain that power.

c. A few scholars have argued that the "nexus of contracts" theory requires corporations to make provision for creditors or displaced employees on the theory that the terms of "implicit" or "express" contracts require directors to take steps to protect the interests of those groups.

Caveat: Most law and economics scholars reject attempts to incorporate provisions of these types in "implicit" contracts.

d. Under the "nexus of contracts" theory, the concept that shareholders "own" the corporation is rejected. Rather, shareholders are viewed as contributors of capital in return for the right to receive the residual return produced by the corporation. Under this theory, shareholders and creditors explicitly share the risk that total revenues will be less than total costs during an accounting period.

e. The central figure in the corporation under the "nexus of contracts" theory is the manager who assembles the contractual components into a successful enterprise.

B. CONSTITUTIONAL INCIDENTS OF THE CORPORATE "PERSONALITY"

A corporation is entitled to some but not all of the constitutional protections available to individual persons. The process of deciding which constitutional protections are available to corporations and which are not is a matter of constitutional construction. The test is whether the protection is a " 'purely personal [guarantee]' " . . . whose " 'historic function' . . . has been limited to the protection of individuals." *First National Bank of Boston v. Bellotti,* 435 U.S. 765, 779, 98 S.Ct. 1407, 1417 (1978).

1. PRIVILEGES AND IMMUNITIES

A corporation is not a citizen of a state or of the United States for purposes of the privileges and immunities clause. *Paul v. Virginia,* 75 U.S. (8 Wall.) 168 (1868). Therefore states may validly impose restrictions on a foreign corporation's activities within the state, *Eli Lilly & Co. v. Sav–On–Drugs, Inc.,* 366 U.S. 276, 81 S.Ct. 1316 (1961), though such restrictions may relate only to *intrastate* activities and may not burden interstate commerce. *Allenberg Cotton Co., Inc. v. Pittman,* 419 U.S. 20, 95 S.Ct. 260 (1974).

2. FREE SPEECH

A corporation has rights of free speech which may not be restricted as such by state statute. *Pacific Gas & Elec. Co. v. P.U.C. of California,* 475 U.S. 1, 106 S.Ct. 903 (1986); *First Nat. Bank of Boston v. Bellotti,* 435 U.S. 765, 98 S.Ct. 1407 (1978); *Consolidated Edison Co. v. Public Service Commission,* 447 U.S. 530, 100 S.Ct. 2326 (1980). In *Austin v. Michigan Chamber of Commerce,* 494 U.S. 652, 110 S.Ct. 1391 (1990), however, the Court upheld a Michigan statute that prohibited corporations from using general corporate funds in support of or in opposition to any candidate in elections for state office.

3. SELF INCRIMINATION AND PRIVACY

A corporation does not have a privilege against self incrimination. *Wilson v. United States,* 221 U.S. 361, 31 S.Ct. 538 (1911); *Wild v. Brewer,* 329 F.2d 924 (9th Cir.1964). It also does not have a right to privacy. *United States v. Morton Salt Co.,* 338 U.S. 632, 70 S.Ct. 357 (1950).

4. DUE PROCESS AND EQUAL PROTECTION

A corporation is protected against deprivations of property without just compensation, *Penn Central Transportation Co. v. City of New York,* 438 U.S. 104, 98 S.Ct. 2646 (1978). A corporation is also entitled to both due process, *Helicopteros Nacionales de Colombia v. Hall,* 466 U.S. 408, 104 S.Ct. 1868 (1984); *Oklahoma Press Pub. Co. v. Walling,* 327 U.S. 186, 66 S.Ct. 494 (1946), and equal protection of the law, *Metropolitan Life Ins. Co. v. Ward,* 470 U.S. 869, 105 S.Ct. 1676 (1985); *Munn v. Illinois,* 94 U.S. (4 Otto) 113 (1876); *Wheeling Steel Corp. v. Glander,* 337 U.S. 562, 69 S.Ct. 1291 (1949).

5. FORMER JEOPARDY AND UNREASONABLE SEARCHES

A corporation is protected from unreasonable searches and seizures, *Marshall v. Barlow's, Inc.,* 436 U.S. 307, 98 S.Ct. 1816 (1978), and can plead former jeopardy as a bar to prosecution, *United States v. Martin Linen Supply Co.,* 430 U.S. 564, 97 S.Ct. 1349 (1977).

C. SOURCES OF LAW

The law of corporations is derived from several sources.

1. STATE INCORPORATION STATUTES

Every state has a general incorporation statute which describes the incorporation process, defines generally the rights, duties, powers and roles of shareholders, directors, and officers within the corporation, and provides rules about fundamental corporate changes. While these statutes vary from state to state, there is a substantial trend toward modernization and liberalization in all states with the result that variations from state to state are declining in importance. Three sources of statutes have been particularly influential:

a. The Model Business Corporation Act prepared and maintained by the Committee on Corporate Laws of the Business Law Section of the American Bar Association. Earlier versions of this statute were published in 1950, 1955, and 1969, and were influential in the enactment of statutes in about 35 states. A major revision was completed in 1984, which has been influential in the enactment of statutes in about 20 states. Most references in this Black Letter are to the 1984 version of the Model Business Corporation Act (originally called the Revised Model Business Corporation Act); it is identified hereafter as "MBCA (1984)". References to the 1969 version are identified as "MBCA (1969)".

b. The Delaware General Corporation Law. This statute is identified hereafter as "Delaware GCL".

c. The statutes of New York, California, and other important commercial states. Because of the commercial importance of these states, their statutes have been influential in the enactment or amendment of statutes in a limited number of smaller states.

2. STATE SECURITIES LAWS

Every state has enacted some form of "blue sky law" that regulates the public distribution of securities within that state. Many of these statutes are similar to, and overlap, the federal Securities Act of 1933.

3. STATE COMMON LAW PRINCIPLES

Because of the importance of statutory provisions in the law of corporations, the common law inheritance of rules and principles is now less important than in some other subjects. Many judicial decisions are interstitial in nature, either supplying supplementary principles when the statutes are silent or construing statutory provisions. Such decisions of course are authoritative. Nevertheless, in some areas broad common law principles are still generally applied on the theory that they define basic rights and duties within a corporation and were not affected by statutory enactments.

4. FEDERAL STATUTES

The Securities Exchange Act of 1934 and the Securities Act of 1933 are the major federal statutes applicable to broad categories of corporations. The 1933 Act regulates the public distribution of securities to investors while the 1934 Act generally regulates securities markets, securities trading, and the public dissemination of information by publicly held corporations. Under these statutes, the Securities and Exchange Commission (SEC) has broad rulemaking power which it has not hesitated to exercise. A significant portion of the law applicable to publicly held corporations is federal in origin, based on these statutes, and rules promulgated thereunder.

a. The "Williams Act" (1970)(relating to cash tender offers) is a part of the Securities Exchange Act.

b. The Insider Trading Sanctions Act (ITSA)(1984) and the Insider Trading and Securities Fraud Enforcement Act (ITSFEA)(1988), both relating to penalties for insider trading, are also part of the Securities Exchange Act.

c. Other federal statutes relating to securities law include the Investment Company Act of 1940 and the Trust Indenture Act of 1939.

5. FEDERAL COMMON LAW

There is no general federal common law of corporations. See *Kamen v. Kemper Financial Services, Inc.,* ___ U.S. ___, 111 S.Ct. 1711 (1991).

a. Prior to 1970 several federal cases and law review commentaries suggested that a "federal law of corporations" was developing under the federal securities acts. However, with a series of restrictive decisions by the United States Supreme Court beginning in about 1975, it became clear that a general federal jurisprudence of corporations has not been created, and federal law applied to corporations must be grounded in the securities acts and regulations. The principal cases involved in the growth and decline of federal corporation law during this period are set forth in Part XV.

b. In the 1980s an argument was made that "a market for corporate control" existed that was interstate in character and beyond the power of states to limit or control. The decision in *CTS Corporation v. Dynamics Corp. of America,* 481 U.S. 69, 107 S.Ct. 1637 (1987), however rejected this argument and broadly held, in near constitutional terms, that state law largely controlled corporations formed under the laws of that state. See part XIV D.

D. FUNCTIONAL CLASSIFICATION OF CORPORATIONS

The basic distinction underlying much of the law of corporations is between the *closely held corporation* (or "close corporation") and the *publicly held corporation* (or "public corporation"). While the same general corporation statutes are often applicable to both classes of corporations, the problems and concerns are usually quite different and in most courses are discussed separately.

1. DEFINITION OF A CLOSELY HELD CORPORATION

A closely held corporation is a corporation with most of the following attributes:

a. It has a few shareholders, all or most of whom are usually active in the management of the business;

b. There is no public market for its shares;

c. Its shares are subject to one or more restrictions on transfer; and

d. It has never registered a public distribution of shares under the federal or state securities acts.

2. DEFINITION OF A PUBLICLY HELD CORPORATION

A publicly held corporation is a corporation with most of the following attributes:

a. Some of its shares are held by members of the general public and the overall number of shareholders is usually large;

b. There is a public market for its shares which may be on a securities exchange or among brokers "over the counter;"

c. The corporation is subject to reporting and disclosure requirements under the securities acts;

d. It has made a distribution of shares to members of the general public.

3. THEORETICAL SIGNIFICANCE OF THE DISTINCTION BETWEEN CLOSELY HELD AND PUBLICLY HELD CORPORATIONS

While many publicly held corporations are relatively large in terms of assets and many closely held corporations are relatively small in terms of assets, the importance of the distinction is not the size of assets as much as the number of shareholders and the marketability of their shares.

a. The presence or absence of a public market for the corporation's shares is the most important difference between the two types of corporations.

   1) A shareholder in a publicly held corporation who is dissatisfied with management may sell her shares on the public market; a shareholder in a closely held corporation may have no place to sell his shares except to other shareholders in a face-to-face transaction in which the other shareholders may be willing to buy only at relatively low prices.

   2) In the publicly held corporation, the value of shares may be more readily estimated because the public market for shares provides a benchmark as to what numerous buyers and sellers believe the shares to be worth; in contrast, in the closely held corporation, there may be no external way to estimate the value of corporate shares.

   3) Because of the nonexistence of a market for shares in the closely held corporation, a minority shareholder may be "locked in" to an unsalable asset and be subject to "freeze out" or "squeeze out" tactics; these concepts have only limited application to publicly held corporations.

   4) Properly drafted share transfer restrictions may require a closely held corporation or its other shareholders to purchase shares of a minority shareholder at a fixed or determinable price and thereby avoid some of the concerns about the lack of marketability of closely held shares.

b. A second major difference is that in a closely held corporation, most of the shareholders are likely to be employed by or earn their livelihood through the corporation's business while in a publicly held corporation, most of the shareholders are not connected with management and have only a limited say in the policies adopted by the corporation. As a result, "ownership" and "control" are likely to be widely separated in a publicly held corporation but closely interconnected in a closely held corporation.

c. A third difference is that the presence of public shareholders unconnected with the business of a publicly held corporation is thought to present a strong case for governmental regulation of internal aspects of a public corporation's affairs, while in a closely held corporation, there is usually thought to be only a relatively weak (or nonexistent) case for governmental regulation of the internal affairs of the corporation.

Caveat: Corporations form a continuum rather than a polar concentration. At the margin there may be uncertainty whether a specific corporation has more of the attributes of a publicly held or a closely held corporation. The issue that must be resolved with respect to such an "in between" corporation may dictate its classification as closely held or publicly held in the specific case, though in some instances a comparison with both publicly and closely held corporations may be helpful. Numerically, the "in between corporation" is quite common, much more numerous than the publicly held corporation.

Example: *Y* Corporation is owned by six persons, three of whom participate full-time in the management of the business. Shares were originally sold to four persons; when one withdrew, he sold his shares to three other investors. Thereafter share transfer restrictions on the shares were imposed by unanimous agreement. The corporation is a closely held corporation.

Example: *AB* Corporation was wholly owned by two brothers in 1969, when they decided to "go public" by selling ten per cent of the outstanding shares through a registered public offering. At the present time, *A* and *B* own 87 per cent of the stock; the balance of the shares are owned by several hundred members of the general public. *A* and *B* continue to operate the business, electing themselves as directors. One brokerage firm "makes a market" in *AB* Corporation stock by quoting bid and asked prices for shares from time to time. Sales, however, are infrequent. *AB* Corporation is a publicly held corporation; if the number of shareholders is over 500 and corporate assets exceed five million dollars, it has additional registration obligations under the Securities Exchange Act of 1934.

Example: *X* Corporation was originally formed and wholly owned by two brothers who died in 1936 and 1938. They left the bulk of their shares to their fourteen children, though one brother made several gifts of shares to trusted employees. Of the fourteen children and employees owning shares, several have died leaving shares to children, nephews, nieces, spouses, etc. By 1980, there are a total of 123 shareholders and no shareholder owns more than 20 per cent of the outstanding shares. There has never been a public offering of the shares and there is no trading in *X* Corporation shares, though a few isolated sales have occurred from time to time. Despite the large number of shareholders, *X* Corporation has more of the characteristics of a closely held corporation than a publicly held corporation, though it is not clearly one nor the other. If the number of shareholders grows to over 500 when it has over five million dollars of assets, it too, like *AB* Corporation, will be obligated to register under the Securities Exchange Act of 1934. Of course, as the number of shareholders increases, the probability that a public market in the corporation's shares will also develop increases.

E. "EFFICIENT" SECURITIES MARKETS

Virtually all modern economic analysis about corporations and corporation law deals with publicly held corporations. This analysis, in turn, largely rests on the hypothesis that securities markets are "efficient." This hypothesis is usually called the "efficient capital market hypothesis" or "ECMH."

1. THE CONCEPT OF AN EFFICIENT MARKET

In an efficient market, there are many purchasers and sellers all seeking to make a profit in the market. Traders seek to take advantage of information, using increasingly sophisticated analysis. As a result, prices move rapidly—indeed almost instantaneously—to reflect all public information that is available about securities traded in that market.

a. This is the "semi-strong" version of the ECMH, which has the strongest empirical support. The "weak" form of the ECMH asserts only that all information contained in past price changes is incorporated into security prices. The "strong" form of the ECMH asserts that even nonpublic information is reflected quickly in security prices.

Caveat: While the evidence in favor of the semi-strong version of the ECMH is generally viewed as persuasive, some anomalies exist that are not explained by that hypothesis. Alternative theories to the ECMH may be developed in the future.

2. INFERENCES THAT MAY BE DRAWN FROM THE ECMH

A number of inferences, some of which are counter-intuitive, may be drawn from the ECMH:

a. Price movements in any one stock are random. It is not possible to predict from a previous transaction whether the next transaction will be higher or lower.

b. Persons who analyze historical changes in prices, usually called chartists, are engaging in futile and irrelevant analysis, because the market price already incorporates that information. Further, since all public information is incorporated in the current price of the shares, one cannot systematically improve one's investment success by studying publicly available information about investment alternatives.

c. It is not possible for a person to develop and apply a trading strategy that consistently outperforms the market.

d. Large institutional investors cannot hope in the long run to maintain portfolios that consistently perform better than the broad-based market indexes.

3. PERSONS WITH NONPUBLIC INFORMATION

Under the semistrong version of the ECMH, it is recognized that persons with undisclosed nonpublic information about a specific security may consistently obtain investment results that outperform the market.

4. JUDICIAL RECOGNITION OF THE ECMH

The ECMH was accepted by the United States Supreme Court as creating a rebuttable presumption that securities investors relied on false public information in *Basic Inc. v. Levinson*, 485 U.S. 224, 108 S.Ct. 978 (1988). The principle that incorporated the ECMH in this case is usually referred to as the "fraud on the market" theory. The ECMH has also been cited and relied upon by the Securities & Exchange Commission and lower federal courts. (See part XV B, infra.)

Caveat: Some writers have argued that the securities market is information-efficient but not value-efficient. In other words, the market may accurately value information but may not accurately value the worth of an entire business.

Caveat: While considerable empirical evidence supporting the validity of the ECMH exists for the broadest securities markets, including the New York Stock Exchange, the market for many publicly held securities is much thinner and less active and there is little empirical evidence as to whether these thinner markets are also efficient. Like the distinction between publicly held and closely held corporations, the "efficiency" of markets may be a matter of degree, and one should not assume that merely because a corporation is classified as "publicly held" an efficient and broad market necessarily exists for its shares.

F. STATE COMPETITION FOR CORPORATIONS

Since the late Nineteenth Century, states have competed to attract businesses to incorporate under their state statutes. Today, the uncrowned winner of this competition is the state of Delaware.

1. ADVANTAGES OF ENCOURAGING LOCAL INCORPORATIONS

The incorporation business provides filing fees and tax revenues for the state, fees for members of the local bar, business for legal stationers, employment in private organizations active in the incorporation business, and the like.

2. SUCCESS OF DELAWARE

Most large publicly held corporations are interstate or national in character and may incorporate in any one of the 50 states. More than half of all such businesses are incorporated in Delaware. Over one-third of all the corporations listed on the New York Stock Exchange are incorporated in Delaware. Every year a number of publicly held corporations incorporated in other states reincorporate in Delaware. There are practically no examples of movement in the opposite direction.

a. The Delaware Legislature and the Delaware Supreme Court are therefore the principal sources of modern corporation law today in terms of the number of corporations directly affected.

3. REASONS FOR SUCCESS OF DELAWARE: RACE FOR THE BOTTOM?

The earliest explanation of Delaware's success was that the Delaware GCL was permissive and permitted management the maximum freedom to operate without constraint. It was also argued that the Delaware judiciary made decisions favorable to management in order to preserve the economic benefits of the incorporation business. In this view, put forth by Professor Cary in 1974, Delaware had won "the race for the bottom."

a. Economists pointed out that if this explanation were accurate, corporations that reincorporate in Delaware should suffer a loss in the value of their publicly traded shares as a result of the efficient capital market hypothesis. Empirical investigations did not reveal such a loss.

b. The Delaware statute and the Delaware judiciary do not appear to be more management-oriented and permissive than the statutes and judiciaries of other states. A comparison of the provisions of the Delaware GCL with the MBCA (1984) and other modern corporation statutes does not reveal significant substantive differences that can be identified as systematically due to promanagement bias. While the importance of the corporation business to the economy of Delaware is obvious to everyone, including the Delaware judiciary, some recent Delaware court opinions stress protection of minority shareholders and hold management responsible for abuses of their position.

4. REASONS FOR SUCCESS OF DELAWARE: THE BEST PRODUCT?

The reason for the popularity and primacy of the state of Delaware may be explained partially by history, partially by the continued efforts by the bar of that state to provide an effective, flexible, and modern body of corporate law, and partially by the familiarity of corporate lawyers around the country with the Delaware GCL. Also contributing to Delaware's primacy is the existence of a sophisticated judiciary and sophisticated filing office that assures reasonable and knowledgeable decision making.

a. The Delaware GCL is flexible and simplifies the problems faced by the corporation in conducting its routine internal business under that statute.

b. There is "more" corporation law in Delaware today than in any other state. As a result, there are fewer areas of uncertainty in Delaware corporation law than in the law of any other state, and corporation lawyers may plan transactions with a relatively high degree of certainty.

c. The sophisticated judiciary, corporate bar, and filing authorities in Delaware are familiar with corporation problems arising in the modern context, particularly in the areas of contests for corporate control and derivative litigation. This sophistication tends to assure that corporate problems are handled fairly and efficiently.

d. Procedures exist in Delaware whereby unsuspected problems may be expeditiously dealt with by amendments to the Delaware GCL. Examples include the enactment of provisions protecting directors from personal liability in certain circumstances (see part XIV B 4, infra) and the enactment of a complex provision dealing with business combinations following takeovers (see part XIII D 2, infra).

e. Delaware case law generally permits corporations to adopt defensive tactics to combat unwanted takeovers.

Caveat: It may be argued that the rules adopted by Delaware in the areas described in parts c, d, and e unreasonably tend to favor management interests and therefore may not be in the best interest of shareholders generally.

5. REASONS FOR SUCCESS OF DELAWARE: OTHER EXPLANATIONS

An alternative explanation for the success of Delaware is that state statutes generally provide an array of incorporation alternatives ranging from "weak" (as in

Delaware) to "strong" (as in California), and that corporations decide where to incorporate based on the most useful statutory provision to them. Delaware's success is due to the large number of corporations that have decided that a "weak" statute best meets their needs.

a. In this view, the competition in state corporation statutes encourages efficiency.

b. Yet another theory views the Delaware statute as a result of the interplay of a variety of interest groups involved with corporations.

G. REVIEW QUESTIONS

I–1. Corporate problems are easy. One should simply visualize the corporation as a separate person and answer the question.

True _______ False _______

I–2. Corporate problems are easy. One should simply view the corporation as a contract among the various participants.

True _______ False _______

I–3. Corporate problems are easy. One should simply assess the situation and decide what is reasonable or fair.

True _______ False _______

I–4. If one person owns all of the stock of a corporation he is that corporation, and all the fictions in this world cannot dispute that fact.

This comment is largely true _______ largely false _______.

I–5. The state grants the corporation its charter and may impose any restrictions it wishes. A corporation therefore has only whatever rights the state chooses to give it.

True _______ False _______

I–6. The rights of preferred shareholders are set forth in articles of incorporation and common shareholders may limit the rights of the preferred shareholders to whatever is set forth in the articles.

True _______ False _______

I–7. The state grants the corporation its charter and its law therefore controls all aspects of the corporation's conduct.

True _______ False _______

I–8. How does a closely held corporation differ from a publicly held corporation?

I–9. Why is it to the advantage of the state in which you live to have a corporation statute that is modern, up-to-date, and reasonably fair to all interests within a corporation?

I–10. Professor Cary argued in a famous 1974 law review article that Delaware is successful in attracting corporations to that state because it won "the race to the bottom." Comment on that argument.

II

FORMATION OF CORPORATIONS

Analysis

A. SELECTION OF STATE OF INCORPORATION

The first question that must be resolved in forming a new corporation is what state should be the state of incorporation. For local or closely held businesses, the choice of the state of incorporation usually comes down to the state in which business is principally conducted or Delaware. In some instances, consideration may be given to incorporation in a state in which the corporation conducts some business but not the state in which business is principally conducted.

1. FACTORS IN SELECTION

There are several factors that enter into the selection of the state of incorporation, and a firm answer cannot be given in the abstract.

a. If a corporation plans to conduct business in state X, the costs of incorporating in Delaware and qualifying to transact business as a foreign corporation in state X are almost always higher than incorporating in state X to begin with.

b. With the "modernization" of state statutes and the elimination of onerous requirements, the disadvantages of local incorporation have tended to diminish or disappear. However, variations do exist in state law, and in some instances restrictive state rules about internal governance may dictate incorporation in a more liberal state.

c. Incorporation in Delaware or another "foreign" state may create later problems; for example, the corporation or its directors may be subject to suit in Delaware or the foreign state even though little or no business is conducted there and none of the directors are present in that state. In addition, state taxation statutes vary widely and may change over time, thereby unexpectedly increasing the cost of operation of a corporation.

d. An advantage of incorporating in Delaware is that there is a lot of "law" available in that state so that many questions can be firmly resolved under Delaware law; the same questions may not have clear answers under the local law.

e. An additional advantage of incorporating in Delaware is that one will deal with filing authorities and courts that are experts on all aspects of corporation law and practice.

2. MECHANICS OF FORMING CORPORATION IN AN UNFAMILIAR STATE

Where a decision has been made to form a corporation in an unfamiliar state, the easiest way for a lawyer to do so is to use a corporation service company. These companies routinely prepare and file the necessary documents to form a corporation in any jurisdiction, and may complete the formation of the corporation and provide additional services (such as obtaining minute books or seals, and preparing and filing tax and other forms required by state law) if requested to do so.

B. VARIATIONS IN STATUTORY REQUIREMENTS AND NOMENCLATURE

1. STATUTORY REQUIREMENTS

It is obviously essential to comply with the specific statutory requirements of the state chosen for the state of incorporation.

a. While numerous variations exist from state to state, there is a surprising degree of uniformity and consistency in most modern statutes. Virtually all onerous substantive requirements have been eliminated in most states.

b. Procedural variations in the incorporation process may still exist in some states. While most states simply require a filing with a state official and nothing more, Delaware and several other states also require a local filing in the county in which the registered office is located. Arizona and several other states require a public advertisement in a newspaper of general circulation of the fact of incorporation. Some states also continue to require the filing of additional documents to establish compliance with various statutory requirements.

Caveat: The consequences of failing to meet these additional requirements may be set forth in the statute itself. For example, Delaware provides that a failure to file locally within the specified period increases the filing fee but does not affect the existence of the corporation. Del. GCL § 103(d).

c. Variations may also exist with respect to filing fees, franchise taxes, stock issuance or transfer taxes, and similar items.

2. NOMENCLATURE

The MBCA (1984) nomenclature is followed in most states. In this nomenclature, the document filed with the secretary of state is called "articles of incorporation." Under earlier versions of the Model Act (and the statutes of a number of states), the secretary of state thereafter issues a document called a "certificate of incorporation" when he or she accepts the articles of incorporation for filing. In the MBCA (1984) (and the statutes of an increasing number of states), the paper work is simplified by requiring the Secretary of State simply to issue a fee receipt as indicating acceptance of the filing.

a. In Delaware and several other states the document filed with the secretary of state is called a "certificate of incorporation."

b. In some states, the document issued by the secretary of state is called a "charter."

C. DOCUMENTS FILED IN THE OFFICE OF THE SECRETARY OF STATE

The basic filing requirement is that articles of incorporation which conform to statutory requirements be filed accompanied by the appropriate filing fee. The state official charged with accepting corporate filings is usually the secretary of state, but some states have differently named filing officers.

1. PROCEDURE UNDER OLDER STATUTES

Under older state statutes, duplicate originals or an original and a copy of the articles of incorporation, must be filed with the secretary of state.

a. To be eligible for filing, articles of incorporation must be verified or acknowledged under oath before a notary public.

b. "Duplicate originals" means that both copies must be manually executed with original notarial seals and the like. As a practical matter, the document is prepared and copies made before it is executed; the original and one copy are then executed and filed. An "original and a copy" means that the original is fully executed and then copied by xerography or similar means so that signatures and seals are reproduced but not original.

c. If the articles of incorporation conform to the statute, the office of the secretary of state attaches the certificate of incorporation to the copy or duplicate original and returns them to the incorporators or their representative.

d. A receipt for the filing fee also usually accompanies the certificate.

2. PROCEDURE UNDER NEWER STATUTES

To reduce the problems of handling many pieces of paper, and to take advantage of modern technology, some states authorize the filing of only a single original executed copy of the articles of incorporation; the incorporators receive only a receipt for the filing fee as the sole evidence of incorporation. Such receipt is the equivalent of a certificate of incorporation. Of course, a certified copy of the original articles on file with the secretary of state may be obtained for a nominal fee.

A few states permit articles of incorporation to be transmitted by telefax rather than manual delivery of "hard" copies.

3. PROCEDURE UNDER THE MODEL BUSINESS CORPORATION ACT (1984)

MBCA (1984) §§ 1.20 and 1.25 standardize and simplify the filing requirements and filing procedures for most documents. Requirements that documents be verified or acknowledged are eliminated; the executing officer must simply designate the capacity in which he or she signs. One exact or conformed copy of the executed document must be filed with the document; the secretary of state attaches the fee receipt (or acknowledgement of receipt if there is no fee) to the copy and returns it to the filing party. The purpose of this procedure is to provide, for the benefit of the corporation, a copy of the filed document which shows on its face that it is an exact copy.

4. DISCRETION OF SECRETARY OF STATE TO REFUSE TO ACCEPT DOCUMENTS FOR FILING

Many state statutes grant the secretary of state (or the administrator of the filing office) authority to refuse to file documents unless they "conform with law" and may also grant that office the power to prescribe forms or to issue regulations relating to the documents being filed.

a. In some states, the secretary of state has been criticized by attorneys on the ground that the rules are unduly technical and that substantive review of portions of articles of incorporation, such as complex provisions creating classes of preferred stock, is unnecessary and disruptive of carefully negotiated financial arrangements.

b. The MBCA (1984) § 1.25 limits the discretion of the secretary of state in reviewing documents submitted for filing. This officer's duty is described as "ministerial" and he or she is directed to file documents even though they contain material not referred to in the Act. MBCA (1984) § 1.21 prohibits the secretary of state from prescribing mandatory forms (with a couple of minor exceptions). MBCA (1984) § 1.30 grants the secretary of state power "reasonably necessary to perform the duties required of him by this Act," but the Official Comment adds that this provision "is not intended to give him general authority to establish public policy." These restrictions on the authority of the secretary of state are narrower than the authority enjoyed by that officer in most states.

Caveat: Some states adopting the MBCA (1984) in substantial part have not adopted these provisions limiting the authority of the secretary of state.

D. INCORPORATORS

Articles of incorporation are executed by one or more persons called "incorporators." Historically, three incorporators who were natural persons were required and many states imposed special residency or other requirements for incorporators. The signatures of incorporators usually had to be verified or acknowledged under oath before a notary public.

1. MODERN ROLE OF INCORPORATORS

The role of incorporators today is a formal one without significant responsibilities, duties, or liabilities. It is generally believed that there is no risk of liability for acting as an incorporator of a corporation. As a result, virtually all states have simplified the requirements with respect to incorporators.

a. Only a single incorporator is required, who in many states may be a corporation, trust, estate or partnership. There are usually no residency requirements for incorporators who are individuals.

b. Requirements of oaths, verifications, and seals have been eliminated in some states by statute or judicial decision. See e.g., *People v. Ford,* 128 N.E. 479 (Ill.1920).

c. Incorporators execute the articles of incorporation and receive back the certificate of incorporation. In most states, they serve no other function.

d. In some states the incorporators meet to complete the formation of the corporation. In jurisdictions that follow earlier versions of the Model Act, the incorporators do not meet and formation of the corporation is completed by initial directors named in the articles of incorporation. MBCA (1984) §§ 2.02(b)(1) and 2.05(a) give each corporation the option of having the formation completed by the incorporators or by initial directors named in the articles of incorporation. The Official Comment to § 2.05 states that "it is expected that initial directors will be named [in the articles of incorporation] only if they will be the permanent board of directors and there is no objection to the disclosure of their identity in the articles of incorporation."

Caveat: Where incorporators actually complete the organization of the corporation, there may be risk of liability if required funds are not actually received, etc.

2. DUMMY INCORPORATORS

Since incorporators have no substantive responsibilities in most states, the practice is widespread of using "dummy" incorporators. These may be a secretary or employee of the law firm creating the corporation, a low level employee of a corporation service company, or any other person unconnected with the future business who is willing to allow his or her name to be used as an incorporator.

E. CONTENT OF THE ARTICLES OF INCORPORATION

1. MANDATORY REQUIREMENTS

There is a clear trend to simplify the mandatory disclosure requirements for articles of incorporation. Today in many states the required information comfortably fits on a post card.

a. Older state statutes generally require the following *minimum* information to appear in every articles of incorporation:

1) The name of the corporation;

2) Its duration, which may be perpetual;

3) Its purpose or purposes which may be, or include, the conduct of any lawful business;

4) The securities it is authorized to issue;

5) The name of its registered agent and the address of its registered office;

6) The names and addresses of its initial board of directors (in states where the initial board completes the formation of the corporation);

7) The name and address of the incorporator or incorporators.

b. Experience has shown that virtually all corporations elect the duration to be "perpetual" and their purposes to be "the conduct of any lawful business." As a result, the MBCA (1984) omits these two provisions, instead providing that every corporation has perpetual duration unless a shorter period is chosen [§ 3.02] and a purpose of engaging in "any lawful business" unless a more limited purpose is set forth in the articles of incorporation [§ 3.01(a)].

2. DISCRETIONARY PROVISIONS

In addition to the required minimum provisions, state statutes permit additional provisions to be included in the articles of incorporation at the election of the corporation.

a. State statutes typically provide that specified rules of corporate governance are automatically applicable unless the corporation elects to eliminate or modify them by specific provision in the articles of incorporation. These are called "opt out" provisions.

Example: In many states each shareholder has preemptive rights (see part V H) and a right to vote cumulatively (see part VII D) unless such rights are specifically limited or excluded by provisions in the articles of incorporation.

b. State statutes also may provide that a corporation may elect to make specific rules of corporate governance applicable by making specific provision in the articles of incorporation for the application of those rules. These are called "opt in" provisions.

Example: In the MBCA (1984), both preemptive rights and cumulative voting are made opt in provisions. [§§ 6.30(a), 7.28(b).] A corporation has these rules of corporate governance only by making specific election to have them. This change was made because it was believed that these rules often constituted traps for the unwary shareholder. Most publicly held corporations eliminate both preemptive rights and cumulative voting on the theory that they greatly complicate the raising of capital and voting for directors and are of little direct benefit in most publicly held corporations.

Example: A publicly held corporation desires that a quorum of shareholders should consist of holders of one third or more of the shares rather than a majority. The statutes of many states provide that a quorum consist of a majority of the outstanding shares but permit the requirement to be reduced to one-third by specific provision in the articles of incorporation. In most states, a similar provision placed only in the bylaws would be ineffective.

c. State statutes authorize additional discretionary provisions to be placed either in the articles of incorporation or the bylaws.

Caveat: Corporate officers and directors are generally more familiar with the bylaws than with articles of incorporation. Where governance provisions are placed in articles of incorporation, it is generally desirable that they also appear in the bylaws so that they will come to the attention of officers and directors. (See part II O.)

Example: A corporation desires to limit the right of directors to obtain indemnification of litigation costs from the corporation. Under the statute of the state of incorporation, the right of indemnification may be limited or excluded by an appropriate provision either in the articles of incorporation or the bylaws. A provision of this nature would normally appear in the bylaws rather than in the articles of incorporation.

Example: A corporation proposes that the board of directors may act only by unanimous vote. Even though such a clause is effective if placed in either the bylaws or the articles of incorporation under the state statute in question, an attorney may recommend that the provision be included in the articles of incorporation because it is unusual and has the potential of creating a deadlock. The provision also should appear in the bylaws.

Example: A closely held corporation plans to create share transfer restrictions that require all shareholders to sell their shares to the corporation upon death or retirement at book value less 25 per cent, a price that is recognized as being artificially low. All shareholders are willing to enter into these restrictions. Such a restriction is valid if placed in the bylaws, but the attorney recommends that the articles of incorporation be amended to include the provision because she wishes to maximize the probability that the restrictions will be enforced in accordance with their terms. Again, the provision should also appear in the bylaws.

d. State statutes generally authorize corporations to include in the articles of incorporation provisions relating to corporate powers. Though it is unnecessary (and, indeed, undesirable) to refer to powers specifically and unambiguously granted to corporations by statute, references to specific powers may be helpful where the state statute is silent or unclear on whether corporations generally possess the specific power.

Example: Old case law in State *X* makes it clear that corporations generally do not have power to act as general partners in general or limited partnerships. The present state incorporation statute contains an oblique reference to "investing in partnerships" but does not specifically authorize a corporation to act as a general partner. A careful attorney recommends that a specific grant of power that the corporation may act as a general partner in a general or limited partnership be routinely included in the articles of incorporation of every corporation she forms. Such a clause effectively broadens the power of the corporation, reduces the likelihood that later transactions may be questioned, and possibly avoids future litigation.

e. Special clauses relating to the purposes of a corporation are sometimes included in articles of incorporation even in states where the statute, like MBCA (1984) § 3.01, automatically grants every corporation the power to engage in any lawful business. (See part II H.)

F. THE CORPORATE NAME

Under most state statutes, a corporate name must (i) contain a reference to the corporate nature of the entity (using the words "corporation," "incorporated," "inc." or similar word), (ii) not be the same as or deceptively similar to a name already in use or reserved for use, and (iii) not imply that a corporation is engaged in a business in which corporations may not lawfully engage. The MBCA (1984) substitutes the test of "distinguishable upon the records of the Secretary of State" for the "same or deceptively similar" test (see 1. below). Secretaries of state maintain lists of names that are reserved or currently in use (and hence unavailable) and also may have internal rules about name availability. As a result, it is desirable to check whether a specific name is available with the secretary of state before it is used.

Example: Articles of incorporation are filed under the corporate name "Chicago Allied Steel Company." The name is rejected because an existing corporation is using the name "Allied Steel Company" and the internal rules of the secretary of state's office require that geographical names be ignored in determining whether names are identical. (Whether or not the secretary of state is correctly construing the statute is usually irrelevant in such situations; it is so much easier to choose another name that is acceptable to the secretary of state than to litigate over name availability that even the most arbitrary rules are unlikely to be tested.)

1. NAME UNIQUENESS

The requirement that each corporation have a unique name is primarily to avoid confusion in such matters as sending tax notices and naming defendants in law suits.

a. In many states, the name requirements are partially designed to prevent unfair competition. These statutes prohibit the use of names that are the "same or deceptively similar"; some states distinguish further between names that are the "same" or "deceptively similar," or merely "similar." The "same" or "deceptively similar" names may not be used under any circumstances while a "similar" name may be used if the proposed corporation obtains a letter of consent from the other corporation. The latter requirement seems clearly based on unfair competition considerations. The following examples are drawn from regulations adopted in a state that follows this pattern:

Example: "Sampson Inc.," "Sampson Company," "Sampson Corporation," and "The Sampson Company" are all "the same."

Example: "Van Lines of North America, Inc." and "North American Van Lines, Inc." are "deceptively similar."

Example: "Chicago Service and Supply, Inc." is similar to "Chicago Service Co." and would need a letter of consent.

Example: "E. G. Williams Electric Company" is not the same, deceptively similar, or similar to "Williams Electric Company" and no letter of consent is required.

Caveat: Not all state agencies might agree with these conclusions.

b. Delaware GCL, MBCA (1984) § 4.01 and the statutes of a few other states have changed the "same or deceptively similar" test to "distinguishable upon the records" of the secretary of state. The MBCA (1984) adopted this standard on the theory that the secretary of state "does not generally police the unfair competitive use of names and indeed, usually has no resources to do so." Confusion "in the absolute or linguistic sense" is the test for name availability under this simpler standard.

Example: "ABC Co.," "ABC Inc.," "AbC Co." and "Abc Inc." would probably not be viewed as distinguishable upon the records of the secretary of state under this standard.

Example: "Transamerica Airlines, Inc." is distinguishable upon the records of the secretary of state from "Transamerica, Inc." and "Trans International Airlines, Inc." *Trans–Americas Airlines, Inc. v. Kenton,* 491 A.2d 1139 (Del.1985).

2. RESERVATION OF NAME

Persons planning to form a corporation may "reserve" an available name for a limited period of time (usually 120 days) for a small fee. MBCA (1984) § 4.02. The reservation of a name permits the preparation of corporate documents, ordering of stationery, etc., with assurance that the proposed name will be available if the articles of incorporation are filed within the period the name is reserved. Reservations of name may not be renewable in some states.

3. REGISTRATION OF NAME

A foreign corporation not transacting business in a state may register its name with the secretary of state to assure that no local business will obtain the right to use its name. MBCA (1984) § 4.03. Registration of a name thus protects the foreign corporation's good will reflected in its name and preserves its option to later expand its operations into the state under its current name. In most states, registration is on an annual basis and may be renewed indefinitely. Some states, however, do not authorize the registration of names of foreign corporations.

4. USE OF ASSUMED NAME BY FOREIGN CORPORATION

Business corporation acts generally do not require a corporation to conduct business in its corporate name. A corporation therefore has the same right as an individual to conduct business under an assumed name so long as the use of the name is not fraudulent and does not constitute unfair competition with some other person already using the same or a similar name.

a. Many states have assumed name statutes that require individuals or corporations using assumed names to file an assumed name certificate with the county clerk or some other state or local official. A corporation that elects to transact business under a name other than its corporate name usually must comply with such a statute in the same way as an individual.

b. A corporation that uses its own official corporate name is not considered to be using an assumed name and therefore is not subject to the filing requirement of assumed name statutes. Assumed name statutes vary widely from state to state, and many states do not have such statutes.

c. A foreign corporation that has not previously registered its name may discover that its own name is not available when it seeks to qualify to transact business in a new state. In this situation, the statutes of many states require the foreign corporation to qualify to transact business under an assumed name in the new state and file an assumed name certificate with the secretary of state. (See part XX.)

G. PERIOD OF DURATION

Modern statutes authorize the corporation to have "perpetual" existence, and while it is possible to specify a shorter period of existence, it is almost never desirable to do so. A period of existence less than perpetual creates the risk that the corporate existence may expire without renewal with uncertain rights and liabilities of participants thereafter. The MBCA (1984) § 3.02 provides that every corporation has a perpetual duration unless a shorter period is specified in the articles of incorporation.

H. PURPOSES

Modern statutes authorize very general purposes clauses, e. g., "the purpose of the corporation is to engage in any lawful business or businesses" without further specification. The use of such clauses, however, is a recent phenomenon. The MBCA (1984) and the statutes of several states go even further and provide that every corporation automatically has a broad "any lawful business" purpose unless a narrower purpose is specified in the articles of incorporation.

1. HISTORY OF PURPOSES CLAUSES

The nature of purposes clauses has evolved over a long period of time, reflecting varying attitudes of mistrust toward the corporation. They were formerly of much greater importance than they are today.

a. In the earliest period, all corporations were formed by special legislative enactment. In effect each purposes clause was separately developed in the legislative process.

b. In the nineteenth and early twentieth centuries corporations could be formed under the early general incorporation statutes only for a limited and specific purpose, e.g., "to conduct a mill for the grinding of wheat, corn, and other grain." Corporations were usually limited to a single specific purpose, though ancillary powers might be implied from such a purposes clause.

Example: A railroad corporation was authorized "to purchase, hold, and use . . . real estate and other property as may be necessary for the construction and maintenance of its road and canal and the stations and other accommodations necessary to accomplish the objects of its incorporation . . ." The U.S. Supreme Court held that a lease of a seaside hotel by the corporation was within this purpose clause and was therefore not ultra vires. *Jacksonville, M., P. Ry. & Nav. Co. v. Hooper,* 160 U.S. 514, 16 S.Ct. 379 (1896).

c. A major advance occurred when state statutes were modernized to permit corporations to include a number of specific purposes clauses. Since the number of such clauses was unlimited, many corporations adopted the practice of including tens or even hundreds of specific purposes clauses routinely in every articles of incorporation. This practice quickly eliminated any significance the purposes clauses might have.

d. Many early statutes restricted the power of corporations to amend articles of incorporation to broaden purposes clauses. These restrictions were gradually eliminated as the practice of using multiple purposes clauses grew. Today, corporations with limited purposes clauses may freely amend them to include whatever purposes are permitted under the applicable state statute.

e. A general purposes clause of the "any lawful business" type is a logical simplification of the practice of using multiple purposes clauses.

2. PURPOSES CLAUSES IN MODERN PRACTICE

In modern practice there is usually little or no reason to have a purposes clause at all, and doctrines based on the premise that purposes clauses are limiting in nature, such as ultra vires or implied powers, have little modern relevance. Purposes clauses may be necessary or desirable in the following situations:

a. A recitation of the purpose of a corporation may be required by a regulatory statute or agency if the corporation is to engage in a specific business.

Example: Professional corporation statutes usually require that a corporation specify in its articles of incorporation which profession it proposes to engage in and permits the corporation to engage only in that one profession.

b. Some persons prefer that articles of incorporation provide some information about the objects of the corporation even though that is not required by modern statutes. A purposes clause that describes in general terms the business in which the corporation plans to engage may be coupled with a clause such as "and any other lawful business" in order to assure that the corporation may enter into new lines of business without going to the expense of amending its purposes clause.

Example: A corporation planning to go into the beer production business might have a purposes clause that states that the purpose of the corporation is to "engage in the business of manufacturing and selling beer, alcoholic and non-alcoholic beverages, and any other lawful business."

3. LIMITED PURPOSES CLAUSE AS A PLANNING DEVICE

A limited purposes clause may be used today (despite broader statutory authorization) as a planning device or to limit corporate activities as a protection for investors. A corporation that pursues a business that exceeds such a limited purposes clause is acting ultra vires. (See part II M below.)

Example: The statute of State *X* provides that every corporation has the power to engage in any lawful business unless a narrower purpose is specified in the articles of incorporation. *A* is an investor in a new corporation which is to be operated by *B* and *C* who are each making much smaller investments. *A* wants to ensure that the corporation will only engage in the retail drug business. He insists that a clause restricting the purposes of the corporation be included in the articles of incorporation. The clause is valid within a limited extent and *A* may be able to enjoin *B* and *C* from engaging in a broader business if the rights of third persons have not intervened.

Caveat: Because of modern rules relating to ultra vires (see part II M), it is doubtful that the narrow purposes clause requested by *A* will effectively limit the activities of the corporation. *A* should seek to establish more effective voting or control devices if he wishes to assure himself that his capital will be invested only in the retail drug business. (See part X B.)

I. SECURITIES

The securities a corporation is authorized to issue must be described in the articles of incorporation. MBCA(1984) § 2.02(a)(2) requires only that the corporation set forth "the number of shares the corporation is authorized to issue." However, § 6.01(a) provides that if a corporation is to issue more than one class of shares, "the articles of incorporation must prescribe the classes of shares and the number of shares of each class that the corporation is authorized to issue." (See part V C.)

The statutes of somewhat more than half of the states also require the articles of incorporation to set forth the par value of the authorized shares, or a statement that the shares are issued "without par value." (See part V B.)

J. INITIAL CAPITALIZATION

Fifty years ago virtually all states required that a corporation have a minimum amount of capitalization before it could commence business. One thousand dollars was the most common amount, but some states selected other amounts.

1. CURRENT TREND

The modern trend is clearly in the direction of eliminating such requirements. Most states today have eliminated all minimum capitalization requirements. The theory behind this trend is that minimum capitalization requirements are arbitrary and unrelated to the true capital needs of the corporation, and therefore do not provide meaningful protection to creditors.

2. FAILURE TO MEET MINIMUM INITIAL CAPITAL REQUIREMENTS

In states that retain minimum capitalization requirements, directors are usually made personally liable, if business is commenced without the required minimum capital.

a. In most states this liability is limited to the difference between the minimum required capitalization and the amount of capital actually contributed.

Example: In a state with a minimum $1,000 capital requirement, a corporation commences business with $700 in capital. The directors are liable for $300; this liability disappears if the corporation thereafter obtains additional capital of $300 or more.

b. A few state statutes have been construed to impose unlimited liability on directors for all debts incurred before the minimum capitalization is paid in.

Example: In such a state, with a minimum $1,000 capital requirement, a corporation commences business with capital of $700. In the course of its business, the corporation thereafter incurs liabilities of $10,000 before any further capital is paid in. The directors are liable for $10,000 and this liability is not eliminated even though thereafter capital contributions of $300 or more are received. E.g., *Sulphur Export Corp. v. Carribean Clipper Lines, Inc.,* 277 F.Supp. 632 (E.D.La.1968). *Tri–State Developers, Inc. v. Moore,* 343 S.W.2d 812 (Ky.1961).

c. There is no requirement that a corporation maintain any specified surplus of assets over liabilities after incorporation.

3. SHARE SUBSCRIPTIONS

Persons may agree to purchase shares in advance of incorporation. Such agreements are called "subscriptions" or "subscription agreements" and the persons agreeing to purchase shares are called "subscribers." Rights and duties with respect to share subscriptions are discussed in part III E.

a. A person subscribing for shares has financial obligations to the corporation and possibly to other subscribers.

b. The incorporator of a corporation need not be a subscriber for shares.

K. REGISTERED OFFICE AND REGISTERED AGENT

The registered office and registered agent at that office must be specified in the articles of incorporation. MBCA (1984) § 5.01. They serve the purposes of providing a location where the corporation may be found (for service of process, tax notices, and the like) and a person on whom process may be served. State statutes require filings with the Secretary of State to reflect changes in the registered office or registered agent, or both. MBCA (1984) § 5.02.

Corporation service companies serve as registered agents for many thousands of corporations in some states. MBCA (1984) § 5.03 addresses how a registered agent may resign as such (presumably because its annual fee has not been paid). The MBCA (1984) also sets forth a a simplified procedure in case the corporation service company itself moves its office to another location within the state, and wishes to avoid having each of its clients file a change of registered office form. MBCA (1984) § 5.02(b).

L. CORPORATE POWERS

MBCA (1984) § 3.02 provides that every corporation "has the same powers as an individual to do all things necessary or convenient to carry out its business and affairs, including without limitation" a list of specific powers. Most states have an enumeration of specific powers but without the quoted, broadening language, which was drawn from the California statute.

1. ENUMERATED POWERS

Every state statute enumerates general powers that every corporation possesses. Generally, it is unnecessary and undesirable to list some or all of these powers in the articles of incorporation. The traditional enumerated powers possessed by corporations under modern statutes include the power:

a. To sue and be sued;

b. To have a corporate seal;

c. To purchase, receive, lend, sell, invest, convey and mortgage personal and real property;

d. To make contracts, borrow and lend money, and guarantee the indebtedness of third persons;

e. To conduct its business within or without the state;

f. To elect or appoint officers or agents, define their duties, fix their compensation, and provide pension, profit sharing, and stock option plans;

g. To purchase shares or interests in, or obligations of, any other entity;

h. To make charitable, scientific or education contributions or donations for the public welfare;

i. To be a partner or manager of a partnership or other venture;

j. To make and alter bylaws for the administration and regulation of its internal affairs.

k. To indemnify directors and officers against liabilities imposed on them while acting on behalf of the corporation, and to provide liability insurance for them.

MBCA (1984), § 3.02(15) also permits a corporation "to make payments or donations, or do any other act, not inconsistent with law, that furthers the business and affairs of the corporation." This power permits corporations to make political donations or contributions to influence elections to the extent permitted by state law.

2. ACTS IN EXCESS OF POWERS

If a corporation does an act which it does not have power to do, it is acting ultra vires. (See part II M.)

3. PARTIAL ENUMERATION OF POWERS

The danger of a partial enumeration of statutory powers in an articles of incorporation is that a negative inference may be drawn that the inclusion of some enumerated powers implies the exclusion of unenumerated ones.

M. ULTRA VIRES

The dictionary definition of "ultra vires" is beyond the scope of the powers of a corporation. It is used to describe acts that exceed either the stated purposes or the powers of the corporation.

Example: A corporation is formed for the purpose of "selling or lending all kinds of railway plant, carrying on the business of mechanical engineers, etc." The corporation contracts to build a railroad in a foreign country. In a famous decision the English courts held the contract to be ultra vires. *Ashbury Railway Carriage & Iron Co. v. Riche*, 7 N.S. Law Times Rep. 450 (1875).

1. THE COMMON LAW ULTRA VIRES DOCTRINE

The early common law view was that an ultra vires transaction was void since the corporation simply lacked the power to enter into the transaction. Such a doctrine, however, led to potentially undesirable results and was gradually modified:

a. A transaction that was purely executory might be enjoined if it was ultra vires with respect to either party.

b. If the transaction was wholly executed by both parties, the transaction cannot be attacked on the ground of ultra vires. *Herbert v. Sullivan*, 123 F.2d 477 (1st Cir.1941).

c. If the transaction was partially executed, ultra vires may be raised, but doctrines of estoppel, unjust enrichment, or pure fairness might mitigate the strict common law view. *Goodman v. Ladd Estate Co.*, 427 P.2d 102 (Or.1967).

d. Ultra vires transactions might be ratified by all the shareholders. See *Lurie v. Arizona Fertilizer & Chemical Co.*, 421 P.2d 330 (Ariz.1966)[corporation entering partnership].

e. Generally, the defense of ultra vires is not available to a corporation in a suit based on tort or in a prosecution for criminal conduct. Such liability, of course, is based on agency principles of respondeat superior.

f. Directors and officers causing the corporation to enter into ultra vires transactions are not automatically liable for losses suffered thereby, though the fact that the conduct was ultra vires might cause courts to be more willing to "pierce the corporate veil" or otherwise impose personal liability on the shareholders. See *Lurie v. Arizona Fertilizer & Chemical Co.*, 421 P.2d 330 (Ariz.1966).

g. The attorney general of the state may attack corporations engaging in ultra vires transactions by injunction, quo warranto, or suits to dissolve the corporation. As a practical matter, such suits by the state are extremely rare.

2. STATUTORY MINIMIZATION OF THE ULTRA VIRES DOCTRINE

The following statute has greatly reduced the importance of the ultra vires doctrine:

"(a) Except as provided in subsection (b), the validity of corporate action may not be challenged on the ground that the corporation lacks or lacked power to act.

"(b) A corporation's power to act may be challenged:

"(1) in a proceeding by a shareholder against the corporation to enjoin the act;

"(2) in a proceeding by the corporation, directly, derivatively, or through a receiver, trustee, or other legal representative, against an incumbent or former director, officer, employee, or agent of the corporation; or

"(3) in a proceeding by the attorney general. . . .

"(c) In a shareholder's proceeding under subsection (b)(1) to enjoin an unauthorized corporate act, the court may enjoin or set aside the act, if equitable and if all affected persons are parties to the proceeding, and may award damages for loss (other than anticipated profits) suffered by the corporation or another party because of enjoining the unauthorized act."

MBCA (1984) § 3.04. Similar statutes are in effect in virtually all states.

Example: A corporation formed for the purpose of dealing in pleasure boats and motors signs a lease to rent a motion picture theater for a long period. The landlord regrets entering the lease and seeks to cancel it on the ground it is ultra vires from the standpoint of the tenant. The landlord loses under the above statute even though the tenant has not amended its articles of incorporation to broaden its purpose. *711 Kings Highway Corp. v. F. I. M.'s Marine Repair Serv., Inc.*, 273 N.Y.S.2d 299 (1966).

Example: A corporation is sued on a guarantee of indebtedness which it made to secure a loan to a customer. Such a guarantee is ultra vires under the law of the state in question. The corporation nevertheless may not defend on the ground that the guarantee is ultra vires since the statute precludes raising ultra vires as a defense. However, a shareholder may conceivably intervene under § 3.04(b)(1) and raise the ultra vires issue in a suit to enjoin the making of such a guarantee. If a shareholder does so, the court has discretion whether or not to enforce the ultra vires contract on the ground of equity or fairness. The plaintiff may also seek to avoid the claim of the intervening shareholder on the ground that he is not in fact acting independently of the corporation and therefore is not equitably entitled to seek to enjoin the action. *Cf. Inter-Continental Corp. v. Moody*, 411 S.W.2d 578 (Tex.Civ.App.1966).

3. OTHER FACTORS MINIMIZING THE IMPORTANCE OF ULTRA VIRES

Three other factors minimize the significance of the ultra vires doctrine today:

a. The use of multiple purposes clauses, and more recently, the use of general purposes clauses;

b. The broadening of the general powers that every corporation possesses by statute; and

c. The power of a corporation to amend its articles of incorporation in order to broaden its purposes to accommodate desirable transactions.

4. MODERN AREAS OF ULTRA VIRES CONCERN

Ultra vires issues may continue to arise in some states on the question whether or not the corporation has power to enter into the following acts:

a. Making political contributions or engaging in activities designed to influence legislation;

b. Granting unusual employee fringe benefits that appear to be unrelated to the value of the services rendered;

c. Entering into partnerships;

d. Making large charitable donations that appear to provide no benefit to the corporation;

e. Guaranteeing indebtedness of others that provide only incidental benefit to the corporation; and

f. Making loans to officers or directors.

Caveat: Even when not expressly referred to, a court may conclude that a corporation implicitly has power to engage in the foregoing acts. E.g. *Union Pac. Railroad Co. v. Trustees, Inc.,* 329 P.2d 398 (Utah 1958) (charitable contribution).

Caveat: Even where state statutes grant the power to enter into such transactions in broad terms, courts may impose a limitation of reasonableness based on public policy or common sense.

Example: A state statute authorizes a corporation to "make donations for the public welfare or for charitable, scientific or educational purposes." A closely held corporation with income in excess of $19,000,000 per year proposes to make a gift of over $500,000 to a charitable corporation controlled by the majority shareholder. The gift is valid; even though the statute should be construed to permit only "reasonable" charitable gifts, the proposed contribution is reasonable under the circumstances. *Theodora Holding Corp. v.*

Henderson, 257 A.2d 398 (Del.Ch.1969). In concluding that a $500,000 gift was reasonable, some reliance may be placed on the federal income tax law that permits the deduction of up to ten percent of taxable income as charitable donations in any year.

Example: After the death of two corporate officers, the board of directors of the corporation gratuitously votes to pay certain bonuses to their widows. Such payments are ultra vires since they are not charitable and, under the specific circumstances, not supported by consideration or justifiable as a species of executive compensation. *Adams v. Smith*, 153 So.2d 221 (Ala.1963). Some courts have disagreed about similar payments, *Chambers v. Beaver–Advance Corp.*, 140 A.2d 808 (Pa. 1958). If a program by which stipends are to be paid to widows or widowers of employees is announced in advance, that plan should be valid as a type of employment compensation.

Example: *X*, an 80 per cent shareholder of corporation Y, causes Y corporation to place a second mortgage on its property to secure a loan made to a corporation that is wholly owned by *X*. Such a mortgage is ultra vires and may be set aside at the suit of the 20 per cent shareholder of Y. *Real Estate Capital Corp. v. Thunder Corp.*, 287 N.E.2d 838 (Ohio Com.Pleas 1972). It was unclear whether the holder of the mortgage had reason to know that Y received no benefit from the mortgage; this transaction may also constitute a breach of fiduciary duty by *X*.

Example: In order to secure passage of legislation, a corporation agrees to make certain payments to local taxing authorities in lieu of taxes; as a result of that agreement, the local taxing authorities withdraw their opposition to the legislation. Such payments are not ultra vires; they are donations to local taxing authorities though not contributions and not lobbying expenditures; *Kelly v. Bell*, 254 A.2d 62 (Del.Ch.1969). The Supreme Court of Delaware affirmed, commenting that personal liability should not be imposed on the directors for such a payment since they exercised a reasonable business judgment in agreeing to make the payment.

N. COMPLETION OF THE FORMATION OF THE CORPORATION

The filing of articles of incorporation is only the first step in forming a corporation.

1. ADDITIONAL STEPS

Lawyers generally are expected to complete the formation of a corporation on behalf of a client. The following additional steps may be necessary to complete the formation of a corporation:

a. Prepare bylaws;

b. Prepare minutes of the various organizational meetings, including waivers of notice or consents to action without formal meetings;

c. Open a bank account;

d. Obtain a minute book and seal;

e. Obtain blank share certificates and make sure they are properly prepared and issued for the consideration specified for those shares;

f. Prepare shareholders' agreement, if any;

g. Obtain necessary tax identification numbers and comply with other state and federal legal requirements;

h. Generally oversee the preparation and execution of the various forms, certificates and other documents.

i. Open a bank account for the corporation;

j. Determine whether the S corporation tax election should be made, and, if so, make that election;

k. Make sure the directors and officers understand the nature of their duties and responsibilities.

These steps may require meetings of the incorporators, the board of directors, or possibly, a meeting of the shareholders. (See parts II D, II N.)

2. CONSEQUENCES OF FAILURE TO COMPLETE FORMATION

The consequences of a partial formation of a corporation usually arise in the context of a suit against officers, directors, or shareholders seeking to hold them liable for an obligation incurred in the name of the corporation. A number of cases hold that no personal liability is created so long as articles of incorporation were properly filed. E.g., *Moe v. Harris,* 172 N.W. 494 (Minn.1919). If personal liability is imposed after the filing of articles of incorporation, the result is likely to be analyzed as a case involving:

a. Promoters' liability (See part III B);

b. Piercing the corporate veil (See part IV); or

c. The failure to comply with a mandatory condition subsequent. This possibility is becoming less common with the simplification of incorporation statutes and the general acceptance of the principle that the corporate existence begins when the articles of incorporation are accepted for filing.

3. THE NEED FOR ORGANIZATIONAL MEETINGS

Organizational documents may consist of "minutes" of meetings prepared by an attorney before the corporation is formed. The question may arise whether it is necessary to actually hold meetings to reflect what the minutes describe.

a. If the corporation is closely held, and there is no disagreement about what is to be done, actual meetings in the physical sense are not usually held.

b. In most states, unanimous written consents may be used instead of minutes to avoid any meeting requirement.

c. If the consent procedure is unavailable, and minutes of meeting must be used, lawyers may insist that an informal meeting actually be held, using the already-prepared minutes as a script.

O. BYLAWS

The bylaws of a corporation are a set of rules for governing the internal affairs of the corporation. They are typically adopted as part of the formation of a new corporation, and may be modified thereafter by the board of directors acting alone or by the shareholders. See MBCA (1984) §§ 10.20—10.22.

1. LEGAL EFFECT OF BYLAWS

Bylaws are binding on intra-corporate matters. They may be viewed as a contract between the corporation and its members, or as a set of binding internal rules of governance.

2. PRACTICAL EFFECT OF BYLAWS

Bylaws essentially are an operating manual of basic rules for the conduct of the ordinary business of the corporation. They may be relied upon by the corporate officers as a checklist in administering the affairs of the corporation.

a. Corporate officers and directors are likely to be more conversant with the bylaws than the articles of incorporation.

b. For this reason, procedural matters and mandatory provisions that appear in the articles of incorporation relating to corporate governance should normally also appear in the bylaws.

P. REVIEW QUESTIONS

II–1. Delaware is the best state in which to incorporate a new business.

True _______ False _______

II–2. Incorporation is an expensive process not suitable for small businesses.

True _______ False _______

II–3. When forming a corporation, it makes no difference who you use as incorporators.

True _______ False _______

II–4. Articles of incorporation may contain only the information specified in the statute.

True _______ False _______

II–5. Why would provisions relating to internal governance that may be included in either the articles of incorporation or by the bylaws ever be included in the articles of incorporation ?

II–6. A corporation must do business under its official name and may not use a fictitious name.

True _______ False _______

II–7. What is the difference between a reserved and a registered name?

II–8. When should a period of duration less than perpetual be elected?

II–9. Corporations must specify the purposes for which they are formed and limit their activities to those purposes.

True ______ False ______

II–10. Corporations should always use the broadest possible purposes clause permitted by the state statute.

True ______ False ______

II–11. Why does a corporation need a registered agent and registered office?

II–12. Should corporate powers ever be listed in articles of incorporation?

II–13. What does ultra vires mean?

II–14. Why do modern statutes restrict or eliminate the doctrine of ultra vires?

II–15. What factors have led to the decline of ultra vires?

II–16. What steps are required to complete the formation of a corporation after articles of incorporation have been filed?

II–17. What is the consequence of filing articles of incorporation and commencing business without completing the organization of the corporation?

II–18. Two lawyers, one practicing real property and estates law and the other specializing in the trial of negligence cases, share an office. Each pays half the rent, the salaries of the employees, the cost of office equipment, supplies, utilities, and the upkeep of the library. They each have their own clients and receive their respective fees. Would they enjoy any advantages, including minimizing their taxes and maximizing their tax benefits, by incorporating? To what extent would they have to change their manner of operations? [This question and answer is drawn from Ballantine, Problems in Law 230 (5th Ed. 1975).]

II–19. What factors enter into the decision to place optional provisions in the articles of incorporation rather than the bylaws?

II–20. If provisions appear in the articles of incorporation it is unnecessary to repeat them in the bylaws.

True _______ False _______

*

III

PREINCORPORATION TRANSACTIONS

Analysis

A. PROMOTERS

"Promoters" are persons who assist in putting together a new business. The term is not one of opprobrium; rather, promoters are often shrewd, visionary individuals who serve important social and economic functions.

1. BASIC FUNCTIONS OF PROMOTERS

In promoting a new venture, promoters:

a. Arrange for the necessary business assets and personnel so that the new business may function effectively. This may include obtaining or renting a plant, assembling work and sales forces, finding sources of raw materials and supplies, finding retail outlets, making long term commitments of various types, and so forth.

b. Obtain the necessary capital to finance the venture. The sources of capital include (i) equity capital contributed by investors, (ii) loans from third parties, either secured or unsecured, and (iii) loans from the investors supplying the equity capital.

c. Complete the formation of the corporation.

2. LOCATION OF DISCUSSION OF PROMOTERS IN THIS OUTLINE

Part B of this section of the outline deals exclusively with problems of contracts entered into by promoters in connection with function (1)(a) above. Problems of capital raising (function (1)(b) above) are discussed in parts III E and V. Promoters' fiduciary duties relating both to promoters contracts and the raising of capital are discussed in part C of this section of the outline. The formation of corporations is discussed in Part II.

B. PROMOTER'S CONTRACTS

Promoters may enter into contracts on behalf of the venture being promoted either before or after articles of incorporation have been filed. Most problems are created by preincorporation contracts since under modern statutes the corporate existence begins when articles of incorporation are accepted for filing, and contracts entered into by the promoter in the corporate name after that date will normally bind only the corporation. The legal consequences of preincorporation contracts entered into by promoters vary, depending in part on the form of the contract itself.

1. CONTRACTS ENTERED IN THE NAME OF A CORPORATION "TO BE FORMED"

In contracts of this type, the promoter enters into a preincorporation contract which on its face shows that the corporation has not yet been formed. A typical form of execution of a contract of this type is:

ABC Corporation, a corporation to be formed by ________ (promoter).

a. Such a contract may be analyzed in several different ways, depending on the facts and the context, which have widely different legal consequences.

   1) The most traditional analysis is that the promoter is personally liable on the contract and is not relieved of liability if the corporation is later formed and adopts the contract. Assuming that the corporation is formed and adopts the contract, both the promoter and the corporation are thereafter severally liable on the contract. Presumably the promoter may look to the newly formed corporation for indemnification if the contract benefits the corporation but the promoter remains personally liable.

   2) A related analysis is that the promoter is personally liable on the contract, but is thereafter relieved of liability if the corporation is later formed and adopts the contract. This is an example of a "novation."

   3) Another possible analysis that leads to a diametrically different result is that the promoter is not personally liable on the contract since the third party intended to deal only with the corporation. While the corporation may become liable if it is later formed and enters into the contract, no one is liable under this analysis until that event occurs.

      Caveat: Under this analysis the third party has made only an offer to the corporation which may be revoked by the third party at any time before the corporation accepts the contract (unless the offer is an option supported by consideration or is otherwise made irrevocable by law).

   4) A final analysis is that the promoter is not personally liable on the contract but has agreed to use her best efforts to cause the corporation to be formed and to adopt the contract. The promoter's "best efforts" promise may be consideration for the third party's promise under the contract. This differs from (3) in that both parties have incurred liability: the promoter may be liable on her promise if no steps are taken to form the corporation though she is not liable on the contract itself.

b. The question of which of these four alternatives is the appropriate one to apply in a specific case depends on the "intention" of the parties; where the intention is not clearly expressed uncertainty may exist as to the appropriate legal analysis. However, most cases find the promoter personally liable on one theory or another. The issue of novation (alternative (2)) is considered further in part III B 4 of this outline.

Example: O'Rorke enters into a contract to build a bridge with "D. J. Geary for a bridge company to be organized and incorporated." O'Rorke is to commence work within 10 days and payments are to be made to him periodically after work is commenced. Geary, as the promoter, is personally liable on the obligation: the fact that payments are required to be made (presumably by Geary personally) before the bridge company is formed indicates an intent that Geary be personally liable. *O'Rorke v. Geary,* 56 A. 541 (Pa. 1903). Accord: *Coopers & Lybrand v. Fox,* 758 P.2d 683 (Colo.App. 1988); *Goodman v. Darden, Doman & Stafford Assoc.,* 670 P.2d 648 (Wash.1983); *Stanley J. How & Associates, Inc. v. Boss,* 222 F.Supp. 936 (S.D.Iowa 1963).

Example: Quaker Hill, Inc. sells nursery stock to a corporation to be formed by Parr and Presba. At the urging of Quaker Hill's representative, the contract is entered into in the name of "Mountain View Nurseries, Inc. by Parr, President" even though Quaker Hill's representative knows no corporation has been formed. Parr and Presba are not personally liable to Quaker Hill because Quaker Hill, by its conduct, clearly indicated its intention to look for payment only to the newly formed corporation. *Quaker Hill, Inc. v. Parr,* 364 P.2d 1056 (Colo.1961). Accord: *Tin Cup Pass Ltd. Partnership v. Daniels,* 553 N.E.2d 82 (Ill.App.1990); *Sherwood & Roberts–Oregon, Inc. v. Alexander,* 525 P.2d 135 (Or.1974); *Stewart Realty Co. v. Keller,* 193 N.E.2d 179 (Ohio App.1962).

Example: In the previous example, before the corporation is formed, Quaker Hill changes its mind and refuses to ship the nursery stock. Quaker Hill is not liable for breach of contract since no contract exists. Since Parr and Presba are not personally liable on the contract, and no corporation has been formed, no one is bound to purchase the nursery stock, and Quaker Hill has effectively revoked its offer to ship the nursery stock.

c. If a lawyer is consulted about the form of a preincorporation contract, he or she should normally recommend that the contract specify expressly who is liable and under what circumstances.

2. CONTRACTS ENTERED INTO IN THE CORPORATE NAME

In these cases, a contract is entered into in the name of a corporation that has not been properly formed. One or both of the parties to the corporation erroneously believe the corporation has been formed. The factual patterns under this heading may vary because the contract may be entered into at various times during the incorporation process. For example, the contract may be entered into when no steps at all toward incorporation have been taken, or it may be entered into after articles of incorporation have been prepared but not filed, or after the articles of incorporation have been mailed to the secretary of state but before the certificate of incorporation is issued. Under earlier statutes, essentially the same problem also arose if the contract was entered into after a certificate of incorporation was issued but before other mandatory steps necessary for incorporation were completed.

a. If a promoter represents that she is acting on behalf of a corporation when she knows no steps have been taken to form a corporation, she is usually personally liable on the contract. This result may be justified on various grounds:

1) A person who purports to act as an agent for a nonexistent principal is personally liable on the contract;

2) A person who purports to act as an agent for a principal warrants his or her authority.

Example: A promoter reserves the name of a proposed corporation but takes no further steps to incorporate. The promoter then purchases hot dogs from a wholesaler on open account, using the corporate name exclusively. The promoter is personally liable for these purchases. *Echols v. Vienna Sausage Mfg. Co.*, 290 S.E.2d 484 (Ga.App.1982).

b. The common law developed concepts of corporations *de facto* and corporations *de jure* to deal with these problems. In a suit brought by a private plaintiff against a promoter, the conclusion that either a *de facto* or a *de jure* corporation existed effectively absolved the promoter of liability.

1) A corporation *de jure* has sufficiently complied with the incorporation requirements so that a corporation is legally in existence for all purposes. A *de jure* corporation exists if there is compliance with all *mandatory* statutory requirements; failure to comply with less important requirements (called *directory* requirements) do not affect the *de jure* status of a corporation. The distinction between mandatory and directory requirements is obviously a matter of degree; *People v. Ford*, 128 N.E. 479 (Ill.1920) holds over the dissent of one Justice that the statutory requirement of a seal is a directory requirement; however, in evaluating this case it should be noted that the contrary conclusion would have called into question the validity of over 4,300 corporations.

Example: Articles of incorporation fail to comply with the statutory requirement that addresses be stated in that two addresses of directors or incorporators are incorrect. All other statutory requirements are complied with. The corporation is a *de jure* corporation.

Example: Under the applicable state statute, articles of incorporation must be filed with the secretary of state and recorded with the county recorder of the county in which the registered office is located. The statute does not set forth the consequences of failure to file locally. A corporation files articles of incorporation with the secretary of state but fails to file locally. Such a corporation is probably not a *de jure* corporation. However, it may be a *de facto* corporation (defined below).

2) A corporation *de facto* is a corporation that is partially but defectively or incompletely formed; it is sufficiently formed, however, to be immune from attack by everyone but the state. Since virtually all litigation in this area involves private plaintiffs rather than the state, a holding that a corporation is *de facto* is virtually as good as a holding that it is *de jure.* The traditional test of *de facto* existence is threefold:

(A) There is a valid statute under which the corporation might incorporate;

(B) There has been a "good faith" or "colorable" attempt to comply with the statute; and

(C) There has been actual use of the corporate privilege.

Example: A corporation files articles of incorporation with the secretary of state but does not file the articles locally as required by statute. In most states the corporation is considered a *de facto* corporation.

Example: A corporation prepares articles of incorporation but because of a clerical mistake by the attorney no filing is ever made with the secretary of state. The corporation is neither a *de facto* nor a *de jure* corporation. *Conway v. Samet,* 300 N.Y.S.2d 243 (1969).

Caveat: The *de facto* doctrine in practice tends to be result-oriented rather than objective.

Example: In a tort case, a defect in formation might be deemed sufficient to prevent the formation of a *de facto* corporation; in a contract case where the third person clearly relied only on the credit of the "corporation," a court might hold on essentially the same facts that a *de facto* corporation existed.

Example: A corporation commences business with less than $1000 in capital, the minimum requirement in the state statute. However, the statute also provides that directors who permit the corporation to commence business with less than the minimum capital are jointly and severally liable only for the difference. The statutory liability should be deemed exclusive. In a suit to impose personal liability on shareholders (other than the directors liable under the statute) an argument that the failure to provide the minimum capital prevents the creation of a *de facto* corporation should be rejected.

Example: The foregoing transaction occurs in a state that does not expressly limit the liability of the directors to the unpaid portion of the minimum capital. No *de facto* corporation was formed and the directors and officers may be held personally liable for all debts or liabilities incurred before the minimum capital is paid in. *Sulphur Export Corp. v. Carribean Clipper Lines, Inc.*, 277 F.Supp. 632 (E.D.La.1968).

Caveat: State statutes may set forth the legal consequences of a failure to comply with some statutory filing requirement; such statutes provide a substitute for the *de facto* doctrine. For another example, see the caveat at part II B 1.

c. Modern statutes substitute a more objective test for the common law *de facto/de jure* distinction. All modern statutes have a provision that states in substance "upon the issuance of the certificate of incorporation the corporate existence shall begin." MBCA (1969) § 50. The MBCA (1984) § 2.03(a) is similar. It provides, "Unless a delayed effective date is specified, the corporate existence begins when the articles of incorporation are filed."

1) Under these provisions it would appear that all transactions entered into in the corporate name after the certificate of incorporation has been issued or the articles of incorporation filed would be corporate obligations.

Example: Articles of incorporation are filed and accepted, and a certificate of incorporation issued. The following day a lease is entered into in the corporate name. However, no further steps are taken to complete the formation of the corporation. No meetings are held, no shares are issued, and so forth. The lease is a corporate obligation, and the person signing the lease is not automatically personally liable thereon since the certificate of incorporation conclusively establishes the existence of the corporation. *Cardellino v. Comptroller of Treasury,* 511 A.2d 573 (Md.App.1986). However, an argument to hold such a person liable may be based on the concept of "piercing the corporate veil." (See part IV.)

(i) These provisions stating when the corporate existence begins do not specifically address the question of the status of obligations entered into in the corporate name before the issuance of the certificate of incorporation (or the filing of articles of incorporation). Statutes addressing this question are discussed immediately below.

(ii) One court declined to rely on the principle that the issuance of the certificate of incorporation establishes the existence of a corporation and applied common law *de facto* principles even though a certificate of incorporation had been issued. *Matter of Whatley,* 874 F.2d 997 (5th Cir.1989)[issue involved competing priorities of security interests or liens].

2) Several state statutes contain a provision based on MBCA (1969), § 139 that addresses the status of preincorporation obligations: "All persons who assume to act as a corporation without authority so to do shall be jointly and severally liable for all debts and liabilities incurred or arising as a result thereof."

(i) Some courts have read § 139 literally to provide that the issuance of the certificate of incorporation is the "bright line" that distinguishes the corporation from the "noncorporation." Under this reasoning, personal liability automatically exists on all obligations that antedate the time the secretary of state issues the certificate of incorporation.

Example: A person mails articles of incorporation to the secretary of state and the following day executes a note in the corporate name on behalf of the corporation. A day after the note is executed, the secretary of state receives the articles of incorporation, reviews them, rejects them, and returns them for correction. Corrections are made and the articles later accepted and the certificate of incorporation issued. In many states the person signing the note is personally liable, though he may be able to avoid liability on the theory of a "corporation by estoppel" described below. *Robertson v. Levy,* 197 A.2d 443 (D.C. App.1964). Accord: *Booker Custom Packing Co., Inc. v. Sallomi,* 716 P.2d 1061 (Ariz.App.1986); *Thompson & Green Machinery Co., Inc. v. Music City Lumber Co., Inc.,* 683 S.W.2d 340 (Tenn.App.1984); *Bowers Building Co. v. Altura Glass Co., Inc.* 694 P.2d 876 (Colo.App.1984); *Cahoon v. Ward,* 204 S.E.2d 622 (Ga.1974); *Timberline Equipment Co. Inc. v. Davenport,* 514 P.2d 1109 (Or.1973).

Caveat: Secretaries of state usually backdate certificates of incorporation or fee receipts to the date the articles of incorporation are filed, in effect ignoring processing time. This practice, which is not uniform, may eliminate some time-of-issuance questions.

Example: The articles of incorporation are filed on May 1, and the corporation executes a promissory note on May 3. On May 4, the secretary of state issues the certificate of incorporation but follows the standard practice in his office of dating it May 1, the date of filing. It is probable that the corporate existence began on May 1 so that the promissory note is solely a corporate obligation.

Example: The articles of incorporation are filed on May 1, but are returned to the incorporators because of the absence of a notarial certificate. The certificate is added, and the same articles are refiled on May 3. Some secretaries of state will issue the certificate of incorporation dated back to May 1. However, if the articles are reexecuted on May 3 so that the notarial certificate bears that date, it is unlikely that a secretary of state would date the certificate earlier than May 3.

(ii) Under § 139, some courts have distinguished between active participants in the "corporation" and passive investors; the latter are not personally liable on transactions entered into before the certificate of incorporation is issued. This view is based on the statutory language referring only to persons "who assume to act" as being liable under § 139. *Timberline Equipment Co., Inc. v. Davenport,* 514 P.2d 1109 (Or.1973).

3) Some statutes contain provisions making the issuance of the certificate of incorporation conclusive of the existence of the corporation but do not contain language similar to that appearing in MBCA (1969) § 139, referring to persons "who assume to act" as corporations. In these states, an argument may be made that the traditional common law concept of

the *de facto* corporation continues to exist because the statute does not purport to deal explicitly with precertificate obligations.

Example: In a state that does not follow the practice of backdating articles of incorporation, an incorporator prepares articles of incorporation on April 1 and mails them to the secretary of state. Because of a delay in the mails the articles are not received until April 5, and a certificate of incorporation is issued on April 7, showing that date as the date of issuance. The corporation enters into a contract on April 4; even though the *de jure* existence of the corporation did not begin until April 7, a corporation *de facto* exists from and after April 1, and only the corporation is liable on the April 4 obligation. *Cantor v. Sunshine Greenery, Inc.*, 398 A.2d 571 (N.J.Super.App.Div.1979).

4) MBCA (1984) § 2.04 provides that "all persons purporting to act as or on behalf of a corporation, knowing there was no incorporation under this Act, are jointly and severally liable for all liabilities created while so acting." This provision is consistent with the results reached in most of the above cases, and is analogous to a similar provision in the Revised Uniform Limited Partnership Act.

d. Some cases have applied a concept of "corporation by estoppel" that appears to be potentially independent of modern statutes and the common law *de facto* corporation concept.

Example: *X* executes articles of incorporation and reasonably but erroneously believes that they have been filed with the secretary of state by his attorney. *X* negotiates the purchase of typewriters in the corporate name and executes notes in the corporate name to pay for them. The seller relies solely on the corporate credit but later discovers that the articles of incorporation were never filed and brings suit against X personally. The seller is "estopped" to deny the existence of the corporation under these circumstances. *Cranson v. IBM*, 200 A.2d 33 (Md.1964). Cf. *Harry Rich Corp. v. Feinberg,* 518 So.2d 377 (Fla.App.1987)[on similar facts, officer not liable under § 139 of MBCA (1969]).

Example: *X* may have a claim over against the attorney for malpractice if held liable on the underlying contract. *Conway v. Samet*, 300 N.Y.S.2d 243 (1969).

1) This is "reverse estoppel" since *X*, the person who made the representation, is being permitted to escape liability while the person who *relied* on the representation is being estopped from disputing the

representation. In normal estoppel cases, only the person *making* a representation is estopped from later denying it.

2) If carried to its logical conclusion, the concept of "corporation by estoppel" would permit shareholders to obtain the benefits of limited liability simply by consistently representing the corporation's existence. Notions of public policy and the need to preserve the incorporation process therefore dictate that only persons who honestly but erroneously believe that articles have been filed should be able to take advantage of the corporation by estoppel concept. RMBCA § 2.04 [described in part c.4 above] accepts this view.

3) If the defendant seeks to avoid liability on the ground that the plaintiff may not sue because it is not a lawful corporate entity, the doctrine of corporation by estoppel is usually applied. *Timberline Equipment Co., Inc. v. Davenport,* 514 P.2d 1109 (Or.1973).

e. This area of the law of corporations reflects the interplay of basically conflicting general principles. In such situations, unpredictability of result and irreconcilable precedents often result, and this area is no exception.

1) The statutes and common sense say—"no certificate of incorporation, no corporation." Under this approach there should be unlimited personal liability for all obligations entered into in the corporate name before the corporation was formed.

2) Where third persons deal on a corporate basis with an apparent corporation, they receive a "windfall" if they may subsequently hold other persons liable.

3) The failure to complete the formation of the corporation usually is discovered long after the transaction in question was entered into. Discovery following the commencement of litigation usually leads to information that reveals that the corporation was not fully formed when the transaction was entered into. Some courts have accepted the "windfall" argument and refuse to impose personal liability even in circumstances where no steps toward incorporation have been taken. E.g., *Frontier Refining Co. v. Kunkel's Inc.,* 407 P.2d 880 (Wyo.1965).

4) The statutes discussed in this part do not appear to create objectively more predictable results than the common law *de facto* doctrine.

3. LIABILITY OF CORPORATION ON PROMOTER'S CONTRACTS

The corporation is not automatically liable on promoters' contracts made for its benefit before it came into existence. Rather, a newly formed corporation may accept or reject all preincorporation contracts.

a. Technically, an acceptance of a preincorporation contract by a corporation is an "adoption" not a "ratification." Ratification assumes that the principal was in existence when the agent entered into the unauthorized contract; hence, when a principal "ratifies" a contract it is deemed bound on the contract from the time the contract was originally entered into. Since the corporation was not in existence when the preincorporation contract was entered into, ratification is not the proper technical term. Some courts, however, loosely use the word "ratification" to describe the corporate adoption of a preincorporation contract.

b. This rule allows subsequent investors in some cases to review promoters' contracts and reject those that seem improvident. However, the rule works unevenly since the time for adoption may occur before the outside investors appear or while the promoter is the dominant force in the newly formed corporation.

c. Adoption may be express or implied and presupposes knowledge of the terms of the contract. However, a recovery in quasi contract is normally available where benefits are accepted even if the contract has not been adopted.

Example: *Z* is given a one-year employment contract involving a salary of $5000 per month by a promoter in the name of a corporation. With knowledge of the terms, the directors of the newly formed corporation accept the benefits of the employment contract for four months. *Z* is then fired. Whether or not the contract was formally adopted by the board of directors, the corporation has adopted the contract and is bound by it. It is therefore liable to *Z* for breach of the employment contract. This is an implied adoption. *McArthur v. Times Printing Co.*, 51 N.W. 216 (Minn. 1892). Accord: *Stolmeier v. Beck,* 441 N.W.2d 888 (Neb.1989); *Kridelbaugh v. Aldrehn Theatres Co.*, 191 N.W. 803 (Iowa 1923).

Example: In the foregoing illustration, the promoter also secretly promises *Z* a year-end bonus of $6,000 as part of his employment contract. The directors of the corporation are unaware of this promise and the circumstances are such as to give the directors no reason to believe that additional compensation was promised. The corporation has not adopted the contract with *Z* and is not bound by the promise to pay the bonus since adoption requires knowledge of the terms of the contract. *Z* has a quasi-contractual claim for the fair market value of his services, which may be greater or less than $5000 per month.

d. Where the contract relates to services leading to the formation of the corporation (e.g., the lawyer's fee for forming the corporation), mere existence of the corporation does not constitute "adoption" of the contract. The lawyer may recover in quasi contract for the reasonable value of his services.

4. RELATIONSHIP BETWEEN PROMOTER'S LIABILITY AND CORPORATE ADOPTION

Generally, corporate adoption of a contract releases the promoter from further liability only if the parties expressly agree that a novation will occur.

Example: The promoter executes a contract with a third party which contains the following clause: "It is understood by the parties hereto that it is the intention of the Purchaser to incorporate. If such incorporation is completed by closing, all agreements, covenants, and warranties contained herein shall be construed to have been made between Seller and the resultant corporation and all documents shall reflect same." The corporation is duly formed and thereafter adopts the contract. Since this clause does not expressly release the promoters from liability upon the adoption of the contract by the corporation, the promoter remains liable as a co-obligor with the corporation. *RKO–Stanley Warner Theatres, Inc. v. Graziano,* 355 A.2d 830 (Pa.1976). It is possible, however, that some courts might construe the last quoted sentence as an indication that the third person intended to look solely to the corporation after its formation and conclude that a novation was intended.

Example: In the foregoing example the corporation is formed but does not adopt the contract. The corporation is not bound despite the language of the agreement. The promoter remains personally liable on the theory that the third person intended someone always to be liable.

a. Williston argued that a novation is almost always contemplated on the theory that the third person usually intends to look solely to the corporation after it is formed.

b. This "complete novation" theory may lead to promoters deciding to form "shell corporations" solely to escape personal liability even after it is clear that the promotion will fail.

Example: A plaintiff testifies, "I understood that I was working for [Mr. Jones] personally until the railroad was organized; and after the railroad was organized, I was working for the railroad, of course." This testimony indicates that a novation was intended and the promoter is not personally liable on the employment contract after the formation of the railroad. *Bradshaw v. Jones,* 152 S.W. 695 (Tex.App.1912).

Caveat: Courts have generally refused to accept Williston's argument and find novations only where there is some clear indication that a novation was actually intended. See *Frazier v. Ash*, 234 F.2d 320 (5th Cir.1956).

C. PROMOTER'S FIDUCIARY DUTIES

Co-promoters of a venture owe fiduciary duties to each other, to the corporation, and to subsequent financial interests in the venture. The duty is essentially the same as the duties owed by a partner to his partnership or to his co-partners, and, in the case of subsequent financial interests, a duty of full disclosure.

1. THE CORPORATION AS THE BENEFICIARY

After the corporation is formed it may obtain from the promoter any benefits or rights the promoter obtained on its behalf.

Example: *A,* a co-promoter, secretly buys land needed by the corporation and sells it to the corporation after it is formed at a profit. The transaction constitutes a breach of fiduciary duty and the corporation may recover the secret profit.

2. CO–PROMOTERS AS THE BENEFICIARY

Co-promoters are essentially partners in the promotion of the venture, and any benefits or rights one promoter obtained must be shared with the co-promoters.

Example: *A*, a co-promoter, secretly buys land needed by the corporation, planning to resell it to the corporation. However, the promotion fails, no corporation is ever formed, and *A* later resells the land to a third person at a profit. Her co-promoters may recover their share of the secret profit.

3. SUBSEQUENT INVESTORS AS THE BENEFICIARY

A major issue relating to promoters' fiduciary duties is the extent to which *subsequent* shareholders or investors are protected by fiduciary duties.

a. According to the "Massachusetts rule" the corporation may attack the earlier transaction if the subsequent sale to public investors was contemplated when the earlier transaction was entered into. *Old Dominion Copper Mining & Smelting Co. v. Bigelow*, 89 N.E. 193 (Mass.1909).

b. According to the "federal rule" the corporation may not attack the earlier transaction since all the shareholders at the time consented to the transaction. *Old Dominion Copper Mining & Smelting Co. v. Lewisohn*, 210 U.S. 206, 28 S.Ct. 634 (1908).

Example: At a time when only *A* and *B* are shareholders of a corporation, *A* and *B* enter into employment contracts" with the corporation.

Thereafter shares are sold to public investors who are unaware of the employment contracts. When they learn of the employment contracts they object on the ground that the compensation to *A* and *B* is excessive. Under the Massachusetts rule the corporation or the subsequent investors may successfully attack the earlier transaction if the subsequent sale to investors was contemplated at the time the employment contracts were entered into; under the federal rule neither can successfully do so.

c. These rules were both established in two cases arising out of a single promotion in the early years of the twentieth century. The "Massachusetts rule" has been followed more widely than the "federal rule."

d. The real issue in these cases is whether there was full disclosure of the promoters' transaction at the time the public investors decided to make their investments. If there was full disclosure, the public investors should have reduced the price they agreed to pay for the shares to reflect the transactions in question.

e. Cases of this nature usually arise in the modern era as "disclosure" or "securities fraud" cases rather than as "promoters fraud" cases. See the discussion in part XV below, particularly the discussion of rule 10b–5.

4. CREDITORS AS THE BENEFICIARY

Fiduciary concepts may also protect creditors against unfair or fraudulent transactions by promoters. *Frick v. Howard*, 126 N.W.2d 619 (Wis.1964). Most of these transactions also may be attacked on the ground they constitute fraud on creditors.

D. AGREEMENTS TO FORM CORPORATIONS

A preincorporation agreement to create a corporation is enforceable to the same extent as any other contract. Modern promotions are usually cast in the form of such a contract.

1. FORM OF CONTRACT

A preincorporation agreement normally sets forth all the basic terms of the business arrangement among the parties. Attachments to the contract may include the proposed articles of incorporation, bylaws, shareholder agreements, and minutes of proposed meetings.

2. SURVIVABILITY OF AGREEMENT

One major issue relating to preincorporation contracts is whether provisions of the agreement that are not incorporated into the governing documents of the corporation survive the formation of the corporation. Since the articles of incorporation, bylaws, shareholder agreements, and minutes of meetings on their face appear on their face to provide a complete set of rules of governance, the contract will normally not survive the formation of the corporation unless specific and precise provisions to that effect are included. Where such provisions are included, they may be enforced so long as they do not violate public policy.

Caveat: To assure that the terms of the preincorporation contract are fully enforceable after the completion of the formation of the corporation, it may be appropriate to have the corporation expressly assume the preincorporation contract or enter into individual contracts with the shareholders to cover matters that appear in the preincorporation contract, such as commitments with respect to the registration of shares if the corporation thereafter makes a public offering, repayment schedules for loans, and other matters that do not normally appear in the governing documents of a corporation.

E. PREINCORPORATION SUBSCRIPTIONS

A preincorporation subscription is a written promise by a person prior to the formation of a corporation to purchase a specific number of shares of the corporation at a specific price after the corporation is formed. Such promises may be obtained by promoters as part of their capital-raising efforts.

1. USE OF PREINCORPORATION SUBSCRIPTIONS

Historically most capital for new ventures was raised through preincorporation subscriptions. Their public use was made impractical by the enactment of the securities acts which impose registration requirements on both the subscription itself and on the subsequent sale of shares. They still may be used in closely held corporations, though simple contractual agreements with the corporation are now more common.

2. ENFORCEABILITY OF PREINCORPORATION SUBSCRIPTIONS IN THE ABSENCE OF STATUTE

Preincorporation subscriptions may be obtained independently of each other. In this event, promises of individual subscribers are not made in consideration of the promises of other subscribers and, since the corporation has not yet been formed, such subscriptions may not be enforceable as contracts. As a result, in the absence of statute, a subscriber might withdraw her subscription at any time before it is accepted by the corporation.

a. In some instances subscriptions may be made in a form that permits an argument that the promises are made in exchange for each other; in these instances preincorporation subscriptions become contractual and therefore irrevocable.

b. A subscription may be conditioned on the occurrence of a specified event and such a subscription is normally not enforceable until the condition occurs.

c. A subscription obtained through fraud may be rescinded in the same manner as a contract.

3. STATUTORY TREATMENT OF PREINCORPORATION SUBSCRIPTIONS

Modern statutes provide that preincorporation subscriptions are irrevocable for a stated period, often six months, without regard to whether they are supported by consideration. MBCA (1984) § 6.20(a). The six month period may be extended or shortened by specific provision in the subscription itself.

a. Modern statutes also provide that calls for payments on subscriptions that have been accepted by the corporation must be uniform. MBCA (1984) § 6.20(b).

b. Modern statutes permit a forfeiture of partial payments on subscriptions in the event later installments are not paid. Notice must be given before a subscription may be forfeited. MBCA (1984) § 6.20(d).

c. All other subscribers may release a subscriber from his or her subscription.

Caveat: These statutory provisions apply only to subscriptions entered into before the corporation is formed. After incorporation, a promise by an investor to subscribe for shares of the corporation is a contract between that investor and the corporation, and is enforceable to the same extent as any other contract.

Caveat: A subscriber becomes a shareholder only upon the payment of the subscription price, though some statutes permit a subscription to be paid with a promissory note, with the shares held in escrow until the promissory note is paid.

F. REVIEW QUESTIONS

III–1. A promoter and an incorporator perform the same functions.

True ______ False ______

III–2. A promoter enters into a contract in the form

"ABC Corporation, a corporation to be formed

"By________."

The promoter is not personally liable on this transaction "because it shows on its face that the corporation is a party."

True ________ False ________.

III–3. A promoter who enters into a contract in the form described in question III–2, even if liable originally on the contract, will certainly be released from liability if the corporation is formed and takes over the contract.

True ________ False ________.

III–4. How do cases involving corporations de facto and by estoppel differ from the promoters' cases?

III–5. The Model Business Corporation Act (1984) abolishes the concept of de facto corporation?

True ________ False ________

III–6. What is a corporation by estoppel and what is wrong with the concept?

III–7. The corporation after it is formed automatically picks up all promoters' contracts.

True ________ False ________

III–8. A and B are promoters. B purchases an inventory of furniture for $60,000 which she represents to A cost $75,000. A agrees to the $75,000 figure. B has breached a duty to A.

III–9. A corporation after it is formed can sue promoters for unfair or fraudulent transactions.

True _______ False _______

III–10. Preincorporation subscriptions for shares are contracts.

True _______ False _______

III–11. D entered into a contract with P for the building of a bridge across the Allegheny river. The contract recited that it was between "P and D for a bridge company to be incorporated." The bridge was built and subsequently the corporation was formed. P sues D personally to recover on the contract contending that D is personally liable inasmuch as the corporation was not in existence at the time the contract was entered into. D contends that in executing the contract he acted for a corporation to be formed and that the corporation and not D is liable on the contract. Is D personally liable to P? Explain your answer.

III–12. A, a promoter of XYZ Publishing Co., engaged M to solicit advertisements for XYZ Publishing Co. prior to its incorporation. M's contract was for one year beginning October first. M started work October first. XYZ was incorporated on October 16. M worked six months and then was discharged by XYZ. XYZ never took formal action through its board of directors to adopt the contract with M but its shareholders, officers and directors knew of the contract and M was paid by the corporation until the time of his discharge. M sues XYZ for breach of contract. XYZ defends on the basis that it was not in existence at the time the contract was made and cannot be bound by acts of its promoters without adoption by the board of directors. Is XYZ liable on the contract?

IV

PIERCING THE CORPORATE VEIL

The phrase "piercing the corporate veil" is a metaphor to describe the cases in which a court refuses to recognize the separate existence of a corporation despite compliance with all the formalities for the creation of a *de jure* corporation. The phrase "piercing the corporate veil" is abbreviated to "PCV" in the balance of this part.

Analysis

A. TRADITIONAL TESTS

The traditional tests for PCV are to "prevent fraud" or to "achieve equity." Many courts add the goals of "preventing oppression" or "avoiding illegality." These tests are all result-oriented and give little indication of the circumstances in which a court will refuse to recognize the separate existence of a corporation.

In deciding whether to PCV, courts have developed concepts (or doctrines) of "shareholder domination," "alter ego," "mere instrumentality," or "identity." These concepts are also result-oriented.

1. DEFINITIONS OF "ALTER EGO" AND "INSTRUMENTALITY"

"Alter ego" literally means "second self." Courts hold that PCV is proper under the alter ego doctrine where (a) such unity of ownership and interest exists between corporation and shareholder that the corporation has ceased to have separate existence, and (b) recognition of the separate existence of the corporation sanctions fraud or leads to an inequitable result. A corporation becomes the "instrumentality" of a shareholder where there has been an excessive exercise of control by the shareholder that leads to wrongful or inequitable conduct that in turn causes the plaintiff a loss.

a. It is unclear whether "alter ego" and "instrumentality" are subdivisions of PCV or whether they are grounds for holding shareholders liable independent of the general tests of "preventing fraud" or "achieving equity."

b. Many courts and commentators view these various doctrines as interchangeable with and essentially the same as the general concept of PCV.

Caveat: In *Castleberry v. Branscum,* 721 S.W.2d 270, 273 (Tex.1986), the Court stated that alter ego is "separate" from other grounds for PCV and applies where "there is such unity between corporation and individual that the separateness of the corporation has ceased and holding only the corporation liable would result in injustice." The court described other grounds for PCV as involving situations where "even though corporate formalities have been observed and corporate and individual property have been kept separately, . . . the corporate form has been used as part of a basically unfair device to achieve an inequitable result."

c. These various tests are particularly unrealistic in a one-person corporation, since, in a sense, a sole shareholder always "dominates" his or her corporation. Similarly, that corporation in the same sense is always an "instrumentality" of the shareholder, as well as the "alter ego" of the shareholder, since there is no one else with an ownership interest in the corporation.

2. JUDICIAL ATTITUDES TOWARD SEPARATE IDENTITY OF CORPORATION

Many courts state that the "general" or "cardinal" rule is that the corporation is separate and independent from its shareholders and that its separate existence should be recognized. *Billy v. Consolidated Machine Tool Corp.,* 432 N.Y.S.2d 879 (N.Y.1980); *Port Chester Elec. Corp. v. Atlas,* 357 N.E.2d 983 (N.Y.1976). Courts also state that one should be "reluctant" to PCV, *Eagle v. Benefield–Chappell, Inc.,* 476 So.2d 716 (Fla.App. 1985), or that PCV should be applied only with "great caution" and in "extreme" circumstances. *Amason v. Whitehead,* 367 S.E.2d 107 (Ga.App.1988); *Farmers Warehouse v. Collins,* 137 S.E.2d 619 (Ga.1964).

3. PUBLICLY AND CLOSELY HELD CORPORATIONS

PCV is almost exclusively a doctrine applicable to closely held corporations. There are no modern examples in which that doctrine has been applied to a publicly held corporation.

Caveat: PCV may be applied to subsidiary corporations owned by a publicly held parent corporation. However, in these cases the separate existence of the subsidiary and not the parent is being ignored.

4. ONE OR TWO PERSON CORPORATIONS

One or two person corporations are treated no differently than other corporations in PCV cases. While PCV is probably more likely to occur in small corporations with one or two shareholders than in corporations with more shareholders, essentially the same tests are applied, and in appropriate cases the separate existence of one or two person corporations will be recognized.

5. MOTIVE FOR INCORPORATION

Motive is unimportant in the sense that the separate corporate existence may be recognized even though the corporation was formed solely for the purpose of avoiding unlimited liability.

Example: *X* is the sole owner of a retail drug business which includes home deliveries. *X* decides to incorporate solely because she fears potential liability for (1) accidents by her delivery trucks and (2) adverse drug reactions from the products she sells. If the corporation is formed and operated consistently with the principles set forth below, its separate corporate existence should be recognized despite the liability-avoiding motive of the sole shareholder behind its formation.

6. BROTHER–SISTER CORPORATIONS

PCV cases are not limited solely to the liability of individual or corporate shareholders for corporate obligations. In appropriate cases, the separate existence of related corporations, i. e., corporations with common shareholders, may be ignored so that the two corporations are treated as a single entity. This may occur even though the common shareholders are not found to be personally liable for corporate obligations under a PCV theory.

7. INACTIVE SHAREHOLDERS

PCV is not an all-or-nothing principle. In appropriate cases, active shareholders may be held liable for corporate debts on a PCV theory but inactive shareholders may be found not to be personally liable on such obligations.

8. ESTOPPEL AGAINST SHAREHOLDERS

PCV is basically an equitable doctrine available to creditors of the corporation whose separate existence is being questioned. It generally is not available to the corporation itself or its shareholders who now regret having formed the corporation; it also may not be available to the bankruptcy trustee of the corporation whose separate existence is being questioned, though individual creditors may be able to assert a claim under the PCV doctrine. *Stodd v. Goldberger*, 141 Cal.Rptr. 67 (Cal.App.1977).

Caveat: A few cases have permitted shareholders to "reverse pierce" and successfully argue that the separate existence should be ignored. E.g. *Roepke Western National Mutual Insurance,* 302 N.W.2d 350 (Minn.1981); *Cargill, Inc. v. Hedge,* 375 N.W.2d 477 (Minn.1985). These cases generally involve attempts to extend statutory protections available to individuals, such as the protection of farm homesteads from seizure by creditors, to property owned by a wholly owned corporation. The courts view these statutory protections as reflecting a strong public policy outweighing the general skepticism by courts of reverse piercing claims.

B. INDIVIDUAL SHAREHOLDER LIABILITY FOR CORPORATE DEBTS

Many PCV cases involve attempts to hold shareholders who are individuals liable for corporate obligations. (The rules relating to *corporate* shareholders are somewhat different and are discussed in the following subsection.)

1. CONSENSUAL TRANSACTIONS

In cases involving *contract* claims the third person has usually dealt voluntarily with the corporation in some way. Hence, absent unusual circumstances he has "assumed the risk" that the corporation will be unable to meet its obligations and should not be able to PCV and hold the shareholders personally liable. Many but not all cases accept this approach.

Example: *X* creates a corporation of which he is sole shareholder with a capital of $1. *Y* sells $50,000 worth of goods to *X*'s corporation on credit without making any credit check and without being misled in any way. *Y* may not recover from *X* on a PCV theory and is limited to his suit against *X*'s corporation. See *Brunswick Corp. v. Waxman,* 599 F.2d 34 (2d Cir.1979); *Texas Industries, Inc. v. Dupuy & Dupuy Developers, Inc.,* 227 So.2d 265 (La.App.1969).

a. "Unusual circumstances" in which shareholder liability for contract claims might be imposed include:

1) The shareholder conducts business in such a way as to cause confusion between individual and corporate finances. See *Zaist v. Olson,* 227 A.2d 552 (Conn.1967).

Example: For convenience, *X* pays all bills of his corporation by his personal checks and reimburses himself at the end of each week by a single corporate check. *X* is probably personally liable on corporate obligations to persons who are aware that bills in the past have been paid from *X*'s personal funds.

Example: The sole shareholder of a corporation lists certain corporate assets on his personal financial statements on the theory that the assets belong to him since he owns all the stock of the corporation. In addition, personal expenditures are paid from corporate accounts and he intermingles business and personal actions and transactions. The shareholder is liable to an employee familiar with these transactions for promised bonuses, vacation pay, and pension and profit sharing benefits. *Anderson v. Chatham,* 379 S.E.2d 793 (Ga.App. 1989).

Caveat: In both of these examples, the plaintiff was personally familiar with the intermingled transactions and may have relied on them. A creditor who was not directly aware of them may also be able to hold the shareholder liable under PCV principles in many states, though such a claim is more difficult to maintain or justify in the absence of detrimental reliance.

2) The third party is in some way misled or tricked into dealing with the corporation.

Example: *X* negotiates a contract directly with *Y*, believing that he is dealing with *Y* on an individual basis. After the deal is concluded in principle, *Y* presents a contract in which his wholly owned corporation is the sole obligor on the contract. *X* does not notice this change. If the change is not conspicuous or *X* is misled in some way, *X* may hold *Y* personally on the contract. However, if the change is conspicuous and there is no deception, it is likely that *X* must look solely to the corporation on the theory that a person who signs a contract without reading it is bound by its contents.

3) The corporation is operated in an unusual way so that:

(i) It can never make a profit;

(ii) Available funds are siphoned off to the shareholder without regard to the needs of the corporation; or

(iii) It is operated so that it is always insolvent. *Iron City Sand & Gravel Div. v. West Fork Towing Corp.*, 298 F.Supp. 1091 (N.D.W.Va.1969); *DeWitt Truck Brokers, Inc. v. W. Ray Flemming Fruit Co.*, 540 F.2d 681 (4th Cir.1976).

Example: A corporation is formed by a group of persons to build houses to be sold to the shareholders. The corporation prices each home at less than cost so that the corporation must ultimately fail. Creditors who are unaware of the pricing practice probably can hold the shareholders individually liable, *Yacker v. Weiner*, 263 A.2d 188 (N.J. Super.Ch.Div.1970), though there is some case law to the contrary, *Bartle v. Home Owners Cooperative*, 127 N.E.2d 832 (N.Y.1955).

Example: *X* forms two corporations, one to manufacture a product and the other to sell it. The price at which the manufacturing corporation sells the products to the selling corporation determines in which corporation the profits will accumulate. *X* conducts the business so that liabilities end up in the selling corporation and assets in the manufacturing corporation. If the distinction between the two corporations is not sharply maintained and creditors believe they are dealing with a single enterprise, both corporations are liable for all corporate obligations. *Holland v. Joy Candy Mfg. Co.*, 145 N.E.2d 101 (Ill.App. 1957); accord, *Ampex Corp. v. Office Electronics, Inc.*, 320 N.E.2d 486 (Ill.App.1974).

Caveat: It is probable that transactions of these types that injure creditors may be attacked directly on the theory that they constitute fraudulent conveyances, frauds on creditors, usurpation of corporate opportunities, or voidable preferences independently of the PCV doctrine. Nevertheless the PCV doctrine is regularly applied to such transactions.

4) The capitalization of the corporation is in some way misrepresented. Of course, an affirmative misrepresentation by the shareholder of the capitalization of his corporation might constitute actionable fraud independent of the PCV doctrine.

Example: A creditor considering an extension of credit to *AB* Corporation requests financial information. A two-week old balance sheet is supplied showing substantial liquid assets and relatively few current liabilities; this balance sheet is accurate as of the time it was prepared, but in the intervening two weeks the shareholders have caused the corporation to make a substantial distribution of liquid assets to themselves as dividends. It is likely that the shareholders would be held personally responsible to the creditor; the theory may be PCV, fraudulent misrepresentation, or a fraud on creditors.

5) The shareholder orally promises unconditionally to be personally responsible for the corporate obligations under circumstances where it is inequitable to permit the shareholder to rely on the statute of frauds.

Example: A supplier to the corporation refuses to make further shipments unless paid in cash on delivery. The shareholder orally promises to pay for the goods personally if the corporation does not as an inducement to encourage the supplier to ship the goods immediately. The supplier ships the goods in reliance on the shareholder's promise. In most jurisdictions, the supplier may enforce the shareholder's promise even though not in writing. This may be based on a PCV analysis, on the "main object" exception to the statute of frauds, on a reliance exception to the statute of frauds, or conceivably on other theories as well. *DeWitt Truck Brokers, Inc. v. W. Ray Flemming Fruit Co.*, 540 F.2d 681 (4th Cir. 1976).

b. Inadequate or nominal capitalization should normally not be a factor in contract cases. Indeed, the formation of a nominally capitalized corporation may be an integral part of a carefully devised plan by the parties to allocate the risk of loss; courts should normally not change such allocation of risks in the absence of fraud or other abuse of the contract process.

Example: *A* agrees to supply widgets to *B* at a specified price for resale. The understanding is that *A* will be paid only out of the proceeds of the resale of the widgets and *B* will not be personally responsible for any deficit or for any unsold widgets. To effectuate this understanding, *B* forms a wholly owned corporation with a capital of one dollar and all sales of widgets are made to or by the corporation. Sales are unprofitable and some widgets are unsalable. *B* is not liable to A on a PCV or any other theory; the application of any such theory would change the allocation of loss agreed to by the parties in an arms-length negotiation.

Example: *A* agrees to supply widgets to *B*'s wholly owned corporation at a specified price for resale. Concerned that *B*'s corporation may lack sufficient assets to pay for the widgets, *A* requests *B* to personally guarantee the payments due from *B*'s corporation. *B* refuses. *A* decides to deal directly with *B*'s corporation anyway. *B* is not liable to *A* on a PCV or any other theory; the application of any such theory would change the allocation of loss negotiated by the parties in an arms length negotiation.

c. Many cases involving voluntary dealings rely on the failure of the corporation and the shareholder to follow corporate formalities as a basis for PCV. This factor is discussed in part B 3 below.

2. NONCONSENSUAL TRANSACTIONS

In cases involving nonconsensual transactions (almost always torts) there is usually no element of voluntary dealing. As a result, one cannot usually argue that the third person "assumed the risk" by dealing with a nominally capitalized corporation.

a. To recognize the separate corporate existence of a nominally capitalized (and therefore judgment proof) corporation engaged in a hazardous activity may shift the risk of loss or injury to some random members of the general public who happen to be injured by the activity.

b. Lack of adequate capitalization should be considered a major factor in PCV in tort cases. While important, most cases that find shareholders liable involve, in addition to inadequate capitalization, some additional justification to PCV.

1) If the capital was originally reasonably adequate in light of the probable risks, a PCV argument is likely to be rejected if unavoidable business reverses have reduced the amount of capital so that the tort creditor cannot be fully compensated.

2) A PCV argument is likely to be accepted where the original capital is nominal or small in light of contemplated business risks.

Example: A corporation is formed to operate a taxicab in New York City with the minimum capitalization and minimum insurance required by law. The cab seriously injures a pedestrian. While the case law is split, some authority would apply a PCV analysis to hold the controlling shareholder liable. Others would require a showing that the policy of the corporation was to distribute all assets to the shareholder as promptly as possible so as to maintain minimum capitalization and insurance. Others require some kind of showing that the shareholder was himself involved in the corporate business. *Walkovszky v. Carlton*, 223 N.E.2d 6 (N.Y.1966). Most cases finding liability involve some aggravating circumstances of the latter types.

Example: A corporation is formed to lease and operate a swimming pool. The corporation is formed but no capital is paid in by the shareholders. A child is drowned at the pool due to the negligence of an employee. An attorney who is an officer and may have been an investor was responsible for forming the corporation and was personally involved in the operation of the corporation. He may be held personally liable for the damages. *Minton v. Cavaney*, 364 P.2d 473 (Cal.1961). Again, aggravating circumstances were involved such as the failure to complete the formation of the corporation, to provide any capital at all, or to follow corporate formalities in connection with the corporate business.

3) A PCV argument is likely to be adopted where the corporation is formed with minimal capital specifically to engage in ultrahazardous activities which cause injury to person or property.

Example: A corporation is formed to do blasting pursuant to a contract. As a result of the blasting operations damage occurs to adjoining property. The shareholders are indirectly involved in decisions as to the conduct of the business: the corporation is nominally capitalized with the bulk of the assets loaned to the corporation by the shareholders. The shareholders are personally liable for the damages caused by the blasting operations. *Western Rock Co. v. Davis,* 432 S.W.2d 555 (Tex. Civ.App.1968).

4) Liability insurance should be viewed as the equivalent of free capital for purposes of PCV in torts cases. This is because such insurance provides readily available funds to tort victims.

c. It is widely believed that many courts are more willing to accept PCV arguments in tort cases than they are in contract cases. A study that counted litigated PCV cases, however, found no evidence to support this belief.

Caveat: Most litigated cases involve only the sufficiency of a complaint to withstand a motion to dismiss rather than review of a judgment on the merits.

d. Shareholders may be personally liable for corporate torts on theories other than PCV.

1) The individual tortfeasor who actually caused the injury is personally liable whether or not he was acting as an agent of the corporation. If he was acting as a corporate agent, the corporation is also liable for the tort under the theory of respondeat superior. If the tortfeasor is also a corporate shareholder, officer or agent, he is liable because he is a tortfeasor and it is unnecessary to argue PCV.

2) If the corporation may be viewed as the agent of a shareholder, the shareholder becomes liable for corporate torts on a respondeat superior theory.

3) In a typical case, however, the tortfeasor is a judgment proof employee, the corporation is also unable to satisfy the claim, and attempts are made to hold shareholders personally liable on a PCV theory.

e. Commentators have suggested that on the basis of economic analysis shareholders should be personally liable for all tort claims not involving voluntary transactions. This proposal has never received serious consideration.

3. FAILURE TO FOLLOW CORPORATE FORMALITIES

In PCV cases, a factor that is often significant if not decisive is the failure to follow corporate formalities.

a. A PCV argument is much more likely to be accepted if the plaintiff can show (in addition to abuse of the corporate form in a contracts case or inadequate capital or liability insurance in a torts case):

1) A failure to complete the formation of the corporation;

2) A failure to contribute capital or to issue shares;

3) A failure to hold elections, meetings and to follow the other trappings of corporate formality;

4) A pattern of decision-making in which shareholders make business decisions much as though they were partners;

5) A failure to designate clearly the capacity of persons who are acting on behalf of the corporation; and

6) A pattern involving the mixing of personal and corporate activities, such as informal loans, use of corporate funds for personal loans, or vice versa.

See generally: *Zaist v. Olson*, 227 A.2d 552 (Conn.1967). Not all cases, however, impose liability merely because of some informality, failures to follow corporate forms, and intermixing of personal and corporate assets. *Zubik v. Zubik*, 384 F.2d 267 (3d Cir.1967).

Caveat: Compliance with corporate formalities may be largely effected by (1) maintaining a paper trail using the unanimous consent procedure provided by modern statutes, and (2) taking steps to assure that the capacity of persons acting on behalf of the corporation is properly identified. Some conduct, however, such as informal loans or the use of corporate funds for personal purposes cannot be cured by a simple paper trail.

b. While a failure to follow corporate formalities may lead to confusion or deception in some cases, liability does not appear to be dependent on a showing that third persons were misled or confused. Reliance on failure to follow formalities to establish PCV may be justified on at two least two different grounds:

1) The failure to follow formalities may indicate that the shareholders treat the corporation as an "alter ego" or "instrumentality" by not maintaining the separate existence of the corporation; or

2) PCV may be viewed as the sanction to assure that corporate formalities are in fact followed as contemplated by statute.

Example: Articles of incorporation are filed but no further steps are taken to complete the corporation. The corporation commences business. The active shareholders are likely to be held personally liable for corporate debts.

Example: The corporation is properly formed in the sense that articles of incorporation are filed, bylaws adopted, shares issued, and minutes of the organizational meetings are prepared. However, thereafter no shareholders' or directors' meetings are held. All decisions are made in the corporate name by the shareholders after talking among themselves. Even though no third party is harmed by such informal conduct or informal decision-making, active shareholders are likely to be held personally liable for corporate debts.

4. ARTIFICIAL DIVISION OF A SINGLE BUSINESS ENTITY

In all PCV cases, an important factor is whether a single business is artificially divided into several different corporations to reduce exposure of assets to liabilities. Professor Berle referred to this phenomenon as the theory of "enterprise entity."

a. The normal response to an artificial division of a single business entity is to hold the entire entity responsible for the debts of the business rather than to hold the shareholders personally liable for such debts.

Example: *X*, the owner of a fleet of taxicabs in New York City, forms a separate corporation for each taxicab, a separate corporation for the garage that services the cabs, and a separate corporation for the paging service that takes telephone calls and relays them to individual cabs. Except for the separate incorporations, the business is operated as a single unit but the shareholder uniformly conducts business in the name of one or more of the corporations. Each corporation is liable for the debts of each other corporation. *Mangan v. Terminal Transp. System*, 284 N.Y.S. 183 (1935), aff'd per curiam, 286 N.Y.S. 666 (1936). Whether or not *X* is personally liable depends on the nature of the claim asserted, the adequacy of the capitalization of the individual corporations, and other factors.

b. Two or more corporations owned by a single shareholder or owned approximately proportionally by several shareholders are often referred to as "brother-sister corporations." Such corporations may also be analyzed as a type of "parent-subsidiary" relationship discussed below.

Example: See the second example in part B 1 a. 3.

C. PARENT CORPORATION'S LIABILITY FOR OBLIGATIONS OF SUBSIDIARY CORPORATION

Many PCV cases involve shareholders who themselves are corporations. In other words, the issue involves the responsibility of a parent corporation for the actions of a subsidiary. Practically every publicly held corporation has numerous subsidiaries engaged in a variety of related or different businesses. Subsidiaries are usually wholly owned by the parent corporation but they may also be partially owned. It is often stated that courts are more likely to PCV when the shareholder is itself a corporation than when the shareholder is an individual, but there is little empirical evidence supporting such an assertion.

1. TYPES OF ISSUES THAT MAY ARISE

PCV in parent/subsidiary context may arise in several ways in addition to the question whether the parent corporation is liable for the debts of a subsidiary:

a. The issue may be whether transactions between parent and subsidiary or between two subsidiaries must be recognized by third persons who are affected by the transaction.

Example: Subsidiary A, a gas pipeline company, is obligated to pay X a royalty based on the sales price of natural gas taken from *X*'s mineral lease. Because of changes in methods of marketing gas, the parent corporation creates Subsidiary B, a gas marketing company, to locate end users for natural gas production. Subsidiary B buys natural gas from Subsidiary A (and also from other suppliers) at a price (essentially a wholesale price) that is less than the price Subsidiary B receives on resale of the gas to end users (essentially a retail price). *X* claims that his royalty should be based on the price Subsidiary B receives for gas, not the amount Subsidiary A receives from Subsidiary B. The test in such cases is whether the price paid by Subsidiary B to Subsidiary A for gas is reasonable, that is, that it is closely related to the prices being paid by unrelated gas marketing companies in the competitive wholesale market for natural gas.

b. The issue may be whether a parent may conspire with its subsidiary, or whether two subsidiaries may conspire together, to violate law or the rights of third parties.

c. The issue may involve a question of statutory construction: e.g., do statutes that refer generally to "corporation," "owner," or "operator" apply to both parent corporations and affiliated or subsidiary corporations.

2. CONFUSION OF AFFAIRS

A parent corporation may be held liable for its subsidiary's obligations if it fails to maintain a clear separation between parent and subsidiary affairs. A failure to maintain a clear separation between affairs of different subsidiary corporations may result in the separate existence of those corporations being ignored as well. Conduct that may lead to parental liability includes:

a. Referring to the subsidiary as a "department" or "division" of the parent;

b. Mixing business affairs, such as using parental stationery to respond to inquiries addressed to the subsidiary;

c. Having common officers who do not clearly delineate the capacity in which they are acting, i. e., a failure to identify "which hat he (or she) is wearing;"

d. Mixing assets, such as having the subsidiary sign a pledge of assets to secure parental indebtedness, transferring funds informally from one entity to the other without the formalities normally involved in a loan, or having a common bank account. *Bernardin, Inc. v. Midland Oil Corp.*, 520 F.2d 771 (7th Cir. 1975).

3. PERMISSIBLE ACTIVITIES

If practices similar to those described in paragraph 2 are avoided, a PCV argument should be rejected even though:

a. One corporation owns all the shares of the corporation;

b. The corporations have common officers or directors; and

c. The corporations file a consolidated tax return or report their earnings to their shareholders on a consolidated basis.

d. The parent corporation maintains a cash management function by which all cash accounts are centralized to obtain the most favorable interest rates and minimize borrowing costs, so long as records are carefully kept and each subsidiary has immediate access to its funds as needed for its operations.

e. The parent corporation provides centralized accounting and legal services for all subsidiaries, charging for such services on an even-handed and reasonable basis.

f. The parent and subsidiary have a common office or share office space so long as the terms of the arrangement are reasonable and the separate identities are maintained by appropriate signs, telephone listings, and the like.

g. The board of directors of the subsidiary consists of employees of the parent, all lines of employee authority in the subsidiary pass through employees of the parent, and the organizational chart of the parent includes the subsidiary. *Berger v. Columbia Broadcasting System, Inc.*, 453 F.2d 991 (5th Cir.1972).

4. FRAUD OR INJUSTICE

Some cases have concluded that in a contract case a parent is liable for its subsidiary's liabilities only upon a showing of "fraud or injustice." *Edwards Co., Inc. v. Monogram Industries, Inc.*, 730 F.2d 977 (5th Cir.1984), rev'g 713 F.2d 139 (5th Cir.1983).

5. CONCLUSION

Most courts appear to apply the same PCV principles to parent/subsidiary relationships as are applied to shareholders who are individuals. With the continued growth of corporate groups in the future, and the increased number of regulatory and environmental laws, it is possible that a unique set of principles for PCV in corporate groups will evolve.

D. USE OF THE SEPARATE CORPORATE EXISTENCE TO DEFEAT PUBLIC POLICY

The flexibility of the corporate fiction often permits it to be used in a way that arguably tends to defeat or undercut statutory policies.

Example: A statute prohibits bank directors from borrowing from their bank. A corporation that is wholly owned by a bank director seeks to obtain a loan from the bank. The argument that the corporate borrower has a separate identity from the shareholder and that therefore the loan may be validly made would defeat a clearly defined public policy expressed in the statute; the loan should therefore be held to violate the statute. This result might be rationalized on the ground that the corporation is the "alter ego" of its shareholder and that a loan to the "corporation" is therefore a loan to the "shareholder."

1. GENERAL PRINCIPLE

The issue in such cases generally revolves more around the strength and purpose of the state public policy than the degree or extent of formation or method of operation of the corporation.

Example: A statute prohibits branch banking, i. e., a bank is prohibited from conducting business at more than one location. A bank buys all the capital stock of another bank and plans to continue the banking business at both the parent and subsidiary bank locations. Whether this violates the anti-branch banking statute depends on an evaluation of the policies underlying that statute, not on an examination of the way in which the parent and subsidiary banks conduct business. If the policy underlying the statute is not a strong one, the parent-subsidiary bank relationship should not be viewed as a violation of the statute.

2. QUALIFICATION OF SHAREHOLDER FOR EMPLOYEE BENEFITS

A corporation may also be used to qualify a person for public benefits available to employees which she would not be entitled to if she conducted business in her own name. The validity of this practice also depends on an evaluation of the policies underlying the grant of benefits.

Example: *X*, a 63–year old farmer learns that his social security benefits may be increased if he establishes a favorable employment record during the last two years before his retirement. Accordingly, he incorporates his farm, becoming the sole shareholder and hires himself as an employee of the corporation to improve his earnings record. The establishment of the corporation to improve a person's social security entitlement is not of itself an improper use of a corporation in light of the purpose of the social security system to assure persons an adequate retirement income. *Stark v. Flemming*, 283 F.2d 410 (9th Cir.1960). However, a court may revise the "salary" downward to a reasonable amount to prevent an artificially high entitlement.

Example: In the foregoing situation, the farmer incorporates in order to obtain unemployment benefits during the winter months when little farm work is done. He "lays himself off" during these slow periods, and files for unemployment compensation. This claim should be rejected since the unemployment benefit system was basically not intended to cover employers or owners of a business. *Roccograndi v. Unemployment Compensation Board of Review,* 178 A.2d 786 (Pa.Super.1962).

3. OTHER POLICY ISSUES

A PCV analysis may also be used to determine whether a parent corporation is bound by a subsidiary's union contract. *United Paperworkers Intern. Union v. Penntech Papers, Inc.*, 439 F.Supp. 610 (D.Me.1977) aff'd 583 F.2d 33 (1st Cir.1978).

E. CHOICE OF LAW IN PIERCING THE CORPORATE VEIL

Some states are more liberal than others in permitting PCV. A question may arise in the case of a migratory corporation—for example a corporation formed in Delaware that is transacting business in Missouri and is sued in Missouri on activities in Missouri—as to whether Delaware or Missouri law should apply in determining whether the court should PCV.

1. HISTORICAL DEVELOPMENT

Until about 1980 no attention was paid to the choice of law issue since there did not seem to be significant variations in the law of PCV from state to state. The few cases in which the choice of law issue was raised generally concluded that the law in each possible state was the same and it was unnecessary to determine which law was applicable.

In many cases arising during this period, the court simply applied the law of the forum without discussing the choice of law issue at all.

2. GENERAL PRINCIPLES

The rule generally followed in the few cases that have addressed the issue is that the liability of a shareholder for the debts of the corporation is a matter of the internal affairs of a corporation, to be governed by the law of the state of incorporation. (See part XX D.)

a. This rule is likely to be followed where the corporation has significant economic ties to the state of incorporation, particularly if the shareholders are themselves residents of the state of incorporation.

b. A Texas statute mandates the application of the internal affairs rule to PCV in the case of foreign corporations authorized to transact business in Texas.

Caveat: Under general conflict of laws principles applicable to torts, a court sitting in the state where the accident or event occurred may determine to apply local law to the PCV issue if the contacts of the corporation with the state of incorporation are minimal, and all significant contacts are with the forum state.

Example: A Delaware corporation operates only in Missouri. All the officers, directors, and shareholders of the corporation are residents of Missouri, the person injured is a resident of Missouri, the accident occurred in Missouri, and the corporation's principal business office and all business activities occur in Missouri. A Missouri court might reasonably conclude that the Missouri law of PCV should apply rather than Delaware law.

F. THE FEDERAL LAW OF PIERCING THE CORPORATE VEIL

Federal courts hold that where the enforcement of a federal statute is involved, and a uniform federal policy of PCV will further the federal policies, the federal courts should establish a federal law of PCV.

Example: The United States brings suit to recover funds from a provider of services under the Medicare program. The provider is a corporation, but the United States seeks recovery from the shareholders of the provider on a PCV theory. The PCV issue should be determined by application of a uniform federal rule under the doctrine enunciated in *Clearfield Trust Co. v. United States,* 318 U.S. 363, 63 S.Ct. 573 (1943). In determining what this federal rule should be, the court may consider not only the federal policy involved, but also the federal decisions applying state PCV principles in diversity cases. *United States v. Pisani,* 646 F.2d 83 (3d Cir.1981).

1. CERCLA

The Comprehensive Environmental Response, Compensation and Liability Act imposes responsibility for clean-up and response costs on all "owners" and "operators" of hazardous waste disposal sites. Much of the current litigation involving the federal law of PCV arises under this statute.

Example: A parent corporation that dominates and manages closely the affairs of a subsidiary that operates a hazardous waste disposal site may be found to have direct responsibility as an "operator" of the site. Alternatively, the same control activity may lead a court to ignore the separate corporate existence of the subsidiary under a PCV theory and hold the parent liable as an "owner." *United States v. Kayser–Roth Corporation,*

724 F.Supp. 15 (D.R.I.1989), aff'd on ground that parent was an "operator," 910 F.2d 24 (1st Cir.1990). *Joslyn Mfg. Co. v. T.L. James & Co.,* 893 F.2d 80 (5th Cir.1990) holds that a parent corporation is not liable as an "owner" under PCV principles where the basic corporate formalities of the subsidiary were maintained, the daily operations were conducted separately, and the corporations had different employees and different employee benefit plans.

G. PIERCING THE CORPORATE VEIL IN TAXATION CASES

Under the Internal Revenue Code the government has broad power to ignore or restructure transactions which have as their sole or principal purpose the avoidance or minimization of taxes.

1. RECOGNITION OF CORPORATION IN GENERAL

Generally, the separate corporate existence of a corporation is recognized for tax purposes if it is carrying on a bona fide business and is not merely a device to avoid taxes.

2. ESTOPPEL AGAINST TAXPAYER

The taxpayer, if he or she selects the corporate form of business, is generally bound by that selection and cannot argue that the separate existence of the corporation should be ignored.

H. PIERCING THE CORPORATE VEIL IN BANKRUPTCY

Under the Federal Bankruptcy Act, courts have considerable flexibility in dealing with corporations and shareholders for the purpose of protecting and preserving the rights of creditors.

1. COMPLETE PIERCING OF THE CORPORATE VEIL

The court may ignore the separate corporate existence and hold the shareholders liable for all corporate obligations.

2. RECLASSIFICATION OF TRANSACTION

The court may refuse to recognize, may reclassify, or change the form of a transaction between shareholder and corporation where it is equitable or reasonable to do so.

Example: A loan by a shareholder to her corporation which is essentially part of the initial capital needed by the corporation to conduct business may be treated as a contribution of equity capital and subordinated. *Costello v. Fazio,* 256 F.2d 903 (9th Cir.1958). On the other hand, where the initial capital is more than nominal and the corporation was organized apparently in good faith, subsequent loans to cover losses should not be subordinated. *In re Mader's Store for Men, Inc.*, 254 N.W.2d 171 (Wis. 1977).

Example: In the previous example, essentially the same result may be reached by rejecting the shareholder's claim in its entirety rather than subordinating it to third party claims.

3. SUBORDINATION

The court may subordinate claims of shareholders to claims of other creditors where the claim of the shareholder is in some sense inequitable. This power was viewed by the Supreme Court as inherent in the bankruptcy jurisdiction of federal courts. *Pepper v. Litton,* 308 U.S. 295, 60 S.Ct. 238 (1939). It is now codified in § 510(c)(1) of the Bankruptcy Act of 1978.

a. The power to subordinate inequitable claims (e.g., for excessive salaries) is known as the "Deep Rock" doctrine from the name of the subsidiary in the leading case applying the doctrine. *Taylor v. Standard Gas & Electric Co.,* 306 U.S. 307 (1939).

Example: A sole shareholder transfers funds to her corporation in the form of loans and backdated deeds of trusts, at a time when the corporation was insolvent. The original capital was about $5,000 while the "loans" aggregated $77,500. The "loans" are in fact capital contributions, the deeds of trust are frauds on creditors, and the shareholder's claims should be subordinated to all other creditors. *In re Fett Roofing & Sheet Metal Co., Inc.,* 438 F.Supp. 726 (E.D.Va.1977), aff'd without opinion 605 F.2d 1201 (4th Cir. 1979).

b. Subordination theoretically simply changes the "order of payment" so that the shareholder's claim may be paid after other creditors are satisfied in full; as a practical matter, however, the claims of other creditors usually exhaust the estate so that if a claim is subordinated under the "Deep Rock" doctrine, it ends up not being satisfied in whole or in part.

c. Where both the parent and subsidiary are bankrupt, proceedings may be consolidated and priorities between the parent's and subsidiary's creditors determined on an equitable basis. *Stone v. Eacho,* 127 F.2d 284 (4th Cir.1942).

I. OTHER USES OF THE PIERCING DOCTRINE

While PCV is usually limited to the principal issue discussed above, the liability of a shareholder for corporate obligations, the same doctrine is sometimes referred to in other contexts. The principles applied in these other contexts appear to be the same as those applied in traditional PCV cases, but the nature of the issue involved dictates whether the doctrine is narrowly or broadly applied.

Example: S, a wholly owned subsidiary of P, transacts extensive business in Louisiana. P does not transact business in Louisiana and is not qualified to transact business in that state. A Louisiana resident attempts to obtain jurisdiction over and service of process on P by serving S in a lawsuit involving a transaction between the Louisiana resident and P that occurred in New York. On a motion to dismiss for want of jurisdiction the plaintiff seeks to apply PCV principles and further argues that S's activities in Louisiana directly benefit P, so that S's contacts with Louisiana should be attributed to P. This effort should fail. *Cannon Mfg. Co. v. Cudahy Packing Co.,* 267 U.S. 333 (1925). P is subject to suit in Louisiana only if the controls exercised over S are such that day-to-day decisions are in fact made by P rather than S. *Quarles v. Fuqua Industries, Inc.,* 504 F.2d 1358 (10th Cir. 1974). While this test may be referred to as PCV, it is more stringent than the test usually applied in shareholder liability cases.

J. REVIEW QUESTIONS

IV–1. How does the piercing the corporate veil concept differ from promoters' transactions, corporations de facto, and similar concepts?

IV–2. X forms a corporation for a risky business solely because of fear of unlimited liability. The corporate veil of X's corporation may be pierced for this reason.

True ______ False ______

IV–3. X forms a corporation with one dollar of capital as permitted by the statutes of his state. The corporation enters into a lease but defaults after six months because of business losses. X is personally liable on the lease.

True ______ False ______

IV–4. In the same situation as question IV–3, the corporation is found liable for a tort committed by an employee in which X did not participate. The corporate form protects X against this liability.

True ______ False ______

IV–5 In the same situation as question IV–3, X commingles business and personal finances and does not keep separate corporate records. X is liable for both liabilities described in questions IV–3 and IV–4.

True _______ False _______

IV–6. X Corporation creates a subsidiary, Y Corporation, with the same officers and directors as X. Because of this confusion of personnel, X Corporation is liable for Y Corporation's debts.

True _______ False _______

IV–7. In question IV–5, X Corporation often refers to Y Corporation as a "division" and transfers money to assist Y Corporation simply by check without formally entering the transaction as a loan in the books of X and Y. X Corporation is liable for Y Corporation's debts.

True _______ False _______

IV–8. X, an individual aged 60, decides to incorporate her own business and employ herself to establish the necessary earnings record for social security purposes. This is a fraud on the Federal Government and X is ineligible for social security benefits.

True _______ False _______

IV–9. P sued A Corporation for damages on the ground that P had been fraudulently induced to enter into a training course contract. P served A Corporation under a state long-arm statute allowing service on "any person who transacts any business" in the state. A Corporation is incorporated in another state and directly transacted no business in the state. However, P contended that A Corporation was doing business because it was a holding company for S which was doing business in the state. The trial court found that A Corporation owned 100 per cent of the stock of S but allowed S's management autonomy as to achievement of goals set in conjunction with A's management; A Corporation provided S with a general financial, legal, tax and administrative services, and acted as its banker but S kept separate books and records, S and A had separate auditors, officers and office staffs. Should the court hold that A was transacting business in the state?

IV–10. D purchased Blackacre for the purpose of mining coal. He formed "A Corporation" and posted on Blackacre a sign, "A Corporation Mines." There was issued to D all of the shares of the corporation except one share which was issued to D's wife. Neither D nor his wife paid any money for these shares. There was no meeting of shareholders, no directors were elected, no corporate control was exercised and no corporate books were kept. The mine was operated as though it were the private business of D: the expenses of the mine were paid by D from his private bank account and the income was deposited in D's private account. One of the employees in the mine is killed as a result of negligence in the mining operations. His executor sues D. Is D liable?

*

V

FINANCING THE CORPORATION

Analysis

D. Debt Securities
- *1. Bonds and Debentures Described*
- *2. Debt Instruments Compared With Preferred Stock*
- *3. Debt/Equity Ratio*
- *4. Hybrid Securities*

E. Tax Advantages of Providing a Portion of the Initial Capital in the Form of Debt

F. Non-tax Advantages of Providing a Portion of the Initial Capital in the Form of Debt

G. Application of the Federal and State Securities Acts
- *1. General Description of Statutory Purpose*
- *2. Cost of Registration*
- *3. Exemptions From Registration*
- *4. Restrictions on Transfer of Unregistered Securities*
- *5. Control Persons and Secondary Distributions*
- *6. What Is a Security?*
- *7. State Blue Sky Laws*

H. Issuance of Shares by a Going Concern
- *1. Preemptive Rights*
- *2. Fiduciary Restrictions on the Oppressive Issuance of Shares*
- *3. Applicability of Securities Acts*

I. Dividends and Distributions
- *1. Dividend Policies in Publicly Held Corporations*
- *2. Dividend Policies in a Closely Held Corporation*
- *3. Legal Requirements for Dividends and Distributions*
- *4. Contractual Restrictions on Dividends and Distributions*

J. Redemptions and Repurchases of Outstanding Shares
- *1. Relationship Between Repurchases and Distributions*
- *2. Reasons for Repurchases of Shares by Publicly Held Corporations*
- *3. Reasons for Repurchases of Shares by Closely Held Corporations*
- *4. Status of Reacquired Shares*
- *5. Redeemable Shares in General*
- *6. Redemptions at Option of Shareholder*
- *7. Fiduciary Duties in Connection With Repurchases of Shares*

K. Illegal Dividends or Distributions
- *1. Protection of Reliance by Directors*
- *2. Recovery by Creditors*

L. Share Dividends and Share Splits
- *1. Definitions*
- *2. Effect of Share Splits or Share Dividends On Market Prices*

A. IN GENERAL

The following are the likely sources of capital for a corporation:

1. EQUITY CAPITAL

"Equity capital" or "equity financing" is capital contributed by shareholders in exchange for shares of stock.

2. LOANS FROM SHAREHOLDERS

Capital loaned by the shareholders to the corporation may be substituted for equity capital in whole or in part. Shareholder loans have many of the characteristics of equity capital and may be treated as equity capital for some purposes.

3. LOANS FROM THIRD PERSONS

The raising of capital through loans from third persons is "debt financing."

a. Debt financing may be either short term, e.g. bank loans or lines of credit for working capital, or long term, e.g. bonds that may have maturity dates 50 or 100 years in the future.

b. Debt financing is distinguishable from loans by shareholders because of the significantly different economic and legal consequences of such loans. For example, there is little likelihood that bona fide loans from third parties will be treated as equity capital; there is a real possibility that shareholder loans will be so treated.

Caveat: Some kinds of highly subordinated bonds usually issued in connection with takeovers, called "junk bonds," have economic characteristics that make them somewhat similar to equity capital. Junk bonds may sometimes be colloquially referred to as "another class of equity" or a "type of common stock."

c. Debt financing is discussed in greater detail in Part V D below.

4. INTERNALLY GENERATED FUNDS

Capital internally generated from the corporation's business through the retention of earnings, creation of reserves, sales of appreciated assets and the like, is a final source of funds for a corporation.

B. THE ISSUANCE OF COMMON SHARES

MBCA (1984) § 2.02(a)(2) provides that the articles of incorporation must set forth "the number of shares the corporation is authorized to issue." MBCA (1984) § 6.01(a) provides that the articles of incorporation must prescribe "the classes of shares and the number of shares of each class" that the corporation is authorized to issue; in addition, if more than one class of shares is authorized, the articles of incorporation "must prescribe a distinguishing designation for each class, and, prior to the issuance of shares of a class, the preferences, limitations, and relative rights of that class must be described" in the articles of incorporation.

1. COMMON SHARES DEFINED

Common shares reflect the residual ownership of the corporation. All corporations must have shares outstanding that reflect this ownership.

a. Common shares have two basic characteristics:

   1) They are entitled to vote for the election of directors and on other matters coming before the shareholders; and

   2) They are entitled to the net assets of the corporation (after making allowance for debts), when distributions are made in the form of dividends or liquidating distributions.

b. When a corporation issues only one class of shares, the shares need no formal designation but they are common shares. They may be designated as "shares," "stock," "capital shares," "common shares," "capital stock" or "common stock." The rights of those shares need not be described in the articles of incorporation since they automatically have the two basic rights of common shares.

c. MBCA (1984) § 6.01(b) permits the essential attributes of common shares to be placed in different classes of shares but requires that classes with each of these attributes must always be authorized. MBCA (1984) § 6.03(b) also requires that at least one share of each class with each of these basic attributes must be outstanding.

2. PAR VALUE

In about 30 states, the articles of incorporation must also state the par value of the shares of each class (or state that the shares are issued "with no par value" or "without par value"). The remaining states, like the MBCA (1984), have eliminated the concept of par value, and the current trend is toward the elimination of this concept in additional states as an historical anomaly.

a. "Par value" is an arbitrary value associated with shares of stock. The par value of shares is set forth in the articles of incorporation and appears on the face of certificates for shares. The complex legal operation of this concept is described in parts 4, 5, 6, and 9 below.

b. Even in states that have eliminated par value, it may be used on an optional basis at the election of the corporation. For example, MBCA (1984) § 2.02(b)(2)(iv) permits the use of par value as a discretionary matter.

1) The Official Comment to the MBCA explains that such provisions may be of use "to corporations which are to be qualified in foreign jurisdictions if franchise or other taxes are computed upon the basis of par value."

2) Optional par value may also be given effect or meaning "essentially as a matter of contract" between the parties. In other words, the par value rules described in parts 4, 5, 6, and 9 below may be elected by the parties if they so desire by creating a par value for shares.

3. AUTHORIZED AND ISSUED SHARES

It is customary in modern corporate practice to authorize a corporation to issue additional shares over what is planned to be issued initially. Additional capital may be needed at a later date, and authorized shares may be issued to raise that capital without amending the articles of incorporation. Shares authorized but not issued may be issued at a later date by the board of directors acting alone without approval of the shareholders.

Example: *A* and *B* plan to contribute $10,000 each for fifty per cent of the stock of a new corporation. The attorney forming the corporation recommends that 500 shares of common stock be authorized and that 100 shares be issued each to *A* and *B* for $100 per share. Three hundred shares have the status of "authorized but unissued shares."

Example: The corporation is to be formed in a state with a par value statute. The attorney forming the corporation recommends that a nominal par value of $1 be assigned to each share and the same number of shares be authorized and issued.

Caveat: Where par value shares are involved, the capital accounts created thereby (described below) are based on *issued* shares, not *authorized* shares. State statutes, on the other hand, may compute taxes either on the basis of authorized shares or on the basis of issued shares.

Example: In the two previous examples essentially the same economic result may be achieved in each example by issuing 10 shares each to A and to B for $1000 per share. There are two differences: (1) the number of authorized but unissued shares of the corporation will be 480 instead of 300; and (2) as described below, if the shares are issued under a par value statute, the transaction will be reflected differently in the capital accounts of the corporation.

Example: The authorized but unissued shares in the previous examples may be later issued by the board of directors at a price then decided upon by the board of directors, though if the shares have a par value, they should not be issued for less than par value (see below). If conditions warrant, the authorized shares may be issued at more (or less) than the original issue price.

4. THE PRICE AT WHICH SHARES ARE ISSUED

a. Under modern statutes such as the MBCA (1984), there is no minimum issue price for shares. The price at which shares are issued is set by the board of directors, and so long as all shares being issued at the same time are issued at the same price, any price may be set by the board.

   Caveat: Many states have constraints on the types of non-cash consideration that may be received for shares. (See part V B 8.)

b. In states with par value statutes, the board of directors may set the price at which shares are issued, but shares should never be issued for less than par value.

   1) The consequence of issuing par value shares for less than par is the creation of "watered shares" and a resulting liability on the part of the recipient to pay to the corporation the difference between par value and what the shareholder actually paid.

   2) It is customary in modern practice to use "low par" or "nominal par" value shares rather than "high par" value shares.

      Example: In the previous examples under par value statutes, the attorney may set the par value of $1 per share but issue the shares at $100 per share. She might theoretically set the par value at any amount up to $100 per share (in the first example) or $1000 per share (in the second example). However, the par value, once set in the articles of incorporation, cannot be thereafter changed except by formal amendment to the articles of incorporation.

      Example: In the first of the previous examples, if the attorney set the par value at the issue price of $100 per share, several undesirable consequences would follow: (i) no shares of the corporation could be thereafter issued by the corporation at less than $100 per share without creating a watered stock liability, (ii) some state taxes are computed on the basis of par value so that a high par value simply increases tax liabilities with no offsetting benefits; and (iii) as described below, the transaction is reflected in the capital accounts of the corporation in a way that is less advantageous to the corporation than if nominal par shares were used.

3) There appears to be no benefit or advantage to the corporation in using a high par value for shares since lenders do not put weight on this factor in deciding whether or not to extend credit.

5. PAR VALUE AND THE CAPITAL ACCOUNTS

Corporation statutes that retain the concept of par value provide that the aggregate of the par values of issued shares constitutes the "stated capital" of the corporation and any excess received for the issuance of shares over stated capital is "capital surplus."

Caveat: The names of the capital accounts used here are those that appear in the MBCA (1969). Some state statutes adopt different terms for these accounts.

Caveat: The names of the capital accounts used in corporation statutes generally differ from the names assigned to accounts by the accounting profession.

Caveat: The concepts set forth in this part are applicable only to states with par value statutes. Under modern statutes such as the MBCA (1984) there are no statutory rules as to how the capital accounts of a corporation should be structured.

Example: When 100 shares of $1 par value shares are issued each to *A* and *B* for $100 per share (or an aggregate of $10,000 each), the balance sheet of the corporation immediately after its formation will be as follows:

Assets		Liabilities	–0–
Cash	20,000		
		Equity Capital	
		Stated Capital	200
		Capital Surplus	19,800
	20,000		20,000

Example: If in this corporation a par value of $100 per share had been assigned, the balance sheet would be as follows:

Assets		Liabilities	–0–
Cash	20,000		
		Capital	
		Stated Capital	20,000
		Capital Surplus	–0–
	20,000		20,000

a. A major advantage of reflecting the bulk of the capital contributions as capital surplus is that under most state statutes stated capital is "locked in" the corporation for the benefit of creditors while capital surplus may be distributed to the shareholders or used to reacquire outstanding shares merely with the approval of shareholders.

Example: In the preceding example, *B* suffers business and gambling reverses and would like to withdraw half of his $10,000 contribution. *A* agrees to this so long as *B*'s shares are reduced correspondingly by the corporation repurchasing 50 of *B*'s shares. Under most state statutes, capital surplus may be used to reacquire outstanding shares but stated capital may not. As a result, a corporation formed under "low par" principles could reacquire one half of *B*'s shares for $5,000, but a corporation formed under "high par" principles could not since it does not have $5,000 of capital surplus. The balance sheet of the "low par" corporation might look like this after reacquiring fifty of *B*'s shares for $5,000:

Assets		Liabilities	-0-
Cash	15,000		
		Equity	
		Stated Capital (150 shares outstanding, 50 treasury shares)	200
		Capital Surplus (5,000 restricted to reflect treasury shares)	14,800
	15,000		15,000

6. THE "NO PAR" ALTERNATIVE TO PAR VALUE SHARES

In most states that have mandatory par value statutes "no par" shares are a permitted alternative. However, in these states, these shares are generally tied into "par value" concepts as described below.

Caveat: The "no par" shares discussed in this part are extensions of "nominal par" value shares discussed above. The discussion in this part does not relate to shares issued under modern statutes such as the MBCA (1984) which have eliminated mandatory par value.

a. No par shares are shares defined in the articles of incorporation as "shares without par value." They may provide some protection against watered stock liability. No par shares may be issued for any amount of consideration specified by the directors; there is no floor below which the price may not be set. However, watered stock liability may continue to arise if property other than cash is the consideration for the issuance of shares or a price is designated but the shares are issued for less than that price. (See V B 8 b.)

Example: The articles of incorporation of a corporation state that the corporation is authorized to issue "500,000 shares of common stock which are without par value." *A* and *B* decide to issue shares for $1,000 of capital. The directors may set the price at which the shares are to be issued, at $.01 per share (in which case 100,000 shares are issued), $1.00 per share (in which case 1,000 shares are issued) or $100 per share (in which case 10 shares are issued).

b. The entire consideration is initially allocated to "stated capital" but in most states the directors may allocate a specified fraction (e.g., one-third) or all the consideration to "capital surplus."

1) If no part of the consideration is allocated to "capital surplus" the no par alternative is treated for accounting purposes like the high par alternative.

2) If all or nearly all of the consideration is allocated to "capital surplus," the no par alternative is treated for accounting purposes like the low par alternative.

c. Where property (other than cash) is received for no par shares, in some states the directors must still specify in dollars the consideration to be received for no par shares. In other states, the directors may simply specify the property to be received without setting a dollar value.

d. "No par" shares have no other significant advantage over "low par" shares in most states and the choice between them is more a matter of custom with the particular attorney than questions of practical or economic significance.

e. Under the since-repealed federal documentary stamp tax, no par shares were valued at the price at which the shares were actually issued while par value shares were valued at par value, no matter what price the shares were actually issued. Some state taxes retain this treatment today, and thus there is a continuing tax inducement to issue low par rather than no par shares in some states.

Caveat: It is important to distinguish conceptually between "no par shares" in states that retain the par value structure, and shares issued in states with statutes that have eliminated par value. The issuance of "no par shares" in par value states affect the stated capital and capital surplus account, may create a watered stock liability in certain circumstances, and may affect the distributions a corporation may lawfully make. States that have eliminated the par value structure have also generally eliminated the mandatory capital accounts and have established rules relating to when distributions may be made that are independent of any allocation of the consideration received when the shares are issued. (See part V I below.)

7. WATERED STOCK

"Watered stock" is a generic term used to describe the issuance of shares at a price below par value.

a. There are three subtypes of watered stock:

   1) "Bonus" shares are shares issued for no consideration at all. Bonus shares are usually issued in connection with the valid issuance of senior securities as an inducement to invest in the senior securities;

   2) "Discount" shares are shares issued for a consideration that is less than the legally established price, either the par value or the price set by the directors; and

   3) "Watered" shares are technically shares issued for property the value of which has been artificially inflated. Historically, many fraudulent transactions took the form of shares issued for overvalued property.

   The phrase "watered stock" has gradually come to refer to bonus or discount stock as well.

b. Several different theories have been developed to explain watered stock liability.

   1) The par value of issued shares was early viewed as a public representation that at least that amount of equity capital has been received by the corporation. From this it may be argued that shareholders who knowingly receive watered shares are involved in a potential misrepresentation to creditors and should be liable to them for any short-fall between the par value and the amount actually paid for shares. This is the historical explanation for "watered stock liability."

   2) Watered stock liability has also been rationalized on the theory that the capital of a corporation is a "trust fund" for creditors who rely on the capital of the corporation when extending credit to it. Under this theory any creditor might bring suit against the recipient of watered shares for failing to make the required payment to this "trust fund." This theory is largely a fiction because:

(i) The capital of a corporation is not a "trust fund" in any meaningful sense. The capital of a corporation may be invested in the business and may be lost if the business does not succeed or increase if the business is successful. No one is liable if the capital is lost; the creditors simply go unpaid. Corporate capital is no more a trust fund for creditors than the assets of an individual may be considered a "trust fund" for his or her creditors; and

(ii) The corporate creditors are no more the "beneficiary" of such a trust than are creditors of an individual debtor.

3) In an early case, the theory of watered stock liability was refined to a "holding out" theory. *Hospes v. Northwestern Mfg. & Car Co.*, 50 N.W. 1117 (Minn.1892). The practical differences between the "holding out" and the "trust fund" or classic theories are that under a "holding out" theory:

(i) Only creditors who extend credit subsequent to the issuance of the watered shares may enforce the liability; and

(ii) Creditors who know that the shares were watered when they extended credit may not recover at all.

(iii) The burden is on the plaintiffs to establish that they qualify under (i) and (ii), but they do not have the burden of establishing that they in fact relied on the capital of the corporation in extending credit.

Caveat: The holding out theory is fictional in the sense that reliance on the capital of the corporation by a creditor is presumed; indeed, the defendants can avoid liability only by making an affirmative showing that the plaintiffs knew that the stock was watered or that they did not rely on the capital of the corporation when they extended credit.

Caveat: In modern practice, creditors almost never rely on par values and capital accounts in determining whether to extend credit. Rather, to the extent they investigate the credit standing of a possible borrower at all, commercial creditors rely on modern credit reporting services or the general reputation of the debtor. Banks usually require a financial statement from the potential debtor, but in analyzing that statement the bank normally pays no attention to par values and capital accounts.

4) Some par value statutes substitute a statutory liability for the common law theories. These statutes obligate every shareholder to pay at least the price set as required by law for shares, and if a shareholder fails to do so,

the corporation or any creditor may enforce this statutory liability. The "price set as required by law" may mean the price set by the board of directors or a price at least equal to the par value of shares.

c) The issuance of watered stock leads to the creation of fictitious assets, or the inflation of asset values, on the balance sheet.

Example: A corporation issues 1,000,000 shares of $10 par value common stock for an aggregate consideration of $5,000,000 in cash. Since the capital accounts automatically reflect a stated capital equal to the number of shares issued (1,000,000) times the par value ($10.00 per share), the asset accounts must be inflated or "watered" in some way if the balance sheet is to balance:

Cash	5,000,000	Liabilities	-0-
"Water"	5,000,000	Equity Capital	
		Stated Capital	10,000,000
	$10,000,000		$10,000,000

Example: In the foregoing example, under some statutes the corporation itself might recover $5.00 per share from each recipient as the basic statutory liability each shareholder owes to the corporation for issuance of shares. This liability may be enforced by the corporation, a creditor, or a bankruptcy trustee or similar representative of the corporation, apparently without limitation. *Bing Crosby Minute Maid Corp. v. Eaton*, 297 P.2d 5 (Cal.1956); *Frink v. Carman Distributing Co.*, 48 P.2d 805 (Colo.1935).

d. Potential watered stock liabilities may make high par value shares unmarketable.

Example: A corporation originally issues shares with a par value of $100 per share at a sales price of $100. The corporation suffers financial reverses so that its outstanding shares are now worth less than $100 per share. The corporation decides to issue additional authorized shares to raise much needed capital; these shares can only be sold at the current market price of $60 per share. Since they are $100 par value shares, any person who purchases the new shares at $60 per share also incurs a potential watered stock liability of $40 per share. Sophisticated investors will naturally refuse to purchase shares under such circumstances and the shares are unmarketable.

Example: In the foregoing situation, the corporation may amend its articles of incorporation to reduce the par value of the authorized shares to

$1 per share or may create a new class of low par value common shares.

e. Depending on the language of the state statute, watered stock liability may also arise if low par value or no par value shares are issued for any price below the price set by the directors for the issuance of such shares. In other words, under some statutes, shares may be viewed as watered whenever the consideration for which the shares are actually issued is less than the price for such shares set by the board of directors. *Milberg v. Baum*, 25 N.Y.S.2d 451 (App.Term 1941) (low par shares); *G. Loewus & Co. v. Highland Queen Packing Co.*, 6 A.2d 545 (N.J.Ch.1939) (no par shares).

Example: The board of directors establishes an issuance price of $100 per share for all shares of common stock. The common stock has a par value of $10. Two years later, the corporation issues shares to X for $50 per share without establishing a different issuance price for the shares. Under traditional watered stock principles, the shares are not watered since the issue price exceeds the par value. Under the statutes of some states, a watered stock liability is created since the shares were issued for less than the consideration set by the board of directors to be received for shares. This liability is avoided if the board of directors determines before issuing the shares for $50 per share that the consideration for which such shares are to be issued should be $50.

Example: The directors set a price of $10 per share for an issue of no par shares. For some reason one shareholder is permitted to buy shares for $8.00. That shareholder has a liability to the corporation for the additional $2.00 despite her contract with the corporation to pay only $8.00.

Example: No par shares may have an advantage where property of highly uncertain value is being contributed because the directors may be able to specify the property that is to be received for the no par shares without setting a dollar value on it.

Caveat: Even where a dollar value must be set for the value of property, the directors' good faith valuation is accepted for purposes of watered stock liability under the statutory provisions that make the determination of the directors as to value conclusive in the absence of fraud. *Johnson v. Louisville Trust Co.*, 293 Fed. 857 (6th Cir. 1923). These statutory provisions are discussed in Part V B 8.

f. Shares issued for no consideration, whether par or no par, may in some cases be cancelled at the suit of other shareholders and votes cast by such shares may be invalidated. *Triplex Shoe Co. v. Rice & Hutchins*, 152 A. 342 (Del. 1930).

8. CONSIDERATION FOR SHARES

When shares are issued for property or services rather than cash, further problems arise.

a. Under many state statutes, only certain types of property qualify as valid consideration for shares. A typical statute provides that consideration may "be paid, in whole or in part, in cash, in other property, tangible or intangible, or in labor or services actually performed for the corporation." MBCA (1969) § 19, 1st par. Many statutes add that "neither promissory notes nor future services shall constitute payment or part payment for the issuance of shares of a corporation." MBCA (1969) § 19, 2d par.

Caveat: In a few states, these statutory provisions are grounded on state constitutional provisions dating from the 19th century that were designed to prohibit the watering of stock.

Caveat: Most states that retain these restrictions on eligible consideration for shares also retain par value provisions. However, these requirements are independent of par value, and some states, including California, have eliminated the par value rules but retained the restrictions on eligible consideration for shares.

b. If ineligible property or services are received for shares, the shares so issued are watered shares.

Example: *A* and *B* agree to form a corporation each to have one half of the stock. *A* is to contribute $100,000 in cash and *B* is to work full time for the corporation without remuneration for one year. The consideration for the shares is recited to be $100,000 each, *A* to pay cash and "*B* to perform services which the board of directors determines to have the value of $100,000 over the next year." B's services are not eligible consideration for the issuance of shares, and if *B*'s shares are issued immediately, they are viewed as having been issued for no consideration at all. A watered stock liability on the part of *B* has been created by which B may be obligated to pay eligible consideration of $100,000 to the corporation despite the agreement by *A* and *B* that *B* is to contribute only services. The amount of this watered stock liability may depend on the par value of the issued shares in some states; in other states, the watered stock liability may be $100,000, the value of the issued shares as determined by the board of directors.

Example: In the previous example, if *B*'s shares are to be issued only after *B* has performed services for one year, no watered stock liability is created. Since the services have been "actually performed," $100,000 of eligible consideration has been received by the corporation. *Eastern Oklahoma Television Co. v. Ameco, Inc.*, 437 F.2d 138 (10th Cir.1971). However, *B* does not have the rights of a shareholder during the period she is rendering services, though *B* may have contract rights against *A*.

Example: In the previous example, if *B*'s shares are to be issued immediately for a promissory note which is to be repaid by the performance of services over the year, a watered stock liability has again been created since promissory notes do not constitute permissible consideration for the issuance of shares. *Cahall v. Lofland*, 114 A. 224 (Del.Ch.1921).

Example: *B*'s shares are to be issued for a one year promissory note for $100,000 secured by a lien on valuable real estate. B plans to repay this note, together with interest, in cash when it comes due. While a promissory note is not eligible consideration for the issuance of shares, some courts have held that a secured promissory note is eligible consideration for shares, since the security granted is itself eligible property, and the transaction does not lend itself to the evil at which the statute is directed. *General Bonding & Cas. Ins. Co. v. Moseley*, 222 S.W. 961 (Tex.1920).

Example: In the previous example, B receives shares in exchange for an unsecured promissory note. Even though the shares are not validly issued because ineligible consideration was received, the note itself is not void and may be sued upon by the corporation.

c. State statutes provide in effect that "in the absence of fraud in the transaction, the judgment of the board of directors * * * as to the value of the consideration received for shares shall be conclusive." MBCA (1969) § 19, 3d par. Provisions of this type are absolutely essential to assure that shares are validly issued, fully paid, and nonassessable.

Example: In the previous example, the board of directors decides to issue *B*'s shares immediately, not for services, but for "six store fixtures having the value of $100,000." In fact, the store fixtures are valueless. If this transaction is not fraudulent, the values established for the store fixtures must be accepted by statute. If the directors have established the valuation of the fixtures in order to defraud another shareholder or a third party, watered stock liability would arise. *See v. Heppenheimer*, 61 A. 843 (N.J.Ch. 1905); *Pipelife Corp. v. Bedford*, 145 A.2d 206 (Del.Ch.1958).

Example: *B'*s shares are to be issued, not for services, but for "secret contract rights." The board of directors establishes in good faith a value of $100,000 for those services. State statutes refer to "intangible" property as qualifying for the issuance of shares, and hence, it is likely that such a transaction involves eligible consideration and the value established for such consideration by the board of directors is conclusive. There is, however, some risk that a court may accept the argument that "secret contract rights" are so ephemeral that they do not qualify as "intangible" property and that therefore the shares were not issued for eligible consideration and are watered.

d. MBCA (1984) § 6.21(b) authorizes shares to be issued for consideration consisting of "any tangible or intangible property or benefit to the corporation, including cash, promissory notes, services performed, contracts for services to be performed, or other securities of the corporation." MBCA (1984) § 6.21(c) provides that "before the corporation issues shares, the board of directors must determine that the consideration received or to be received for shares to be issued is adequate. That determination by the board of directors is conclusive insofar as the adequacy of consideration for the issuance of shares relates to whether the shares are validly issued, fully paid, and nonassessable." MBCA (1984) § 6.21(d) provides that "when the corporation receives the consideration for which the board of directors authorized the issuance of shares, the shares issued therefor are fully paid and nonassessable."

1) The corporation may escrow shares issued for future services or benefits or a promissory note until the consideration is received. MBCA (1984) § 6.21(e).

2) The Official Comment to § 6.21 states that "in the realities of commercial life, there is sometimes a need for the issuance of shares for contract rights or such intangible property or benefits."

3) The traditional rules relating to eligible and ineligible consideration for shares create anomalous results that are eliminated by MBCA (1984) § 6.21.

Example: Jane Fonda agrees to make a film in exchange for a twenty-five per cent interest in the film. Under traditional rules she could not be issued shares upon the execution of her contract; on the other hand, a bank might lend the new corporation $10,000,000 solely on the basis of Jane Fonda's contract. Under § 6.21, shares could be issued to Ms. Fonda in exchange for her contract to perform services.

Example: John D. Rockefeller could not give his promissory note for shares even though his note is "as good as gold." On the other hand, someone else, owning John D.'s promissory note, could acquire shares for John D.'s note. Under § 6.21, Rockefeller's promissory note may serve directly as consideration for shares.

e. If shares are issued for services already performed or to be performed, the fair value of the shares so received is subject to federal income tax at ordinary income tax rates. This tax liability may create cash flow problems for the shareholder who normally must find the cash to pay the tax from sources other than the shares.

f. The contribution of property to a corporation in exchange for its shares is not a taxable disposition of the property contributed, if immediately after the exchange the persons contributing the property own at least 80 per cent of the voting and nonvoting shares of the corporation. This nonrecognition of gain is limited to transactions in which no property other than shares is received by the contributor and the liabilities assumed by the corporation to which the property is subject do not exceed the basis of the property in the hands of the contributor. I.R.C. § 351. No gain or loss is recognized by the corporation in connection with the raising of capital by the issuance of shares. I.R.C. § 1032.

Caveat: If I.R.C. § 351 is not applicable, a shareholder who contributes appreciated property to the corporation is taxed on the appreciation in the same manner as though he had sold the appreciated property to an unrelated person.

9. TREASURY SHARES

"Treasury shares" are shares of the corporation that were once lawfully issued but have been reacquired by the corporation and held in its "treasury."

a. Under traditional statutes, treasury shares have an intermediate status between being issued and unissued. They are not outstanding for purposes of voting, quorum determinations or dividend payments. They are viewed as "issued" for other purposes.

b. Treasury shares are widely used by corporations formed under par value statutes to avoid the rules set forth in this part of the outline.

1) Treasury shares, having once been issued for more than par value, may be resold by the corporation without regard to the relationship between the sales price and par value.

2) Treasury shares, having once been issued for an eligible consideration, may be resold by the corporation in exchange for future services,

promissory notes, or other consideration that is not eligible consideration for the issue of new shares.

3) Stated capital is not reduced by the par value of treasury shares; such shares are reflected on the financial statements by a special entry showing that they are held as treasury shares and restrictions are placed on the earned surplus and/or capital surplus accounts to reflect that the purchase price for the treasury shares has been charged to those accounts. Accounting for treasury shares is complicated; it is based on the assumption that those shares are not permanently retired but will be reissued at a later date.

Example: Corporation A, a publicly held corporation, wishes to contribute 10 shares as a door prize for a benefit for an employee who has been seriously injured in an automobile accident. It may not use authorized but unissued shares for this purpose under the state statute that permits shares to be issued only for "money or property actually received or services actually performed." Corporation A may lawfully contribute 10 treasury shares for this purpose.

Caveat: One court has applied the limitations on the issuance of authorized shares to the reissuance of treasury shares. *Public Inv. Ltd. v. Bandeirante Corp.,* 740 F.2d 1222 (D.C.Cir.1984). This result reached by the court is reasonable on the facts of that case, but it is not consistent with generally understood principles relating to treasury shares.

Caveat: Treasury shares are only shares of the issuing corporation that have been repurchased by the corporation. If the corporation acquires shares of *other* corporations, those shares are held in the "treasury" of the acquiring corporation, but they are investments, not "treasury shares."

c. MBCA (1984) § 6.31(a) eliminates the concept of treasury shares by providing that when a corporation acquires its own shares, they automatically become authorized but unissued shares. This change was made in recognition of the fact that with the elimination of restrictions on the issuance of shares, there is no reason to retain the concept of treasury shares.

C. SENIOR SECURITIES

Common shares are the residual ownership interests in the corporation. Corporations may also issue other classes of shares. Shares that have rights that must be satisfied before the common shares are entitled to distributions are called "senior securities."

Senior securities are often described as "preferred" shares, and a traditional classification of shares is between "common" and "preferred" shares. The MBCA (1984) does not use the terms "common shares" and "preferred shares" since it is possible to create classes of shares that have some characteristics of both types of shares. These terms, however, are widely used in corporate practice and have well understood meanings.

1. PREFERRED SHARES

"Preferred" means that shares have preference over common shares either as to dividends or on liquidation or both. A "preference" simply means that the preferred shares are entitled to a payment of a specified amount before the common shares are entitled to anything. Most preferred shares have both dividend and liquidation preferences; most traditional preferred shares are nonvoting shares that are limited to a right to receive a specified amount and no more, no matter how profitable the corporation.

a. Preferential rights are defined in the articles of incorporation, and the attributes of preferred shares may include some rights normally associated with common shares.

Example: A "$3.50 preferred" means that the preferred share is entitled to a dividend preference of $3.50 per share before any dividend may be paid on the common shares. Such a share is not entitled to, and will never receive more than, $3.50 per share no matter how much is available for distribution. The $3.50 payment is a dividend, however, and is discretionary with the board of directors. Unlike interest, it is not a debt owed by the corporation.

Example: In the prior example the preferred share may also be entitled to a preferential liquidating payment of $75.00. On liquidation, $75.00 must be first set aside for the holder of each such share and nothing may be paid on the common until the $75.00 is paid to the holders of the preferred. On the other hand, once the preferred receives $75.00 it is not entitled to, and will never receive anything more no matter how much is available for distribution. The question whether unpaid preferential dividends must also be satisfied in liquidation depends on the language of the articles of incorporation. *Matter of Chandler & Co.*, 230 N.Y.S.2d 1012 (1962).

Example: Preferred shares may be entitled to vote on specific matters or to vote generally. They may be entitled to vote only upon the occurrence of a specified event such as the omission of preferred dividends for a specified period. Preferred shares may also be entitled to additional distributions of dividends or liquidation payments by specific provision in the articles of incorporation.

b. A dividend preference may be noncumulative, cumulative, or cumulative-to-the-extent-earned.

1) A cumulative dividend that is not paid in one year carries over to the next and must be satisfied in addition to the current year's preferred dividend before any dividend can be paid on the common stock in the second year.

Example: A preferred carries a $5 cumulative dividend. Because of shortage of working capital, the directors do not declare (in technical terms, they "omit") the dividend for three years. In the fourth year a dividend is declared: however, $20 in dividends must be paid to the holders of the preferred before any common dividend may be paid.

2) A noncumulative dividend treats each year as a unit; a noncumulative dividend not paid in any year is gone.

Example: If the foregoing preferred were noncumulative, the directors could pay a dividend on the common in the fourth year after paying only the $5.00 current dividend on the preferred. Indeed, an attempt to pay past noncumulative dividends could probably be enjoined by the common shareholders as a violation of their rights.

Caveat: In New Jersey, equitable principles have been held to limit the power of the corporation to omit entirely the payment of noncumulative dividends when earnings are sufficient to "cover" the dividend.

Example: A New Jersey corporation omits a noncumulative dividend of $1.00 per share in 1990 even though earnings of the corporation that year exceed $1.00 per share for each share of preferred. A "dividend credit" has attached to these earnings, and in 1992 the corporation may not pay a dividend on common shares without satisfying not only the noncumulative dividend for 1992 but also the unpaid dividend for 1990. This New Jersey "dividend credit" rule has not been adopted elsewhere. See *Sanders v. Cuba R. Co.*, 120 A.2d 849 (N.J.1956); *Lich v. United States Rubber Co.*, 39 F.Supp. 675 (D.N.J.1941); compare *Guttmann v. Illinois Central R. Co.*, 189 F.2d 927 (2d Cir.1951).

3) A cumulative-to-the-extent-earned dividend is cumulative only to the extent earnings exist; in any year if earnings fail to cover the preferred

dividend, the portion of the dividend that is not covered does not cumulate and is gone.

Example: The New Jersey "dividend credit" rule is essentially an example of a cumulative-to-the-extent-earned dividend. In other states a cumulative-to-the-extent-earned dividend exists only if specific provision is made for such a dividend in the articles of incorporation.

c. Preferred shares may be made *redeemable* at a price set forth in the articles of incorporation. When shares are redeemed they are reacquired by the corporation and either disappear or become treasury shares. Upon redemption, the holder of redeemable shares is entitled only to the "redemption price" set forth in the articles of incorporation.

Example: Preferred shares sold for $50.00 per share may be made redeemable at the option of the corporation at $60.00 per share plus unpaid cumulative dividends. The corporation may at any time thereafter at its option elect to redeem those shares at $60 per share plus the unpaid dividends, if any.

Example: Under most state statutes, it is permissible to make shares redeemable at the option of the holder rather than the option of the corporation. Such shares have many characteristics of a demand promissory note. Such shares may be used instead of a debt instrument for financing when the lender is a corporation and desires to take advantage of the credit for intercorporate dividends under the Federal income tax law. The S.E.C. requires preferred shares redeemable at the option of the holder to be shown on balance sheets as a separate category under neither the "debt" nor "equity" accounts.

d. Preferred shares may be made *convertible* at the option of the holder into common or other shares at a ratio set forth in the articles of incorporation. The securities into which the convertible shares may be converted are called the "conversion securities" and the ratio is called the "conversion ratio".

Example: A corporation issues preferred shares that are convertible into two shares of common. The "conversion ratio" is therefore 2 for 1. Any preferred shareholder may deliver shares of the preferred stock to the corporation and receive two shares of common for each share of preferred; upon the conversion, the shares of preferred disappear.

1) Conversion ratios are usually protected against "dilution" that may occur if the conversion securities are increased through a share split, share dividends, or recapitalizations.

Example: In the prior example, while the preferred is outstanding, the conversion security is split on a 3 for 1 basis. If the preferred's conversion right is protected against dilution, the conversion ratio is changed to 6 for 1. See *Merritt–Chapman & Scott Corp. v. New York Trust Co.*, 184 F.2d 954 (2d Cir. 1950).

Example: In the prior example, if the preferred's conversion right is not protected against dilution, the preferred share's conversion ratio remains at 2 for 1, and as a result of the stock split, the value of the conversion right has been reduced by 2/3ds.

Caveat: Many state statutes prohibit "upstream conversions," that is the creation of a right of common to convert to preferred, or either common or preferred to convert to debt. The MBCA (1984) permits upstream conversions on the theory that they are potentially less damaging to creditors and other senior security holders than the redemption of shares for cash.

e. Preferred shares issued by corporations whose common shares are publicly traded may themselves be publicly traded. Publicly traded preferred shares are typically *cumulative* and *redeemable.*

1) If the shares are also *convertible,* the corporation may "force" a conversion by calling the preferred for redemption at a time when the market price of the conversion security is greater than the redemption value of the convertible security.

Example: A preferred share is redeemable at $70 per share and convertible into common on a two for one basis. When the market price of the common is $45 per share the shares are called for redemption. This is a forced commission since the value of the conversion security ($90) exceeds the redemption price ($70).

2) The conversion right typically continues to exist for a limited period after the call for redemption is announced; since it is obviously to the financial advantage of each shareholder to convert his or her shares in a forced conversion before they are redeemed, one would normally expect all the preferred shareholders to convert their shares.

Caveat: In practice, some convertible shares are usually not converted because of inadvertence, the shares have been lost, etc. As a result, holders of such shares receive the lower redemption price rather than the conversion shares with a higher value.

Example: In *Zahn v. Transamerica Corp.*, 162 F.2d 36 (3d Cir.1947), convertible shares were called without disclosing that it would be advantageous for minority shareholders to elect to convert shares. The corporation thereby violated a duty owed to the minority shareholders to adequately advise shareholders of their rights. See *Speed v. Transamerica Corp.*, 235 F.2d 369 (3d Cir.1956).

f. Preferred shares are "participating" if they are entitled to share in excess declarations of dividends or excess distributions in liquidation along with common shares. Because they are "open-ended," participating preferred shares have some characteristics of a class of common shares.

Example: In *Zahn v. Transamerica Corp.*, 162 F.2d 36 (3d Cir.1947), a corporation created a class of preferred stock called "Class A stock." Class A stock was entitled to a dividend of $3.20 per year plus the right to share equally with the common stock in all declarations of dividends in excess of $4.80 per share. In effect, $3.20 was first paid to the Class A stock, then $1.60 to the common, and excess distributions were shared equally on a share-for-share basis. The Class A stock was a participating preferred. In the absence of specific provision, it is unlikely that a dividend-participation right of this nature would be construed to include an implied liquidation-participation right on the same terms. *Squires v. Balbach Co.*, 129 N.W.2d 462 (Neb.1964).

g. In states with par value statutes, preferred shares are assigned a par value (or are issued "without par value") in the same way as common shares and are subject to the same rules as common shares in this regard.

h. A corporation may issue several classes of preferred shares, each having varying dividend and other rights specified in the articles of incorporation. While a class of preferred shares may be junior to other classes of preferred, it is nevertheless a preferred stock since it is preferred in comparison to common stock.

Caveat: Names of classes of preferred stock give no information as to their relative priorities. A class of shares with only nominal or unimportant preferential rights may be given a formal designation such as "Senior preferred shares" which may give the impression that its preferential rights are greater than they actually are.

Caveat: A class of shares with preferential rights may be called "Class A common" or be given some other designation that does not use the word "preferred" and does not indicate that it has preferential rights.

i. The 1980s saw the development of novel classes of preferred shares. Most of these novel preferreds were designed to give corporate holders the benefit of the tax credit for intercorporate dividends while providing economic terms more similar to debt instruments.

Example: Corporations may issue classes of preferred stock with floating or adjustable dividend rates that vary with market interest rates, the prime rate, or some similar measure.

Example: Corporations may issue classes of preferred shares that require the corporation to reset the dividend rate and other rights of the preferred if its market price declines below a set value to restore the market price of the preferred to that value.

2. PREFERRED ISSUED IN SERIES

Most state statutes authorize the creation of "series" of preferred shares, the financial and other terms of which may vary from series to series.

a. Specific authorization to create one or more series of preferred shares out of a larger class of preferred shares must appear in the articles of incorporation.

b. The board of directors is vested with authority to set the terms of each series from time to time by resolution. Some statutes limit the discretion of the board in certain respects. MBCA (1984) § 6.02 does not contain restrictions in this regard.

1) The preferred shares that may be issued in series are called "blank shares" since the board may "fill in" the terms.

2) The theory is that the board of directors may set the financial terms of the series just before the shares are marketed in order to obtain the best price for the shares.

3) It usually is not practical to create a new class of preferred shares by amendment to the articles of incorporation within the same short time span because of the need for a shareholders' meeting to approve the amendment.

Caveat: Even though the justification for series usually refers to the time problems of marketing a new issue of preferred shares, series may be used for purposes other than financing.

Antitakeover devices known as "poison pills" are usually created by the board of directors pursuant to the power to create series of shares in order to avoid having a shareholders' vote on the desirability of such an issue. Usually there is no time pressure to create a poison pill series of preferred shares.

c. A formal certificate describing the terms of the series must be filed with the secretary of state after the series has been established. This certificate becomes a formal amendment of the articles of incorporation even though it does not require action by the shareholders.

d. From an economic and legal standpoint, there is no difference between "classes" and "series" of shares. The differences are in nomenclature and in their method of creation.

   1) The rights of a class or of a series depends on the terms of the articles of incorporation or resolution creating them.

   2) The MBCA (1984) § 6.02 permits the board of directors to fix the terms of "classes" as well as "series" of shares if that power is granted the board of directors by the articles of incorporation.

3. CLASSIFIED COMMON STOCK

Common stock may be issued in different classes. Under the MBCA (1984) and most state statutes there are virtually no restrictions or limitations on the rights of common shares that may be varied from class to class. Because of this flexibility, classes of common shares are widely used as planning devices in closely held corporations.

a. A class or classes of nonvoting common shares may be created under the statutes of most states.

b. In many states, classes may be created with identical financial rights but with multiple or fractional votes per share.

c. Limited case law also permits the creation of a class of shares with full voting power but with little or no financial interest in the corporation. *Stroh v. Blackhawk Holding Corp.,* 272 N.E.2d 1 (Ill.1971); *Lehrman v. Cohen,* 222 A.2d 800 (Del.1966).

d. Different classes of common shares are usually designated by alphabetical notation, e.g "Class A common," "Class B common," etc.

e. When used as a planning device, usually all class A shares are issued to one shareholder, all class B shareholders to another shareholder, and so forth.

Example: Class A common may have twice the dividend right per share of Class B common. This arrangement permits two shareholders to share equal voting control by issuing the same number of class A and class B shares, but unequal dividend rights.

Example: A class of shares may be created with one tenth of the liquidation right per share of another class.

Example: Classes of shares may be created each with the right to elect two directors. This arrangement permits a shareholder who owns less than 50 per cent of all the outstanding shares to have representation on the board, and if only two shareholders are involved, to elect one-half of the board of directors.

4. EQUIVALENCE OF SHARES WITHIN A CLASS OR SERIES

All shares of a class or series must have identical preferences, limitations, and relative rights with those of other shares of the same series or class (except to the extent shares of a class may be divided into series).

Caveat: It is unclear in many states whether classes or series of shares may be created that have rights that may distinguish between holders of the same class of shares on the basis of outside events. These classes or series are used as defensive tactics against takeovers, treating the aggressor differently than other shareholders. (See part XIII E 9, infra.)

D. DEBT SECURITIES

Debt securities are bonds, and debentures, and in some instances longer term promissory notes. They are subsumed under the generic terms "bonds" or "debt securities."

1. BONDS AND DEBENTURES DESCRIBED

Bonds and debentures are typically long-term debt instruments. A bond is a secured debt while a debenture is unsecured. Bonds may be secured by liens on all or specific parts of the property of the issuer.

a. Bonds and debentures are unconditional written obligations to pay a specific amount at a future date.

b. Bonds and debentures are usually negotiable instruments.

1) Historically they were payable to bearer and the obligation to pay periodic interest was represented by coupons which were themselves negotiable instruments payable to bearer.

2) Because of changes in the tax law, most bonds or debentures today are issued in registered form with interest payments being paid directly by check to the owner. Registered debt instruments are negotiable by endorsement rather than by mere delivery.

3) While significant number of bearer and registered debt securities still are outstanding, most publicly held bonds and debentures are held today in book entry form. (See part XI D.)

c. The rights of bondholders or debenture holders are set forth in a trust indenture which typically vests in a trustee the rights to enforce the terms of the indenture, including the right to foreclose on security. The rights and duties of the trustee are defined in the indenture. *United States Trust Co. v. First Nat. City Bank*, 394 N.Y.S.2d 653 (App.Div.1977).

d. Bonds or debentures are usually issued in units of $1,000 or larger round numbers. If they are publicly traded, the price for such securities is a function of the general level of interest rates in the economy and the risk of default for the specific issue.

1) Bonds or debentures are usually issued at or close to the face amount $1,000 per unit. Market prices of debt instruments thereafter fluctuate with market conditions. When the bond matures the issuer must repay the face amount, which is sometimes referred to as the "par value" of a debt instrument.

2) The fixed relationship between the face amount of a bond or debenture and the amount the issuer must pay each year in interest is called the "coupon rate." When market prices fluctuate an investment in a bond will yield an effective return of return that may be greater or less than the coupon rate.

Example: A $1,000 bond with an 8 per cent coupon is trading at par. That means that the market price is $1,000 and the yield on the purchase of such a bond is 8 per cent per year, the same as the coupon rate.

Example: A bond has a coupon rate of 8 per cent per year. Market interest rates are 10 per cent for a bond of similar risk and maturity. The market price of the bond is less than $1,000 so that an investor who purchases the bond will receive approximately 10 per cent on the amount needed to purchase the bond.

3) Bonds or debentures are usually redeemable by the corporation at a premium over the face amount of the instrument. They may be

convertible into common stock at the election of the holder. Convertible debentures may trade at a multiple of the underlying price of the conversion security rather than as a true debt instrument.

Example: In *Van Gemert v. Boeing Co.*, 520 F.2d 1373 (2d Cir.1975), *cert. denied*, 423 U.S. 947, 96 S.Ct. 364, convertible debentures were called for redemption giving the minimum notice to holders required by the trust indenture. The conversion was "forced" in the sense that the conversion securities were worth significantly more than the redemption price. The court held that the corporation owed a duty to convertible debenture holders to give them reasonable notice so that bondholders could elect to convert. In this case a significant number of bondholders failed to exercise the conversion privilege. Contra: *Meckel v. Continental Resources Co.*, 758 F.2d 811 (2d Cir.1985). See also *Broad v. Rockwell International Corp.*, 642 F.2d 929 (5th Cir.1981).

f. The 1980s saw the development of numerous types of novel debt instruments.

1) Zeroes are debentures that do not bear interest. They are issued at deep discounts from par and the entire interest component is reflected in the discount.

2) Income bonds are debt instruments, but the obligation to pay interest is conditioned on the existence of earnings to cover the interest.

3) Participating bonds are debt instruments, but the obligation to pay interest fluctuates with the earnings of the corporation.

4) PIK (payment in kind) bonds pay interest in the form of promissory notes or additional bonds for a stated period of time.

5) Reset bonds are debentures that require the issuer to adjust ("reset") the interest rate on a specific date in the future if the bonds are selling below par value so as to return the bonds' market value to par value.

6) Junk bonds are bonds that are below investment grade and trade much as though they were a class of equity security.

Example: One type of junk bond is a "fallen angel," a debt instrument that was originally of investment grade but has ceased to qualify because of lack of earnings by the issuer. Most modern junk bonds, however, were issued as such as part of the takeover movement in the 1980s.

g. A promissory note is a negotiable instrument representing an unconditional promise to pay that may be secured or unsecured. A bond or debenture is a type of promissory note but those instruments differ from a traditional promissory note in that:

1) A promissory note is usually payable to the order of the creditor; and

2) The obligation to pay interest is not represented by coupons;

3) There is no trust indenture or trustee;

4) Promissory notes are not usually publicly traded.

2. DEBT INSTRUMENTS COMPARED WITH PREFERRED STOCK

Bonds or debentures are debt securities. They differ from preferred stock, which is an equity security, from a legal standpoint in several basic respects:

a. Interest on bonds or debentures is an unconditional obligation of the corporation while dividends on preferred stock are discretionary with the board of directors.

b. A bond or debenture usually has a maturity date at which time the principal becomes due while preferred stock never becomes due. A debenture without a maturity date (called a "consol") is not unknown but is extremely rare in the United States.

c. A bond or debenture may have legal rights of foreclosure on default of payments while a preferred stock does not.

d. Bonds or debentures are created pursuant to indentures that usually appoint a trustee to handle the rights of security holders whereas preferred stock is created by provision in the articles of incorporation of the corporation.

Despite these legal differences the economic differences between these two types of securities may be slight, depending on the specific terms of the two instruments being compared.

3. DEBT/EQUITY RATIO

a. The ratio between a corporation's equity capital and its long term debt is called the corporation's debt/equity ratio.

Example: A corporation is capitalized with $50,000 of long-term bonds carrying an interest cost of 10 per cent per year and 1,000 shares of common stock issued for $10 each, or an aggregate capital of

$10,000. The debt/equity ratio of the corporation is 5:1[$50,000 of debt to $10,000 of equity].

b. The Miller–Modigliani theorem states (with certain simplifying assumptions) that the aggregate value of a corporation's securities (the market value of its equity securities plus the market value of its debt securities) is independent of the corporation's debt/equity ratio.

c. A debt/equity ratio of greater than 4:1 between shareholder debt and equity increases the risk that a court will treat the debt as equity capital and disallow corporate deductions for interest.

d. A corporation with a high debt/equity ratio is called a "thin corporation."

4. HYBRID SECURITIES

"Hybrid" securities are securities that have some of the attributes of debt and some of the attributes of preferred stock.

a. The major problem with such securities is uncertainty as to whether the instrument will be treated as equity or debt for tax purposes. *John Kelley Co. v. C.I.R.*, 326 U.S. 521, 66 S.Ct. 299 (1946).

b. Marketability of hybrid securities may also be complicated by uncertainty as to the "true" nature of the instrument.

E. TAX ADVANTAGES OF PROVIDING A PORTION OF THE INITIAL CAPITAL IN THE FORM OF DEBT

Persons who contribute the initial capital of the corporation usually desire to lend a portion of that capital to the corporation. There are both tax and non-tax advantages in doing this.

Caveat: The tax advantages described in this section are generally not applicable where the corporation has elected to be taxed as an S corporation.

a. Interest on debt is deductible by the corporation while dividends on common or preferred shares are not. Thus the use of debt may allow the shareholders some return from the corporation without incurring the double taxation on dividends that is a feature of current federal income taxation of C corporations.

b. A repayment of debt may be a tax-free return of capital rather than a taxable dividend. The use of debt may therefore permit the tax-free return of a portion of a shareholder's investment.

Caveat: A partial redemption of a taxpayer's common or preferred shares gives rise to ordinary income or capital gain.

c. Since the existence of shareholder debt in the capital structure reduces taxes, the shareholder usually desires the greatest amount of debt possible in the structure.

Caveat: The Internal Revenue Service has general power to reclassify excessive debt as equity contributions for tax purposes. Generally, if the debt is excessive, it is reclassified as equity in its entirety. Hence, there can readily be "too much of a good thing" in the wholesale creation of debt. See *Taft v. C.I.R.,* 314 F.2d 620 (9th Cir. 1963).

F. NON–TAX ADVANTAGES OF PROVIDING A PORTION OF THE INITIAL CAPITAL IN THE FORM OF DEBT

Non-tax advantages of providing a portion of the initial capital in the form of debt include:

a. An important advantage of debt financing is that it simplifies non-tax planning where some investors are contributing more capital than others.

Example: *A* proposes to contribute $10,000 in cash; *B* proposes to contribute $6,000 in property of various types. A and *B* desire each to own 50 per cent of the shares. In order to equalize contributions, the attorney suggests that common shares be issued to reflect the $6,000 contribution by *A* and *B*, and that *A* separately lend the corporation $4,000. The terms of repayment of this loan, the interest rate, and the rate of compensation for services are matters for negotiation.

b. Debt financing may permit the shareholders to obtain parity with general trade creditors if the business fails. See the "Deep Rock" doctrine, part IV H 3; *Costello v. Fazio,* 256 F.2d 903 (9th Cir.1958).

c. Loans from third persons provide leverage for the equity investors and may permit them to increase the value of their investment.

1) Leverage arises when the venture earns more on each borrowed dollar than the interest cost of borrowing that dollar.

Example: A corporation is capitalized with $50,000 of long-term bonds carrying an interest cost of 10 per cent per year and 1,000 shares of common stock issued for $10 each, or an aggregate capital of $10,000. The $5,000 interest cost of the bonds must be paid each year whether or not there are earnings. The effect of leverage is shown by comparing the rate of return on total dollars invested ($60,000) with the rate of return on the common shares at various levels of hypothetical income (after paying the $5,000 of interest):

(1) Income (before interest expense)	(2) Earnings Per Total Dollar Invested	(3) Earnings Per Share (after interest expense)
2,000	0.03	−.03
5,000	0.08	0
20,000	0.33	1.50
50,000	0.83	5.00

Example: In the previous illustration under ideal market conditions, any enhanced value of the common stock because of the advantages of leverage would be precisely matched by a decline in value of the bonds.

Caveat: Since World War II, the United States has suffered an inflationary spiral. If inflation continues, debt financing is attractive because the loans will ultimately be repaid with inflated dollars. The competition for loans in these circumstances may cause higher interest rates which will offset, either wholly or partially this advantage of debt financing.

G. APPLICATION OF THE FEDERAL AND STATE SECURITIES ACTS

When raising capital, the possible impact of the federal Securities Act of 1933, 15 U.S. C.A. § 77a, and the state securities acts ("blue sky laws") must always be considered.

1. GENERAL DESCRIPTION OF STATUTORY PURPOSE

The Securities Act of 1933 is designed to protect the public investor from fraudulent or misrepresented promotions or sales of securities by issuers in interstate commerce. The state blue sky laws serve a similar purpose for public distributions of securities within each state.

a. These statutes generally require a registration of a securities issue before it may be publicly sold. Registration involves submission of detailed information about the offering, its review by the SEC, and public dissemination of that information to potential investors in the form of a prospectus or offering circular.

b. The goal is full disclosure of all relevant facts about the securities being sold. The federal Securities Act is a full disclosure statute: no governmental evaluation of the investment quality of securities is involved.

Caveat: Many state blue sky statutes also are pure disclosure statutes. Several, however, involve "merit review," i.e. they authorize the administrator to refuse to permit the sale of a security in the state if the transaction is not fair, just or equitable even if all information is accurately disclosed.

c. The sale of unregistered securities when registration is required gives rise to substantial civil liabilities to purchasers of the securities and may give rise to criminal prosecution as well.

d. The leading cases relating to the obligations of persons preparing and signing registration statements are *Escott v. BarChris Const. Corp.,* 283 F.Supp. 643 (S.D.N.Y.1968), and *SEC v. National Student Marketing Corp.,* 457 F.Supp. 682 (D.D.C.1978).

e. The role of lawyers in the disclosure process is discussed in *Escott* and in *In the Matter of Carter & Johnson,* SEC Rel. 17597 (1981).

2. COST OF REGISTRATION

The registration process, particularly at the federal level, is so expensive as to be impractical for most small and medium-sized (e.g., up to say, $2,000,000) public offerings. The current minimum cost of a full scale registration by a corporation that has never previously registered a public offering exceeds $100,000, and a figure of $200,000 or more in expenses and underwriting fees may be more realistic.

3. EXEMPTIONS FROM REGISTRATION

Because of the cost of registration, attention must be focused on the availability of exemptions for a particular offer. At the federal level, there are several exemptions from the registration requirement:

a. Regulation D is the SEC's principal "small offering" exemption. It contains three exemptions, together with accompanying definitions, terms, and conditions.

1) Rule 504 exempts offers by corporations of up to $1,000,000 in any one year. The offers may not be made by general solicitation or general advertising, and securities sold must be subject to restrictions on resale, except in states where the offer is registered under state law and that law requires delivery of a disclosure document.

2) Rule 505 exempts offers by corporations of up to $5,000,000 in any one year if the number of unaccredited investors is less than 35 and no general solicitation or general advertising is used. Under rule 505, there is no limit on the number of accredited investors. Specified information about the issue must be given to all unaccredited investors.

3) Rule 506 permits offers in unlimited amounts to accredited investors and to not more than 35 unaccredited investors. Each purchaser who is not an accredited investor must have (or the issuer must reasonably believe such purchaser to have) such knowledge and experience in financial and business matters that the purchaser is capable of evaluating the merits and risks of the prospective investment. No general solicitation or general advertising may be used, and specified information must be delivered to each purchaser who is not an accredited investor.

4) Rule 501(a) lists eight categories of "accredited investors:" institutional investors; private business development companies; tax exempt organizations; directors, executive officers or general partners of the issuer; purchasers of more than $150,000 of the securities; natural persons with a net worth of $1,000,000 or with an income in excess of $200,000 per year (or joint annual income in excess of $300,000); trusts with total assets of $500,000 or more; or entities owned by accredited investors. The issuer must have reasonable grounds to believe and must believe that a purchaser at the time of sale falls into one of these categories.

5) A notice of sale must be filed with the SEC on Form D with respect to sales exempt under Regulation D.

6) Minor or insignificant deviations from the requirements of Regulation D do not cause a loss of the entire Regulation D exemption.

b. Section 4(2), 15 U.S.C.A. § 77d, exempts "transactions by an issuer not involving any public offering." Offerings not complying with Regulation D may nevertheless be exempt under section 4(2) if they meet the tests established by the case law for the availability of the exemption. The test is not dependent on the mathematical number of offerees; the basic requirement is that all offerees must have sufficient access and sophistication so that they do not need the protection of the act. *SEC v. Ralston Purina Co.,* 346 U.S. 119, 73 S.Ct. 981 (1953).

1) Regulation D relates to investors or *purchasers* of securities, the section 4(2) exemption requires *offerees* to meet the requirements of access and sophistication.

2) Large private offerings of securities to sophisticated institutional investors are called private placements; in the aggregate private placements involve billions of dollars each year. Such placements are normally exempt under rule 506 as well as under section 4(2).

c. Regulation A, adopted by the SEC under section 3(b) of the Securities Act (which authorizes the SEC to exempt issues of less than $5,000,000 where the SEC determines that registration "is not necessary in the public interest and for the protection of investors"), exempts offerings of up to $1,500,000 upon following a simplified registration process, including filing with a regional office of the SEC rather than in Washington. This simplified registration process is colloquially known as "Reg A;" its use has declined since the adoption of Regulation D.

d. Section 4(6) of the Securities Act, added in 1980, exempts offerings or sales solely to one or more accredited investors if the aggregate amount does not exceed $5,000,000 and there is no advertising or public solicitation. Most offerings exempt under this section are also exempt under Regulation D, but there are a number of technical differences.

e. Section 3(a)(11) of the Securities Act exempts securities which are part of an issue offered and sold only to persons resident within a single state where the issuer is incorporated and doing business in that state. Section 3(a)(11) should be read in conjunction with Rule 146 that describes the SEC's position with respect to that exemption.

Caveat: This so-called "intrastate exemption" is very narrowly and restrictively construed. A single offer of a security to a nonresident totally destroys the availability of the exemption.

f. Rule 701 provides an exemption for specified offers of securities by an employer to employees as compensation plans or pursuant to employment contracts. Such shares may not exceed the maximum of $500,000 or 15 per cent of the employer's assets but never more than $5,000,000, and must be made subject to limitations on resale.

Caveat: Rule 701 is applicable to employers that are not registered under the Securities Exchange of 1934. For companies that are registered under the 1934 Act, a simplified registration process on Form S–8 is available to register securities to be issued to employees.

4. RESTRICTIONS ON TRANSFER OF UNREGISTERED SECURITIES

The availability of several exemptions from registration under the Securities Act of 1933 is dependent on the ultimate investors having certain knowledge or sophistication, or being residents of specific states. In order to ensure that persons acquiring securities are the ultimate investors and do not buy them with a view toward further distribution to persons who might destroy the availability of the exemption, SEC regulations and accepted corporate practice require restrictions to be imposed on resale of securities sold pursuant to many exemptions. Securities that must be made subject to such restrictions are called "restricted securities."

a. The restrictions are noted on certificates issued pursuant to the exemption and "stop transfer" orders are issued to the transfer agent, the person handling transfers of the corporation's securities. Under these certificate notations and "stop transfer" orders, the shareholder may be required to establish to the satisfaction of the issuer or its transfer agent that the proposed transfer is consistent with the original exemption. Notations may also appear on book entry statements of brokerage firms.

b. A person who buys shares with a view toward further distribution is called an "underwriter." An underwriter may be either a large commercial organization in the securities business (typically investment bankers who handle the distribution of an entire public issue of securities) or equally an individual planning to resell securities he or she originally acquired.

c. Restricted securities include shares originally sold pursuant to the private offering exemptions (§ 4(2) or Regulation D). Such shares may be resold pursuant to rules 144 or 144a.

   1) Rule 144 basically provides a safe harbor for sales of restricted securities after a two-year holding period upon compliance with requirements covering the availability of current public information about the issuer, the manner of sale, volume limitations, and the filing of form 144 with the SEC.

   2) Sales during the two-year holding period may be consistent with the original exemption (though not protected by rule 144) if there is a bona fide change in circumstances justifying the decision to sell the securities.

   3) Rule 144 also provides that sales after a holding period of three years are generally free of restriction.

   4) Rule 144a allows resales of certain restricted securities exclusively to "qualified institutional buyers" for their own accounts. The theory is that these are very large transactions that do not affect the general public and the institutions involved are able to fend for themselves and obtain the informational equivalent of registration.

5. CONTROL PERSONS AND SECONDARY DISTRIBUTIONS

A secondary distribution is a public distribution of unregistered shares by a person other than the issuer.

a. Secondary distributions arise in two basic contexts:

1) Under the Securities Act of 1933, a person who is in control of a registrant (referred to as a "control person") is subject to registration requirements upon the sale of his or her shares of the issuer. The registration requirements are substantially the same as those applicable to the registrant itself; and

2) A person holding unregistered shares obtained from the issuer in a transaction that is exempt from registration may seek to resell them publicly; such sales are also a kind of secondary distribution that may require registration.

b. Secondary distributions must be registered unless an exemption is available. They are often registered in conjunction with or as part of a subsequent registration of an issue by the issuer itself. Persons acquiring unregistered shares from an issuer routinely request the issuer to agree to register such shares, or more commonly, to include any proposed secondary distribution in the next public issue registered by the issuer.

6. WHAT IS A SECURITY?

The Securities Act of 1933 and state blue sky laws are used to police a variety of marginal investment schemes which may not involve "securities" in the traditional sense.

a. Securities acts define "security" broadly, usually referring to "investment contracts" and "other instruments" that evidence an investment. These phrases have been judicially defined to include within the scope of "security" any contract, transaction or scheme whereby a person invests money *in a common enterprise* and *is led to expect profits solely from the efforts of others.*

1) "Solely" has not been construed literally; a scheme may involve a security even if the investor is required to put forward a small amount of individual effort.

2) Golf club memberships, condominiums, scotch whiskey in warehouses, chain letter or pyramid schemes, fractional royalty interests, earthworm farms, commodity options, and other schemes have all been held to constitute "securities" in some circumstances.

Example: An owner of a citrus grove sells land in "units" consisting of a row of trees per "unit." The original owner usually enters into a contract with the investor purchasing the unit by which the owner agrees to provide services such as cultivation, pruning, insect control, and protection from freezing. The owner also usually harvests and markets the crop, dividing the proceeds with the investors purchasing the units. The units constitute "securities" even though an investor theoretically might cultivate and harvest his own row of trees on his own and use or sell the crop as he sees fit. *S. E. C. v. W. J. Howey Co.*, 328 U.S. 293, 66 S.Ct. 1100 (1946).

b. Since such investment schemes are almost never registered as securities, these cases make unlawful the public sale of most such schemes.

c. In *Landreth Timber Co. v. Landreth,* 471 U.S. 681, 105 S.Ct. 2297 (1985), the Supreme Court rejected the so-called "sale of business doctrine" and held that the sale of all or a majority of the shares of a closely held corporation constituted the sale of a "security" subject to the federal securities acts. Even though the majority interest in the business arguably did not meet the *Howey* test, the Court held that common stock was plainly within the class of instruments Congress intended to include within the category of "securities."

1) The holding in cases such as *Landreth* is of importance primarily because it makes available the protections of federal antifraud provisions to all sales of closely held shares (assuming that the facilities of interstate commerce are used) even where the purchaser is intent on acquiring control of the business rather than making a passive investment.

2) In *Reves v. Ernst & Young*, 494 U.S. 56, 110 S.Ct. 945 (1990), the Court held that promissory notes were presumptively a "security," but that presumption may be rebutted by a showing that the following criteria were met: the transaction in which the note in question was issued was not of a type that normally utilized securities for raising capital, the distribution of the note was not one that was likely to give rise to common trading for speculation or investment by the general public, the expectation of the trading public as to whether the note in question was within the coverage of the securities acts, and whether other regulatory schemes provide protection to the investing public similar to that provided by the securities acts.

7. STATE BLUE SKY LAWS

The provisions of most state "blue sky" statutes roughly parallel the federal securities acts.

a. Some state statutes do do not require registration of issues sold within the state but only contain antifraud provisions.

b. Some states impose substantive standards over and above the "full disclosure" philosophy of the Securities Act of 1933. These states impose a merit review standard that permits distributions to be registered and sold in the state only if their terms are "fair, just, and equitable."

c. The private offering and other exemptions in state statutes are often more numerical and objective than the corresponding exemptions in the Federal Act.

d. Generally, the registration requirements of the state statutes are in addition to and not in substitution of the requirements of the Securities Act of 1933.

   1) A national distribution of new securities may require registration in fifty states as well as with the SEC.

   2) The state registration process, known as "blue skying an issue" is greatly simplified by reason of the fact that most states have integrated or coordinated their registration process with the federal process. This is known as "registration by coordination." Other types of registration at the state level are "registration by notification" for issuers that regularly raise capital publicly and "registration by qualification."

   3) Registration by qualification is imposed on public distributions that are exempt from federal registration, e.g., under the intrastate exemption or Regulation D. The SEC has integrated its Regulation D rules for small local offerings with registration under the blue sky statutes to minimize duplicative or overlapping requirements.

e. Publicly held corporations that file regular reports with the SEC under the Securities Exchange Act of 1934 may usually utilize the information previously filed in such reports in registering new issues of securities under the Securities Act of 1933. Regulations authorizing this use of previously filed material are called the Integrated Disclosure Program and corporations that may take advantage of the most favorable provisions of these regulations are called seasoned companies.

H. ISSUANCE OF SHARES BY A GOING CONCERN

Shares issued by a going concern create unique problems because issuance of new shares affects outstanding shareholders. Shares issued at bargain prices or otherwise than in proportion to prior holdings may "dilute" the financial interests or voting power of existing shareholders, or both.

1. PREEMPTIVE RIGHTS

The classic common law protection for existing shareholders are "preemptive rights."

a. Preemptive rights give holders of outstanding shares the right to subscribe and pay for a proportionate part of any new issue of securities by the corporation at the price established by the board of directors. *Stokes v. Continental Trust Co.*, 78 N.E. 1090 (N.Y.1906).

b. If all shareholders exercise their preemptive rights no dilution occurs and the additional capital needed by the corporation is entirely raised from its present shareholders.

Example: Several years ago, a corporation was formed with an authorized capital of 250 shares with a par value of one dollar each. Shares were issued for a consideration of $10 each as follows: *A*—100 shares, *B*—100 shares, and *C*—50 shares. The corporation has been a financial success, and *A* and *B* decide to amend the articles of incorporation to increase the number of shares by 200 to 450 shares, and issue to themselves 100 shares each at $50 per share. *C* was the owner of 20 per cent of the original shares (50/250) and therefore has a preemptive right to acquire 20 per cent of the new shares at the same price as the shares being acquired by *A* and *B*—$50 per share. If C exercises her preemptive right, she will be entitled to purchase 40 shares at $50 per share, and after the new shares are issued, will continue to own 20 per cent of the outstanding shares: she will own 90 shares while B and C will each own 180 shares.

c. There are substantial exceptions to and limitations on modern preemptive rights:

1) Preemptive rights are discretionary. In many states, they are an "opt out" option, so that a corporation has preemptive rights unless a specific provision excluding them appears in the articles of incorporation. MBCA (1984) § 6.30, and the statutes of several states make preemptive rights an "opt in" provision: corporations have preemptive rights only, and to the extent, they specifically so designate.

As an aid to draftsmen, MBCA (1984) § 6.30 contains a model provision relating to preemptive rights that may be elected by a simple clause, e.g. "This corporation elects to have preemptive rights." This model provision may be modified as appropriate. It deals with the scope of preemptive rights and other issues, such as waiver and resale of securities offered preemptively but not purchased.

2) Preemptive rights in some states may not apply to treasury shares (i.e., shares that were once issued but have been reacquired by the corporation).

(i) The theory underlying this limitation is that the dilution represented by treasury shares has already occurred and existing shareholders should have no complaint if a prior dilution is restored.

(ii) Some modern statutes specifically extend preemptive rights to treasury shares and case law in some states rejects this exception in the absence of express statutory language. *Fuller v. Krogh*, 113 N.W.2d 25 (Wis.1962).

Caveat: This issue does not arise under MBCA (1984) since that statute treats previously issued shares as authorized but unissued shares when they are reacquired by the corporation.

3) Preemptive rights do not extend to shares issued for property, including shares of other corporations. MBCA (1984) § 6.30(b)(3)(iv).

(i) This exemption is based on considerations of practicability or necessity.

(ii) Some courts have construed this exemption narrowly since in many instances the corporation could sell shares for cash, recognizing the preemptive right, and use the cash to acquire the property. *Dunlay v. Avenue M Garage & Repair Co.*, 170 N.E. 917 (N.Y.1930).

4) Preemptive rights do not extend to authorized but unissued shares to the extent they represent part of the contemplated initial capitalization of the corporation. MBCA (1984) § 6.30(b)(3)(iii) [six months after incorporation]. This exemption is based on the assumption that preemptive rights extend only to new issues of shares after the corporation has raised its initial capital.

5) Preemptive rights do not extend to shares of different classes unless the other class is convertible into the class held by the shareholder. MBCA (1984) §§ 6.30(b)(5), (b)(6), (c).

Example: Common shareholders do not have a preemptive right to acquire shares of preferred stock unless the preferred is convertible into common.

Example: Preferred shareholders may have a preemptive right to acquire new preferred shares of the same class. They do not, however, have preemptive rights to acquire common shares. Some early case law to the contrary, e. g., *Thomas Branch & Co. v. Riverside & Dan River Cotton Mills, Inc.*, 123 S.E. 542 (Va. 1924), has been overruled by statutory provisions defining the preemptive right.

d. Preemptive rights serve little purpose in publicly held corporations since they complicate the raising of capital. Also, the availability of a public market for shares renders the preemptive right less important since any shareholder may add to his or her shareholdings simply by purchasing shares in the open market.

2. FIDUCIARY RESTRICTIONS ON THE OPPRESSIVE ISSUANCE OF SHARES

Where preemptive rights are unavailable (either because the transaction falls within an exception to the preemptive right or because the right itself has been eliminated by the corporation), the power of the board of directors to issue new shares on terms that are unfair to minority shareholders may be limited by a general fiduciary duty. *Schwartz v. Marien*, 335 N.E.2d 334 (N.Y.1975); *Ross Transport, Inc. v. Crothers*, 45 A.2d 267 (Md. 1946).

a. This fiduciary duty also extends to bad faith issuances of shares where preemptive rights exist but circumstances are such that it is unreasonable to expect the minority shareholder to exercise his preemptive right.

Example: X, a 20 per cent shareholder is not involved with management. With the specific intent of reducing X's interest in the corporation, the board of directors (at the request of the majority shareholder) proposes to issue new shares that will require X to invest $100,000 in cash if she exercises her preemptive right to retain her current percentage interest. The management-connected shareholders plan to pay for their portion of the new issue by cancelling loans they have previously made to the corporation. X declines to purchase the additional shares. As a result of the new issue, X 's proportional interest in the corporation is reduced to less than one per cent. Some courts have enjoined transactions of this type on the theory that they are oppressive and serve no business purpose. *Katzowitz v. Sidler*, 249 N.E.2d 359 (N.Y.1969). Not all courts have agreed, however, though factual differences may partially explain the result. *Hyman v. Velsicol Corp.*, 97 N.E.2d 122 (Ill. App.1951).

b. Issuance of shares to controlling shareholders at unfair prices may be set aside even though the transaction has a valid business purpose. *Adelman v. Conotti Corp.*, 213 S.E.2d 774 (Va.1975); *Bennett v. Breuil Petroleum Corp.*, 99 A.2d 236 (Del.Ch.1953).

c. Transactions that affect the balance of power within a corporation may also be set aside if they have no apparent business purpose. *Schwartz v. Marien*, 335 N.E.2d 334 (N.Y.1975).

d. If there is a good faith business purpose and no personal benefit to controlling shareholders, shares may be issued on terms that benefit one class at the expense of another. *Bodell v. General Gas & Electric Corp.*, 140 A. 264 (Del. Ch.1927).

e. Bad faith transactions which reduce the proportional interest of minority shareholders are called "squeeze outs" or "freeze outs."

f. The broad fiduciary duty recognized in *Donahue v. Rodd Electrotype Co. of New England, Inc.*, 328 N.E.2d 505 (Mass.1975) may also be applied to these issues. See parts V J 7, X E 4.

3. APPLICABILITY OF SECURITIES ACTS

The federal and state securities acts are applicable to shares issued by a going concern.

I. DIVIDENDS AND DISTRIBUTIONS

A "dividend" is a payment out of current or past earnings; other distributions, to the extent permitted, may be called "capital distributions," "distributions in partial liquidation" or by other names that indicate that they are distributions of capital, not distributions of earnings.

Caveat: Terminology is not precise; a liquidating distribution may be referred to as a "liquidating dividend" even though the payment constitutes a return of capital.

Dividends or distributions typically are discretionary with the board of directors.

Example: A corporation announces that it has ceased paying dividends and probably will not resume dividends for at least five years in order to accumulate funds for expansion and modernization. Shareholders have no basis for objecting to such a policy even if the corporation had a policy of paying dividends in the past. *Berwald v. Mission Development Co.*, 185 A.2d 480 (Del.1962).

1. DIVIDEND POLICIES IN PUBLICLY HELD CORPORATIONS

Publicly held corporations generally adopt stable dividend policies that permit regular periodic distributions even though corporate income fluctuates. Changes in dividend payment rates by publicly held corporations are publicly announced, not made lightly, and tend to reflect only important or apparently permanent changes in earnings experience.

Example: A publicly held corporation establishes and publicly announces a "regular" dividend of $0.25 per quarter. This rate will be retained despite fluctuations in earnings; in the event of a temporary decline in earnings, the "regular" dividend may be "omitted" for one or two quarters and then resumed consistent with the general philosophy of preserving a stable dividend policy.

Example: In the prior situation, the corporation suffers a loss in one year but continues to pay the regular dividend of $0.25 per quarter. If the corporation has accumulated undistributed earnings from earlier years, the payment is a dividend out of those earlier years' accumulated earnings for tax and accounting purposes.

Example: If excess cash accumulates, the corporation may declare a "special" or "extra" dividend of perhaps $1.50 per share. A special dividend carries with it no promise that anything more than the regular dividend will be paid in the future.

Caveat: Miller and Modigliani have established that (with certain simplifying assumptions) the value of a corporation's common shares is independent of the dividend policy adopted by the corporation. Under these assumptions, the retention of corporate earnings increases the market value of the corporation's common shares by precisely the amount the payment of a dividend would have reduced that value.

2. DIVIDEND POLICIES IN A CLOSELY HELD CORPORATION

In a closely held corporation dividend policies are directly influenced by the tax status of the corporation.

a. In a corporation that is subject to C corporation tax rules the dividend policy generally adopted is "no dividends." The payment of dividends carries a higher tax cost than the payment of the same amount in the form of salaries, rents or other payments that are deductible by the corporation.

   1) If the entire income of the corporation can be distributed to shareholders in tax deductible form, the income of the corporation has been "zeroed out."

   2) The disadvantage of dividends in C corporations is that they lead to double taxation: the corporate income is subject to the corporate income tax and amounts paid in dividends to shareholders are subject to a second tax when the dividends are included in the individual shareholders' tax returns.

   3) If the corporate income cannot be zeroed out, it is generally advantageous to permit corporate earnings to accumulate in the corporation rather than paying out the excess income in the form of dividends.

   4) The Internal Revenue Code contains a penalty tax applicable to corporations that unreasonably accumulate surplus. Section 531 imposes the penalty tax on accumulations that exceed the "reasonable needs of the business" but a minimum accumulation of $250,000 is permitted in any

case. This penalty tax may often be avoided by the corporation agreeing to pay a dividend.

Caveat: Because of the changes in tax law made in 1986, this surtax is rarely applied since zeroing out to the maximum extent possible is now the most advantageous tax policy for C corporations.

b. In a corporation that has elected S corporation treatment, all corporate income is directly taxed to the shareholders, whether or not distributed, so that payment of dividends has little or no effect on the aggregate tax bills.

1) Since shareholders must pay income tax on S corporation earnings allocated to them, whether or not distributed, it is customary in S corporations to make sufficient distributions to cover the income tax liability that the allocation of corporate income creates.

c. The distribution of corporate income in the form of salaries, rent, etc. may give rise to internal dispute and dissatisfaction since some shareholders may receive larger payments than others and the payments may bear no relationship to relative shareholdings.

Example: Some shareholders are excluded entirely from management and receive nothing with respect to their shares. Virtually all the corporate income is used to pay salaries to officers and employees who are either shareholders connected with the management or family members of such shareholders. As a result, the favored shareholders benefit from substantially the entire corporate income.

1) Excluded shareholders would naturally prefer distributions in the form of dividends despite the additional tax cost.

2) Some shareholders may be excluded entirely from participation in the management of the corporation, and the corporation may adopt a no dividend policy, in an effort to "soften up" minority shareholders and persuade them to sell their shares at a low price either to the corporation or to other shareholders. This tactic is referred to as a "freeze out."

3) Freeze out tactics may lead to litigation seeking the payment of a dividend or other relief against the controlling shareholders.

d. Suits to compel the payment of a dividend have been successful only rarely since the payment of dividends is generally a matter of business policy for the directors to establish and is generally not subject to review by courts. *Sinclair Oil Corp. v. Levien,* 280 A.2d 717 (Del.1971). It is clear that a court has authority to order that a dividend be paid in an appropriate case.

1) Where courts have ordered dividends to be paid, the plaintiff has been able to show (i) the availability of surplus cash not needed in the corporate business and (ii) affirmative indications of bad faith on the part of management. *Keough v. St. Paul Milk Co.,* 285 N.W. 809 (Minn.1939); *Dodge v. Ford Motor Co.,* 170 N.W. 668 (Mich.1919); *Miller v. Magline, Inc.,* 256 N.W.2d 761 (Mich.App.1977).

2) Excessive compensation to insiders is an indication of bad faith.

Example: A corporation pays "bonuses" to four of its employees who constitute the original incorporators but not to one person who later became an employee and a shareholder. The "bonuses" are computed on the basis of the excess earnings of the corporation and without a review of the employment performance of any of the employees. The "bonuses" are disguised dividends and are not pro rata; as a result the shareholder who did not receive a dividend may recover his pro rata share. *Murphy v. Country House, Inc.,* 349 N.W.2d 289 (Minn.App.1984).

3) Where a dividend is judicially declared, the court establishes the amount as an issue of fact. *Patton v. Nicholas,* 302 S.W.2d 441 (Tex.Civ.App.1957).

e. Language in some corporate charters have been construed as requiring the mandatory payment of dividends, particularly on preferred stock, *Crocker v. Waltham Watch Co.,* 53 N.E.2d 230 (Mass.1944); *New England Trust Co. v. Penobscot Chemical Fibre Co.,* 50 A.2d 188 (Me.1946); *Arizona Western Insurance Co. v. L.L. Constantin & Co.,* 247 F.2d 388 (3d Cir.1957).

1) The desirability of such a construction is questionable as a matter of policy since mandatory dividends may injure creditors.

2) Some courts have refused to treat apparently mandatory language as creating an unqualified right to a dividend. *L.L. Constantin & Co. v. R.P. Holding Corp.,* 153 A.2d 378 (N.J.Super.Ch.Div.1959).

3. LEGAL REQUIREMENTS FOR DIVIDENDS AND DISTRIBUTIONS

State statutes impose widely varying tests for the legality of dividends and distributions.

a. The tests may differ depending on whether the state retains par value concepts, or whether, like the MBCA (1984), it has eliminated par value and the related concepts of "stated capital" and "capital surplus."

b. MBCA (1984) § 6.40 imposes two tests to determine whether a distribution may be lawfully made:

1) An "equity insolvency" test that requires the corporation to be "able to pay its debts as they become due in the ordinary course of business" after giving effect to the distribution; and

2) A "balance sheet" test that prohibits a distribution if, after giving it effect, "the corporation's total assets would be less than the sum of its total liabilities plus * * * the amount that would be needed" to satisfy preferential liquidation rights of other classes of shares.

c. All states apply some form of equity insolvency test for distributions. In Massachusetts, that is the sole test. Other states combine that test with some form of balance sheet test as described below.

1) The theory of state statutes generally is to permit dividends to be paid from earnings but not from capital. Implementation of this theory requires reliance on the balance sheet in general, and on the equity accounts within that balance sheet in particular.

2) Many states follow the MBCA (1969) and permit dividends to be paid only out of "earned surplus," a term that is defined as the sum of net accumulations of income from all earlier periods reduced by dividends paid in earlier years and similar items.

(i) States with an "earned surplus" test for dividends, also usually permit non-dividend distributions out of capital surplus or other surplus accounts but not from stated capital. In effect, the capital accounts created from the par value concept control the extent to which distributions of capital may be made in these states.

Caveat: This subsection describes the 1969 Model Act restrictions on dividends or distributions. Some states still have statutes based on the 1950 Model Act that refer to distributions of capital or other surplus as "partial liquidations."

(ii) Identification of the source of distributions from surplus accounts may be required.

3) Other states permit dividends or distributions that do not "impair capital" or use a similar phrasing. Rather than treating "dividends" and "distributions" separately and defining when each may be paid, these statutes set aside an irreducible core (the "capital" of the corporation) and prohibit distributions from that core.

Caveat: Statutes that permit dividends only out of "earned surplus" but then permit distributions from capital surplus or other surplus accounts probably come out at about the same place as statutes that broadly permit all dividends or distributions that do not "impair capital."

Caveat: State statutes, particularly from non-Model Act states, may not fit neatly into the above classification. Determining the precise restrictions applicable to distributions in non-Model Act states may not always be easy since the language may not address some issues. Some states, furthermore, have unique provisions. California, for example, requires capital to be preserved equal to five-fourths of the corporation's liabilities.

4) The validity of certain kinds of transactions that affect the dividend-paying or distribution-making capacity of a corporation depends on the language of the specific statute:

(i) "Quasi reorganizations" are bookkeeping entries by which deficits of earned surplus are eliminated by the transfer of capital or other surplus to earned surplus; future earnings are thereafter available for the immediate payment of dividends.

(ii) "Nimble dividends" are dividends paid out of current earnings even though a deficit in earned surplus may exist from prior years. *United States v. Riely,* 169 F.2d 542 (4th Cir.1948). In states that permit nimble dividends, current earnings may be used to pay dividends even though a capital deficit exists because of the issuance of watered stock. *Goodnow v. American Writing Paper Co.,* 69 A. 1014 (N.J.Err. & App.1908). See also *Morris v. Standard Gas & Electric Co.,* 63 A.2d 577 (Del.Ch.1949), applying the Delaware statute which prohibits a nimble dividend if the value of corporate capital is less than the capital represented by the capital stock.

(iii) "Reevaluation surplus" is surplus created by the directors' decision to "write up" the value of appreciated assets; distributions of "reevaluation surplus" are permitted in some states. *Randall v. Bailey,* 23 N.Y.S.2d 173 (1940); *Dominguez Land Corp. v. Daugherty,* 238 P. 697 (Cal.1925).

(iv) Surplus may also be created by recognizing and placing a value on goodwill or other intangible assets not previously shown in the corporation's books; the use of such surplus for distributions has been permitted in some cases. *Randall v. Bailey,* 23 N.Y.S.2d 173 (1940).

(v) "Reduction surplus" is surplus created by the reduction of stated capital by amendment to the articles of incorporation or by the retirement of shares; the use of such surplus for distributions is permitted by some state statutes only with the consent of the shareholders.

Caveat: These various concepts are not recognized in all states. They have no applicability in states that have adopted statutes like the MBCA (1984) that eliminate the legal capital accounts from the statute.

Caveat: The ability to create artificial capital surplus by writing up assets, and to transmute "stated capital" into "capital surplus" by amending articles of incorporation to reduce the par value of outstanding shares, makes it relatively easy for a corporation to adjust its accounts to permit the making of any distribution it wishes that is consistent with the insolvency test.

Caveat: Perhaps in no other area of corporation law is the appearance of firm regulation more deceptive than in the area of statutory controls over distributions.

4. CONTRACTUAL RESTRICTIONS ON DIVIDENDS AND DISTRIBUTIONS

Because state statutes provide few practical restrictions on distributions and therefore little or no protection for creditors, major creditors regularly impose contractual restrictions on dividends and distributions in loan agreements. Such agreements provide more meaningful restrictions than state statutes.

Example: *ABC* Company plans to borrow $15,000,000 from *X* Life Insurance Company. The loan is in the form of a sale of bonds in a private placement. *X* Life Insurance Company declines to make the loan unless *ABC* Corporation agrees to the following limitations on dividends and distributions:

(a) *ABC* Corporation may pay a regular dividend of $0.25 per share per quarter if its annual income in the preceding year was $5,000,000 or more.

(b) *ABC* Corporation may pay an extra or special dividend not to exceed $1.00 per share if its net earnings exceed $25,000,000 and not to exceed $2.00 per share if its earnings exceed $50,000,000 in the preceding year.

(c) No other dividend or distribution or redemption or reacquisition of shares by *ABC* Corporation may be made without the prior written approval of *X* Life Insurance Company.

(d) Earnings shall be determined in accordance with generally accepted accounting principles as determined by outside independent auditors.

J. REDEMPTIONS AND REPURCHASES OF OUTSTANDING SHARES

A corporation may repurchase its own shares by negotiating for the purchase with a shareholder. A redemption of shares by a corporation is a reacquisition that occurs pursuant to the terms of the shares themselves, with the redemption price established by, or in the manner specified by, the articles of incorporation. Redemptions are usually at the option of the issuer but may also be at the option of the holder.

A redemption or repurchase by a corporation of some of its outstanding shares has the same economic effect as a dividend or distribution to the shareholders whose shares are redeemed or purchased. A redemption or repurchase may also affect the relative voting interests of the remaining shareholders.

1. RELATIONSHIP BETWEEN REPURCHASES AND DISTRIBUTIONS

When a corporation repurchases or redeems some of its own shares, the assets of the corporation are reduced by the purchase price of the shares but the shares of itself that are owned by the corporation are not assets. (This can be appreciated most easily by comparing the status of repurchased shares with the status of authorized but unissued shares.)

Example: A, B, and C are the sole shareholders of ABC Corporation. Each own 100 shares. They decide that each of them will sell 10 shares back to the corporation for $100 per share, or a total of $1,000 each. When the sale is completed, each shareholder continues to own one-third of the outstanding shares (90 shares each) and the corporation is $3,000 poorer. The shareholders are each $1,000 richer in the sense that the proceeds are available for personal use.

a. The legal restrictions applicable to dividends are also generally applicable to share repurchases or redemptions. MBCA (1984) §§ 6.40, 1.40(6).

b. Unlike a distribution, a redemption or repurchase may affect the voting power of the remaining shares.

Example: In the prior example, C decides to retire and ABC Corporation agrees to repurchase all of her shares for $10,000. The repurchase increases the voting power of A and B from 33 ⅓ per cent each to 50 per cent each, and the corporation is $10,000 poorer.

2. REASONS FOR REPURCHASES OF SHARES BY PUBLICLY HELD CORPORATIONS

Share repurchases may occur in publicly held corporations for several reasons: e.g., to provide shares for employee share purchase plans, for the acquisition of other businesses, or to eliminate the interest of major shareholders without affecting the market for the shares.

a. Such repurchases are often made in the public market at current market prices and create relatively few problems, unless they occur in the context of a struggle for control, e.g., *Cheff v. Mathes,* 199 A.2d 548 (Del.1964); *Unocal Corp. v. Mesa Petroleum Co.,* 493 A.2d 946 (Del.1985); or as part of a plan to force out all public shareholders (a "going private" transaction). *Kaufmann v. Lawrence,* 386 F.Supp. 12 (S.D.N.Y.1974).

b. Repurchases of shares by a corporation on the securities markets may affect the price of shares. In order to avoid market manipulation, the SEC has promulgated regulations under the Securities Exchange Act of 1934 relating to such repurchases.

3. REASONS FOR REPURCHASES OF SHARES BY CLOSELY HELD CORPORATIONS

Since there is no public market for shares in closely held corporations, a shareholder who wishes to sell his or her shares has only limited options: usually the only interested potential buyers are other shareholders or the corporation itself.

Caveat: If the shares are the subject of a buy/sell agreement, the shareholder is required to sell the shares either to the corporation or the remaining shareholders pursuant to the terms of that agreement.

Caveat: In some situations, third parties may be possible purchasers of closely held shares. If the shares reflect working control of the business, the shares may be readily salable. If the shares reflect a minority interest, normally a third party is willing to purchase them only upon an agreement with the corporation and the controlling shareholders that assures that the third party will be able to resell the shares at a later time.

a. There is no public market price by which the fairness or reasonableness of repurchase prices for minority shares can be judged.

b. Repurchases or shares in closely held corporations are usually designed to permit a shareholder to withdraw from the corporation and liquidate his or her investment.

c. When the other shareholders are willing to acquire the interest of the shareholder who wishes to sell, repurchases by the corporation are often simpler and more convenient than pro rata purchases by the remaining shareholders.

1) The corporation may acquire life insurance policies on the lives of its shareholders to have funds available to acquire their shares on their death.

2) Repurchases of shares by a corporation do not create taxable income to the remaining shareholders even if earnings and profits of the corporation are used to repurchase the shares. Therefore, repurchases of shares are usually more favorable from a tax standpoint than direct purchases by the other shareholders (who must use after-tax dollars to make the purchase).

3) If several shareholders are to remain involved with the corporation, repurchase by the corporation solves the problems that may arise if some shareholders find it difficult or impossible to raise the funds to purchase their pro rata part of the shares.

4) Repurchases by the corporation may be made on the installment basis over a period of years with the shareholder accepting promissory notes of the corporation for the bulk of the purchase price.

(i) The payment of the purchase price by the corporation over time may allow the corporation to pay for the shares out of expected future earnings.

(ii) The relative priority of debt so created as opposed to trade creditors is discussed below.

d. In order for a corporation to repurchase its own shares, the corporation must meet the same tests that are applicable to a contemplated dividend or distribution by the corporation of the purchase price. (See part V I.)

1) In most states, the corporation must have available earned or capital surplus from which the purchase may be made and the corporation not be rendered insolvent by the transaction.

2) Where the corporation repurchases shares and all or a part of the purchase price is deferred and represented by promissory notes, these tests may be applied in either of two ways:

(i) Only once, at the time of the original sale at which the promissory notes are issued; or

(ii) Sequentially at the time of each payment on the notes.

3) The early case law generally tested the validity of each payment separately; *In re Trimble Co.,* 339 F.2d 838 (3d Cir.1964); *Robinson v. Wangemann,* 75 F.2d 756 (5th Cir.1935); *Mountain State Steel Foundries,*

Inc. v. C.I.R., 284 F.2d 737 (4th Cir.1960) (holding that a promissory note covered by earned surplus when it came due was enforceable even if not covered by earned surplus at the time it was issued).

4) MBCA (1984) § 6.40(e) and some cases take the position that the tests should be applied only once, at the time of the original purchase. *Williams v. Nevelow*, 513 S.W.2d 535 (Tex.1974).

  (i) Under this approach promissory notes representing the purchase price of shares are considered to be no different from any other ordinary corporate obligation, and are enforceable on a parity with other creditors even if there is no surplus to cover the note at the time of payment.

  (ii) The theory is that the corporation might obtain a loan from a third party and use the proceeds to repurchase the shares, and such a loan would clearly be on parity with other creditors. The same should be true of a loan made by the selling shareholder.

  (iii) The opposing theory is that the selling shareholder knows that each payment on the notes is essentially a distribution by the corporation and should be evaluated as though it were a distribution.

  (iv) California apparently takes an intermediate position and invalidates the note if there is not available earned surplus at the time of payment but allows a lien securing the note to be enforced. *Matter of National Tile & Terrazzo Co., Inc.*, 537 F.2d 329 (9th Cir.1976).

5) Contractual obligations by the corporation to repurchase shares at fixed prices are enforceable despite the potential unfairness to other shareholders.

Example: The corporation's president persuades *X* to purchase shares of the corporation by promising that the corporation will repurchase them at cost at any time. At this time, the price of the shares is about $45 per share. This promise is enforceable even though the price of the shares thereafter plummets to $15 per share. *Grace Securities Corp. v. Roberts*, 164 S.E. 700 (Va.1932).

4. STATUS OF REACQUIRED SHARES

Reacquired shares under most statutes are classed as "treasury shares." Under the MBCA (1984) and some state statutes, they are classed as authorized but unissued shares. (See part V J 4.)

5. REDEEMABLE SHARES IN GENERAL

State statutes expressly permit corporations to issue preferred shares that are redeemable by the corporation upon terms set forth in the articles of incorporation.

a. In many states common shares may not be made redeemable at all or may be made redeemable only if there exists another class of common shares that is not redeemable. See *Lewis v. H.P. Hood & Sons, Inc.*, 121 N.E.2d 850 (Mass. 1954).

b. MBCA (1984) § 6.01(c)(2) permits redeemable common shares without limitation or restriction.

c. If redeemable shares have voting power, the redemption may affect control of the corporation. Such redemptions, however, have been permitted if made in good faith. *Hendricks v. Mill Engineering & Supply Co., Inc.*, 413 P.2d 811 (Wash.1966).

d. Some commentators have argued that redeemable voting shares should be prohibited as a matter of public policy because of the coercive threat the power of redemption may create.

e. The corporation may purchase redeemable shares from individual shareholders at a negotiated price below the redemption price without necessarily triggering the redemption obligation. *Snyder v. Memco Engineering & Mfg. Co., Inc.*, 257 N.Y.S.2d 213 (App.Div.1965).

6. REDEMPTIONS AT OPTION OF SHAREHOLDER

MBCA (1984) and the statutes of many states permit shares to be made redeemable at the option of the shareholder. In some states the statutes are silent on this question; presumably, such rights are permitted if not specifically prohibited.

a. Such shares have some of the characteristics of a demand promissory note.

b. Such shares are a financing device that is more attractive than debt where the supplier of capital is a corporation in that a dividend is entitled to the dividend received credit under the federal income tax law.

7. FIDUCIARY DUTIES IN CONNECTION WITH REPURCHASES OF SHARES

Donahue v. Rodd Electrotype Co. of New England, Inc., 328 N.E.2d 505 (Mass.1975) holds that controlling shareholders have a strict fiduciary duty and a duty "of utmost good faith and loyalty" to minority shareholders when redeeming shares.

a. *Donahue* involved a situation where shares owned by the father of the majority shareholder had been redeemed by the corporation but the corporation offered to redeem shares owned by minority shareholders only at a much lower price. The court held this conduct violated the fiduciary duty that the majority shareholder owed to the minority. Many post-*Donahue* cases support this holding on similar facts. E.g., *Estate of Meller v. Adolf Meller Co.*, 554 A.2d 648 (R.I.1989); *Sundberg v. Abbott*, 423 N.W.2d 686 (Minn.App.1988); *Balvik v. Sylvester*, 411 N.W.2d 383 (N.D.1987). But see *Toner v. Baltimore Envelope Co.*, 498 A.2d 642 (Md.1985), where the court rejected a *per se* rule that any difference in price was improper and held that an examination of all relevant facts was necessary.

b. The *Donahue* opinion has been widely cited and relied upon by courts in other jurisdictions in a variety of different contexts. See part X E 4.

K. ILLEGAL DIVIDENDS OR DISTRIBUTIONS

Generally, assenting directors are liable for an illegal dividend or distribution; shareholders who receive such a dividend or distribution are liable to repay it only if they knew it was unlawful when they received it. *Reilly v. Segert,* 201 N.E.2d 444 (Ill. 1964); MBCA (1984) § 8.33.

1. PROTECTION OF RELIANCE BY DIRECTORS

Directors who rely on the records of the corporation and the opinion of the corporation's accountant in good faith in determining whether a dividend or distribution may be made, usually do not incur liability for an illegal dividend. See MBCA (1984) § 8.33.

2. RECOVERY BY CREDITORS

Liability for illegal dividends or distributions generally run to the corporation rather than to individual creditors. *Schaefer v. DeChant,* 464 N.E.2d 583 (Ohio App.1983). Creditors may be able to force a defaulting corporation into bankruptcy or receivership in order to compel the corporation to recover illegal dividends or distributions for the benefit of creditors.

L. SHARE DIVIDENDS AND SHARE SPLITS

Unlike dividends or distributions that are payable in cash or property, a share dividend or share split does not dissipate corporate assets. In effect, the total number of shares having claims to the corporate pool of assets is increased but the pool of assets is itself neither increased nor decreased.

Share dividends or splits differ from share repurchases or share redemptions. When shares are repurchased or redeemed, the size of the corporate pool of assets is reduced by the purchase price for the shares and the number of shares having claim to the remaining assets is reduced by the number of repurchased or redeemed shares.

1. DEFINITIONS

A share dividend differs from a share split in degree rather than in kind.

a. In par value states, a share split differs from a share dividend in accounting treatment. In a share split, the par value of each old share is divided among the new shares while in a share dividend the par value of each share is unchanged and the stated capital of the corporation is increased by the number of shares issued as a dividend.

b. The New York Stock Exchange defines a "stock dividend" to be a distribution of less than 25 per cent of the outstanding shares (as calculated prior to the distribution); a "partial stock split" is defined to be a distribution of 25 per cent or more but less than 100 per cent of the outstanding shares (as calculated prior to the distribution) and a "stock split" is defined to be a distribution of 100 per cent or more of the outstanding shares (as calculated prior to the distribution).

   1) MBCA (1984) § 6.23 refers only to "share dividends" and does not use the phrase "stock splits."

c. A share dividend is usually described as a percentage increase while a share split is described in the form of a "new-for-old" ratio.

   Example: A corporation declares a 6 per cent stock dividend. Each shareholder's holdings are increased by one share for every 16 ⅔ shares held; fractional shares may be paid in cash or in the form of scrip which may be sold for cash. In par value states, funds must be transferred from earned surplus (or some other account) to stated capital to reflect the increase in the number of outstanding shares.

   Example: A corporation declares a 2–for–1 stock split. Each shareholder is issued one new share for each share held; as a result, each shareholder has two shares where before he or she had one. In par value states, the par value of or capital represented by each share is cut in half and as a result, the aggregate stated capital is not increased by the stock split.

d. In a stock split, the regular dividend rate is adjusted, though the combined rate on the new shares may be somewhat greater than the rate on the old shares. No change in dividend rate is normally made as a result of a share dividend.

   Example: In a 2–for–1 split, the corporation announces the regular dividend rate of $0.50 quarterly on the old shares will be replaced by a $0.30 quarterly rate on the new. The new rate is the equivalent of $0.60 quarterly rate on the old shares, and the effect is an increase of 10 cents per share in the regular quarterly dividend rate.

Example: The corporation declares a 6 per cent share dividend. The old dividend rate of $0.50 quarterly is retained on a per share basis; total quarterly dividends will therefore increase 6 per cent as a result of the increase in the number of shares.

2. EFFECT OF SHARE SPLITS OR SHARE DIVIDENDS ON MARKET PRICES

The market price of new shares after a stock split may be somewhat greater than the price of the old shares.

a. This may partially be explained by the dividend increase though partially it may be a psychological reaction by the market.

Example: In the preceding example, the shares before the split sold for $20 per share. The new shares sell for about $13.00 per share. Only part of this increase can be explained by the dividend increase.

b. A share dividend rarely has a noticeable effect on market prices.

3. SHAREHOLDER ATTITUDES TOWARD SHARE DIVIDENDS OR SPLITS

Many shareholders may sell shares received as a dividend or in a split without realizing that they are thereby reducing slightly their proportional interest in the corporation.

4. TREATMENT OF SHARE DIVIDENDS AND SPLITS AS PRINCIPAL OR INCOME

Since share dividends or splits have some characteristics of income and some of principal, it is not surprising that litigation has arisen over the proper classification of such distributions in various contexts. In most of these situations, the intention of the creator of the interest, if clearly expressed, controls; litigation arises because no intention is expressed or the expression is ambiguous.

a. A recurring question that arises in trusts or testamentary bequests is whether a share dividend should be awarded to the life tenant or to the remainderman.

1) One view is that share dividends should be classified as income and not principal if earnings are capitalized to reflect the dividend. *In re Fosdick's Trust,* 152 N.E.2d 228 (N.Y.1958).

2) A second view is that share dividends should be classified as income to the extent they are paid out of income that accrued subsequent to the creation of the life interest. This is referred to as the Pennsylvania rule.

3) A third view is that share dividends should be treated as income up to an amount equal to six per cent of the principal each year.

4) A fourth view is that all share dividends should be treated as principal. This is referred to as the Massachusetts rule.

b. A similar issue is whether a testamentary gift of a specified number of shares should be deemed to carry with it shares later received in a share split. Again, the intent of the testator ultimately controls: did he or she intend to give a specified number of shares or a specified interest in the corporation? Where intent is ambiguous or uncertain, diversity of views may prevail. *Compare In re Marks' Estate,* 255 A.2d 512 (Pa.1969) with *In re Howe's Will,* 224 N.Y.S.2d 992 (App.Div.1962).

M. REVIEW QUESTIONS

V–1. How does a corporation obtain its capital?

V–2. What function does par value serve today?

V–3. Why doesn't the use of no par shares solve all problems of corporate capitalization?

V–4. Watered stock is a historical concept that has no practical importance today.

True ______ False ______

V–5. What does the MBCA (1984) do about par value?

V–6. In what sense is preferred stock preferred?

V–7. What is the difference between a bond and debenture?

V–8. In these days of inflation, Ben Franklin's old statement that "the best corporation is a debt-free corporation" is more true than ever.

True _______ False _______

V–9. So long as one offers shares to fewer than 35 persons, there can be no problem under the federal or state securities acts.

True _______ False _______

V–10. What are preemptive rights?

V–11. A corporation that eliminates preemptive rights may issue shares at any time in the future at any price the directors decide appropriate.

True _______ False _______

V–12. Why is a repurchase of outstanding shares by a corporation similar to a dividend?

V–13. Creditors should always impose restrictions on dividends by contract. The protection given creditors by the legal restrictions on making distributions or paying dividends by state corporation statutes are almost totally illusory.

True _______ False _______

V–14. A publicly held corporation decides to pay a dividend in the form of shares of stock rather than in the form of money. As a matter of economics, there is no significant difference in these two types of distributions.

True _______ False _______

V–15. Commerce, Inc. is incorporated in a state with a par value statute; it has a single class of shares listed on the New York Stock Exchange. It has recently engaged in an extensive mail-order sales campaign in order to stimulate its sagging economic fortunes. Commerce, Inc., although it had a large accumulated deficit in earned surplus from losses from prior years, declared and paid a dividend out of its net profits for last year. Commerce, Inc. was not insolvent at the time of the declaration or payment of the dividend.

Commerce, Inc. now finds itself in deep financial trouble. Plagued by creditors and unable to meet presently due liabilities, it files a petition in bankruptcy. Its bankruptcy trustee sues both the directors and the shareholders of Commerce, Inc. who received the dividend. What are the potential liabilities of the directors who authorized the dividends and the shareholders who received them? Would it make any difference if Commerce, Inc. were incorporated in a state that has enacted the MBCA (1984)? [This question and answer is drawn in part from Ballantine, Problems in Law 241 (5th Ed.1975).]

V–16. B owned a mining claim worth $100,000. She formed X corporation in a state with a par value statute and transferred to X the mining claim for shares having a par value of $250,000. The corporation became insolvent and R was appointed its receiver. R sued B for $150,000. May R recover? Explain your answer.

V–17. P entered into an agreement with D Corporation whereby P agreed to sell to D 150 shares of D's stock for $40,000. D Corporation was to pay the purchase price in installments of $1,000 every 3 months. At the time of the purchase D Corporation has sufficient surplus to make the purchase without impairing capital. After the corporation had paid $13,000 on the purchase price it became insolvent. Is P entitled to file a claim for $27,000 as a creditor in a subsequent bankruptcy?

V–18. X corporation has been in business for 10 years, has made substantial profits every year, and yet has never paid a dividend. In addition to its capital of $2,000,000 it has accumulated $8,000,000 surplus without clear plans to expand its business. Of its $10,000,000 in assets, $2,000,000 is cash. Z, a stockholder, sues to have the court order the board of directors of X to declare a dividend. Should the order issue?

VI

THE STATUTORY SCHEME OF MANAGEMENT AND CONTROL

Analysis

A. THE STATUTORY SCHEME IN GENERAL

Traditional state corporation statutes provide an idealized distribution of the powers of management and control among the three tiers of a corporation—shareholders, directors and officers.

Caveat: This part outlines the broad statutory principles of corporate management and control; later parts describe in detail the roles and functions of shareholders (part VII), directors (part VIII), and officers (part IX). The discussion in this part is more theory than reality.

1. SHAREHOLDERS

The shareholders are viewed as the ultimate owners of the corporation. Ownership, however, is separated from control and management. Shareholders have only limited powers of management and control in the corporation, including:

a. The power to select directors.

b. The power to remove directors.

1) At common law shareholders could remove directors only for cause.

2) In most state statutes this power has been broadened to permit removal without cause. *Scott County Tobacco Warehouses, Inc. v. Harris*, 201 S.E.2d 780 (Va.1974). See MBCA (1984) § 8.08; Del. GCL § 141(k) [if board is classified (see part VII D 4 c) directors may be removed only for cause unless certificate of incorporation provides to the contrary].

c. The power to make recommendations to the board of directors about business and personnel matters. *Auer v. Dressel*, 118 N.E.2d 590 (N.Y.1954).

Caveat: Even though shareholders may make recommendations, they do not have direct power to implement them.

Caveat: Regulations adopted by the Securities and Exchange Commission require registered publicly held corporations to submit certain proposals to shareholders. (See part XII, below.) If the SEC regulations are inapplicable it is doubtful whether a shareholder may compel a proposal to be submitted to the shareholders for their consideration. *Carter v. Portland General Electric Co.*, 362 P.2d 766 (Or.1961).

d. The power to amend or repeal bylaws. MBCA (1984) § 10.20. But see *Somers v. AAA Temporary Services, Inc.*, 284 N.E.2d 462 (Ill.App.1972) holding that under the Illinois statute then in effect, the shareholders lose power to amend bylaws to the extent authority to do so is vested in the board of directors.

Under the MBCA provision and the statutes of most states, shareholders would not lose their power to amend bylaws under the circumstances of this case.

e. In conjunction with the board of directors, the power to approve fundamental corporate changes:

   1) Amendments to articles of incorporation [MBCA (1984) § 10.03];

   2) Mergers, consolidations or compulsory share exchanges with other corporations [MBCA (1984) § 11.03];

   3) Sales of substantially all the assets of the corporation not in the ordinary course of business [MBCA (1984) § 12.02]; and dissolution [MBCA (1984) § 14.02].

f. The power to inspect corporate books and records for proper purposes. MBCA (1984) § 16.02.

g. The power to select the corporate auditor (in corporations subject to SEC regulation).

h. Where an internal struggle for control exists, the power to definitively resolve which faction shall be entitled to manage the corporation, *Campbell v. Loew's Inc.*, 134 A.2d 852 (Del.Ch.1957).

   Caveat: State statutes authorize the shareholders rather than the directors to establish the consideration for which shares are to be issued if the power to do so is reserved to the shareholders by the articles of incorporation. See MBCA (1984) § 6.21(a). As a practical matter, this option is almost never exercised, and that function is performed by the board of directors.

2. DIRECTORS

In the statutory scheme directors are not viewed as agents or representatives of shareholders but as persons with independent authority, independent fiduciary duties, and some tenure to office. These characteristics of the role of directors are created by statute, not by decision of the shareholders.

In general terms, the board of directors of a corporation is entrusted with the general power of management of its business and affairs. All significant business decisions are generally entrusted to the directors, *Continental Securities Co. v. Belmont*, 99 N.E. 138 (N.Y.1912), though they may delegate authority to make many decisions to corporate officers or agents.

a. Traditional business corporation acts state that powers of the corporation "shall be exercised by," and the business and affairs of a corporation "shall be managed by," the board of directors. Some state statutes retain this traditional language.

1) This description more or less accurately reflects the role of the board of directors in smaller, closely held corporations where it is usually feasible for boards of directors directly to manage and oversee the business and affairs of the corporation.

2) In closely held corporations, most or all of the directors are usually substantial shareholders in the corporation. They also usually serve as the principal officers of the corporation.

b. In most states, this statutory language has been modified to state that the powers of the corporation may be "*exercised by or under authority of*" and its business and affairs may be "*managed by or under the direction of*" the board of directors. See MBCA (1984) § 8.01; Del. GCL § 141(a).

1) The broader language "under the authority of" and "under the direction of" more or less accurately reflects the role of the board of directors in large publicly held corporations where detailed control and management of huge aggregations of assets is performed by professional managers.

2) In publicly held corporations, a majority of the directors are usually not officers of the corporation, and usually neither the officers nor the directors are substantial shareholders of the corporation.

(i) The board of directors selects the corporate officers and has the power to remove them. The board also may employ employees or agents, or create new officers and employ persons to fill them. It is customary for boards of directors to delegate the power of employing lower level employees and agents to the corporate president or other officers.

(ii) Certain corporate decisions are peculiarly within the discretion of the board directors. These functions, such as determining the amount that should be distributed as dividends to shareholders, are specifically assigned to the board's discretion by statute.

3. OFFICERS

The officers of the corporation in the idealized statutory scheme have a limited role: they carry out the policies and decisions of the board of directors. They are not themselves the formulators of policy.

a. While officers have limited authority to bind the corporation by their actions within the scope of their responsibilities, this power is not broadly construed.

b. The essence of the statutory scheme is that discretionary power within the corporation is in the board of directors not the officers or shareholders.

c. In most corporations the actual roles and discretion of officers is greater than contemplated by the statutory scheme. The modern statutes relating to the roles of directors (described in Part VI A 2. b)) indirectly support this greater role and discretion.

B. ATTEMPTS TO VARY THE STATUTORY SCHEME

Attempts to reallocate the corporate powers in ways significantly different from the statutory scheme historically have been viewed with suspicion and many have been held to be against public policy and unenforceable.

1. STRICT COMMON LAW APPROACH

The strict common law approach was that agreements between shareholders that attempted to resolve questions that are the responsibility of the board of directors were against public policy as expressed in the corporation statute and therefore were unenforceable and may be ignored by the other parties to the agreement. *McQuade v. Stoneham,* 189 N.E. 234 (N.Y.1934).

Example: In a corporation with more than 30 shareholders, two shareholders, *A* and *B,* together own a majority of the voting shares. A and B enter into a written agreement that provides: (a) They will vote for themselves as two of the three directors; (b) They will establish and maintain *A* as president and *B* as vice president; (c) The salary of the president will be $50,000 per year and the salary of the vice president will be $40,000 per year. A and B have a falling out and B is summarily discharged. B has no claim against A for breach of contract, since the agreements referred to in (b) and (c) invade the discretionary power of the board of directors and are unenforceable. The agreement (a) does not interfere with the discretion of directors (since the selection of directors is purely a function of the shareholders) and is therefore not subject to attack on the same ground. Its enforceability depends on whether it is severable from the unenforceable portions of the agreement.

Example: *C* agrees to invest in a corporation only if the other two shareholders, *A* and *B,* agree that the corporation will not borrow in excess of $10,000 without the prior consent of *C. A* and *B* agree in writing to this proposal and *C* purchases the shares. Since borrowing money is within the discretionary power of the board of directors to manage the business, the agreement by the shareholders is against public policy and unenforceable. The board of directors may ignore the agreement and borrow money in excess of $10,000 without obtaining the prior consent of *C.* See *Burnett v. Word, Inc.,* 412 S.W.2d 792 (Tex.Civ.App.1967).

2. RELAXATION OF STRICT COMMON LAW APPROACH

As illustrated by the foregoing examples, the strict common law rule sometimes leads to significant injustice because apparently reasonable and sensible contracts are invalidated. As a result, the same court that decided *McQuade* shortly thereafter modified the strict common law approach by holding that contracts which involved only slight impingements on the statutory scheme and hurt no one should not be invalidated under this general principle. *Clark v. Dodge,* 199 N.E. 641 (N.Y.1936).

a. Courts state that the common law approach is primarily intended to protect minority shareholders who are not parties to the contract by assuring that they receive the protection of the unfettered best judgment of the board of directors.

b. *Clark v. Dodge* states that if all the shareholders are parties to the contract, somewhat broader impingements on the discretion of the directors should be permitted. However, major impingements that radically change the locus of power or scheme of corporate governance are not permitted even if all the shareholders agree.

c. Major impingements on the statutory scheme appear to be invalid under these early cases because a corporation must follow the substance of the statutory scheme if it is to be a corporation at all.

Example: It is likely that some courts might consider the veto in the second example above to be a "slight impingement."

Example: All the shareholders agree that the corporation should pay dividends of $50,000 per year if there are funds available after the board of directors has set aside whatever funds it believes necessary for future contingencies and growth. In most states such an agreement today would be deemed a "slight impingement" and the agreement would be held valid.

Example: All the shareholders agree that all internal decisions within the corporation shall be made as though the shareholders were partners and that the corporation shall not have a board of directors. Absent specific statutory authorization, such an agreement is more than a "slight impingement" and is not enforceable.

Example: All the shareholders agree that directors must agree to and accept all transactions that a majority of the shareholders approve. Such an agreement is more than a "slight impingement" and is not binding on the board of directors.

Example: A shareholder's agreement providing that each shareholder has an option to purchase shares offered by other shareholders also contains provisions relating to the naming of officers and the fixing of their compensation. These provisions were in fact never implemented. The court may ignore the provisions dealing with the officers (which violate the statutory scheme) and enforce the balance. *Triggs v. Triggs,* 385 N.E.2d 1254 (N.Y.1978).

d. Some courts have relaxed even further the test for invalidating such agreements, and appear to be prepared to uphold substantially any shareholders agreement, so long as all shareholders agree to it. *Galler v. Galler*, 203 N.E.2d 577 (Ill.1964).

3. ORDERS AND DIRECTIONS OF MAJORITY SHAREHOLDERS

The directors are not agents of the shareholders and may not be compelled to approve transactions merely because a majority or even all the shareholders approve them. *Continental Securities Co. v. Belmont*, 99 N.E. 138 (N.Y.1912).

a. The sole remedy of the majority shareholders in this situation is to elect different directors.

Example: *A*, owner of a majority of the shares of a corporation, desires that the corporation buy a piece of land. The directors decline. *A* cannot compel the directors to do so but may elect more compliant directors at the next election of directors and resubmit the proposal then. *Automatic Self-Cleansing Filter Syndicate Co., Ltd. v. Cuninghame*, 2 Ch. 34 (Ct.App.Eng.1906).

b. Even though the shareholders may not order the directors to approve a transaction, they may recommend a transaction and urge its approval by the board.

Example: *A*, in the above example, may properly bring before a shareholder's meeting a resolution urging the directors to approve the land purchase. *Auer v. Dressel*, 118 N.E.2d 590 (N.Y.1954).

c. The majority shareholder may also seek to remove the directors and elect more compliant directors.

1) At common law directors could be removed only for "cause," a term that implies dishonesty, misconduct, or incompetence. Hence, at common law the selection of more compliant directors would have to await the next

annual meeting. *Auer v. Dressel,* 118 N.E.2d 590 (N.Y.1954); *Campbell v. Loew's, Inc.,* 134 A.2d 852 (Del.Ch.1957).

2) In most states today, shareholders may remove directors without cause; in such states, the majority shareholders may immediately remove the present board and elect different directors willing to enter into the transaction. *Scott County Tobacco Warehouses, Inc. v. Harris,* 201 S.E.2d 780 (Va.1974). See MBCA (1984) § 8.08; Del.Gen.Corp.Law, § 141(k).

Example: *A*, in the above example, calls a special shareholder's meeting the purpose of which is stated to be the removal of the directors without cause; at that meeting A removes the recalcitrant directors, and elects himself and friends to the board of directors; the land purchase may then be reconsidered by the new board of directors.

d. The justification for requiring removal of the old board and election of a new is that directors owe fiduciary duties to the corporation, to creditors and to minority shareholders.

1) A director should not be compelled to follow the wishes of a majority shareholder if she believes the transaction breaches a fiduciary duty and may thereby create personal liability.

2) The election of successor directors imposes fiduciary duties on them and they must decide whether the desired transaction is consistent with their duties.

4. DELEGATION OF DUTIES

The directors may not delegate their entire duties of management to third persons and agreements entered into by the corporation which purport to do so may be unenforceable as against public policy.

Example: A corporation enters into a management contract with a third person which vests "sole and exclusive power to manage all affairs of the corporation" in that third person for a period of 25 years. Such an agreement is against public policy and unenforceable. *Sherman & Ellis, Inc. v. Indiana Mutual Cas. Co.,* 41 F.2d 588 (7th Cir.1930); *Kennerson v. Burbank Amusement Co.,* 260 P.2d 823 (Cal.App.1953).

Example: A corporation enters into a management contract of the general type described in the previous example but the agreement reserves to the board of directors the power to fire the third person for "cause." It is doubtful that such a limited power would save such an agreement from invalidity.

Example: A corporation enters into a management contract of the general type described in the previous example but the agreement reserves to the board the power to review the performance of the manager annually and to replace him if the board considers it appropriate. This qualification probably makes the agreement valid since the delegation of authority is no longer total.

5. DIRECTORS' VOTING AGREEMENTS

The directors may not enter into agreements among themselves relating to how they will vote.

Example: *A* and *B* are directors. They agree that *B* will support proposals presented by *A* and that *A* will support proposals presented by *B*. Such an agreement is against public policy and unenforceable, though, of course, *A* and *B* may vote together on a voluntary basis.

6. TESTAMENTARY DIRECTIONS

Majority shareholders may seek to guide the fortunes of their corporation after their death by testamentary directions to their trustees. Such directions are generally unenforceable on the ground they restrict the discretion of directors, though the inflexibility of testamentary directions may indicate a broader basis for their invalidity.

Example: Z, a 68 per cent shareholder has power to elect the entire board of directors of A Corporation. *Z*'s last will and testament bequeaths his shares in *A* Corporation to a testamentary trust and directs his trustees (i) to elect themselves as directors, (ii) to name Z's widow chairman of the board of A Corporation at a salary of $10,000 per month, and (iii) to elect Z's son as president, at a salary of $8,000 per month. Instructions (ii) and (iii) violate public policy and are unenforceable. *Matter of Hirshon*, 233 N.Y.S.2d 1018 (App.Div.1962), *modified* 192 N.E.2d 174 (N.Y.1963).

Caveat: If trustees name themselves as directors, testamentary instructions may create unavoidable conflicts between the duty of the trustee to follow the directions of the testator and the duty of a director to make decisions based on the best interests of the corporation. Testamentary trustees/directors faced with such a conflict may petition a court for instructions, but this is an expensive and cumbersome process, particularly if there is an appeal.

C. THE STATUTORY SCHEME AS AN IDEALIZED CORPORATE MODEL

The statutory scheme is an idealized model of corporate governance that, in some respects, does not accurately reflect the structure of power in either the very large, publicly held corporation, where shares may be owned by thousands or millions of shareholders, or in the very small corporation, with very few shareholders.

1. THE PUBLICLY HELD CORPORATION

In the publicly held corporation, the power of management is in fact vested not in the board of directors but in the full time, professional corporate officers and employees. This group is usually referred to as "management."

a. Management has the detailed knowledge about business affairs necessary to make business decisions. The board of directors usually consists of a majority of outsiders, who have only limited knowledge of business affairs, and several members of management. The outside persons are usually referred to as "outside directors" or "independent directors".

b. The board of directors meets only periodically while management is a full time professional staff.

c. The board of directors does not have its own staff or independent sources of information but is dependent on management to decide which issues should be brought to the board and what information should be given to the board.

   Example: When Penn Central went into bankruptcy the board of directors had not been advised of the steadily deteriorating financial position of the railroad or of the plans of the management to file for receivership. As a result, the board was as shocked and surprised as the ordinary man-in-the-street.

d. While the board of directors theoretically selects the chief executive officer (CEO) and other top management, in practice, the current CEO may name his successor and the board in effect may ratify that selection.

e. New members of the board of directors are usually selected by the management; in many corporations the outside members of the board of directors have a substantial voice in the selection process. As a practical matter, the shareholders have an opportunity only to vote for or against the persons so designated, thereby in effect ratifying the choices previously made.

f. Most shareholders vote by proxy in publicly held corporations based on information provided by the corporation. The number of shareholders who attend shareholders' meetings in person are usually an infinitesimal proportion of all the shareholders. Most shareholders routinely vote in favor of management's recommendations.

2. THE CLOSELY HELD CORPORATION

The statutory scheme also does not accurately reflect the manner of operation of corporations owned by a very small number of shareholders.

a. Such corporations are usually called "close corporations" or "closely held corporations".

b. The shareholders in close corporations are usually simultaneously officers and directors. Business decisions may be made by consensus and without regard to whether the person is acting as officer, director, or shareholder.

c. Requirements of meetings, appointments, elections, and so forth are all likely to be considered meaningless formalities. Indeed, many such corporations go for years without ever having a formal shareholders' or directors' meeting.

d. A number of states have adopted statutes relaxing the statutory requirements applicable to closely held corporations. (See part VI D 2 below; see also parts X D, X G.)

3. INTERMEDIATE CORPORATIONS

There are many corporations that do not have the characteristics of the publicly held corporation or of the closely held corporation. These "in between" corporations may have some characteristics of either type of corporation, and in many such corporations, the idealized statutory scheme may be a reasonable description of the allocation of power and control within the corporation.

D. STATUTORY MODIFICATION OF TRADITIONAL RULES

Many states have adopted statutes that modify to some degree the common law rules set forth in Part B, above. These statutes fall into two broad categories:

1. STATUTES GENERALLY PERMITTING MODIFICATION OF THE ROLE OF THE BOARD OF DIRECTORS

The statutes of many states permit any corporation to modify the traditional role of its board of directors by appropriate provision in its articles of incorporation. The provision may permit a corporation to dispense entirely with the board of directors and have the business and affairs managed directly by its shareholders or place restrictions on the discretion of directors.

a. Typical is Del. GCL § 141(a): "The business and affairs of every corporation * * * shall be managed by or under the direction of a board of directors *except as may be otherwise provided in this chapter or in its certificate of* *incorporation. If any such provision is made in the certificate of incorporation, the powers and duties conferred or imposed upon the board of directors by this chapter shall be exercised or performed to such extent and by such person or persons as shall be provided in the certificate of incorporation.*

Example: Lehrman and Cohen each own 50 per cent of the stock of X Corporation. They have numerous disagreements and finally agree that Danzansky, X Corporation's general counsel, whom they both trust, shall be given the power to vote as a director to break any deadlocks on the board of directors. An appropriate provision in the articles of incorporation granting Danzansky a tie breaking vote on the board of directors is valid. Cf. *Lehrman v. Cohen,* 222 A.2d 800 (Del.1966).

b. MBCA (1984) § 8.01(c) contained a provision similar to Del. GCL § 141(a), but that subsection was repealed in 1991 and a more general provision, § 7.32, discussed below, was substituted.

2. STATUTES APPLICABLE ONLY TO SPECIALLY DEFINED CLOSE CORPORATIONS

The statutes of about 12 states contain special provisions applicable only to electing close corporations. These statutes permit an electing close corporation, among other things, to dispense entirely with the board of directors to restrict the discretion of directors, and to permit the business and affairs of the corporation to be conducted as though it were a partnership. See Del. GCL §§ 341—355; part X D.

a. A "close corporation" is defined in these statutes, usually as a corporation with less than 35 shareholders.

b. A close corporation elects to become subject to these special statutes by including a provision stating to the effect that "This corporation is an electing close corporation" in its articles of incorporation.

c. Where the board of directors is eliminated under the Delaware Close Corporation Statute, the shareholders are referred to as "managing shareholders" and have the rights and duties of directors. *Graczykowski v. Ramppen,* 477 N.Y.S.2d 454 (App.Div.1984).

d. In *Zion v. Kurtz,* 405 N.E.2d 681 (N.Y.1980), the court upheld an agreement under these statutes between two shareholders that the corporation would not enter into transactions or new business without the consent of both shareholders despite the fact that no reference to the agreement appeared in the articles of incorporation and the corporation had not elected close corporation status. The court viewed these omissions as technical and subject to the power of the court to order the articles of incorporation reformed. The vote was 4–3; the dissenters argued that public notice of electing close corporation status and of agreements restricting the power of directors was essential for their validity under these statutes.

Caveat: If this approach is followed, these special close corporation statutes validate most shareholder agreements in non-electing corporations.

3. SECTION 7.32 OF THE MODEL BUSINESS CORPORATION ACT (1984)

In 1991, the Committee on Corporate Laws withdrew the provisions in the MBCA (1984) that appeared to permit limited flexibility in the statutory scheme, and replaced them with a new, more general, section 7.32, entitled "Shareholder Agreements".

a. Section 7.32 rejects "the older line of cases" relating to statutory norms and adds an "element of predictability currently absent" from the MBCA (1984). It recognizes that "many of the corporate norms" contained in corporation statutes were designed with an eye towards public companies where management and share ownership are quite distinct.

b. Section 7.32 validates virtually all shareholders' agreements relating to corporate governance and the business arrangement, including:

   1) Governance of the entity;

   2) Allocation of the return from the business, and

   3) Other aspects of the relationships among shareholders, directors, and the corporation.

   This is a broad but not universal mandate. Agreements that affect third parties and agreements that violate fundamental principles of public policy may not be validated.

   Example: The official comment to § 7.32 suggests that a provision in a shareholders' agreement that the directors have no duty of care or loyalty is not within the scope of that section.

c. The agreement must be unanimously approved by the shareholders; it may appear in the articles of incorporation, the bylaws, or a shareholders' agreement.

d. The existence of the agreement must appear on the share certificates or information statements reflecting shares. A purchaser of shares without notice of the existence of the agreement has the sole remedy of recission within 90 days after learning of the existence of the agreement.

e. An agreement under § 7.32 is valid for 10 years unless otherwise provided in the agreement. It automatically terminates if the shares of the corporation become publicly traded on a national securities market.

E. REVIEW QUESTIONS

VI–1. What is the "statutory scheme" or "statutory norm" in the law of corporations?

VI–2. In a corporation with two shareholders, it is silly to talk about the statutory scheme. The shareholders should simply run the corporation in the same way that they run a partnership.

True _______ False _______

VI–3. X corporation has a provision in its articles of incorporation that states, "no act of the board of directors of this corporation concerning the management of its business affairs shall be of any effect unless consented to or ratified by a unanimous vote of all its shareholders." A, B and C were the sole shareholders and the sole directors of X corporation. They had earlier elected A president, *B* vice president and C secretary-treasurer of the corporation. They now meet as a board of directors and vote to relieve C of his duties as secretary-treasurer and make B secretary-treasurer in addition to his being vice president. C votes against his removal as secretary-treasurer and contends that he cannot be removed under the above charter provision without unanimous vote of the shareholders, and he being one, does not consent to his own removal. C brings suit against A and B to compel them to admit him to the office of secretary-treasurer and to compel them to deliver to him the books of such office. What result?

*

VII

SHAREHOLDERS' MEETINGS, VOTING, AND CONTROL ARRANGEMENTS

Analysis

A. SHAREHOLDERS' MEETINGS

The rules with respect to shareholders' meetings are rather straight-forward. There is a considerable degree of uniformity from state to state in these statutory requirements.

1. ANNUAL MEETINGS

Annual meetings are required to be held for the purpose of electing directors and conducting other business. The time and place of the annual meeting may be specified in or fixed in accordance with the bylaws. The failure to hold an annual meeting does not affect the validity or continued existence of the corporation. The failure to hold an annual meeting also does not affect the incumbency of sitting directors. (See part VIII, F; MBCA (1984) § 7.01.)

2. SPECIAL MEETINGS

All meetings other than the annual meeting are special meetings. Such meetings may be called by the board of directors, and under many state statutes by the President, the holders of a specified number of shares (often 10 per cent), and other persons named in the bylaws. MBCA (1984) § 7.02.

3. NOTICE

Shareholders who are entitled to vote must be given written notice of annual or special meetings as provided in the statute or in the bylaws. Many statutes require at least ten but not more than fifty days' notice. MBCA (1984) § 7.05 requires 10 to 60 days notice.

a. The purposes of a special meeting must be stated in the notice and the business to be conducted at that meeting is limited to that specified in the notice. MBCA (1984) § 7.02(d). No purposes of an annual meeting need be stated and any relevant business may be conducted at such a meeting.

b. Notice may be waived by a written document executed before, at, or after the meeting in question. MBCA (1984) § 7.06.

c. In the absence of statute or SEC regulation, there is no common law requirement that matters not required to be considered by shareholders be noticed or submitted to a vote of shareholders. *Carter v. Portland General Electric Co.*, 362 P.2d 766 (Or.1961).

B. QUORUM AND VOTING REQUIREMENTS

In order for action to be taken at a shareholders' meeting, there must be a quorum at the meeting and the action must be approved by the required percentage of the votes of shareholders.

1. QUORUM REQUIREMENTS

A quorum at a meeting is typically a majority of the voting shares though some statutes allow the quorum to be reduced either without limitation or to a specified fraction (e.g. one third) by provision in the articles of incorporation. Earlier versions of the Model Act allowed the quorum to be reduced to one third; MBCA (1984) § 7.25(a) permits the quorum requirement to be reduced without limitation.

Example: A quorum by statute consists of a majority of the voting shares. A corporation has 100 shares outstanding and 52 shares are represented at the meeting. A quorum is present and therefore a majority of those present—27 shares—may validly approve actions unless a greater percentage is required by the statute or bylaws.

a. Statutes permit the quorum requirement to be increased up to and including unanimity. Unanimity is a popular control device in closely held corporations since it assures minority participation in the election of directors and other important decisions.

   1) A unanimity requirement for a quorum enables any shareholder to prevent undesired action simply by refusing to attend the meeting. It thereby increases the likelihood of deadlock.

   2) A unanimity quorum requirement is usually accompanied by the creation of a voting device or plan that assures that a minority shareholder is entitled to elect at least one person to the board of directors.

b. Shares represented by proxy are deemed present for purposes of a quorum. *Duffy v. Loft, Inc.*, 151 A. 223 (Del.Ch.1930).

c. The majority view is that if a quorum is once present, the meeting may continue even though a faction leaves the meeting in an effort to break the quorum. *Levisa Oil Corp. v. Quigley,* 234 S.E.2d 257 (Va.1977) (minority view). MBCA (1984) § 7.25(b) codifies the majority view.

2. SHARES ENTITLED TO VOTE; CLASS VOTING

Shares entitled to vote at a meeting generally are outstanding common shares (except non-voting common shares). Classes or series of preferred shares may be entitled to vote if appropriate provision is included in the articles of incorporation.

a. Treasury shares (i. e., shares once outstanding but reacquired by the corporation) and shares owned by a majority-owned subsidiary of the corporation are not eligible to vote under most state statutes.

b. Classes or series of nonvoting shares may be entitled to vote on specific matters that affect the rights of that class or series in ways specified by statute.

1) Most state statutes define such voting as "class voting." The MBCA (1984) uses the phrase "voting by voting groups" to describe the same concept. See MBCA (1984) § 1.40(26).

2) Where class voting on a specific matter is required, that matter is approved only if it receives the necessary affirmative votes from shareholders of that class as well as the necessary affirmative votes of all shares entitled to vote generally on matters coming before the meeting.

3) On most matters requiring class voting, the statutes require a supermajority vote. (See part XIX.)

c. Under the MBCA (1984) only shares may vote. The statutes of some states permit corporations to grant voting power to bond or debenture holders. See Del. GCL, § 221. Authorization for nonshareholders to vote under these statutes must appear in the articles of incorporation of the corporation.

3. THE VOTE REQUIRED TO APPROVE A MATTER

The traditional rule is that the affirmative vote of a majority of the votes present at a meeting at which a quorum is present is necessary to adopt a measure.

a. The MBCA (1984) § 7.25(c) changes the approval requirement from a simple majority to "the votes cast * * * favoring the action exceed the votes cast opposing the action." This change was designed to eliminate the negative way the traditional rule treated abstentions.

Example: Assume a corporation has 100 shares of a single class outstanding, all entitled to cast one vote each. A quorum consists of 51 shares. If 60 shares are represented and the vote on a proposed action is 28 in favor, 23 opposed and 9 abstaining, the action is not adopted under the traditional language of most statutes since the affirmative vote by 28 shares is not a majority of the shares present. On the other hand, if the 9 abstaining shares were not present at all, the action would have been approved since 51 shares were present and 28 voted in favor of the proposal.

b. An abstention may be reflected by casting of a blank ballot, or by casting a ballot marked "abstention" or by casting no ballot at all.

c. MBCA (1984) § 7.28 establishes a plurality vote requirement for the election of directors in order to take into account the possibility of three or more factions competing for directorships. Earlier versions of the Model Act and the statutes of many states do not contain a special rule for elections of directors.

Caveat: The MBCA (1984) phrases quorum and voting requirement in terms of "voting groups" in order to apply these requirements separately in situations where different classes of shares are entitled to vote separately on an issue. In most meetings, there is only one voting group, the group consisting of all shares entitled by the articles of incorporation to vote on the matter, acting on a matter.

4. SUPERMAJORITY QUORUM AND VOTING REQUIREMENTS

Statutes generally allow the quorum and voting requirements to be increased up to and including unanimity. See MBCA (1984) § 7.27.

a. A case finding such an increase in voting or quorum requirements to be against public policy, *Benintendi v. Kenton Hotel*, 60 N.E.2d 829 (N.Y.1945), was promptly rejected by legislative enactment.

b. Supermajority requirements may be imposed in closely held corporations to ensure that a minority shareholder has a veto power over matters coming before the shareholders.

Example: An owner of 20 per cent of the outstanding shares may obtain a veto power by insisting that the articles of incorporation provide that a quorum consists of 90 per cent of the outstanding shares and that actions to be approved must be voted upon affirmatively by all shareholders present at a meeting at which a quorum is present.

Caveat: Supermajority provisions increase the prospect of a deadlock at the shareholders' level because any minority shareholder may be able to block action.

c. Supermajority requirements are also used as defensive weapons to protect publicly held corporations against unwanted takeover attempts.

Example: A publicly held corporation amends its articles of incorporation to provide that if any person obtains a majority of the outstanding shares of a corporation without the approval of the board of directors, the voting requirement for all actions by the shareholders is increased to seventy per cent. This provision deters takeovers because an outsider does not obtain voting control of the corporation unless he either obtains approval of the current board of directors or purchases over seventy per cent of the outstanding shares of the corporation.

d. Statutes require a supermajority vote for fundamental corporate actions, including amendments to articles of incorporation, mergers, mandatory share exchanges, dissolution, and similar transactions.

1) The MBCA (1984) requires an absolute majority of all outstanding shares while other statutes may require a higher percentage of the votes (typically 2/3ds).

2) Older statutes may permit nonvoting as well as voting shares to vote on that matter.

3) If the statute permits individual classes or series to vote separately on a fundamental corporate action, the supermajority vote requirement must be met both within the class or series and within the class of voting shareholders generally.

5. UNANIMOUS CONSENT TO ACTION TAKEN WITHOUT A MEETING

Under most state statutes, a written consent signed by all the shareholders is as valid as an action taken at a meeting. MBCA (1984) § 7.04. The requirement of unanimity ensures that this provision is used only by corporations with relatively few shareholders.

6. MAJORITY CONSENT TO ACTION TAKEN WITHOUT A MEETING

In Delaware and a few other states, a consent signed by the percentage of shares needed to approve a transaction is effective. Del. GCL § 228. This majority-consent procedure may be used in publicly-held as well as closely-held corporations and permits a purchaser of a majority of the shares of a publicly held corporation immediately to replace the board of directors and take control of the corporation.

Example: A corporation with 120,000 shares outstanding receives a consent signed by holders of 61,000 shares in a state with a majority-consent procedure. The consent removes the current board of directors without cause and replaces them with different individuals. The action is validly taken. No account is taken of the quorum requirement in this computation.

a. Because of the possible usefulness of the majority consent procedure in takeover struggles, many Delaware corporations have sought to limit the use of the majority consent procedure by defining and limiting in their bylaws the manner in which the majority consent procedure operates. *Datapoint Corp. v. Plaza Securities Co.*, 496 A.2d 1031 (Del.1985); *Empire of Carolina, Inc. v. Deltona Corp.*, 514 A.2d 1091 (Del.1985); *Allen v. Prime Computer, Inc.*, 540 A.2d 417 (Del.1988)

b. A consent solicitation in a large publicly held corporation has many of the characteristics of a disputed election. See *Blasius Industries, Inc. v. Atlas Corp.*, 564 A.2d 651 (Del.Ch.1988).

7. MULTIPLE OR FRACTIONAL VOTES PER SHARE

Under older statutes the rule is one vote per share (except possibly for nonvoting shares). A number of state statutes now permit multiple or fractional votes per share. In these states all computations must be based on an aggregate-votes rather than aggregate-voting shares basis. MBCA (1984) §§ 6.01, 7.21.

Example: Articles of incorporation provide that for purposes of determining a quorum, a shareholder has one vote for each share owned up to fifty shares and one vote for each twenty shares owned in excess of fifty shares, but no shareholder may cast more than one fourth of all the votes at a meeting (except as proxy for other shareholders). The provision, which prevents a single shareholder from constituting a quorum no matter what size his holdings, is valid under the Delaware GCL. *Providence & Worcester Co. v. Baker*, 378 A.2d 121 (Del.1977).

a. Publicly held corporations with strong minority interests held by a single family have created classes of shares with multiple votes per share as an antitakeover device. Shares with multiple votes are assigned to family members; these shares may be sold to third persons only after conversion to shares with a single vote per share.

b. The SEC adopted a rule designed to limit the use of such shares, but in an important decision the Second Circuit held that this Rule exceeded the powers of the SEC since it did not relate to disclosure matters. *Business Roundtable v. SEC,* 905 F.2d 406 (D.C.Cir.1990). The SEC rule invalidated in this case is known as the "one share one vote" rule.

8. MANIPULATION OF MEETING DATES FOR ULTERIOR PURPOSES

Cases are divided on whether a court should intervene if the persons in control of a corporation manipulate the meeting date in order to avoid a proxy fight or in order to make a successful proxy fight more difficult.

a. *Schnell v. Chris–Craft Industries, Inc.,* 285 A.2d 437 (Del.1971) holds that such manipulation may constitute a breach of fiduciary duty by the persons in control of the corporation. See *Stahl v. Apple Bancorp., Inc.,* 579 A.2d 1115 (Del.Ch.1990) [decision to defer meeting date and rescind record date when faced with threatened proxy fight and tender offer not a breach of duty when no proxies had been solicited and the place of meeting not yet established]; see also *Alabama By–Products Corp. v. Neal,* 588 A.2d 255, 258 (Del.1991) [*Schnell* "should be reserved for those instances that threaten the fabric of the law or which by an improper manipulation of the law would deprive a person of a clear right."]

b. *In re Unexcelled, Inc.,* 281 N.Y.S.2d 173 (App.Div.1967) permits such manipulation based on a literal reading of the applicable business corporation act.

C. RECORD OWNERSHIP AND RECORD DATES

Eligibility to vote shares at a shareholders' meeting is determined by "record ownership" on a specified date, called the "record date."

1. RECORD OWNERSHIP

Corporations issue certificates representing shares in the name of designated persons and the names and addresses of those persons are recorded in the records of the corporation. That person is called the "record owner."

a. A person who buys shares from a current shareholder obtains possession of the certificate (along with an executed power of attorney from the old owner) and presents the certificate to the corporation, which cancels the old certificate and issues a new certificate in the name of the purchaser. The purchaser thereby becomes the new record owner.

b. A person may acquire ownership of shares without acquiring the certificates or going through the mechanics of arranging new certificates to be issued so that she can become the record owner. A person who owns shares but is not the record owner" is called the "beneficial owner".

   1) Where beneficial and record ownership are divided, the record owner has mere naked title to the shares and may be compelled to transfer that title to the beneficial owner by delivering certificates and/or executing the necessary power of attorney to enable the beneficial owner to become the record owner.

   2) Many shares of publicly held corporations are not held by the record owner. Rather ownership by the beneficial owner is reflected only by a book entry in the records of a brokerage firm.

2. RECORD DATE

Persons entitled to vote at a meeting are the record owners on a specific date called the "record date." The record date may be established by the board of directors; if it does not do so the record date is the date of the notice of the meeting. MBCA (1984) § 7.07.

a. Shares may be transferred on the books of the corporation after the record date, but persons who become record owners after the record date do not thereby obtain the power to vote.

b. Even though the record owner on the record date has legal authority to vote the shares at the meeting, the person who is the beneficial owner on the date of the meeting may compel the record owner to vote as the beneficial owner directs. This is usually done by requiring the beneficial owner to execute a blank proxy appointment form in favor of the beneficial owner. A court may compel the record owner to execute such a proxy appointment form.

c. Under many statutes, an entitlement to vote may be established by "closing the transfer books" on a specific date, thereby refusing to recognize subsequent transfers of securities and in effect freezing the transfer books until after the meeting. This is practically never used today in modern corporations and was eliminated as an option in the MBCA (1984).

d. Rules relating to record dates and record ownership are designed to simplify the meeting for the corporation which deals exclusively with the record owners and does not concern itself with the identity of the beneficial owner. *Salgo v. Matthews,* 497 S.W.2d 620 (Tex.Civ.App.1973).

e. MBCA (1984) § 7.23 authorizes corporations to establish procedures to recognize beneficial owners as owners of shares.

f. The SEC has adopted regulations that establish a procedure by which issuers of publicly held shares may communicate directly with assenting beneficial owners of shares held in book entry form by brokerage firms on behalf of their customers. The brokerage firms must poll their customers stating that their identities and addresses will be provided to the issuer unless the beneficial owner objects to that disclosure.

   1) Beneficial owners who do not object are known as "NOBOs" (nonobjecting beneficial owners).

   2) An issuer may be compelled to create a list of NOBOs at the request of a person also seeking the shareholders' list as a prelude to mounting a takeover attempt. *Sadler v. NCR Corporation,* 928 F.2d 48 (2d Cir.1991).

3. VOTING LIST

Corporations must prepare an accurate voting list of the record owners entitled to vote at a meeting. This list must be available for inspection at the meeting, and under most statutes must also be available for inspection for a period of time before the meeting. MBCA (1984) § 7.20. The failure to prepare this list does not affect the validity of any action taken at a meeting. Some state statutes impose a penalty on the corporate officer who is obligated to prepare a voting list but fails to do so.

4. MISCELLANEOUS VOTING RULES

Statutes of many states set forth rules as to who may vote shares in certain circumstances. MBCA (1984) § 7.24 contains more elaborate rules than most statutes. Older statutes provide:

a. Shares owned by a trustee may be voted by the trustee only if the shares are transferred to his or her name.

b. Shares held by an administrator, executor, guardian or conservator may be voted directly by him or her without transfer of the shares to his or her name. (Unlike a trustee, such fiduciaries have official evidences of their appointment.)

c. Shares held by a receiver may be voted directly by the receiver without transfer of the shares to his or her name if the order of appointment specifically authorizes the receiver to vote shares.

d. A shareholder who pledges shares may continue to vote them until the shares are transferred to the name of the pledgee, who thereafter may vote the shares.

5. INSPECTORS OF ELECTION

Disputes as to entitlement to vote are usually resolved by inspectors of election who may be granted discretionary authority to resolve disputes on the basis of the statutory voting rules and the records of the corporation. *Salgo v. Matthews,* 497 S.W.2d 620 (Tex.Civ.App.1973).

Caveat: Inspectors of election do not have authority to determine who are beneficial owners and permit them to vote. Rather their decisions are based solely on the records of the corporation.

D. CUMULATIVE VOTING

Elections of directors may be by cumulative voting or straight voting. In about six states constitutional or statutory provisions mandate cumulative voting in all elections of directors; in most states, however, each corporation may elect by appropriate provisions in its articles of incorporation whether or not to have cumulative voting. MBCA (1984) § 7.28.

In elections for directors, all directors run at large and not for or by places. Shareholders vote for candidates; they may not vote against a candidate except by voting in favor of other candidates.

1. STRAIGHT VOTING

In straight voting a shareholder may cast the number of votes equal to the number of shares he or she holds for candidates for each position to be filled on the board of directors.

Example: A shareholder with 30 voting shares in an election to fill three directorships may cast up to 30 votes for each of three candidates.

a. Under straight voting, shareholders holding a majority of the voting shares will elect the entire board of directors.

b. Straight voting is simple and easy to understand. As a result, it is widely used in publicly held corporations.

2. CUMULATIVE VOTING

In cumulative voting each shareholder determines the aggregate number of votes he or she may cast in an election by multiplying the number of shares he or she holds by the number of positions to be filled. Each shareholder may cast that number of votes for one or more candidates. MBCA (1984) § 7.28(a).

Example: In the foregoing example, the shareholder with 30 shares may cast an aggregate of 90 votes since there are three positions to be filled. Under cumulative voting she may cast all 90 votes for a single candidate or divide them between two or more candidates as she sees fit.

a. Since in directoral elections, all candidates run at large and not for or by places, cumulative voting permits minority shareholders to elect one or more directors in certain circumstances.

Example: In the foregoing example, if the shareholder with 30 shares votes all 90 votes for herself, she will be elected to the board unless three other candidates receive 91 or more votes each. If the other shareholders own a total of 85 shares, they cannot prevent her election. The other shareholders may cast 255 votes (3 × 85) but that is not enough to give each of three candidates 91 votes each. They may give candidate *X*, and *X*, 91 votes each, but they then have only 73 remaining votes to give to *X*, and hence cannot prevent the election of the minority shareholder as the third director.

b. The basic formula for determining whether a single block of shares may elect a director under cumulative voting is

$$\frac{S}{D + 1} + 1$$

where *S* equals the total number of shares voting and *D* equals the number of directors to be elected. The analogous formula to elect *N* directors is

$$\frac{nS}{D + 1} + 1.$$

3. ADVANTAGES AND DISADVANTAGES OF CUMULATIVE VOTING

The claimed advantages of cumulative voting are that it is more democratic, that it permits minority representation, and that it permits the election of a "watchdog director" to oversee the majority's management of the corporation. The claimed disadvantages are that it increases partisanship and divisiveness on the board, and that it is complex and confusing to shareholders.

Example: Bruce and Howard each own 12,500 shares of a family corporation. Bruce is the president and has pretty much run matters for several years. The board of directors consists of three directors—Bruce, Howard, and Bruce's wife, Eva. In prior years the board was elected by straight voting, but cumulative voting is required provided that one shareholder announces he plans to vote cumulatively. The statute provides that directors are elected by a plurality of the vote. At the election, Howard announces that he plans to vote cumulatively, but Bruce does not change his voting strategy and casts his votes as follows:

Bruce	—12,500
Eva	—12,500
Sarah X	—12,500.

Howard casts his votes cumulatively as follows:

Howard	—18,750
Clara (Howard's wife)	—18,750.

Howard and Clara are validly elected and now control the corporation. There is a three way tie for the third place on the board of directors and no third director was elected. See *Stancil v. Bruce Stancil Refrigeration, Inc.,* 344 S.E.2d 789 (N.C.App.1986).

4. MINIMIZATION OF THE EFFECT OF CUMULATIVE VOTING

Several devices minimize the impact of cumulative voting:

a. In states where cumulative voting is not required, a majority or other specified percentage of the shareholders may amend the articles of incorporation to eliminate cumulative voting entirely. *Maddock v. Vorclone Corp.,* 147 A. 255 (Del.Ch.1929).

b. The majority shareholders may be able to remove without cause the director or directors elected by the minority. MBCA (1984) § 8.08(a). However, the statutes of most states avoid circularity by limiting the power to remove a director elected by cumulative voting to situations where the vote to retain the director is insufficient to have elected him if the vote were cast in an election for directors in which cumulative voting was permitted. MBCA (1984) § 8.08(c).

Example: In the first example under part VII D 2, the shareholder with 30 shares has elected one director; the shareholders with 85 shares have elected two directors. The shareholders with 85 shares call a special meeting of shareholders to remove the minority director without cause, as shareholders may do under the state statute in question. On the removal motion, the minority shareholder casts her 30 shares against the removal. Since that vote would have been enough to elect one director at an election of directors, the removal motion fails even though 85 shares were voted in favor of it and on other issues a simple majority of the shareholders may resolve all questions.

c. Under many state statutes, if the board of directors consists of nine or more members, the board may be "classified" or "staggered" so that members are elected for two or three year terms with one half or one third being elected each year. MBCA (1984) § 8.06.

1) While the formal justification for classification is to ensure continuity of service on the board of directors, *Bohannan v. Corporation Com'n*, 313 P.2d 379 (Ariz.1957), the practical justification is usually more closely related to its impact on cumulative voting. *Stockholders Committee v. Erie Technological Products, Inc.*, 248 F.Supp. 380 (W.D.Pa.1965).

Example: A publicly held corporation incorporated in a state in which cumulative voting is mandatory has 10,000,000 voting shares outstanding and a board of directors consisting of 17 members. If all members of the board are elected each year, a bloc of 555,555 shares is sufficient to elect one director. If the board is "classified" or "staggered" so that six members are elected in each of two years and five are elected in the third year, it takes a bloc of 1,428,572 shares to elect a single director. A "public interest" organization might be able to find one half million sympathetic votes but find that one and one half million votes is beyond its vote generating capacity.

2) In the 1980s staggering the board of directors and preventing removal of directors without cause became a popular defense against unwanted takeover attempts in publicly held corporations, since these provisions prevent the purchasers of a majority of the shares through a cash tender offer from immediately replacing a majority of the board of directors.

Example: In the prior example, if directors cannot be removed without cause, an outside aggressor who purchases more than 5,000,000 voting shares cannot elect a majority of the entire board of directors until at least two annual elections of directors have been held.

Caveat: One case, *Wolfson v. Avery,* 126 N.E.2d 701 (Ill.1955) has invalidated a staggered election system on the ground that it violates the right of cumulative voting granted by the state constitution.

Caveat: One case, *Humphrys v. Winous Co.,* 133 N.E.2d 780 (Ohio 1956) upheld a staggered election system that placed only a single director in each class. Such a plan effectively destroys cumulative voting in that corporation and is prohibited under the statutes of all states, the Ohio statute having been amended to reverse this decision.

3) Some state statutes provide that a board of directors consisting of three or more members may be classified if cumulative voting is not permitted; if cumulative voting is permitted, the board may be classified only if it consists of nine or more members.

d. The board might be permanently reduced in size to reduce the impact of cumulative voting in much the same way as "staggering" the board does.

Example: In the mathematical formula relating to cumulative voting set forth earlier, reduction of the number of directorships to be filled reduces the size of the denominator of the fraction and therefore increases the value of that fraction.

e. Work of the board may be delegated to committees and the minority-elected director may not be named to committees.

f. The board may be "stage managed" so that all important decisions are made beforehand through informal discussions that do not include the minority-elected director. The meeting thereafter is entirely *pro forma,* without discussion, and conducted with a "quick gavel."

E. PROXY VOTING

A proxy is the grant of authority by a shareholder to someone else to vote his shares. The relationship is one of principal and agent.

1. TERMINOLOGY

Depending on the context, the term "proxy" may refer to the piece of paper granting the authority, to the grant of authority itself, or to the person holding the authority. The MBCA (1984) uses the term "proxy" in the last sense; it uses the phrase "proxy appointment" in the first sense and "appointment form" in the second sense. See MBCA (1984) § 7.22.

2. PREVALENCE

Voting by proxy is the norm in publicly held corporations where the large number of shareholders make personal voting impractical. Voting by proxy is less universal but still widely used in closely held corporations when a shareholder will not be personally present at a meeting.

Caveat: The use of proxies in registered public corporations is regulated in detail by the Securities and Exchange Commission; such regulation is described below in part XII.

3. FORMAL REQUIREMENTS

A proxy appointment must be in writing. Under many statutes a proxy appointment is valid for eleven months only, thus necessitating a new solicitation for every annual meeting. Under MBCA (1984) § 7.22(c) a proxy appointment is valid for a longer period if specified in the appointment form (but such an appointment would normally be revocable).

4. REVOCABILITY

Proxy appointments are generally revocable. Where revocable, the act of revocation may consist of any action inconsistent with the continued existence of the grant of authority.

Example: A shareholder executes a proxy appointment form solicited by management on April 1. Four days later he executes a competing appointment form on behalf of an insurgent group. The later appointment revokes the earlier one and the shares may be voted by the proxy named by the insurgent faction.

Example: A shareholder executes an appointment form but later decides to attend the meeting in person. If she votes in person, her act constitutes a revocation of the earlier proxy appointment.

5. IRREVOCABLE PROXY APPOINTMENTS

A proxy appointment is revocable even if it is stated to be irrevocable and even if consideration for the appointment is paid. *Stein v. Capital Outdoor Advertising, Inc.,* 159 S.E.2d 351 (N.C.1968).

Example: A shareholder executes an appointment form that states it is irrevocable for five years. The appointment is valid for five years under the MBCA (1984) but it may be revoked at any earlier time.

a. A purchased vote is generally thought to be against public policy and unenforceable.

   1) The New York Business Corporation Law, § 609(e), expressly prohibits a shareholder from selling his vote.

2) Case law involving purchased votes has usually invalidated the proxy appointment but the cases are not numerous.

3) In *Schreiber v. Carney,* 447 A.2d 17 (Del.Ch.1982), the court refused to invalidate an arrangement in which a major shareholder contracted, for a consideration, to vote its shares in the same manner as a majority of the independent shareholders. There was full disclosure of the arrangement to the independent shareholders.

b. To be irrevocable a proxy appointment must (i) state that it is irrevocable; and (ii) be "coupled with an interest." Examples of appointments that are "coupled with an interest" include:

1) A proxy who is a pledgee under a valid pledge of the shares;

2) A proxy who is a person who has agreed to purchase the shares under an executory contract of sale;

3) A proxy who is a person who has lent money or contributed valuable property to the corporation;

4) A proxy who is a person who has contracted to perform services for the corporation as an officer; and

5) A proxy appointment given in order to effectuate the provisions of a valid pooling agreement (described in the following part).

c. Some courts have upheld irrevocable proxy appointments that do not squarely fall within any of the above categories or meet the above requirements. Some statutes define the five situations described above as the only ones in which an irrevocable proxy appointment may be recognized.

F. SHAREHOLDER VOTING AGREEMENTS

Agreements among shareholders that they will vote their shares cooperatively or as a unit are called "pooling agreements" and are generally enforceable. MBCA (1984) § 7.31.

1. SCOPE OF VALID SHAREHOLDERS AGREEMENTS

Shareholder voting agreements are valid so long as they relate to issues, such as the election of directors, on which shareholders may vote. *E. K. Buck Retail Stores v. Harkert,* 62 N.W.2d 288 (Neb.1954); *Weil v. Beresth,* 220 A.2d 456 (Conn. 1966); *Ringling Bros.-Barnum & Bailey Combined Shows, Inc. v. Ringling,* 53 A.2d 441 (Del.1947). If the agreement deals with issues that are within the discretion of directors, the agreement may be invalid on the basis of principles discussed earlier (see part VI).

Example: Two shareholders agree that in the future (i) they will vote for each other as directors, (ii) they will use their best efforts to elect one as president and the other as secretary, and (iii) they will cause the corporation to pay each of them a salary of $10,000 per month. The first agreement is a valid pooling agreement; the other two are invalid unless enforceable under special statutes. Whether or not the first agreement is severable depends on the language of the agreement and the extent to which the valid portions standing alone are sufficient to effectuate the underlying purpose of the agreement.

2. FORMAL REQUIREMENTS

A few states have adopted statutes regulating pooling agreements, limiting the period during which a pooling agreement may continue (e. g., to ten years), requiring that copies of the pooling agreement be deposited at the principal office of the corporation, and so forth. However, in most states, the pooling agreement is a contractual voting device that has few procedural prerequisites and may continue indefinitely.

3. DETERMINATION OF HOW POOLED SHARES SHOULD BE VOTED

Pooling agreements may provide directly for the manner in which shares are to be voted, that is, for or against a specified proposal or motion. Or such matters may be the subject of subsequent negotiation and decision of the shareholders with some method of determining how the shares are to be voted in the event of a failure to agree. Resolution of disagreements is usually by arbitration, an arbiter, or by a decision of some person mutually trusted by all the participants.

4. ENFORCEMENT OF POOLING AGREEMENTS

Enforcement of a pooling agreement creates special problems since the shares are registered in the names of the individual shareholders on the books of the corporation.

a. In one leading case the Delaware Supreme Court enforced a pooling agreement by disqualifying the shares sought to be voted in violation of the agreement. *Ringling Bros.-Barnum & Bailey Combined Shows, Inc. v. Ringling,* 53 A.2d 441 (Del.1947). The effect of this was to defeat the purpose of the agreement since the disqualified votes were essential if the parties to the pooling agreement were to remain in control of the corporation.

b. Some state statutes specifically address the enforcement issue by authorizing specific performance of pooling agreements. See MBCA (1984) § 7.31(b).

c. New York makes irrevocable a proxy granted in connection with a pooling agreement. To take advantage of this enforcement device, the agreement should contain specific reference to the irrevocable nature of the proxy appointment, and should designate who may exercise the irrevocable proxy and under what circumstances.

G. VOTING TRUSTS

Voting trusts are a device by which the power to vote may be temporarily but irrevocably severed from the beneficial title to shares. Voting trusts are formal arrangements by which shares are registered in the name of one or more voting trustees on the books of the corporation.

1. COMMON LAW ATTITUDE

At common law there was great suspicion of voting trusts. While this attitude has been partially reversed by state statutes specifically recognizing and validating such trusts, some of the rules discussed below can be traced to early judicial hostility to the voting trust device. See generally *Tankersley v. Albright*, 514 F.2d 956 (7th Cir.1975), refusing to grant summary judgment on the validity of a common law voting trust.

On the other hand there has been some recognition that a voting trust should be viewed as simply another control mechanism that may in certain situations be the subject of abuse but generally is not more subject to criticism than other control devices. This perspective is most clearly set forth in *Oceanic Exploration Co. v. Grynberg,* 428 A.2d 1 (Del.1981).

2. STATUTORY REQUIREMENTS

State statutes uniformly recognize the validity of voting trusts that meet statutory requirements. See MBCA (1984) § 7.30. The most common such requirements are the following:

a. The agreement may not extend beyond ten years.

b. The agreement must be in writing.

c. A counterpart of the agreement must be deposited with the corporation at its registered office, to be subject to the right of inspection by (i) shareholders or (ii) holders of a beneficial interest in the trust.

d. Some states have imposed the further requirement that the essential purpose of the trust must be a proper one. Such a requirement probably serves little substantive purpose since carefully prepared testimony may validate a trust otherwise vulnerable while an unusually forthright or honest witness may inadvertently give testimony that leads to invalidation of the entire trust.

Example: The person creating a voting trust and persuading other shareholders to deposit their shares in the trust testifies that the purpose was to secure control of the corporation and thereby to preserve her employment with the corporation. This is not a proper purpose for a voting trust, and a trust formed for this purpose is invalid in some states.

Example: In the previous example, the creator of the trust testifies that its purpose was to assure the continued benefit of skilled and experienced management to the corporation. This is a proper purpose of a voting trust and a trust created for this purpose would be valid in the same state.

e. Because of the common law attitude toward voting trusts, discussed above, a voting trust agreement that fails to comply with all statutory requirements is considered invalid in its entirety in most states. Even though these requirements are basically simple ones that may be easily complied with, a number of cases have arisen in which these requirements have been ignored.

f. An arrangement that has most of the characteristics of a voting trust must fully meet the applicable statutory requirements if it is to be upheld even though it is formally a voting agreement or proxy arrangement rather than a voting trust. *Abercrombie v. Davies*, 130 A.2d 338 (Del.1957).

g. A voting trust may be set aside if later events cause its essential purpose to fail. *Selig v. Wexler,* 247 N.E.2d 567 (Mass.1969).

3. FINANCIAL RIGHTS WITHIN THE VOTING TRUST

Voting trust agreements usually provide that all dividends or other corporate distributions pass through to the beneficial owners of the shares so that all attributes of ownership other than the power to vote remain in the beneficial owners. Trustees may issue voting trust certificates to represent the beneficial interests; these certificates may be traded much as shares of stock are traded.

4. USES OF VOTING TRUSTS

Voting trusts may be used for a wide variety of purposes, including:

a. The preservation, retention or securing of control in a closely held corporation.

b. Assurance of temporary stability in control of a corporation coming out of bankruptcy or receivership or being created as the result of divestment from another corporation pursuant to the anti-trust laws. *Brown v. McLanahan,* 148 F.2d 703 (4th Cir.1945).

c. Elimination of a troublesome shareholder from participation in control of a corporation.

d. Obtaining credit, when required by creditors as a condition of providing needed financing to the corporation.

5. VOTING TRUSTS IN PUBLICLY HELD CORPORATIONS

Voting trusts are generally considered to be inconsistent with corporate democracy in corporations with publicly traded securities. The New York Stock Exchange usually refuses to list for trading a security that is partially held in a voting trust.

6. POWERS OF TRUSTEES OF VOTING TRUSTS

The power of trustees to vote on fundamental corporate depends on the specific language of the voting trust, *Clarke Memorial College v. Monaghan Land Co.,* 257 A.2d 234 (Del.Ch.1969). Some decisions have imposed equitable limitations on the power of trustees to approve damaging fundamental changes despite clear and broad language in the governing document. *Brown v. McLanahan,* 148 F.2d 703 (4th Cir.1945).

H. CLASSES OF SHARES AS A VOTING DEVICE

A device that permits the complete divorce of voting power from the ownership of a significant financial interest in the corporation without restriction or limitation is the creation of classes of shares with disproportionate voting and financial rights.

1. MODERN STATUTES

In most states, no limitation is placed on the creation of classes of shares without voting rights, with fractional or multiple votes per share, with power to select one or more directors, or with limited financial interests in the corporation. MBCA (1984) § 6.01. As a result classes of shares offer a high degree of flexibility and adaptability.

Example: Two shareholders each own 50 per cent of the stock of a corporation. After a series of disputes or disagreements, they agree to restructure the corporation. Two classes of shares are created, each with the power to elect two directors. Each shareholder holds all the shares of one class of shares. In addition a third class of shares, consisting of one share is issued to the corporation's attorney. The third class has a par value of $10 per share, is not entitled to receive dividends, may be redeemed at any time by unanimous vote of the other shareholders for its par value, and may receive only its par value upon dissolution of the corporation. This third class has the power to elect one director. A class with such limited financial rights and significant voting rights is a valid class of shares. *Lehrman v. Cohen,* 222 A.2d 800 (Del.1966).

Example: A corporation is to have two shareholders, one putting in $100,000, the other $50,000. They desire to share equally in control but in the ratio of their contributions (2:1) for financial purposes. The following plan is adopted: an equal number of shares of two classes of common stock, Class A common and Class B common, are authorized. Each class is entitled to elect two directors, but the dividend and liquidation rights of the Class A are twice those of Class B. The corporation then issues all the Class A common to one shareholder for 100,000 dollars and all the Class B common to the other shareholder for 50,000 dollars. If shares with multiple votes per share are authorized in the particular state, the shares may be identical in all financial respects, with the class received by the smaller contributor having two votes per share.

Example: A minority shareholder wishes to be assured of being treasurer of the corporation and to have a veto over all amendments to the articles of incorporation. The following plan is adopted: a special class of common shares is issued to the minority shareholder, and the articles of incorporation provide that (1) the treasurer must be a holder of that class of shares, and (2) the articles may be amended only by an affirmative vote of two-thirds of each class of shares, voting by classes. In other respects the classes have equal rights.

Example: There are three shareholders, each contributing the same amount of capital, but *C* is also contributing the basic idea and wants the same voting power as *A* and *B* combined. To effectuate this structure, voting and non-voting common shares (with equal dividend and liquidation rights) are issued in the following amounts:

Shareholder	Shares	
	Voting	Non–Voting
A	50	50
B	50	50
C	100	–0–

Example: *A, B,* and *C* are each contributing the same amount of capital, but *A* wants to be sure that *B* and *C* will not combine to oust him and cut off his income. The attorney suggests that *A* execute a five-year employment contract with the corporation guaranteeing him the specified income, renewable for a second five years at the option of *A*. To assure that *A* is assured of a right to participate in the board deliberations, three classes of stock are created, one for each shareholder, with each class having the power to elect one director.

I. SHARE TRANSFER RESTRICTIONS

Share transfer restrictions are contractual restrictions on the free transferability of shares. The most common kind of restrictions are option or buy/sell agreements that require a shareholder to offer his or her shares to the corporation or to other shareholders at a predetermined price upon the occurrence of specified events. Share transfer restrictions are increasingly the subject of statutory recognition. See MBCA (1984) § 6.27. They serve important functions in several different areas of modern corporate practice.

1. USE IN CLOSELY HELD CORPORATIONS

In the closely held corporation share transfer restrictions typically constitute contractual obligations to offer shares either to the corporation or to other shareholders, or to both successively, on the death or retirement of the shareholder or before she sells or disposes of the shares to other persons.

a. The restriction may take the form of—

1) An option running in favor of the corporation or shareholders to purchase at a designated or computable price shares owned by another shareholder upon the occurrence of a triggering event. *Allen v. Biltmore Tissue Corp.*, 141 N.E.2d 812 (N.Y.1957) (purchase option at original purchase price enforceable).

2) A mandatory buy-sell agreement obligating the corporation or shareholders to purchase the shares at a designated or computable price shares owned by another shareholder upon the occurrence of a triggering event.

3) A right of first refusal, giving the corporation or the shareholders an opportunity to meet the best price the shareholder has been able to obtain from third parties before selling to those parties.

b. The choice between these three forms of share transfer restrictions depends on the business needs of the shareholders.

Example: An option or a right of first refusal does not guarantee the shareholder a specified price, whereas a buy-sell agreement does.

Example: Because of the limited marketability of blocs of minority shares in a closely held corporation, a right of first refusal may not be practical since no outsider is likely to offer to purchase a minority bloc except at a significant discount.

c. Share transfer restrictions enable participants in the venture to decide who may participate in the venture. In effect they achieve the corporate equivalent of the partnership notion of *delectus personae.*

d. Share transfer restrictions ensure a stable management and protect against an unexpected change in the respective proportionate interests of the shareholders which might occur if one shareholder is able to quietly purchase shares of other shareholders.

e. Share transfer restrictions may materially simplify the estate tax problems of a deceased shareholder.

1) If the corporation or other shareholders are obligated to purchase the shares owned by the deceased shareholder (a buy-sell agreement) the estate is assured that a large, illiquid asset will be reduced to cash.

2) Either an option or a buy-sell agreement, if established in good faith, is accepted by the Internal Revenue Service as establishing the value of the shares for Federal estate tax purposes, thereby avoiding disputes with the tax authorities over valuation of closely held shares.

Example: *A* and *B* are brothers without families of their own or other close relatives. They enter into a buy/sell contract by which each agrees that the corporation will buy the shares of a deceased shareholder at a price of $50 per share. *A* dies at a time when it is clear that the shares are worth much more than $50.00. The agreement is not binding on the Internal Revenue Service since the contract indirectly benefits the natural object of the decedent's bounty and appears to be a device to minimize estate taxes.

Example: *A* and *B* are unrelated individuals each with families that include small children. They enter into the same agreement as in the previous example. If the agreement is binding on the shareholder's estate (as it normally would be) it is also binding on the Internal Revenue Service.

Caveat: Since closely held shares are not traded on a market, there is no reliable basis on which value can be determined. The Internal Revenue Service is apt to take an optimistic attitude as to the value of closely held shares in the absence of an agreement establishing the value.

f. Share transfer restrictions may be imposed to ensure the continued availability of the S corporation election, e.g., to ensure that the thirty-five shareholder maximum is not exceeded and that shares are not transferred to an ineligible shareholder which causes the loss of the S corporation election.

g. Share transfer restrictions in the form of buy-sell agreements may be used as a device to resolve deadlocks arising from equal voting power being held by two persons or factions.

2. USE IN PUBLICLY HELD CORPORATIONS

In a publicly held corporation, share transfer restrictions are used to prevent violations of the federal Securities Act where the corporation has issued unregistered shares pursuant to an exemption which would be lost if the shares are transferred to ineligible persons.

a. Share transfer restrictions are imposed on unregistered shares that are acquired by individual investors, warning that transfers are prohibited.

b. Instructions are placed with the transfer agent to refuse to accept unregistered shares for transfer, unless the transferee can establish to the satisfaction of the issuer or its transfer agent that the transfer does not cause loss of the exemption. Typically, this requires an opinion of counsel, affidavits by the purchaser or transferee, and possibly the acceptance of further restrictions on transfer by the purchaser or transferee.

c. Share transfer restrictions in publicly held corporations thus usually take the form of flat prohibitions on transfer.

d. Shares subject to restrictions on transfer are called "restricted securities." Rule 144 under the Securities Act of 1933 is the principal rule establishing when restricted securities may be sold on the public market; it basically establishes a two-year holding period requirement.

Caveat: A corporation may at the same time have securities outstanding that are publicly traded and freely transferable and restricted securities that may be transferable only upon compliance with substantial safeguards.

3. OTHER USES

Share transfer restrictions may be imposed where there are substantive limitations on who may be a shareholder or where governmental authorities wish to review, and possibly limit, who is participating in the ownership of a business.

Example: It may be unethical for persons who are not attorneys to share in the profits of a law practice. A professional corporation that is engaged in the practice of law may therefore impose share transfer restrictions prohibiting the conveyance or transfer of shares to a person who is not an enrolled attorney.

Example: The New York Stock Exchange for many years reserved the right to determine who may participate in the ownership of brokerage firms. This restriction was usually imposed by a share transfer restriction that prohibited transfers of shares of brokerage firms to persons without the prior consent of the Exchange. *Ling and Co. v. Trinity Sav. and Loan Ass'n,* 482 S.W.2d 841 (Tex.1972).

4. STRICT CONSTRUCTION

Share transfer restrictions are restraints on alienation and many courts have stated that they therefore should be strictly construed.

Example: An option or buy/sell agreement that applies to sales or donations of shares to "third persons" will usually not be violated by a transfer or gift to children or grandchildren.

Example: A restriction against sales "to the public" may not prohibit a sale to another shareholder.

Example: A prohibition against sale to an "officer-stockholder" may not prohibit a sale to a corporation owned by an officer-stockholder.

Example: A restriction without specific language of survivability may expire on the death of a shareholder. *Vogel v. Melish*, 196 N.E.2d 402 (Ill.App. 1964).

Caveat: Commentators point out that share transfer restrictions serve important roles within corporations and criticize the strict construction approach. As a result a trend toward a more liberal approach appears to be developing. *Bruns v. Rennebohm Drug Stores, Inc.*, 442 N.W.2d 591 (Wis. App.1989). When creating share transfer restrictions, however, an attorney must assume the worst and draft the clause on the assumption that a court will adopt the traditional strict construction approach.

5. PERMISSIBLE RESTRAINTS

At common law, the validity of a share transfer restraint depends on whether it "unreasonably restrains or prohibits transferability." An "unreasonable" restraint may be apparent on the face of the restraint or it may be found in the circumstances in which the restraint is applied.

Example: An outright prohibition on transfers of shares is invalid.

Example: A restriction imposed by bylaw or charter amendment cannot apply to previously outstanding shares unless the particular shareholder assents to the restriction. *B & H Warehouse, Inc. v. Atlas Van Lines, Inc.*, 490 F.2d 818 (5th Cir.1974). [There is some contrary authority but MBCA (1984) § 6.27(a), second sentence, codifies the result reached in *B & H Warehouse.*]

Example: Restrictions which prohibit transfers unless consent of the directors or other shareholders is first obtained are of doubtful validity since consent may be arbitrarily withheld. *Rafe v. Hindin,* 288 N.Y.S.2d 662 (App.Div.1968) (consent arrangement invalid).

a. The common law view about the enforceability of share transfer restrictions has caused several states to adopt legislation broadening the types of restrictions that may be enforced.

1) Delaware GCL § 202(c), for example, expressly validates restrictions that

(i) Require the prior consent by the corporation or the holders of a class of securities to a proposed transfer,

(ii) Require the approval of the proposed transferee by the corporation, or

(iii) Prohibit a transfer to designated persons or classes of persons, if such designation "is not manifestly unreasonable."

2) Delaware GCL § 202(d) provides that a restriction imposed to insure the continued availability of the S corporation election or any other tax advantage to the corporation is "conclusively presumed" to be for a reasonable purpose.

3) MBCA (1984) § 6.27 follows the broad outline of the Delaware statute. It authorizes share transfer restrictions to maintain the legal status of the corporation (e.g. under subchapter S or the integrated close corporation statutes), to preserve exemptions under securities laws, or "for any other reasonable purpose."

4) Both the Delaware GCL and MBCA (1984) expressly authorize traditional share transfer restrictions in the form of buy/sell or option agreements without limitation.

6. DURATION OF RESTRAINTS

There is no outer limitation on the duration of share transfer restrictions. It is probable that a restriction remains enforceable without regard to the rule against perpetuities or similar notions of "reasonableness" of duration.

a. Valid restraints normally continue so long as the need or justification for them exists.

b. Share transfer restrictions may terminate in several ways.

1) By express agreement of the shareholders involved.

Example: All shareholders decide to sell their shares to an outside purchaser despite a restriction against sales to "third persons" unless the shares are first offered to the corporation. The restriction is abandoned by agreement.

2) By abandonment or disuse.

Example: Shares are sold or transferred by two or three shareholders in isolated transactions without compliance with the restrictions and without objection by the various parties. The restrictions probably have been abandoned and later sales or transfers may be made free of the restrictions.

7. FORMALITIES AND NOTICE

Proper formalities must be followed when creating valid share transfer restrictions if they are to be binding on persons who may be unaware of them.

a. Most restrictions on transfer appear in the bylaws of the corporation; they may also appear in the articles of incorporation or in a contract between the corporation and shareholders, or among the shareholders themselves. MBCA (1984) § 6.27(a), first sentence.

b. Statutes require that a reference to a restriction be placed or "noted" on the face or back of share certificates subject to the restriction. MBCA (1984) § 6.27(b).

1) Article Eight of the Uniform Commercial Code adds that the reference or notation on the shares must be "conspicuous" if the restriction is to be enforceable against a person without actual knowledge of the restriction. MBCA (1984) §§ 6.27(b), 1.40(3) contain the same requirement.

Example: A printed heading in capitals or larger of other contrasting type or color is "conspicuous" under the UCC and MBCA (1984).

2) A person who knows of the valid restriction before she buys the shares is bound by the restriction, whether or not the above procedural requirements have been followed. MBCA (1984) § 6.27(b), last sentence.

3) Copies of restrictions appearing in contracts but not in articles of incorporation or bylaws may have to be filed with the corporation and be available for inspection under the statutes of some states.

8. TRADITIONAL SHARE TRANSFER RESTRICTIONS: OPTION OR BUY–SELL AGREEMENTS

By far the most common share transfer restriction is an agreement that upon a triggering event, the shareholder will offer his or her shares to the corporation or to other shareholders. In an option agreement, the offer must be made but the corporation or shareholders are not required to purchase the shares. In a buy/sell agreement, the purchasers are contractually committed to make the purchase.

a. The option or obligation to purchase the shares usually run either to the corporation or to some or all of the shareholders. MBCA (1984) §§ 6.27(d)(1), (d)(2), however, allows them to run to "the corporation or other persons (separately, consecutively, or simultaneously)". The choice is a matter of convenience.

1) The advantages of restrictions running to the corporation are:

(i) The corporation may be able to raise the necessary cash more easily than the shareholders individually.

(ii) The proportionate interests of the remaining shareholders are necessarily unaffected by a corporate acquisition of shares.

(iii) If life insurance is to be used to provide funds to purchase shares on the death of a shareholder, it is usually simplest to have the corporation pay the premium and own the policies on the lives of each shareholder rather than having each shareholder attempt to insure the life of every other shareholder.

(iv) Purchase by the corporation may be more attractive from a tax standpoint.

2) The disadvantages of restrictions running to the corporation are:

(i) If the corporation lacks the necessary legal capital to lawfully repurchase the shares at the time the repurchase is to be made, the restriction may be unenforceable.

Caveat: In this situation, the agreement may require the shareholders or some of them to agree to buy the shares if the corporation is not legally permitted to do so.

(ii) In an option arrangement running to the corporation alone, the corporation may decline to purchase, and anticipated control arrangements may be adversely affected.

(iii) Interested shareholders may generally participate in the decision whether or not the corporation should purchase and may vote their own self-interest. *Boss v. Boss,* 200 A.2d 231 (R.I.1964).

3) A disadvantage of having share transfer restrictions run to other shareholders is that one or more of the shareholders may be unable or unwilling to purchase their allotment of shares.

(i) The proportionate interests of the remaining shareholders will be affected if some purchase and some do not.

(ii) The agreement may provide that shares not purchased should be reoffered proportionately to the remaining shareholders.

(iii) In the absence of such a reoffer requirement it is likely that all unpurchased shares are thereafter considered free of all repurchase obligations.

(iv) If the number of shareholders is large the mechanics of having restrictions run to shareholders become complicated, and it usually is preferable for the restrictions to run to the corporation.

(v) An offer made simultaneously to all the shareholders may be withdrawn if some decline to accept. *Helmly v. Schultz,* 131 S.E.2d 924 (Ga.1963).

4) A shareholder may not always desire that his shares be offered proportionately to the other shareholders.

Example: A controlling shareholder with a son and daughter who are minority shareholders may wish to provide that all shares be first offered to his son and then to his daughter (or vice versa) rather than be offered proportionately. In this situation, the share transfer restriction becomes part of the shareholder's testamentary plan of disposition of his property.

b. The price provisions of shareholder option or buy-sell agreements raise the most difficult and important problems in drafting option or buy/sell agreements.

1) Closely held shares by definition have no market or quoted price, and one simply cannot refer to a "fair," "reasonable," or "market" price.

2) Since it usually is impossible to know whose shares will be first offered for sale under such an agreement, the basic goal in establishing such a mechanism is to be as fair as possible.

3) The following methods are widely used to establish a purchase price:

(i) A stated price. *Allen v. Biltmore Tissue Corp.,* 141 N.E.2d 812 (N.Y.1957).

(ii) Book value.

(iii) Capitalization of earnings.

(iv) Best offer by an outsider.

(v) Appraisal or arbitration, either by trained, impartial appraisers or arbitrators, or by directors or other shareholders.

(vi) A percentage of net profits to be paid for a specified number of years following the event which triggers the sale.

c. Any price fixed in the agreement or by periodic negotiation is enforceable in the absence of fraud, overreaching, or breach of fiduciary duty. *Yeng Sue Chow v. Levi Strauss & Co.,* 122 Cal.Rptr. 816 (App.1975); *In re Mather's Estate,* 189 A.2d 586 (Pa.1963).

Example: Two shareholders agree that the shares of the one who dies first shall be bought by the other at $1.00 per share. That agreement is enforceable even though at the time of death the shares are worth over $1000 per share.

Example: In the foregoing example, a court may deem the grossly inadequate price to necessitate a careful examination of the circumstances surrounding the execution of the agreement. Indications of overreaching or reliance by one shareholder on the other may constitute grounds for setting the argument aside for "unconscionability" or "fraud."

Example: A contract provides for the periodic adjustment of a fixed purchase price. A willful refusal by a younger shareholder to renegotiate the price under such an agreement might be considered fraudulent. A convenient "forgetfulness" on the part of such a shareholder might also be grounds for setting aside the obsolete price. See *Collins v. Universal Parts Co.,* 260 So.2d 702 (La.App.1972).

Example: The two shareholders agree that if they have a dispute over policy, A will set a price on his shares, and B will have the option either to purchase A's shares at that price or sell her shares to A at that price. The agreement is enforceable.

d. "Book value" is by far the most popular method of valuation.

1) This value may be computed by a simple division of a balance sheet figure by the number of outstanding shares and tends to increase as the profitability of the business increases.

2) Courts may order adjustments in this value to reflect reality and avoid a "blind adherence" to whatever figures are set forth in the books of the corporation. *Aron v. Gillman,* 128 N.E.2d 284 (N.Y.1955); *Jones v. Harris,* 388 P.2d 539 (Wash.1964).

3) Book value is based on the application of specific accounting conventions to corporate transactions and as a result book value may not be a realistic estimate of value. Carefully drafted agreements may require adjustments to be made from the corporation's accounting records, and in extreme situations a court may require book value to be adjusted to be a more realistic estimate of value in the absence of specific directions as to how the calculation should be made.

Example: An accounting convention requires assets to be valued at historical cost rather than current market value. A corporation which owns real estate acquired decades earlier at a low price may have a book value that considerably understates the true liquidating value of the assets.

Example: Investments in readily marketable securities may be shown on the books at cost even though current market values may be obtained from the financial tables of any newspaper.

Example: Accounting conventions permit corporations to include certain things as assets which may never be realized on liquidation; for example costs of initial formation or of "good will" acquired in connection with the purchase of another business. It may be appropriate to eliminate such "assets" from the balance sheet before computing book value.

Example: If a corporation utilizes accelerated depreciation schedules for tax purposes, it may be desirable to specify that straight line depreciation should be used to compute book value for valuation purposes.

Example: If inventory is valued on a LIFO ["last-in first-out"] basis for tax purposes, it may be desirable to require the inventory to be valued at a more realistic figure before computing book value.

e. Appraisal of the value of closely held stock is designed to determine the price at which a ready willing and able buyer and seller would agree upon as the sale price of the shares. Prior purchases and sales of the shares, if any, may be influential in making this determination. In the absence of reliable prior sales, appraisal usually is based on a capitalization of earnings.

Example: If a corporation has average earnings of $50,000 a year over the last three years, and it is reasonable to capitalize those earnings at ten per cent, the capitalized value of the corporation is $500,000

Example: If the reasonable capitalization ratio were eight per cent, the business would be valued at $625,000 (625,000 × .08 = 50,000); if it were fifteen per cent, it would be valued at $333,333 (333,333 × .15 = 50,000).

1) The most appropriate capitalization ratio may be justified by the appraiser on the basis of earnings ratios of comparable publicly held businesses, the appraiser's general experience with valuing businesses in the particular industry, or simply the appraiser's intuitive "feel" as to how risky a specific business is.

2) Valuation based on capitalization of earnings may also be affected by different assumptions about the level of average earnings in the future, and whether different assets should be capitalized at different rates.

3) An appraiser or arbitrator will usually take into account all the various possible methods of valuation. He may consider, for example, (i) book value, (ii) capitalized value, (iii) estimated liquidation value if the assets were sold and (iv) sales prices of shares in isolated transactions in the past. He may take an average of these values, or if three closely agree, may base his valuation on only those three.

4) After the value of the overall business is obtained, a tentative per share value is usually obtained by a simple division by the number of outstanding shares.

   (i) Complications may arise if senior securities must be valued.

   (ii) The appraiser or arbitrator may find it appropriate to apply one or more discounts from the tentative per share value in order to reflect lack of marketability, the minority status of the shares in question if they have no chance of sharing in control, and a variety of other factors that may affect the value of the shares

J. REVIEW QUESTIONS

VII–1. If a corporation does not impose larger quorum and voting requirements than specified in the statute, what is the minimum number of shares necessary to enact an ordinary resolution at a shareholders meeting?

VII–2. May a corporation create shares with more or less than one vote per share?

VII–3. What is the difference between record ownership and beneficial ownership?

VII–4. Why does a corporation need to set a record date for voting at a meeting or for payment of dividend?

VII–5. Cumulative voting permits minority representation on the board.

True _______ False _______

VII–6. The opposite of cumulative voting is noncumulative voting.

True _______ False _______

VII–7. In a struggle for control, shareholder A gives a proxy appointment to the management faction. A week later A receives a solicitation from the insurgent faction and also signs their proxy appointment form. Which appointment form will control?

VII–8. A proxy appointment may be made irrevocable if it is supported by consideration and is stated to be irrevocable.

True _______ False _______

VII–9. What is the difference between a pooling agreement and a voting trust?

VII–10. Why are share transfer restrictions commonly used in closely held corporations?

VII–11. Are share transfer restrictions ever used in publicly held corporations?

VII–12. The president of Compliance Corp. calls a special meeting of shareholders expressly for the purposes of considering a merger with Ready, Ltd., and such other matters as might come before the meeting. Notice to such effect is sent to all shareholders. At the meeting the holders of a majority of shares are present.

Two shareholder-directors, N.E. Gative and Ken Servative, voice strong opposition to the merger. A shareholder then proposes that Gative and Servative be removed as directors without cause. This proposal is passed by a majority vote. L. I. Berl and Red Stamp are then elected as successor directors. The shareholders decide that the board should retain counsel and continue negotiation with Ready, Ltd., concerning the proposed merger. Several months later, the plan of merger is finalized, approved by the board of directors, and proposed to the shareholders of Compliance Corp. The plan receives the necessary shareholder vote of both Ready, Ltd. and Compliance Corp.

Meanwhile, prior to the filing of the articles of merger, Gative and Servative commence an action to enjoin the merger and for their reinstatement as directors. What result? [This question and answer are drawn from Ballantine, Problems in Law 236 (5th Ed. 1975).]

VII–13. The shareholders of D Corporation request in writing that the president of the corporation call a meeting for the following purposes: (1) to vote upon a resolution endorsing the administration of the former president who had been removed by the directors and demanding that he be reinstated as president; and (2) to vote upon a proposal to hear charges against certain directors and vote upon their removal. The president refuses to call the meeting on the ground that neither of the proposals are proper for a meeting of the shareholders. Will an order in the nature of mandamus lie to require the president to call the meeting?

VIII

DIRECTORS

Analysis

H. Directors' Liability for Actions
  1. Avoidance of Liability by Filing Written Dissent
  2. Resignation
  3. Statutory Limitation of Liability

I. Reliance on Opinion of Others
  1. Scope of Protected Reliance

J. Committees of the Board of Directors
  1. Types of Committees and Their Authority
  2. Executive Committee
  3. Audit Committee
  4. Nominating Committees
  5. Compensation Committees
  6. Public Policy Committees
  7. Litigation Committees

K. Review Questions

A. NUMBER AND QUALIFICATIONS OF DIRECTORS

In most states today the board of directors may consist of one or more members. MBCA (1984) § 8.03(a). Residential or shareholding requirements for directors, while once common, have been largely eliminated. MBCA (1984) § 8.02. The MBCA (1984) states expressly that only individuals may serve as directors; in some European legal systems an entity may serve as a director but there appears to have been no recent attempt to broaden state statutes to permit this practice.

1. NUMBER

Historically, three directors were required and a few states retain this requirement.

a. The New York Business Corporation Law, § 702, and the statutes of a few other states allow boards of one or two directors only where there are one or two shareholders.

b. Most states simply state that the board may consist of one or more members without qualification.

c. The number of directors is usually established in the bylaws; if the bylaws are silent the number may be set by the statute as either the minimum permitted in the state or the number of initial directors set forth in the articles of incorporation.

2. CHANGE IN THE SIZE OF BOARD OF DIRECTORS

The number of directors may be increased or decreased by amendments to the bylaws, but a decrease does not have the effect of eliminating or shortening the term of any sitting director.

a. Since the directors generally have power to amend bylaws, the board of directors in effect has power to determine its own size under most state statutes.

b. MBCA (1984) § 8.03(b) and the statutes of a few states impose limits on the extent to which a board of directors may utilize its power to amend bylaws to increase or decrease its own size without shareholder approval. The MBCA prohibits an increase or decrease of more than 30 per cent except by action of the shareholders.

1) MBCA (1984) § 8.03(c) permits corporations to create a variable-sized board of directors: the shareholders or the bylaws establish a maximum and minimum size and authorize the board of directors to determine the actual size within those limits from time to time.

2) A variable-size board of directors may be useful in a publicly held corporation subject to the MBCA (1984) because it gives the board of

directors needed flexibility in deciding to add one or more specific individuals to the board when necessary or not to fill vacancies as they occur, yet minimizes the possible manipulation of the size of the board to serve narrower purposes and preserves the ultimate power of the shareholders over the size of the board.

c. Some cases recognize that bylaws setting the number of directors may be amended informally.

Example: The shareholders elect four directors when the bylaws specify that the board shall consist of only three directors. In some states, this constitutes an implied amendment of the bylaws.

Caveat: This is not a desirable practice since it injects future uncertainty as to the number of directors to be elected and reduces the value of the written bylaws.

B. MEETINGS, QUORUM, NOTICE AND RELATED MATTERS

Regular meetings of the board occur at the times specified in the bylaws. Special meetings may be called by the persons specified in the bylaws.

1. NOTICE

No notice of regular meetings is required. MBCA (1984) § 8.22(a). Special meetings may be called upon two days notice unless a longer or shorter notice is required or permitted by the bylaws. MBCA (1984) § 8.22(b).

2. QUORUM

A quorum of directors consists of a majority of the directors except that a greater number may be specified by the bylaws. MBCA (1984) § 8.24(b) and the statutes of a few states permit the bylaws to reduce a quorum to one-third of the board of directors.

a. Generally, only lawfully elected directors may be counted toward quorum or voting requirements. *Dillon v. Scotten, Dillon Co.*, 335 F.Supp. 566 (D.Del. 1971).

b. Directors personally interested in the transaction may not be counted towards quorum or voting requirements unless the articles of incorporation specifically so provide. *Sterling v. Mayflower Hotel Corp.*, 93 A.2d 107 (Del.1952).

c. A board of directors may act on a specific matter only if a quorum is present when the action is taken. MBCA (1984) § 8.24(c). Most state statutes are silent on this matter.

Caveat: This rule for directors' action is the opposite of the rule prescribed for shareholders. MBCA (1984) § 7.25(b) provides that at a shareholders meeting, once a quorum is present the meeting may proceed to its conclusion and the withdrawal of one or more shareholders does not destroy the quorum. The opposite rule is established for directors in MBCA (1984) § 8.24(c).

d. The board of directors may sometimes be able to act even though a quorum is not present where vacancies exist and the action to be taken is the filling of such vacancies. Depending on the language of the specific statute, this power may exist:

1) Only when the number of directors *in office* is less than a quorum; or

2) When the number of directors *acting* is less than a quorum even though the number *in office* is greater than a quorum. *Jacobson v. Moskowitz,* 261 N.E.2d 613 (N.Y.1970).

Example: A board consists of eleven members. A quorum is six. Because of deaths and resignations the number in office is five. Under both constructions, the five remaining directors may meet and fill the six vacancies.

Example: In the prior example, the number in office is eight. The remaining directors are bitterly divided, five-three, and the three minority directors refuse to attend meetings in order to prevent the existence of a quorum and the approval of actions that they do not favor. Under statutes of the second type, the five directors, even though less than a quorum, may fill the vacancies. Under statutes of the first type, the five directors could not act because the number of directors in office (eight) is more than a quorum.

3) MBCA (1984) § 8.10(a)(3) adopts position 1) above.

e. Some courts have treated a willful refusal to attend a meeting as a breach of fiduciary duty. *Gearing v. Kelly,* 182 N.E.2d 391 (N.Y.1962). However, other courts have recognized this tactic as part of a struggle for control and have held that it should not be treated as improper.

f. In closely held corporations, an important planning device that creates a veto power on the part of minority shareholders is to increase the quorum requirement for the board of directors to all the directors, and to require unanimous votes to approve specific actions.

1) If a minority shareholder has power to elect at least one director, these provisions assure minority participation on all directoral matters.

2) These provisions increase the likelihood of a deadlock.

3. VOTING

Directors vote on a per capita basis. A majority vote of those present at a meeting where a quorum is present is necessary for the board to act. MBCA (1984) § 8.24(c). The bylaws may increase the vote necessary for approval of an action up to and including unanimity.

a. Del. GCL § 141(d) permits certificates of incorporation to provide that some directors may have a fractional vote rather than a per capita one. Presumably fractional votes may mirror the relative shareholdings of individual shareholders.

b. In closely held corporations, an important control device is to provide a unanimity requirement for all directoral action.

4. OBJECTION TO NOTICE

A director waives objection to the adequacy of notice of a meeting by attending the meeting, unless he or she attends for the sole purpose of objecting to the transaction of any business and does not participate in the business undertaken at the meeting. Even minimal participation is likely to be construed as a waiver. MBCA (1984) § 8.23(b).

C. COMPENSATION

Directors traditionally serve without compensation, it being assumed that their financial interest in the corporation or feelings of prestige encourage them to serve on a gratuitous basis. Increasingly, in publicly held corporations, directors are receiving significant and substantial compensation as inducements to serve and to devote substantial attention to corporate affairs. See MBCA (1984) § 8.11.

D. REMOVAL AND RESIGNATION OF DIRECTORS

1. REMOVAL OF DIRECTORS

Directors may be removed by shareholders, with or without cause, under the statutes of most states. MBCA (1984) § 8.08. Articles of incorporation, however, may limit the power of removal to removal for cause. Removal by judicial action is also authorized under the statutes of some states.

a. The power to remove directors without cause tends to assure fealty by the board to the majority shareholder.

b. Many publicly held corporations have eliminated the power of shareholders to remove directors without cause as a defensive measure against unwanted takeovers. This provision is usually coupled with the staggering of the election of directors.

c. Under the statutes of some states, a court may also remove a director for cause specified in the statute, upon the petition of a specified percentage of the shareholders. MBCA (1984) § 8.09, for example, permits court removal for "fraudulent or dishonest conduct, or gross abuse of authority or discretion." Removal for cause by judicial action is appropriate in at least two types of situations:

   1) In a publicly held corporation, a judicial proceeding to remove a director for cause, when the director refuses to resign, may be simpler and less expensive than holding a shareholders' meeting to remove the director, an action that must be preceded by a proxy solicitation.

   2) Judicial removal may also be used in a closely held corporation where the director charged with misconduct declines to resign and possesses the voting power as shareholder to prevent his removal.

2. RESIGNATION OF DIRECTORS

The resignation of directors in most states is not expressly covered by statute. MBCA (1984) § 8.07 permits resignation either immediately or at a future date; a resignation at a future date permits the departing director to participate in the selection of his or her successor.

E. FILLING OF VACANCIES

Vacancies created by resignation, death or removal of a director, may be filled either by the board of directors or the shareholders. MBCA (1984) § 8.10(a). Under older statutes, vacancies created by increasing the size of the board could only be filled by the shareholders, but most modern state statutes permit all vacancies to be filled by the board of directors without regard to the way the vacancies were created.

F. TERM OF OFFICE

Directors serve for the term for which they were elected and a director continues to serve, despite the expiration of her term, until her successor "is elected and qualifies or until there is a decrease in the number of directors." MBCA (1984) § 8.05(e).

1. HOLDOVER DIRECTORS

If directors are not elected at an annual meeting for any reason, or the required annual meeting is never held, the directors then in office "hold over" until their successors are selected.

a. This follows directly from the language of the corporation statute.

b. This principle applies (1) where meetings are held erratically, if at all, and (2) in deadlock situations where the shareholders are evenly divided and unable to elect successors. *Gearing v. Kelly*, 182 N.E.2d 391 (N.Y.1962).

Example: *A* and *B* are the sole shareholders in a corporation, each owning fifty per cent of the shares. There are four directors, elected by straight voting, two in effect having been named by *A* and two by *B*. One of *A* 's directors dies, and the vacancy is validly filled by the board of directors by a 2 to 1 vote with a person acceptable to *B* but not to *A*. The person so elected remains in office indefinitely since in the next election for directors the election will be deadlocked when *B* casts votes for three or four directors.

Example: In the foregoing example, directors are to be elected by cumulative voting. By casting all his votes for two candidates, *A* is able to restore the prior two-two division of the board and the hold-over director provision will have no application.

G. DECISIONS MUST BE MADE AT MEETINGS

The common law rule is that the power invested in directors to control and manage the affairs of a corporation is not "joint and several," but "joint only," and that directors may take action only "as a body at a properly constituted meeting."

1. RATIONALE

The theory is that shareholders are entitled to a decision reached only after group discussion and deliberation. Views may be changed as a result of discussion, and the sharpening of minds as a result of joint deliberation improves the decisional process.

2. IMPLICATIONS

This rule leads to several subsidiary conclusions:

a. The independent, seriatim approval of an act by each director individually, is not effective directoral action. *Baldwin v. Canfield*, 1 N.W. 261 (Minn.1879), mod. 1 N.W. 276 (Minn.1879).

b. Directors may not vote by proxy.

c. Formalities as to notice, quorum, and similar matters must be fully adhered to.

3. MODERN STATUS OF THE RULE

The common law rule will likely be applied today in situations where it appears that no benefit was received from the transaction by the corporation. *Hurley v. Ornsteen,* 42 N.E.2d 273 (Mass.1942); *Mosell Realty Corp. v. Schofield,* 33 S.E.2d 774 (Va.1945).

a. The rule has the undesirable consequence of permitting a corporation to use its own internal procedural defects as a sword to undo undesired transactions. E.g., *Mosell Realty Corp. v. Schofield,* 33 S.E.2d 774 (Va.1945). This basic injustice is heightened because a person dealing with a corporation usually has no way of verifying that formalities were in fact completely and fully followed.

b. Several exceptions have been created, including "estoppel," "ratification," and "acquiescence." E.g., *Meyers v. El Tejon Oil & Refining Co.,* 174 P.2d 1 (Cal. 1946).

Example: The directors of a corporation informally agree that a particular transaction is desirable. Even though such informal directoral action is ineffective to formally authorize the transaction under the common law rule, it constitutes acquiescence in and ratification of the very same transaction, thereby binding the corporation. *Sherman v. Fitch,* 98 Mass. 59 (1867); *Phillips Petroleum Co. v. Rock Creek Mining Co.,* 449 F.2d 664 (9th Cir.1971); *Mickshaw v. Coca Cola Bottling Co.,* 70 A.2d 467 (Pa.Super.1950).

c. Most state statutes allow the board of directors or a committee of the board to participate in a meeting by conference telephone or similar communications equipment which enables all persons participating in the meeting to hear each other at the same time. See MBCA (1984) § 8.20(b).

1) Such participation constitutes "presence" in person at a meeting so as to satisfy the quorum requirement.

2) This provision may be of considerable practical usefulness where directors are widely scattered, or where one or more of them are distant from the location where regular meetings are held.

3) The fact that specific statutory authorization was felt to be necessary for a common sense idea such as telephonic meetings shows that the common law rule that directors can act only in meetings has some continued vitality.

d. The rigid requirement that all directoral decisions must be made at a duly convened meeting makes very little sense today when applied to a close corporation where all the shareholders are active in the business. In that situation even the requirement of a formal meeting is likely to be considered a meaningless formality.

e. Most state statutes now permit directors to act by unanimous written consent without a formal meeting. MBCA (1984) § 8.21.

1) A written consent has the same effect as a unanimous vote.

Caveat: An informal action, not evidenced by a written consent, has been held to be invalid on the ground that the statute has "preempted the field." *Village of Brown Deer v. Milwaukee,* 114 N.W.2d 493 (Wis.1962). This holding is also consistent with the traditional common law rule.

2) This modest and sensible provision solves many problems created by the common law rule that directors' actions must be taken at meetings. It requires, however, that a written consent be prepared and be executed, requirements that are often not met in informally run closely held corporations.

Caveat: The unanimous consent procedure is not available if one director is unwilling to sign the consent. Even though that director is in the minority, a formal meeting of the board of directors should thereafter be held to approve the transaction.

H. DIRECTORS' LIABILITY FOR ACTIONS

Individual directors are sometimes faced with the issue of responding to a decision by a majority of the board of directors to authorize the corporation to enter into transactions which the director feels to be precipitate, risky, or illegal. Caution is required in this respect because in some circumstances the director may be held personally responsible even though he or she in fact objected to the transaction and actually voted against it.

1. AVOIDANCE OF LIABILITY BY FILING WRITTEN DISSENT

Statutes provide that a director is presumed to have assented to an action unless he or she in fact votes against the action and that his or her dissent appears in the written minutes or a written dissent is thereafter timely filed. MBCA (1984) § 8.24(d).

a. Under this provision, an abstention or silence when an oral vote on a motion is taken is the equivalent of voting in favor of the action.

b. A director who did not speak up against the action at the time it was voted upon may not later claim that she voted against the action.

c. A written dissent must be filed with the secretary of the meeting or the secretary of the corporation by certified mail within a short period after the meeting.

d. These requirements may have a psychological effect upon the other directors who realize that at least one director considers the conduct sufficiently questionable so as to seek legal protection.

e. These requirements may also afford notice to shareholders or others examining the records that the transaction should be examined carefully because at least one director questioned the propriety of the transaction.

2. RESIGNATION

The director fearing liability may resign as director, though if the resignation occurs after the objectionable transaction is approved, liability may be avoided only if the director files the appropriate dissent.

3. STATUTORY LIMITATION OF LIABILITY

The statutes of many states permit corporations to limit the liability of directors by specific provision in articles of incorporation. See part XIV B 4.

I. RELIANCE ON OPINION OF OTHERS

Depending on the language of the specific state statute, a director may be able to avoid liability in some situations by showing that he or she relied on the opinion of others in good faith. MBCA (1984) § 8.30(b).

1. SCOPE OF PROTECTED RELIANCE

Generally, a reliance defense is not available to a director who has actual knowledge about, or expertise with respect to, the issue in question. MBCA (1984) § 8.30(c). Statutes permit reliance on one or more of the following:

a. The written opinion of legal counsel for the corporation (though, as a practical matter, reliable and unqualified written opinions may be difficult to obtain on questionable transactions).

b. Financial reports prepared by the corporation or by its auditors or accountants.

c. Statements by officers or employees of the corporation with respect to matters within their authority.

d. Reports by committees of the board other than committees on which the director serves.

J. COMMITTEES OF THE BOARD OF DIRECTORS

Where a board of directors is large, it may be convenient to appoint one or more committees to perform certain of the functions of the board of directors. MBCA (1984) § 8.25. The committee may specialize on one area of concern to the board, e.g., a committee on executive compensation or an audit committee, or may function as a substitute for the full board between meetings of the full board, i. e., an executive committee.

1. TYPES OF COMMITTEES AND THEIR AUTHORITY

MBCA (1984) § 8.25 deals only with committees composed exclusively of members of the board of directors which are authorized to exercise functions of the board of directors.

a. Boards of directors may create advisory committees that may consist of directors and possibly other people as well, e.g. members of management or members of the general public. These committees may render advice or make recommendations to the board of directors. MBCA (1984) § 8.25 does not deal with advisory committees; it applies only to committees of the board exercising directoral functions in lieu of the board of directors.

b. A committee formed under MBCA (1984) § 8.25 may be created only by a majority of the directors in office (or the larger number required by a supermajority provision if one has been adopted). This is a supermajority provision since the normal vote needed to adopt a proposal in the board of directors is a majority of the directors present at the time a quorum is present.

c. A committee formed under MBCA (1984) § 8.25 must have two or more members.

d. The creation of a committee and the delegation to it of authority does not of itself constitute compliance with the directors' statutory duty of care.

e. MBCA (1984) § 8.25(e) lists eight functions that must be exercised by the full board of directors and may not be delegated to a § 8.25 committee.

   1) This list is not based on the traditional ordinary/extraordinary matters distinction but is designed to prevent delegation of matters that have immediate and irrevocable effect (such as the declaration of a dividend), matters that may become irrevocable without swift action, and matters that will cause changes of position by others that cannot be rectified.

Example: Nondelegable functions include authorization of dividends, approval or recommendation to shareholders of fundamental actions such as mergers, amendments to articles of incorporation, and the like, amendment of bylaws, approval of reacquisitions of shares or the sale of shares, and the creation of classes or series of shares out of blank shares.

2) All other matters may be decided by committees acting on behalf of the board of directors.

Example: A derivative suit is filed by a shareholder seeking to set aside a transaction between the corporation and a trust created by the chief executive officer for the benefit of her children. A demand is made on the board of directors, and the board responds by creating a § 8.25 committee of outside disinterested directors to determine whether maintenance of that suit is in the best interests of the corporation. The committee decides that it is not in the best interests of the corporation to pursue this litigation and that a motion to dismiss the litigation with prejudice should be filed; this decision has the same force as though it were made by the board of directors itself. As to the circumstances when such a motion should be granted see part XVIII D 1.

2. EXECUTIVE COMMITTEE

An executive committee generally provides oversight over general corporate matters during periods when the board of directors is not sitting.

a. Executive committees usually consist only of directors who are employees or executives of the corporation.

b. Under older statutes, an executive committee may be created only if specific provision therefor appears in the articles of incorporation or bylaws. Under the MBCA (1984) § 8.25, any committee, including an executive committee, may be created by a corporation unless the articles of incorporation or bylaws specifically provide otherwise.

c. Some statutes that specifically refer to executive committees impose limitations on the powers of such committees apparently to ensure that there will not be a "run away" committee.

d. Delegation of authority to an executive committee generally does not relieve the board of directors, or any member, of any responsibility imposed upon it or them.

3. AUDIT COMMITTEE

Publicly held corporations have audit committees; such committees are now required by SEC regulation. Audit committees perform functions such as the following:

a. Recommend the accounting firm to be employed by the corporation as its independent auditor.

b. Consult with the accounting firm so chosen to be the independent auditors with regard to the plan of audit.

c. Review, in consultation with the independent auditors, the report of audit and the accompanying management letter of response, if any.

d. Consult with the independent auditors (out of the presence of management) with regard to the adequacy of the internal accounting controls and similar matters.

e. Report to the full board of directors the results of the audit and make recommendations for changes to improve the adequacy of the control processes.

4. NOMINATING COMMITTEES

Most publicly held corporations now have nominating committees.

a. The role of the nominating committees usually depends on the board of directors and its relation to the Chief Executive Officer (CEO).

b. In some corporations, the nominating committee has a significant voice in the selection of candidates to serve on the board of directors. In other corporations, the CEO continues to have the predominant voice in the selection of candidates.

c. Nominating committees may perform some or all of the following functions:

   1) Establish qualifications for directors.

   2) Establish procedures for identifying possible nominees who meet these criteria.

   3) Review the performance of current directors and recommend, where appropriate, that sitting directors be removed or not reappointed.

   4) Recommend the appropriate size and composition of the board of directors.

5. COMPENSATION COMMITTEES

Most publicly held corporations also have compensation committees to resolve issues of compensation and retirement benefits. Again, in a specific corporation the committee's role depends on the board of directors and its relation to the CEO, though virtually all compensation committees consist entirely of nonmanagement directors. Such committees may perform some or all of the following functions:

a. Review and approve (or recommend to the full board) the annual salary, bonus and other benefits, direct and indirect, of the CEO, other management directors and other designated members of senior management.

b. Review and submit to the full board of directors recommendations concerning new executive compensation or stock plans.

c. Establish, and periodically review, the corporation's policies in the area of so-called management perquisites.

d. Review compensation policies relating to members of the board of directors.

e. Review the operation of retirement plans for employees.

f. Review conflict of interest transactions between the corporation and a director.

Caveat: The audit, nominating and compensation committees are particularly important when assessing the balance of power between management and the board of directors in a publicly held corporation. As described subsequently in part IX, CEOs in the past have tended to dominate boards of directors; the extent to which the board of directors has developed independence from the CEO varies widely from corporation to corporation. As the independence of the board of directors increases, the power and importance of these committees has also increased.

6. PUBLIC POLICY COMMITTEES

Some publicly held corporations have created public policy committees to review such matters as the charitable activities of the corporation, the role of the corporation in community affairs, political activities by the corporation (to the extent permitted by public policy), equal opportunity policies established by the corporation, and non-financial policies such as worker safety, environmental impact, and product safety.

7. LITIGATION COMMITTEES

When derivative litigation is filed by a shareholder on behalf of the corporation, a litigation committee composed of disinterested directors may be created to review the litigation and determine whether its pursuit is in the best interest of the corporation. Within a broad range courts respect the decision of an independent litigation committee and may dismiss derivative litigation based on the decision of such a committee. (See generally part XVIII.)

K. REVIEW QUESTIONS

VIII–1. Directors who are unavoidably absent should vote by proxy.

True _______ False _______

VIII–2. Directors may only act collegially in meetings.

True _______ False _______

IX

OFFICERS

Analysis

F. Officers' Liability on Corporate Obligations
- *1. Express Guarantee*
- *2. Confusion of Roles*
- *3. Statutory Liability*
- *4. Personal Participation in Tortious Conduct*
- *5. Authority*

G. Corporate "Notice" or "Knowledge"
- *1. General Rule*
- *2. Agent Acting Adversely to Principal*
- *3. Corporate Criminal Responsibility*

H. Tenure of Officers and Agents
- *1. Employment Contracts in General*
- *2. Lifetime Employment Contracts*
- *3. Discharge for Cause*
- *4. Compensation Patterns*

I. Review Questions

A. STATUTORY DESIGNATIONS OF CORPORATE OFFICERS

State corporation statutes contain only skeletal provisions dealing with corporate officers. The officers of a corporation, and the functions they are to perform, are usually defined in the bylaws or in resolutions adopted by the board of directors rather than by statute.

1. TRADITIONAL STATUTES

A typical statute of a generation ago—MBCA (1969), for example—merely states that each corporation shall have a president, a treasurer, a secretary, and (usually) one or more vice-presidents.

a. Under these statutes a person may fill two or more offices simultaneously except the offices of president and secretary. This exception apparently was based on the belief that execution of documents required signatures of two officers, one executing the document and the other attesting to the execution.

b. These statutes also grant unlimited authority to the board of directors to create such additional offices as the board deems appropriate.

2. FLEXIBLE MODERN STATUTES

MBCA (1984) § 8.40(a) and Del. GCL § 142 do not designate any specific officer titles. Each grants the corporation freedom to determine which officers it chooses to have. These statutes are based on the view that little purpose is served by statutorily designated titles and problems of implied or apparent authority may be thereby created.

a. Both statutes recognize that there must be an officer performing the functions usually associated with the office of the corporate secretary under traditional statutes. See MBCA (1984) §§ 8.40(c), 1.40(20); Del. GCL § 142(a).

b. Both statutes permit any individual to hold two or more offices at the same time without limitation or restriction (except as may be expressed in the articles of incorporation or bylaws). MBCA (1984) § 8.40(d); Del. GCL § 142(a), last sentence.

B. NON-STATUTORY OFFICERS

Boards of directors or bylaw provisions may create new or different offices under both types of statutes. These various offices are sometimes created by specific provisions in the bylaws; more commonly they are discretionary with the board of directors, being created or eliminated by simple resolution.

1. PUBLICLY HELD CORPORATIONS

Publicly held corporations use functional designations: "Chairman of the Board of Directors," "Chief Executive Officer" (CEO), "Chief Financial Officer" (CFO), "Chief Legal Officer" (CLO), and "Chief Operations Officer" (COO).

a. If the corporation is formed in a state that requires that every corporation have a "president," the person holding that office may be a senior officer but subordinate to other officers, such as the CEO and COO.

2. ASSISTANT OFFICERS

Most corporations find it convenient to designate assistant officers, particularly assistant secretaries or treasurers.

C. AUTHORITY OF OFFICERS IN GENERAL

Corporate officers, including the president, have relatively little inherent power by virtue of their offices. The principal repository of inherent power to conduct the business and affairs of the corporation is in the board of directors, not the officers.

1. SOURCES OF AUTHORITY

Corporate officers may draw authority from the following sources:

a. The statutes (to a limited extent).

b. The articles of incorporation (though provisions dealing with officers in this document are uncommon).

c. The bylaws (which usually outline the functions of officers in some detail). (See part C 2, below.)

d. General resolutions of the board granting authority to officers.

e. Specific resolutions of the board authorizing the corporate officers to enter into specific transactions reviewed and approved by the board. (See part C 4, below.)

f. Many cases recognize that some authority may be implied from the office held by the person acting. This is referred to as implied or inherent authority. (See part C 2, below.)

g. Many cases find that authority exists in specific circumstances by the application of amorphous doctrines such as ratification, estoppel, or implied consent inferred from inaction by the board of directors.

Caveat: It may be unclear whether authority implied on the basis of informal conduct or acquiescence is implied actual authority or apparent authority.

2. INHERENT AUTHORITY FROM DESCRIPTION OF OFFICE

The bylaws of the corporation usually describe in general terms the roles of traditional corporate officers. The brief descriptions that follow, taken from typical bylaw provisions, define the authority of corporate officers.

a. The president is "the principal executive officer of the corporation," and, subject to the control of the board, "in general supervises and controls the business and affairs of the corporation." He or she is the proper officer to execute corporate contracts, certificates for securities, and other corporate instruments.

b. The vice president performs the duties of the president in his absence or in the event of his death, inability or refusal to act. Vice presidents act in the order designated at the time of their election, or in the absence of designation, in the order of their election. Vice presidents may also execute share certificates or other corporate instruments.

c. The secretary keeps the minutes of the proceedings of shareholders and the board of directors, sees that all notices are duly given as required by the bylaws, is custodian of the corporate records and of the corporate seal, sees that the seal of the corporation is properly affixed on authorized documents, keeps a register of the names and post office addresses of each shareholder (if there is no transfer agent), attests to the execution by the president or vice president of certificates for shares of the corporation, important contracts, and other documents, and has general charge of the stock transfer books of the corporation if there is no transfer agent.

d. The treasurer has "charge and custody of and is responsible for" all funds and securities of the corporation, and receives, gives receipts for, and deposits, all moneys due and payable to the corporation. The treasurer may be required to give a bond to ensure the faithful performance of his duties.

3. INHERENT AUTHORITY OF THE PRESIDENT

Laymen often believe that the president of a corporation has wide discretion to enter into not only ordinary business transactions, but extraordinary transactions as well.

a. Most courts have held that this view is erroneous. The traditional position is that the president has only limited authority which extends only to minor, ordinary, routine transactions. *Black v. Harrison Home Co.*, 99 P. 494 (Cal. 1909); *In re Westec Corp.*, 434 F.2d 195 (5th Cir.1970).

1) Many of the cases taking this position are relatively old.

2) The theory underlying this position is that the locus of power to approve more significant transactions is in the board of directors, not the president. *Schwartz v. United Merchants & Manufacturers*, 72 F.2d 256 (2d Cir.1934).

3) This traditional construction of the president's authority may lead to injustice since persons relying on appearances may discover that their reliance was ill-advised.

4) Persons aware of the traditional rule are forced to demand an exhibit of the president's authority before dealing with him.

b. There is a general trend to broaden the implied authority of the president.

1) Some courts have concluded that a president presumptively has any powers which the board of directors could give him.

2) Others have held that the president has authority to enter into transactions "arising in the usual and regular course of business," and have construed that phrase broadly.

Example: The corporate president hires a salesman on a commission basis that is customary in the industry. Since the hiring of agents and employees is within the regular course of business, most courts today would find the president has inherent authority to bind the corporation to this transaction.

Example: The president of the corporation negotiates a settlement of a lawsuit in which the corporation is a defendant. The settlement involves the payment of a material amount. That action exceeds the inherent authority of the president. *Covington Housing Development Corp. v. City of Covington*, 381 F.Supp. 427 (E.D.Ky.1974), aff'd 513 F.2d 630 (6th Cir.1975). The board of directors should approve the settlement. A similar rule applies to the decision to file a major lawsuit that may have important business impact.

Example: The president of a corporation promises a 30 year old person a pension of $1,500 per year commencing in thirty years if he will leave his present employment and become an employee of the corporation. Such a promise is within the inherent authority of the president. *Lee v. Jenkins Bros.*, 268 F.2d 357 (2d Cir.1959).

Caveat: Even though many cases reflect the broadening of the inherent authority of the president of a corporation, the scope of the president's inherent power is uncertain in application and reliance on inherent authority therefore is risky. See the examples in part 4 b below.

4. DETERMINATION OF AN OFFICER'S AUTHORITY

A person dealing with a corporate officer who purports to represent the corporation generally must satisfy himself or herself of the officer's authority.

a. Reliance on the officer's oral representations is hazardous because usually an agent's representations about his or her own authority are not binding on the principal.

b. Reliance on the office, e. g., dealing with the "President" of a corporation, is also hazardous because of the common law view described above that such offices carry with them only very limited authority to bind the corporation.

Example: The president of an oil drilling corporation orders 45 miles of 4⅝″ plastic pipe. Without more, it cannot be determined whether or not such a transaction is within the president's actual or apparent authority; litigation may be necessary to establish the liability of the corporation.

Example: In the preceding example, the corporation is a multi-billion dollar publicly held corporation. The president is also the CEO and the corporation follows the practice of having business matters conducted by the management with the board of directors serving only an oversight role. The president has actual authority to enter into a transaction of this nature.

Example: In the preceding example, the corporation receives and uses the pipe. Without regard to the authority of the president, the corporation is liable to pay for the plastic pipe under principles of quasi contract or unjust enrichment.

c. The simplest and most foolproof way to ensure that the corporation is bound by a transaction is to require the person purporting to act for the corporation to deliver, prior to the closing of the transaction, a certified copy of a resolution of the board of directors authorizing the transaction in question. The certificate should be executed by the secretary or an assistant secretary of the corporation, the corporate seal should be affixed, and the certificate should recite the date of the meeting.

1) There is no reason to go behind the certificate and attempt to ascertain whether or not the stated facts are true. The corporation is estopped to deny the truthfulness of facts stated in the secretary's certificate, since keeping and certifying corporate records is within the actual authority of the secretary. *In re Drive-In Development Corp.*, 371 F.2d 215 (7th Cir.1966).

2) The binding nature of the certificate rests on an estoppel. Therefore a detailed inquiry into the circumstances behind the certificate may be counterproductive since it may develop information that may destroy the basis of estoppel.

3) If one knows (or should know) that the representations are untrue, one cannot rely on estoppel.

4) The small size of many transactions may make any formality, including a certified resolution, uneconomic.

D. APPARENT AND IMPLIED AUTHORITY OF OFFICERS

Where the authority of a person purporting to act for a corporation has not been specifically created by action of the board of directors, the following doctrines may be available to a third person seeking to hold the corporation on a transaction entered into by the person in the corporate name.

1. RATIFICATION

The board of directors of a corporation may learn that an officer has entered into a transaction in the past without being specifically authorized to do so. If the board of directors does not promptly attempt to rescind or revoke the action previously taken by the officer, the corporation is bound on the transaction on a theory of "ratification." *Scientific Holding Co., Ltd. v. Plessey Incorporated,* 510 F.2d 15 (2d Cir.1974). Ratification may arise merely from knowledge of the transaction and failure to disaffirm or rescind it; it is particularly likely to arise where the corporation retains some benefit from the transaction.

2. ESTOPPEL OR UNJUST ENRICHMENT

When elements of retention of benefits by the corporation and/or known reliance by the third party on the existence of the contract are added, "estoppel" or "unjust enrichment" might be applied. "Estoppel" differs from "ratification" mainly in that attention is placed on reliance by third persons, and the inequitableness of permitting the corporation to pull the rug out from under such persons.

Caveat: These doctrines are most commonly applied in situations involving silence and acquiescence; they may, however, be applicable to affirmative conduct as well.

Example: A corporation may expressly ratify a transaction, or a corporation may be estopped to deny that a transaction was authorized if it expressly creates the appearance of authority but withholds actual authority.

Example: One or more directors know that a third person is relying on the authority of the president in approving a questionable transaction. If the directors do not speak up until after it turns out that the result of the transaction is unfavorable to the corporation, the failure to speak up promptly constitutes ratification. *Yucca Mining & Petroleum Co. v. Howard C. Phillips Oil Co.*, 365 P.2d 925 (N.M.1961).

Caveat: Courts are reluctant to find ratification of an unauthorized act by an officer where the act is fraudulent, unfair to minority shareholders, or against public policy.

3. IMPLIED AUTHORITY

Implied authority arises when a third person seeks to hold the corporation on a current transaction by showing that the directors accepted or ratified prior similar transactions in the past.

a. The acquiescence of the board of directors indicates that an actual grant of authority was informally made. *Hessler, Inc. v. Farrell*, 226 A.2d 708 (Del. 1967).

b. The same facts which support a finding of ratification of transaction A_1 may be used to find implied authority for a later similar transaction, A_2.

4. APPARENT AUTHORITY

Apparent authority exists where there is conduct on the part of the principal that leads a reasonably prudent third person to suppose that the agent has the authority he purports to exercise.

a. The classic example of apparent authority involves the third person who knows that an officer has exercised authority in the past with the consent of the board of directors and continues to rely on the appearance of authority.

b. Apparent authority involves conduct on the part of the *principal* [that is, the corporation] which creates the appearance of authority; a mere representation by a corporate officer that he possesses the requisite authority is not sufficient. However, relevant corporate conduct may consist of silence, or of acquiescence in and ratification of acts performed in the past.

c. Apparent authority differs from implied actual authority. For apparent authority, the third person must show that she was aware of the prior acts or holding out and that she relied on appearances, while implied actual authority may be found even in the absence of knowledge on the part of the third person.

Caveat: The same conduct may often tend to prove either implied actual authority or apparent authority.

Example: A corporate president has purchased pipe from a supplier four times in the past; each time the corporation has routinely paid for the pipe. The fifth time, involving a transaction of the same general order of magnitude, the corporation declines to accept or pay for the pipe. In a suit for damages, a court may rest a decision against the corporation on either apparent authority or implied actual authority and may rely on the prior transactions to justify either conclusion.

E. FIDUCIARY DUTIES OF OFFICERS

Corporate officers and agents owe a fiduciary duty to the corporation of honesty, good faith, and diligence. The scope of an officer's or agent's obligation to the corporation is determined in part by the nature of his employment with the corporation. The duty of subordinate officers or agents is narrower than the analogous duty of a director.

1. GENERAL DUTIES OF ALL OFFICERS OR AGENTS

An officer or agent should act for the sole benefit of the corporation and give to it her best uncorrupt business judgment.

a. Full disclosure of possibly conflicting transactions may be required.

b. The officer or agent may hold in trust for the corporation profits made personally in competition with, or at the expense of, the corporation.

2. LIABILITY FOR EXCEEDING AUTHORITY

A corporate officer or agent may also be liable to the corporation if he or she exceeds his or her actual authority and binds the corporation in a transaction with a third person.

Caveat: If the corporation is to be bound, the transaction must be within the officer's or agent's apparent authority.

3. STATUTORY IMPOSITION OF DUTY OF CARE

MBCA (1984) § 8.42 imposes a duty of care on officers analogous to the duty of care imposed on directors. Other duties of officers are not codified. State statutes permitting corporations to limit monetary liability for due care violations may cover officers as well as directors. See part XIV B 4.

F. OFFICERS' LIABILITY ON CORPORATE OBLIGATIONS

A corporate officer or employee who acts within the scope of her authority as the corporation's representative in a consensual transaction is not personally liable on the transaction if she acts solely as an agent. However, personal liability may be imposed on an officer or employee in several circumstances.

1. EXPRESS GUARANTEE

The officer or employee may expressly guarantee the performance by the corporation, intending to be personally bound on the obligation. Such a guarantee may be written or oral, and may or may not be supported by consideration, depending on the sequence of events and what is requested.

a. To be enforceable, a guarantee must be supported by consideration.

b. Whether or not a guarantee must also be in writing depends on the proper scope of the provision of the statute of frauds dealing with promises to answer for the indebtedness of another.

Example: The president of a corporation makes an oral promise to a supplier of merchandise that she will personally agree to pay for goods if they are delivered. Such an oral promise is generally not enforceable but, depending on the circumstances, it might be enforced despite the statute of frauds on the theory that the president was the primary obligor or that the "main purpose" of the transaction was to benefit the president.

2. CONFUSION OF ROLES

The officer or employee may not intend to be personally bound, but may in fact become so by creating the impression that she is negotiating on an individual rather than corporate basis, or the agreement is executed in such a way as to indicate personal liability.

a. If a person negotiates a transaction without disclosing that she is acting on behalf of a corporation, there is personal liability to the third person on general agency principles relating to undisclosed principals.

b. If the existence of the corporation is disclosed, joint liability of the corporation and the officer may be created because of carelessness in the manner of execution.

Example: An officer executes a document in the name of, and on behalf of, a corporation as follows:

ABC Corporation

By ______________________________
President

The officer is not personally liable on the obligation since the form of execution unambiguously indicates that only the corporation is liable.

Example: In the previous example, the form of execution is as follows:

ABC Corporation

______________________________, President.

This form of execution is ambiguous since the corporation and the president may be either joint obligors or the president may have intended to sign only in a representative capacity. *Harris v. Milam,* 389 P.2d 638 (Okl.1964).

Caveat: The word "president" alone does not resolve the ambiguity since it may be an identification of the individual obligor or an indication that he or she signed only as a representative of the corporation.

Example: Whitcomb is the director of a nonprofit corporation called "Response to Hunger Network." Whitcomb contacts Benjamin Plumbing, Inc. to obtain a quotation for some plumbing work. The letter requesting the quotation is on church letterhead and signed "William K. Whitcomb, For Response to Hunger Network." The acceptance of Benjamin Plumbing's quotation was signed by Whitcomb, followed by the typed words, "William K. Whitcomb, Canning Committee—RHN." This letter was on letterhead captioned "RESPONSE TO HUNGER NETWORK." Whitcomb is personally liable on the plumbing contract, since neither the letter requesting the quotation nor the acceptance of that quotation indicates that Whitcomb was acting on behalf of a corporation. *Benjamin Plumbing, Inc. v. Barnes,* 470 N.W.2d 888 (Wis.1991).

Caveat: In cases involving ambiguous forms of execution, courts appear to be more willing to allow corporate officers to testify about the "real intention of the parties" in executing general contracts than in executing promissory notes. This principle, however, is not applicable when the existence of the corporation does not appear at all in the form of execution.

3. STATUTORY LIABILITY

Liability may arise because imposed by statute. For example, some state statutes impose personal liability for corporate obligations if officers fail to pay franchise taxes or to publish a notice upon incorporation.

Example: The Internal Revenue Code of 1954 provides for a personal penalty of one hundred per cent of the tax if a corporation fails to pay over income taxes withheld from employees. This penalty tax may be imposed on "any person required to collect, truthfully account for, and pay over" the tax. (I.R.C. § 6672.)

4. PERSONAL PARTICIPATION IN TORTIOUS CONDUCT

A corporate officer is personally liable if he or she personally participates in tortious conduct.

5. AUTHORITY

A corporation officer may be personally liable on contracts or other obligations entered into in the name of the corporation if the officer exceeds his or her actual authority to bind the corporation. The corporation is bound if the action is within the officer's apparent authority but in that situation may have an action over against the officer for exceeding his or her actual authority.

G. CORPORATE "NOTICE" OR "KNOWLEDGE"

A corporation can "know" or "have notice of" something only if one or more persons who represent the corporation know or have notice of the thing. The issue is the circumstances in which personal knowledge is to be imputed to the corporate entity.

1. GENERAL RULE

Knowledge acquired by a corporate officer or employee while acting in furtherance of the corporate business or in the course of employment is imputed to the corporation.

Example: If the president knows of a transaction, the corporation ratifies it if the corporation accepts the benefits of the transaction, even though one or more directors or other officers may not know the details of the transaction.

Example: Service of process on an authorized agent of the corporation supports a default judgment against the corporation even though the agent fails to forward the papers to the corporation's attorney.

2. AGENT ACTING ADVERSELY TO PRINCIPAL

Difficult problems arise when it is sought to impute knowledge of an agent to the corporation if the agent is acting adversely to the corporation. Generally, information or knowledge may be imputed from an agent who has ultimate responsibility for the transaction to his corporation even if the agent is acting adversely to and in fraud of the corporation.

Example: A corporate president learns that a low level employee is defrauding the corporation and "cuts himself in on the action" by demanding a percentage of the fraudulent gains. The president's knowledge is imputed to the corporation even though the president does not disclose his knowledge to the directors.

3. CORPORATE CRIMINAL RESPONSIBILITY

An agent's wrongful intention may be imputed to a corporation so that a corporation may be subject to civil or criminal prosecution, including prosecution for traditional crimes such as murder or rape. For the corporation to be prosecuted such acts must be connected with, or be in furtherance of, the corporation's business.

H. TENURE OF OFFICERS AND AGENTS

Corporate officers and agents serve at the will of the person or group having authority to elect or appoint the officers or agents. Corporate officers are elected by the board of directors, and may be removed by the board of directors with or without cause. MBCA (1984) § 8.43(b). Agents appointed by officers or other agents may be discharged by the persons with authority to employ them.

1. EMPLOYMENT CONTRACTS IN GENERAL

An officer or agent may be given an employment contract, and removal of such an officer or agent may give rise to a cause of action for breach of contract.

a. The mere election or appointment of an officer or agent, even for a definite term, does not of itself give rise to a contract right. MBCA (1984) § 8.44(a).

b. Corporate bylaws usually provide that specified named officers, such as the president, vice president, secretary, and treasurer, are elected by the board of directors for a term of one year. A provision of this nature generally does not limit the power of a corporation to grant an officer an employment contract extending beyond the term of office.

   1) Despite the contract, the officer may be relieved of her duties at any time. But see the sharply divided opinions of the New York Court of Appeals in *Staklinski v. Pyramid Elec. Co.*, 160 N.E.2d 78 (N.Y.1959). Of course, the corporation may be liable for breach of contract for the premature termination of the employment period if the officer is discharged without cause. MBCA (1984) § 8.44(b).

2) Long-term employment contracts for officers may be upheld on the same theory applied to other long-term contracts, e. g., long term leases that "bind" subsequent boards of directors. *Staklinski v. Pyramid Elec. Co.*, 160 N.E.2d 78 (N.Y.1959); *In re Paramount Publix Corp.*, 90 F.2d 441 (2d Cir.1937).

3) Even if the bylaw provision is deemed to be a restraint on the power of the board of directors to give an officer a long term employment contract, an employment contract for more than one year may be deemed to be an implied amendment of the bylaws. *Realty Acceptance Corp. v. Montgomery*, 51 F.2d 636 (3d Cir.1930). The board of directors may first amend the bylaws and then enter into a long-term employment contract. This assumes that the board of directors has power to amend the bylaws, as most boards of directors do.

Caveat: At least one court has invalidated a long-term employment contract as being inconsistent with the bylaw provision that limits the term of officers. It is not clear in this case whether or not the board of directors had the power to amend bylaws. *Pioneer Specialties, Inc. v. Nelson,* 339 S.W.2d 199 (Tex.1960).

2. LIFETIME EMPLOYMENT CONTRACTS

The claim that an officer or agent has been given a lifetime employment contract by a corporation has been treated with hostility by courts. Such contracts are usually oral and arise within the context of a family-run business.

a. While such a contract is not within the one year provision of the statute of frauds, courts feel that the factual basis for such an open-ended commitment is inherently implausible.

b. Lifetime employment contracts may subject a corporation to a substantial liability which may run for a long and indefinite period during which circumstances may substantially change.

c. Many cases that have refused to enforce such arrangements have done so on the ground the officer making the arrangement had neither actual nor apparent authority to enter into such an arrangement. See: *Lee v. Jenkins Bros.*, 268 F.2d 357 (2d Cir.1959).

3. DISCHARGE FOR CAUSE

An officer or employee with an employment contract may always be discharged for cause.

a. "Cause" may consist of facts of dishonesty, negligence, refusal to obey reasonable orders, refusal to follow reasonable rules, or a variety of other acts such as engaging in an unprovoked fight.

b. In effect, such conduct constitutes a breach of an implied (or express) covenant in the employment contract.

c. Of course, if an officer does not have an employment contract, it is irrelevant as a legal matter whether or not "cause" for discharge exists.

4. COMPENSATION PATTERNS

Employees sometimes request that they be compensated on a basis that reflects (a) corporate earnings or profits or (b) the market behavior of the corporation's shares rather than at a flat rate. No particular legal problem is raised by such contracts so long as the total amount of compensation is not so excessive as to constitute waste. (See part XIV D, infra.)

a. The major question arising with respect to bonus arrangements based on corporate earnings and profits usually is one of computation. Profits may be computed in various ways, and differences may be material. The simple phrase "net profits," for example, is often ambiguous and its meaning may be elusive.

b. Corporate officers and employees may also be paid in shares of stock. More commonly, compensation is in the form of options to purchase shares or plans by which employees may purchase shares at advantageous prices. Also popular are plans that measure compensation on the basis of stock prices but do not involve the actual purchase of shares. These plans include phantom stock plans and stock appreciation rights.

   1) Such arrangements are designed to give employees a long term investment interest in their employer. They are more common in publicly held corporations (where a market for shares exists) than in closely held corporations.

   2) Long term employees of closely held corporations may be permitted to buy a small number of shares of the corporation as an incentive. Typically, these shares are subject to an agreement by the corporation to repurchase them when the employment arrangement ends.

c. Employment contracts for highly paid personnel usually provide for deferred compensation, fringe benefits, reimbursement of business expenses, and other tax-related benefits. Such benefits may also be provided to lower-paid employees on a more limited basis.

d. In closely held corporations, an employment agreement may be an integral part of the basic understanding between minority and majority shareholders.

   1) Terms relating to employment are often placed in shareholders' agreements so that they will be binding on all the other shareholders as well as on the corporation.

2) If there is disagreement between majority and minority shareholders, in the absence of an employment agreement the majority may exclude the minority totally from the corporation and its business.

I. REVIEW QUESTIONS

IX–1. The reason that most persons believe that the president of a corporation has considerable authority is that the president is the most important person within the corporation and owns the most shares. Does this view accurately reflect the power of a president in a corporation?

IX–2. An officer of a corporation cannot be given an employment contract for a period that exceeds the term for which the person was elected.

True ______ False ______

IX–3. M is the president of P Corporation. P Corporation entered into a contract with D Corporation (which owned ½ the stock of P Corporation) to distribute D Corporation's products. D Corporation failed to deliver the product. M suggested to the board of directors of P Corporation that suit be instituted against D Corporation. A resolution to such effect was defeated by a majority of P Corporation's board of directors. M then instituted suit against D Corporation on behalf of P Corporation. Did M have power to institute the action in light of the decision by P Corporation's board of directors?

IX–4. A, the president of D Corporation, without the consent of D Corporation's board of directors entered into a contract with P Corporation for the purchase of 45 miles of 6⅝″ gas pipe. D Corporation refused to accept the pipe and P Corporation sued for breach of contract. At the trial the judge charged the jury that the corporation is bound by the act of the president in signing a contract. Is the jury charge correct?

*

X

MANAGEMENT OF THE CLOSELY HELD CORPORATION

Analysis

A. CHARACTERISTICS OF A CLOSELY HELD CORPORATION

A "close corporation" or "closely held corporation" is a corporation with a few shareholders. In such a corporation unique management problems arise because of the relationship that necessarily exists among shareholders. For a discussion of definitions and the relationship of close corporations to other types of corporations, see part I D.

1. SHAREHOLDER PARTICIPATION IN MANAGEMENT

The management of a close corporation is usually associated with the principal shareholders, or with all the shareholders.

a. The majority shareholders may name the board of directors, and through them, the officers and employees.

b. Usually they name themselves to all important (and the highest salary-paying) positions.

c. Normally, minority shareholders also wish to participate in management. A major aspect of close corporation planning is to develop devices that assure minority shareholders of meaningful participation in management despite the power of majority shareholders to name a majority or all of the directors and all officers and employees.

2. INFORMALITY OF MANAGEMENT

The controlling shareholders usually operate the business in an informal manner, more as though it were a partnership rather than a corporation.

a. In many closely held corporations, shareholders' meetings are held infrequently if at all. Unanimous consents may be prepared to record who is serving on the board of directors from time to time.

b. Formal directors meetings may also be held infrequently. In many closely held corporations, meetings consist of informal discussions or simple decision making by the majority shareholder (who may be the sole director of the corporation) or by the controlling shareholders. The controlling shareholders may or may not consult with other officers, directors, or shareholders.

c. The attorney for a closely held corporation should assure that minimal records are kept as to the identity of shareholders, directors, and officers, the manner of their election or appointment, and the periods they serve. The attorney should also assure that documents executed on behalf of the corporation clearly reflect corporate execution by the persons who hold the positions described in the form of execution.

d. Closely held corporations are often called "incorporated partnerships" to reflect the close similarity in management that exists between partnerships and closely held corporations.

3. LACK OF MARKET FOR MINORITY SHARES

Since a close corporation has only a relatively small number of shareholders, there is no public trading in, or public market for, its shares.

a. Potential purchasers of minority blocks of shares usually must be found among the corporation, present shareholders, or rarely, among outsiders willing "to take a gamble."

b. The market for minority blocks of closely held shares is at worst non-existent and at best a buyer's market.

1) There are few alternative purchasers and therefore little or no incentive for buyers to offer reasonable prices for shares.

2) Minority shares may have some value because they constitute a nuisance and may serve as the basis for litigation.

c. If the shares offered for sale constitute a controlling interest, they are readily salable to outsiders interested in running the business in which the corporation is engaged.

d. If the minority shares offered for sale represent the balance of control between factions, they are readily salable to one faction or another.

e. Transferability of shares is usually restricted by contractual restrictions limiting free transferability. A shareholder desiring to sell his shares may have to comply with the restrictions before offering shares to outsiders.

4. DIVIDEND POLICY

In a closely held corporation dividend policies may be established that favor controlling shareholders.

a. Dividend policies are directly influenced by the tax status of the corporation.

1) In a corporation that is subject to C corporation tax rules the dividend policy generally adopted is "no dividends." The payment of dividends carries a higher tax cost than the payment of the same amount in the form of salaries, rents or other payments that are deductible by the corporation. (See part V I 2.)

(i) The disadvantage of dividends in C corporations is that they result in double taxation: the corporate income is subject to the corporate income tax and amounts paid in dividends to shareholders are subject to a second tax when the dividends are included in the individual shareholders' tax returns.

(ii) If all the corporate income is distributed in the form of salaries, rents, or other deductible payments, the income is said to be "zeroed out." If the income cannot be zeroed out, it is generally advantageous to permit corporate earnings to accumulate in the corporation rather than paying out the excess income in the form of dividends.

2) In a corporation that has elected S corporation treatment, all corporate income is directly taxed to the shareholders, whether or not distributed, so that payment of dividends has little or no effect on the aggregate tax bills.

(i) Since shareholders must pay income tax on S corporation earnings allocated to them, whether or not distributed, it is customary in S corporations to make sufficient distributions to cover the income tax liability that the allocation of corporate income creates.

(ii) Additional distributions may be made in the form of salaries, rent, etc. to controlling shareholders or their designees that are deductible by the corporation in the calculation of its taxable income. Such distributions may give rise to internal dispute and dissatisfaction since some shareholders may receive larger payments than others and the payments may bear no relationship to relative shareholdings.

b. In a closely held corporation, the controlling shareholders may divert the bulk of the corporate income to themselves by adopting a "no dividend" policy, refusing to employ the minority shareholders in the business, and paying the bulk of the earnings to themselves in the form of salaries, bonuses, pension fund contributions, and fringe benefits (free use of automobiles, country club memberships and the like).

1) In extreme cases these policies permit the minority shareholders no return at all on their investment and interest in the corporation.

2) These policies may be adopted in an effort to "soften up" minority shareholders and persuade them to sell their shares at a low price either to the corporation or to other shareholders.

3) This tactic is referred to as a "freeze out."

4) Freeze out tactics may lead to litigation seeking the payment of a dividend or other relief against the controlling shareholders.

Caveat: Unreasonable payments of salaries, bonuses, or fringe benefits may be disallowed as corporate deductions by the Internal Revenue Service. Minority shareholders may use these tax determinations in an effort to obtain a court order requiring the payment of a dividend or the return of the excess funds to the corporation. See e.g. *Wilderman v. Wilderman,* 315 A.2d 610 (Del.Ch.1974).

5. WIDESPREAD USE OF SHAREHOLDERS AGREEMENTS

In closely held corporations there is widespread use of shareholders' agreements whenever there is more than one shareholder in the corporation.

a. An important function of shareholders' agreements is to assure that minority shareholders may be able to dispose of their shares when they die, retire, or wish to leave the corporation. This is usually effected by the execution of a binding buy/sell agreement. (See parts V J 3, VII I.)

   1) Persons considering the acquisition of a minority position in a closely held corporation normally demand an enforceable buy/sell agreement guaranteeing that the investor may exit from the investment at a predetermined or objectively determinable price.

   2) Such agreements provide considerable practical protection for minority shareholders, though the terms of a buy/sell agreement may make an actual exit unattractive.

b. A second important function of shareholders' agreements is to assure minority shareholders that they will have an effective voice in corporate affairs. A variety of control arrangements may be established to ensure that the minority shareholders may veto transactions they view to be undesirable, or to assure that they may exit from the corporation if they object to a transaction.

c. A third important function of shareholders' agreements is to assure minority shareholders that they will be entitled to a financial return from their investment.

   1) An employment contract with the corporation is the simplest device to assure a financial return.

   2) In the absence of an effective contract, the position of minority shareholder within the corporations is totally dependent on the good will of the controlling shareholders.

d. A final important function of shareholders' agreements is to facilitate estate planning for shareholders. (See part VII I 1.)

6. **NO COMPULSORY DISSOLUTION**
Minority shareholders in a close corporation ordinarily have no power to force a dissolution of the corporation.

   a. Dissolution may occur voluntarily under state statutes only with the consent of a majority or greater fraction of the outstanding shares.

   b. In this respect a close corporation differs significantly from a partnership, in which each partner possesses an inherent power to dissolve the partnership.

7. **FREEZEOUTS**
In the absence of a binding shareholders agreement, the foregoing factors may readily result in a freezeout of minority shareholders in which they are on the one hand "locked in" the corporation for a long period of time, and on the other hand excluded from management and deprived of any return on their investment.

   a. Over a period of time in which deaths, withdrawals, or fallings out are likely, the possibility that adverse and hostile interests will develop within a closely held corporation is fairly high.

   b. Advance planning, usually in the form of a buy/sell agreement, may avoid freezeouts.

      1) Advance planning may not occur in family businesses which have devolved down through one or two generations, particularly when deaths of controlling shareholders occur unexpectedly and without adequate planning.

      2) Advance planning also may not occur in any corporation in which the participants enter the venture fully trusting each other.

      3) Advance planning also may not occur where trusted employees are permitted to purchase small amounts of stock in the corporation, the assumptions usually being that they are totally loyal to the controlling shareholders and their stock will be repurchased by the corporation when the employment ends.

B. DEVICES THAT PERMIT SHARING OF CONTROL IN CLOSELY HELD CORPORATIONS

In the absence of special statutory treatment of closely held corporations, such corporations must establish control devices through the use of traditional and accepted shareholder control techniques.

1. TRADITIONAL CONTROL TECHNIQUES DISCUSSED ELSEWHERE

The following control techniques, all discussed earlier, may appropriately be used as control devices in close corporations.

a. Shareholder voting agreements (see part VII F).

b. Voting trusts (see part VII G).

c. Irrevocable proxy appointments (see part VII E 5).

d. Share transfer restrictions (see part VII I).

e. Multiple classes of shares (see part VII H).

f. Employment agreements between shareholders and the corporation (see part IX H).

g. Increased requirements for a quorum and for approval of actions by shareholders (see part VII B 1; VII B 4).

h. Increased requirements for a quorum and for approval of actions by directors (see part VIII B 2 f, VIII B 3 b).

2. SUPERMAJORITY QUORUM AND VOTING REQUIREMENTS

Minority participation may be assured by increased voting and quorum requirements in order to give minority interests effectively a veto power (items g. and h. immediately above). This veto power may be applicable at the shareholder level, at the board of directors level, or at both levels.

a. Increased quorum and/or voting requirements are usually referred to as supermajority requirements.

b. It is usually important to increase both the quorum requirement and the minimum vote requirement to make sure that it is impossible for the corporation to act without the assent of the minority shareholder.

c. Usually unanimity is imposed for both the quorum and voting requirements, but in some circumstances a lesser percentage may be sufficient to give the desired veto power.

Example: A 25 per cent shareholder may feel secure if an 80 per cent quorum and voting requirement is imposed. However, it is essential that decisions permitting the issuance of additional voting shares themselves be subject to this supermajority requirement if the 25 per cent shareholder is to be fully protected.

d. Creation of a veto power through these devices greatly increases the possibility of deadlock within the corporation.

3. LEGAL PROBLEMS CREATED BY INFORMAL MANAGEMENT IN THE CLOSE CORPORATION

In most small closely held corporations, corporate matters are likely to be resolved by unanimous consent with a minimum of formality and no regard for statutory niceties. Meetings may be held infrequently, if at all, corporate records may be kept on an erratic basis, and decisions may be made without any recognition that the corporation theoretically consists of different layers with different rights and responsibilities.

a. The failure to follow corporate formalities creates several possible legal issues:

1) Will the ignoring of corporate formalities result in the corporate veil being "pierced" and the participants being held personally liable on corporate obligations? (See part IV.)

2) Will the participants' control arrangement be unenforceable because it violates the "statutory norms"? (See part VI.)

3) Will decisions that are made informally and without following the statutory norms be binding on the corporation and third parties? (See part VIII G).

C. JUDICIAL RECOGNITION OF THE SPECIAL PROBLEMS OF THE CLOSE CORPORATION

The traditional view was that all corporations should be governed by essentially the same rules set forth in the corporation statutes, and that no special rules could or should be developed for the closely held corporation. See, e.g. *Kruger v. Gerth*, 210 N.E.2d 355 (N.Y.1965).

1. DISSENTING VIEWS

Beginning in the 1960's this traditional view was challenged by several individual judicial opinions urging a more relaxed and more realistic treatment of the closely held corporation. See the dissenting opinions in *Kruger v. Gerth*, 210 N.E.2d 355 (N.Y.1965). These views usually urged:

a. Application of a greatly broadened fiduciary duty between shareholders in a closely held corporation;

b. Relaxation of the traditional statutory norms to permit more flexible control arrangements within the closely held corporation;

c. Recognition that closely held corporations were "incorporated partnerships," and the selective application of partnership principles, including freedom to dissolve, to closely held corporations; and

d. Enactment of statutory provisions designed expressly for the benefit of closely held corporations. (See part X D.)

2. JUDICIAL ACCEPTANCE IN ILLINOIS AND MASSACHUSETTS

Strong and influential decisions favoring special judicial treatment of closely held corporations are *Galler v. Galler*, 203 N.E.2d 577 (Ill.1964) and *Donahue v. Rodd Electrotype Co.*, 328 N.E.2d 505 (Mass.1975).

a. *Galler* applied a relaxed standard of statutory norms to uphold a reasonable control arrangement and strongly urged special statutory treatment for the closely held corporation.

b. *Donahue* applied a broad fiduciary duty, not unlike that existing between partners in a general partnership, to shareholders in a closely held corporation. (See part X E 4.)

c. The fiduciary duty of shareholders created in Massachusetts in *Donahue,* (see part X E 4) extends to management duties as well as financial ones.

Example: A minority shareholder has a veto power over certain transactions because of a unanimity requirement. The shareholder exercises this power arbitrarily to prevent the payment of all dividends, thereby causing the corporation to incur a penalty tax for unreasonable accumulation of surplus. The minority shareholder has breached his duty to the other shareholders. *Smith v. Atlantic Properties, Inc.,* 422 N.E.2d 798 (Mass.App.1981).

d. Decisions in a number of other states have accepted the general principles of these two leading cases.

D. STATUTES RELATING TO MANAGEMENT OF CLOSE CORPORATIONS

Many states have adopted statutes relating to management problems within the closely held corporation. These statutes in a broad sense may be traced to judicial dissatisfaction with the application of traditional corporation law principles to such corporations. They fall into two general categories: statutes of general applicability dealing with variations in management structure and special statutes for closely held corporations that require an election by the corporation.

1. GENERAL STATUTES PERMITTING THE ELIMINATING OF THE BOARD OF DIRECTORS

The statutes of many states permit any corporation to modify the traditional role of its board of directors by appropriate provision in its articles of incorporation. The provision may permit a corporation to dispense entirely with the board of directors and have the business and affairs managed directly by its shareholders or place restrictions on the discretion of directors. As a practical matter, this option is almost solely utilized by closely held corporations. (See part VI D 1.)

a. Typical is Del. GCL § 141(a): "The business and affairs of every corporation * * * shall be managed by or under the direction of a board of directors *except as may be otherwise provided in this chapter or in its certificate of incorporation. If any such provision is made in the certificate of incorporation, the powers and duties conferred or imposed upon the board of directors by this chapter shall be exercised or performed to such extent and by such person or persons as shall be provided in the certificate of incorporation.*

Example: Lehrman and Cohen each own 50 per cent of the stock of X Corporation. They have numerous disagreements and finally agree that Danzansky, X Corporation's general counsel, whom they both trust, shall be given the power to vote as a director to break any deadlocks on the board of directors. An appropriate provision in the articles of incorporation granting Danzansky a tie breaking vote on the board of directors is valid. Cf. *Lehrman v. Cohen,* 222 A.2d 800 (Del.1966).

b. MBCA (1984) § 8.01(c) contained a provision similar to Del. GCL § 141(a), but that subsection was repealed in 1991 and a more general provision, § 7.32, discussed below, was substituted. (See part X D 3.)

2. STATUTES APPLICABLE ONLY TO SPECIALLY DEFINED AND ELECTING CLOSE CORPORATIONS

The statutes of about 12 states contain special statutes applicable only to electing close corporations. The Committee that approved the MBCA (1984) adopted a "Model Close Corporation Supplement" that was based on these statutes.

a. These statutes are intended to permit electing close corporations to manage their affairs with essentially the same freedom as if they were partnerships and to simplify problems of dissension, deadlock, and shareholder succession.

b. The definition of an eligible corporation usually involves the following elements:

   1) The number of shareholders may not exceed a specified number (ranging from as low as 10 in some states to 35 or even 50 in others).

2) The corporation never has made a registered public offering of shares.

3) Share transfer restrictions must be imposed on all outstanding shares limiting their free transferability.

4) Notations must be placed on all certificates describing which special provisions the corporation has elected to make applicable.

c. A corporation that meets the foregoing qualifications may become a statutory close corporation by including in its articles of incorporation a statement to the effect that "this corporation is a statutory close corporation."

d. While there is considerable variation in the special state statutes relating to close corporations, they generally provide the following:

1) Agreements that restrict the discretion of directors are specifically validated if they are set forth in the articles of incorporation.

2) The corporation may elect to dispense with the board of directors entirely.

(i) If this option is elected, the liabilities otherwise imposed on directors are imposed on the shareholders as if they were directors.

(ii) The corporation may elect to conduct its affairs "as though it were a partnership."

(iii) Where the board of directors has been eliminated under the Delaware close corporation statute, the shareholders are referred to as "managing shareholders" and have the rights and duties of directors. *Graczykowski v. Ramppen,* 477 N.Y.S.2d 454 (App.Div.1984).

3) These statutes also permit an electing close corporation, among other things, to eliminate bylaws, to broaden the power to create share transfer restrictions, and in some states to permit the creation of mandatory buyouts upon the death of a shareholder.

4) These statutes contain special provisions to resolve dissension or deadlock, such as the appointment of receivers, custodians or provisional directors. (See part X G.)

e. In *Zion v. Kurtz,* 405 N.E.2d 681 (N.Y.1980), the court upheld an agreement between two shareholders that the corporation would not enter into transactions or new business without the consent of both shareholders (an option permitted under the Delaware special close corporation statute) despite the fact that no reference to the agreement appeared in the articles of incorporation and the corporation had not elected close corporation status.

The court viewed these omissions as technical and subject to the power of the court to order the articles of incorporation reformed. The vote was 4–3; the dissenters argued that public notice of agreements restricting the power of directors was essential for their validity under these statutes.

f. Even though several states have adopted special close corporation statutes and this development has been widely praised, the actual experience in California, Delaware, Florida and Texas indicates that this election is not widely used.

1) It is probable that most attorneys are able to work out basic control relationships under the general corporation statutes and therefore do not feel it is necessary to use or experiment with these largely untried statutes.

2) The sheer complexity of some of these statutes may also have discouraged their widespread use. Some close corporation statutes are complex and prolix; much of the complicated language is addressed to problems related to eligibility, i. e., which corporations are eligible to take advantage of these special provisions and what happens when an electing corporation loses its eligibility.

g. Some lawyers may be concerned that the use of the close corporation election may have adverse tax consequences or may result in the possible loss of the shield of limited liability. The statutes of some states expressly attempt to negate this result. The Model Close Corporation Supplement, for example, provides that liability for corporate debts should not be imposed on shareholders merely because the corporation has adopted informal procedures for shareholder management of the corporation that are authorized by these special statutes.

h. Despite the broad remedial purposes underlying modern close corporation statutes, some courts have given them narrow and literalistic readings not consistent with the underlying purposes. E. g., *Blount v. Taft*, 246 S.E.2d 763 (N.C.1978). Other courts have been more generous. See e.g. *Zion v. Kurtz*, 405 N.E.2d 681 (N.Y.1980).

Caveat: These statutes, while generally applauded in academic commentary, do not appear to be widely used in practice.

3. SECTION 7.32 OF THE MODEL BUSINESS CORPORATION ACT (1984)

In 1991, the Committee on Corporate Laws withdrew provisions in the MBCA (1984) that permitted limited flexibility in the statutory scheme, and replaced them with a new section 7.32, entitled "Shareholder Agreements" which provides significant freedom to closely held corporations to organize in any way they wish.

a. Section 7.32 rejects "the older line of cases" relating to statutory norms and adds an "element of predictability currently absent" from the MBCA (1984). It recognizes that "many of the corporate norms" contained in corporation statutes were designed with an eye towards public companies where management and share ownership are quite distinct.

b. Section 7.32 validates virtually all shareholders' agreements relating to corporate governance and business arrangements, including agreements relating to:

   1) Governance of the entity;

   2) Allocation of the return from the business; and

   3) Other aspects of the relationships among shareholders, directors, and the corporation.

c. Section 7.32 creates a broad but not universal mandate to customize the management of closely held corporations. Agreements that affect third parties and agreements that violate fundamental principles of public policy may not be validated.

   Example: The official comment to § 7.32 suggests that a provision in a shareholders' agreement that the directors have no duty of care or loyalty is not within the scope of that section.

d. The agreement under § 7.32 must be unanimously approved by the shareholders; it may appear in the articles of incorporation, the bylaws, or a shareholders' agreement.

e. The existence of an agreement under § 7.32 must appear on the share certificates or information statements reflecting shares. A purchaser of shares without notice of the existence of the agreement has the sole remedy of recission within 90 days after learning of the existence of the agreement.

f. An agreement under § 7.32 is valid for 10 years unless otherwise provided in the agreement. It automatically terminates if the shares of the corporation become publicly traded on a national securities exchange or public market for securities.

g. The existence or performance of an agreement under § 7.32 is not a ground for imposing personal liability on a shareholder for the acts or debts of a corporation "even if the agreement or its performance treats the corporation as if it were a partnership or results in failure to observe the corporate formalities otherwise applicable to the matters governed by the agreement." MBCA (1984) § 7.32(f).

Caveat: A corporation may be taxed as a partnership rather than as a corporation if a § 7.32 agreement creates sufficient partnership characteristics.

E. DISSENSION AND DEADLOCK WITHIN THE CLOSE CORPORATION

Many small corporations at one time or another in their history are wracked by dissension or deadlock; advance planning may help to reduce or eliminate such disagreeable incidents.

1. DISSENSION

"Dissension" refers to internal squabbles, fights, or disagreements typically in a corporation which has a clearly defined controlling shareholder or shareholders.

a. Dissension may arise in any corporation in which one shareholder or faction of shareholders has effective working control and the power to exclude other shareholders from meaningful participation in management or the economic benefits of the business.

b. Typically, the minority faction is in a weak position, and may be subject to freezeouts.

c. In states which do not have a clearly defined fiduciary duty that prevents freeze outs (see part X E 4), attorneys may counsel minority shareholders to adopt obstructionist tactics, including litigation, in an effort to improve their bargaining position.

d. Such tactics are likely to increase the enmity and friction within the corporation.

2. DEADLOCK

"Deadlock" refers to control arrangements that effectively prevent the corporation from acting or making decisions.

a. Deadlocks typically involve two factions or two shareholders in a control structure that does not permit either faction to have effective working control. It is possible for a corporation with more than two factions to become deadlocked if each individual shareholder and/or director has a veto power but that is much less common.

b. A corporation is potentially subject to deadlock if:

1) Two factions own exactly fifty per cent of the outstanding shares;

2) There are an even number of directors, and two factions each have the power to select the same number; or

3) A minority shareholder has retained a veto power in one of the ways previously described.

c. A deadlock may occur either at the shareholders' level or at the directors' level.

1) If the shareholders are deadlocked, the corporation may continue to operate under the guidance of the board of directors in office when the deadlock arose. The general rule is that directors serve until their successors are qualified; if the deadlock prevents a subsequent election, those in office remain in office indefinitely.

Example: Two shareholders each own 50 per cent of the outstanding shares. Shares are not entitled to vote cumulatively. There are four directors, A, her spouse, Mr. A, B, and her spouse, Mr. B. Mr. B resigns as a result of marital discord with B. Control of the corporation has been turned over permanently to A and Mr. A. In subsequent elections, an attempt by B to elect two directors (and return to parity on the board) can itself be deadlocked by A.

Example: In the foregoing example, A and Mr. A, acting as directors, fill the vacancy by electing their son, XX. Even though A and Mr. A may not constitute a quorum of directors, under the statutes of many states they may fill a vacancy. B is now outvoted on the board, three to one. There may be no way for her to return to parity since XX remains in office until his successor is elected and all such elections continue to be deadlocked. See *Gearing v. Kelly*, 182 N.E.2d 391 (N.Y.1962).

Example: In the foregoing example, if cumulative voting is permitted, B may restore her former position by dividing her votes between herself and Mr. B. However, if an odd number of directors were to be elected, cumulative voting leads to a deadlock in any attempt to fill a vacancy in the last position on the board of directors.

2) A deadlock at the directoral level may prevent the corporation from functioning at all, though more commonly the president or general

manager may continue to operate the business, often to the complete exclusion of the other faction.

3. VOLUNTARY BUYOUTS AS A REMEDY FOR DISSENSION OR DEADLOCK

The most practical solution for a corporation that is deadlocked or wracked with dissension is usually for one faction to buy out the other.

a. It is ordinarily preferable to preserve a going corporation rather than to dissolve it. The business and assets of a corporation, including intangible good will, are ordinarily worth more as a unit than fragmented.

b. It sometimes may be possible for parties to work out a sale after the dissension or deadlock has arisen.

c. The more logical solution, however, is to address the problem of possible dissension or deadlock when the parties are in amity and to work out an agreement in advance by which one faction buys out the other at a fair price in the event a serious disagreement arises. Such an agreement is usually cast as a buy/sell agreement. (See part VII I.) Such an arrangement must resolve several basic questions:

1) Who is to buy out whom if both desire to continue the corporate business? Often the senior should buy out the junior, though if the age discrepancy is large, it may be more sensible to reverse the order and have the junior buy out the senior.

2) An agreement may provide that one shareholder sets a price at which she is willing to buy out the other shareholder or to sell her own shares, and the other shareholder has the election to buy or sell.

3) What events trigger the power to buy? Some kind of objective standard as to what constitutes dissension or deadlock sufficient to trigger the buyout obligation is usually desirable, such as the failure to agree on a slate of directors for some specified period.

4) Which pricing formulas should be used and which should be avoided? Because of the likelihood of dissension, the formula chosen should not rely on a cooperative effort to set the price. Also, the formula should yield as "fair" a price as possible rather than one that arguably creates a bargain for one faction or the other.

5) May the person who is bought out form a competing business, and if so, where and on what terms? A non-competition agreement is enforceable if it is reasonable under the circumstances.

6) In the event a buy-out has not been prepared in advance or cannot be worked out after the dissension or deadlock arises, the traditional remedy is involuntary dissolution, discussed below. (See part X F.) *In re Security Finance Co.*, 317 P.2d 1 (Cal.1957).

7) A number of innovative alternative remedies, less draconian than dissolution, have been evolved by state statutes and by judicial decisions. These alternative remedies are also discussed in part X F, below.

d. General corporation statutes in many states, and special close corporation statutes may contain mandatory buy-out provisions that can be elected by a corporation.

4. FIDUCIARY DUTIES AMONG SHAREHOLDERS AS A REMEDY FOR UNFAIR TREATMENT OF MINORITY SHAREHOLDERS

The traditional view is that shareholders have no fiduciary duty as such to each other, and that transactions that are unfair to minority shareholders cannot generally be attacked as a breach of a duty of loyalty or good faith owed by a majority shareholder.

a. Massachusetts has developed a fiduciary duty theory in this context. In *Donahue v. Rodd Electrotype Co.,* 328 N.E.2d 505 (Mass.1975) the court analogized the close corporation to a partnership and held that a "strict" fiduciary duty existed and that controlling shareholders owed a duty of the "utmost good faith and loyalty" to the minority.

Example: *Donahue* involved a situation where shares owned by the father of the majority shareholder had been redeemed by the corporation but the corporation offered to redeem shares owned by minority shareholders only at a much lower price. The court held this conduct violated the fiduciary duty that the majority shareholder owed to the minority. Many post-*Donahue* cases support this holding on similar facts. E.g. *Estate of Meller v. Adolf Meller Co.,* 554 A.2d 648 (R.I.1989); *Sundberg v. Abbott,* 423 N.W.2d 686 (Minn.App.1988); *Balvik v. Sylvester,* 411 N.W.2d 383 (N.D.1987). But see *Toner v. Baltimore Envelope Co.,* 498 A.2d 642 (Md.1985), where the court rejected a *per se* rule that any difference in price was improper and held that an examination of all relevant facts was necessary.

b. The *Donahue* opinion has been widely cited and relied upon by courts in other jurisdictions. See also *68th Street Apts., Inc. v. Lauricella,* 362 A.2d 78 (N.J. Super.1976), *Knaebel v. Heiner,* 663 P.2d 551 (Alaska 1983), *Russell v. First York Savings Co.,* 352 N.W.2d 871 (Neb.1984) (overruled on other grounds, *Van Pelt v. Greathouse,* 364 N.W.2d 14 (Neb.1985)). To the extent a tort of "freeze out" is recognized, it can be traced to the *Donahue* case.

Example: Minority shareholders in a closely held corporation establish (1) that they requested but were denied employment with the corporation, (2) the corporation never paid dividends, (3) compensation to the majority shareholders and their families in the form of salary, bonuses, and pension benefits was excessive, and (4) majority shareholders offered to buy out minority's shares at an unreasonably low price. A violation of the *Donahue* fiduciary duty has been established and the majority's conduct is unlawful. *Sugarman v. Sugarman,* 797 F.2d 3 (1st Cir.1986); *Crowley v. Communications for Hospitals, Inc* 573 N.E.2d 996 (Mass.App.1991).

c. *Donahue* was followed in Massachusetts by *Wilkes v. Springside Nursing Home, Inc.*, 353 N.E.2d 657 (Mass.1976) in which the court ordered reinstatement of a minority shareholder to the corporate payroll after he had been fired in violation of his expected treatment. The *Wilkes* court recognized, however, that the controlling faction needed "some room to maneuver" and that the group's "selfish interest" should be balanced against its fiduciary duty. Following this decision, the Massachusetts courts have continued to struggle to establish the line between appropriate majority action and breaches of the *Donahue* fiduciary duty.

1) In *Hallahan v. Haltom Corp.,* 385 N.E.2d 1033 (Mass.App.1979), the court ordered shares acquired by an equal co-owner of shares in an effort to change the balance of power to be returned to the seller at cost.

2) In *Leader v. Hycor, Inc.,* 479 N.E.2d 173 (Mass.1985) the court upheld a "reverse stock split" at the ratio of one new share for each 4,000 old shares, with fractional shares to be purchased for cash at a specified amount per share.

3) In *Goode v. Ryan,* 489 N.E.2d 1001 (Mass.1986), the court held that the *Donahue* duty did not permit the estate of a minority shareholder to compel the corporation to repurchase its shares in order to simplify the settlement of the estate. In this case, there was no prior contractual obligation to repurchase the shares.

4) In *Evangelista v. Holland,* 537 N.E.2d 589 (Mass.App.1989), the court held that a preexisting contract for the corporation to repurchase minority shares on the death of a shareholder at a set price should be enforced despite the argument that *Donahue* required the corporation to negotiate a price closer to the current value of the shares owned by the deceased shareholder. The court stated that there was a "mutuality of risk" and no violation of the *Donahue* duty.

d. Other cases recognize a fiduciary duty may exist but do not follow the implications of the strict *Donahue*) duty. *Zidell v. Zidell, Inc.,* 560 P.2d 1091 (Or.1977), and *Masinter v. WEBCO Co.,* 262 S.E.2d 433 (W.Va.1980).

e. Not all cases embrace the *Donahue* fiduciary concept. See *Toner v. Baltimore Envelope Co.,* 498 A.2d 642 (Md.1985).

5. MINORITY DISSOLUTION PROVISIONS

The Model Close Corporation Supplement, and the statutes of a few states permit corporations to elect special dissolution provisions that permit a minority shareholder to compel the dissolution of a corporation. In the absence of specific statutory authorization, a minority dissolution right may be created through the use of a voting trust or other device that permits the minority shareholder to compel the majority shareholder to vote in favor of dissolution under specified circumstances.

F. THE TRADITIONAL JUDICIAL REMEDY FOR DISSENSION OR DEADLOCK: INVOLUNTARY DISSOLUTION

The traditional remedy for problems of dissension and deadlock when no buyout has been agreed to is involuntary dissolution by judicial decree at the request of a shareholder. In order to obtain dissolution a petitioning shareholder must establish that statutory grounds for dissolution have been met. In addition, the court may withhold this remedy on equitable grounds.

1. STATUTORY GROUNDS FOR INVOLUNTARY DISSOLUTION

Generally, dissolution may not be available to a shareholder unless he or she can establish that the situation comes within the precise language of the statute.

a. There is no general common law right of involuntary dissolution and statutes authorizing this remedy are strictly construed. *Johnston v. Livingston Nursing Home, Inc.,* 211 So.2d 151 (Ala.1968); *Kruger v. Gerth,* 210 N.E.2d 355 (N.Y.1965); *Nelkin v. H. J. R. Realty Corp.,* 255 N.E.2d 713 (N.Y.1969).

b. Statutory grounds for involuntary dissolution vary to some extent from state to state. The following provisions, taken from the MBCA (1984) § 14.30, are fairly typical:

1) The acts of the directors or those in control of the corporation are "illegal, oppressive, or fraudulent;" or [MBCA (1984) § 14.30(2)(ii)]

2) The directors are deadlocked in the management of the corporate affairs, the shareholders are unable to break the deadlock and "irreparable injury to the corporation is threatened or being suffered, or the business and affairs of the corporation can no longer be conducted to the advantage of

the shareholders generally, because of the deadlock;" or [MBCA (1984) § 14.30(2)(i)]

3) The shareholders are deadlocked in voting power, and have failed to elect successors to directors whose terms have expired during a period that includes at least two consecutive annual meeting dates; or [MBCA (1984) § 14.30(2)(iii)]

4) The corporate assets are being "misapplied or wasted." [MBCA (1984) § 14.30(2)(iv)]

c. The word "oppressive" does not necessarily mean "imminent disaster;" it has been construed to mean lack of fair dealing or fair play, and in any event is a question for the trier of fact to resolve. *Mardikos v. Arger,* 457 N.Y.S.2d 371 (1982); *White v. Perkins,* 189 S.E.2d 315 (Va.1972); *Gidwitz v. Lanzit Corrugated Box Co.,* 170 N.E.2d 131 (Ill.1960).

d. Some statutes appear to adopt more lenient standards for authorizing involuntary dissolution.

Example: Wisconsin authorizes dissolution if the corporation is deadlocked so that "its business can no longer be conducted with advantage to its shareholders." Refusal to dissolve a deadlocked corporation that is unable to elect directors may itself be an abuse of discretion under this statute. *Strong v. Fromm Laboratories, Inc.,* 77 N.W.2d 389 (Wis.1956).

Example: The California statute authorizes dissolution if "reasonably necessary for the protection of the rights or interests of any substantial number of the shareholders, or of the complaining shareholders." Dissolution may be ordered under this statute even in the absence of deadlock, mismanagement, or unfairness. *Stumpf v. C. E. Stumpf & Sons, Inc.,* 120 Cal.Rptr. 671 (Cal.App.1975).

e. Even if statutory grounds for involuntary dissolution are established, courts generally view that remedy as being discretionary with the court rather than automatic. *Wollman v. Littman,* 316 N.Y.S.2d 526 (App.Div.1970); *In re Radom & Neidorff, Inc.,* 119 N.E.2d 563 (N.Y.1954).

1) Other remedies short of involuntary dissolution may sometimes be available and courts have declined to order dissolution until such other remedies have been tried. *Jackson v. Nicolai–Neppach Co.,* 348 P.2d 9 (Or. 1959); *Masinter v. WEBCO Co.,* 262 S.E.2d 433 (W.Va.1980).

2) Discretion is built into involuntary dissolution statutes which generally provide that courts "may" grant dissolution upon finding that grounds exist.

3) The ultimate remedy of dissolution may benefit one faction of shareholders at the expense of another in an unfair manner.

Example: If a single shareholder's personal abilities largely explain the corporation's success, she may well desire dissolution followed by liquidation. By performing services on behalf of the corporation, the dominant shareholder is in effect sharing the fruits of her abilities with other shareholders who may be making little or no direct contribution. If the corporation were dissolved, presumably the dominant shareholder could buy in the operating assets at a favorable price and thereafter continue to operate the business without sharing the fruits with anyone. It is unlikely that the minority shareholders will obtain the true value of their shares in this scenario. If the dominant shareholder simply abandons the corporation and starts a new business in competition with it, she may be subject to suit for unfair competition or usurpation of corporate opportunity. Hence, she may desire dissolution. This appears to have been the situation in *In re Radom & Neidorff, Inc.*, 119 N.E.2d 563 (N.Y.1954), in which dissolution was denied even though statutory grounds existed.

2. A NEW ALTERNATIVE REMEDY: JUDICIALLY ORDERED BUYOUTS

A significant modern trend is the increased recognition that courts may order a buyout of shares rather than involuntary dissolution in order to resolve problems of dissension or deadlock. Buyout orders are specifically authorized by statute in some states, and may be viewed as part of the inherent judicial power in states where they do not have express statutory sanction.

a. In a substantial number of cases since 1970, courts have ordered a buyout remedy in involuntary dissolution suits even when not expressly authorized by statute. See e.g. *Balvik v. Sylvester,* 411 N.W.2d 383 (N.D.1987); *Davis v. Sheerin,* 754 S.W.2d 375 (Tex.App.1988).

b. In 1991, MBCA (1984) § 14.34 was added to the Model Act expressly authorizing an involuntary buyout of shares owned by a shareholder who has filed a petition for involuntary dissolution under § 14.30.

1) § 14.34 is applicable to all corporations whose shares are not traded on national securities exchanges or public securities markets.

2) The price at which the shares are to be sold is the fair value of the shares. The parties are given an opportunity to reach a voluntary agreement as to the price, but if they fail to reach agreement on the price, the court determines the fair value of the shares.

3) If the court establishes the fair value of the shares, it may also establish terms for the purchase, including payment in installments and appropriate security.

4) After an involuntary dissolution suit is filed, the corporation or any shareholder may elect to purchase the shares. If one or more shareholders make this election, the remaining shareholders are entitled to purchase on a pro rata basis.

5) Once the election is made, the shareholder originally petitioning for dissolution may not withdraw the suit.

6) If a judicially ordered purchase does not occur within ten days of the order, the corporation is to be voluntarily dissolved.

Caveat: There has been little experience with such statutes, and it is not clear that they provide a significant benefit over a privately arranged transaction.

c. In some states, the remedy of mandatory buyout is available only to corporations that have elected close corporation status.

G. ALTERNATIVE REMEDIES FOR DISSENSION AND DEADLOCK

A variety of alternative remedies short of dissolution exist. Some are authorized specifically by special close corporation statutes; some may be part of a court's inherent discretion to fashion an appropriate remedy in litigation generally.

1. RECEIVERSHIPS

Some statutes contemplate the appointment of a receiver as an interim measure before dissolution is decreed; courts in some states may appoint receivers for deadlocked corporations within specific statutory authority.

a. If a corporation is placed in receivership, control passes from the hands of the deadlocked shareholders to a court-appointed receiver; even if the business and assets are preserved during the receivership, it is unlikely that the cause of deadlock will be corrected and the business ever returned to its owners. In such situations, dissolution is usually the ultimate step in the receivership.

b. In some states, receivership contemplates a winding up of corporate affairs from the outset.

c. Receivership may encourage the warring shareholders to reach an agreement by which one agrees to buy out the other's interest; in such situations, the receivership may be terminated when sale is consummated. *Shaw v. Robison*, 537 P.2d 487 (Utah 1975).

2. CUSTODIANS

Some state statutes authorize courts to appoint custodians for corporations that are deadlocked or otherwise threatened with irreparable injury. See e.g. Del. GCL § 226. A custodian differs from a receivership in that the goal is to continue the business of the corporation and not to liquidate it or distribute its assets. If a custodian is appointed and the cause of the deadlock or irreparable injury is not eliminated, a custodianship may be converted into a receivership.

a. This provision is designed to provide a simpler, more flexible and less drastic solution to deadlocked corporations than either the appointment of a receiver or dissolution. *In re Jamison Steel Corp.*, 322 P.2d 246 (Cal.App.1958); *Giuricich v. Emtrol Corp.*, 449 A.2d 232 (Del.1982).

b. The mere threat of the appointment of a custodian has a strong stimulus to quarreling shareholders to make some kind of a mutual accommodation.

c. It is doubtful that the appointment of a custodian can cure a deep-seated and fundamental difference of views between equally divided shareholders. A buyout or involuntary dissolution may be the only ultimate remedies.

Example: Two shareholders each own 50 of the stock of a corporation. One shareholder is in control of the board of directors and the deadlock prevents the other shareholder from attaining parity. A custodian may be appointed under Del.C. § 226(a)(1) despite the absence of irreparable injury. *Giuricich v. Emtrol Corp.*, 449 A.2d 232 (Del. 1982).

3. PROVISIONAL DIRECTORS

A provisional director is an impartial person appointed by a court to serve on the board of directors of a corporation if the board itself is so divided that it cannot make decisions "with the consequence that the business and affairs of the corporation can no longer be conducted to the advantage of the shareholders generally." See e.g. Del. GCL § 353.

a. Provisional directors are usually authorized only in the case of corporations that have elected close corporation status. (See part X D 2.)

b. A petition for the appointment of a provisional director may be made by one-half of the directors or by a specified fraction of the voting shareholders.

c. A provisional director may be removed by majority vote of the voting shareholders.

Caveat: While shareholders may not wish to have outsiders take over the business of the corporation through a receivership or custodian, or participate in management as a provisional director, these remedies generally may not be disclaimed in advance by a corporation.

4. BUYOUTS

Court ordered buyouts are a logical solution to problems of dissension or deadlock. They may be specifically authorized by statute, particularly in the case of special close corporation statutes, or in the absence of specific statutory authority, under the inherent authority of courts to fashion effective remedies.

5. ADDITIONAL REMEDIES AUTHORIZED BY THE CLOSE CORPORATION SUPPLEMENT

The Model Close Corporation Supplement, § 41, expressly authorizes remedies in addition to the appointment of a custodian or provisional director for electing close corporations, including:

a. The performance, prohibition, alteration, or setting aside of any action of the corporation or of its shareholders, directors, or officers of or any other party to the proceeding;

b. The cancellation or alteration of any provision in the corporation's articles of incorporation or bylaws;

c. The removal of any individual as a director or officer;

d. The appointment of any individual as a director or officer;

e. An accounting with respect to any matter in dispute;

f. The payment of dividends;

g. The award of damages to any party.

H. ARBITRATION AS AN ALTERNATIVE TO JUDICIAL INTERVENTION

Mandatory arbitration is sometimes used as a device to avoid a deadlock short of dissolution.

1. WHAT TYPES OF DISPUTES ARE ARBITRABLE?

Modern arbitration statutes contain virtually no restrictions on the types of disputes that may be resolved pursuant to arbitration.

a. In considering the desirability of arbitration, two questions should be considered:

   1) What kinds of controversies is the arbitrator likely to face?

   2) What kinds of solutions will he or she be permitted to adopt?

b. Many disputes leading to deadlock in a closely held corporation involve personality conflicts or broad differences in policy. An arbitrator may have no criteria for resolving such disputes, and even if he or she does resolve a specific dispute, it is unlikely that the decision will cure the basic disagreement which led to the original deadlock.

   Example: A minority shareholder in a corporation deadlocked because of an unanimity requirement seeks arbitration of a claim that the majority shareholder should be removed as director. A decision by the arbitrator to remove the majority shareholder in effect turns control of the corporation over to the minority shareholder, and because there is an unanimity requirement for the election of directors, the turnover of control is permanent, or at least until dissolution can be compelled pursuant to statute or a buyout otherwise arranged. Even if the majority shareholder has committed acts which constitute cause for removal, it is doubtful whether an arbitrator should favor permanently one faction over another in a pure struggle for control. *Application of Burkin,* 136 N.E.2d 862 (N.Y.1956).

   Example: In the foregoing example, a derivative suit for damages against the majority shareholder might be a more appropriate remedy than removal.

   Caveat: Courts routinely order arbitration in close corporation disputes when provided for by contract without consideration of the probable success of the arbitration. E.g., *Moskowitz v. Surrey Sleep Products, Inc.*, 292 N.Y.S.2d 748 (App.Div.1968).

c. Ultimately, if deep personal or policy conflicts continue, dissolution appears to be the only suitable remedy because arbitration cannot cure the root cause of the disagreement.

2. THE ADVANTAGES OF ARBITRATION

The advantages of arbitration are speed, cheapness, informality (as contrasted with a court proceeding), and the prospect of a decision by a person with knowledge and experience in business affairs. Where the reason for deadlock is a question not involving basic personal or policy matters, arbitration may satisfactorily resolve a dispute and permit the corporation to continue.

Example: The issue in disagreement is whether a corporation should exercise an option to purchase in a lease of real property. Such an issue is arbitrable. *Vogel v. Lewis*, 268 N.Y.S.2d 237 (App.Div.1966), aff'd 224 N.E.2d 738 (N.Y.1967).

3. ALTERNATIVE DISPUTE RESOLUTION (ADR)

While intra-corporate disputes in the close corporation would appear to be well suited for resolution by ADR techniques such as mediation or minitrial, there is no reported incident of the successful use of these techniques in this area.

I. REVIEW QUESTIONS

X–1. In a closely held corporation the shareholders today have essentially the same fiduciary duties to each other as partners in a partnership.

True ______ False ______

X–2. So long as an even division of shares between two shareholders is avoided, there is no possibility of a deadlock in a corporation.

True ______ False ______

X–3. Why isn't dissolution an adequate solution to deadlock and oppression problems in the closely held corporation since it appears to be an adequate solution for the same problems in the case of a partnership?

X–4 Are there better solutions to the deadlock problem than dissolution?

X–5. Every state should adopt a close corporation statute, since the experience in the states that have enacted them indicate that they are almost widely and universally used.

True _______ False _______

XI

CORPORATE GOVERNANCE AND THE PUBLICLY HELD CORPORATION

Analysis

A. CONTROL OF THE PUBLICLY HELD CORPORATION

The large publicly held corporation bears little relationship to the theoretical structure contemplated by state business corporation acts (Part VI) or to the actual structure of closely held corporations (Part X). The issues with respect to who controls large publicly held corporations and for whose benefit they are operated are among the most controversial today in corporation law. These issues are usually referred to under the title "corporate governance."

1. LIMITED ROLE OF SMALL SHAREHOLDERS

The number of voting shares in the large publicly held corporation is so large that the votes of any single small investor are almost always irrelevant on any issue.

a. With respect to the election of directors, the small shareholder is presented with a list of candidates for directors and she may vote for them or withhold her vote for some or all of them.

b. Since the overwhelming majority of the shareholders are going to vote in favor of the proposed directors, it really does not make very much difference whether or not she exercises her franchise.

Example: Phillips Petroleum Corporation, a large energy corporation in 1990 had sales of over $13 billion dollars and 277,180,511 common shares outstanding and held by investors. With the price of Phillips common stock at roughly $30 per share, a person owning one tenth of one per cent of Phillips shares (27,718 shares) would have an investment in Phillips of more than $830,000. One tenth of one per cent of the outstanding vote shares is not sufficient to give the shareholder a significant voice in corporate affairs.

Example: A shareholder who owns 300 shares of Phillips common stock may or may not authorize those shares to be voted for nominees for directors. It is inconceivable that 300 votes will affect the election of any nominee.

Caveat: Proxy appointments from small shareholders are cumulatively significant in establishing the existence of a quorum.

2. THE INCREASED SIGNIFICANCE OF INSTITUTIONAL INVESTORS

For many years the small shareholder was thought to epitomize the public shareholder. However, largely since World War II the institutional investor has grown tremendously in importance.

a. Institutional investors include pension and retirement funds, insurance companies, banks, foundations and university endowments, and investment companies, both closed end and mutual funds.

b. As of 1991, institutional investors own more than 50 per cent of all shares listed on the New York Stock Exchange. In many listed companies, a relatively small number of institutional investors—under 30—own an absolute majority all outstanding voting shares.

Example: In the case of Phillips Petroleum Company, one shareholder, Bankers Trust Company, alone owns beneficially more than 25 per cent of all Phillips shares. Most of these shares are owned by Bankers Trust as trustee for the Phillips thrift and long term savings plans for its employees.

c. The growth of institutional investors' portfolios in a sense has increased the broad base of ownership of the means of production in modern society. However in terms of the power to control, the growth of holdings by institutional investors represent a narrowing of the base, since relatively few persons now determine how large blocks of shares are voted.

d. Despite the potential voting power of institutional investors, historically they have not been active in the control and management of publicly held corporations. They have viewed their roles to be passive investors and by and large have not attempted to influence management decisions.

e. This passive attitude appears to be changing as some institutional investors have taken increased interest in issues of corporate governance, particularly those that affect financial returns to the investors. (See part XI C 3.)

Example: CALPERS, the California Public Employees Retirement System, is one of the largest pension funds. It has been a leader in seeking to increase the voice of large shareholders in decisions relating to corporate governance.

3. WHO SELECTS THE DIRECTORS?

The real decision as to who will be elected directors is made not in the shareholder election process, but at some earlier point when an internal decision within the corporation is made as to which candidates should be presented by the corporation to the shareholders as candidates for election to the board of directors.

a. Shareholders basically ratify this selection when they vote for directors.

(1) As a matter of policy, most institutional investors routinely support management's nominees for directors. In a few recent instances, individual institutional investors have refused to do so.

(2) Except in the rare case of a proxy fight, shareholders are presented with no choice as to whom to vote for. They may withhold their vote but may not vote for persons not on management's slate.

b. Historically, the slate of candidates was prepared or approved by the Chief Executive Officer (CEO). This practice permitted the CEO to "stack" the board of directors with friends.

c. This practice is gradually changing as the use of nominating committees has grown. (See part VIII J 4.)

(1) Nominating committees are usually composed primarily of outside directors not affiliated with management. The CEO, however, is usually the chairman of the nominating committee, or at least a member of that committee, and one or more inside directors may also serve on the nominating committee.

Caveat: Even in corporations that have created nomination committees, the CEO may still have considerable control over who is nominated to be a director on the management's slate.

(2) Many corporations have not created nominating committees to oversee the nomination process.

d. In some instances, a corporation has consulted with large institutional investors before picking new outside directors.

4. WHO RUNS THE BUSINESS?

Professional management, not the board of directors, runs the business. The board of directors does not participate directly in management but serves a limited role of oversight.

a. Executive management in a large publicly held corporation is itself hierarchical and bureaucratic. Businesses may be divided into subunits or "profit centers" with a considerable degree of discretion and independence.

(1) The home office provides centralized services in a variety of areas, including accounting, legal, capital management, pension and incentive plan administration, etc.

(2) The CEO has ultimate responsibility for the successful management of the enterprise.

(i) The CEO stands at the apex of the bureaucratic organization of the corporation.

(ii) As a practical matter in very large enterprises, the CEO may have little to do with day-to-day operations but be involved with financial and long term planning.

B. WHAT DOES THE BOARD OF DIRECTORS LOOK LIKE AND WHAT DOES IT DO?

A great deal of attention has been focussed on the board of directors of publicly held corporations. Historically, the board was viewed largely as a rubber stamp for management. While that was at least partially true at some earlier time, the modern board of directors is largely composed of persons unaffiliated with incumbent management and may act independently of the management on many matters.

1. COMPOSITION OF BOARDS OF DIRECTORS IN PUBLICLY HELD CORPORATIONS

The board of directors consists partly of management representatives ("inside directors") and partly of outsiders who are not officers or employees of the corporation and whose detailed knowledge of corporate affairs must of necessity be limited ("outside directors").

a. The Chief Executive Officer (CEO) is usually the chairman of the board of directors, though in some corporations these positions may be held by different people.

b. Inside directors are top level executives employed by the corporation. Since they are subordinate to the CEO in the executive suite they are generally assumed to largely reflect and support the CEO's policies.

c. Outside directors are predominantly CEOs (or retired CEOs) of other corporations, though they also include well known public figures, educators, politicians, business school deans, university presidents, and others. Experience with management of complex bureaucratic structures and lack of prior economic involvement with the corporation are usually desirable characteristics for outside directors.

1) Some analysis divides outside directors into "affiliated" and "non-affiliated" outside directors.

2) An "affiliated" outside director is one who has a substantial economic or business interest in the corporation, e. g. the corporation's outside counsel or a representative of its investment banker. An affiliated outside director is viewed as lacking the independence of a non-affiliated director.

3) The modern trend is strongly in the direction of having a majority of the board of directors consist of outside directors who are not affiliated with the corporation.

2. FUNCTIONS OF THE BOARD OF DIRECTORS IN PUBLICLY HELD CORPORATIONS

Studies suggest that the actual functions of boards of directors in publicly held corporations are as follows:

a. They provide general review and oversight of management.

b. They select the CEO and may replace the CEO if overall performance is unsatisfactory. (See part XI B 5.)

c. They assure that the corporation has in place a working auditing and accounting system.

d. They provide advice and counsel to management.

e. They provide intellectual discipline for management (which must appear before the board and present views and defend recommendations).

f. They act in crisis situations, such as where the CEO unexpectedly dies or is incapacitated, or where the affairs of the corporation are in such bad financial shape that a change of CEOs seems desirable.

3. WHAT BOARDS OF DIRECTORS DO NOT DO

By and large boards of directors do *not* perform the following functions:

a. They do not establish objectives, strategies and policies of the corporation.

b. They do not ask discerning or "tough" questions at meetings of the board.

c. They do not select high level corporate officers other than the CEO.

d. They do not decide what the corporation does.

e. They do not control the agenda of the board of directors.

4. WHY IS THE USE OF OUTSIDE DIRECTORS ENCOURAGED?

Outside directors serve on important committees—auditing, compensation, and nominating. (See parts VIII J 3–5.) They also serve other important roles in corporate governance.

a. A variety of factors has contributed to the growth of importance of outside directors.

   1) There was widespread disclosure of corporate misconduct during the 1970s, particularly following the Watergate scandal. Directors were blamed for failing to exercise independent oversight over management.

2) The Securities and Exchange Commission and the national securities exchanges have urged corporations to "broaden" their boards to include more outside directors.

3) The New York Stock Exchange requires listed companies to have audit committees made up exclusively of directors "independent of management and free from any relationship that . . . would interfere with the exercise of independent judgment as a committee member." *New York Stock Exchange Listed Company Manual,* § 303.00.

4) Courts hold that defensive tactics to avoid unwanted takeovers are more likely to be upheld as valid exercises of business judgment if they are approved by outside directors without involvement by inside directors who have large financial stake in the defeat of the takeover. (See part XIII E, F.)

5) Courts give respect to decisions by outside directors that derivative litigation against the corporation and its officers should not be pursued. (See part XVIII D.)

b. Along with the trend toward more outside directors is heightened realization of the duties and responsibilities of directors.

c. The wider use of committees of boards of directors consisting primarily or exclusively of outside directors may gradually shift the locus of power in publicly held corporations away from management and toward the outside directors.

Caveat: Because modern boards of directors consist predominantly of outside directors, they meet relatively infrequently (perhaps eight or ten times per year) for meetings that last only a few hours. Such a part-time board, consisting primarily of outside directors who have their own companies to manage, cannot be expected to assume the full management role contemplated by traditional corporation statutes.

5. THE ROLE OF THE BOARD OF DIRECTORS IN SELECTING THE CEO

Selection of the CEO, review of his or her performance, and removal where performance is unsatisfactory, are the most important functions of the board of directors.

a. In many publicly held corporations, the management tends to be a self-perpetuating body. Incumbent management usually recommends the successor to the incumbent CEO, and that recommendation is traditionally accepted by the board of directors.

1) The willingness of the board to accept management recommendations depends in part on the success of the retiring CEO and in part the relationship between the CEO and the individual members of the board of directors.

2) Major shareholders may also have an important voice in the selection, review and replacement of the CEO, but the ultimate responsibility rests with the board of directors.

3) The recent trend is for boards of directors to exercise independence in reviewing recommendations by incumbent management and the outgoing CEO as to who should be named CEO.

b. CEOs in many corporations rise gradually through the corporation's ranks until ultimately selected as the top manager by the board of directors on the recommendation of the outgoing CEO.

c. Many other factors, however, may enter into the selection process.

1) Personalities, loyalties, business relationships and the like may give considerable power to persons such as bankers, advisers, corporate counsel, and the like that is not dependent on the number of shares held or voted by them.

2) A potential CEO has a greater chance of approval by the board of directors if that person has served on the board of directors as an inside director or has had opportunities to become known to individual directors.

d. There are many recent examples of an outsider being named as CEO by the board of directors.

e. Where there is no single controlling block of shares, there always remains the possibility that a majority of the board of directors may agree to remove the CEO over his or her objection. Such actions occur rarely but are becoming increasingly common during the 1990s.

Example: Canion, the CEO and founder of Compaq Computer Corporation, in 1991 announced a gradual plan to reduce prices, improve the product line, and reduce personnel costs in order to restore that company's profitability and traditional position in the personal computer business. Concluding that the proposal was too gradual and too slow, the board of directors requested Canion's resignation when he proved to be unwilling to speed up drastically his proposed changes.

Example: In 1990, Stewart, the CEO of Lone Star Industries was forced to resign after an investigation revealed excessive expenses running into the millions of dollars were charged to Lone Star.

C. THE ROLE OF SHAREHOLDERS IN THE PUBLIC CORPORATION

Shareholders, of course, have the ultimate power to determine who controls the business. Again a great deal of attention has been given to the roles that shareholders play, the roles they should play, and the implications of the growth of institutional investors in the modern American economy.

1. BERLE AND MEANS VIEW

Berle and Means in 1933 wrote an influential book that pictured shareholders as a large group of disorganized small shareholders who tended to vote blindly in favor of management or as management recommends.

a. Because management had total control of the enterprise in this view, the business was operated for the benefit of the managers rather than for the benefit of the shareholders.

b. This control, according to Berle and Means, could be traced to several factors:

   1) Management has control of the "proxy solicitation machinery" and views of management are routinely brought before the shareholders as the experienced voice of those actually managing the business. Persons seeking to challenge incumbent management must communicate with shareholders largely at their own expense. Hence, overthrow by way of a proxy fight is apt to be expensive and unlikely to be successful.

   2) There is natural self-selection by shareholders. Most small shareholders consider their financial interest in their own investment as paramount, and if they are dissatisfied with the management of their corporation, they may sell their shares. Thus, shareholders unhappy with management tend to disappear by a process of self-elimination, and the remaining shareholders tend to be pro-management. This is often referred to as the "Wall Street Option".

c. The early development of institutional investors arguably supported the Berle and Means thesis since institutional investors typically voted large numbers of shares in favor of management. Since they viewed themselves as investors, not controllers, institutional investors were viewed as natural allies of management.

   Caveat: Whatever the early attitude of institutional investors, it is clear that during the 1980s a considerable amount of militancy developed on the part of some institutional investors which sought greater participation in corporate governance.

2. LIMITATIONS ON MANAGEMENT CONTROL: LAW AND ECONOMICS

The law and economics movement argued that the Berle and Means thesis was fundamentally flawed. Management control, was not limitless, it was argued, and the current system works pretty well.

a. The divergence in interest between managers and shareholders is an illustration of the phenomenon that arises naturally whenever one person has the responsibility to manage assets on behalf of other persons.

   1) The natural tendency of managers to favor their own private interests to those of shareholders may lead to "stealing" or "shirking," terms that generally refer to any conduct favoring the manager's self-interest over the interests of shareholders.

   2) The losses incurred by shareholders from stealing and shirking are called "agency costs" by economists.

b. Shareholders may reduce agency costs by monitoring the performance of managers or by devising incentive systems that encourage managers to maximize the wealth of shareholders.

   1) The mandatory disclosure requirements of the SEC (see part XII) permit monitoring; the use of independent auditors to report to the shareholders is another type of monitoring.

   2) Incentive devices that link managers' natural self interest to shareholder wealth maximization include stock purchase plans, stock option plans, bonuses based on overall profitability, and the like.

c. There are also significant market forces that work in the direction of assuring that management devotes its efforts to maximization of shareholder wealth rather than their personal wealth.

   1) These markets include a market for managerial talent, the market for corporate control, and the securities market itself.

      (i) The market for managerial talent rewards successful managers with employment opportunities in prestigious, well paid positions.

      (ii) The market for corporate control threatens managers who do not effectively maximize shareholder wealth with hostile takeovers through cash tender offers and the resultant loss of desirable positions.

(iii) A poor operating performance in terms of profits will result in depressed share prices and dissatisfied shareholders; these may lead indirectly to the ouster of management through a tender offer or similar maneuver.

Caveat: While commentators agree that these market forces operate to some extent as the economist predicts, there is considerable disagreement as to the effectiveness of these market forces in curbing abuses. Economists argue that these forces have substantial effect; other academics express skepticism largely based on anecdotal stories of excessive compensation or benefits.

Caveat: In the 1980s purchase-type takeovers of large publicly-held corporations were very common. In a significant number of cases, such a purchase was followed by the replacement of the board of directors and management.

(iv) Cash purchase-type takeovers have become rare during the 1990s but may resume in the future.

(v) Involuntary purchase-type takeovers determine corporate control through economic incentives to shareholders to sell their shares to aggressive outside interests.

(vi) Many purchase-type takeovers during the 1980s were based on borrowed funds, and the unwillingness of lenders to continue to make loans for this purpose spelled the end of the takeover movement of the 1980s.

d. Nonmarket forces also may tend to discipline management.

1) Ineffective management may lead members of the financial community—commercial bankers, investment bankers, etc. who have great power—to limit or dry up the sources of the corporation's long and short term financing.

2) If management conduct is sufficiently egregious and operating results are poor, one or more shareholders may launch a proxy fight seeking to replace the board of directors and thereafter the CEO.

3) A "palace coup" is a possibility, particularly if there are large blocks of shares not participating in management.

4) A shareholder's derivative suit may be filed if management's compensation is excessive or if there has been self-dealing transactions.

5) Institutional investors may seek to negotiate with management when they believe compensation or benefits have become excessive.

6) In 1991 there has been a considerable amount of negative publicity about excessive management compensation, particularly invidious comparisons with compensation levels for top management in Japan and other highly competitive industrialized nations.

7) The presence of large institutional shareholdings increases the possibility that an investor acquire or obtain voting control over a sufficiently large bloc of shares to permit the taking over of a publicly held corporation without making a public offer to purchase shares.

3. THE ROLE OF INSTITUTIONAL INVESTORS IN CORPORATE GOVERNANCE

The growth of institutional investors' shareholdings (see part XI A 2) has been accompanied by increased interest on the part of many institutional investors in matters of corporate governance.

a. This increased interest is due to several factors:

1) Institutional shareholdings have become so large that it is no longer possible to exercise a "Wall Street option" and simply sell shares to other investors. Only other institutional investors have the capacity to absorb high volumes of shares without devastating effects on market prices.

Example: Where institutional investors hold shares that are not widely traded, particularly in the over-the-counter market, there have been price declines in a single day of more than 50 per cent. Such declines may usually be traced to decisions by a few institutional investors to dispose of their holdings at whatever price is available.

2) Many institutional investors handle funds that ultimately belong to individual members of the general public in the form of pensions, life insurance proceeds, savings, or financial investments.

(i) These institutional investors therefore have fiduciary duties to maximize the returns to pensioners and others.

(ii) During the takeover movement of the 1980s, many of these institutional investors felt it necessary to accept tender offers at prices higher than the market price for shares.

(iii) Management's natural interest is to oppose outside takeover attempts, and many institutional investors concluded that it was not in their best interests to support management in the development of increasingly sophisticated defensive techniques that resulted in the defeat of tender offers at attractive prices.

3) Institutional investors recognize that they have the power, if they band together, to effectively control many large publicly held corporations.

Example: In a struggle for control, the blocs controlled by institutional investors may be the critical swing blocs, and by deciding to sell or not to sell the investors effectively determine who will control the corporation.

Example: Institutional investors have objected to management decisions to implement "shark repellent" defenses designed to make unwanted takeover attempts more difficult. This attitude reflects growing recognition that shark repellent defenses make takeovers more difficult, tend to entrench incumbent management, and are not in the best interests of shareholders, since they deprive shareholders of the opportunity to obtain premiums over market price for their shares in connection with takeover attempts.

b. The increased activism of institutional investors has taken several forms. Corporate management has opposed, or at least been very skeptical of, these developments.

1) Institutional investors have sometimes made informal recommendations or suggestions to corporate management, particularly in the context of takeovers. These recommendations or suggestions have been generally ignored.

2) Institutional investors have withheld their votes for incumbent directors in some instances.

3) Institutional investors have submitted shareholder proposals (see part XII) for inclusion in proxy statements. Some of these proposals have been approved and others have received very substantial percentages of the vote, calling management's attention forcefully to the dissatisfaction of large shareholders.

Caveat: In 1991 CALPERS decided to forego this approach at least temporarily, in favor of direct discussions with management.

4) Direct discussions between institutional investors and management have occurred in a number of instances.

5) Rather than facing a proxy fight on shareholders' proposals, some corporations have agreed voluntarily to give institutional investors

representation on the board of directors or otherwise adopt proposals, such as confidential voting procedures, favored by institutional investors.

6) In 1992 the SEC was considering amendments to its proxy regulations to make it easier for institutional investors to communicate with each other and to influence management.

4. SHAREHOLDER WEALTH MAXIMIZATION AS EXCLUSIVE GOAL OF CORPORATIONS

The traditional view is that the objective of a corporation is to maximize the wealth of its shareholders. This view is expressed in early cases, *Dodge v. Ford Motor Co.,* 170 N.W. 668, 684 (Mich.1919), and is the basic premise or tenet on which the entire analysis of the corporate governance by the law and economics movement is based.

a. Statutes in approximately thirty states now allow the board of directors and management to take into account the interests of "constituencies" other than shareholders in making decisions on behalf of the corporation.

   1) Constituencies may include employees, customers, suppliers, creditors, communities, and states in which the corporation has facilities or plants.

   2) These alternative constituencies are usually called "stakeholders" in the corporation to distinguish them from shareholders.

   3) Most of these statutes permit, but do not require, directors and managers to consider the interests of stakeholders. Connecticut requires directors and managers to do so.

b. These statutes were enacted, usually without extensive consideration, by state legislatures in response to fears of corporations incorporated in those states that they might be subject to unwanted takeover bids.

   1) Management of threatened companies believed that these statutes might permit them to turn down and defeat cash tender offers at above-market prices by relying on the interests of other stakeholders.

   2) There have been no reported instances of the actual application of these statutes.

c. These statutes have been widely criticized from several different perspectives. They have also had their defenders.

   1) Law and economics scholars have criticized these statutes because in their eyes economic efficiency is maximized if the managers are required to

maximize the return to "residual" claimants, i.e. the shareholders. They also argue that stakeholders may usually protect themselves by contract.

2) The Committee on Corporate Laws and the Business Roundtable have criticized these statutes because they increase uncertainty and raise the specter of possible lawsuits brought by other stakeholders who are not protected by director or management decisions.

3) The statutes have been defended as being consistent with the shareholders' long term profit interest and as merely stating what many directors and managers already feel to be the case: that duties are owed to these other Constituencies despite the legal theory to the contrary.

d. Shareholder wealth maximization is itself a difficult goal to apply in light of the diversity of shareholders, the ease with which shares may be traded, the diversification of investors' portfolios, and the development of options and so-called derivative securities.

D. NOMINEE AND BOOK ENTRY REGISTRATION

Corporation statutes assume that owners of shares record their identities in the share transfer records of the corporation and thereby become record owners of shares. Developments largely since 1970 have led to the development of book entry and nominee registration of ownership so that today only a minority of publicly held shares are held of record by the beneficial owners of the shares.

1. NOMINEE REGISTRATION BY INSTITUTIONAL INVESTORS

Large institutional investors developed the practice of holding securities in the names of *nominees*, usually a partnership of employees using names such as "Abel and Company." This practice began as early as the 1920s.

a. This practice developed for innocuous reasons: to avoid onerous transfer requirements placed on corporations or fiduciaries selling shares.

b. A single institutional investor often uses several different nominees.

c. The names of nominees used by institutional investors are generally known so that the issuer knows which institutions are the beneficial owners of shares registered in the names of nominees. Also, many institutional investors report publicly the shares owned in their portfolios.

2. "STREET NAME" REGISTRATION

Also at a relatively early time, traders and speculators in securities developed the practice of holding shares registered in "street names." The "street" referred to is

Wall Street, and the "names" referred to are the names of well known brokerage companies with offices on Wall Street.

a. Shares registered in street name are endorsed in blank by the registered owner and are transferred by delivery, usually between brokerage firms, to reflect transactions entered into over the New York or other stock exchanges.

b. Where a speculator purchases shares with a view toward a prompt resale, she will normally not want the shares registered in her own name.

c. Street name shares are bearer securities, but the problem of theft is not a serious one since most transfers of street name securities are between brokers.

d. Where shares are registered in street name, the corporation does not know who the beneficial owner is; indeed, it may not even know in which brokerage firm the shares are currently held.

e. Today, the transfer of shares held in book entry form is as simple as transfers of shares held in street name, and in addition has the advantage of eliminating the physical movement of bearer securities between offices.

3. BOOK ENTRY REGISTRATION

In the late 1960s, the securities trading industry faced a crisis in the "back office" when trading volume increased and the old method of completing securities transactions by delivering street name and other certificates was unable to handle the increased volume. A new system of recording share ownership developed from this crisis.

a. Central clearing corporations were created in the 1970s to facilitate trading in securities. Within a central clearing corporation, all shares are held of record by the central clearing corporation, and off-setting trades among members are netted on a daily basis. Each member's account with the central clearing corporation for any specific security is charged only with the daily net change. This process virtually eliminates transfers of certificates and substitutes book entries for other evidence of beneficial ownership of securities.

b. The principal central clearing corporation today is the Depository Trust Company (DTC) that handles transactions for securities traded on the New York Stock Exchange and other markets. Shares held by DTC are registered in the name of a nominee, Cede and Co., and certificates, if they exist at all, are held by DTC.

   1) Membership in DTC includes leading brokerage firms and banks.

   2) Shares owned by members of DTC and customers of those members are reflected only by book entry in the records of DTC.

c. Shares owned by customers of brokerage firms are reflected only by book entry in the records of the brokerage firm. Shares borrowed by customers to effect short sales are also reflected only by book entry in those records.

1) A customer's only evidence of the shares beneficially owned by her is the monthly statement from the brokerage firm.

2) A customer may receive a certificate for shares only by specifically requesting it. Some brokerage firms impose a charge to compensate for the extra paperwork involved in procuring a certificate registered in the name of the beneficial owner.

3) All transactions in a specific stock by customers of any member firm each day are netted together by the member firm and only the net balance is reported to DTC. Appropriate changes in the book entries showing each customer's current portfolio are made.

4) More than 60 per cent of all shares owned by members of the general public are now reflected by book entry rather than registration on the books of the issuer.

5) The system of book entry is ultimately dependent on the insurance provided to investors by the Securities Investors Protection Corporation, against financial failure of individual brokerage firms. SIPC insurance protects against loss of value from financial collapse of brokerage firms only.

d. In the book entry system, dividends or other distributions are wired by the issuer to DTC and in turn wired to member brokerage firms and banks. As a result, dividends on book entry shares appear on the customer's statement as having been credited on the payable date for the dividend or distribution.

e. The book entry system is highly efficient and has permitted the securities industry to handle trading days involving hundreds of millions of shares per day.

1) One potential disadvantage is that it places two intermediaries—DTC and the brokerage firm—between the issuer and the beneficial owner.

2) Book entry also complicates the distribution of proxy statements, annual reports, and other documents by the issuer to beneficial owners, particularly those requiring action in a brief period of time. (See part XII.)

f. Book entry is becoming more and more widely used and the number of shares represented by certificates issued to beneficial owners continues to decline.

g. MBCA (1984) § 7.23 authorizes corporations to establish, on a voluntary basis, procedures by which the corporation may recognize beneficial owners of street name or nominee-owned shares, thereby avoiding the need to communicate through different layers or tiers of record and non-beneficial owners.

   Caveat: This provision is experimental and there has been no experience with how it might work in practice.

h. The SEC has also addressed this problem by requiring brokers to supply issuers with lists of beneficial owners who do not object to their identities being disclosed to the issuers. This list is called the NOBO list. (See part XII.)

E. REVIEW QUESTIONS

XI–1. What is the "Wall Street Option" in publicly held corporations?

XI–2. In a publicly held corporation, who selects the directors?

XI–3. The major role of directors in the publicly held corporation is to establish general business policies for the corporation.

True ______ False ______

XI–4. A major function of directors is to decide who is to run the business, that is to select the chief executive officer.

True ______ False ______

XI–5. What is "book entry registration?"

XI–6. How does "street name" registration differ from "book entry?"

XI–7. What are institutional investors?

XI–8. Do institutional investors usually support management or insurgents?

XII

SEC DISCLOSURE REQUIREMENTS AND PROXY REGULATION

Publicly held corporations have obligations to disclose information to shareholders and to members of the general public. These disclosure obligations are closely tied in with the regulation of the solicitation of proxies by these corporations. Most modern law in these areas is of federal rather than state origin. Periodic reporting requirements are set forth in the Securities Exchange Act of 1934. The basic provision of federal law relating to proxy solicitation is section 14(a) of the 1934 Act, which makes it unlawful for any person to use the mails or any means or instrumentality of interstate commerce or the facilities of a national securities exchange to solicit proxies with respect to covered corporations "in contravention of such rules and regulations as the [Securities and Exchange] Commission may prescribe as necessary or appropriate in the public interest or for the protection of investors." Pursuant to this rather boundless grant of authority to regulate proxies, the SEC has issued the comprehensive and detailed regulations which form the bulk of this chapter.

Analysis

A. CORPORATIONS SUBJECT TO FEDERAL PERIODIC DISCLOSURE AND PROXY REGULATION RULES

This section deals with two different sets of requirements: the requirement that corporations make periodic public disclosures (described in part B) and the requirement that corporations comply with the SEC proxy regulations (described in part C).

1. CORPORATIONS SUBJECT TO PERIODIC DISCLOSURE REQUIREMENTS

Corporations that have registered a public offering of securities under the Securities Act of 1933 (see part V G) or are required to register under section 12 of the Securities Exchange Act of 1934 are subject to the public disclosure requirements described in part B.

2. CORPORATIONS SUBJECT TO THE SEC PROXY REGULATIONS: SECTION 12 REGISTRATION

Only corporations that are required to register under section 12 of the Securities Exchange Act of 1934 are subject to federal proxy regulations. Section 12 is applicable to all corporations (1) having securities that are registered on a national securities exchange, or (2) having assets in excess of $5,000,000 and a class of equity securities held of record by 500 persons or more. The SEC has by regulation increased the $1,000,000 minimum appearing in section 12 to $5,000,000.

Example: Corporation X has 400 shareholders of record holding common stock, and another 400 shareholders of record holding preferred stock, but no shares are registered on a national securities exchange. The preferred shares were sold pursuant to a 1933 Act registration. Corporation X is not required to register under section 12 even though it has an aggregate of 800 shareholders since no class of shares is held by 500 persons. It is, however, subject to the periodic disclosure requirements.

Example: Corporation Y has 520 shareholders of record of common shares and $7,000,000 of assets. The shares are traded infrequently by a single broker/dealer in Topeka, Kansas. Corporation Y is required to register under section 12 even though shares are not traded on any exchange. It is therefore subject to both the periodic disclosure and proxy regulation requirements.

Example: Corporation Z has $100,000,000,000 in assets and 440 common shareholders. Corporation Z has never made a public offering of shares. Corporation Z is not required to register under section 12 and is not subject to SEC periodic reporting or disclosure requirements.

Example: Corporation *Z's* shareholders increase in number because of gifts of shares to children and grandchildren until there are 525 common shareholders. Corporation Z must register under section 12 and therefore becomes subject to both the proxy regulation and periodic disclosure requirements.

Example: In the previous examples, corporations X and Z have previously made registered public offerings under the Securities Act of 1933. Even though they are not required to register under section 12 of the 1934 Act they must comply with the periodic disclosure requirements.

Caveat: Most corporations that make an initial public offering of shares under the Securities Act of 1933 are also required to register under section 12 of the 1934 Act because they meet the 500 shareholder and $5,000,000 of assets requirements as a result of the public offering. It is possible, however, that a corporation making a public offering may not meet these minimum requirements. Similarly it is possible for a corporation to become subject to section 12 of the 1934 Act without ever making a public offering under the 1934 Act. See the above examples relating to corporation Z.

3. TERMINATION OF SECTION 12 REGISTRATION

Once a corporation is required to register under section 12, it remains subject to that section even though the number of shareholders drops below 500; registration under section 12 may be terminated only if the corporation has no class held of record by more than 300 persons. A corporation may also terminate registration if its assets are valued at less than $5,000,000 on the last day of its fiscal year for the last three years and it has no class held of record by more than 500 persons.

B. PERIODIC DISCLOSURE REQUIREMENTS

Companies subject to the SEC periodic reporting and disclosure requirements are obligated to file periodic reports with the SEC. These reports, which are subject to detailed formal requirements by SEC regulation, are designed to update on a continuing basis the information that is publicly available about the company. These reports are publicly available: they are placed in SEC reading rooms and are widely distributed by electronic means to investors, brokerage firms, and the like. Information in these reports also form the basis of reports and stories in financial and other newspapers and magazines.

1. FORM 10–K

Form 10–K is an annual report to the SEC designed basically to provide the same information about the issuer that appears in a 1933 Act registration statement. It must include full audited financial statements. If the information required in the 10–K overlaps with information in proxy statements or annual reports (discussed below) the information may be omitted from the 10–K.

2. FORM 10–Q

Form 10–Q is a quarterly report containing unaudited interim financial data. It must also disclose material nonrecurring events that occurred during the quarter, such as commencement of significant litigation.

3. FORM 8–K

Form 8–K is a report that must be filed only when a reportable event occurs. A reportable event generally involves matters of major significance such as changes in control, material acquisitions or dispositions of assets, changes in the certifying accountant, and resignations of directors.

4. OTHER FORMS

The SEC has promulgated other forms for use in a variety of specialized circumstances. For example, Form SR must be filed describing the expenses attributable to, and the use of funds acquired through, a public offering. Form 10–C is applicable to corporations having a class of securities quoted on NASDAQ that undergoes a name change or has changes in excess of 5 per cent in the number of securities of the class that is quoted on NASDAQ.

C. FEDERAL REGULATION OF PROXIES

The justification for the federalization of the proxy solicitation process in corporations registered under section 12 of the 1934 Act was the absence of meaningful state regulation over nation-wide solicitations of proxies prior to 1934.

1. CONSTITUTIONAL BASIS FOR REGULATION

The constitutional basis for federal proxy regulation is the use of the mails or an instrumentality in interstate commerce. As a practical matter, it is probably impossible to solicit a large number of proxies in connection with a security registered under section 12 without some use of the mails or facilities of interstate commerce.

2. PROXY STATEMENTS

The SEC proxy regulations (rule 14a–3) provide that with certain exceptions a solicitation of a proxy appointment must be accompanied or preceded by the delivery of a proxy statement setting forth detailed information about the persons making the solicitation, about the background of all nominees, and in connection with solicitations by management, about remuneration and other transactions with management and with others, and about any matter on which the vote of shareholders is sought.

a. These proxy statements are a major source of shareholder information about corporate affairs.

b. The public disclosure documents referred to in part XII B are filed with the SEC and are publicly available. The proxy statements are sent directly to shareholders in connection with the solicitation of proxies by management.

3. FORM OF PROXY APPOINTMENTS

SEC regulations under § 14(a) of the 1934 Act prescribe the form of proxy appointments and prohibit certain devices such as undated or post-dated appointments or broad grants of discretionary power to proxy holders. Shareholders must be given the option to vote for candidates for directors (or withhold a vote for some or all of the candidates). Proxies must actually vote the shares as shareholders direct for the election of directors and on other issues presented for decision to the shareholders.

4. PRESOLICITATION REVIEW

The SEC conducts a presolicitation review process for proxy documents. Drafts of proxy statements and other soliciting materials (such as letters, press releases, and the like), must be filed with the SEC at least ten days prior to the date it is proposed to mail definitive copies to securities holders.

a. Because the period for evaluation is short, as a practical matter the SEC review is based on an analysis of the filing and whatever else is in the Commission's files relating to the filing company.

b. Most courts have recognized that this preliminary SEC review of proxy solicitation material should not be given great weight in subsequently evaluating the sufficiency of the disclosures.

c. While the SEC does not pass upon the accuracy or adequacy of the disclosures, it does indicate that revisions should be made if it concludes that some materials are incomplete or inaccurate.

5. WHAT IS A SOLICITATION?

The SEC has consistently argued, and most courts have agreed, that the definitions of "solicitation" and "proxy" should be broadly construed to ensure the widest protection provided by the proxy regulations.

Example: An authorization to obtain a list of shareholders signed by 42 shareholders is a solicitation subject to the proxy regulations. *Studebaker Corp. v. Gittlin*, 360 F.2d 692 (2d Cir.1966).

Example: Advertisements urging the approval or disapproval of certain transactions may constitute solicitations, though some courts have disagreed. E. g., *Brown v. Chicago R. I. & P. Ry.*, 328 F.2d 122 (7th Cir.1964).

6. EXEMPT PROXY SOLICITATIONS

The SEC proxy regulations exempt certain narrow classes of solicitations. The principal exceptions are:

a. Solicitations to less than 10 persons;

b. Solicitations by brokers to beneficial owners to obtain instructions on how to vote the shares;

c. Solicitation by a beneficial owner to obtain a proxy appointment form from the record holder;

d. Newspaper advertisements that describe only how holders may obtain copies of the proxy documents;

e. Proxy advice furnished by a person who renders financial advice in the ordinary course of business and receives no special remuneration for the proxy advice.

Caveat: In 1990, the SEC received a request from CALPERS to make changes in the proxy regulations that would permit, among other things, institutional investors to contact more than 10 other institutional investors with respect to shareholder issues without requiring compliance with the SEC proxy rules. Many of these proposals are opposed by management of publicly held corporations and it is uncertain what changes, if any, the SEC will make in these regulations.

7. CORPORATIONS THAT NEED NOT SOLICIT PROXIES

Most publicly held corporations find it necessary to solicit proxies if there is to be a quorum at a shareholders' meeting.

a. Most corporate officers and directors in the aggregate own only a minute fraction of the outstanding shares.

b. As a practical matter, the number of shares voted by shareholders who appear personally at a meeting is also usually numerically insignificant.

c. In some corporations subject to registration under section 12, a quorum may be represented by a single person or by a relatively few persons who may be expected to be physically present at the meeting. Such persons typically are allied with management.

   1) In such corporations, management may conduct its business without any solicitation of public shareholders.

2) Section 14(f) of the Securities Exchange Act of 1934 requires such corporations to supply shareholders with information "substantially equivalent" to the information that would have been required if a proxy solicitation to its shareholders had been made.

8. PROBLEMS CREATED BY BOOK ENTRY AND NOMINEE HOLDINGS

The widespread practice of holding shares in book entry form or in the names of nominees creates problems for the SEC proxy disclosure process since the beneficial owners of such shares are not the record owners and do not directly receive the required proxy statements or annual reports.

a. SEC regulations require brokers and dealers to transmit proxy material to the beneficial owners of shares, and either:

1) Execute proxy forms in blank (and deliver them to the beneficial owners so that the shares may be voted by them) or

2) Solicit directions as to how to vote the shares and directly vote them as the beneficial owners direct.

b. Stock exchange rules and SEC regulations require brokers and dealers to transmit proxy information to beneficial owners if the solicitor of proxies reimburses the expenses of the broker or dealer. Issuers must provide registered owners who are nominees with sufficient copies of the proxy material so that a copy can be transmitted to each beneficial owner.

c. SEC regulations require brokerage firms that hold shares of customers in book entry form to determine whether the customers object to disclosure of their names to the issuer in order to permit direct communication between issuer and beneficial owner.

1) Beneficial owners who do not object are known as NOBOs.

2) Many brokerage firms recommend that customers do not elect to become NOBOs in part because of concern that the customers may be solicited by other brokerage firms if their names appear on a NOBO list.

3) A corporation may be required to prepare a NOBO list and make it available to a shareholder for inspection. *Sadler v. NCR Corp.,* 928 F.2d 48 (2d Cir.1991).

d. Studies by the SEC reveal that these devices work reasonably efficiently and that there are not widespread abuses of the proxy solicitation process as a result of the nominee and book entry registration practices.

e. MBCA (1984) § 7.23 proposes an alternative device that permits corporations to establish procedures to treat beneficial owners of shares as traditional record owners, thereby minimizing the routine transfer of voting-related documents by nominees and others. This section is experimental in nature.

f. Private organizations have proposed creating computerized beneficial ownership lists to simplify the communication problems between issuer and beneficial owner. These proposals have not been implemented.

9. ANNUAL REPORTS

The proxy regulations indirectly require the distribution of annual reports since rule 14a–3(b) provides that if a solicitation is made on behalf of management relating to an annual meeting of shareholders at which directors are to be elected, the proxy statement must be accompanied or preceded by an annual report of the corporation. This is the only basis in many states to require the distribution of annual information to shareholders.

10. SHAREHOLDER PROPOSALS

Rule 14a–8 of the SEC regulations establishes an elaborate procedure by which a shareholder may submit one proposal each year for inclusion in the registrant's proxy statement.

a. If the proposal is an appropriate one for shareholder action, the registrant is required to include the proposal even if opposed to it.

b. The shareholder submitting the proposal must have owned for a period of at least one year either (i) one per cent of the outstanding shares or (ii) shares with a market value of at least $1,000. The shares may be owned beneficially or of record. As a practical matter, the sole qualifier is the market value test.

c. A shareholder submitting a proposal may also submit a supporting statement which the registrant is required to publish if the proposal and the supporting statement do not exceed 500 words in the aggregate. Management may explain the basis of its opposition to a proposal without limitation on the number of words.

d. Proposals that fail in one year may be resubmitted within the following five years only if they meet the following standards:

   1) If submitted only one time during the last five years, it received at least 3 per cent of the total number of votes cast on the proposal;

   2) If submitted two times within the last five years, it received at least 6 per cent of the total number of votes cast at its last submission; and

3) If submitted three or more times during the last five years, it received at least 10 per cent of the total number of votes cast at its last submission.

e. Because shareholders may seek action on proposals of dubious relevance or propriety, or simply for personal publicity, the SEC has imposed specific requirements and limitations on shareholders' proposals. A proposal may be omitted if:

1) It is not a proper subject for action by security holders under the law of the registrant's domicile;

2) It would require the registrant to violate any state, federal or foreign law, if implemented;

3) It is contrary to any of the SEC's proxy regulations;

4) It relates to the redress of a personal claim or grievance against the registrant, its management, or any person, or is designed to result in a benefit to the proponent or to further a personal benefit not shared with other security holders;

5) It deals with operations which account for less than 5 per cent of the registrant's total assets or 5 per cent of its net earnings and gross sales for its most recent fiscal year "and is not otherwise significantly related" to the registrant's business;

6) It deals with a matter that is beyond the registrant's power to effectuate;

7) It deals with a matter relating to the conduct of ordinary business operations of the registrant;

8) It relates to an election to office;

9) It is moot (presumably because the registrant has substantially implemented the proposal);

10) It is either counter to a proposal by management or substantially the same as a proposal by another shareholder which will be included in the proxy materials;

11) It relates to specific amounts of cash or stock dividends.

f. The SEC has issued numerous rulings applying many of these exclusions; as a result, phrases such as "proper subject" or "ordinary business operations" have been given considerable practical content, and the tests are not as vague and open-ended as the language might indicate. In *S.E.C. v. Transamerica Corp.*,

163 F.2d 511 (3d Cir.1947) the court rejected an argument that a "proper subject" should be construed restrictively or legalistically.

Example: Important business-related proposals are "proper subjects" for shareholder action under state law if they are phrased as recommendations to the board of directors rather than specific directions to the corporation.

Example: A proposal to institute cumulative voting must be included in a proxy statement.

Example: A proposal that an electric utility not build a nuclear power plant may not be omitted on the ground that it involves only "ordinary business operations."

Example: A proposal that the bylaws of an oil company be amended to disqualify OPEC citizens from service on the board of directors may be omitted from the proxy statement since one OPEC citizen was already a director and running for reelection so that the proposal related to an election to office. *Rauchman v. Mobil Corporation,* 739 F.2d 205 (6th Cir.1984).

Example: A proposal that the corporation cease all dealings with the Union of South Africa until it changes its racial policies must be included in the proxy statement. Numerous other social issues have been the subject of shareholder proposals, ranging from control of radioactive emissions to eliminating the sale of war toys and prohibiting political contributions by the corporation.

Example: In 1989, the SEC upheld the right of a neo-Nazi group to include a resolution in AT & T's proxy statement calling on AT & T to dismantle its affirmative action program. In 1991, the SEC held by a 3–2 vote that CAPITAL CITIES/ABC could omit a proposal that required the registrant to report on its equal employment opportunity programs, including data on workforce composition and affirmative action timetables and programs. The SEC held that this proposal could be omitted on the ground it dealt with the ordinary business operations of the registrant.

Caveat: Some SEC Commissioners have expressed concern that the numerous social policy proposals being included in proxy statements provide little or no benefit to shareholders generally. This view may explain the CAPITAL CITIES/ABC vote.

g. The best-known rule 14a–8 case is *Medical Committee for Human Rights v. S.E.C.,* 432 F.2d 659 (D.C.Cir.1970), vacated as moot 404 U.S. 403, 92 S.Ct. 577

(1972). The court held reviewable an SEC decision during the Viet Nam war that permitted the omission of a shareholder's proposal relating to the manufacture of napalm; the Court strongly intimated that proposals of this nature should be permitted to be considered by shareholders.

h. Institutional investors have proposed a number of shareholders' proposals. In many instances, these proposals were voluntarily implemented by the registrant and were not voted on by shareholders. In other instances these proposals were either adopted outright or received significant shareholder support. Proposals made by institutional investors include: confidential voting (approved outright by shareholders of two companies during 1990 and voluntarily implemented by management at several others), independent tabulation of votes, requiring shareholder approval for poison pills and other defensive tactics relating to takeovers, requiring shareholder approval of management compensation arrangements following a takeover (so-called golden parachutes), requiring issuers to opt out of undesirable provisions of state law, and requiring the redemption of poison pills when faced with a desirable tender offer.

i. In light of recent institutional activity under rule 14a–8, the SEC is considering a variety of amendments to this rule.

j. Some academic commentary during the 1980s and early 1990s has been critical of the shareholder proposal rule.

D. FALSE AND MISLEADING STATEMENTS IN PROXY COMMUNICATIONS

Rule 14a–9 makes it unlawful to solicit proxy appointments by communications that contain "any statement which, at the time and in the light of the circumstances under which it is made, is false or misleading with respect to any material fact, or which omits to state any material fact necessary in order to make the statements therein not false or misleading."

1. PRIVATE CAUSE OF ACTION

This broad prohibition creates a private cause of action by shareholders. *J. I. Case Co. v. Borak*, 377 U.S. 426, 84 S.Ct. 1555 (1964). In that case the Court held that rule 14a–9 created a private cause of action since, "private enforcement of the proxy rules provides a necessary supplement to Commission action. As in antitrust treble damage litigation, the possibility of civil damages or injunctive relief serves as a most effective weapon in the enforcement of the proxy requirements."

2. NATURE OF POST-BORAK LITIGATION

Since *Borak* there has been a substantial volume of private litigation under rule 14a–9. Such litigation is within the exclusive jurisdiction of the federal courts and state "security for expenses" statutes are inapplicable. This litigation has been largely shaped by three other leading Supreme Court decisions:

a. In *Mills v. Electric Auto–Lite Co.*, 396 U.S. 375, 90 S.Ct. 616 (1970), the Court held:

   1) It is not necessary to show that the omission of a material fact actually influenced votes; rather, it is enough to establish that the vote itself was an essential step in the transaction being questioned, and

   2) If a material omission is established, the plaintiff's attorney is entitled to recover attorney's fees from the issuer even though no dollar recovery appears likely.

b. In *TSC Industries, Inc. v. Northway, Inc.*, 426 U.S. 438, 96 S.Ct. 2126 (1976), an opinion widely read as narrowing the scope of the private cause of action under rule 14a–9, the Court:

   1) Defined a "material fact" to be "an omitted fact if there is a substantial likelihood that a reasonable shareholder *would* consider it important in deciding how to vote;"

   2) Rejected the competing test that would have defined material fact to be a fact "which a reasonable shareholder *might* consider appropriate;" and

   3) Held that it was error to grant summary judgment on the issue whether the misleading statements involved in this case were "material" under the above tests. Thus, while the difference between the rejected and adopted tests may seem primarily semantic, the Court's distinction appears to constitute a warning to lower courts to limit rule 14a–9 to substantial misstatements; prior to this decision some courts had tended to find relatively minor misstatements or omissions to be "material" and therefore violations of rule 14a–9.

      Example: In a proposed sale of a corporation, the proxy statement does not disclose that the largest single shareholder needs funds immediately in order to meet estate tax liabilities. Whether such an omission meets the test of materiality set forth in *TSC Industries v. Northway* is an issue that should be submitted to a jury and not resolved on a motion for summary judgment. *Mendell v. Greenberg,* 927 F.2d 667 (2d Cir.1990).

c. In *Virginia Bankshares, Inc. v. Sandberg,* ___ U.S. ___, 111 S.Ct. 2749 (1991), the Court held that (1) a statement couched in terms of opinion or belief may nevertheless be materially misleading in violation of rule 14a–9, but that (2) a false statement in a proxy solicitation does not meet a test of "causal necessity" if it is addressed solely to shareholders whose combined votes are not sufficient to prevent the action being taken.

1) A statement of opinion or belief that "The Plan of Merger has been approved by the Board of Directors because it provides an opportunity for the Bank's public shareholders to achieve a high value for their shares" when in fact the directors did not hold the belief that a high value was being offered was a materially misleading statement.

2) In a cash out merger (see part XIX) the corporation solicits proxies from all shareholders even though the controlling shareholder owns 85 per cent of the outstanding shares and only a majority vote is needed to approve the merger. Since the minority shareholders' vote could not affect the outcome of the vote, the materially misleading statement about "high value" did not meet the test of "causal necessity" and could not be made the basis of a private suit brought by minority shareholders under Rule 14a–9.

3) In *Scattergood v. Perelman,* 945 F.2d 618 (3d Cir.1991), the court extended the "causal necessity" argument to encompass misstatements appearing in communications with shareholders prior to the actual delivery of the proxy statement.

Caveat: False statements in proxy statements may also invalidate transactions under Rule 10b–5 (see part XV B) and state law (see part XIX B).

3. REMEDIES IN RULE 14a–9 CASES

In an appropriate rule 14a–9 case, the court has several alternative remedies.

a. A court may issue a temporary restraining order (TRO) to enjoin the distribution of proxy material, the voting of the proxies themselves, or the holding of the meeting.

1) A TRO would normally terminate after all misstatements or deficiencies in the proxy solicitation material under rule 14a–9 have been corrected.

2) In many cases the plaintiff does not seek a TRO because he or she is unable or unwilling to post the bond that may be required if the proxy solicitation involves approval of a merger or other significant transaction.

b. In the absence of a TRO, the meeting may be held, the proxies voted, and the transaction consummated before there is a judicial determination of whether or not the proxy solicitation material violates rule 14a–9. Thereafter, if a material omission in connection with a vote necessary to effectuate a transaction is established, the court may:

1) "Unwind" the merger;

2) Award money damages;

3) Do nothing.

c. Under *Mills*, attorney's fees might be awarded even if the transaction in question is not set aside or damages not awarded. The prospect of an award of attorneys' fees encourages vigorous prosecutions of violations of rule 14a–9 even if substantial relief seemed remote.

Caveat: The narrowed definition of materiality in *TSC Industries* coupled with the refusal to grant summary judgment on the issue of liability in that case, have significantly decreased the likelihood that attorney's fees will be awarded in close cases. Further, any award of attorney's fees is likely to be deferred until after the end of a long and expensive trial on the merits. From the standpoint of plaintiffs' attorneys, these factors make vigorous prosecution of close cases less attractive.

E. PROXY CONTESTS

SEC regulations with respect to proxy contests are described in the following chapter. (See part XIII B.)

F. REVIEW QUESTIONS

XII–1. Since the solicitation of proxy appointments is an internal function of corporate management, this subject is largely governed by state law.

True ______ False ______

XII–2. When is a corporation subject to federal proxy regulation?

XII–3. When is a corporation subject to SEC periodic disclosure requirements?

XII–4. What is the constitutional basis for federal regulation of proxies?

XII–5. How does federal proxy regulation attempt to assure the transmission of complete and adequate information about corporate affairs to shareholders?

XII–6. If a corporation includes false or misleading statements in its proxy solicitation statement, may the individual shareholders object and bring suit if the statement is used to obtain shareholder approval of a transaction?

XII–7. In a suit by a shareholder, does the false or misleading statement have to be material and, if so, how is "materiality" defined?

XII–8. May a shareholder plaintiff obtain attorneys' fees in a suit described in question XII–6 if his suit is successful?

XII–9. May the prohibitions on false or misleading statements be avoided by phrasing them in terms of opinion or estimate rather than fact?

XII–10. A minority shareholder in a publicly held corporation subject to SEC regulation requests that the corporation include in its proxy statement a proposal that the corporation not develop nuclear energy facilities. May the corporation reject out of hand such a request?

XII–11. Even though a corporation is required to include a shareholder proposal in its proxy statement, history demonstrates that most such proposals that are presented by individuals are rejected by large pluralities. Why is any attention paid at all to such proposals?

XII–12. Have any shareholder proposals ever been adopted?

XII–13. Expansion, Ltd. is a growing corporation that speculates in the recent boom in rural real estate. Its success has been erratic. The acquisition of Hideaway Ranch, Inc., a popular tourist resort, became its next objective. To this end, Expansion bought 39 percent of Hideaway's shares from a few large shareholders and then proposed a merger to the Hideaway management, which was inclined to support the merger, particularly because of Expansion's promise to retain them in managerial capacities in Expansion, the surviving corporation. Hideaway solicited proxies for the proposed merger and received the necessary shareholder vote. However, the proxy material failed to disclose Expansion's erratic past or its speculative plans; nor did it mention the commitment made to Hideaway management. Under the merger Hideaway shareholders received two shares of Expansion for each of their Hideaway shares. No independent appraisal was made. An examination of Expansion's history reveals that its shares rarely reached a value as high as referred to in the prospectus. Expansion's securities are registered under section 12 of the federal Securities Exchange Act of 1934 but Hideaway's are not.

What rights and remedies might be available to Jack Case, a shareholder of Hideaway who dissented and is now seeking appraisal?

XII–14. Assume that Hideaway is a publicly held corporation registered under section 12 and Expansion does not attempt to complete the merger until after it has acquired more than 50 per cent of Hideaway stock, thereby assuring that the merger will be approved. If the proxy statement fails to make the disclosures referred to in question 13, will Case be able to bring a suit under the federal proxy regulations?

XIII

PROXY FIGHTS, TENDER OFFERS AND OTHER CONTESTS FOR CONTROL

Contests for control of publicly held corporations may take a variety of forms; during the 1980s the takeover movement was in full swing and new forms evolved rapidly in response to increasing sophistication in takeover defenses. This movement has come to a halt in the 1990s largely as a result of the collapse of the junk bond market and the drying up of sources of credit and lendable funds available for takeovers.

The contests for control discussed in this chapter are alternative to consensual transactions such as mergers or the purchase of assets or shares discussed in Chapter XIX. If a corporation is approached with a proposal that it be purchased or merged in a consensual transaction, but declines to do so, the aggressor may adopt one or more of the tactics discussed in this chapter.

Analysis

A. PRINCIPAL FORMS OF CONTESTS FOR CONTROL

Contests for control may take several different forms. These forms may be divided into the following broad categories:

1. PROXY FIGHTS OR PROXY CONTESTS

In a proxy fight a nonmanagement faction (the "insurgents") seek to obtain sufficient proxies from other shareholders to oust incumbent management. Management usually conducts a competing proxy solicitation. (See part XIII B.)

2. PURCHASE TYPE TAKEOVERS

In purchase type takeovers, the outside aggressor (sometimes called the "offeror") makes a public offer to purchase shares directly from tendering shareholders, bypassing the board of directors. Usually the offeror seeks enough shares to ensure voting control; if more shares are tendered than called for, the offeror may take pro rata or may take all shares tendered. (See part XIII C.)

a. Such an offer is usually called a "cash tender offer."

b. The ultimate goal of the aggressor is usually to obtain all of the shares of the target corporation, and a second transaction to acquire the balance of the outstanding shares usually shortly follows a successful acquisition of control.

c. Most modern takeovers have involved cash tender offers.

3. EXCHANGE OFFERS

An exchange offer differs from a cash tender offer in that the aggressor offers a package of its own securities—often a combination of cash, debt, and equity securities—for the securities of the target corporation.

a. Such an offer is subject to the registration and disclosure requirements of the Securities Act of 1933.

b. Because shareholders of the target receive paper rather than cash, acquisition by exchange offer is much less common than acquisition by an offer to purchase shares for cash.

4. "BEAR HUG" TRANSACTIONS

A "bear hug" is a forced embrace of the directors of a target corporation to persuade them to accept voluntarily a merger or other amalgamation which permits the take-over to proceed.

Example: A target corporation is approached by an aggressor with a proposal that it be merged voluntarily into the aggressor. The board of directors of the target corporation declines to consider such a transaction; a merger is therefore impractical since approval of the board of directors is required before a proposed statutory merger may be submitted to shareholders. (See part XIX B.) The aggressor however states that if the directors refuse to consider a merger, the aggressor will make a cash tender offer for the voting shares of the target at an attractive price. The board of directors, fearing that the offer may succeed, reopens negotiations with the aggressor, and a mutually satisfactory merger transaction is worked out and is subsequently approved by the shareholders. That is a successful "bear hug."

5. UNCONVENTIONAL PURCHASE-TYPE OFFERS

Several cases have involved attempts to acquire a majority of the target's shares by unconventional means such as the private negotiated purchases of shares owned by institutional investors or substantial minority shareholders or by a campaign of open market purchases. The major issue involved in these unconventional purchase-type acquisitions is whether they are subject to the same disclosure and legal requirements as cash tender offers.

B. PROXY CONTESTS

In a proxy contest, insurgents compete with management in an effort to obtain proxy appointments. In the classic proxy fight the goal of insurgents is to elect a majority of the board of directors and thereby obtain control, but in some cases contests are waged solely to obtain representation on the board.

1. MODERN USES OF THE PROXY CONTEST

The classic proxy fight was designed to wrest control away from the incumbent management by an insurgent faction. While some modern proxy fights follow this pattern, most modern proxy fights involve different goals.

a. In some tender offers, the offeror has launched a proxy fight in an effort to compel the board of directors of the target to withdraw poison pills or other takeover defenses that prevent the completion of a purchase-type takeover.

b. In the case of attempted takeovers of very large targets, the aggressor may acquire a substantial minority position by tender offer and then launch a proxy contest in an effort to elect a majority of the board of directors or persuade directors to deal directly with the aggressor.

c. A proxy fight may also be launched by an individual or one or more institutional investors in an effort to get management's attention to the fact that institutional investors own a substantial percentage of the corporation's shares and are unhappy with incumbent management's policies.

2. MANAGEMENT ADVANTAGES IN PROXY FIGHTS

Management's advantages in a proxy fight include:

a. Insurgents may have to go to court to get the current list of shareholders and the NOBO list (see part XII C 8 c);

b. Within a broad range, management may finance its solicitation from the assets of the corporation, while the insurgents must finance their campaign from outside sources; and

c. For the reasons discussed earlier (see part XI, B), shareholders may have a pro-management bias.

Caveat: While management has significant advantages in a traditional proxy contest, insurgents are sometimes successful, thereby demonstrating that such advantages are not insurmountable. With the continued concentration of shares in institutional ownership and the interest of institutional investors in matters of corporate governance, successful proxy contests may become even more common.

3. INSURGENT TACTICS

An insurgent group, desiring to contest management control, usually first purchases a substantial block of shares in the open market before openly announcing its intentions. However, under the Williams Act (see part XIII D 1 b) it must make a public SEC filing if it acquires over 5 per cent of the corporation's securities. Following this acquisition, it must conduct what is essentially a political campaign to persuade shareholders to vote in their favor.

a. A shareholders' and NOBO list may be essential so that substantial shareholders may be identified and contacted personally.

1) A court proceeding under state law (see part XVII) may be necessary to obtain these lists.

2) In addition to a court proceeding under state law, an insurgent faction has limited rights under SEC rule 14a–9, which requires management to provide minimal assistance to insurgent factions. Rule 14a–9 provides that:

(i) Each issuer must either mail to all shareholders the documents prepared by the insurgents at the insurgents' expense no later than the time management mails its proxy solicitation to shareholders, or

(ii) The corporation may provide the shareholder with a reasonably current list of names and addresses by which the shareholder can substantially duplicate the mailing by management.

3) Many institutional investors regularly disclose publicly their entire portfolios showing their beneficial ownership in all corporations.

b. Specialized proxy contest firms are available to assist both management and insurgents in the campaign.

c. Large shareholders may be courted individually; with the modern growth of institutional investors, the support of this segment of the financial community may be essential if a proxy fight is to have a chance of succeeding.

d. Such a campaign may be expensive, running into the hundreds of thousands or millions of dollars.

4. CORPORATIONS SUBJECT TO PROXY CONTESTS

The traditional view was that proxy fights were not feasible in the very large corporation with hundreds of thousands or millions of shareholders, since the cost of solicitation was believed to be prohibitive. This view is changing.

a. The most likely candidate for a proxy fight was thought to be a small or medium-sized publicly held company with a poor earnings record and, often, elderly management that has not paid attention to shareholders' relations.

b. In several takeover attempts against very large corporations, however, proxy fights have been threatened as part of the aggressor's strategy. Where an aggressor is contemplating the purchase of a multi-billion dollar company, often in large part for cash, the cost of solicitation of even millions of shareholders may be viewed as a relatively modest expenditure.

5. REGULATION OF PROXY CONTESTS

Proxy contests in corporations subject to section 12 of the Securities Exchange Act of 1934 are subject to regulation by the Securities and Exchange Commission under its proxy regulations.

a. State law may also be applicable to proxy contests but there are few reported state cases dealing with proxy fights. See, however, *Salgo v. Matthews*, 497 S.W.2d 620 (Tex.Civ.App.1973).

b. SEC regulations require all "participants" in a proxy contest (including nonmanagement groups) to file specified information with the SEC and the securities exchanges at least five days before a solicitation begins.

1) "Participant" is defined to include anyone who contributes more than $500 for the purpose of financing the contest.

2) Information that must be disclosed includes the identity and background of the participants, their interests in securities of the corporation, when they

were acquired, financing arrangements, participation in other proxy contests, and understandings with respect to future employment with the corporation.

3) Copies of presolicitation material, such as advertisements, press releases, and letters must be submitted to the SEC.

c. These regulations reject the view that such contests should be viewed as political contests with each side free to hurl charges with comparative unrestraint on the assumption that the opposing side may refute misleading charges. Rather, each participant's statements are subject to objective standards of accuracy and truthfulness. *SEC v. May*, 229 F.2d 123 (2d Cir. 1956).

6. WHO PAYS THE COSTS OF PROXY CONTESTS

The corporation usually pays the costs of the defense of a proxy contest. Where a change in control occurs, the corporation may also pay the costs of the successful campaign to oust incumbent management.

a. There appears to be no doubt that the corporation should pay for the cost of printing and mailing the notice of meeting, the proxy statement required by federal law, and the proxy appointment forms themselves. These are legitimate corporate expenses because without the solicitation of proxies it is likely that no quorum of shareholders could be obtained.

b. Most courts have allowed management also to charge to the corporation the reasonable expenses of educating shareholders if the controversy involves a "policy" question rather than a mere "personal" struggle for control. *Rosenfeld v. Fairchild Engine and Airplane Corp.*, 128 N.E.2d 291 (N.Y.1955); *Levin v. Metro–Goldwyn–Mayer, Inc.*, 264 F.Supp. 797 (S.D.N.Y.1967).

1) Virtually every issue may be dressed up as a "policy" rather than "personal" issue.

2) "Education" usually favors the management's side of the controversy.

c. The effect of a. and b. is probably to permit the deduction of all reasonable management expenses. Some judges have unsuccessfully suggested that a narrower test should be applicable to the reimbursement of management expenses.

d. Successful insurgents may also seek to have the corporation reimburse their expenses. The reimbursement of successful insurgents has been permitted if:

1) Approved by the shareholders, and

2) The dispute involved "policy" rather than "personalities." *Rosenfeld v. Fairchild Engine and Airplane Corp.*, 128 N.E.2d 291 (N.Y.1955).

e. As a result the corporation ends up paying for the expenses of both sides if the insurgents are successful. Some judges have unsuccessfully argued that insurgents' reimbursement should be prohibited.

f. Unsuccessful insurgents may perform a socially useful function, since proxy fights can be viewed as basically desirable phenomena that help to rid corporations of inefficient or ineffective management.

1) Not surprisingly, however, there appears to be no instance where management has voluntarily paid unsuccessful insurgents, except in connection with a settlement of the controversy that allowed incumbent management to retain control of the enterprise.

2) A proposal to require reimbursement of unsuccessful insurgents would have to be carefully structured to avoid possible abuse, particularly encouraging groundless proxy fights.

7. DEFENSIVE TACTICS IN PROXY CONTESTS

Incumbent management faced with a proxy contest may use its control over corporate affairs in an attempt to defeat the insurgents. The validity of such tactics are judged by whether a reasonable business purpose exists for the corporate action independent of the effect on the proxy contest.

Example: A board of directors has authority to set the annual meeting date within certain parameters set forth in the bylaws. The board elects to move the meeting date forward as much as possible solely to make the successful solicitation of proxies by the insurgents more difficult. Such action is invalid because there is no proper business purpose and may be set aside. *Schnell v. Chris–Craft Indus., Inc.*, 285 A.2d 437 (Del. 1971).

Example: Shortly before a scheduled meeting of shareholders at which a proxy fight is to be resolved, the board of directors learns that the "election is too close to call." The board of directors announces that the election is deferred several months and a new record date is established. Since the delay does not benefit shareholders generally and requires the dissident faction to make a new solicitation, the change in meeting date may be enjoined. *Aprahamian v. HBO & Co.,* 531 A.2d 1204 (Del.Ch. 1987).

Caveat: Not all cases agree with these holdings. Cases holding that management may generally exercise powers granted to it without regard to the purpose of the action tend to be older cases.

C. PURCHASE–TYPE TAKEOVERS

Purchase-type takeovers are usually commenced by a cash tender offer for a controlling interest in the target, followed by a "mop up" transaction that permits the aggressor to obtain all the outstanding publicly held shares issued by the target. However, many variations in this pattern exist.

1. CASH TENDER OFFERS IN GENERAL

In a cash tender offer, the outside aggressor ("offeror") invites shareholders to tender their shares for purchase by the aggressor at a price specified by the aggressor. No approval of the board of directors is required for such a transaction.

a. The price is set at a premium over current market price so as to attract tenders. In many tender offers during the latter part of the 1980s, the premium was set at 50 per cent or more over the current market price of the shares.

b. The offeror usually seeks sufficient shares to ensure control over the corporation. In many tender offers, however, the offeror seeks to purchase all the outstanding shares and announces it will accept all shares tendered to it, either unconditionally or on condition that a minimum number is tendered.

c. A number of substantive rules have been established by the Williams Act and SEC regulation with respect to tender offers. For example, tender offers must remain open for specified periods, shares previously tendered may be withdrawn during specified periods, if the price is increased during an outstanding tender offer, the higher price must be paid for all shares previously tendered, a person making a tender offer must purchase only through the offer and may not make private purchases while the offer is outstanding, oversubscribed cash tender offers must be accepted pro rata rather than on a first-come-first-bought basis, and so forth.

d. An aggressor may complete a tender offer and then immediately announce a new tender offer in an effort to acquire additional shares.

2. ROLE OF ARBITRAGERS

When a cash tender offer is made, the open market price for the shares increases dramatically close to or above the tender offer price. Persons owning shares thus have the choice of selling their shares in the open market (usually at a discount from the tender offer price) or tendering their shares. Most shares sold on the open market are ultimately tendered because of the activities of "risk arbitragers."

a. Risk arbitragers are speculators who purchase shares in the open market at prices below the tender offer price in order to tender them and profit by the difference between the two prices.

b. In many tender offers, the volume of transactions effected by risk arbitragers has been very substantial.

c. Risk arbitragers are the natural allies of aggressors since they profit only if the transaction is consummated.

d. As a result of activities of arbitragers, institutional investors, and speculators generally, the conventional belief during the late 1980s was that a corporation that was "put into play," i.e. made the subject of a cash tender offer, would be purchased by some one and would not remain independent.

e. When competing bids seemed likely, the market price for shares subject to a tender offer might temporarily exceed the price offered in the tender offer.

3. MOP UP TRANSACTIONS

No tender offer ever obtains all of the outstanding shares of a target. Even where a partial cash tender offer is successfully completed, the offeror usually desires to acquire all of the minority shares not purchased through the tender offer. The outstanding minority shares are usually acquired in a cash out merger (see part XIX) that compels minority shareholders to accept the proferred terms (or follow the statutory dissent and appraisal procedure).

4. FRONT END LOADED TRANSACTIONS

In some instances, an offeror may announce in advance that if the offer is successful it will thereafter acquire the balance of the shares in a transaction that is binding on all minority shareholders. During the late 1970s, the terms of the second transaction were sometimes announced in advance as being considerably less favorable than the terms of the original acquisition of the shares.

a. The purpose was to apply pressure to shareholders to tender promptly into the original tender offer.

b. This two step procedure is usually called a "front end loaded transaction" or a "two tier" acquisition.

c. Front end loaded transactions were widely criticized as being unfair to small shareholders who might be unable to tender into the original offer. They were also criticized as creating a kind of "prisoners' dilemma" that resulted in decisions to tender even though the offer was not in the shareholders' best interests if they could act in concert.

d. Several states enacted "fair price" statutes that required second step transactions to be executed at the same price as the original offer.

Caveat: Front end loaded transactions were widely discussed during the 1970s and early 1980s but their use quickly died out during the early 1980s. All recent mop up transactions have apparently been at the same price as the tender offer which transferred control of the target to the aggressor.

5. LEVERAGED BUYOUTS

A leveraged buyout is an acquisition of a target through borrowed funds which are repaid out of the earnings and assets of the target. Many takeover transactions during the late 1980s involved leveraged buyouts, and the spectacular collapse of some leveraged buyout transactions contributed to the end of the takeover boom.

a. In a leveraged buyout, the offeror creates a new corporation (Newco) to acquire the shares of the target. The Newco receives the minimum equity capital required from the offeror and borrows the balance of the purchase price for all the outstanding shares of the target. The tender offer is made in the name of Newco so that the target becomes a subsidiary of Newco.

b. Following the acquisition of the shares of the target (and the subsequent mop up merger) the target and Newco may be merged so that the target's assets become responsible for and available to service the takeover debt of Newco. Alternatively, the separate existence of the target as a subsidiary of Newco may be retained, but the target may formally guarantee the payment of the debt of Newco (an "upstream guarantee").

c. In effect a leveraged buyout results in recapitalization of the target by the massive substitution of debt for equity capital.

d. The acquisition debt may be paid down by the sale of assets by the recapitalized target or out of its earnings or cash flow.

e. If incumbent management forms a part of the group that makes the cash tender offer, the transaction may be called a management buyout, an "MBO" or a "going private" transaction.

f. After a leveraged buyout, the Newco/target corporation may no longer meet the reporting requirements of section 12 of the Securities Exchange Act of 1934. However, several companies acquired through leveraged buyouts in the early 1980s later made public offerings of equity securities and thus again became publicly held corporations.

6. MISCELLANEOUS TAKEOVER TECHNIQUES

Not all purchase type takeovers involve classic cash tender offers. A variety of other techniques have been experimented with as ways to acquire control of a target corporation. The principal legal issue involved in such transactions is generally whether it should be viewed as a cash tender offer subject to the requirements of the Williams Act.

Example: A simultaneous offer to purchase shares of the target corporation made to some 40 institutional and other investors by telephone in a single evening is a tender offer that must be registered under the Williams Act. *Wellman v. Dickinson,* 682 F.2d 355 (2d Cir.1982).

Example: A "widespread solicitation of public shareholders in person, over the telephone and through the mails," by agents and employers is also a tender offer and must be registered under the Williams Act. *Cattlemen's Investment Co. v. Fears,* 343 F.Supp. 1248 (W.D.Okl.1972).

Example: A purchase of a single 30 per cent block of shares followed by an offer to purchase shares owned by all directors of the company plus purchases on the open market over a securities exchange is not a tender offer. *Nachman Corp. v. Halfred, Inc.,* Fed.Sec.L.Rep. (CCH) 94,455 (N.D.Ill.1973), *Hanson Trust PLC v. SCM Corp.,* 774 F.2d 47 (2d Cir.1985).

a. A plan of buying shares through routine transactions on a securities exchange designed to acquire control of a publicly held corporation is not a tender offer. *Kennecott Copper Corp. v. Curtiss–Wright Corp.,* 584 F.2d 1195 (2d Cir.1978).

b. An offer to purchase shares from a small number of institutional investors and arbitragers immediately after a cash tender offer has been withdrawn is not a continuation of the cash tender offer. This transaction is called a "street sweep." The SEC has strongly opposed this conclusion, going to the extent of considering regulations to extend the time of a tender offer to cover such transactions.

Example: A corporation withdraws a tender offer after a spirited contest. Minutes thereafter it offers to purchase shares from a limited number of risk arbitragers who have assembled large blocks of shares. This does not constitute a tender offer. *Hanson Trust PLC v. SCM Corp.,* 774 F.2d 47 (2d Cir.1985).

D. REGULATION OF CASH TENDER OFFERS AND RELATED TRANSACTIONS

In the late 1960s, numerous cash tender and public exchange offers were largely based on the element of surprise, virtually blitzkrieg tactics. The element of surprise was largely eliminated by the Williams Act (discussed below). During the takeover boom of the 1980s, cash take-over offers were usually successful because of the large premiums over market price that were being offered, the willingness of institutional investors to tender in order to show portfolio profits, and the activities of speculators who would take substantial market positions in the target stock and then tender that stock to the offeror. The success of the takeover movement itself spawned increasingly sophisticated defensive tactics and the enactment of state statutes designed to make such takeovers increasingly difficult.

1. THE WILLIAMS ACT

The Williams Act amends the Securities Exchange Act of 1934 and applies to cash tender offers for corporations with securities registered under section 12 of the 1934 Act. The general goal of the Williams Act is not to either favor or disfavor takeovers but to assure full disclosure of proposed transactions and provide a fair set of rules for the struggle for control of the corporation.

a. Disclosure of information by any person who makes a cash tender offer for a registered company is required. Disclosure must include information as to the source of funds used in the offer, the backgrounds of the persons involved in the offer, the purpose for which the offer is made, plans the aggressor may have if successful, and any contracts or understandings it has with, or with respect to, the target corporation.

b. Disclosure of similar information is required by any person or group who acquires more than 5 per cent of the outstanding shares of any class of stock of a registered company, whether or not a tender offer is in progress or is contemplated.

   1) In *Rondeau v. Mosinee Paper Corp.*, 422 U.S. 49, 95 S.Ct. 2069 (1975) the Court held that an issuer could not use the failure to make this filing as a basis for enjoining the later voting of the stock.

   2) Filing is required of a "group" that is formed with a view toward acquisition of control if the group's holdings exceed 5 per cent. *GAF Corp. v. Milstein*, 453 F.2d 709 (2d Cir.1971).

c. Similar information must be disclosed by:

   1) Issuers making an offer for their own shares, or

   2) Issuers in which a change of control is proposed through seriatim resignations of directors.

d. Miscellaneous substantive restrictions are imposed on the mechanics of a cash tender offer. (See part XIII C 1 c.)

e. Section 14(e) imposes a broad prohibition against the use of false, misleading or incomplete statements in connection with a tender offer.

1) Section 14(e) is patterned after rule 10b–5 and adopts the same standards of materiality, scienter, and disclosure. The Supreme Court has held that section 14(e), like rule 10b–5, only relates to nondisclosure or deception and does not affect unfair practices generally. *Schreiber v. Burlington Northern, Inc.,* 472 U.S. 1, 105 S.Ct. 2458 (1985).

Example: A plan to use the target's cash to pay for the target's shares must be disclosed. *General Host Corp. v. Triumph American, Inc.,* 359 F.Supp. 749 (S.D.N.Y.1973). If disclosed, the plan does not violate section 14(e) even if the transaction constitutes waste or injures creditors.

2) In *Piper v. Chris–Craft Industries, Inc.,* 430 U.S. 1, 97 S.Ct. 926 (1977), the Court held that a defeated tender offeror does not have standing to sue for damages under this provision of the Williams Act. Injunctive relief may not be foreclosed by this decision.

3) Tendering shareholders have standing to seek injunctive relief and, probably, damages. *Lowenschuss v. Kane,* 520 F.2d 255 (2d Cir.1975).

4) The Supreme Court in *Chris–Craft* specifically left open the question whether a nontendering shareholder might have standing to sue an offeror. *Plaine v. McCabe,* 797 F.2d 713 (9th Cir.1986) and other cases hold that such a shareholder does have standing.

5) An issuer has standing to enjoin violations of section 14(e), acting on behalf of shareholders. *Polaroid Corp. v. Disney,* 862 F.2d 987 (3d Cir. 1988).

2. STATE TAKEOVER STATUTES

Most states have enacted statutes dealing with the regulation of takeovers of publicly held corporations incorporated in those states. Unlike the Williams Act, these statutes in fact are largely designed to protect such corporations against aggressors.

a. State statutes enacted before 1982 generally imposed hearing requirements and fairness standards on all cash tender offers made with respect to corporations with significant contacts with the state. The Illinois statute of this type was held unconstitutional in *Edgar v. MITE Corporation,* 457 U.S. 624, 102 S.Ct. 2629 (1982) on the grounds it was preempted by the Williams Act and also as involving unreasonable burdens on interstate commerce. Following this decision, pre–1982 state statutes were either abandoned or held unconstitutional by lower courts.

b. New attempts by states to impose restrictions on tender offers began promptly after the decision in *MITE.* These statutes are usually referred to as "post-*MITE*" statutes and apply only to corporations incorporated in the state in question. They all build on the admitted power of states to regulate the internal affairs of domestic corporations.

1) These statutes were upheld in near constitutional terms of state power and authority over domestic corporations in *CTS Corporation v. Dynamics Corp. of America,* 481 U.S. 69, 107 S.Ct. 1637 (1987).

2) The most important of these statutes is Delaware GCL § 203. This complex statute provides that if a person acquires 15 per cent or more of a corporation's voting stock, that person may not enter into mergers or other specified transactions with the corporation unless (a) the person acquires 85 per cent or more of the corporation's stock, or (b) the transaction is approved by the board of directors and at least 2/3ds of the shares other than the shares held by the person acquiring the stock.

(i) Section 203 is of great importance because so many publicly held corporations are incorporated in Delaware.

(ii) More than twenty-five other states, including New York, have adopted similar statutes.

3) Indiana pioneered the "control share acquisition" type of statute, the statute actually considered and upheld in *CTS.*

(i) In this type of statute, shareholder approval must be obtained for purchases by a single shareholder that break through the 20 per cent, 33 per cent, and 50 per cent levels. If a shareholder fails to obtain such permission, the acquired shares lose the right to vote and may be reacquired by the corporation upon terms set forth in the statute.

(ii) A person seeking to acquire additional shares that break through the specific level must give notice to the corporation and the proposed transaction must be submitted to shareholders for approval. Shares owned by the acquiring person and by corporate management may not be counted in this vote.

(iii) Under the Ohio statute, the effect of a negative vote is that the purchase of shares may not be completed.

(iv) Some doubt has been expressed by commentators whether the Indiana type of statute actually deters takeovers.

4) Pennsylvania provides that if a shareholder acquires more than 20 per cent of the voting shares of a corporation, other shareholders have the

right to compel that shareholder to acquire their shares at a "fair value." This statute is similar to the rule in England.

5) More than 30 states have adopted statutes authorizing boards of directors to consider constituencies other than shareholders when making decisions. (See part XI C 4.) These are generally viewed as being motivated by a desire to make takeovers of domestic corporations more difficult.

Caveat: All these state statutes are applicable only to corporations that are incorporated in the state in question and also registered under section 12 of the Securities Exchange Act of 1934.

Caveat: The constitutionality of the Delaware statute has not been considered by the United States Supreme Court but has been upheld in several lower court decisions. Many persons believe the mandatory buy-out feature of the Pennsylvania statute is of doubtful constitutionality and that statutes of the Delaware/New York type will definitely be upheld.

E. DEFENSIVE TACTICS

Numerous defensive tactics have been devised in order to defeat or deter takeover bids. They increased in sophistication particularly during the 1980s. By 1990, more than 90 per cent of all publicly held corporations have installed defensive armament against unwanted takeover attempts. The most popular and successful defense is the poison pill, discussed below.

1. EARLY TESTS

The courts addressed defenses to takeover attempts before the wave of takeovers during 1980s. The early test of propriety adopted by the courts to evaluate defensive tactics was purely one of underlying purpose: if the actions of the board of directors were motivated by a belief that the transaction was reasonable and necessary to maintain what the board believed to be the security and integrity of the corporation, the transaction is proper and protected by the business judgment rule. If, on the other hand, the board or management acted solely or primarily because of the desire to perpetuate itself in office, the transaction was improper and may be invalidated. *Cheff v. Mathes*, 199 A.2d 548 (Del.1964).

a. The selfish motive of self-perpetuation is usually called "entrenchment." Entrenchment transactions are not protected by the business judgment rule because the directors are not acting in order to further what they believe to be the best interests of the corporation.

b. This early test may be criticized on the ground that it is possible to dress up virtually every transaction with a "proper business purpose."

c. A number of cases have applied the entrenchment doctrine to invalidate modern takeover defenses.

d. The validity of defensive transactions is largely governed by state law. Attempts to attack such transactions under rule 10b–5 (discussed in part XV B) appear to be foreclosed by the United States Supreme Court decisions in *Santa Fe Industries, Inc. v. Green,* 430 U.S. 462, 97 S.Ct. 1292 (1977) [which limits rule 10b–5 to cases of deception rather than unfairness or breach of fiduciary duty] and *Schreiber v. Burlington Northern, Inc.,* 472 U.S. 1, 105 S.Ct. 2458 (1985) [extending the same limitation to suits under 14(e) of the Williams Act]. On the other hand, some of the transactions described below have been successfully attacked by regulations promulgated under the Williams Act.

2. CREATING LEGAL OBSTACLES TO THE TAKEOVER

A target corporation may create legal obstacles to the takeover.

a. A target might buy a business that increases the chances that the threatened takeover will give rise to anti-trust problems. *E.g. Panter v. Marshall Field & Co.,* 646 F.2d 271 (7th Cir.1981).

b. A target might acquire and hold a business that requires governmental approval for its transfer, e.g. a parent corporation owning a life or casualty insurance subsidiary.

3. PORCUPINE PROVISIONS

Amendments may be made in articles of incorporation or bylaws that make it difficult for an offeror who acquires a majority of the voting shares to obtain working control of the board of directors and the management of the target. These are sometimes referred to as "porcupine provisions."

a. Provisions might be added making it difficult for an offeror who acquires a majority of the voting shares to replace the board of directors.

1) Articles of incorporation or bylaws may be amended to provide that directors may be removed only for cause.

2) Articles of incorporation or bylaws may be amended to provide for the staggering of the board of directors and the election of only 1/3 of the board of directors each year.

3) Articles of incorporation or bylaws may be amended to require supermajority votes to amend bylaws or take other actions that might affect other takeover defenses.

4. SUPERVOTING STOCK

Articles of incorporation may be amended to provide for supervoting stock (stock with multiple votes per share) and "placing" or "parking" that stock in the hands of members of the founding families or other persons friendly to the incumbent management.

a. Supervoting stock is generally made non-transferable but convertible into regular voting common stock that is transferable. A person holding supervoting stock is thus unable to convey the supervoting privilege but may sell the shares after they are converted into ordinary voting stock.

b. Supervoting stock permits a target corporation to make itself completely takeover-proof.

Caveat: The SEC attempted to prevent the use of supervoting stock by enacting rule 19c–4 that prohibited national securities exchanges and associations from listing stocks that violate a fundamental "one share/one vote" principle. In *Business Roundtable v. S.E.C.*, 905 F.2d 406 (D.C.Cir.1990), the court invalidated this rule on the ground that it exceeded the power of the SEC to promulgate, but national securities exchanges continued to voluntarily comply with the rule.

Caveat: The correctness of the *Business Roundtable* holding is open to question.

c. Instituting suit to enjoin the offer for violations of the Williams Act, the antitrust laws or on other grounds. E. g., *Corenco Corp. v. Schiavone & Sons, Inc.*, 488 F.2d 207 (2d Cir.1973).

5. WHITE KNIGHTS

A corporation facing an undesired takeover attempt may seek to find a more congenial suitor, a "white knight." In order to assure the white knight's success, the target may seek to negotiate exclusively with the white knight and in addition may grant the white knight a "lockup."

6. LOCKUPS

Lockups involve entering into transactions with friendly persons on favorable terms to make takeovers difficult or unattractive. Lockups may involve the sale of shares at bargain prices or the grant of options to purchase shares at current market prices.

a. A corporation faced with an unwanted tender offer may create employee stock ownership or stock option plans (ESOPs), with a trustee friendly to incumbent management, and distribute a significant number of shares to that trustee. *E.g. NCR Corp. v. American Tel. & Tel. Co.*, 761 F.Supp. 475 (S.D.Ohio 1991); *Shamrock Holdings, Inc. v. Polaroid Corp.*, 559 A.2d 278, 290 (Del.Ch.1989).

1) A typical ESOP is a trust which purchases shares of the corporation's stock from either the corporation itself and/or its existing shareholders.

2) If a shareholder sells 30 per cent or more of its shares to an ESOP it can defer federal income taxes on the sale by reinvesting the proceeds in stocks or bonds of a U. S. company under IRC § 1042.

3) Typically, the ESOP borrows money from a bank or from another third party to pay for the shares. The ESOP amortizes the loan with periodic tax-deductible contributions by the corporation to the ESOP. Dividends paid to ESOP participants, or dividends paid to the ESOP and used to pay the ESOP debt on the acquired shares can be tax deductible by the corporation pursuant to IRC § 104(k).

4) If the ESOP acquires more than 50 percent of the corporation's stock, the lender may be able to exclude part of the interest income from taxation (IRC § 133) which enables the lender to charge the ESOP a lower rate of interest.

5) Subject to the prohibited transaction and fiduciary rules of ERISA, the existing owners may continue to maintain control of the corporation, even if they sell more than a majority interest, by providing that shares owned by the ESOP will be voted by the ESOP trustee, who can be an officer or other individual friendly to the existing shareholders.

6) ESOPs may be leveraged or unleveraged.

   (i) If unleveraged, the corporation issues a number of shares which are immediately allocated to the ESOP participants. The corporation receives a tax deduction equal to the value of the shares contributed from time to time.

   (ii) In a leveraged ESOP, the ESOP acquires a large block of shares which are allocated to the participants as the ESOP debt is repaid. The corporation receives a tax deduction only as the shares are allocated and equal only to the value of the shares when first acquired by the ESOP.

7) Most ESOPs require the trustee to vote unallocated shares in the same proportion that the already-allocated shares are voted. The effect of this, if the number of ESOP members is small is greatly to magnify the voting power of the covered employees, and thus improve the effectiveness of the ESOP as an antitakeover device.

Example: A publicly-held corporation, incorporated in Panama, is threatened with a takeover attempt. It issues two large blocks of its shares, one to a wholly-owned subsidiary, and the other to an Employee Stock Option Plan (ESOP), the trustees of which are directors of the corporation. Neither transaction is protected by the business judgment rule because of self-interest. In addition, circularly-owned shares (i. e. shares owned by a subsidiary of the issuing corporation) cannot usually be voted under American law (see MBCA (1984) § 7.21(b)) and the court extended that ban to a Panamanian corporation whose principal business was in New York. The ESOP was viewed as "solely a tool of management self-perpetuation" without serving any legitimate corporate purpose. The grant of a preliminary injunction barring the voting of both blocks of shares was affirmed. *Norlin Corp. v. Rooney, Pace Inc.,* 744 F.2d 255 (2d Cir.1984).

b. Before an unwanted tender offer is made a corporation may find a white knight and sell to that white knight shares at current market prices, or grant it options to purchase shares at current market prices. E.g. *Smith v. Van Gorkom,* 488 A.2d 858 (Del.1985). Transactions of this nature protect unsuccessful white knights since if a competing bidder appears and acquires the target at a higher price, the white knight may tender the acquired shares for purchase under the competing bid.

c. A corporation facing an unwanted tender offer may sell or grant options to purchase desirable assets or business lines ("crown jewels") to a favored bidder at a bargain price. *E.g. Hanson Trust PLC v. ML SCM Acquisitions, Inc.,* 781 F.2d 264 (2d Cir.1986). This type of lockup is designed to discourage the competing bidder by making the target less attractive.

7. GREENMAIL

A target corporation facing an unwanted tender offer may seek to buy off the aggressor by repurchasing its shares at a premium over market. E.g. *Heckmann v. Ahmanson,* 214 Cal.Rptr. 177 (1985); *Cheff v. Mathes,* 199 A.2d 548 (Del.1964).

a. Such purchases are usually referred to as "greenmail."

b. In 1987, the Internal Revenue Code was amended to impose a 50 percent nondeductible excise tax on greenmail payments (in addition to the normal income tax payable on sales of shares).

c. Some state statutes also prohibit greenmail-type repurchases.

8. MANIPULATION OF THE TARGET'S SHARE PRICE

A corporation facing an unwanted tender offer may seek to defeat it by driving up the price of its shares to make the takeover price unattractive.

a. The target may buy back its own shares in the open market for ostensibly proper reasons; such transactions drive up the price and make a purchased takeover more difficult. *Bennett v. Propp*, 187 A.2d 405 (Del.Ch.1962); *Herald Co. v. Seawell*, 472 F.2d 1081 (10th Cir.1972).

Caveat: Advance disclosure of such purchases is required under rule 13e–1 under the Williams Act, and in addition there is a risk that the corporation may be charged with improper market manipulation.

b. The target may declare an extraordinary dividend or announce an increase in its earnings or regular dividends.

9. SELECTIVE TRANSACTIONS THAT EXCLUDE THE OFFEROR

A target may make a selective offer to repurchase or redeem its own shares in exchange for debt obligations but limit the offer by excluding shares acquired by or behalf of the offeror.

a. A selective offer of this type may be devastating to the tender offer since the aggressor may end up owning a corporation saddled with immense debts.

b. In *Unocal Corp. v. Mesa Petroleum Co.,* 493 A.2d 946 (Del.1985), the Delaware Supreme Court upheld this type of transaction on the basis of an expanded business judgment rule, discussed below.

c. Shortly thereafter, the SEC adopted rule 14d–10, usually called the "all holders rule" that requires equal treatment of all shareholders of the same class.

10. POISON PILLS

Poison pills are new issues of stock that increase in rights if any person makes a cash tender offer or acquires more than a specified percentage of shares.

a. Poison pills are technically a new series of preferred shares that are distributed to common shareholders in the form of a dividend. The new series is usually created by the board of directors without shareholder action.

b. The increase in rights occurs upon a triggering event: either an outsider making a cash tender offer for shares of the corporation or a person acquiring more than a specified percentage of the common stock, perhaps 25 per cent.

1) Before a triggering event occurs, the board of directors may redeem the poison pill preferred at a nominal cost.

2) After a triggering event occurs, the preferred is generally not redeemable.

c. The increased rights of the holders of the poison pill preferred may consist of "flip in" or "flip over" rights.

1) Flip in rights permit the holder to purchase additional shares or debt securities of the target at a bargain price, to sell shares back to the target at high prices, or to exchange the poison pill preferred for valuable packages of debt and securities issued by the target.

2) Flip over rights permit the holder to purchase shares of the aggressor at a bargain price if there is a subsequent merger or other defined transaction between the target and the aggressor.

3) Most modern poison pills contain both flip in and flip over provisions, either of which results in unacceptable dilution of the interest of the aggressor.

d. The principal case approving the issuance of poison pill preferred is *Moran v. Household International, Inc.,* 500 A.2d 1346 (Del.1985).

e. The basic effect of a poison pill is to compel the aggressor to negotiate with the board of directors to neutralize the pill through redemption of the poison pill rights.

11. POISON PILL DEBT

A target may enter into loan agreements with creditors that contain restrictions that may thwart attempted takeovers. Such debt is referred to as "poison pill debt."

12. LEVERAGED RECAPITALIZATIONS

A target may seek to make itself unattractive by engaging in a leveraged recapitalization or "leveraged recap." Where a leveraged buyout is proposed, the target is in effect doing what the aggressor is proposing to do.

a. The target may sell off some lines of business and distribute the proceeds, together with any excess cash, directly to shareholders in the form of an extraordinary dividend.

b. The target may sell debt securities or borrow funds from commercial sources and distribute those funds or proceeds in the form of an extraordinary dividend.

c. The target may declare a dividend in the form of debt—corporate promissory notes or debentures payable to the shareholders.

d. A leveraged recapitalization may be submitted to the shareholders for their approval. It may be in the form of a recapitalization in which old stock is retired and new stock is issued when the extraordinary distribution is made. This stock is called "stub" stock.

Caveat: A distribution of cash in a leveraged recapitalization normally exceeds earned and capital surplus; it may be necessary to write up the value of assets and create revaluation surplus to make the transaction lawful in legal capital states.

Caveat: Following a leveraged recapitalization, the corporation will be highly leveraged; if it fails to meet its increased debt obligations, the leveraged recapitalization may be attacked on the ground that it constitutes a transfer in fraud of creditors.

F. LEGAL PRINCIPLES RELATING TO DEFENSIVE TACTICS

A large number of recent cases have considered the validity of defensive tactics in different contexts. No general theory has developed.

Caveat: In the following decisions particular weight should be given to the Delaware decisions because of the importance of that state as the state of incorporation of publicly held corporations. However, it cannot be assumed that other states will automatically accept principles established in the Delaware cases.

1. BUSINESS JUDGMENT RULE IN GENERAL

Early cases took the position that defensive tactics were simply a matter of the exercise of the business judgment of the directors and such decisions were immune from judicial review under the business judgment rule. *E.g. Panter v. Marshall Field & Co.,* 646 F.2d 271 (7th Cir.1981). (See part XIV B.)

Example: In *Gearhart Industries, Inc. v. Smith International, Inc.,* 741 F.2d 707 (5th Cir.1984), upheld a "poison pill" preferred (issued in the context of a takeover struggle) under the business judgment rule and Texas law.

a. Two courts have applied New Jersey law to conclude that the board of directors may not adopt "poison pill" preferred stock that materially changes the voting rights of shareholders without approval of the shareholders. *Asarco, Incorporated v. Court,* 611 F.Supp. 468 (D.N.J.1985); *Minstar Acq. Corp. v. AMF,* Inc., 621 F.Supp. 1252 (S.D.N.Y.1985). The second case also invalidates a "scorched earth" plan under which the target corporation granted excessive amounts of compensation to high-level employees.

Caveat: As a result of these two decisions, corporations have not attempted to create "voting poison pills," i.e. series of preferred shares in which voting rights change upon the occurrence of a triggering event.

b. In *Unocal Corp. v. Mesa Petroleum Co.,* 493 A.2d 946 (Del.1985), upholding an exchange offer of debt for stock that excluded the aggressor from participation, the Delaware Supreme Court developed a sliding scale business judgment rule: "A further aspect is the element of balance. If a defensive measure is to come within the ambit of the business judgment rule, it must be reasonable in relation to the threat posed. This entails an analysis by the directors of the nature of the takeover bid and its effect on the corporate enterprise."

Example: This sliding scale test authorizes the board of directors to consider such factors as the inadequacy of the price offered, nature and time of the offer, questions of illegality, and the impact on other constituencies as part of its evaluation of defensive measures under the business.

c. In *Moran v. Household International, Inc.,* 500 A.2d 1346 (Del.1985), upholding the adoption of a "poison pill" as a defensive tactic in advance of a specific takeover attempt, the court reasoned that the poison pill did not prevent all takeover attempts, and that the management's invocation of the poison pill in response to a specific takeover attempt could be considered when the occasion arose.

d. In *Revlon, Inc. v. MacAndrews & Forbes Holdings, Inc.,* 506 A.2d 173 (Del. 1985), the Delaware Supreme Court held that a "lock up" agreement that favored one contestant in a takeover attempt over another was invalid and should be enjoined since the board of directors had resolved to sell the corporation and, upon making that decision, the board had an obligation to get the best possible price for shareholders and could not arbitrarily favor one contestant over another. The board of directors, in other words, has to conduct an auction to insure that shareholders receive the best possible price.

e. In *Paramount Communications, Inc. v. Time, Inc.,* 571 A.2d 1140 (Del.1989), the Delaware Supreme Court held that where the *Revlon* auction requirement was not applicable, the board of directors (if acting in an informed manner) may adopt a strategy that does not maximize shareholder value in the short term. While the precise scope of the freedom thus given to directors to defeat attractive take over proposals is a matter of debate, this holding seems inconsistent with the premise underlying the *Revlon* decision that the goal of director action should be to maximize the gain of shareholders.

1) It is unclear whether the rejection of short term profit maximization by the board of directors must be framed in terms of long term profit maximization or whether directors may point to other corporate considerations, such as the interests of other constituencies.

2) *Paramount* is widely believed to legitimate the "just say no" defense. (See part XIII F 3.)

2. AUCTIONS AND THE REVLON PRINCIPLE

Many takeover attempts during the 1970s and 1980s were contested by two or more different aggressors seeking to take over the target. In *Revlon, Inc. v. MacAndrews & Forbes Holdings, Inc.,* 506 A.2d 173 (Del.1985), the Delaware Supreme Court held that a "lock up" agreement that favored one contestant in a takeover attempt over another was invalid and should be enjoined since the board of directors had resolved to sell the corporation and, upon making the decision, the board must seek to obtain the best possible price for shareholders and may not arbitrarily favor one contestant over another.

a. The Court held that the duty of the board of directors changes when it "becomes apparent" the target is to be sold. Before that time, the board of directors may be a defender of the target. However, when the decision to sell is made, the board of directors becomes auctioneers charged with getting the best price for the shareholders at the sale of the company. *E.g. Ivanhoe Partners v. Newmont Mining Corp.,* 535 A.2d 1334 (Del.1987).

   Caveat: In a later case discussed below, *Paramount Communications, Inc. v. Time Inc.,* 571 A.2d 1140 (Del.1990), the court referred to the "radically altered state" that triggers *Revlon* duties and defined when those duties arose as the time when the corporation is "put up for sale" or when it commences "an active bidding process seeking to sell itself or to effect a business reorganization involving a clear break-up of the company" or when "in response to a bidder's offer, [it] abandons its long-term strategy and seeks an alternative transaction involving the breakup of the company."

b. Following *Revlon,* courts in Delaware and elsewhere struggled with additional basic questions: How is a *Revlon* auction to be conducted? *E.g. Mills Acquisition Co. v. MacMillan, Inc.,* 559 A.2d 1261 (Del.1989). When may the board conclude that the auction has ended? *E.g. Cottle v. Storer Communication, Inc.,* 849 F.2d 570 (11th Cir.1988). If an offer at an attractive price is received, must the board conduct an auction or may it accept the offer subject to a "market check" that assures that the best price has been obtained? *E.g. Barkan v. Amsted Industries, Inc.,* 567 A.2d 1279 (Del.1989).

c. The *Revlon* principle seems to establish the primacy of the interests of shareholders in making takeover decisions.

3. THE "JUST SAY NO" DEFENSE

The "just say no" defense states that a board of directors may establish a policy that the corporation is not for sale, and may therefore refuse to discuss or negotiate with possible acquirers. If the defensive armament of poison pills and other devices is impregnable, recognition of the "just say no" defense would theoretically permit the board of directors to reject all proposed transactions, no matter how favorable they may be for shareholders.

a. In *City Capital Assoc. v. Interco Inc.*, 551 A.2d 787 (Del.Ch.1988) and *Grand Metropolitan Public Ltd. Co. v. Pillsbury Co.*, 558 A.2d 1049 (Del.Ch.1988), the Delaware Chancery Court enjoined the use and compelled the redemption of poison pills on the ground that they had exhausted their utility to shareholders.

1) These cases both involved all cash offers at a price that most shareholders indicated they wished to accept. In *Pillsbury*, for example, nearly 90 per cent of the shareholders had signified their desire to sell their shares to the aggressor by tendering them.

2) These decisions were justified under the *Unocal* test that the threat of an all cash offer was mild and did not justify the defensive tactic of the imposition of a totally-blocking poison pill by the board of directors.

3) In *Amanda Acquisition Corp. v. Universal Foods Corp.*, 708 F.Supp. 984 (E.D.Wis.1989), the court refused to require the redemption of a poison pill, distinguishing *Pillsbury* in part of the ground that only 27 per cent of Universal Foods' shareholders had tendered their shares as compared to more than 87 per cent in *Pillsbury*.

b. The "just say no" defense received its clearest recognition in *Paramount Communications, Inc. v. Time Inc.*, 571 A.2d 1140 (Del.1989), where the Delaware Supreme Court upheld the right of the board of directors, acting in an informed manner, to follow a preplanned long-term corporate restructuring in preference to an all cash offer from a third party.

c. There has been speculation that *Paramount* in effect accepts the "just say no" defense because it should be relatively easy to maintain "on the shelf" future plans that may be used to justify a refusal to redeem a poison pill or dismantle other defenses.

Caveat: The Delaware cases referred to in this section generally, and the *Paramount* decision in particular, tend to be fact specific; great attention is paid by the court to the detailed facts of the specific takeover and the result is justified in terms of those facts. Thus, broad generalization from the language of these opinions may not be reliable.

G. ECONOMIC ANALYSIS OF CASH TAKEOVER BIDS

There has been extensive consideration of the causes and effects of the takeover movement of the 1970s and 1980s. Much of the analysis favoring takeovers was written during the 1980s when numerous transactions were occurring. In the early 1990s, financing for takeovers dried up and (either concomitantly or as a result), a number of highly leveraged companies created during the takeover boom filed for bankruptcy under chapter 11. Other highly leveraged companies avoided bankruptcy by negotiating with creditors and by infusing substantial amounts of equity into the capital structure of the company. The arguments discussed below reflect the earlier analysis more than the recent events.

1. ARGUMENTS BASED ON INEFFICIENT MANAGEMENT

The law and economics movement views takeover bids as part of the market for corporate control which is an important element in improving the quality of management by weeding out inefficient managers and assuring that undervalued or underutilized assets are redeployed in a more efficient manner.

Example: A leading article written in 1981 suggests that management should never interfere or attempt to defeat a cash tender offer, but should simply stand aside and let the shareholders determine what is in their best interest.

Example: Empirical studies of stock price movements show that the adoption of defensive tactics or the enactment of state takeover statutes reduce the market value of outstanding shares.

Example: It is argued that the willingness of aggressors to pay a premium over market price indicates that the efficient capital market has downgraded the value of the corporation under existing management presumably because of its deficiencies.

a. These simple law and economics arguments have their problems.

1) Takeovers occur in waves and tend to be concentrated in specific industries at any one time; the improvement in efficiency argument cannot explain these patterns.

2) Many takeovers occur apparently because the target is efficiently managed: the aggressor announces in advance that it plans to retain incumbent management.

3) Some studies show that the securities market is information efficient but is not value efficient, so that the market price of shares may not accurately measure the worth of a business when sold as a single unit.

2. OTHER BENEFITS

Economists and others have also suggested that takeovers may provide "synergistic" benefits by combining complementary businesses.

1) One undeniable fact was that the wealth of shareholders of target corporations is increased by a successful takeover. The wealth of

shareholders of aggressors is not significantly increased and may even be decreased, but the net wealth of both groups of shareholders is increased by a takeover.

2) The wealth of "stakeholders" and other constituencies appears to be decreased by many takeovers, though it is unlikely that simply the net gain to shareholders can be explained as a redistribution of wealth from stakeholders to shareholders.

3. THE BUILDING OF EMPIRES

A more skeptical explanation is that the trend represents "empire building" by managers of aggressors who believe that various advantages arise from size:

a. Greater remuneration;

b. Greater prestige and psychic income;

c. Greater protection from takeovers; and

d. Enhanced market power.

Caveat: The empire building hypothesis is rejected by law and economics scholars on the ground that in the absence of demonstrated economic efficiency of larger empires, they must necessarily collapse.

H. ECONOMIC ANALYSIS OF LEVERAGED BUYOUTS

The creation of highly leveraged corporations through leveraged buyouts and leveraged recapitalizations has also been applauded and criticized by economists. The arguments suggested below also largely antedate the apparent collapse of many LBO companies.

1. LBOS AS THE WAVE OF THE FUTURE

Professor Jensen has argued that increased leverage in capital structures is the wave of the future, since it assures shareholders that cash flow is directed to the reduction of debt (and indirectly used for the benefit of shareholders) rather than wasted in discretionary projects.

a. Anecdotal examples reveal that a business that has been acquired through a leveraged or management buyout may be operated more efficiently than before the buyout.

b. The optimistic assessment by Professor Jensen does not appear to be borne out by recent events.

2. THE TAX EXPLANATION FOR LBOS

The tax advantages obtained by the substitution of debt for equity (with deductible interest reducing the business's tax liability to zero) have been cited as a partial explanation.

a. Highly subordinated debt has many characteristics of equity securities but payments on such debt is deductible.

b. It is unlikely that tax savings fully explain LBOs.

3. NEGATIVE EXPLANATIONS FOR LBOS

Many persons have criticized these transactions on the ground that they represent excessive indebtedness and the payment of too high a price for the business. Other persons have argued that high fees paid to investment advisers, lenders, and attorneys explain the LBO movement. In other words, the motivating force for LBOs is greed.

a. The activities of Drexel Burnham Lambert and Michal Milken are cited as examples of the illegal and fraudulent conduct that occurred during the later stages of the takeover boom in which LBOs predominated.

b. A substantial number of companies that have gone through leveraged buyouts or leveraged recapitalizations have found themselves unable to meet their debt obligations and have filed for reorganization under chapter 11 of the Bankruptcy Code. These examples may show that many LBOs were not based on sound economic principles.

3. LBOS AS TRANSFERS IN FRAUD OF CREDITORS

Some courts have held that the leveraged buyout or leveraged recapitalization transaction was itself a fraudulent transfer with respect to creditors since the transaction made the corporation insolvent and unable to pay its obligations as they matured. *E.g. Wieboldt Stores, Inc. v. Schottenstein,* 94 B.R. 488 (N.D.Ill.1988); *Crowthers McCall Pattern, Inc. v. Lewis,* 129 B.R. 992 (S.D.N.Y.1991).

a. The result is that the leveraged buyout transaction or leveraged recapitalization may be voidable and some or all of the cash paid out by the corporation in that transaction may be recoverable.

b. Directors who approved the leveraged buyout or leveraged recapitalization transaction may have liability under state law.

c. Some academic commentary has criticized cases holding or suggesting that the fraudulent transfers statutes should apply to leveraged buyouts on the ground that inadequate weight is being given to the benefits of such transactions.

I. REVIEW QUESTIONS

XIII–1. In a successful proxy fight in which the insurgents triumph, who pays the expenses and costs?

XIII–2. The argument has been made that all proxy fight contestants should have their expenses reimbursed by the corporation. What is the basis of this argument and what is its weakness?

XIII–3. How are proxy contests regulated?

XIII–4. What is a tender offer and how are they regulated?

XIII–5. How does a takeover by cash tender offer differ from a takeover by merger?

XIII–6. What is the "Williams Act"?

XIII–7. Why have states adopted statutes dealing with tender offers despite the existence of the Williams Act?

XIII–8. What role is played in takeover attempts by risk arbitragers?

XIII–9. What is a leveraged buyout?

XIII–10. What are "porcupine provisions"?

XIII–11. What is a "poison pill"?

XIII–12. The decisions by the Supreme Court of Delaware on permissible defensive tactics in takeovers are hopelessly confused; the court wavers from one side to another.

True ________ False ________

XIII–13. What is the "just say no" defense?

XIII–14. P is a dissident shareholder who is attempting to replace the management of corporation X. X's bylaws provide that the annual meeting shall be held on January 11 of each year. The board of directors in accordance with statutory provisions allowing the directors to change the date of the annual meeting have advanced the date to December 8 of the prior year. P brings an action against X Corporation for an injunction preventing the advancement of the meeting date. P contends that management has attempted to use the provisions of law and the corporate machinery to perpetuate itself in office and to obstruct the efforts of the dissident stockholder to undertake a proxy contest against management. These contentions are not disputed. Management contends that it has complied strictly with the provisions of state law in changing the date which is all that is required. Is P entitled to an injunction?

XIV

DUTIES OF DIRECTORS, OFFICERS, AND SHAREHOLDERS

Directors, officers, and shareholders owe duties to the corporation and to other interests within the corporation. To some extent these duties are defined by unique roles within the corporation. These duties are generally created by state law but the federal securities statutes also impose duties that are similar to, and partially overlap, state created duties.

Analysis

A. DUTIES IN GENERAL

The following is a brief description of the scope of fiduciary duties owed by directors, officers, and shareholders to the corporation and to other interests within the corporation.

1. DIRECTORS

Directors have the broad responsibility of overseeing the management of the corporation. They occupy a unique position within the corporate structure, and owe both a duty of care and a high degree of fidelity and loyalty to the corporation. The relationship between director and corporation is a unique one.

a. The duties of directors are sometimes analogized to those of a trustee of a trust.

   1) Directors of corporations are not strictly trustees, since they are not automatically liable for consequences of actions which exceed their powers. Further, the area of their discretion and judgment is considerably greater than that possessed by traditional trustees.

   2) The directors' duties of fidelity and loyalty are essentially the same as a trustee's duties. *Guth v. Loft, Inc.*, 5 A.2d 503 (Del.1939); *Litwin v. Allen*, 25 N.Y.S.2d 667 (Sup.Ct.1940).

   3) Directors may enter into transactions with the corporation under some circumstances.

b. In most instances, directors owe duties to the corporation as a whole rather than to individual shareholders or to individual classes of shareholders. However, if a director deals with a shareholder directly, or if she acts in a way which injures a specific shareholder, she may become directly liable to that shareholder.

c. Directors need not be full-time employees of the corporation and are not required to devote their efforts exclusively to the corporation. (Of course, a full-time employee may also be a director, but the role of director as such is not a full-time responsibility.)

2. OFFICERS AND AGENTS

The duties owed by corporate officers and agents to the corporation depends to some extent on the position occupied by the officer or agent and the type of liabilities that are being imposed.

a. A full-time, high-level managing officer may owe substantially the same duties to the corporation as a director.

b. Agents or employees in subordinate or limited positions owe a correspondingly lesser degree of duty, though even the lowest agent owes the principal certain minimum duties of care, skill, propriety in conduct, and loyalty in matters connected with his agency.

c. A distinction also may be made between full-time and part-time officers or agents in some contexts.

3. SHAREHOLDERS

Since shareholders as such have no power to manage the business and affairs of the corporation and do not perform services for the corporation, their fiduciary relationship to the corporation differs from the relationship of a director or officer.

a. Many cases state that a shareholder owes no fiduciary duty to his corporation. Such statements, however, are too broad, since shareholders, particularly controlling shareholders, clearly owe a duty to their corporation or their fellow shareholders in some circumstances.

  1) A number of states hold that controlling shareholders in a closely held corporation owe a duty to other shareholders that is akin to that owed by partners to each other. See e.g. *Matter of T.J. Ronan Paint Corp.* [Doran], 469 N.Y.S.2d 931, 936 (App.Div.1984); *Fender v. Prescott,* 476 N.Y.S.2d 128 (App.Div.1984). See also the cases discussed in part X E 4.

  2) Controlling shareholders also owe duties to creditors, holders of senior securities and minority shareholders when they transfer control of the corporation to a third party. (See part XV D.)

b. Minority shareholders do not have an open license to abuse or sell their voting power, or exercise it fraudulently.

c. Shareholders are not subject to the same conflict-of-interest rules as directors. For example, shareholders may usually vote their shares in favor of ratification of their own self-dealing transactions but a director should not participate in an analogous decision by the board.

B. DUTY OF CARE OF OFFICERS AND DIRECTORS

A director or officer owes a duty to the corporation to exercise reasonable care in performing his or her duties with respect to the corporation's affairs.

1. GENERAL TESTS

MBCA (1984) § 8.30 states that the standard test for directors' duty of care is that the duties must be discharged

"(1) in good faith;

"(2) with the care an ordinarily prudent person in a like position would exercise under similar circumstances; and

"(3) in a manner he reasonably believes to be in the best interests of the corporation."

a. A similar test that is often quoted in judicial opinions is the exercise of that degree of diligence, care and skill "which ordinarily prudent [persons] would exercise under similar circumstances in their personal business affairs." See *Selheimer v. Manganese Corp. of America,* 224 A.2d 634 (Pa.1966).

b. This standard of care is justified on different grounds.

   1) A stricter test might discourage persons from becoming directors.

   2) Courts feel that they should not second-guess corporate managers with the benefit of hindsight.

c. A number of old cases state that bank directors owe a higher degree of care than directors of ordinary business corporations. E. g., *Bates v. Dresser,* 251 U.S. 524, 40 S.Ct. 247 (1920). On the other hand, there is dicta in more recent cases to the effect that bank directors should not be treated differently in this regard.

   Caveat: As a result of the numerous bank and savings and loan failures during the 1980s, litigation against directors and officers of those organizations is pending in many different states. It is questionable whether these old bank director cases will be applied in this modern setting.

2. THE BUSINESS JUDGMENT RULE

Section 4.01(c) of the Principles of Corporate Governance prepared by the American Law Institute provides:

"A director or officer who makes a business judgment in good faith fulfills his duty under this Section [establishing the duty of care] if:

"(1) He is not interested in the subject of his business judgment;

"(2) He is informed with respect to the subject of his business judgment to the extent he reasonably believes to be appropriate under the circumstances; and

"(3) He rationally believes that his business judgment is in the best interests of the corporation."

a. This is usually referred to as "the business judgment rule."

1) The business judgment rule states that honest business decisions made in good faith and on the basis of reasonable investigation are not actionable, even though the decision is mistaken, unfortunate, or even disastrous. *Shlensky v. Wrigley*, 237 N.E.2d 776 (Ill.App.1968) [decision not to play night games at Wrigley Field]; *Kamin v. American Express Co.,* 383 N.Y.S. 2d 807 (1976), aff'd on opinion below, 387 N.Y.S.2d 993 [decision to pay dividend in property on which tax loss was available].

2) The relationship between the duty of care and the business judgment rule is the subject of disagreement. The business judgment rule may be viewed as a "safe harbor" under the broader duty of care, or it may be an articulation of the duty of care in the context of affirmative decision-making by the board of directors, or it may be "purely aspirational."

b. The business judgment rule is not applicable unless a decision has been made. The "failure to direct" cases discussed below are evaluated under the general due care standard, not the business judgment rule.

Caveat: A decision not to take action is itself a decision that may be protected by the business judgment rule.

c. The business judgment rule relates to directoral responsibility for the results of decisions. A rule that is closely related to the business judgment rule prevents the validity of the directors' decisions themselves from being questioned or set aside by a court if the requirements of the business judgment rule are met. This principle is sometimes referred to as the "business judgment doctrine" to contrast it with the "rule" that protects directors from liability.

d. If the decision is illegal, the business judgment rule is not a shield. *Miller v. American Tel. & Tel. Co.*, 507 F.2d 759 (3d Cir.1974).

e. Issues relating to dividend policies and distributions are often stated to be peculiarly appropriate for the application of the business judgment rule. *Kamin v. American Express Co.*, 383 N.Y.S.2d 807 (Sup.Ct.1976).

3. SMITH v. VAN GORKOM AND ITS CONSEQUENCES

Prior to 1985, relatively few cases imposed liability upon directors for failure to comply with their duty of care.

a. An early case imposing liability upon a bank director for unreasonable or imprudent actions is *Litwin v. Allen,* 25 N.Y.S.2d 667 (1940), and several other early cases involving bank directors also imposed liability. These cases, however, appeared to be exceptions to a general principle that the duty of care and the business judgment rule effectively immunized directors from liability for their decisions.

b. *Smith v. Van Gorkom,* 488 A.2d 858 (Del.1985) imposed liability upon the directors of Trans Union Corporation for accepting an outside offer to purchase the corporation without investigating whether a higher price might be obtained and without making an investigation into the value of Trans Union's business. The directors relied on the opinion of Van Gorkom, the CEO, that the price being offered was a reasonable one and approved a sale of the corporation within a three day period with virtually no discussion of possible alternatives and no assistance from outside experts.

   1) The Delaware Supreme Court held that the test for applying the business judgment rule was "gross negligence." However, it concluded that the business judgment rule did not protect the directors of Trans Union since they had been grossly negligent in not adequately informing themselves of the transaction they approved.

   2) The corporation was sold at $55 per share. While the sale was pending it received an inquiry that indicated that a sale at $60 per share might be possible. Since there were more than 12,000,000 shares outstanding, the potential liability of the directors arising from this $5 differential was more than $60,000,000.

   3) The court decided that all directors, outside as well as inside directors, were responsible for the potential loss to shareholders but did not consider the measure of damages.

c. The decision in *Smith v. Van Gorkom* raised a great outcry in part because it was decided at the height of the takeover boom involving immense transactions.

   1) The possibility of director liability with respect to such transactions was a deterrent to any outside person agreeing to serve as a director.

   2) Directors' and officers' liability insurance premiums soared (see part XVI), though whether caused by the *Van Gorkom* decision or independent factors was disputed.

   3) It was feared that the decision would lead to super cautious decision-making by directors, on creating a "paper trail" that would appear to

demonstrate informed decision-making, and on increased reliance on opinions of experts, including legal counsel.

4). Many commentators were appalled that liability could be imposed on directors for simply following the recommendation of the CEO for whom they had great respect.

4. DIRECTOR LIABILITY STATUTES

In 1986, in direct response to the *Van Gorkom* decision, the Delaware legislature enacted § 102(b)(7) that authorized certificates of incorporation to contain:

> "A provision eliminating or limiting the personal liability of a director to the corporation or its stockholders for monetary damages for breach of fiduciary duty as a director, provided that such provision shall not eliminate or limit the liability of a director (i) for any breach of the director's duty of loyalty to the corporation or its stockholders, (ii) for acts or omissions not in good faith or which involve intentional misconduct or a knowing violation of law, (iii) under [the section of the Delaware GCL making directors liable for unlawful distributions] or (iv) for any transaction from which the director derived an improper personal benefit. No such provision shall eliminate or limit the liability of a director for any act or omission occurring prior to the date when such provision becomes effective."

The requirement that such a provision appear in a certificate of incorporation means a shareholders' vote is necessary if the liability of directors is to be eliminated or limited.

a. Virtually all states have enacted similar statutes since 1986. A few states, including Indiana, have adopted "self executing statutes" that automatically limit the liability of directors without requiring an amendment to the articles of incorporation.

b. The Corporate Governance Project of the American Law Institute originally proposed a "cap" on monetary damages rather than an outright shield against such liability. Only Virginia followed this approach, and it subsequently permitted, as an alternative, the outright elimination of liability by an elective provision in the articles of incorporation. The final version of the Corporate Governance Project follows the revised Virginia approach.

c. Thousands of corporations incorporated in Delaware, including most publicly held corporations, have taken advantage of § 102(b)(7) and eliminated directoral liability to the maximum extent permitted by that section.

d. This section makes it clear that the directors of a corporation adopting an appropriate provision are not personally liable for damages even in the case of gross negligence. *In re Data Products Corporation Shareholders Litigation,* ___

A.2d ___ (Del.Ch.1991); *John Hancock Capital Growth Management, Inc. v. Aris Corp.*, ___ A.2d ___, 1990 WL 126656 (Del.Ch.1990).

e. Future litigation probably will concentrate on the scope of the exceptions set forth in Del. GCL § 102(b)(7). For example, the plaintiffs in *John Hancock Capital Growth Management* argued unsuccessfully that their suit was not precluded by § 102(b)(7) because it presented a claim based on a breach of the duty of loyalty.

f. Section 102(b)(7) only applies to suits for "monetary damages." Suits for equitable relief to enjoin a transaction are not precluded by that section. As a result litigation in due care cases continue to arise despite the enactment of § 102(b)(7). A few state statutes apply to suits for equitable relief as well as to suits for monetary damages.

g. MBCA (1984) § 2.02(b)(4) adopts an opt-in clause permitting the elimination or limitation of liability of directors. The exceptions, however, are narrower than Del. GCL § 102(b)(7): liability may not be eliminated or limited for "(A) the amount of a financial benefit received by a director to which he is not entitled; (B) an intentional infliction of harm on the corporation or the shareholders; (C) a violation of section 8.33 [relating to illegal distributions]; or (D) an intentional violation of criminal law."

5. FAILURE TO DIRECT

Sometimes the claim is made that a director should be liable for mismanagement because he or she totally failed to direct. Liability based on such claims, if established, is not precluded by the business judgment rule [since no judgment or decision was made] or presumably by § 102(b)(b)(7) [because such conduct would be an act or omission "not in good faith or which involve intentional misconduct or a knowing violation of law"].

a. The director may be aged, ill, resident of a distant state, or merely lazy or unduly trusting. He or she may feel that he was elected only as a figurehead or as an accommodation and was not intended to have any significant function.

   1) This is generally not a defense: When a person agrees to be a director she accepts certain responsibilities and obligations, and if these are too burdensome, the proper course is to resign rather than fail to meet them.

   2) The test of skill and prudence is based on an average person of reasonable intelligence and competence.

   3) A director is not considered to be acting in good faith if she has or should have knowledge concerning the matter in question that would cause such reliance to be unwarranted.

Example: A director who is an attorney does not object to a transaction even though she knows it probably violates the antitrust laws. Her duty must be evaluated on the basis of the legal knowledge she has as a lawyer; she may thus be liable even though a non-lawyer director in the same situation would not be.

4) There is some recent case law on failure to direct cases. *Francis v. United Jersey Bank,* 432 A.2d 814 (N.J.1981), imposed liability on an elderly woman for misappropriations committed by her sons. The defendant had received financial statements showing the transactions but had made no attempt to prevent them. In this case, the defendant had received a small part of the misappropriated amounts personally; there is thus an element of self dealing in this case.

b. Causation may be a difficult burden for plaintiffs in failure to direct cases. *Barnes v. Andrews,* 298 Fed. 614 (S.D.N.Y.1924), holds that a director who was negligent in failing to direct can be held liable only if the plaintiff shows a causal relationship between his failure and some specific loss.

Example: *Allied Freightways, Inc. v. Cholfin,* 91 N.E.2d 765 (Mass.1950) holds that a housewife-director is not liable for losses suffered by a corporation as a result of her husband's defalcations because her negligence was not the "proximate cause" of the loss, it being doubtful that she could have prevented the loss in any event.

c. Defendants in "failure to direct" cases may also be able to rely in some cases on the principles (i) that directors, in the absence of other information, may assume that managers and officers are honest, and (ii) that directors may rely in good faith on information, opinions, reports or statements prepared by responsible corporate officials, counsel, or committees of the board of directors. See MBCA (1984) § 8.30(b).

d. In summary, only a few cases impose liability on non-bank directors for total failure to direct. In the most important modern case of this type (*Francis v. United Jersey Bank,* 432 A.2d 814 (N.J.1981)) there was an element of self dealing which may explain the result reached in that case.

6. KNOWING AUTHORIZATION OF WRONGFUL ACT

Liability has sometimes been imposed where the director knowingly authorizes or participates in a wrongful act. In these cases, neither the business judgment rule nor Del. GCL § 102(b)(7) helps the defendants because of the "good faith" requirement.

Example: Personal liability has been imposed on directors where they authorize the improper use of corporate funds, knowing that the use is not in furtherance of corporate affairs, or where they assent to the corporation's use of a financial statement to obtain credit when they know that it is false or fraudulent.

a. Directors have been held liable for a tortious or unlawful act of the corporation if they personally participated in the act.

b. Attempts to hold non-participating directors or officers personally liable for antitrust fines imposed on the corporation, or for bribes, improper payments or illegal campaign contributions made by the corporation, have generally been unsuccessful. *Graham v. Allis–Chalmers Mfg. Co.*, 188 A.2d 125 (Del.1963).

1) There was evidence in some of these cases of the directors' or officers' personal involvement in the conduct or payments in question.

2) A partial explanation is that potential liability in such cases may be enormous, running into the millions of dollars, and totally out of proportion to the wrongfulness of the directors' conduct.

3) In some cases, particularly those involving campaign contributions or improper payments, it was felt that the corporation benefitted from the payments.

4) In *Miller v. American Telephone & Telegraph Co.*, 507 F.2d 759 (3d Cir. 1974), the court upheld a shareholder's complaint against AT & T that that corporation had failed to try to collect a debt of $1,500,000 owed to the company by the Democratic National Committee for communications service provided during the 1968 Democratic Convention. The decision was based in part on a statute prohibiting campaign contributions by corporations to political parties.

Caveat: The cases on which this part of the outline are based all antedate § 102(b)(7) of the Del. GCL.

c. Directors are not automatically liable if they approve an act that turns out to be ultra vires.

7. RELIANCE ON EXPERTS AND COMMITTEES

MBCA (1984) § 8.30(b) permits directors to rely on information, opinions, reports, or statements, including financial statements and other financial data prepared or presented by responsible corporate officers, employees, legal counsel, public accountants, or committees of the board of directors.

a. Reliance on materials presented by others is absolutely essential, as a practical matter, for outside directors who are remote from the day-to-day affairs of the corporation.

b. Reliance is justified only if the director "reasonably believes" that the officers or directors are "reliable and competent" on the matters presented, and in the case of legal counsel, public accountants, and other professionals, the director "reasonably believes" that the matters are within the person's professional or expert competence.

c. A director may also rely on the reports of committees of the board of directors (of which the director is not a member) if the director "reasonably believes" the committee merits competence.

d. If the director makes a judgment that the source of information on which she proposes to rely is reliable and competent, then the decision to rely is itself protected by the business judgment rule.

8. APPLICATION OF THE BUSINESS JUDGMENT RULE TO CONFLICT OF INTERESTS IN GENERAL

A modern trend in corporation law is the recognition of a role for the business judgment rule in the resolution of a variety of issues in which one or more directors have a direct and significant financial interest.

a. A director who is financially interested in a transaction is usually referred to as an "interested director" or a "disqualified director." A decision by such a director on the transaction in which he is interested is not protected by the business judgment rule.

b. Not all directors may be interested in a specific transaction. These directors are usually called "disinterested directors" or "independent directors." The question is whether disinterested directors may make a decision with respect to the transaction in question that is itself entitled to business judgment rule protection, thereby validating the transaction in which the director is interested.

   Caveat: Where all the directors are interested, some courts have permitted the election or appointment of additional directors who are disinterested and permit the new directors to pass on the transaction in question.

c. The major argument against the uncritical application of the business judgment rule in such cases is concern about "structural bias," the fear that directors by virtue of their close working relationships and mutual trust and confidence will not make truly independent and objective evaluations of such transactions on behalf of the corporation.

   1) The concern has been expressed in terms that the directors "will look out for their own," or, "there but for the grace of God, go I." See Comment,

The Propriety of Judicial Deference to Corporate Boards of Directors, 96 Harv.L.Rev. 1894 (1983).

2) Many lawyers familiar with modern boards of directors discount the "structural bias" concern, arguing that disinterested directors today have the independence and strength to put aside concerns of friendship or sympathy and make objective decisions as to whether it is in the best interests of the corporation to pursue such claims.

d. The business judgment rule may be applied (or be sought to be applied) in the following types of interested director transactions, among others:

1) Approval of self-dealing transactions, discussed in part XIV C;

2) Release of corporate opportunities so that individual directors may take advantage of them, discussed in part XIV E;

3) The installation of antitakeover defenses, discussed in part XIII F 1;

4) The auction of the corporation when in the *Revlon* mode, discussed in part XIII F 2;

5) Approval of executive compensation, discussed in part XIV D;

6) Dismissal of derivative suits in which interested directors are named as parties defendant, discussed in part XVIII D;

7) Decisions on behalf of subsidiary corporations in freeze out transaction, discussed in part XIX B.

C. SELF-DEALING

Self-dealing transactions have produced a steady stream of litigation. In many such cases, personal liability has been imposed on directors. Most states have adopted legislation dealing with this subject. See MBCA Subchapter F, §§ 8.60—8.63.

1. DEFINITION

A self-dealing transaction is one between a director and his corporation. Most such transactions are directly between director and corporation, but some may be indirect, e. g., transactions between a relative of the director and the corporation, between two corporations with a common director, or between a parent corporation and its partially-owned subsidiary.

2. THE DANGER OF SELF-DEALING TRANSACTIONS

The danger of self-dealing transactions between a corporation and a director is the risk that the corporation may be treated unfairly in the transaction, since the director's selfish interest may outweigh his or her loyalty to the corporation.

a. When a self-dealing transaction is questioned, the director must usually justify the propriety and fairness of the transaction; the burden of proof is thus shifted from the person questioning the transaction to the interested director.

b. The form the transaction takes is not significant.

Example: The same test is applicable to all of the following transactions: the sale of corporate property to a director, the sale of property to a director's spouse, the sale of property by a director to a corporation, a contract between the corporation and a director for the director to perform services such as selling stock or managing the business, and a loan by a director to her corporation. [The tests are discussed below.]

c. The early common law took the position that because of the risk inherent in self-dealing transactions, all such transactions were automatically voidable at the election of the corporation. *Stewart v. Lehigh Valley R. Co.*, 38 N.J.L. 505 (1875). Such a rule has been abandoned since many self-dealing transactions are entirely fair and reasonable; indeed, in many situations directors may give their corporations terms that are more favorable than the corporation might obtain elsewhere. *Robotham v. Prudential Ins. Co. of America*, 53 A. 842 (N.J. Ch.D.1903).

Example: Loans by directors to the corporation are often made when the corporation could not borrow elsewhere or could borrow only on terms that are considerably less favorable than the terms offered by the director; such transactions should obviously be encouraged.

3. THE MODERN TEST FOR SELF-DEALING TRANSACTIONS IN ABSENCE OF STATUTE

The test for self-dealing transactions developed by the courts in absence of statute combines procedural and substantive requirements essentially as follows:

a. If the court feels the transaction to be *fair to the corporation*, it is upheld. The burden of proving fairness is on the self dealing director and requires full disclosure of the dual interest of the director.

b. If the court feels that the transaction involves *fraud, undue overreaching* or *waste of corporate assets* it is set aside or the directors are otherwise required to restore the status quo before the transaction.

c. If the court feels that the transaction is not clearly fair to the corporation but does not involve fraud, overreaching or waste of corporate assets, the transaction is upheld where the interested director can convincingly show that the transaction was approved (or ratified) by a disinterested majority of the board of directors without participation by the interested director, or by a majority of the shareholders after full disclosure of all relevant facts.

Example: A fair transaction is not ratified either by disinterested directors or by the shareholders. It may nevertheless not be set aside.

Example: All the directors are interested in a fair transaction; they ratify the transaction but shareholder ratification is not sought. It may not be set aside. *Wiberg v. Gulf Coast Land & Development Co.*, 360 S.W.2d 563 (Tex.Civ.App.1962).

Caveat: Tests established by some authorities would require ratification or approval even for fair transactions. If this test is applied, the transactions in the above examples would be voidable.

Example: The director and majority shareholder misappropriates corporate funds for personal purposes. The disinterested directors approve the transaction. The transactions may nevertheless be set aside since the payments are unlawful and constitute waste.

Caveat: There is a possibility that the informal use of corporate funds may be justified as compensation if the amount is reasonable and there is prior understanding as to the amount of such withdrawals over a period of time.

Example: In the previous example, the transaction is submitted to the shareholders and approved by holders of 87 per cent of the voting shares. Since the transaction involves unlawful conduct or waste it may be set aside on suit brought by a nonconsenting shareholder: the partial ratification is not binding on the other shareholders.

Example: In the previous example, the transaction is submitted to the shareholders and approved by all of them. The transaction may not be set aside by a shareholder; creditors or preferred shareholders may be able to set it aside if they can show injury to or fraud on creditors.

Example: A majority of disinterested directors approve a transaction consisting of the sale of land by the corporation to a director. The price is close to, but lower than, the corporation's asking price; the land has been on the market for a year at the asking price without any serious offers. The approval by the disinterested directors if preceded by full disclosure makes the transaction immune from attack by shareholders. In the absence of full disclosure the transaction is voidable. *State ex rel. Hayes Oyster Co. v. Keypoint Oyster Co.*, 391 P.2d 979 (Wash.1964).

Caveat: Where approval by disinterested directors is sought, the interested director, if present, should not be counted toward the quorum requirement, and she should not vote on or participate in the discussion of the merits of the transaction. She also should not informally "lobby" disinterested directors in an effort to persuade them to support the transaction. Any of these actions on the part of the interested director may make the transaction voidable by the corporation and require the interested director to establish the fairness of the transaction if it is questioned.

Example: A majority of directors approve a musical program for radio advertising unaware that the wife of the CEO is to be one of the performing artists. The performer is competent and receives no special treatment or prominence. No duty has been breached since the transaction does not involve self dealing. *Bayer v. Beran,* 49 N.Y.S.2d 2 (1944).

d. Two recurring issues relating to common law ratification are who may be considered disinterested for purposes of ratification, and what degree of specific knowledge or notice is required to constitute an effective ratification. There is a tendency in cases to relax these requirements in situations where the transaction appears to be fair and to stiffen them when the transaction seems questionable.

e. Where a subsidiary corporation has minority shareholders, transactions between parent and subsidiary may injure the minority shareholders of the subsidiary.

4. RATIFICATION BY SHAREHOLDERS

Ratification by shareholders of a transaction between a director and the corporation may validate a self-dealing transaction.

a. At common law, interested directors may vote their shares as shareholders in favor of the transaction. *North–West Trans. Co. v. Beatty*, 12 App.Cas. 589 (Eng.1887); *Gamble v. Queens County Water Co.*, 25 N.E. 201 (N.Y.1890).

b. A shareholder who is also a creditor may vote his or her shares in favor of a transaction which benefits him or her as a creditor. *Allaun v. Consolidated Oil Co.,* 147 A. 257 (Del.Ch.1929).

c. Not all self-dealing transactions may be ratified by majority vote. Transactions that involve fraud, undue overreaching, or waste of corporate assets (e. g., a director using corporate assets for personal purposes without paying for them) can only be ratified by a unanimous vote, and even then, may be attacked by preferred shareholders or representatives of creditors if the corporation becomes insolvent. *Schreiber v. Bryan*, 396 A.2d 512 (Del.Ch.1978).

5. STATUTORY TREATMENT OF SELF-DEALING TRANSACTIONS

Statutes in many states address the issue of self-dealing transactions. Most such statutes are similar to old MBCA (1984) § 8.31, Director Conflict of Interest:

"(a) A conflict of interest transaction is a transaction with the corporation in which a director of the corporation has a direct or indirect interest. A conflict of interest transaction is not voidable by the corporations solely because of the director's interest in the transaction if any one of the following is true:

"(1) the material facts of the transaction and the director's interest were disclosed or known to the board of directors or a committee of the board of directors and the board of directors or committee authorized, approved, or ratified the transaction;

"(2) the material facts of the transaction and the director's interest were disclosed or known to the shareholders entitled to vote and they authorized, approved, or ratified the transaction; or

"(3) the transaction was fair to the corporation.

"(b) For purposes of this section, a director of the corporation has an indirect interest in a transaction if (1) another entity in which he has a material financial interest or in which he is a general partner is a party to the transaction, or (2) another entity of which he is a director, officer, or trustee is a party to the transaction and the transaction is or should be considered by the board of directors of the corporation.

"(c) For purposes of subsection (a)(1), a conflict of interest transaction is authorized, approved, or ratified if it receives the affirmative vote of a majority of the directors on the board of directors (or on the committee) who have no direct or indirect interest in the transaction, but a transaction may not be authorized, approved, or ratified under this section by a single director. If a majority of the directors who have no direct or indirect interest in the transaction vote to authorize, approve, or ratify the transaction, a quorum is present for the purpose of taking action under this section. The presence of, or a vote cast by, a director with a direct or indirect interest in the transaction does not affect the validity of any action taken under subsection (a)(1) if the transaction is otherwise authorized, approved, or ratified as provided in that subsection.

"(d) For purposes of subsection (a)(2), a conflict of interest transaction is authorized, approved, or ratified if it receives the vote of a majority of the shares entitled to be counted under this subsection. Shares owned by or voted under the control of a director who has a direct or indirect interest in the transaction, and shares owned by or voted under the control of an entity described in subsection (b)(1), may not be counted in a vote of shareholders to determine whether to authorize, approve, or ratify a conflict of interest transaction under subsection (a)(2). The vote of those shares, however, shall be counted in determining whether the transaction is approved under other sections of this Act. A majority of the shares, whether or not present, that are entitled to be counted in a vote on the transaction under this subsection constitutes a quorum for the purpose of taking action under this section."

a. Section 8.31 was withdrawn in 1988 and replaced by sections 8.60—8.63, discussed below. Section 8.31 is quoted because it is similar to most state statutes currently in effect dealing with self dealing transactions. Provisions of these statutes, however, vary widely.

b. These statutes are usually understood as simply exonerating or removing a cloud from self-dealing transactions based on the early common law rule of automatic voidability. "It merely removes an 'interested director' cloud when its terms are met and provides against invalidation of an agreement 'solely' because such a director or officer is involved." *Fliegler v. Lawrence,* 361 A.2d 218, 222 (Del.1976).

c. These statutes provide room for the business judgment rule. The conditions for approval set forth in §§ 8.31(a)(1) and 8.31(c) are similar to the requirements of the business judgment rule. In *Marciano v. Nakash,* 535 A.2d 400 (Del.1987), the Delaware Supreme Court stated that under § 144 of the Delaware GCL "approval by fully-informed disinterested directors * * * or disinterested stockholders * * * permits invocation of the business judgment rule and limits judicial review to issues of gift or waste with the burden of proof upon the party attacking the transaction."

d. Compliance with these statutes generally require full disclosure of both the existence of conflicting interests and the details of the transaction.

e. Old MBCA (1984) § 8.31 excluded interested shareholders from voting to approve conflict-of-interest transactions but many state statutes do not expressly do so.

   1) In *Fliegler v. Lawrence,* 361 A.2d 218 (Del.1976), interested shareholders voted to ratify a transaction as literally permitted by Del. GCL § 144. The court applied an "intrinsic fairness" test and set aside the transaction, stating that "nothing in the statute sanctions unfairness * * * or removes the transaction from judicial scrutiny." At 222.

2) As a practical matter, shareholder approval of self-dealing transactions is almost never sought in publicly held corporations. Directoral approval is the usual pattern.

3) Shareholder approval is practical in the case of closely held corporations, and the limited case law on shareholder approval is based entirely on transactions involving those corporations.

f. Proof of fairness of a complex transaction may be difficult and expensive, involving a protracted trial. Hence there is a strong incentive on all parties to obtain review and approval of the transaction by directors or shareholders rather than requiring the interested director to establish the fairness of the transaction.

g. Claims that a transaction constitutes waste, or involves fraud, ultra vires conduct, or were not properly approved are not affected by compliance with these statutes.

h. Under the California statute (which differs significantly from MBCA § 8.31 in that fairness is the sole test for invalidity), unfair or unreasonable transactions may not be validated. *Remillard Brick Co. v. Remillard–Dandini Co.,* 241 P.2d 66 (Cal.App.1952); *Kennerson v. Burbank Amusement Co.,* 260 P.2d 823 (Cal. App.1953).

6. INDIRECT CONFLICTS OF INTEREST

Transactions between corporations with common directors may lend themselves to the same evil as self-dealing transactions between a director and his corporation, since the interest of a common director may be small in one corporation and large in the other.

a. Many indirect conflicts of interest, however, are inadvertent: two corporations with a common director may enter into arms' length transactions with each other without the common director, the board of directors, or high level management of either corporation being aware of it. As a result, old MBCA § 8.31(b) defines an indirect conflict of interest as one in which the "transaction is or should be considered by the board of directors." The new subchapter F follows the same pattern. (See part XIV C 8.)

b. The common law standard for evaluating transactions between corporations with common directors is one of manifest unfairness (or "entire fairness") to one corporation. *Globe Woolen Co. v. Utica Gas & Electric Co.,* 121 N.E. 378 (N.Y.1918); *Chelrob, Inc. v. Barrett,* 57 N.E.2d 825 (N.Y.1944); *Ewen v. Peoria & E. Ry. Co.,* 78 F.Supp. 312 (S.D.N.Y.1948); *Shlensky v. South Parkway Building Corp.,* 166 N.E.2d 793 (Ill.1960); *Case v. New York Central R. Co.,* 204 N.E.2d 643 (N.Y.1965); *Chasin v. Gluck,* 282 A.2d 188 (Del.Ch.1971).

c. The role of the common director in approving the transaction may be relied upon in evaluating a transaction, e. g., *Puma v. Marriott*, 283 A.2d 693 (Del. Ch.1971).

7. REMEDIES

Rescission is normally the proper remedy for a voidable transaction. In such a suit, the corporation must be prepared to return any consideration received by it in the transaction. Normally, it may not simultaneously retain the consideration and in effect seek to reduce the price by attacking the validity of the transaction.

Example: A director sells valuable real estate at a fair price to her corporation in exchange for promissory notes and cash. However, the transaction is voidable by the corporation because the interested director actively lobbied individual members of the board of directors to approve the transaction. The corporation simply refuses to make payments on the promissory notes, claiming that the price was too high. This is not a proper remedy for the corporation: It must either rescind (and return the land) or not rescind (and pay the stipulated price). It may not in effect renegotiate the transaction or have the court set a lower price for the land. *New York Trust Co. v. American Realty Co.,* 155 N.E. 102 (N.Y.1926).

8. SUBCHAPTER F OF THE MODEL BUSINESS CORPORATION ACT (1984)

In 1988, the Committee on Corporate Laws withdrew § 8.31, discussed above, and substituted a new and more comprehensive statute dealing with conflict of interest transactions. This new treatment appears in sections 8.61—8.63, and is usually referred to as "Subchapter F" since it is subchapter F of chapter 8.

Caveat: Chapter F is a complex and elaborate statute that cannot be easily summarized. The following comments and examples describe only the broad outlines of this statute.

a. Subchapter F is structured similarly to § 8.31: a conflict of interest transaction is not voidable by the corporation if (a) it has been approved by disinterested directors or shareholders, or (b) the interested director establishes the fairness of the transaction. Unlike § 8.31, however, Subchapter F is designed to create a series of bright line principles that increase predictability and enhance practical administration.

b. Subchapter F deals only with "transactions" between a director and the corporation.

Example: Chapter F does not deal with non-transactional policy decisions, e.g. whether the corporation should establish a divisional headquarters in a director's home town.

c. Section 8.60(1) defines a "conflicting interest" in terms that are exclusive: section 8.60(1)(i) defines a direct conflicting interest to be when "the director knows at the time of commitment that he or a related person is a party to the transaction or has a beneficial interest in or so closely linked to the transaction and of such financial significance to the director or a related person that the interest would reasonably be expected to exert an influence on the director's judgment if he were called upon to vote on the transaction." Section 8.60(1)(ii) adds limited classes of indirect interests to the definition of "conflicting interest:" transactions that would in the normal course of events be brought to the board of directors for decision and involve (i) an entity of which the director is a director, general partner, agent, or employee or (ii) an entity that controls, is controlled by, or is under common control with one of those entities or (iii) a person who is a general partner, principal, or employer of the director.

Section 8.60(2) defines a "related person" to include spouses, children, grandchildren, siblings, parents, and any trust of which the director is a trustee.

Example: If D (a director of X Co.) is a major creditor of Y Co., and the issue is some transaction between X Co. and Y Co., D's creditor interest in Y Co. may possibly influence D's vote as a director of X Co. However, this transaction does not fall within the definition of "conflicting interest" and therefore is not governed by Subchapter F.

d. A "director's conflicting interest transaction" is defined in § 8.60(2) to be a transaction effected or proposed to be effected by the corporation respecting which a director of the corporation has a conflicting interest. This definition is also exclusive; § 8.61(a) provides that a court may not enjoin, set aside or award damages or impose another sanction with respect to a transaction that is not a "director's conflicting interest transaction" on the ground that the director has a personal interest in the transaction.

Example: D, a director, votes to approve a transaction between the corporation and D's cousin. Since a cousin is not a "related person," the transaction is not a director's conflicting interest transaction and may not be invalidated on the ground of conflict of interest.

Example: D, a director, votes to approve a transaction between the corporation and the president of a golf club D desperately wishes to join. The transaction is not a director's conflicting interest transaction and may not be invalidated on the ground of conflict of interest.

Caveat: Subchapter F deals only with claims based on conflict of interest. The transactions described above may be attacked on the ground they were not approved at a lawful meeting, or that they constitute fraud or waste.

e. Section 8.61(b)(1) provides squarely that approval of a transaction by disinterested directors, following full disclosure by the interested director, is protected by the business judgment rule and § 8.30.

Caveat: The Official Comment to this section is unusual in that it stresses the substantive requirements of the business judgment rule, stating that if the transaction is approved "merely as an accommodation to the director with the conflicting interest," that approval would not be given preclusive effect under the business judgment rule. Similarly, if the terms of a director's conflicting interest transaction are "manifestly unfavorable to the corporation," that fact "would be relevant" to the question whether the approval of the transaction was in "good faith."

Example: The board of directors of a manufacturing corporation approves a cash loan to a director, the terms of which—the duration, security, and interest rate—are at prevailing commercial rates. The loan, however, is not made in the course of the corporation's ordinary business and its effect is to require a commitment of limited working capital that would otherwise have been used in furtherance of the corporation's business activities. The loan is not protected by subchapter F since the board of directors did not comply with the requirement of § 8.30(a) that the action be, in the board's reasonable judgment, in the best interests of the corporation.

9. LOANS TO DIRECTORS OR OFFICERS

Most state statutes contain a provision restricting or prohibiting loans to directors or officers. MBCA (1984) § 8.32 contained a liberalized prohibition similar to these state statutes, but that section was withdrawn in 1988 when subchapter F was approved. That subchapter now governs loans to directors or officers.

Example: A corporation desires to provide low cost housing loans for officers, employees and directors who are compelled to relocate as a result of a decision to change the location of the home office. Under the statutes of some states, such loans are unlawful if made to directors or officers even though the program benefits the corporation and the loans proposed to be made to officers and directors are consistent with loans granted to lower level employees. Compensation arrangements with the officers and directors, however, may be adjusted to give substantially the same benefits as the prohibited loans. Such loans are valid under subchapter F if the requirements of that subchapter are met.

10. EXONERATORY PROVISIONS FOR SELF-DEALING TRANSACTIONS IN ARTICLES OF INCORPORATION

Provisions may be placed in the articles of incorporation of a corporation which attempt to validate transactions between directors and the corporation which otherwise might be voidable under the above principles. These clauses are not construed literally, and do not validate fraudulent or manifestly unfair acts. *Spiegel v. Beacon Participations,* 8 N.E.2d 895 (1937). Such clauses may, however,

a. Permit an interested director to be counted in determining whether a quorum is present, and

b. Exonerate transactions between corporation and director "from adverse inferences which might be drawn against them." *Everett v. Phillips,* 43 N.E.2d 18 (N.Y.1942).

Caveat: There is no express statutory authorization for provisions exonerating directors from the duty of loyalty. Compare the provisions relating to the duty of care authorized by Del. GCL § 102(b)(7), discussed in part XIV B 4.

D. EXECUTIVE COMPENSATION

Executive compensation for most employees may be set administratively without direct participation by the board of directors. However, some senior executives also serve as directors of the corporation. The establishment of a director's compensation involves a specific application of the principles relating to self-dealing. In addition, the board of directors must in any case review and approve the compensation paid to the CEO, who is invariably a director and usually is also chairman of the board of directors. Most publicly held corporations have created compensation committees composed of nonmanagement directors to review all compensation issues for highly compensated executives.

1. TEST FOR EXCESSIVE COMPENSATION

Courts are reluctant to inquire into issues of executive compensation in publicly held corporations. In such corporations, the test for excessive compensation is whether the payments are so large as to constitute spoliation or waste. *Rogers v. Hill,* 289 U.S. 582, 53 S.Ct. 731 (1933).

Example: A bylaw duly approved by the shareholders provides that a stated percentage of the profits are to be set aside each year and paid as a bonus to specified executive officers. Twenty-five years later, the business of the corporation has increased many-fold; the profits payable to the executive officers under the bylaw are roughly ten times higher than the compensation payable by comparable corporations to comparable officers. The payments constitute waste and may be reduced by the court to a reasonable amount.

Example: A corporation creates a non-discriminatory pension plan for its employees, including its chief executive officer. Because of his nearness to retirement and large pension that he commands, over $10,000,000 of the initial payment of $14,000,000 is attributable to the inclusion of the CEO in the plan, an amount far in excess of reasonable compensation. The plan also constitutes waste. *Fogelson v. American Woolen Co.*, 170 F.2d 660 (2d Cir.1948).

Example: A chief executive of a corporation receives a salary of $4,000,000 per year. This salary is at the high end of the range of salaries for chief executive officers for corporations of an equivalent size in the same industry. The salary is not so out of line as to constitute waste.

Caveat: During the 1990s there has been increased criticism of the salaries paid to senior executives, particularly CEOs. Levels of executive compensation is of direct concern to institutional investors who are substantial shareholders in publicly held corporations. This approach, rather than judicial intervention, seems more appropriate to deal with this issue if indeed it needs to be dealt with.

2. COMPARISON WITH TESTS UNDER INTERNAL REVENUE CODE

In closely held corporations large salary payments are usually designed to limit the "double tax problem" of doing business as a C corporation. (See part V I 4.) The IRS may disallow a deduction for unreasonable salaries (treating the excess as a dividend). The test in the tax cases is whether the compensation is for services and is reasonable. *Charles McCandless Tile Service v. United States*, 422 F.2d 1336 (Ct.Cl.1970), *Herbert G. Hatt,* 28 T.C.M. (CCH) 1194 (1969).

a. In a closely held corporation, excessive compensation paid a controlling shareholder may be recovered by the corporation (at the suit of a minority shareholder) if the compensation is unreasonable. *Fendelman v. Fenco Handbag Mfg. Co.*, 482 S.W.2d 461 (Mo.1972). In this respect, an adverse tax determination is evidence of unreasonableness. *Wilderman v. Wilderman*, 315 A.2d 610 (Del.Ch.1974).

b. In the publicly-held corporation, on the other hand, a reasonableness test for measuring excessiveness of compensation for fiduciary purposes has been rejected as being unworkable and involving courts in business decisions with respect to which courts have little or no competence. *Heller v. Boylan*, 29 N.Y.S.2d 653 (1941).

3. COMPENSATION BASED ON STOCK PERFORMANCE

Courts have generally upheld compensation arrangements based on the price or value of shares. Economists generally applaud these arrangements because they tend to align management's selfish interests with the maximization of shareholder wealth.

a. Stock option plans, stock purchase plans, and stock bonus plans may have special tax benefits. Such plans are generally upheld if approved by disinterested directors or by shareholders, and the benefits being conferred bear a reasonable relationship to the services being performed. *Beard v. Elster,* 160 A.2d 731 (Del.1960); *Eliasberg v. Standard Oil Co.,* 92 A.2d 862 (N.J.Super.Ch. Div.1952).

b. A "phantom stock" plan provides compensation that is computed over a period of time as though the officer had owned a specified number of shares. Each year bookkeeping entries are made to reflect "dividends," "stock splits" and similar transactions; when the employee retires or leaves the employment of the corporation, an additional amount equal to the hypothetical increase in market price of the hypothetical shares is paid to him or her. Such an arrangement is a legitimate form of compensation. *Lieberman v. Koppers Co., Inc.*, 149 A.2d 756 (Del.Ch.1959); *Berkwitz v. Humphrey,* 163 F.Supp. 78 (N.D. Ohio 1958).

c. Stock appreciation rights (SAR's) are bonus payments computed on the basis of growth of value of the corporation's shares. In recent years bonus payments based on the attainment of a predetermined goal (e. g. ten per cent increase in gross sales of the division) have become popular. These are referred to as performance unit payments (PUP's).

d. Employee share ownership plans (ESOPs) are an extremely popular compensation device available to employees at all levels. Such plans have some tax benefits and may be used as an antitakeover device. (See part XIII E 6.)

e. Nonqualified retirement plans for executives are usually contractual in nature, individually negotiated, and not funded in advance by the corporation. Funds may be placed in revocable trusts to fund such plans: these plans usually provide that they become irrevocable upon a change in control (a "rabbi trust").

4. NEED FOR BENEFIT TO CORPORATION

The doctrine of consideration requires that services be given or promised in exchange for compensation. A post-death payment to the estate of a deceased employee or surviving spouse not made pursuant to a preexisting plan has sometimes been attacked on this ground. *Adams v. Smith,* 153 So.2d 221 (Ala. 1963); *Alexander v. Lindsay,* 152 So.2d 261 (La.App.1963).

Caveat: The court usually can find some way to avoid this technical objection to the enforceability of a compensation arrangement if it wishes to do so. Regular pension or profit sharing plans, for example, are not subject to this objection because they are part of an overall plan of compensation entered into while services are being performed.

Example: A retiring employee agrees to be available for consultation after his retirement at the corporation's request in exchange for specified payments for life. The employee is never requested to consult. The payments are nevertheless supported by consideration. *Osborne v. Locke Steel Chain Co.*, 218 A.2d 526 (Conn.1966).

E. CORPORATE OPPORTUNITIES

The corporate opportunity doctrine requires a corporate director to render to Caesar at the best possible price that which is Caesar's.

1. GENERAL TEST

As a fiduciary, a director owes a duty to further the interest of the corporation and to give it the benefit of her uncorrupted business judgment. She may not take a secret profit in connection with corporate transactions, compete unfairly with the corporation, or take personally profitable business opportunities which belong to the corporation.

a. Very often the application of the doctrine of corporate opportunity to a specific situation ultimately comes down to a judicial evaluation of business ethics.

b. If the opportunity is not a "corporate opportunity" the director may take advantage of it personally for his or her own private gain and need not share it with the corporation or with other participants in the corporation.

2. WHEN IS AN OPPORTUNITY A "CORPORATE OPPORTUNITY?"

Several competing tests exist as to when an opportunity should be considered a corporate opportunity.

a. An early test was that the opportunity must involve "property wherein the corporation has interest already existing or in which it has an expectancy growing out of an existing right." Many modern courts refer to this language. E. g., *Burg v. Horn,* 380 F.2d 897 (2d Cir.1967); *Litwin v. Allen,* 25 N.Y.S.2d 667 (1940). However, this is a narrow test of corporate opportunity and has been rejected by some courts for this reason. E. g., *Kerrigan v. Unity Sav. Ass'n,* 317 N.E.2d 39 (Ill.1974).

b. A test that has been adopted by some courts is that the opportunity must in some sense arise out of the line of the corporation's business as it is then conducted. The "line of business" test compares the closeness of the opportunity to the types of business in which the corporation is engaged. The closer it is, the more likely it is to be a corporate opportunity. This test tends to be expansive and has been categorized as "too broad." *Burg v. Horn*, 380 F.2d 897 (2d Cir.1967).

c. Another influential test simply applies the test of fairness or "intrinsic fairness" to the transaction in question. *Schreiber v. Bryan*, 396 A.2d 512 (Del. Ch.1978).

d. The test established by a leading Minnesota case combines a "line of business" test with the pervasive issue whether it is unfair for the director under the circumstances to take advantage personally of the opportunity. *Miller v. Miller*, 222 N.W.2d 71 (Minn.1974).

e. The Corporate Governance Project of the American Law Institute defines a corporate opportunity for a principal senior executive or director who is a full-time employee as an opportunity that is reasonably closely related to the business in which the corporation is engaged.

1) Opportunities offered to any director or principal senior executive in the belief that they would be offered to the corporation or which arise out of the use of corporate information or property, are also corporate opportunities under the test set forth in this Project.

2) *Klinicki v. Lundgren*, 695 P.2d 906 (Or.1985) adopts this definition even though in 1985 it was a tentative test subject to revision by the American Law Institute.

Example: A corporation is planning to build a new plant at a specified location. An officer buys up a portion of the land on which the plant is to be built and resells it at a profit to the corporation without disclosing his identity. The opportunity is a corporate opportunity under all the above tests and the officer must account to the corporation for his entire profit.

Example: A corporation is in the boat building business and does not buy or sell used boats. The corporate president learns that a used boat is for sale at a favorable price. She buys the boat personally and resells it profitably. The used boat is not a corporate opportunity under any of the above tests and she need not account to the corporation for her profit.

3. FACTORS CONSIDERED IN EVALUATING WHETHER AN OPPORTUNITY IS A CORPORATE OPPORTUNITY

A number of factors are considered in evaluating the director's decision to take advantage of an opportunity.

a. Whether there were prior negotiations with the corporation about the opportunity;

b. Whether the opportunity was offered to the corporation or to the director as an agent of the corporation;

c. Whether the director disclosed the opportunity to the corporation or took advantage of it secretly;

d. Whether the director learned of the opportunity by reason of his or her position with the corporation;

e. Whether the director used corporate facilities or property in taking advantage of the opportunity;

f. Whether as a result of taking advantage of the opportunity the director is competing with the corporation or thwarting corporate policy (*Zidell v. Zidell, Inc.*, 560 P.2d 1091 (Or.1977));

g. Whether the director acquired at a discount claims against the corporation when the corporation could have done so (*Weissman v. A. Weissman, Inc.*, 97 A.2d 870 (Pa.1953); *Manufacturers Trust Co. v. Becker*, 338 U.S. 304, 70 S.Ct. 127 (1949));

h. Whether the need of the corporation for the opportunity was substantial; and

i. Whether the director was involved in several ventures and the opportunity in question was not uniquely attributable to one such venture. (*Johnston v. Greene*, 121 A.2d 919 (Del.1956)).

Example: The president of a corporation operating a retail department store learns that a competitive store is for sale two blocks away. He secretly buys the competing store, and uses his knowledge of inventory control and relations with suppliers to make the new store more competitive. The new store is a corporate opportunity and the president must account for his profit.

Example: In the previous example, the corporation has previously decided not to expand into new locations in the community in question. The competing store is not a corporate opportunity but the president may be liable for conversion of trade secrets or unfair competition if he improves the competitive nature of the store on the basis of proprietary information obtained from the corporation. *Lincoln Stores v. Grant*, 34 N.E.2d 704 (Mass.1941).

Caveat: Commentators have suggested that the benefits of free and unfettered competition dictate that the scope of corporate opportunities should be narrowly confined.

4. REJECTION OF CORPORATE OPPORTUNITY

Even if an opportunity is a corporate opportunity, directors may take advantage of it if the corporation elects not to do so. *Zidell v. Zidell, Inc.*, 560 P.2d 1091 (Or. 1977).

a. The corporation may voluntarily relinquish a corporate opportunity, though such a relinquishment is a self-dealing transaction and is scrutinized by the courts on the basis of principles described earlier, see part XIV C; *Johnston v. Greene*, 121 A.2d 919 (Del.1956).

b. A persuasive reason for the relinquishment helps to make it clear that the corporation voluntarily decided not to pursue the opportunity.

Example: The corporation operating the retail department store referred to above receives a proposal from the competing store that it purchase the competing store's business; the board of directors of the department store reviews the proposal and decides that under the circumstances it would be unwise to expand the corporation's business. The opportunity is no longer a corporate opportunity and individual directors may thereafter take advantage of the opportunity and purchase the competing store.

c. As is the case with self-dealing transactions generally, effective approval by the board of directors requires compliance with the standards of the business judgment rule as applied to self dealing transactions. (See XIV C.) Requirements include full disclosure of all the surrounding facts by the interested directors and their non-participation in the decision-making process.

5. INABILITY OF CORPORATION TO TAKE ADVANTAGE OF OPPORTUNITY

Directors may take advantage of a corporate opportunity if the corporation is unable or incapable of taking advantage of the opportunity.

Example: A third person refuses to deal with the corporation but is willing to deal with one or more directors individually. The opportunity is not a corporate opportunity.

a. Most courts permit directors to take advantage of a corporate opportunity if the corporation is financially unable to capitalize on the opportunity. *A. C. Petters Co. v. St. Cloud Enterprises, Inc.*, 222 N.W.2d 83 (Minn.1974).

1) When courts permit a director to utilize a corporate opportunity on this basis, they require a convincing showing that the corporation indeed lacks the independent assets to take advantage of its opportunity.

2) Directors do not have the obligation to lend funds to the corporation in order to permit it to take advantage of a corporate opportunity.

3) The "financial inability" defense is troublesome since it may tempt directors to refrain from exercising their strongest efforts on behalf of the corporation if they thereafter may take advantage personally of a profitable opportunity. *Irving Trust Co. v. Deutsch*, 73 F.2d 121 (2d Cir. 1934).

b. The Corporate Governance Project of the American Law Institute does not recognize a defense of financial inability, and *Klinicki v. Lundgren,* 695 P.2d 906 (Or.1985) accepts this position. Under this approach, before a director or officer may take advantage of an opportunity, the corporation must voluntarily renounce its interest in the opportunity or unreasonably fail to act on the proposal.

c. A rigid rule prohibiting directors from taking advantage of a corporate opportunity may be overstrict since directors would have to forego an opportunity entirely if they are unable to persuade the corporation to forego the transaction and are unwilling to lend the necessary funds to the corporation.

Caveat: If the opportunity is sufficiently attractive, the corporation should normally be able to borrow funds to develop the opportunity on the security of the opportunity.

6. DIRECTOR'S COMPETITION WITH THE CORPORATION

Directors may engage in a similar line of business in competition with the corporation's business where it is done in good faith and without injury to the corporation. A director is not a full-time employee and may utilize his or her time as the director sees fit.

a. Cases have found a competing director or officer guilty of a breach of fiduciary duty on several possible theories: conflict of interest, corporate opportunity, misappropriation of trade secrets or customer lists, or wrongful interference with contractual relationships. *Duane Jones Co. v. Burke*, 117 N.E.2d 237 (N.Y.1954).

b. Tort concepts of unfair competition in this area are close to fiduciary duties.

c. Judicial notions of fairness or fair play seem dominant, and cases require a close appraisal of the fiduciary's conduct in light of ethical business practice. *Aero Drapery of Kentucky, Inc. v. Engdahl*, 507 S.W.2d 166 (Ky.1974). (See also the examples in part XIV E 3 above.)

F. THE FAIRNESS TEST

Minority shareholders in a corporation may be injured by a variety of transactions authorized by the controlling shareholder or by the board of directors elected by such shareholders. The test usually applied to such transactions is "fairness" or "intrinsic fairness." However, to an increasing extent, courts are willing to accept the decision of disinterested directors as to the reasonableness of such transactions under the business judgment rule.

1. TRANSACTIONS WITH A PARTIALLY OWNED SUBSIDIARY

A clear example of a potentially injurious transaction is a transaction between a corporation and its partially owned subsidiary. The minority shareholders of the subsidiary are injured by any transaction that in effect transfers assets from the subsidiary to the parent on less than a fair and equivalent exchange.

a. The parent corporation usually has the power to nominate and elect all the directors of the subsidiary and thereby to name all members of the subsidiary's management.

b. If the transaction involves a proportionate distribution of assets by the subsidiary to all of its shareholders, the minority has no basis for complaint on the ground of domination of the management by the parent corporation.

c. The proper standard for evaluating transactions between parent and subsidiary is that it must be "entirely fair" or "intrinsically fair" to the subsidiary.

Example: Plaintiffs are minority shareholders of a corporation which is 97 per cent owned by the parent corporation. They attack decisions (1) to pay large dividends by the subsidiary to ease the cash needs of the parent (the plaintiffs received their proportionate share of these distributions) and (2) to cause the subsidiary not to pursue claims for breach of contract against the parent or other subsidiaries of the parent. The question of the excessive dividends should be evaluated by the "business judgment rule" since all shareholders are being treated proportionately. However, the refusal to enforce the contract claim should be judged on the basis of an "intrinsic fairness" test since it obviously involves self-dealing—the parent received something from the subsidiary "to the exclusion and detriment of the minority shareholders." *Sinclair Oil Corp. v. Levien,* 280 A.2d 717 (Del.1971).

Caveat: Problems of this type arise only when there are minority shareholders of the subsidiary. They do not arise when the subsidiary is 100 per cent owned by the parent corporation.

d. A common problem is the allocation of tax benefits resulting from the filing of a consolidated return. As a result of the consolidation of the financial operations of the subsidiary with the parent, it is possible that valuable tax benefits owned by the partially owned subsidiary are realized by the parent corporation. *Case v. New York Central R. Co.,* 204 N.E.2d 643 (N.Y.1965).

   1) Some courts have refused to consider claims based on the filing of consolidated returns apparently on the theory that there are plusses and minuses involved in consolidation and it is not clear that a single transaction should be taken in isolation. See *Meyerson v. El Paso Natural Gas Co.,* 246 A.2d 789 (Del.Ch.1967); *Alliegro v. Pan American Bank,* 136 So.2d 656 (Fla.App.1962).

   2) In order to avoid conflicts of interest in this situation, parent corporations usually enter into tax sharing agreements with their partially owned subsidiaries, requiring each subsidiary to pay the portion of the total tax shown on the consolidated return resulting from the subsidiary's operations and requiring the parent corporation to compensate the subsidiary for any tax benefits utilized by the parent to reduce or eliminate its tax obligation as reflected in the consolidated return.

e. Because of conflict of interest problems, a parent corporation with a partially owned subsidiary may place outside unaffiliated directors on the board of the subsidiary.

   1) When a transaction between subsidiary and parent is proposed, the subsidiary may be represented solely by the outside directors. In this way, the transaction may be subject to the business judgment rule rather than the rule of "intrinsic" or "entire" fairness.

   2) In some instances, a majority of the subsidiary's board of directors may consist of unaffiliated outside directors.

f. A parent corporation with a partially owned subsidiary may lawfully eliminate the minority shareholders in the subsidiary through a cash out merger, thereby making the subsidiary wholly owned rather than partially owned. (See part XIX B.)

2. MISCELLANEOUS TRANSACTIONS

The fairness test is applicable to a variety of transactions which defy precise categorization and are best illustrated by example. These situations also generally involve duties of controlling shareholders or of directors named by controlling shareholders.

Example: Preemptive rights are excluded in X Co; directors elected by a controlling shareholder cause X Co. to issue to the controlling shareholder new or treasury shares that increases her ownership from 62 per cent to 90 per cent of all outstanding shares. The shares are issued at a bargain price. The transaction is unfair to minority shareholders since it dilutes their economic interest and may be set aside.

Example: In the previous example, the price for the additional shares is fair but the purpose is to give the controlling shareholder enough shares to approve unusual corporate transactions. The transaction is unfair since it has no valid business purpose and dilutes the voting power of the minority shareholders. The transaction may be set aside.

Example: Directors of a corporation know that inventory owned by the corporation has appreciated greatly in value over the value reflected on the books of the corporation. To obtain the greatest portion of this appreciation for itself, the directors elected by the majority shareholder cause the corporation to call for redemption at $80 per share a class of convertible preferred shares. If the called shares were converted into common they would have a value of $160 per share because of the appreciation in value of the inventory. The corporation does not disclose the inventory appreciation to the preferred shareholders, and, as a result, most of the holders of the preferred shares elect to have their holdings redeemed at $80.00 per share. This transaction violates a duty of fairness owed to the minority shareholders: in effect, the directors must fully and fairly disclose the financial consequences of the alternatives available to the preferred shareholders and not mislead them.*Zahn v. Transamerica Corp.*, 162 F.2d 36 (3d Cir.1947); *Speed v. Transamerica Corp.*, 235 F.2d 369 (3d Cir.1956).

Caveat In the previous example, the directors' decision whether or not to call the preferred is itself not subject to a fairness test. Since the preferred shareholders do not have the power to elect directors, they should realize that when they acquire shares that are subject to redemption that the decision to redeem may be based solely on what maximizes the wealth of the common shareholders. The directors must treat the preferred holders fairly only in the sense of not misleading them as to which option they should elect.

Example: In the previous example, before the preferred is called the directors elected by the common shareholders declare extra dividends on the common shares reflecting most of the inventory appreciation, after making the required provision for the senior securities. The holders of senior securities cannot complain of the extra dividends paid to the common shareholders.

Example: The directors in a closely held corporation agree to repurchase shares owned by the father of the majority shareholder at a price of $600.00 per share. Previously, the corporation offered to repurchase shares of other minority shareholders at $300.00 per share. The transaction is voidable unless the other minority shareholders are also given an opportunity to sell shares to the corporation at the favorable price. Cf. *Donahue v. Rodd Electrotype Co.*, 328 N.E.2d 505 (Mass.1975).

Example: A majority of the directors of a corporation have been named by the bank supplying most of the credit needed by the corporation to operate and the other directors have acquiesced in the prior credit transactions. The credit instruments require the majority shareholders to grant the bank an irrevocable proxy appointment that continues so long as credit is outstanding. The bank has named its own officers to be a majority of the directors of the corporation. The bank decides it needs a pledge of all the corporate assets as security for a further loan that has been applied for. This pledge does not require shareholder approval under state law. The shareholders should be advised of the demand and the board of directors should not simply authorize the pledge; a failure to give the notice to shareholders makes the transaction voidable. *Wright v. Heizer Corp.*, 560 F.2d 236 (7th Cir.1977).

3. TRANSACTIONS DISCUSSED ELSEWHERE

The fairness test is potentially applicable in a number of other contexts discussed elsewhere in this Black Letter. In many of these areas the appropriate use of disinterested directors may permit the transactions to be evaluated under the business judgment rule rather than the "entire fairness" standard. These areas are:

a. Self dealing transactions. Part XIV C 5, 8.

b. Corporate opportunities. Part XIV E 4.

c. Freeze-out transactions. Part XIX B.

d. Discontinuance of derivative litigation. Part XVIII D.

G. STATE STATUTORY LIABILITIES

State business corporation acts may impose personal liability on directors for transactions that violate specific statutory provisions. This liability is usually in addition to other liabilities and not dependent on bad faith.

1. ACTS FOR WHICH LIABILITY IS IMPOSED

While provisions vary from state to state, liability for the following actions are typical:

a. Paying dividends or making distributions in violation of the act or in violation of restrictions in the articles of incorporation. See MBCA (1984) § 8.33. Liability is usually limited to the excess of the amount actually distributed over the amount which could have been distributed without violating the act or restriction.

b. Authorizing the purchase of its own shares by a corporation in violation of the act. The liability is usually limited to the consideration paid for such shares which is in excess of the maximum amount which could have been paid without violating the statute.

c. Distributing assets to shareholders during the dissolution and winding up of the corporation without paying and discharging, or making adequate provision for the payment and discharge of, all known debts, obligations, and liabilities of the corporation.

d. Permitting the corporation to commence business before it has received the minimum required consideration for its shares. The liability is usually limited to the unpaid part of the minimum required capitalization and the liability terminates when the required consideration has actually been received.

e. Permitting the corporation to make a loan to an officer or director, or to make a loan secured by shares of the corporation when such transactions are prohibited. The liability is limited to the amount of the loan until it is repaid.

Caveat: Many of these liability provisions appear in older statutes that contain restrictive requirements that have been eliminated from more modern statutes. Most modern state statutes, like the MBCA (1984), do not contain minimum capital requirements for new corporations, and either do not prohibit loans to officers and directors or loans secured by shares of the corporation, or have greatly relaxed older prohibitions against such loans. Where the restrictions have been eliminated, the reason for the liability provisions has been also.

2. **DIRECTORS WHO ARE LIABLE**
Business corporation acts usually provide that joint and several liability is imposed on all directors present at the meeting at which the action in violation of the statute is taken, unless a director's negative vote is duly entered in writing in the corporate records or the secretary is notified in writing by registered mail of the negative vote.

3. **DEFENSES**
Statutes imposing strict liability may relieve directors of liability if in the exercise of ordinary care, they

   a. Relied in good faith upon written financial statements of the corporation represented to be correct by appropriate corporate officials [MBCA (1984) § 6.40(d)]; or

   b. Relied in good faith on book values in determining the amounts available for distribution; or

   c. Relied in good faith upon the written opinion of an attorney for the corporation [MBCA (1984) § 8.30(b)].

4. **PRACTICAL IMPORTANCE OF STATUTORY LIABILITY**
There has been virtually no litigation over the scope of the statutory liabilities for unlawful distributions or the scope of the defenses described in this subsection.

H. REVIEW QUESTIONS

XIV–1. What is meant by a "duty of care"?

XIV–2. What is meant by "the business judgment rule?" By the "business judgment doctrine"?

XIV–3. A director offers to sell his corporation a piece of land owned by a family trust at a questionable price. What standards are applicable to determine the validity of such a transaction?

XIV–4. If the board of directors in the previous question conclude that the transaction is in the best interests of the corporation, may the transaction be protected against later attack by a dissatisfied shareholder?

XIV–5. What rule is applicable to determine the validity of a transaction between two corporations with common directors?

XIV–6. May the shareholders ratify a self dealing transaction that does not meet the standard of fairness?

XIV–7. Today many executives in publicly held corporations receive executive compensation of more than a million dollars per year. Is this self dealing? What is the standard for determining the validity of such very large compensation?

XIV–8. How may executive compensation be tied directly to the performance of the stock in the stock market?

XIV–9. What is meant by the doctrine of "corporate opportunity"?

XIV–10. What is the test for determining when an opportunity is a corporate opportunity?

XIV–11. May a director take advantage of a corporate opportunity if the corporation is unable or unwilling to do so?

Yes ______ No ______

XIV–12. A corporation enters into a transaction with its subsidiary of which it owns 98 per cent of stock. Which standard should be applied to such a transaction, the business judgment rule or the fairness standard of self-dealing transactions?

XIV–13. Corporation A owns 93 per cent of the outstanding shares of Corporation B. The remaining 7 per cent of the shares are held by 50 individuals. Corporation A desires to raise capital for itself by pledging certain liquid assets of Corporation B. May it do so?

XIV–14. A corporation has two classes of authorized shares: 1,000 preferred shares and 3,000 common shares. Outstanding are: (1) 1,000 noncumulative $100 par value preferred shares with full voting rights with a liquidation preference of $200 per share, the preferred shares are redeemable at $105 per share and each share is convertible into two common shares; and (2) 1,000 common shares without par value with full voting rights.

The corporation has net assets of $210,000, of which $105,000 is earned surplus. It is about to dissolve. What should the board of directors do in fairness to both classes? [This question and answer is drawn from Ballantine, Problems in Law 238 (5th Ed. 1975).]

XIV–15. A is a large corporation with over 30,000 employees at 100 plants scattered around the country or overseas. The corporation and certain employees have entered pleas of guilty to indictments charging violations of the federal anti-trust laws. Ds are directors of the corporation who were not charged with any violation of the anti-trust laws in the proceeding against the corporation. P brings an action on the corporation's behalf to hold Ds liable for the losses sustained by the corporation by reason of the violations of its employees. There is no evidence presented to the effect that Ds knew or had any knowledge that would have put them on notice that violations were occurring. Are Ds liable to the corporation?

Yes ______ No ______

XIV–16. X corporation, a mining company, entered into a contract with M corporation, a smelting company, which provided that M should smelt all of X's ore for a period of 10 years at a specific price per ton of ore. The price agreed to be paid by X to M was 10 per cent higher than the regular and customary price for smelting. A, B and C were directors of X corporation and also of M corporation. When this contract came up for approval before the boards of directors of the two corporations, the directors A, B and C, refrained from voting, but the contract was approved by the board of directors of X corporation because the directors other than A, B and C, were advised that A, B and C wanted such contract approved. The metal market was dropping when this contract was made and continued to drop thereafter. Usually the price of smelting drops with the market. The X corporation elected a new board of directors which made an investigation and found that the contract with M was causing the company to lose money. The new board voted to cancel the contract with M and brought suit for a declaratory judgment to determine that the cancellation was legal. M's defense is that the contract is valid because the directors who were common to both corporations, A, B and C, abstained from voting on the contract. Is the defense valid at common law? Under modern conflict of interest statutes?

a) At common law?

Yes ______ No ______

b) Under modern statutes?

Yes _______ No _______

XIV–17. X corporation, in which D is the majority stockholder but not on the board of directors, is engaged in mining copper. X corporation is in very precarious financial shape, being barely able to meet its day-to-day obligations as they come due. D completely controls the board of directors of X corporation and regularly consults with members of the board and visits X's mining operation. D learns that a vein of ore that X is mining runs directly into B's property which adjoins X's property. An opportunity to buy B's property arises and without mentioning the opportunity to X corporation, D buys B's mines for $100,000 cash. T, a minority stockholder in X, sues D on behalf of the corporation to compel him to turn over to X at cost the mining property he purchased from B. D's defense is that B would sell his property only for cash and that at the time D bought the mines from B the X corporation was unable to raise more than $10,000 in cash. Is the defense valid?

XV

DUTIES RELATING TO THE PURCHASE OR SALE OF SHARES

Analysis

A. STATE LAW REGULATING TRANSACTIONS IN SHARES BY AN OFFICER OR DIRECTOR

The state law relating to transactions in corporate shares by directors and officers (or by the corporation itself) has been largely overshadowed by the development of federal law, particularly rule 10b–5 and section 16(b), discussed at length in this chapter. However, with the restrictions imposed on rule 10b–5 by Supreme Court decisions (also described below), greater attention may be paid in the future to state law in this area.

1. INSIDER TRADING

An officer or director of a corporation may have knowledge about corporate affairs which will affect the price or value of the corporate shares before it becomes known to the general public or to other shareholders. As a result, the director or officer may be tempted to make a personal profit by either purchasing or selling shares (depending on the nature of the information) without disclosing the information. Such trading is called "insider trading." State common law did not develop a simple test for handling insider trading. Most cases permitted such trading in the absence of fraud. *Goodwin v. Agassiz*, 186 N.E. 659 (Mass.1933). However, liability has been imposed on several common law theories.

a. If an affirmative misrepresentation was made by the insider, normal fraud principles dictate that the defrauded person might rescind the transaction or sue for damages.

b. Where certain facts are of critical importance and peculiarly within the knowledge of the insider, some courts find an affirmative duty to disclose these "special facts." No definition is offered as when facts are "special." *Strong v. Repide*, 213 U.S. 419, 29 S.Ct. 521 (1909); *Taylor v. Wright*, 159 P.2d 980 (Cal. App.1945). This may be viewed as an extension of fraud concepts, but it quickly became a significantly easier burden to establish than fraud.

c. Kansas early adopted a stricter rule of fiduciary duty to protect all outsiders, *Hotchkiss v. Fischer*, 16 P.2d 531 (Kan.1932), though the difference between these cases and the cases applying the "special facts" rule appears to be one of degree. Apparently, only Kansas has adopted this broad rule.

d. The broadest common law rule is set forth in *Diamond v. Oreamuno*, 248 N.E.2d 910 (N.Y.1969) where the court permitted the corporation to recover losses avoided by insiders by selling their securities before the announcement of negative information.

   1) Relying on analogies with the federal securities laws, the court in effect concluded that inside information was corporate property and the insider should not be permitted to profit from the use of that corporate property even though the corporation was not injured thereby.

2) This view has not been widely accepted. It has been rejected by two courts. *Schein v. Chasen*, 313 So.2d 739 (Fla.1975); *Freeman v. Decio*, 584 F.2d 186 (7th Cir.1978) (Indiana law). Two federal district courts have concluded that New Jersey probably would recognize the *Diamond* principle. *In re ORFA Securities Litigation*, 654 F.Supp. 1449 (D.N.J.1987); *National Westminster Bancorp NJ v. Leone*, 702 F.Supp. 1132 (D.N.J.1988).

3) In *People v. Florentino*, 456 N.Y.S.2d 638 (N.Y.Crim.Ct.1982), the court upheld a criminal proceeding against an attorney who, while representing issuers of securities in takeover attempts, purchased shares of target companies before the takeover was announced.

Caveat: The state law of insider trading has not developed fully because federal law has sharply circumscribed insider trading and most insider trading cases have been brought under federal law. (See part XV B, below.)

2. PURCHASE AT A DISCOUNT OF CLAIMS AGAINST THE CORPORATION

A corporate officer or director generally may purchase claims against a solvent corporation at a discount though in some circumstances the opportunity to acquire a claim at a discount may itself be a corporate opportunity. *Weissman v. Weissman Inc.*, 97 A.2d 870 (Pa.1953).

a. Different principles are applicable where the corporation is insolvent. Corporate directors should then attempt to settle or discharge claims against the corporation on the best possible terms from the corporation's standpoint in order to benefit other creditors and the shareholders rather than seeking to share personally in the distribution.

b. Claims validly bought at a discount when a corporation is solvent may share at face value in a subsequent distribution in insolvency or bankruptcy. *Manufacturers Trust Co. v. Becker*, 338 U.S. 304, 70 S.Ct. 127 (1949).

3. PURCHASE OR SALE OF SHARES IN COMPETITION WITH THE CORPORATION

In some circumstances an officer or director may sell personal stock in competition with the corporation when it is attempting to raise capital by selling additional shares.

a. The opportunity to sell shares to a third person in this situation is usually a corporate opportunity and subject to attack by the corporation.

b. *Brophy v. Cities Service Co.*, 70 A.2d 5 (Del.Ch.1949) applies this principle in the converse situation where an insider buys shares knowing that the corporation is planning to reacquire shares in the near future.

4. PURCHASE OR SALE OF SHARES IN CONNECTION WITH STRUGGLES FOR CONTROL

If outsiders are seeking to wrest control of a publicly held corporation away from incumbent management, the incumbents may purchase or sell shares in order to preserve their position. Most such transactions involve the corporation rather than officers or directors. A variety of such transactions and the legal principles applicable to them are discussed in part XIII D.

B. RULE 10b-5

Rule 10b-5, promulgated by the Securities and Exchange Commission under section 10(b) of the Securities Exchange Act of 1934, is the source of most current principles relating to transactions in securities by officers, directors, and others. It reads as follows:

> "It shall be unlawful for any person, directly or indirectly, by the use of any means or instrumentality of interstate commerce, or of the mails or of any facility of any national securities exchange,
>
> "(1) to employ any device, scheme, or artifice to defraud;
>
> "(2) to make any untrue statement of a material fact or to omit to state a material fact necessary in order to make the statements made, in light of the circumstances under which they were made, not misleading, or
>
> "(3) to engage in any act, practice, or course of business which operates or would operate as a fraud or deceit upon any person,
>
> in connection with the purchase or sale of any security."

1. HISTORY OF THE RULE

Rule 10b-5 was originally promulgated because the express antifraud remedy sections in the federal securities acts applied only to buyers of securities, and the SEC wished to extend remedies to sellers of shares to insiders.

a. The history of rule 10b-5 has some of the attributes of a roller coaster: a dizzying growth until about 1975 followed by a decline as the Supreme Court sharply limited the growth of the jungle of case law.

   1) In analyzing rule 10b-5 cases it is important to note the date the case was decided.

   2) Despite the post-1975 decline, rule 10b-5 is still the most widely cited and applied antifraud provision in the federal securities acts.

2. RULE 10b–5 IS FEDERAL LAW

Rule 10b–5 is a federal regulation and suits arising under it are based on federal law. This has both procedural and substantive implications when compared to the analogous state law.

a. Even though it is a regulation adopted by the SEC, rule 10b–5 has the same force as a federal statute; its violation may be made the basis of a criminal prosecution or civil suit.

b. Federal court jurisdiction exists under the federal question doctrine.

c. Suit may be brought only in federal court; state courts do not have jurisdiction to adjudicate rule 10b–5 claims.

d. State security for expenses statutes (see part XVIII, C) and other restrictive state procedural rules are not applicable.

e. The procedures in federal court may be simpler than in state courts and the discovery rights broader.

f. There is nationwide service of process in rule 10b–5 suits under section 27 of the Securities Exchange Act, and broad venue provisions. *Securities Investor Protection Corp. v. Vigman*, 764 F.2d 1309 (9th Cir.1985).

g. The doctrine of pendent jurisdiction permits the joinder of both state and federal claims arising from the same transaction in a rule 10b–5 suit but a rule 10b–5 claim cannot be joined with a state cause of action in a state court.

h. The substantive principles under rule 10b–5 are more fully developed and probably more favorable to plaintiffs than the correlative principles of state law.

   1) Many rule 10b–5 cases arise on motions to dismiss; courts are reluctant to close off plausible sounding allegations without a trial so that pro-plaintiff decisions are numerous.

   2) There are more rule 10b–5 precedents than state court precedents and hence "more law" on which to build one's case.

   3) There may be a feeling (that is perhaps changing) that federal judges are more sympathetic to minority shareholder complaints than state court judges.

i. A private cause of action is created by rule 10b–5 so that a person injured by a transaction that violates the rule has direct recourse to the federal courts.

Kardon v. National Gypsum Co., 73 F.Supp. 798 (E.D.Pa.1947), *supplemented* 83 F.Supp. 613 (E.D.Pa.).

j. Rule 10b–5 is applicable to any "security," including those issued by closely held as well as publicly held corporations. *Landreth Timber Co. v. Landreth*, 471 U.S. 681, 105 S.Ct. 2297 (1985).

k. Rule 10b–5 is applicable to every transaction using the facilities of interstate commerce or the mails. Section 3(a)(17) of the Securities Exchange Act of 1934 provides that the term "interstate commerce" includes "intrastate use of (A) any facility of a national securities exchange or of a telephone or other interstate means of communication or (B) any other interstate instrumentality."

3. LIMITING PRINCIPLES ON RULE 10b–5

United States Supreme Court decisions impose significant substantive rules governing the scope of rule 10b–5:

a. *Ernst & Ernst v. Hochfelder*, 425 U.S. 185, 96 S.Ct. 1375 (1976) holds that a private plaintiff under rule 10b–5 must allege and prove "scienter," that is, "intentional wrongdoing" or a "mental state embracing intent to deceive, manipulate or defraud."

1) The Court rejected several lower court holdings that mere "negligence" was sufficient.

2) The Court reserved the issue whether in some circumstances recklessness might satisfy the scienter requirement. Later decisions by lower federal courts have almost unanimously held that "recklessness" or "severe recklessness" satisfies the scienter standard. *Broad v. Rockwell Intern. Corp.*, 642 F.2d 929 (5th Cir.1981); *Keirnan v. Homeland, Inc.*, 611 F.2d 785 (9th Cir.1980).

3) The Court also reserved the question whether a lesser standard of conduct might satisfy rule 10b–5 in cases where relief was being sought directly by the SEC (as contrasted with suits for damages brought by private plaintiffs). This issue was resolved against the SEC in *Aaron v. SEC*, 446 U.S. 680, 100 S.Ct. 1945 (1980), holding that scienter must be established in SEC-instituted suits also.

b. *Santa Fe Industries, Inc. v. Green*, 430 U.S. 462, 97 S.Ct. 1292 (1977) holds that rule 10b–5 is limited to situations involving deception. Unfair transactions that are adequately disclosed cannot be attacked under rule 10b–5.

c. *Blue Chip Stamps v. Manor Drug Stores*, 421 U.S. 723, 95 S.Ct. 1917 (1975) holds that only persons who are purchasers or sellers of securities may bring suit as plaintiffs.

1) This doctrine is based on the early decision in *Birnbaum v. Newport Steel Corp.,* 193 F.2d 461 (2d Cir.1952) and is sometimes referred to as the "Birnbaum doctrine" or "Birnbaum rule."

2) The opinion also contains exceptionally strong dicta criticizing federal securities law litigation in general.

d. Claims may be made under rule 10b–5 even though under the same factual situation a claim might also be made under the more specific provisions of the Securities Act of 1933 or other sections of the Securities Exchange Act of 1934. *Herman & MacLean v. Huddleston,* 459 U.S. 375, 103 S.Ct. 683 (1983).

4. RULE 10b–5 AS AN ANTIFRAUD PROVISION

A private cause of action exists under rule 10b–5 on behalf of every person who buys or sells securities as a result of fraud or misrepresentation. Since the rule is applicable to both closely and publicly held shares and since it is triggered by the use of a facility of interstate commerce, rule 10b–5 is a far-reaching antifraud provision that is applicable to virtually all securities transactions, including many cases in which an unsophisticated attorney may not realize that a federal cause of action exists.

Example: The president of a small Colorado corporation offers to purchase the shares owned by a Colorado shareholder on the basis of a misrepresentation or a failure to disclose "material" facts about the corporation. The transaction involves a single telephone call, made by the president of the corporation from one floor in a Denver office building to the shareholder on another floor in the same building. The transaction is covered by rule 10b–5.

Example: A purchaser of all of the outstanding shares of a closely held corporation claims that she entered into the purchase because of false or misleading statements by the seller; the purchaser also claims that the seller failed to state material facts as to the value of the corporation. A claim under rule 10b–5 is stated since shares of a closely held corporation are "securities" under the Securities Exchange Act of 1934. *Landreth Timber Co. v. Landreth,* 471 U.S. 681, 105 S.Ct. 2297 (1985). It is not relevant that the purchase involved a business that the purchaser planned to operate herself.

a. Rule 10b–5 proscribes not only affirmative misrepresentations and half-truths but also failures to disclose "material facts necessary in order to make the statements made, in light of the circumstances under which they were made, not misleading."

1) Rule 10b–5 is an antifraud provision, not a full disclosure provision. While mere silence may constitute a violation, *Speed v. Transamerica*

Corp., 99 F.Supp. 808 (D.Del.1951), *supplemented* 100 F.Supp. 461 (D.Del.), the silence must arise in a context where there is a requirement to speak. Such a requirement exists in three situations:

(i) Disclosure is required if undisclosed information renders previous public statements by the corporation misleading;

(ii) Disclosure is required if the corporation has reason to believe that individuals are engaged in trading in the securities markets on the basis of information that has not been disclosed; and

(iii) Disclosure is required if there are rumors swirling through the brokerage community that are generally (but incorrectly) being attributed to the issuer.

Example: A corporation learns that it and its managers are to be indicted for paying a bribe. It discloses this information when required to by SEC regulation but does not disclose it immediately. The failure to disclose this information immediately is not a violation of rule 10b–5 since there is no duty to disclose. *Roeder v. Alpha Industries, Inc.,* 814 F.2d 22 (1st Cir.1987).

Caveat: Under SEC regulations, there is a duty to disclose potential indictments in the corporation's next 10K. *Roeder* holds only that there is no duty to disclose immediately under rule 10b–5.

Example: A corporation makes a major mineral find in Canada. As rumors begin to develop it issues a press release prepared by an officer who knowingly understates the true dimensions and importance of the find. The corporation violates rule 10b–5 if it fails to make an immediate correction of the misstatements in the press release.

Caveat: The New York Stock Exchange listing agreement for corporations imposes an affirmative contractual duty on listed corporations to disclose promptly all material developments. In appropriate cases trading may be suspended while an appropriate disclosure statement is prepared and disseminated.

2) A projection or forward looking statement made by the issuer is misleading if it is not made with a reasonable belief that it is accurate.

b. The test of what is "material" is whether a reasonable person would attach importance to the information in determining a course of action—in other words, if the information would, in reasonable and objective contemplation, effect the value of the securities, it should be considered "material." *SEC v. Texas Gulf Sulphur Co.*, 401 F.2d 833 (2d Cir.1968); *TSC Industries, Inc. v. Northway, Inc.*, 426 U.S. 438, 96 S.Ct. 2126 (1976) [§ 14(a) case].

Example: Information concerning the existence and status of preliminary negotiations with respect to a merger may or may not material depending upon a balancing of the probability that the merger will occur and the anticipated magnitude of the event in light of the totality of the corporation's activity. *Basic, Inc. v. Levinson,* 485 U.S. 224, 108 S.Ct. 978 (1988).

c. If the misrepresentation relates to a publicly traded security, a purchaser or seller may be able to recover without establishing knowledge of or reliance on the misrepresentation. *Basic Inc. v. Levinson,* 485 U.S. 224, 108 S.Ct. 978 (1988). The theory is that investors rely on the efficiency of the securities markets in establishing an appropriate price for shares; a misrepresentation made in a public manner therefore misleads all investors.

1) This principle is generally referred to as the "fraud on the market theory." In *Basic,* the Court adopted this theory to the extent of creating a rebuttable presumption of reliance, thereby shifting the burden of showing a lack of reliance to the defendants.

Caveat: A dissenting opinion questioned the wisdom of the Court adopting an economic theory as the basis of decision when it has not been universally accepted.

2) This principle is based on an earlier United States Supreme Court decision holding that in a case of a failure to disclose a material fact, proof of reliance on the failure to disclose may be inferred and need not be separately established. *Affiliated Ute Citizens v. United States,* 406 U.S. 128, 92 S.Ct. 1456 (1972).

3) This principle has also been extended to cases where a person invests in a newly issued security on the belief that an unlawfully issued security could not be marketed. *T.J. Raney & Sons, Inc. v. Fort Cobb Irrigation Fuel Authority,* 717 F.2d 1330 (10th Cir.1983), cert. denied 465 U.S. 1026, 104 S.Ct. 1285 (1984).

4) A false or misleading press release by the corporation may give rise to liability based on the "fraud on the market theory."

d. If disclosure is impractical, a person with material information who is subject to a disclosure requirement must forego the transaction.

e. A transaction in violation of rule 10b–5 may be rescinded by the innocent party, or damages may be computed on the assumption that the contract had not been entered into.

5. RULE 10b–5 AS A PROHIBITION AGAINST INSIDER TRADING

Rule 10b–5 is also applicable to transactions in shares of publicly held corporations effected anonymously over securities exchanges or through brokers. As a result, rule 10b–5 is also a broad prohibition against trading on the basis of insider information.

a. The basic principle that trading on inside information violates rule 10b–5 was established in *In re Cady Roberts, Inc.,* 40 S.E.C. 907 (1961), and *S.E.C. v. Texas Gulf Sulphur Co.,* 401 F.2d 833 (2d Cir.1968), cert. denied 394 U.S. 976, 89 S.Ct. 1454 (1969).

b. The Insider Trading Sanctions Act of 1984 ("ITSA") and the Insider Trading and Securities Fraud Enforcement Act of 1988 ("ITSFEA") legislatively recognize this principle and impose a civil penalty of up to three times the insider's profit for violations of the insider trading prohibitions. Other sanctions, including criminal prosecution for willful violations, also potential are available.

Caveat: The current policy of the federal government is to view insider trading as a serious offense that should be prosecuted vigorously, both civilly and criminally. This is true despite extensive academic commentary that suggests that insider trading harms no one and may be beneficial in several ways.

c. In anonymous transactions it is usually impractical for the person with material information to disclose the material facts. That is a corporate function.

1) *SEC v. Texas Gulf Sulphur Co.,* supra, holds that officers, directors, and employees of an issuer who know of a material favorable development as a result of their position with the corporation violate rule 10b–5 if they purchase shares or options to purchase shares before the information is released.

Example: The president of a corporation learns of an adverse corporate development. Before it is announced he sells his shares in the company. The president has violated rule 10b–5 irrespective of any violation of state law.

2) *SEC v. Texas Gulf Sulphur Co.*, also holds that insiders must wait until the information has been reasonably disseminated to the investing public through wire services and the like before they may trade.

Example: In the previous example, the corporate president holds a press conference to announce a major favorable development. Immediately after the press conference and before the information is widely disseminated he calls his broker and places an order to buy shares. The president has violated rule 10b–5.

3) *SEC v. Texas Gulf Sulphur Co.* suggests that "tippees," i.e. persons who obtain material information before it is publicly released have an obligation not to trade on that information.

Caveat: Several aspects of the holding in *SEC v. Texas Gulf Sulphur Co.* have been affected by later holdings of the United States Supreme Court. The liability of tippees is one such area. (See part XV B 5 b.)

4) The New York Stock Exchange has published guidelines as to when it is appropriate for an insider to purchase shares of her own corporation. These guidelines suggest periodic investment purchases (e. g., buying a few shares every month) or limiting transactions to brief periods after public information is released.

5) Under § 20A of the Securities Exchange Act of 1934 (added by ITSFEA) a person violating the insider trading prohibitions is liable to contemporaneous traders of the security even though there is no privity between the insider and the person trading.

(i) Liability under § 20A is limited to the total profit gained or loss avoided by the person violating the insider trading prohibitions, and is further reduced by any disgorgement of profits ordered by a court at the instance of the SEC.

(ii) Earlier cases were sharply split over whether such an action might be maintained at all, and if so, how damages should be measured.

d. Rule 10b–5 applies, literally, to "any person." The rule therefore appears to apply to "tippees" who are not directly connected with the issuer as well as traditional insiders. As a result of two United States Supreme Court decisions, *Chiarella v. United States,* 445 U.S. 222, 100 S.Ct. 1108 (1980), and *Dirks v. SEC,* 463 U.S. 646, 103 S.Ct. 3255 (1983), however, this broad language should not be taken literally.

1) Rule 10b–5 clearly applies to prohibit insider trading by lower level corporate employees as well as officers and directors. *SEC v. Texas Gulf Sulphur Co.,* supra.

   Example: A geologist employed by a mining company learns of a major ore strike before information is publicly announced. A purchase of shares before this information is publicly announced constitutes a violation of rule 10b–5.

2) Persons who receive inside information from the issuer in connection with duties to the issuer—e.g. accountants, investment banking firms or law firms— are "constructive insiders" and subject to the same rules as a corporate officer, director, or employee. *Dirks v. SEC,* 463 U.S. 646, 103 S.Ct. 3255, n. 14 (1983).

   Example: A brokerage firm obtains information about a corporation in connection with a contemplated debt financing before the information is generally available. The brokerage firm violates rule 10b–5 if it purchases or sells corporate securities before the information is released. *Shapiro v. Merrill Lynch, Pierce, Fenner & Smith, Inc.,* 495 F.2d 228 (2d Cir.1974).

   Example: To avoid inadvertent violations of rule 10b–5 in this connection brokerage firms attempt to maintain a firm internal separation between underwriting and sales activities. This internal separation is called a "Chinese wall."

   Example: The office manager of a law firm learns that a client is about to become the subject of a tender offer. The office manager calls her broker and purchases shares of the client. The office manager has violated rule 10b–5. *SEC v. Musella,* 578 F.Supp. 425 (S.D.N.Y.1984).

   Caveat: Under ITSFEA the law firm in the previous example may be liable for a civil penalty since at the time of the violation it "directly or indirectly controlled the person who committed the violation." In order to recover from a controlling person, the SEC must establish either that the controlling person "knew or recklessly disregarded the fact that such controlled person was likely" to violate the Act or "knowingly or recklessly failed to establish, maintain or enforce" policies or procedures designed to prevent insider trading.

3) *Chiarella v. United States, supra,* involved a criminal prosecution of a "blue collar" printer employed by a legal printing firm who purchased

shares on the basis of information obtained from the documents he had access to at his place of employment.

(i) The majority set aside the conviction on the ground that the defendant had not violated any duty to the general public or to the issuer by such transactions.

(ii) The possibility that the conviction might be upheld on the theory that the employee violated a duty to his employer was strongly urged in a dissenting opinion but was not addressed by the majority since it was not raised below.

(iii) The theory that a violation of duties owed to an employer or other private parties might be the basis of a violation of the Securities Acts is known as the "misappropriation theory."

(iv) Subsequent lower courts have generally accepted the misappropriation theory. *United States v. Newman,* 664 F.2d 12 (2d Cir.1981), cert. denied 464 U.S. 863, 104 S.Ct. 193 (1983); *S.E.C. v. Materia,* 745 F.2d 197 (2d Cir.1984), cert. denied 471 U.S. 1053, 105 S.Ct. 2112 (1985) [printing firm employee]; *SEC v. Cherif,* 933 F.2d 403 (7th Cir.1991); *Rothberg v. Rosenbloom,* 771 F.2d 818 (3d Cir.1985), rev'd on other grounds after remand, 808 F.2d 252 (1986); *SEC v. Clark,* 915 F.2d 439 (9th Cir.1990); *SEC v. Willis,* 737 F.Supp. 269 (S.D.N.Y.1990) [psychiatrist learning information from patient].

(v) In *Carpenter v. United States,* 484 U.S. 19, 108 S.Ct. 316 (1987), the Court upheld the conviction of a Wall Street Journal editorial writer who told friends that certain companies would be favorably commented upon in the "Heard on the Street" column. The friends successfully traded on that information; Winans, the editorial writer, was convicted of criminal violations of the insider trading prohibitions under the misappropriation theory. He was also convicted under the federal mail fraud statute.

(A) The Court affirmed the conviction of Winans on the misappropriation theory by an equally divided court, thereby leaving the status of this theory uncertain.

(B) The Court affirmed the mail fraud conviction by a vote of 8–0. With this powerful remedy available to the SEC for violations similar to Winans' the concern for prompt resolution of the validity of the misappropriation theory has diminished.

(vi) In *United States v. Chestman,* 947 F.2d 551 (2d Cir.1991), a majority of the *en banc* court held that the misappropriation theory did not apply to the improper disclosure of inside information by a family member to a broker since neither marriage nor family relationship of themselves created a fiduciary duty not to disclose inside information between the insider and the family member making the disclosure.

(vii) Following *Chiarella,* the SEC adopted rule 14e–3, that makes it unlawful for any person who wrongfully obtains advance information about a cash tender offer to use that information in securities transactions. The validity of this rule was upheld by the Second Circuit *en banc* in *United States v. Chestman,* 947 F.2d 551 (2d Cir. 1991). This rule is a clear application of the "disclose or abstain" approach and would clearly cover the printer in *Chiarella.*

4) As indicated earlier, *SEC v. Texas Gulf Sulphur Co.* suggests that "tippees," i.e. persons who obtain material information before it is publicly released have an obligation not to trade on that information.

(i) In *Dirks v. S.E.C.,* 463 U.S. 646, 103 S.Ct. 3255 (1983), the Court held that a tippee violates rule 10b–5 only if the tipper provided the information in breach of a fiduciary duty. A breach of fiduciary duty may be established for this purpose by showing that the insider disclosed the information for the purpose of obtaining an improper benefit, and the tippee is aware of that purpose.

Example: A corporate officer provides information to the writer of an industry newsletter in order to get a "reputational benefit." The writer violates rule 10b–5 if he trades on the basis of that information. *S.E.C. v. Gaspar,* 1985 Fed. Sec.L.Rep. (CCH) 92,004 (S.D.N.Y.1985).

Example: The CEO of a publicly held corporation provides material inside information to his mistress, who trades on the basis of this information. The SEC charged Paul Thayer, then Deputy Secretary of Defense, with a violation of rule 10b–5 on the basis of this "close personal relationship."

Example: While taking a sunbath on the bleachers at a high school track meet, the coach of the University of Oklahoma football team overhears a corporate officer describe to the officer's spouse a corporate matter that involves material information. The football coach subsequently trades profitably on the basis of this information. If the corporate officer is unaware of the football coach's presence at the time of the conversation, there is no expectation of benefit and therefore no breach of fiduciary duty. The football coach is a pure eavesdropper and his trading does not violate rule 10b–5. *S.E.C. v. Switzer,* 590 F.Supp. 756 (W.D.Okl.1984).

Caveat: An eavesdropper may be liable for trading on inside information with respect to a tender offer or takeover bid under rule 14e–3, discussed below. That is because rule 14e–3 is not based on rule 10b–5 and is more broadly phrased.

(ii) The "tipper," the person providing the inside information to the tippee is also liable for unlawful insider trading by the tippee.

e. In 1984 Congress enacted ITSA which authorizes the SEC to recover treble damages for violations of the insider trading rules described above. ITSFEA, enacted in 1988, increased criminal penalties for willful violations of the securities acts or regulations from $100,000 and five years for individuals to $1,000,000 and 10 years; penalties for defendants other than natural persons were increased from $100,000 to $2,500,000.

1) ITSFEA adds a "bounty" provision permitting awards to informants of amounts not to exceed 10 per cent of the penalties recovered.

2) By the enactment of ITSA and ITSFEA, Congress has reaffirmed the basic policy of enforcing sanctions against insider trading despite theoretical economic arguments that such trading injured no one.

3) In numerous proceedings since the enactment of this legislation, the SEC has settled suits against persons violating the insider trading rules under which the defendants agree to repay not only the profits obtained but also penalties ranging from an amount equal to the profits obtained to an amount equal to triple the profits obtained.

4) The SEC has pursued individuals making relatively small profits as well as the major figures in the insider trading scandals of the 1980s in which penalties in the hundreds of millions of dollars were obtained.

5) The SEC regularly brings criminal proceedings against persons charged with improper insider trading and prison terms have been assessed in a number of cases.

6. RULE 10b–5 AS A PROTECTION AGAINST DECEPTION OF THE CORPORATION IN CONNECTION WITH THE ACQUISITION OR DISPOSITION OF SHARES

Rule 10b–5 is potentially applicable when a corporation issues or acquires its own shares since the phrase "purchase or sale" is broad enough to cover such transactions.

a. If shares are issued or acquired by a corporation as a result of deception or a failure of some persons to disclose material facts to the corporation, the corporation may have a claim under rule 10b–5, and this claim may be asserted derivatively by a minority shareholder. *Drachman v. Harvey*, 453 F.2d 722 (2d Cir.1971).

Example: Stock options granted to officers who knew of a major favorable development may be cancelled if the recipients do not advise the members of the option committee of the development. *SEC v. Texas Gulf Sulphur Co.*, 401 F.2d 833 (2d Cir.1968).

b. A rule 10b–5 violation also occurs if the corporation is fraudulently induced to issue shares for inadequate compensation even though such conduct also constitutes a violation of state-created fiduciary duties.

7. RULE 10b–5 AS A REGULATOR OF CORPORATE PUBLICITY

A corporation may violate rule 10b–5 if it issues a false or misleading press release and investors rely on this release in securities trading. *SEC v. Texas Gulf Sulphur Co.,* 401 F.2d 833 (2d Cir.1968). This is a variation of the "fraud on the market" doctrine. (See part XV B 4.)

a. While the *Birnbaum* rule requires that the plaintiff be a purchaser or seller of shares, there is no similar requirement for defendants: a person may violate rule 10b–5 even though he neither purchases nor sells a security.

b. Scienter is required under *Hochfelder* and *Aaron* (see part XV B 3 a). Pre-*Hochfelder* cases held that an evil intent or wrongful purpose was unnecessary.

Caveat: A misleading statement that was negligently prepared might be as injurious to a "free and open public market" for securities as a statement published with scienter, *SEC v. Texas Gulf Sulphur Co.*, 401 F.2d 833 (2d Cir.1968), but the requirements of *Hochfelder* must be met if a rule 10b–5 violation is to be found.

c. Disclosure of pending merger negotiations has been a particularly troublesome issue. *Greenfield v. Heublein, Inc.,* 742 F.2d 751 (3d Cir.1984) held that disclosure was required only when an "agreement in principle" had been reached and that prior to that time a general denial was not misleading, but *Basic Inc. v. Levinson,* 485 U.S. 224, 108 S.Ct. 978 (1988) rejected this approach and held that the existence of preliminary merger discussions could not be denied if they actually existed and were "material."

1) According to the Supreme Court, the materiality of preliminary negotiations depends on an assessment of the specific facts involved.

2) Extremely preliminary inquiries presumably would not be material.

3) The practical problems in this area may cause issuers to adopt a "no comment" policy with respect to all inquiries about merger negotiations.

d. Individual shareholders who rely on a corporate press release that is issued in violation of rule 10b–5 may recover damages from the corporation. *Mitchell v. Texas Gulf Sulphur Co.*, 446 F.2d 90 (10th Cir.1971).

1) A class action on behalf of all persons who purchased during the period of the misrepresentation may be permitted. *Basic Inc. v. Levinson,* 485 U.S. 224, 108 S.Ct. 978 (1988); *Blackie v. Barrack*, 524 F.2d 891 (9th Cir.1975).

2) Obviously, the potential liability to the corporation as a result of a false press release may be very substantial and the scope of this liability is still developing. See *Green v. Occidental Petroleum Corp.*, 541 F.2d 1335 (9th Cir.1976), Sneed, J. concurring.

3) Justice White, dissenting in *Basic, Inc. v. Levinson,* 485 U.S. 224, 108 S.Ct. 978 (1988), suggests that major problems in this area arise because of the imposition of monetary liability on defendants who do not themselves trade in the security involved.

e. The financial analyst who "touts" a stock without disclosing that he is financially interested in it also violates rule 10b–5. *Zweig v. Hearst Corp.*, 594 F.2d 1261 (9th Cir.1979).

f. Some pre-*Basic* decisions have been reluctant to conclude that press releases issued by corporations have in fact been false or misleading or that a corporation has an affirmative duty to disclose a specific event before it issues a press release, see e. g. *State Teachers Retirement Board v. Fluor Corp.,* 654 F.2d 843 (2d Cir.1981). These courts refer to the business judgment rule but there may also be concern about the scope of potential liability if the opposite result were reached.

C. SECTION 16(b) OF THE SECURITIES EXCHANGE ACT

Section 16(b) of the Securities Exchange Act of 1934 is an *in terrorem* provision designed to prevent specified persons from trading in a corporation's securities on an in-and-out basis on the strength of inside information.

1. PURPOSE OF SECTION 16(b)

Section 16(b) was enacted in 1934 as part of the Securities Exchange Act. There is not extensive legislative history, though it appears that the purposes of the section were (1) to prevent covered persons from unfairly profiting from inside information that may have a temporary market effect, and (2) to prevent in-and-out transactions that might be used to manipulate securities prices.

2. SCOPE OF SECTION 16(b)

The scope of § 16(b) can best be described by contrasting it to rule 10b–5.

a. Section 16(b) is applicable only to corporations registered under § 12 of the Securities Exchange Act—corporations (1) with securities traded on a national securities exchange or (2) with assets of more than $5,000,000 and more than 500 shareholders of record of any class of equity security. Rule 10b–5 is applicable to all corporations, registered and unregistered.

b. Section 16(b) is only applicable to officers, directors and ten per cent shareholders of the issuer. Rule 10b–5 covers geologists, brokers, tippees and others.

Caveat: Attribution rules apply to § 16(b) so that transactions in the name of spouses, relatives or nominees may be attributed to an officer, director, or ten per cent shareholder.

1) In 1991, the SEC adopted a systematic set of rules under the reporting requirements of § 16(a) identifying which officers are subject to § 16(a). Officers covered by § 16 include officers referred to in the corporation's 10K and officers designated by the corporation as having significant policy making roles. Effectively these regulations determine the scope of § 16(b) as well as § 16(a) since persons exempt from the reporting requirements of § 16(a) are, by regulation, also exempt from § 16(b).

2) Before these regulations were promulgated, the case law was in confusion as to whether a literal or a functional approach should be followed, i.e. whether persons identified as officers should be subject to § 16(b) even though they performed no executive functions, and whether persons without the title of an officer but who did perform executive functions should be subject to that section. See e.g. *Winston v. Federal Express Corporation,* 853 F.2d 455 (6th Cir.1988); *C.R.A. Realty Corp. v. Crotty,* 878 F.2d 562 (2d Cir.1989).

c. Section 16(b) is applicable only to offsetting purchases and sales or sales and purchases of an equity security of the issuer within any six-month period. Rule 10b–5 may be violated by a single purchase or a single sale.

Example: If there is a sale on January 1, § 16(b) is applicable if there is an offsetting purchase made at any time from six months before to six months after January 1. However, a purchase made six months plus one day after the sale cannot be matched under § 16(b).

d. The sequence of § 16(b) transactions—that is sale-and-purchase or purchase-and-sale—or the fact that different certificates are involved in the two transactions, does not affect § 16(b) liability.

Example: In the previous example, a sale made on the following May 1 will be matched with the January 1 purchase even though the shares actually sold on May 1 had been owned for five years.

e. The words "purchase" and "sale" in § 16(b) are construed broadly. In the case of unusual transactions, the test is not a dictionary one; rather, an unusual transaction is considered a "purchase" or a "sale" for purposes of § 16(b) if it is of a kind that can possibly lend itself to the speculation encompassed by § 16(b).

Example: Under some circumstances, a gift may be a sale, as may be a redemption, conversion or a simple exchange of shares pursuant to a merger or consolidation.

Example: The acquisition of a warrant to acquire a security may be a purchase of the underlying security.

Example: The purchase of a derivative security (such as a put or call) may be the purchase or sale of the underlying security. In 1991, the SEC adopted a new set of regulations systematically treating derivative securities under § 16(b).

f. Section 16(b) creates an automatic liability; it is unnecessary to show actual use of inside information. In contrast, rule 10b–5 requires proof of scienter.

Example: A sale for entirely justifiable reasons—e. g., unexpected medical expenses—triggers § 16(b) if there has been an offsetting purchase within the previous six months.

g. Recoveries under § 16(b) are always payable to the corporation. In contrast, rule 10b–5 authorizes private damage recovery in many situations by buyers or sellers.

h. "Profits" are computed so as to squeeze out all possible profit.

1) The computation involves matching the highest sale price with the lowest purchase price, the next highest sale price with the next lowest purchase price, and so forth so long as a profit is shown; all loss transactions are ignored.

Example: A director buys 100 shares for $60.00 per share on January 10 (1/10) and sells them for $50.00 per share on January 19 (1/19). On April 5 (4/5) the same director buys 100 shares for $10.00. All purchases and sales take place within a six-month period. The highest sale price of $5,000 (1/19) is matched with the lowest purchase price of $1,000 (4/5) to produce a

§ 16(b) profit of $4,000. As a matter of common sense, most people would feel that these transactions were not profitable. *Gratz v. Claughton,* 187 F.2d 46 (2d Cir.1951).

2) The United States Supreme Court has never passed on this rather draconian measure of recovery.

i. Section 16(a) requires all persons subject to section 16 to file reports with the SEC. The first report must describe the person's initial ownership of the issuer's shares and subsequent reports must be filed each month showing acquisitions and dispositions of such securities. The SEC publishes this information so that it is possible to locate § 16(b) violations from the public record.

1) The 1991 regulations significantly change the reporting requirements under § 16. Exemptions from reporting were eliminated and virtually all transactions in the issuer's securities must be reported.

(i) Deferred reporting of exempt and immaterial transactions is provided for.

(ii) The Securities Enforcement Remedies and Penny Stock Reform Act of 1990 authorizes the SEC to issue administrative orders (after notice and hearing) requiring compliance with § 16(a). Failure to comply may lead to a fine of up to $100,000 for each day a natural person fails to comply with the SEC's order.

(iii) Corporations are required to disclose failures to comply with § 16(a) by its officers, directors, or ten per cent shareholders.

j. Even though all § 16(b) profits are recoverable by the corporation, corporations may be reluctant to enforce § 16(b) against its own officers, directors, and substantial shareholders. § 16(b) expressly recognizes that enforcement by private shareholders may be necessary.

1) There is a significant amount of such litigation.

2) This litigation is often basically champertous. Attorneys regularly review § 16(a) filings to locate possible § 16(b) violations; they then arrange for a person to purchase shares of the issuer in order to qualify the person to act as plaintiff.

3) Suits are brought solely for the award of attorneys' fees; the plaintiffs are nominal and have no interest in the outcome.

4) This litigation is the principal enforcement device of § 16(b).

5) It is unlikely that many violations of § 16(b) escape detection under these circumstances.

k. The SEC has authority to exempt classes of transactions from § 16(b). It has exercised this authority in a number of circumstances. The most important is rule 16b–3, relating to stock option plans, stock purchase plans, and compensation plans of various types that are based on stock prices. This rule is a conditional exemption that contains a significant amount of substantive regulation.

l. Like rule 10b–5, the jurisdiction of § 16(b) suits is exclusively federal.

3. APPLICATION OF SECTION 16(b) IN TAKEOVER SITUATIONS

The foregoing statement of principles gives little picture of the substantial volume and variety of § 16(b) litigation. During the 1970s, the United States Supreme Court struggled with the application of this section to takeover situations where an unsuccessful aggressor acquires over ten per cent of the target's shares and then sells that interest or has it "merged out" within six months thereafter. In the following decisions, inconsistent approaches and vigorous dissents are evident:

a. *Reliance Elec. Co. v. Emerson Elec. Co.*, 404 U.S. 418, 92 S.Ct. 596 (1972), holds that a 13.2 per cent shareholder could dispose of its holding by first selling 3.2 per cent subject to § 16(b) and thereafter dispose of the balance free of § 16(b) since it was then less than a ten per cent shareholder.

b. *Kern County Land Co. v. Occidental Petroleum Corp.*, 411 U.S. 582, 93 S.Ct. 1736 (1973) holds that a complex series of transactions including an "involuntary" merger and a voluntary option to sell securities were not "sales," and therefore not covered by § 16(b).

c. In *Foremost–McKesson, Inc. v. Provident Securities Co.*, 423 U.S. 232, 96 S.Ct. 508 (1976), the Court finally "solved" the application of § 16(b) to the unsuccessful tender offeror by holding that the initial purchase that puts the aggressor over ten per cent was not a § 16(b) purchase.

4. SECTION 16(b) AND TRADING PARTNERSHIPS

In *Blau v. Lehman*, 368 U.S. 403, 82 S.Ct. 451 (1962), a partner in Lehman Brothers was a director of the issuer. Unknown to him, Lehman Brothers engaged in purchases and sales of the issuer's stock (but never became a ten per cent holder). The Court held that the partnership might be considered a director only if the partnership "deputized" the partner to represent the partnership on issuer's board of directors. See *Feder v. Martin Marietta Corp.*, 406 F.2d 260 (2d Cir.1969).

5. SECTION 16(b) AND TRADING IN DIFFERENT CLASSES OF SECURITIES

The securities the purchase and sale of which are matched under § 16(b) must generally be of the same class. There is normally no meaningful basis for computing profits by matching a sale of common with a purchase of preferred.

a. If the preferred is convertible into common and is trading at or close to the conversion price, matching may be permitted since the two securities are trading as economic equivalents.

Caveat: In *Gund v. First Florida Banks,* 726 F.2d 682 (11th Cir.1984), the court matched sales of convertible debentures with purchases of common stock even though the two were not trading as market equivalents. The court computed "profits" by comparing the actual purchase price of the common stock with the highest price the common attained within six months before or after the debentures were sold.

b. The 1991 regulations adopted by the SEC contain carefully drawn, definitive regulations relating to trading in derivative securities (puts and calls) along with the underlying equity securities.

6. SECTION 16(b) IN PERSPECTIVE

It seems clear that people do not knowingly violate § 16(b); the penalties are simply too great. Most violations appear to be a result of ignorance rather than the actual misuse of inside information.

a. Most inadvertent violations probably are a result of the failure to keep track precisely when the six month period ends. Other causes of inadvertent violations include a failure to appreciate how broadly the words "purchase" and "sale" are construed in the case of unusual transactions, uncertainty as to whether a specific person is within § 16(b), the failure to recognize that attribution rules may apply, and uncertainty as whether a resignation followed by an immediate sale may be viewed to be within § 16(b).

b. Despite its shortcomings and erratic imposition of liability, § 16(b) effectively eliminated the evil of in-and-out trading by pools composed in part of officers and directors that existed prior to 1934.

D. SALE OF CONTROL SHARES

When a controlling shareholder sells her interest to third persons, she is selling more than the property represented by her shares. Control of a going business in which other persons—minority shareholders, senior security holders, and unsecured creditors—may have a substantial interest is also being sold. A controlling shareholder has duties towards these interests.

1. CONTROL PREMIUMS

Shares owned by a controlling shareholder command a premium over other shares simply because they represent the power to control the business, to designate the corporate officers, to establish salaries, to establish business policies, and so forth.

a. This premium is usually referred to as the "control premium" and may be expressed as a per share differential or as an additional lump sum payment for the controlling shares. Shares which carry with them control of the corporation are often referred to as "control shares."

b. A "controlling" shareholder usually owns more than 50 per cent of the shares. However, a shareholder with less than 50 per cent of the outstanding shares may be a "controlling" shareholder if the remaining shares are widely held and fragmented.

c. Following the sale of control shares, control of the board of directors may be transferred by the seriatim resignation of directors so that each vacancy is filled by the directors in office, either "new" or "old."

Caveat: If the corporation is registered under section 12 of the Securities Exchange Act of 1934, a change of control in this fashion must be publicly disclosed to the voting shareholders and to the SEC.

2. TESTS FOR SALE OF CONTROL

Many cases attest that generally a controlling shareholder may sell controlling shares for whatever price he or she can obtain.

a. The virtually unanimous position of courts is that there is nothing inherently wrong in receiving a premium for control shares. *Zetlin v. Hanson Holdings, Inc.,* 397 N.E.2d 387 (N.Y.1979); *Tryon v. Smith,* 229 P.2d 251 (Or.1951); *McDaniel v. Painter,* 418 F.2d 545 (10th Cir.1969). However, since the seller and buyer are not the only persons interested in a sale of control shares, courts have imposed duties on the selling shareholder with respect to investigating the honesty of the purchaser.

b. A controlling shareholder who sells his shares to unscrupulous third persons who thereafter "loot" the corporation may be liable for the loss suffered by the corporation.

1) Some cases take the position that the controlling shareholder has a duty to make a reasonable investigation of potential purchasers in every case and to refuse to transfer control to them if the investigation reveals that they may not be honest, responsible persons. *Gerdes v. Reynolds,* 28 N.Y.S.2d 622 (1941); *DeBaun v. First Western Bank and Trust Co.,* 120 Cal.Rptr. 354 (Cal.App.1975).

2) Some cases take the position that the controlling shareholder has a duty to investigate potential purchasers only if the shareholder has reason to believe the purchasers may loot the corporation. *Claggett v. Hutchinson,* 583 F.2d 1259 (4th Cir.1978); *Swinney v. Keebler Co.,* 480 F.2d 573 (4th Cir.1973).

3) The Corporate Governance Project of the American Law Institute, § 5.16(b), sets the test as "when it is apparent from the circumstances that the purchaser is likely to violate" a duty of fair dealing.

Example: Danger signs include, (1) an obviously excessive price for the shares willingly paid, (2) an unusual interest in the liquid and readily salable assets owned by the corporation, (3) insistence by the buyers on an immediate transfer of control, (4) insistence by the buyers that the liquid assets be made available immediately, (5) little interest by the purchasers in the operation of the corporation's business, and (6) the insistence that the purchase be handled with dispatch. *Swinney v. Keebler Co.*, 480 F.2d 573 (4th Cir.1973) holds that on the facts of that case no duty to investigate arose even though with hindsight several of these factors existed.

4) If the duty of reasonable investigation is not met, liability may be imposed on the sellers based on their negligence. Recovery is based on the damage suffered, i. e., the amount looted by the purchasers rather than by the purchase price paid or the amount of the control premium. *DeBaun v. First Western Bank & Trust Co.*, 120 Cal.Rptr. 354 (Cal.App.1975).

5) In effect the sellers become the guarantors of the honesty of purchasers they do not fully investigate.

6) Investment companies that have liquid and readily salable assets are a likely target for looting but many looting cases involve regular business corporations.

Example: Common shares of *X* Investment Company trade in the range of $1.00–$2.00 per share based on the net asset value per share after making due allowance for the claims of creditors and preferred shareholders. An anonymous offer to buy the controlling shares at $3.00 per share is received through an intermediary. If the controlling shareholders accept this offer without investigation, they may be liable if the purchasers wrongfully convert the assets of *X* Investment Company to their own use. Under the circumstances there is no way to justify a price significantly in excess of the net asset value of the shares except to assume that a portion of the value attributable to the interests of the creditors and preferred shareholders will be converted to benefit the new controlling common shareholders.

c. Outside of arguments based on possible looting, courts have not evolved consistent theories about the propriety of a controlling shareholder receiving a control premium.

1) As indicated above, most cases allow the controlling shareholder to retain the control premium.

2) A few cases have compelled the controlling shareholder to share the control premium with minority shareholders on several theories.

(i) Some of these cases contain broad statements to the effect that a director owes a fiduciary duty to the corporation and to the minority shareholders. E. g., *Perlman v. Feldmann*, 219 F.2d 173 (2d Cir.1955). Such statements are little more than make-weight since they do not explain when the premium may be recovered and when it may not.

(ii) Some cases have permitted the recovery of a control premium on a theory of "corporate action" or usurpation of corporate opportunity.

Example: The purchaser first offers to buy the assets of the corporation at an attractive price; the controlling shareholder suggests that the transaction be recast in the form of a purchase of the controlling shares. The favorable sale opportunity may be a corporate opportunity belonging to all the shareholders, rather than to the majority shareholder. The facts of *Perlman v. Feldmann* may be explained on this basis.

Caveat: The Corporate Governance Project of the American Law Institute rejects this argument on the ground that the majority shareholder is free to decline the offer in its entirety and therefore the minority shareholders have no power to require that the transaction be completed as proposed.

(iii) Some cases have viewed the control premium as being for the sale of a corporate office rather than for the sale of stock. Since a sale of office is against public policy, the excess payment may be recovered by the corporation for the benefit of the minority shareholders. This argument proves too much since all sales of control stock at a premium may be analyzed in this fashion.

Example: A contract provides that part of the purchase price for the sale of control shares is payable only upon the immediate transfer of corporate office. A sale of office may be inferred from this contract provision.

(iv) A shareholder owning or controlling less than a majority of the shares may have effective working control of the corporation when other shareholders are numerous and disorganized. Generally such a shareholder is viewed as a controlling shareholder, but if her interest is very small, the sale of that interest at a premium may be viewed as a sale of control alone.

Example: A selling shareholder holds 28.3 per cent of the shares of a publicly held corporation. The contract provides for a control premium and the seriatim resignation of directors to permit the immediate transfer of control. This agreement is not of itself against public policy. *Essex Universal Corp. v. Yates*, 305 F.2d 572 (2d Cir.1962).

Example: The selling shareholder owns three per cent of the outstanding shares. The contract provides for a control premium and the seriatim resignation of directors to permit the immediate transfer of control; the price greatly exceeds the market value of the shares being sold. An improper sale of office may be inferred from these circumstances. *Petition of Caplan*, 246 N.Y.S.2d 913 (1964).

(v) Some cases have imposed liability for a control premium on a theory of nondisclosure or misrepresentation.

Example: A controlling shareholder contracts to sell more shares than she owns, planning to purchase the additional shares from other shareholders; if she purchases the additional shares without disclosing the resale contract, she is liable under rule 10b–5 or state law.

Example: A controlling shareholder contracts to sell his shares for $1,500 per share. The purchaser offers to buy minority shares at the same time at $300 per share. The controlling shareholder permits the $300 offer to be made without disclosing that he is receiving five times as much per share. One court has held that this nondisclosure makes the transaction improper and the minority shareholders may share in the control premium. *Brown v. Halbert*, 76 Cal.Rptr. 781 (Cal.App.1969).

(vi) Some cases have imposed liability for the control premium on the basis of the extreme unfairness of the transaction.

Example: The majority shareholders of a savings and loan association create a holding company and exchange their shares for holding company shares. Minority shareholders in the association, however, are not permitted to exchange their shares for holding company shares. The holding company then makes a public offering of its own shares and an active market is created for its shares. The minority shareholders of the association are excluded from this market since they continue to own S & L shares rather than holding company shares. This conduct violates the majority's fiduciary responsibility to treat the minority fairly. *Jones v. H. F. Ahmanson & Co.*, 460 P.2d 464 (Cal.1969).

Example: In the *Ahmanson* case, the plaintiffs were permitted to measure damages based either on the appraised value of the "exchange shares" when the holding company was created or the value such shares had on the date litigation is commenced. This option gives the plaintiffs a risk-free election with the benefit of hindsight.

(vii) A noncontrolling shareholder who is also a director has been held to be not subject to the same duties as a controlling shareholder. *Treadway Companies, Inc. v. Care Corp.*, 638 F.2d 357 (2d Cir.1980).

d. Where a control premium is recoverable, courts have permitted either the corporation or the minority shareholders to recover, depending on the theory adopted.

1) If the theory of recovery is looting, corporate opportunity, corporate action, or the sale of corporate office, logically only the corporation should recover and a suit by a shareholder should be considered exclusively derivative in nature.

2) If the theory is misrepresentation or violation of rule 10b–5, the minority shareholders should recover in their own right.

3) A corporate recovery indirectly enriches the purchaser of control who paid the premium. Because of this, *Perlman v. Feldmann* allowed the minority shareholders to recover directly even though the theory adopted in that case apparently was corporate opportunity which would dictate solely a corporate recovery. (See generally part XVIII, H.)

3. EVALUATION OF SALE OF CONTROL TRANSACTIONS

Law review commentators in the 1950s and 1960s suggested that the best rule is that all control premiums should be shared with all shareholders in every sale of control case.

a. These commentators essentially argue that since shares of stock are fungible, the control premium represents the pure power to control which should be a corporate asset available to all shareholders.

b. More recent commentators have argued that transactions based on a control premium are desirable since they permit transactions to occur that benefit not only the purchaser of control but also shareholders in the corporation. These arguments are based on economic analysis.

c. Limited empirical studies involving the sale of control in publicly held corporations indicate that shareholders have not been injured by sale of control transactions.

4. GRANT OF VOTING POWER TO NON-VOTING SHARES

A form of control premium is also involved in cases where a class of voting shares agrees to share the voting power with a larger class of nonvoting common in exchange for a larger "slice of the equity." *Honigman v. Green Giant Co.*, 309 F.2d 667 (8th Cir.1962). Such transactions have been approved where the additional equity is not excessive, or to put it a different way, where the transaction seems fair.

E. REVIEW QUESTIONS

XV–1. What is meant by "insider trading?"

XV–2. Are the rules relating to insider trading based on state or federal law?

XV–3. Should not every transaction by an insider that is based on personal use of non-public information subject to attack on the theory that it involves misuse of corporate assets?

Yes ______ No ______ Uncertain ______

XV–4. Rule 10b–5 is applicable only to publicly held corporations that are subject to registration under section 12 of the Securities Exchange Act of 1934?

True _______ False _______

XV–5. A Colorado corporation has three shareholders, all of whom reside in Denver. Its business is located in Denver and all of its sales are made to Denver residents. The majority shareholder defrauds minority shareholders by inducing them to sell shares on the basis of false representations. This transaction involves only Colorado law and not rule 10b–5.

True _______ False _______

XV–6. What kinds of transactions are subject to rule 10b–5?

XV–7. What limiting factors have been applied to rule 10b–5?

XV–8. How does section 16(b) of the Securities Exchange Act differ from rule 10b–5?

XV–9. How are profits to be determined in a section 16(b) case?

XV–10. A person who owns a controlling interest in the shares of a corporation may sell those shares for any price that she can get.

True _______ False _______

XV–11. Why not adopt a rule that control is a corporate asset and that the profit from its sale must be divided among all shareholders?

XV–12. Dynamic, Inc. is a successful computer component manufacturer whose excellent engineering staff is developing a seemingly matchless production technique. Partially because of its engineering expertise, Dynamic, Inc.'s shares, which are registered under section 12(g) of the Securities Exchange Act of 1934 and actively traded over-the-counter, sell at about $180 per share. Ian Sider, director and vice president of Dynamic, Inc., learns at a board of directors' meeting that the cream of the engineering staff of Dynamic, Inc. is threatening to leave and establish their own computer operation. Rather than wait to see if the threat materializes, Sider calls his broker and directs the sale of his 10,000 shares of Dynamic, Inc. The shares are sold for $170 per share.

One week later the disgruntled engineering faction publicly announces its intention to leave. The shares of Dynamic, Inc. drop to $100 per share. Ben Taken, a new shareholder of Dynamic, Inc., who purchased one day prior to the public announcement for $175 per share, consults you as to possible recourse against Sider. What is your advice? [This question and answer is drawn from Ballantine, Problems in Law 239 (5th Ed. 1975).]

XV–13. Maggie M. is a paralegal with the law firm of Jones and Smith, a firm with a substantial corporate practice. She is asked to work on certain documents from which she infers that Apex Corporation is to announce the successful settlement of a major lawsuit. Maggie M. tells her boyfriend about what she has learned and together they purchase calls on Apex Corporation stock. Has Maggie M. violated Federal law? Has her boyfriend?

XV–14. In the situation described in question XV–14, would it make any difference if the information Maggie M. obtained related to a takeover bid by a client of Jones and Smith and Maggie M. bought stock in the target corporation?

XV–15. Peter Jones is a vice president of Apex Corporation. His college roommate, John Smith, is a stock broker and old personal friend. Peter Jones tells Smith of the successful settlement of the law suit; Jones then purchases calls on Apex Corporation Stock. Has either Peter Jones or John Smith violated Federal law?

XV–16. X corporation was a manufacturer of steel. Because of wartime conditions steel was in short supply and a grey market existed with respect to it although there were government controls on prices. D, the controlling shareholder of X, sold his stock to Y corporation at a premium over the price which non-control shares could command. Y was an end-user of steel and used its control of X to allocate steel to itself at the government prices. P, a minority shareholder of X, brings a derivative action on behalf of the corporation against D for breach of D's fiduciary duty. Is D liable to the corporation?

XVI

INDEMNIFICATION AND LIABILITY INSURANCE

"Indemnification" simply means the corporation reimburses a defendant who is a present or former corporate officer or director for expenses incurred in defending against an asserted claim or prosecution. If indemnification is allowed at all, it normally covers legal fees and other expenses; in some instances it may also cover amounts paid in settlement, amounts needed to satisfy a judgment entered against defendant officers or directors, or even the amount of a criminal fine. Liability insurance for directors and officers (usually called "D & O insurance") is also commercially available to a limited extent.

Analysis

A. INDEMNIFICATION AND PUBLIC POLICY

There are basic policy questions posed by indemnification.

1. POLICIES FAVORING INDEMNIFICATION

Policy justifications for indemnification of officers and directors include:

a. It encourages responsible persons to accept the position of director; and

b. It encourages innocent directors to resist unjust charges;

c. It discourages groundless shareholder litigation.

Caveat: Given litigation costs today, few responsible persons would be willing to serve as directors in the absence of indemnification.

2. POLICY LIMITATIONS ON INDEMNIFICATION

There can be little objection to indemnification of expenses if a director is totally absolved of liability or misconduct. *In re E. C. Warner Co.,* 45 N.W.2d 388 (Minn. 1950). At the other extreme, indemnification against liabilities imposed on some kinds of wrongful acts clearly violates public policy. The policy issue raised is to sort out the situations where indemnification is proper and should be encouraged and situations where it is against public policy and should be prohibited.

Example: Liability is imposed under section 16(b) of the Securities Exchange Act of 1934. Indemnification is not permitted since it would create circularity, and vitiate the public policy underlying that section.

Example: The defendant is found guilty of wrongful misconduct and is held liable to a third person in damages for such misconduct. In view of the finding that the defendant was guilty of wrongful misconduct, neither indemnification of expenses nor against the judgments themselves should be permissible.

B. SCOPE OF INDEMNIFICATION UNDER MODERN STATE STATUTES

State statutes attempt to work out a compromise of these various competing considerations. Statutes on indemnification vary from skeletal authorization to elaborate procedural and substantive requirements, largely based on either the Delaware GCL or on one of the more recent versions of the indemnification provisions of the Model Business Corporation Act: section 5 of the 1969 Model Act, section 5 as amended in 1979, or MBCA (1984) §§ 8.50 thru 8.58.

Caveat: The MBCA (1984) provisions approved in 1984 are based directly on the 1979 amendments to section 5 of the MBCA, but are reorganized and broken down into nine different sections to simplify the structure. Experience with the 1969 Model Act indicated that a number of problems were not adequately addressed by that statute. The Delaware statute is similar to the 1969 Model Act. In other states, indemnification provisions vary widely; some are modeled after the 1960 version of the Model Act, or even earlier statutes. Some are considerably more permissive than the Model Act.

1. INDEMNIFICATION WHEN THE DEFENDANT HAS BEEN SUCCESSFUL IN THE PROCEEDING

Under most modern statutes a defendant is entitled to indemnification *as a matter of statutory right* if "he is wholly successful, on the merits or otherwise." MBCA (1984) § 8.52.

Example: A defendant prevails because of the statute of limitations or because of pleading defects. He is entitled to indemnification as a matter of right.

Example: In a criminal securities case, a defendant pleads *nolo contendere* on one count in a plea bargain that results in the dismissal of other counts. *Merritt–Chapman & Scott Corp. v. Wolfson,* 321 A.2d 138 (Del.Super. 1974) holds that the defendant is entitled to indemnification for expenses with respect to the dismissed counts. It is doubtful if this was the intention of the statutory draftsmen, and the Model Business Corporation Act (1984) reverses this result by requiring the defendant to be "wholly" successful on the merits or otherwise. MBCA (1984) § 8.52.

a. The language "on the merits *or otherwise*" may result in some directors being entitled to indemnification even though they were successful because of a procedural defense that does not go to the merits of the claim against the director. In some of these instances, further investigation might show that the director had engaged in conduct that would have prevented indemnification if the procedural defense had not been available.

   1) The award of indemnification in this situation is justified on the ground that it is unreasonable to require the successful director to litigate the merits of his or her claim in order to establish a right to indemnification.

   2) It also is assumed that in most cases in which a nonsubstantive defense is established, e. g. the statute of limitations, that the director or officer also has a substantive defense that is never reached.

b. The California statute does not include the phrase "or otherwise," thereby limiting mandatory indemnification to cases where the director or officer establishes his innocence on the merits.

c. If a director is entitled to mandatory indemnification but the corporation refuses to make the required payment, the director may petition a court for an order compelling the payment of indemnification. MBCA (1984) § 8.54(1). If such an order is entered, the director is entitled also to recover expenses incurred in obtaining the order.

2. PERMISSIVE INDEMNIFICATION

Under modern statutes, indemnification is permitted *as a matter of discretion but not as a matter of right* in a variety of situations upon certain findings being made as to the conduct of the person. Directors cannot compel corporations to grant indemnification for conduct falling within the category of permissive indemnification. *Tomash v. Midwest Technical Development Corp.,* 160 N.W.2d 273 (Minn.1968). Permissive indemnification is authorized in the following situations:

a. Liabilities that may be indemnified against include "the obligation to pay a judgment, settlement, penalty, fine (including an excise tax assessed with respect to an employee benefit plan), or reasonable expenses incurred with respect to a proceeding." MBCA (1984) § 8.50(4).

b. The test for whether indemnification is permitted depends on whether or not the conduct was in the person's "official capacity." See MBCA (1984) § 8.50(5).

   1) For actions in the official capacity of a person, indemnification is permitted only if the person acted in good faith and can establish that she reasonably believed that her conduct was *in* the corporation's best interest. MBCA (1984) § 8.51(a)(2)(i).

   2) For all other actions, indemnification is permitted only if the person acted in good faith and can establish that she reasonably believed that her conduct "was *at least not opposed to*" the corporation's best interest. MBCA (1984) § 8.51(a)(2)(ii).

   3) In the case of a director, "official capacity" means only "the office of director in a corporation." In the case of an individual other than a director, "official capacity" means only the office in the corporation or the employment or agency relationship undertaken by that individual for or on behalf of the corporation. All relationships other than the foregoing do not involve actions in "official capacity."

   Example: A director serves at the request of the corporation as an officer of a trade association. That service is not in the official capacity of the director.

c. In the case of a criminal proceeding, the person, in addition to the tests of subpart b, must have had no reasonable cause to believe her conduct was unlawful. MBCA (1984) § 8.51(a)(3).

d. Even though an individual arguably meets these standards, indemnification is not permitted in two situations:

1) In a suit or proceeding by or in the name of the corporation in which the person is adjudged liable to the corporation; and

2) In a proceeding charging the receipt of an improper personal benefit in which the person is adjudged liable for receiving that personal benefit.

Example: A director is named as a defendant in a derivative suit brought in the name of the corporation claiming that the director improperly diverted a corporate opportunity to her own personal advantage. The director thereafter settles the case, agreeing to return the opportunity to the corporation but not admitting that she violated her duty to the corporation. The suit involves an action by the director in her "official capacity;" she is entitled to indemnification of her expenses in connection with the suit if she can establish that she acted in good faith and that her conduct was in the corporation's best interest. In no event is she entitled to indemnification for the amount paid over to the corporation in the settlement of the claim.

Example: The director in the foregoing example does not settle but litigates the matter to a conclusion. If she is "adjudged" liable to the corporation, she is not eligible for indemnification of her expenses. If she is successful "on the merits or otherwise" she is entitled as a matter of right to indemnification.

Example: A director is charged with violation of rule 10b–5 in connection with sales of shares on the open market allegedly on the basis of inside information. Sales of stock are not in the director's official capacity and the standard for eligibility for indemnification is that the director acted in good faith and that she reasonably believed that her conduct "was at least not opposed to" the corporation's best interests. If the director settles the case she is eligible to have both her expenses and the amount of the settlement indemnified by the corporation if it is determined that her conduct met this standard.

Example: In the previous example, if a court concludes that the sales violated rule 10b–5, the director has received an improper personal benefit and is not eligible for indemnification despite her good faith and reasonable belief that her conduct was not opposed to the corporation's best interests. The director, however, may request court approval for indemnification under MBCA (1984) § 8.54.

Example: The CEO of the corporation concludes that it is in the best interest of the corporation to pay a bribe in order to obtain a defense contract. After the contract is obtained, an investigation occurs and the CEO is prosecuted and indicted. Since he knew that his conduct was unlawful, the CEO is not entitled to indemnification without regard to his good faith and the belief that the bribe was in the best interests of the corporation.

Example: A director is requested to serve as a trustee of an employee benefit plan. As a trustee, she votes in favor of a ruling that deprives certain striking employees of benefits under the plan. In this regard, she reasonably believes that her decision is in the interests of the participants and beneficiaries of the plan. If she is thereafter sued individually by employees who were denied benefits as a result of the ruling, both the director's expenses and any judgment entered against her may be indemnified by the corporation. See MBCA (1984) § 8.51(b).

Caveat: MBCA (1984) § 8.51(c) provides that the termination of a proceeding by judgment, order, settlement, plea of nolo contendere, or similar terminating event is not "of itself" determinative that the director did not meet the foregoing standards of conduct.

Caveat: In all cases where a person is not eligible for indemnification under the specific MBCA (1984) provisions, the person may petition a court for a determination that the person "is fairly and reasonably entitled to indemnification in view of all the relevant circumstances" even though the specific requirements of the indemnification statute are not met. MBCA (1984) § 8.54.

3) Some states permit indemnification in suits in which the person is adjudged liable to the corporation, despite the obvious circularity that is involved.

e. Many corporations, by bylaw provision, grant a contractual right of indemnification in all cases in which indemnification is permissive. Such a provision is valid. MBCA (1984) § 8.58(a), Official Comment. Some state statutes make this the default rule—i.e. that all corporations must indemnify in all permissive cases unless the articles of incorporation provide the contrary.

f. Corporations may generally "opt out" of indemnification statutes by restricting or eliminating indemnification in the articles of incorporation or the bylaws. A corporation may do this in order to conserve limited resources or to limit the rights of former directors or officers to demand indemnification.

3. "AUTHORIZATION" AND "DETERMINATION" OF INDEMNIFICATION

MBCA (1984) § 8.55 distinguishes between a "determination" of indemnification and an "authorization" of indemnification. A "determination" relates to the eligibility of the officer or director for indemnification under the tests set forth above while an "authorization" is a corporate judgment that an appropriate use of corporate resources is to pay the director or officer the amount so "determined."

a. A "determination" may be made:

1) By the board of directors by majority vote of a quorum consisting exclusively of directors who are not parties to the proceeding. MBCA (1984) § 8.55(b)(1).

2) If a quorum cannot be obtained, by a majority vote of a committee designated by the board of directors that consists of two or more members who are not parties to the proceeding. Directors who are parties to the proceeding may participate in this selection process. MBCA (1984) § 8.55(b)(2).

3) By the shareholders, but shares owned by or voted under the control of directors who are parties to the proceeding may not vote on the determination. MBCA (1984) § 8.55(b)(4).

4) By special legal counsel. According to the Official Comment, such counsel "should normally be counsel having no prior professional relationship with those seeking indemnification, should be retained for the specific occasion, and should not be either inside counsel or regular outside counsel." Such counsel may be selected by:

(i) The board of directors or a committee of the board meeting the requirements described in subparts 1) or 2) above.

(ii) If there are not sufficient disinterested directors to select the special legal counsel, then the full board of directors, by a majority vote of all directors, including those who are parties to the proceeding may select the special counsel. MBCA (1984) § 8.55(b)(3). This is justified by a principle of necessity.

Caveat: Despite comments in the literature that the use of special legal counsel is widespread for this purpose, the more common practice is to have determinations made by a committee of the board of directors.

b. "Authorization" of indemnification cannot be made by special legal counsel, but may be made by the directors or shareholders who may "determine" eligibility for indemnification under part a. If special legal counsel is employed, indemnification may be authorized by the persons or groups entitled to select the counsel. MBCA (1984) § 8.55(c).

c. Issues relating to the reasonableness of expenses must also be resolved by the persons or groups "authorizing" indemnification and not by special legal counsel "determining" eligibility for indemnification.

4. COURT-APPROVED INDEMNIFICATION

MBCA (1984) § 8.54(2) recognizes that a person ineligible for indemnification under the technical requirements of the statute may in some circumstances be fairly entitled to indemnification, and provides that a person otherwise not eligible for indemnification may petition a court (which may be either the court in which the proceeding occurred or another court) for a determination that the person is "fairly and reasonably" entitled to indemnification.

a. Court-approved indemnification is limited to the indemnification of reasonable expenses.

Example: A director is named as a defendant in a suit charging violation of the insider trading rules because of sales by the defendant of more than 100,000 shares of stock in a two-month period. After a trial, the court concludes that with respect to the sales of 99,800 shares, the director did not violate the insider trading rules since he did not have material inside information when the sales were made; with respect to the sale of 200 shares, however, the court concludes that a violation of rule 10b–5 occurred. The latter holding renders the defendant director ineligible for indemnification under the statute; a court, however, might conclude that the director is fairly and equitably entitled to indemnification of his expenses since the violation of rule 10b–5 was minor in comparison to the essential vindication of the defendant on the bulk of the litigation.

b. A corporation may avoid the obligation imposed by court-ordered indemnification by an appropriate provision in the articles of incorporation.

5. ADVANCES FOR EXPENSES

MBCA (1984) § 8.53 authorizes a corporation to pay or reimburse the expenses of a proceeding as they are incurred without waiting for a final determination that the person is eligible for indemnification. This provision recognizes that as a practical matter, adequate legal representation and adequate preparation of a defense often requires substantial payments of expenses before a final determination. If advances were not permitted less affluent officers and directors might be unable to finance their own defense. On the other hand, advances for expenses may lead to payments to defendants who are ultimately determined to be ineligible for indemnification.

a. In the absence of specific statutory authorization to make such advances, a court may not order them. *Gross v. Texas Plastics, Inc.,* 344 F.Supp. 564 (D.N.J.1972), aff'd mem. 523 F.2d 1050 (3d Cir.1975).

b. A director seeking advance indemnification must furnish the corporation a written affirmation of the director's good faith belief that he or she meets the standard of conduct that permits indemnification, MBCA (1984) § 8.53(a)(1), and a written undertaking to repay the advance if it is ultimately determined that the director did not meet the applicable standard of conduct. MBCA (1984) § 8.53(a)(2).

Caveat: The written undertaking must be unlimited and general, but need not be secured and may be accepted without regard to the financial ability of the defendant to make repayment. MBCA (1984) § 8.53(b). The theory is that discrimination in the availability of advances for expenses should not be based on the outside wealth of defendants or on their ability to file acceptable security.

c. Before making a specific advance, a determination must be made that on the basis of the facts then known to those making the determination, indemnification is not precluded. MBCA (1984) § 8.53(a)(3). This determination is to be made by the persons entitled to make indemnification determinations under MBCA (1984) § 8.55, discussed above.

Caveat: Advances for expenses are also subject to the authorization of indemnification by appropriate corporate officers. MBCA (1984) § 8.53(c).

d. Some state statutes relax significantly the determinations that must be made before advances for expenses may be authorized that appear in the MBCA (1984). In some states, such advances have become almost automatic.

6. INDEMNIFICATION OF OFFICERS, EMPLOYEES, AND AGENTS

The foregoing provisions relate specifically to directors. Different principles may be applicable to officers, employees and agents of a corporation, who may have broader rights of indemnification based on contract, specific corporate action, or general principles of agency. MBCA (1984) § 8.56.

Caveat: Indemnification under these broader principles are subject only to limitations of public policy.

Example: An officer and an employee of a corporation are indicted personally for antitrust violations; they plead nolo contendere at the request of the corporation. The corporation may properly indemnify them for the fines imposed on them. *Koster v. Warren,* 297 F.2d 418 (9th Cir.1961). The court stated in this case that an agreement in advance to indemnify all employees convicted of antitrust violations might be against public policy.

a. While the indemnification of an officer, agent or employee who is not a director is not subject to the limiting principles applicable to indemnification of directors, a corporation has the same *discretionary* right to indemnify an officer, employee or agent of the corporation as it has to indemnify directors. MBCA (1984) § 8.56(2).

b. An *officer* of the corporation (but *not* employees or agents generally) has the same right to *mandatory* indemnification as a director and also may apply for court-ordered indemnification to the same extent as a director. MBCA (1984) § 8.56(1). The purpose of this provision is to authorize the assistance of officers but not to extend a duty to indemnify lower level personnel within the corporation unless the corporation is willing to make the payments.

c. A *director* who is also an officer, agent or employee of the corporation has only the indemnification rights of directors under this chapter. The purpose of this limitation is to ensure that all directors are treated alike with respect to indemnification.

Caveat: Many state statutes do not contain this restriction. In these states presumably an officer/director has the broader indemnification rights of an officer.

7. MODIFICATION OF STATUTORY INDEMNIFICATION POLICIES

Statutes based on the Delaware statute or on the 1969 Model Act provide that the indemnification statute is not exclusive. That means that corporations may include broader indemnification provisions in their articles of incorporation or bylaws if they wish to do so.

a. In states with non-exclusive statutes, the only limitation on indemnification rights granted by contract or bylaw provision is public policy.

b. MBCA (1984) § 8.58(a), in contrast, makes the statute exclusive but provides that a contractual or voluntary provision relating to indemnification that goes beyond the statute "is valid only if and to the extent the provision is consistent with this subchapter."

1) The Official Comment to MBCA (1984) § 8.58 states that the quoted language "is believed to be a more accurate description of the limited validity of nonstatutory indemnification provisions."

2) As a practical matter there may be little difference between the Model Act and non-exclusive statutes, since public policy probably does not permit indemnification significantly broader than that permitted by the Model Act.

Example: A bylaw provision provides that indemnification decisions shall be made by an outside committee consisting of law professors with no interest in the proceeding. That provision is valid under both types of statutes.

Example: A corporation agrees to grant indemnification on a mandatory basis whenever it may do so on a voluntary basis. The provision is valid under both types of statutes.

8. INDEMNIFICATION OF WITNESSES

MBCA (1984) §§ 8.50–8.58 applies only when a director is made a "party" to a proceeding, i.e. whether the director "was, is, or is threatened to be made a named defendant or respondent in a proceeding." MBCA (1984) § 8.50(6).

a. MBCA (1984) § 8.58(b) states that it does not limit the power of a corporation to pay or reimburse the expenses of a director in connection with an appearance as a witness in a proceeding, assuming that the director is not a "party."

b. Most statutes are silent on whether indemnification of expenses of directors who are not parties to litigation is permitted.

c. The power to indemnify when the statute is silent may be implicit in the general powers of a corporation.

9. NOTIFICATION OF INDEMNIFICATION

MBCA (1984) § 16.21(a) requires the corporation to notify shareholders of all indemnifications or advances of expenses to defendants in connection with suits brought by or in the name of the corporation.

a. The notification must be in writing and must be given with or before the next annual notice of the meeting.

b. The statutes of many states do not require notice to be given shareholders in these situations.

10. INDEMNIFICATION IN FEDERAL PROCEEDINGS

Indemnification of liabilities incurred under federal statutes may raise additional questions of public policy.

a. The Securities and Exchange Commission has long taken the position that it is against public policy for a corporation to indemnify officers or directors against liabilities imposed by the Securities Act of 1933. Rule 460, 17 C.F.R. § 230.460 (1985), provides that acceleration of a registration statement may be denied unless a waiver of rights to indemnification is filed assuring that a claim to indemnification against 1933 Act liabilities will be submitted to a court for final determination.

b. Some cases indicate that indemnification is also more narrowly permitted against liabilities imposed by federal securities acts than under common law or state statutory provisions, *Globus v. Law Research Serv. Inc.,* 418 F.2d 1276 (2d Cir.1969), *cert. denied* 397 U.S. 913, 90 S.Ct. 913 (1970), including indemnification against negligent conduct by officers or directors of investment companies. *S.E.C. v. Continental Growth Fund, Inc.,* 1964 Fed.Sec.L.Rep. (CCH) 91,437 (S.D.N.Y. Oct. 7, 1964). See also *Gould v. American–Hawaiian Steamship Co.,* 387 F.Supp. 163 (D.Del.1974), vacated on other grounds 535 F.2d 761 (3d Cir.1976).

C. D & O LIABILITY INSURANCE

"D & O" [directors' and officers'] liability insurance is a relatively new phenomenon. It provides useful but limited protection against costs and liabilities for negligence, for misconduct not involving dishonesty or knowing bad faith, and for false or misleading statements in disclosure documents. Most persons today would decline to serve as a director of a publicly held corporation unless protected by a D & O policy.

1. STRUCTURE OF D & O POLICIES

D & O policies are complementary to indemnification. Most publicly held corporations provide both indemnification and insurance for its directors.

a. D & O insurance is "claims made" insurance. It insures only for claims that are presented to the insurer during the period of insurance (and a short period thereafter if the insurance is not renewed). When the period of insurance ends, if no claim has been made the insurer has no responsibility for events occurring during the period.

b. D & O insurance consists of two different parts.

1) The "Corporate Reimbursement" portion of the policy insures the corporation against payments it is obligated or permitted to make to officers or directors under its indemnification obligations. This portion of

the policy does not insure the corporation against direct claims made by shareholders or others.

Example: The corporation issues a press release that contains false statements and violates rule 10b–5. It is sued by shareholders who sold shares before the press release was corrected. Claims made in those suits against the corporation are not covered by the insurance policy.

Example: An officer is also named as a defendant in the shareholder suits described in the previous example. The officer retains a lawyer and incurs other expenses in connection with her defense. These expenses are indemnifiable and the corporation actually indemnifies the officer. The indemnification payments are covered by the insurance policy.

2) The "Directors and Officers" portion of the policy insures directors and officers against obligations that are not indemnifiable by the corporation but which are not within the insurance exclusions of the policy.

Example: A director is named as a defendant in a derivative suit filed on behalf of the corporation by a minority shareholder. The suit is settled by the director agreeing to pay a small sum to the corporation. The corporation is not permitted to indemnify the director for this payment in settlement in most states because of circularity. The amount paid in settlement, however, is covered by the D & O insurance policy.

2. INSURABLE RISKS

Companies writing D & O liability insurance write policies that cover only insurable risks in the traditional sense. This limitation largely eliminates the public policy issues that are raised by broad indemnification clauses.

3. POLICY EXCLUSIONS

The Directors and Officers portion of D & O policies contain important exclusions from coverage.

a. There is an exclusion for failing to disclose contingent liabilities on the application for insurance. A misrepresentation or omission by the corporation may invalidate the D & O coverage for all officers and directors. *Bird v. Penn Central Co.*, 341 F.Supp. 291 (E.D.Pa.1972).

b. There is an exclusion for transactions for personal profit or advantage, for illegal remuneration, for dishonesty, or wrongful misconduct, for acts in bad faith with knowledge thereof, for ERISA violations, for section 16(b) liabilities, or for failure to maintain other types of insurance.

4. POLICY COVERAGE AND PREMIUMS

D & O policies are purchased by the corporation for all its officers and directors. The cost of the premium is shared: a typical pattern is for the corporation to pay 90 per cent and the covered persons 10 per cent. This division in cost reflects the fact that D & O insurance largely protects the corporation against liabilities that fall within the corporation's obligation to indemnify officers and directors under statute or bylaw provisions.

5. STATE STATUTES

Many state statutes specifically authorize corporations to purchase D & O insurance. See MBCA (1984) § 8.57. Where no statutory authorization exists, the power to purchase such insurance is usually thought to be implicit in the general corporate power to provide executive compensation. Corporate bylaws often specifically authorize the purchase of such insurance.

6. CAPTIVE INSURANCE AND SELF-INSURANCE

A few states permit corporations to create captive insurance subsidiaries or to self-insure through trusts or other devices. These are not true insurance arrangements because the critical element of insurance: spreading risk over many insureds, is missing. They are permitted in some states because D & O insurance was effectively unavailable during part of the 1980s in some industries.

D. REVIEW QUESTIONS

XVI–1. What does "indemnification" mean?

XVI–2. Should not all indemnification be considered to be against public policy?

XVI–3. Is it against public policy to indemnify a defendant who has been found guilty of criminal or improper conduct?

XVI–4. What is "D & O insurance?"

XVI–5. Should not D & O insurance be prohibited as being against fundamental public policy?

Yes _______ No _______

XVII

BOOKS AND RECORDS

Analysis

6. What Is a "Proper Purpose?"
7. Inspection Rights of Beneficial Owners
H. Review Questions

A. MANDATORY RECORD KEEPING REQUIREMENTS

All state statutes require each corporation to maintain a record of its shareholders to determine entitlement to vote, to dividends, and so forth. In addition, many statutes require each corporation to keep certain minimum records, such as minutes of meetings, books and records of account, and so forth, set forth in the statute. The Model Business Corporation Act (1984), unlike most state statutes, contains detailed rules with respect to the maintenance of minimum records.

1. RECORD OF SHAREHOLDERS

The record of shareholders is often referred to as the "list of shareholders" or "shareholders' list." With the development of computerization, the record of shareholders may not be kept in traditional written form. MBCA (1984) § 16.01(c) requires only that a corporation maintain "a record of its shareholders, in a form that permits preparation of a list of the names and addresses of all shareholders, in alphabetical order by class of shares showing the number and class of shares held by each."

a. When inspection of the record of shareholders is demanded, MBCA (1984) § 16.03(d) permits the corporation to provide a list of shareholders compiled no earlier than the date of the demand.

b. Many states require a voting list to be compiled immediately before the meeting (see part VII C 3). This is a different document than the internal record of shareholders; the voting list is a physical list that is automatically open to inspection for a limited period of time during or immediately before a meeting.

c. The record of shareholders consists of the names of record owners only; it does not attempt to list beneficial owners. Where shares are held in the names of nominees, only the name of the nominee appears.

1) Many institutional investors publish their investment portfolios. In the case of publicly held companies, this information may provide revealing and useful information as to beneficial owners of shares of portfolio companies.

2) Book entry ownership of shares of publicly held companies reduces significantly the value of the record of shareholders maintained by the corporation since the record owner of such shares is a nominee of the clearing corporation. (See part XI D.)

(i) SEC regulations require beneficial owners of shares held in book entry form to indicate whether they object to disclosure of their identities to issuers; a list of shareholders who do not object is called a NOBO list.

(ii) Courts may view a NOBO list [or a COBO list, "consenting beneficial owners"] as the equivalent of a record of shareholders for disclosure purposes. See *Sadler v. NCR Corporation,* 928 F.2d 48 (2d Cir.1991).

d. There has been a substantial volume of litigation over whether records of shareholders in publicly held corporations must be produced in connection with proxy fights and takeover attempts. Much of this litigation predates the widespread use of nominees and book entry ownership.

1) A list of names and addresses of numerous well-to-do individuals who are shareholders of record is itself valuable, and may be salable to mail solicitation firms.

2) Litigation dealing with attempts to obtain the record of shareholders often involves the "proper purpose" test. (See part XVII G.)

3) Courts probably tend to be more lenient in granting access to the record of shareholders than to other books and records but the right to obtain a record of shareholders is not unlimited.

e. Federal proxy regulations give alternative access to the record of shareholders. Rule 14a–7 requires a corporation either to supply a copy of the record of shareholders or to mail solicitations to shareholders on behalf of a shareholder upon payment of the postage by that shareholder. Corporations usually elect the latter alternative.

2. MANDATORY AND DISCRETIONARY RECORDS

MBCA (1984) § 16.01(a) requires every corporation to "keep" certain basic records, such as minutes of meetings and records of actions taken by directors and shareholders. MBCA (1984) § 16.01(b) and (c) require every corporation to "maintain" "appropriate accounting records" and a record of shareholders.

a. "Keep" is used in the sense of permanent historical records while "maintain" is used in the sense of current records.

b. MBCA (1984) § 16.01(e) also requires that specified records be kept at its principal office where they may be inspected by shareholders. MBCA (1984) § 16.02(a). (See part XVII G 5.)

c. Many state statutes have somewhat analogous statutory provisions. These provisions vary widely from state to state and no state statute contains the detail of MBCA (1984). Provisions relating to accounting records, in particular, vary widely. The 1969 Model Act, for example, required corporations to keep "correct and complete books and records of account." MBCA (1969) § 52.

d. MBCA (1984) § 16.01(d) permits a corporation to "maintain" records in other than written form if they can be converted into written form within a reasonable time. Many state statutes have analogous statutory provisions, that vary widely from state to state.

e. Most records maintained by corporations, e.g. financial records, tax returns, samples of advertising, are not required to be retained by the corporation statutes, but their retention may be required by other statutes. Depending on their character and the purpose of the shareholder, discretionary records may be subject to inspection by a shareholder.

B. MANDATORY FINANCIAL DISCLOSURE TO SHAREHOLDERS

MBCA (1984) § 16.20 requires every corporation to furnish shareholders with annual financial statements, containing at a minimum an income statement, a balance sheet, and a statement of changes in shareholders' equity.

1. AUDITING REQUIREMENTS

These financial statements do not need to be prepared by an accountant or by following GAAP or other accounting principles; if not prepared in accordance with GAAP, they must contain a description of the basis on which they were prepared and describe whether they were prepared in a manner consistent with the statements for the preceding year.

Caveat: If GAAP statements are prepared for any purpose they must be provided to shareholders.

2. FINANCIAL DISCLOSURE REQUIREMENTS IN GENERAL

An increasing number of states require some kind of mandatory financial disclosure to shareholders.

a. Some non-MBCA states require disclosure of franchise tax reports or other documents that provide basic financial information.

b. Many non-MBCA states have no mandatory disclosure requirements for financial information.

c. Publicly held corporations registered under section 12 of the Securities Exchange Act of 1934 must make public financial statements prepared in accordance with detailed SEC regulations. This information is of course available to shareholders.

C. OTHER MANDATORY DISCLOSURE REQUIREMENTS

MBCA (1984) § 16.21 requires disclosure to shareholders of transactions involving issuance of shares for promissory notes or promises of future services and indemnification transactions in proceedings in which the corporation is a party. MBCA (1984) § 16.01(e)(7) also requires corporations to maintain a copy of its most recent annual report at its principal office where it is available for inspection by shareholders.

MBCA (1984) § 16.22 requires every corporation to file an annual report with the Secretary of State. The annual report must disclose the nature of the corporation's business, the identity of its directors and officers, and the number and classes of outstanding shares.

Most states do not contain these disclosure requirements, though many states require disclosure of various types of information, usually by way of a required annual report of the corporation. There is great diversity of requirements in this regard.

D. INSPECTION BY THE PUBLIC

Corporations that are not registered under the federal securities acts generally need not make public disclosures except to the extent required by corporation and state tax statutes.

1. DOCUMENTS AVAILABLE AT THE SECRETARY OF STATE'S OFFICE

Documents available at the Secretary of State's office include articles of incorporation, designations of registered offices and registered agents, assumed name certificates, and articles of merger. The MBCA (1984) requires every corporation to file an annual report with the Secretary of State containing current information about the corporation's business, directors, and capitalization.

2. DOCUMENTS AVAILABLE AT OTHER STATE OFFICES

Some states require annual reports to be filed with a state office that are publicly available. Information may also be publicly available from franchise tax returns and other filings, but in most states relatively little information is available.

3. INFORMATION AVAILABLE ABOUT PUBLICLY TRADED CORPORATIONS

Considerable information is normally obtainable from the SEC about a corporation that is registered under the federal Securities Exchange Act or has filed a registration statement under the federal Securities Act of 1933. Information may also be obtained from state securities ("blue sky") commissions if the corporation has filed a registration statement under the state blue sky laws.

E. INSPECTION BY THE GOVERNMENT

The government of the state of incorporation has broad visitorial powers under many state incorporation statutes, but as a practical matter, those powers are seldom exercised. Specific state or federal offices may also have visitorial powers under substantive statutes.

F. INSPECTION OF BOOKS AND RECORDS BY DIRECTORS

A director has a broad right of inspection of books and records.

1. JUSTIFICATION FOR INSPECTION RIGHT

A director is a manager of the corporation and owes certain duties to it and to all the shareholders. A director has a duty to adequately acquaint himself or herself with the business and affairs of the corporation.

2. SCOPE OF DIRECTORS' INSPECTION RIGHT

Some decisions state that the directors' right of inspection is absolute and unqualified. See *Pilat v. Broach Systems, Inc.*, 260 A.2d 13 (N.J.Super.Law Div. 1969); *Brenner v. Hart Systems, Inc.,* 493 N.Y.S.2d 881 (App.Div.1985); *Davis v. Keilsohn Offset Co.,* 79 N.Y.S.2d 540 (App.Div.1948). Other courts, however, have sometimes denied inspection rights to directors where it was clear that the director was acting with manifestly improper motives and adequate information prepared by unbiased persons was available to the directors. The ALI Corporate Governance Project adopts the latter view, stating that a judicial order to enforce the director's inspection right should be issued "unless it is proved that the information to be obtained by exercise of the right is not reasonably related to the performance of directorial functions and duties, or that the director or his agent is likely to use the information in a manner that would violate his fiduciary to the corporation and that such use would not be effectively prevented by a judicial order prohibiting him from using the information in that manner." *Principles of Corporate Governance,* § 3.03.

G. INSPECTION BY SHAREHOLDERS

The right of a shareholder to inspect corporate books and records is considerably narrower than the right of a director, and rests on an entirely different theoretical base.

1. JUSTIFICATION FOR INSPECTION RIGHT

A shareholder has a financial interest in the corporation and the common law recognizes a right to inspect books and records to protect this interest. However, the shareholder is not charged with management responsibility, is not subject to a broad fiduciary duty, and may have conflicting or inconsistent financial interests;

as a result, a shareholder's right to inspect is limited to inspections for "proper purposes."

2. SOURCES OF THE SHAREHOLDERS' RIGHT OF INSPECTION

A shareholder may have either a common law or a statutory right of inspection. In some states shareholders may have both a common law and a statutory right, i. e. the statutory right supplements but does not supplant the common law right. A shareholder may also have rights of discovery if he or she is in litigation with the corporation and, to the extent the corporation is required to make disclosure to the public generally, shareholders also have the rights of members of the general public. In many states, shareholders also have a special statutory right to inspect a list of shareholders before or during a shareholder's meeting. MBCA (1984) § 7.20.

a. The right of shareholders to inspect books and records is not subject to elimination by provisions in articles of incorporation. *State ex rel. Cochran v. Penn–Beaver Oil Co.,* 143 A. 257 (Del.1926).

b. Most litigation seeking inspection of books and records by shareholders relates to inspecting a current record of shareholders.

3. THE SHAREHOLDERS' COMMON LAW RIGHT OF INSPECTION

A common law inspection right is available to any shareholder of record who establishes a proper purpose for examining the books and records of the corporation. The burden of proof of a proper purpose is on the shareholder. *Fleischer Dev. Corp. v. Home Owners Warranty Corp.,* 856 F.2d 1529 (D.C.Cir.1988).

a. From the standpoint of the corporation, a shareholder's demand to inspect the corporation's books and records is almost certain to be viewed as a hostile and threatening act.

b. The practice has therefore developed of routinely denying all requests for common law inspection and compelling the shareholder to affirmatively establish a proper purpose in every case, relying on whatever pretext may be available for the denial, and putting the shareholder to his or her proof as to purpose.

4. DEVELOPMENT OF THE ORIGINAL STATUTORY RIGHT OF INSPECTION

In an effort to make the right of inspection available without recourse to litigation in every case, the statutes of many states supplement the common law right of inspection with a statutory right of inspection which may include a "penalty" on corporate officers who arbitrarily refuse to permit proper examination of books and records. The 1969 Model Business Corporation Act contains a provision of this type.

a. The statutory right of inspection is typically available to persons (a) who have been shareholders of record for at least six months prior to the demand or (b) who own at least five per cent of the outstanding shares of the corporation.

b. The statutory right of inspection, like the common law right, also requires a showing of "proper purposes" for the inspection which must be stated in the shareholder's written demand. However, in the event a shareholder qualifies for the statutory right of inspection, the corporation has the burden of showing the plaintiff does not have a proper purpose.

c. Some of these statutes specifically provide that a record of shareholders need not be produced if the applicant has offered to sell or assisted another person in the sale or offering for sale of a shareholders list within the preceding five years.

d. Under many statutes a corporate officer or agent who refuses to grant a statutory right of inspection is liable for a "penalty" equal to a specified per cent of the value of the shares owned by the shareholder or some other fixed amount.

1) A corporation or officer may avoid imposition of the penalty only by showing reasonable grounds for the denial of inspection. Other grounds may be set forth in the statute as defenses.

2) As a practical matter, such penalty provisions are rarely enforced because the basic test of eligibility—a proper purpose—is a vague and uncertain one. While the potential of a substantial penalty probably has a healthful, *in terrorem* effect, there are few reported cases in which a penalty has been actually imposed.

e. The relationship between the common law right of inspection and these statutory rights of inspection is not clear in many states.

5. MODEL BUSINESS CORPORATION ACT (1984) INSPECTION RIGHT

MBCA (1984) §§ 16.01 through 16.04 adopts a somewhat different approach toward enforcement of shareholders' inspection rights than set forth in the traditional statutes discussed above.

a. Shareholders have an unrestricted and unqualified right to inspect certain fundamental documents that the corporation must preserve at its principal office. MBCA (1984) § 16.02(a). This right of inspection is absolute and not subject to a proper purpose limitation. The documents are listed in MBCA (1984) § 16.01(e) and include:

1) Articles or restated articles of incorporation;

2) Bylaws;

3) Resolutions creating classes or series of shares;

4) Minutes of shareholders' meetings and records of action taken by consent of the shareholders for the past three years;

5) Written communications to shareholders within the past three years, including financial statements required to be provided to shareholders (MBCA (1984) § 16.20, 16.21);

6) A list of the names and business addresses of directors and officers; and

7) The corporation's most recent annual report (MBCA (1984) § 16.22).

b. MBCA (1984) § 16.02(b) authorizes a shareholder to inspect and copy additional records only upon a showing of "proper purpose" and good faith, and upon providing a statement setting forth "with reasonable particularity his purpose and the records he desires to inspect." The records must be directly connected with that purpose. The records subject to this additional inspection right include:

1) Excerpts from minutes of the board of directors, records of actions of committees of the board of directors, and minutes of shareholders meetings more than three years old (and therefore not available under a. above);

2) Accounting records of the corporation; and

3) The record of shareholders.

Caveat: The classes of records available for inspection under MBCA (1984) § 16.02 are narrower than the scope of inspection permitted by many courts under earlier statutes. Some courts, for example, have permitted inspection of correspondence or internal records that do not fall within any of the categories set forth in § 16.02.

Example: Accounting records might be construed in an appropriate case to include receipts, vouchers, bills and other documents evidencing the financial condition of the corporation.

Example: Accounting records in an appropriate case might also be construed to include accounting records of a subsidiary or other venture controlled by the corporation.

Caveat: Unlike the statutory rights of inspection discussed in the previous section, MBCA (1984) does not condition inspection on the ownership of shares for a specified period or of a specified percentage.

c. The rights of inspection set forth in MBCA (1984) § 16.02 are expressly made nonexclusive of all other inspection rights. MBCA (1984) § 16.02(e). Further, they may not be restricted or eliminated by provisions in the articles of incorporation or bylaws. MBCA (1984) § 16.02(d).

d. The scope of the inspection right, including the right to have copies made by photographic, xerographic, or other means, is defined in MBCA (1984) § 16.03. The corporation may impose a reasonable charge for making copies of records but may not limit the inspection right to the right to make longhand copies or notes with respect to the contents of the books and records. MBCA (1984) §§ 16.03(b), (c). The shareholder is entitled to be accompanied by her attorney or accountant. MBCA (1984) § 16.03(a).

Caveat: Most earlier statutes are silent on many of the issues discussed in MBCA (1984) § 16.03. Many statutes, however, contemplate inspection by agent or attorney. Court decisions, further, tend to construe broadly the inspection rights of shareholders, once established, to include copying by machine, etc.

e. A shareholder who is denied the right of inspection may seek a summary judicial order compelling the inspection. MBCA (1984) § 16.04. Further, the court must order the corporation to pay the shareholder's costs in compelling inspection unless the corporation "proves that it refused inspection in good faith because it had a reasonable basis for doubt about the right of the shareholder to inspect the records demanded." MBCA (1984) § 16.04(c). The Official Comment states that this language establishes a "partially objective standard, in that the corporation must be able to point to some objective basis for its doubt that the shareholder was acting in good faith or had a purpose that was proper."

Example: The corporation learns that a shareholder demanding a right of inspection has improperly used information obtained from the corporation in the past and refuses to permit the inspection. If the shareholder establishes a good faith and proper purpose for this inspection, a court should order the inspection. The corporation, however, should not be required to pay the shareholder's expenses in obtaining the order compelling the inspection since the corporation has a reasonable basis for doubting the shareholder's good faith because of the shareholder's prior misuse of corporate information.

f. A court may impose restrictions on the use of information by the shareholder. MBCA (1984) § 16.04(d). It may, for example, prohibit the shareholder from disclosing it to a competitor. Courts have the inherent power to restrict the use of information obtained by shareholders independent of specific statutory authority to do so. See, e.g. *CM & M Group, Inc. v. Carroll,* 453 A.2d 788 (Del.1982); *Helmsman Management Services, Inc. v. A & S Consultants, Inc.,* 525 A.2d 160 (Del.Ch.1987).

6. WHAT IS A "PROPER PURPOSE?"

The basic test of inspection by shareholders is a "proper purpose." If the common law right of inspection is involved, the shareholder must affirmatively show a proper purpose; if the shareholder qualifies for the statutory right of inspection, the corporation has the burden of establishing an absence of proper purpose and may be subject to penalty if it fails to do so after denying inspection.

a. A purpose is proper if it is directed toward obtaining information bearing upon or seeking to protect the shareholder's interest and that of other shareholders of the corporation. A shareholder may have a proper purpose even though he or she is unfriendly to management.

Example: A shareholder demands a list of shareholders in order to communicate with other shareholders about matters of corporate concern; e. g., to solicit proxies, to initiate a proxy contest, to publicize mismanagement, to discuss a derivative suit, to discuss proposals of management, or to form a protective committee. These are all proper purposes. *General Time Corp. v. Talley Industries, Inc.,* 240 A.2d 755 (Del.Ch.1968).

Example: The mere fact that the shareholder making the request is a competitor of the corporation does not necessarily make his or her purpose improper though such a demand may raise suspicions.

Example: It is not a proper purpose to seek the list in order to communicate one's own personal social or political views to shareholders. *State ex rel. Pillsbury v. Honeywell, Inc.,* 191 N.W.2d 406 (Minn.1971).

Example: Inspection is demanded to determine the worth of the shareholder's holdings. Such a purpose is proper.

Example: Inspection is demanded to seek reasons for a decline in profits and to communicate with other shareholders. Such purposes are proper.

Example: A desire to obtain trade secrets for a competitor is not a proper purpose.

Example: Probably idle curiosity is not a proper purpose, though it is a rare shareholder who cannot allege a more specific purpose that would be considered proper.

b. Obviously, substantial and difficult factual issues of predominant motive and intent underlie this determination. A careful coaching of a shareholder's testimony may lead to the conclusion that the purpose for inspection is proper, while an outspoken or unusually forthright shareholder may run into difficulty.

7. INSPECTION RIGHTS OF BENEFICIAL OWNERS

A person who is a beneficial owner of shares but not the record owner has a common law right of inspection. Whether or not a beneficial owner has a statutory right depends on the precise wording of the statute. Under the MBCA (1984) § 16.02(f), a beneficial owner of shares has a statutory right of inspection.

a. Under some state statutes, pledgees or judgment creditors have a statutory right to inspect.

b. Holders of voting trust certificates also have a statutory right to inspect under the MBCA (1984) and many state statutes.

H. REVIEW QUESTIONS

XVII–1. What is the test for determining the propriety of a shareholder's demand to inspect corporate records?

XVII–2. If the test is a "proper purpose", why are further restrictions on the right of inspection necessary?

XVII–3. What is the test for a director's right to inspect?

XVII–4. To what extent must a corporation provide routine information to all shareholders, such as financial reports and the like?

XVII–5. The shareholders of X corporation adopt a bylaw which requires that all shareholders, as a condition precedent to a right to inspect the books of the corporation, give at least three months notice before the proposed inspection. The bylaw further provides that inspection should be granted only if the purpose of the inspection is approved by the board of directors. The state corporation statute provides for a traditional statutory right of inspection but is silent on whether the right may be limited in any way by the corporation. P, a shareholder of X, demands the right to inspect the books of X within two weeks of the date of the demand and states that his purpose for inspection is to determine whether there has been mismanagement, a purpose that is clearly proper under applicable state law. The demand is refused by the directors under the above bylaw because it is untimely. P seeks a writ of mandamus to compel the officers and directors to permit his inspection of the books. Should the writ issue?

XVIII

SHAREHOLDER LITIGATION

The term "shareholder litigation" primarily refers to litigation brought by a shareholder in connection with his capacity or role as shareholder.

Analysis

- D. *Defenses in Derivative Suits*
  1. *Application of the Business Judgment Rule to Dismiss Derivative Litigation*
  2. *Dismissal for Failure to Meet Procedural Requirements*
  3. *Miscellaneous Substantive Defenses*
  4. *Disqualification of the Plaintiff*
- E. *Derivative Suits in Federal Courts*
  1. *Classification of Parties for Diversity Purposes*
  2. *Pendent Jurisdiction*
- F. *Miscellaneous Procedural Problems*
  1. *Necessary Party*
  2. *Combination of Claims*
  3. *Multiple Suits*
  4. *The Role of Corporate Counsel*
  5. *Jury Trials*
  6. *Merger of Corporate Defendant*
  7. *Collateral Estoppel*
- G. *Settlement of Derivative Suits*
  1. *The Nature of Settlement Negotiations*
  2. *Judicial Approval*
  3. *Judicial Review of Settlements*
  4. *Notice and Hearing on Settlement*
  5. *Derivative Pursuit of Secret Settlement*
  6. *Settlement of Underlying Claim*
  7. *Res Judicata Effect of Settlement*
- H. *Recovery in Derivative Suits*
  1. *Justification of Rule*
  2. *Exception Where Wrongdoers Are Major Shareholders*
  3. *Other Relief*
- I. *Res Judicata*
  1. *Final Judgment on the Merits*
  2. *Settlements*
  3. *Dismissal of Suit*
- J. *Litigation Expenses*
  1. *Creation of a Fund*
  2. *Non–fund Cases*
  3. *Amount of Plaintiffs' Attorneys' Fees*
  4. *Defendants' Expenses*
- K. *Review Questions*

A. "DIRECT," "DERIVATIVE," AND "CLASS" LITIGATION

The basic distinction in shareholder litigation is between "direct" and "derivative" litigation, since different procedural rules apply to these categories. A third, overlapping, category deals with "class" litigation.

1. "DIRECT" DEFINED

A direct suit involves the enforcement by a shareholder of a claim based on injury to the shareholder directly as an owner of shares.

Example: Suits to recover dividends, to examine corporate books and records, and to compel the registration of a securities transfer are all direct suits.

Example: A suit to compel the payment of a dividend may be either direct, *Knapp v. Bankers Securities Corp.*, 230 F.2d 717 (3d Cir.1956), or derivative, *Gordon v. Elliman*, 119 N.E.2d 331 (N.Y.1954) (a case later overruled by statute).

Example: A suit alleging that it was improper for a majority shareholder to vote on a resolution authorizing the corporation to issue additional shares to the majority shareholder states a direct claim—it prevents the dilution of the voting power of the complaining shareholder's shares.

Example: A suit alleging a conspiracy of the directors to use their powers to depress the market price of the shares so that they can buy them at less than fair value states a direct claim since such action does not injure the corporation as such.

Example: A suit alleging that a plan of merger or reorganization was designed to dilute a shareholder's voting power states a direct claim. *Eisenberg v. Flying Tiger Line, Inc.*, 451 F.2d 267 (2d Cir.1971).

2. "DERIVATIVE" DEFINED

A derivative suit is an action brought by one or more shareholders to remedy or prevent a wrong to the corporation as such rather than to the shareholders personally.

Example: A suit brought to compel a director to restore property wrongfully taken from the corporation is a derivative claim.

Example: Suits to recover improperly paid dividends from third parties or to require a controlling shareholder to account for a premium received on the sale of shares have been held to be derivative since the benefit inures to the corporation.

Example: A suit charging officers and directors with misapplication of corporate assets or other breaches of duty is derivative in character.

a. In a derivative suit, the plaintiff shareholders do not sue on a cause of action belonging to themselves as individuals. They sue in a representative capacity on a cause of action that belongs to the corporation.

b. In a derivative suit, the real party in interest is the corporation. In effect, the shareholder is suing as a champion of his corporation.

c. For most procedural purposes, however, the corporation is treated as a defendant. *Koster v. Lumbermens Mut. Cas. Co.*, 330 U.S. 518, 67 S.Ct. 828 (1947).

3. "CLASS SUITS"

A class suit is typically a direct suit in which one or more shareholder plaintiffs purport to act as a representative of a class or classes of similarly situated shareholders, for injuries to the members of the class as such.

a. A class suit is typically direct and not derivative: all shareholders of a particular class (or all shareholders) are claiming they were injured by an act which did not itself injure the corporation. *Green v. Wolf Corp.*, 406 F.2d 291 (2d Cir.1968).

b. A derivative action, however, usually has some aspects of a class action since a shareholder, when suing to right a wrong done to the corporation, is also suing to protect the interest of all other shareholders.

4. PRACTICAL APPLICATION OF DISTINCTIONS

Different procedural and substantive rules are applicable to direct and derivative claims. Unfortunately, however, the line between the two types of claims is sometimes hazy.

a. Anything that harms the corporation also harms the shareholders by reducing the value of their shares. However, a shareholder may not transmute a derivative claim into a direct one merely by alleging a direct reduction in value of shares owned because of injury to the corporation. *Armstrong v. Frostie Co.*, 453 F.2d 914 (4th Cir.1971).

1) Where an injury is done to the corporation each shareholder is made whole if the corporation recovers damages from the wrongdoer.

2) A derivative action brought in the corporation's name avoids a multiplicity of suits by shareholders.

3) Damages recovered by the corporation derivatively are available for the payment of the corporation's creditors while a direct recovery by shareholders might adversely affect creditors; a direct recovery for a derivative injury has a mandatory dividend feature.

b. In some situations a single claim may give rise to both a direct and a derivative claim, or careful pleading may affect the categorization.

Example: A suit claiming a conspiracy to injure the business of a corporation states a derivative claim. If it is alleged that the conspiracy is to compel a shareholder to sell her shares at less than real value, a direct claim may be alleged. See *Green v. Victor Talking Machine Co.,* 24 F.2d 378 (2d Cir.1928).

Example: A suit claiming the corporation issued shares without honoring preemptive rights is direct; however, it may also arguably be derivative if it is alleged in the same transaction that the corporation was induced to issue shares for inadequate consideration through fraud or a violation of federal securities law. *Shaw v. Empire Sav. & Loan Ass'n.*, 9 Cal.Rptr. 204 (Cal.App.1960).

B. EVALUATION OF DERIVATIVE LITIGATION

There are two diametrically opposed views as to the social value of modern derivative litigation.

1. A MAJOR DETERRENT TO MISCONDUCT

One view is that derivative litigation is one of the major bulwarks against overreaching and misconduct by corporate insiders. A number of judges have expressed this view as have many academic writers.

a. Statistical studies of derivative litigation reveal that most cases are settled and that the corporation and shareholders receive some benefit, either in the form of monetary recovery or changes in procedure or practice.

b. The problem with these studies is that they do not distinguish nuisance settlements from substantial ones.

2. A DEVICE FOR THE ENRICHMENT OF THE PLAINTIFFS' BAR

The opposing view is that most derivative litigation is without substantive merit and is instituted for the benefit of plaintiffs' attorneys.

a. This view is often stated by attorneys who represent corporations that are involved in derivative litigation. They rely on personal experience, on impressions, and on anecdotal evidence.

b. Litigation instituted for the settlement value of cases and for the benefit of the plaintiffs' attorneys is called "strike suits."

c. Empirical studies based on stock price movements following the announcement of the institution or settlement of derivative litigation are not conclusive, but they tend to support the view that most derivative litigation does not have favorable impact on stock prices.

3. ROLE OF PLAINTIFFS' ATTORNEYS

Most derivative litigation is attorney-fueled litigation. Plaintiffs' attorneys find possible litigation situations and then seek to find a plaintiff in whose name suit may be brought.

a. Plaintiffs' attorneys advance the litigation costs to pursue the litigation and as a result have a financial interest in the litigation that exceeds that of any single plaintiff.

b. The litigation is directed and conducted by the plaintiffs' attorneys who are motivated at least in part by their financial interest in the litigation.

4. LITIGATION AND SETTLEMENT

Most derivative litigation is settled and does not go to final judgment.

a. In settlement negotiations, fees to be paid to plaintiffs' attorneys are normally a major element to be resolved. Agreements as to fees must be approved by the court as part of the settlement process. (See part XVIII G.)

b. Derivative litigation is often settled without any payment of money by third party defendants to the corporation but by the corporation agreeing to make changes in procedures and practices.

C. PREREQUISITES FOR MAINTAINING DERIVATIVE SUITS

MBCA (1984), subchapter 7D, §§ 7.40 through 7.47, is a recently revised statutory provision dealing with procedural and substantive requirements of derivative litigation.

The Federal Rules of Civil Procedure also contain elaborate procedural requirements for derivative suits (rule 23.1) which are similar to those set forth in subchapter D in some respects, though the underlying policies differ significantly. Many states have adopted statutes or rules similar to the federal rules in whole or in part. In diversity suits, state principles may be applied by federal courts under the *Erie* principle. *Hausman v. Buckley*, 299 F.2d 696 (2d Cir.1962).

1. DEMAND ON THE CORPORATION AND THE DIRECTORS

Generally, in a derivative suit, the plaintiff must allege and prove a good faith effort to first obtain redress from the corporation on the claim. A demand on the board of directors is the traditional device to satisfy this requirement.

a. The traditional rule is that a demand must be made unless it would be futile because members of the board of directors are interested in the transaction in question and a demand would in effect require the directors to sue themselves.

1) Statutes generally require that the plaintiff allege in the complaint either that a demand has been made on the board of directors or that such a demand would be futile.

2) Historically, this was only a pleading requirement: the worst that could happen if a demand on the directors was not made on the ground that it was futile, but the court concludes that it should have been made, was that a demand could be made at that time. The demand requirement did not affect the progress of the litigation.

3) Except in Delaware, it is still true that in many derivative suits no prior demand is made on directors, the plaintiff alleging circumstances that arguably makes a demand futile. Cases, however, have required more than *pro forma* allegations and have dismissed suits in which the reasons given for not making a demand are conclusionary. *In re Kauffman Mut. Fund Actions*, 479 F.2d 257 (1st Cir.1973); *Grossman v. Johnson,* 674 F.2d 115 (1st Cir.1982); *Gonzalez Turul v. Rogatol Distributors, Inc.,* 951 F.2d 1 (1st Cir.1991).

4) In Delaware, the most important single state with respect to derivative litigation, the demand required/demand futile distinction has become the touchstone for a substantive issue that is outcome-determinative in many cases: should a decision made by independent directors that the derivative litigation not be pursued be thereafter given preclusive effect under the business judgment rule?

(i) This substantive issue is discussed at length in part XVIII D 1, below.

(ii) Because of the importance of this substantive decision, many Delaware cases consider the circumstances when a demand is required and when it is excused. Litigation over the demand issue in Delaware is time-consuming since it requires a virtual trial and subsequent appeal on a critical issue that must be resolved before discovery is undertaken and the merits are addressed. Judge Easterbrook, concurring in *Starrels v. First Nat. Bank of Chicago,* 870 F.2d 1168 (7th Cir.1989) has stated that the Delaware demand rule creates more litigation than it avoids. See also *Kaplan v. Wyatt,* 484 A.2d 501 (Del.Ch.1984), aff'd on other grounds 499 A.2d 1184 (Del.1985).

b. MBCA (1984) § 7.42 avoids the problems created in Delaware by requiring that a demand be made on the board of directors or the corporation in every case.

Caveat: Section 7.42 requires that the demand be made on the "corporation." The demand should be addressed to the board of directors if the issue is one to be dealt with by the board; if the issue may be dealt with by an officer of the corporation, the demand may be addressed to the chief executive officer or the secretary of the corporation.

c. The Corporate Governance Project of the American Law Institute also requires a demand in virtually every case.

d. Rule 23.1 of the Federal Rules of Civil Procedure requires that a plaintiff must "allege with particularity the efforts, if any, made by the plaintiff to obtain the action he or she desires from the directors or comparable authority and the reasons for his or her failure to obtain the action or for not making the effort." In *Kamen v. Kemper Financial Services, Inc.,* ___ U.S. ___, 111 S.Ct. 1711 (1991), the Court held that the demand futility exception, as defined in the law of the state of incorporation, applies to derivative suits brought under federal statutes. State law also controls in suits brought on the basis of diversity of citizenship. *RCM Securities Fund Inc. v. Stanton,* 928 F.2d 1318 (2d Cir.1991).

2. DEMAND UPON SHAREHOLDERS

MBCA (1984) 7.42 does not require a demand on shareholders. The Federal Rules of Civil Procedure and the statutes of several states provide that if a demand on shareholders is not made, the plaintiff must show some adequate reason for not making the effort. Expense, or difficulty, may be justifiable reasons.

a. Massachusetts appears to have adopted the most stringent rule, requiring a demand in every case where a majority of shareholders are not wrongdoers. *S. Solomont & Sons Trust Inc. v. New England Theatres Operating Corp.*, 93 N.E.2d 241 (Mass.1950); *Pomerantz v. Clark*, 101 F.Supp. 341 (D.Mass.1951).

b. While some cases have required a demand on shareholders even when the cost would be substantial, many cases have held that such an act may be omitted on one ground or another. *Levitt v. Johnson*, 334 F.2d 815 (1st Cir.1964). Courts generally have proceeded on a case-by-case basis, not requiring a demand when there are thousands of shareholders, and considering other factors such as the motives of the plaintiff, the number of shareholders joining in the action, and the proximity to the next shareholders' meeting.

c. If a demand is made on shareholders, and the shareholders reject the maintenance of the suit, the suit may nevertheless be brought by the minority shareholder. *Rogers v. American Can Co.*, 305 F.2d 297 (3d Cir.1962).

Example: An allegation that the wrongdoers own a majority of the shares and hence favorable shareholder action is unlikely is an adequate reason.

Example: An allegation that the number of shareholders is so large that it is unreasonable to require the plaintiff to incur the expense of what is essentially a proxy solicitation when there is little chance of success is an adequate reason.

Example: An allegation that the acts complained of cannot be ratified by the shareholders, so that action by the shareholders is useless has been held to be an adequate reason for not making a demand on shareholders. *Mayer v. Adams*, 141 A.2d 458 (Del.1958). Essentially contra is *Claman v. Robertson*, 128 N.E.2d 429 (Ohio 1955).

3. CONTEMPORARY OWNERSHIP

MBCA (1984) 7.41(1) provides that a person may not commence a derivative suit unless he "was a shareholder of the corporation at the time of the act or omission complained of occurred or became a shareholder through transfer by operation of law from one who was a shareholder at that time."

a. This is usually referred to as the "contemporary ownership rule."

b. Rule 23.1 of the Federal Rules of Civil Procedure has a similar requirement. In the federal courts the contemporaneous ownership rule is designed primarily to prevent the collusive establishment of diversity of citizenship. *Hawes v. Oakland,* 104 U.S. (14 Otto) 450 (1881).

c. In MBCA (1984) 7.41 and analogous state statutes relating to derivative litigation, the contemporaneous ownership rule has been justified as necessary to prevent the "buying of a lawsuit."

1) If buying a lawsuit is the concern, the contemporaneous ownership requirement might be safely liberalized to allow suit by plaintiffs who discover the facts giving rise to the lawsuit only after becoming a shareholder. *Pollitz v. Gould,* 94 N.E. 1088 (N.Y.1911). California has adopted this approach. Cal.Corp.Code 800(b)(1).

2) Most state statutes, however, have not accepted this liberalizing principle. See *Goldie v. Yaker*, 432 P.2d 841 (N.M.1967); *Jepson v. Peterson*, 10 N.W.2d 749 (S.D.1943).

3) Concern about abuses of shareholder litigation explains the reluctance to relax the contemporaneous ownership rule. On the other hand, where a suit seems reasonable, the "time of the transaction" has been construed flexibly to permit suit to be maintained. *Maclary v. Pleasant Hills, Inc.*, 109 A.2d 830 (Del.Ch.1954).

d. A principle related to the contemporaneous ownership rule prohibits a shareholder who purchases all or substantially all the shares of a corporation at a fair price from having the corporation then bring suit against the selling shareholders on grounds of prior corporate mismanagement. *Bangor Punta Operations, Inc. v. Bangor & Aroostook R. Co.*, 417 U.S. 703, 94 S.Ct. 2578 (1974); *In re REA Express, Inc.*, 412 F.Supp. 1239 (E.D.Pa.1976); *Courtland Manor, Inc. v. Leeds*, 347 A.2d 144 (Del.Ch.1975); *Capitol Wine & Spirit Corp. v. Pokrass*, 98 N.Y.S.2d 291 (App.Div.1950). This is an equitable principle that bars a suit by the corporation after the sale rather than simply barring a shareholder from serving as a plaintiff.

e. A shareholder plaintiff who sells or disposes of his or her shares during the pendency of derivative litigation loses the right to maintain or continue the suit. *Tenney v. Rosenthal*, 160 N.E.2d 463 (N.Y.1959).

f. A shareholder plaintiff who is "cashed out" by a merger, receiving cash for his or her shares, may not continue the suit. *Lewis v. Anderson*, 477 A.2d 1040 (Del.1984); *Kramer v. Western Pacific Industries, Inc.*, 546 A.2d 348 (Del.1988).

4. SECURITY FOR EXPENSES

Security-for-expenses statutes require certain plaintiff shareholders in derivative suits to provide the corporation with "security for the reasonable expenses, including attorney's fees" which the corporation or other defendants may incur in connection with a derivative suit. These statutes also authorize the corporation or the individual defendants to recover their expenses from such security in some circumstances.

a. The constitutionality of this type of statute was upheld in *Cohen v. Beneficial Indus. Loan Corp.*, 337 U.S. 541, 69 S.Ct. 1221 (1949).

b. Under statutes requiring security-for-expenses, the amount of the security is fixed by the court in light of the expenses for which the corporation may be liable, including not only the direct expenses of the corporation, but also the expenses of other defendants for which the corporation may become liable by indemnification or otherwise.

1) The amount of the required security may be very substantial, running into the tens or hundreds of thousands of dollars. The security is usually in the form of a bond with sureties, though it also may be in the form of cash or marketable securities.

2) Since the plaintiffs may be unable or unwilling to post security, this requirement often creates a major obstacle to the successful prosecution of a derivative suit.

Example: A decision that the securities-for-expenses statute is applicable and setting the amount of the security at $75,000 may well be the decision that effectively terminates the litigation.

c. Shareholder plaintiffs who are required to post security-for-expenses are defined in different ways in state statutes.

1) In the older statutes (where the purpose to discourage derivative litigation is most manifest), the size of the plaintiff's holding is determinative.

(i) A typical provision is that plaintiffs must post security-for-expenses unless their holdings are more than five per cent of the outstanding shares or exceed a specified market value, e. g., $25,000. MBCA (1969) § 49.

(ii) Intervening shareholder plaintiffs may have their shares counted toward meeting the statutory minima. *Sorin v. Shahmoon Industries, Inc.*, 220 N.Y.S.2d 760 (1961). However, a solicitation of shareholders for this purpose may be deemed a proxy solicitation subject to the proxy solicitation rules adopted by the Securities Exchange Commission. *Studebaker Corporation v. Gittlin,* 360 F.2d 692 (2d Cir. 1966).

Caveat: A different rule is applicable in the federal courts in diversity cases where only plaintiffs who own shares at the time of the wrong may serve as plaintiffs. *Kaufman v. Wolfson,* 136 F.Supp. 939 (S.D.N.Y.1955).

(iii) A corporation may not issue additional shares to reduce the plaintiff's holdings to less than 5 per cent and then seek security-for-expenses. *Roach v. Franchises Intern., Inc.*, 300 N.Y.S.2d 630 (App.Div.1969).

2) Some modern statutes require security-for-expenses only upon a court finding that the suit was apparently brought without reasonable cause or seems patently without merit.

d. Security-for-expenses statutes often do not define when the corporation may actually look to the security for reimbursement; rather, they usually state in effect that "[t]he corporation may have recourse to such security in such amount as the court thereafter determines."

1) Under such statutes, courts usually allow reimbursement only if the plaintiff is unsuccessful and they conclude that the suit was brought without reasonable cause.

2) Where reimbursement is allowed, an unsuccessful shareholder plaintiff posting security-for-expenses ends up paying the expenses of both sides of the litigation.

3) If no security is posted and the case is dismissed, the plaintiff is not liable for the defendant's expenses in securing the dismissal. *Tyler v. Gas Consumers Ass'n*, 231 N.Y.S.2d 15 (1962).

e. Security-for-expenses statutes are applicable to suits in federal court based on state-created causes of action.

1) This is a direct application of the *Erie* principle.

Example: A claim in federal court based solely on diversity of citizenship is subject to the security-for-expenses requirement.

2) Security-for-expenses statutes are not applicable to suits in federal court based on violations of the federal securities acts.

Example: A suit is brought under rule 10b–5. The state security-for-expenses statute is not applicable.

Caveat: If a state claim is brought in federal court in connection with a federal claim under the doctrine of pendent jurisdiction, it is subject to the security-for-expenses requirement.

f. Security-for-expenses statutes are not applicable to direct class actions brought either in the federal or state courts. *Eisenberg v. Flying Tiger Line, Inc.*, 451 F.2d 267 (2d Cir.1971); *Knapp v. Bankers Securities Corp.*, 230 F.2d 717 (3d Cir.1956).

g. The stated purpose of security-for-expenses statutes is to deter "strike" suits, that is, suits brought not to redress an injury to the corporation but in the hope of securing a settlement profitable to the plaintiff shareholders and their attorneys.

1) Most statutes do not distinguish between "strike" suits and bona fide shareholder suits but are applicable to all shareholder suits brought by shareholders whose holdings are less than the specified amount.

(i) Such statutes have the effect of making all such suits more difficult and reflect an antipathy toward shareholder derivative litigation.

(ii) Such statutes also probably have the incidental effect of encouraging suits to be brought under the federal securities laws rather than under state law.

h. The MBCA (1984) does not contain a security-for-expenses statute even though earlier versions of the Model Act did. The decision to eliminate this requirement was made in part on the ground that basing the requirement on the size or value of the plaintiff's holdings rather than on the apparent good faith of the claim arguably unreasonably discriminated against small shareholders.

i. MBCA (1984) § 7.46(2) provides that the court, upon termination of a derivative suit, may require the plaintiff to pay "any defendant's reasonable expenses (including counsel fees) incurred in defending the proceeding if it finds that the proceeding was commenced or maintained without reasonable cause of for an improper purpose."

1) MBCA (1984) § 7.46(3) also permits the court to impose costs incurred by defendants as a result of the filing of a pleading, motion or other paper that "was not well grounded in fact, after reasonable inquiry, or warranted by existing law or a good faith argument for the extension, modification or reversal of existing law and was interposed for an improper purpose, such as to harass or to cause unnecessary delay or needless increase in the cost of the litigation."

2) The Official Comment to § 7.46 states that these sections were added to parallel Federal Rule of Civil Procedure 11.

3) Section 7.46 also reflects distrust of plaintiff attorneys in derivative litigation.

5. VERIFICATION

Rule 23.1 of the Federal Rules of Civil Procedure require that a derivative complaint must be "verified." A plaintiff shareholder may verify his complaint even though she may not understand all aspects of the transactions being complained of if serious fraud is charged and the plaintiff has reason to believe that serious misconduct occurred. *Surowitz v. Hilton Hotels Corp.*, 383 U.S. 363, 86 S.Ct. 845 (1966).

D. DEFENSES IN DERIVATIVE SUITS

Defenses in derivative suits may be grouped into three broad classes.

1. APPLICATION OF THE BUSINESS JUDGMENT RULE TO DISMISS DERIVATIVE LITIGATION

One of the most controversial applications of the business judgment rule today is whether a disinterested majority of the board of directors (or a disinterested committee of the board of directors) may determine that as a matter of business judgment a derivative suit brought by a shareholder seeking recovery by the corporation from other directors or officers of the corporation should not be pursued because it is not in the best interests of the corporation.

Caveat: For a discussion of the business judgment rule in general, see part XIV B 2.

Caveat: Where a derivative suit seeks recovery by the corporation from third persons unrelated to the corporation, it is clear that a decision of the directors not to pursue such litigation is protected by the business judgment rule. The difficult issue occurs when the third party defendants are directors or officers of the corporation itself.

a. The first decisions on this issue involved suits in which shareholders sought to recover improper foreign payments or domestic political contributions from the directors or officers who authorized them (or who failed to prevent them). The courts initially accepted with little reservation the conclusion that dismissal of derivative litigation was no different than other questions resolved by disinterested directors as a matter of business judgment. *Gall v. Exxon Corp.,* 418 F.Supp. 508 (S.D.N.Y.1976); *Auerbach v. Bennett,* 393 N.E.2d 994 (N.Y. 1979); *Burks v. Lasker,* 441 U.S. 471, 99 S.Ct. 1831 (1979).

Caveat: For the reasons discussed in Chapter XIV, it is doubtful that the plaintiffs in these cases would have prevailed if a trial on the merits had been held.

b. The major argument against the uncritical application of the business judgment rule in such cases is concern about "structural bias," the concern that directors will be motivated by friendship and mutual respect that has developed between directors so that the independent directors "will look out for their own," or adopt a "there but for the grace of God, go I" approach that will not lead to an impartial and independent judgment. See Comment, The Propriety of Judicial Deference to Corporate Boards of Directors, 96 Harv. L.Rev. 1894 (1983).

1) Many lawyers familiar with modern boards of directors discount the "structural bias" concern, arguing that disinterested directors today have the independence and strength to put aside concerns of friendship or sympathy and make objective and impartial decisions as to whether it is in the best interests of the corporation to pursue such claims.

2) In virtually every reported instance in which the question of dismissal has been referred to an independent litigation committee, the committee has concluded that it was in the best interest of the corporation not to pursue the matter and to dismiss the litigation.

c. Either the board of directors itself (excluding, however, directors who are defendants in the proceedings) or a special litigation committee composed of outside directors who are not involved in the actions complained of investigates the matters complained of in the shareholders' complaint.

1) Where a litigation committee is formed, it is usually delegated the power of the board of directors to formulate the policy of the board of directors with respect to the matters complained of.

2) The board of directors or committee may hire independent counsel to investigate the matters complained of and make a report with recommendations as to what position the board of directors or the litigation committee should take.

3) If the board of directors or litigation committee concludes that it is not in the best interests of the corporation to pursue the derivative suit, the corporation files a motion to dismiss the shareholders' suit on the ground that the decision whether or not to pursue litigation is itself a business decision subject to the business judgment rule.

Caveat: If this is a proper application of the business judgment rule, the decision to discontinue the litigation under the business judgment rule is binding on the plaintiff shareholders who never obtain a decision on the merits of their lawsuit and may only litigate questions such as whether the board or committee were truly independent and whether the board or committee reasonably informed itself in good faith of the facts before reaching its decision.

Example: Exxon learns that over $50,000,000 of questionable payments have been made by an Italian subsidiary. A minority shareholder brings a derivative suit against persons who were directors when the payments were made; some defendants knew of the payments while others did not. A committee of uninvolved directors is formed to review the desirability of pursuing this litigation; the committee decides that it is in the best interests of the corporation not to pursue the claim and the corporation moves that it be dismissed. If the committee meets the requirements of the business judgment rule, this decision must be accepted and the case should be dismissed. *Gall v. Exxon Corp.*, 418 F.Supp. 508 (S.D.N.Y.1976).

Example: In the previous example, the plaintiff may obtain a hearing in an effort show that the committee was not a "disinterested" committee; if so, its conclusion would not be protected by the business judgment rule.

Example: Sanford is the President of Duke University, the former governor of North Carolina, a personal friend of J.B. Fuqua, the dominant shareholder in Fuqua Industries, and a director of that corporation. J.B Fuqua is a trustee of Duke University who has made a number of contributions to that University. J.B. Fuqua is named a defendant in a derivative suit alleging that he and other directors (but not Sanford) have taken a corporate opportunity in purchasing shares of Triton, Inc. common stock. Sanford is named a committee of one to review the allegations and recommend action to be taken. Held, Sanford's recommendation that the litigation be dismissed is not entitled to business judgment rule protection as a matter of law, since Sanford is not clearly an independent director whose decision is entitled to the protection of that rule. *Lewis v. Fuqua,* 502 A.2d 962 (Del.Ch. 1985).

Caveat: The more common practice is to have a committee of two or more directors, in part in order to avoid the result reached in the foregoing example.

d. The Delaware courts have developed a complex set of rules with respect to the dismissal of derivative litigation. The test for the application of the business judgment rule depends predominantly on whether the case is a "demand excused" or a "demand required" case.

1) *Zapata Corp. v. Maldonado,* 430 A.2d 779 (Del.1981), holds that where a demand on directors is excused, a court may exercise its own "independent business judgment" to determine whether litigation should be dismissed over the objection of the plaintiff solely on the basis of the business judgment of directors.

Example: In the previous example involving Exxon, if all the directors were involved in the payments so that a demand on the board of directors was excused, under *Zapata v. Maldonado* the court may exercise its own independent business judgment as to whether it is in Exxon's best interest to pursue the litigation.

2) *Aronson v. Lewis,* 473 A.2d 805 (Del.1984), holds that the *Maldonado* approach is only applicable in "demand unnecessary" or "demand futile" cases. Where demand is required, then the decision whether or not to

pursue the litigation is vested in the board of directors under Delaware law, and the business judgment rule controls. There is no room for the judicial exercise of "independent business judgment" under *Maldonado* if the independent litigation committee or the board of directors has made a decision to discontinue the litigation that is protected by the business judgment rule.

3) The test for demand futility under *Aronson* is two-fold: (A) whether on the basis of the particular facts alleged there is a reasonable doubt that the board of directors has the independence and disinterestedness necessary for application of the business judgment rule, and (B) whether the facts alleged with particularity, when taken as true, support a reasonable doubt that the challenged transaction was the product of a valid exercise of business judgment.

(i) Later Delaware cases restate the test in somewhat different terms. *Levine v. Smith,* 591 A.2d 194, 205–206 (Del.1991)[citations omitted; emphasis in original]:

"The premise of a shareholder claim of futility of demand is that a majority of the board of directors either has a financial interest in the challenged transaction or lacks independence or otherwise failed to exercise due care. On either showing, it may be inferred that the Board is *incapable* of exercising its power and authority to pursue the derivative claims directly. When lack of independence is charged, a plaintiff must show that the Board is either dominated by an officer or director who is the proponent of the challenged transaction or that the Board is so under his influence that its discretion is 'sterilize[d].'

"Assuming a plaintiff cannot prove that directors are interested or otherwise incapable of exercising independent business judgment, a plaintiff in a demand futility case must plead particularized facts creating a reasonable doubt as to the 'soundness' of the challenged transaction sufficient to rebut the presumption that the business judgment rule attaches to the transaction."

(ii) To avoid the business judgment rule the plaintiff must overcome one of these two hurdles. If both conditions are met, a demand is required and the decision of the board or committee is thereafter entitled to the protections of the business judgment rule.

(iii) The decision as to whether demand is futile must be made on the basis of the "particularized facts" set forth in the pleadings without the benefit of discovery. "Conclusory" allegations are insufficient.

(iv) If plaintiff makes a demand, that is of itself a concession by the plaintiffs that the case is a demand required case, and the rules described above apply. *Stotland v. GAF Corp.,* 469 A.2d 421 (Del. 1983); *Spiegel v. Buntrock,* 571 A.2d 767 (Del.1990).

(v) If the board of directors appoints a special litigation committee with the ultimate power of decision, that is a concession by the board of directors that it is interested, and if a later decision by the board of directors with respect to that litigation is made, that decision is not entitled to business judgment rule protection. *Abbey v. Computer & Communications Technology Corp.,* 457 A.2d 368 (Del.Ch.1983).

(vi) Most Delaware cases since *Aronson* have concluded that demand is required and therefore that the business judgment rule is applicable to the decision of the independent litigation committee or board of directors to discontinue the litigation.

Example: Fink, the owner of 47 per cent of stock of Meyers, is 75 years old. He enters into an employment agreement with Meyers at $150,000 per year plus a bonus of 5 per cent of its pre-tax profits over $2,400,000. The contract is for five years, renewable thereafter by Fink on a year to year basis. After termination, Fink is to become a consultant to Meyers, at an annual salary of $150,000 per year for three years, $125,000 per year for the next three years, and $100,000 per year thereafter for life. Compensation is not to be affected by Fink's inability to perform services. It is alleged that a demand would have been futile because Fink has personally selected and approved each director of Meyers. All the directors are named as defendants in the derivative suit. Held, the complaint should be dismissed for failing to make a demand. The allegations of control by Fink do not contain "particularized facts" and are "[conclusions] devoid of factual support." *Aronson v. Lewis,* 473 A.2d 805 (1984).

Example: Perot becomes a director and the largest shareholder of General Motors Corporation when he sells his shares of EDS to GM. Management differences develop between Perot and other GM directors and officers; Perot becomes increasingly vocal about his disagreements and states he is no longer a "company man." Perot and GM then negotiate a sale of Perot's stock in GM to GM at a substantial premium over market value; Perot agrees to stop criticizing GM management, to refrain from engaging in a proxy contest against the board of directors of GM for five years, and not to compete with EDS for a specified period. The terms of the transaction are reviewed by a Special Review Committee composed of outside directors of GM and approved. Held, the complaint does not set forth particularized allegations of waste, the purchase of shares at a premium may be the reasonable exercise of business judgment, and the "hush mail" provisions do not alone establish an improper motive. Therefore demand is required, and the decision of the board of directors to buy out Perot is based on the exercise of business judgment and more intensive judicial review is improper. *Grobow v. Perot,* 539 A.2d 180 (Del. 1988); *Levine v. Smith,* 591 A.2d 194 (Del.1991).

Example: A corporation facing a takeover bid arranges with its ESOP to purchase 30 per cent of the corporation's shares through a bank loan secured by a lien on the corporation's assets. This transaction effectively shifts control of the corporation to the ESOP and commits the corporation to a disposition of most of its cash and a substantial portion of its assets. Held, the negative consequences of the transaction are so great that there is reasonable doubt that the decision to enter into the transaction is the product of business judgment. *RCM Securities Fund, Inc. v. Stanton,* 928 F.2d 1318 (2d Cir. 1991).

4) The demand futile/demand required distinction has led to extensive pre-trial skirmishing in the Delaware courts since the issue is not a procedural one, but a substantive one that is likely to be outcome determinative: is the decision by the independent litigation committee protected by the business judgment rule? Some judges have questioned the desirability of the Delaware approach. (See part XVIII C 1 a.)

5) The Delaware law of demand futile/demand required must be followed by federal courts in cases based on substantive federal law or diversity of citizenship that involve Delaware corporations. *Kamen v. Kemper Financial Services, Inc.,* ___ U.S. ___, 111 S.Ct. 1711 (1991); *RCM Securities Fund, Inc. v. Stanton,* 928 F.2d 1318 (2d Cir.1991).

e. The MBCA (1984) § 7.42 requires a written demand on directors in all cases. Section 7.44 does not tie the business judgment rule issue to the requirement of a demand but expands on the general standard of due care of § 8.30 in the context of dismissal of derivative litigation.

f. The Corporate Governance Project of the American Law Institute also requires demand in virtually all cases. In addition, it permits limited judicial review of the decision to dismiss derivative litigation prior to discovery.

g. A few courts have accepted the principle of *Maldonado* without apparently restricting it to demand excused cases.

1) *Joy v. North,* 692 F.2d 880 (2d Cir.1982)[Connecticut law], was the first such case.

2) *Miller v. Register & Tribune Syndicate, Inc.,* 336 N.W.2d 709 (Iowa 1983) holds that where a majority of the directors are named as defendants, the board of directors may not establish a litigation committee with the power of the board to terminate derivative litigation. Rather, the board must apply to a court for the appointment of a trustee or receiver if it wishes to discontinue the litigation.

3) In *Alford v. Shaw,* 358 S.E.2d 323 (N.C.1987) the court held that it was error to "rely blindly on the report of a corporation-appointed committee which assembled such materials on behalf of the corporation." The decisions in *Auerbach* and *Aronson* therefore should not be followed and courts should apply their independent business judgment when reviewing such decisions.

2. DISMISSAL FOR FAILURE TO MEET PROCEDURAL REQUIREMENTS

A suit may be dismissed if there is a failure to comply with requirements which are peculiar to such suits.

Example: A failure to make a demand on the directors, or a failure to post security-for-expenses when required to do so, will result in the dismissal of the suit.

3. MISCELLANEOUS SUBSTANTIVE DEFENSES

Defenses which would have been available to third party defendants if the corporation had sued directly on the claim that is the underlying basis of the derivative suit are also defenses to the derivative litigation.

Example: The action may be barred by the statute of limitations or statute of frauds. Such defenses usually may only be raised by the third party defendants, not the corporate defendant.

Example: A defense based on ratification of the transaction by directors or shareholders may be available if the transaction is voidable rather than void, or if it falls within the business judgment rule. Such defenses may arise from director or shareholder action after the claim is presented by the plaintiff, and usually may be raised by the corporate defendant as well as the individual defendants.

4. DISQUALIFICATION OF THE PLAINTIFF

Another class of defenses are those available against the specific shareholder plaintiff but which may not be available against other shareholder plaintiffs. Derivative suits basically involve two separate claims: first, the substantive claim by the corporation against a third person and second, the claim by the shareholder that he or she should be permitted to represent or champion the corporation. The defenses in this class go to the latter issue.

Example: Laches may bar some shareholders but not others from acting as plaintiff.

Example: If the plaintiff actually participated in the wrongful transaction, or assented to it, he or she may be estopped from questioning the transaction. Shares owned by such a disqualified person are called "tainted shares" or "dirty stock" and even innocent transferees of such shares may be estopped from questioning the transaction.

E. DERIVATIVE SUITS IN FEDERAL COURTS

In recent years, the bulk of shareholder class and derivative litigation has been brought in the federal courts, usually under the federal securities laws, but also often on the basis of diversity of citizenship.

1. CLASSIFICATION OF PARTIES FOR DIVERSITY PURPOSES

For purposes of diversity in derivative suits, if it appears on the face of the pleadings and by the nature of the controversy that the corporation is antagonistic to the enforcement of the claim, the corporation is aligned as a defendant. *Smith v. Sperling*, 354 U.S. 91, 77 S.Ct. 1112 (1957).

2. PENDENT JURISDICTION

Plaintiffs are often able to state a cause of action under both federal and state law.

a. Suits involving such situations are usually brought in the federal courts since the concept of "pendent jurisdiction" permits the federal courts to determine both the federal and state claim in a single proceeding even in the absence of diversity of citizenship.

b. State courts do not have jurisdiction over claims arising under the federal securities acts, and thus cannot adjudicate all claims for relief in a single proceeding.

c. The preference for the federal forum also may be based on more generous discovery rights, nationwide service of process under the federal securities acts, the avoidance of state security-for-expense statutes, and other procedural advantages.

d. Substantive advantages that are sometimes cited—e.g. a belief that federal courts are more sympathetic to minority plaintiffs than state courts and the greater liberality of federal securities law—are doubtful.

F. MISCELLANEOUS PROCEDURAL PROBLEMS

The shareholder plaintiff and the corporate defendant both have unique roles in derivative litigation: the shareholder is a nominal plaintiff while the corporation is a nominal defendant but the real plaintiff. These unique roles lead to a variety of procedural issues.

1. NECESSARY PARTY

The corporation is a necessary party; without it the action cannot proceed. *Dean v. Kellogg*, 292 N.W. 704 (Mich.1940).

2. COMBINATION OF CLAIMS

The power to mix personal and derivative claims in a single law suit is often restricted or prohibited.

a. The plaintiff shareholder may not combine individual or direct actions with a derivative action in the same suit, though some exceptions have been permitted.

b. The plaintiff shareholder may not be subject to personal counterclaims.

c. The defendant corporation may be limited in the defenses it may assert on behalf of its codefendants. *Otis & Co. v. Pennsylvania R. Co.*, 57 F.Supp. 680 (E.D.Pa.1944).

3. MULTIPLE SUITS

Since a derivative suit has class as well as derivative aspects, multiple derivative suits may be filed by several different shareholders.

a. In the absence of other considerations, the suit first filed should proceed while later actions may be stayed, dismissed, or consolidated with the initial suit. *Schiff v. Metzner*, 331 F.2d 963 (2d Cir.1964).

b. Counsel for the shareholder first bringing suit is usually permitted to control the litigation from the plaintiff's standpoint. The court, however, may designate an attorney for another shareholder as the principal counsel for plaintiffs.

c. Intervention by other shareholders is permitted and indeed may be encouraged if for some reason the representation of the original plaintiff shareholder may be considered questionable or inadequate.

4. THE ROLE OF CORPORATE COUNSEL

Even though the corporation is technically a defendant, its interest in the litigation is usually adverse to the interest of the other defendants.

a. The same lawyer normally may not represent the defendant corporation as well as other defendants. *Cannon v. U. S. Acoustics Corp.*, 398 F.Supp. 209 (N.D.Ill.1975); *Marco v. Dulles*, 169 F.Supp. 622 (S.D.N.Y.1959). Such multiple representation may be permitted only if it is clear that there is no possible conflict. *Seifert v. Dumatic Industries, Inc.*, 197 A.2d 454 (Pa.1964).

b. The attorney-client privilege between corporation and counsel may not be invoked by current management, who may be the real defendants in the suit. *Garner v. Wolfinbarger*, 430 F.2d 1093 (5th Cir.1970).

c. An attorney involved in an investigation of wrongdoing for a client may be disqualified to serve later as a derivative plaintiff based on that wrongdoing. *Richardson v. Hamilton Intern. Corp.*, 469 F.2d 1382 (3d Cir.1972); *Cannon v. U. S. Acoustics Corp.*, 398 F.Supp. 209 (N.D.Ill.1975).

d. Corporations must appear through counsel. They cannot appear *in proper person* or be represented by a lay officer. *Union Sav. Ass'n v. Home Owners Aid, Inc.*, 262 N.E.2d 558 (Ohio 1970).

5. JURY TRIALS

Derivative suits are equitable in nature, a categorization which may be significant in resolving procedural questions. In *Ross v. Bernhard*, 396 U.S. 531, 90 S.Ct. 733 (1970), the United States Supreme Court held that a right to jury trial may exist in derivative suits brought in federal courts where the issue is of a "legal" (as contrasted with an "equitable") nature.

6. MERGER OF CORPORATE DEFENDANT

If the independent existence of the corporate defendant disappears by merger or similar transaction during the pendency of the suit, the suit is dismissed unless the surviving entity is added as a party defendant. *Niesz v. Gorsuch*, 295 F.2d 909 (9th Cir.1961).

a. Statutes may provide for the continuation of litigation against the surviving entity.

b. Shareholders of the new or surviving entity may be able to sue that entity derivatively on the same claim.

c. In the case of a "cash out" merger in which the plaintiff shareholder receives cash and ceases to be a shareholder, the plaintiff may no longer maintain the suit.

7. COLLATERAL ESTOPPEL

Defendants in a derivative suit may be prohibited from relitigating issues as to violations of securities acts resolved adversely to them in a prior proceeding brought by the SEC or other governmental agency. *Rachal v. Hill*, 435 F.2d 59 (5th Cir.1970).

G. SETTLEMENT OF DERIVATIVE SUITS

Historically, the secret settlement of shareholders' suits was viewed as a serious evil. The settling shareholder sometimes received substantial sums which in fact were payments to ignore a corporate wrong. Suits brought solely for their settlement value are usually called "strike suits."

1. THE NATURE OF SETTLEMENT NEGOTIATIONS

The settlement of a derivative suit generally involves negotiation between the attorneys for the plaintiffs, the corporation, and the individual defendants. Negotiations may involve a number of issues.

a. The amounts, if any, to be paid by the individual defendants to the corporation.

b. Changes in procedures, if any, to be made by the corporation to prevent recurrence of improper conduct.

c. The amount to be paid to the plaintiffs' attorneys, either out of funds to be paid to the corporation by the individual defendants or by the corporation directly from its own assets.

d. Whether the corporation or the individual defendants will affirmatively support the fees to be paid to the plaintiff's attorneys.

2. JUDICIAL APPROVAL

The problem of secret or corrupt settlements has now been largely resolved by bringing the process of settlement of derivative or class suits under judicial control.

a. Such suits may not be dismissed or compromised without the approval of the court.

b. Notice of the proposed dismissal or compromise must be given to shareholders or members in such manner as the court directs.

3. JUDICIAL REVIEW OF SETTLEMENTS

In exercising discretion to review proposed settlements, courts consider whether the proposed settlement is reasonable, fair and adequate. *Saylor v. Bastedo,* 594 F.Supp. 371 (S.D.N.Y.1984); *Lewis v. Newman,* 59 F.R.D. 525 (S.D.N.Y.1973); *Perrine v. Pennroad Corp.,* 47 A.2d 479 (Del.1946); *Shlensky v. Dorsey,* 574 F.2d 131 (3d Cir.1978). Among the factors considered are:

a. The size of the potential recovery and the size of the suggested settlement.

b. The probability of ultimate success.

c. The complexity, expense and likely duration of the litigation.

d. The financial position of the defendants.

e. The amount proposed to be awarded as fees to the plaintiffs' attorneys. Courts appear to be increasingly willing to inquire closely into the fees being sought by the plaintiffs' attorneys.

4. NOTICE AND HEARING ON SETTLEMENT

Shareholders are entitled to notice of, and may appear at the hearing on, a proposed settlement and object to its terms.

5. DERIVATIVE PURSUIT OF SECRET SETTLEMENT

Courts have held that where a secret settlement has led to a payment to a derivative plaintiff, other shareholders may bring a derivative suit in the name of the corporation against the settling shareholder to recover the payment. *Clarke v. Greenberg,* 71 N.E.2d 443 (N.Y.1947).

6. SETTLEMENT OF UNDERLYING CLAIM

A corporation may itself settle a claim that is in litigation without court approval and without the consent of the plaintiffs' attorneys, but that settlement itself may be made the basis of a later derivative suit. *Wolf v. Barkes,* 348 F.2d 994 (2d Cir. 1965).

7. RES JUDICATA EFFECT OF SETTLEMENT

See the discussion in part XVIII F below.

H. RECOVERY IN DERIVATIVE SUITS

A recovery in a derivative suit is usually payable to the corporation rather than to individual shareholders on a pro rata basis or to the plaintiff.

1. JUSTIFICATION OF RULE

This principle normally protects fully the interest of shareholders and creditors alike, and does not involve the court in making a business judgment as to whether corporate funds should be distributed as a kind of dividend to some or all of the shareholders.

2. EXCEPTION WHERE WRONGDOERS ARE MAJOR SHAREHOLDERS

If an individual wrongdoer who is required to satisfy the judgment obtained in the derivative suit is also a significant shareholder, a corporate recovery permits that defendant to share indirectly in, and, if a controlling shareholder, to control the use of, the recovery.

a. In a few instances, courts have been persuaded to grant shareholders a pro rata recovery in this type of situation in order to limit the recovery to "innocent" shareholders or to prevent the "guilty" shareholder from "benefitting from his own wrong."

Example: In *Perlman v. Feldmann,* 219 F.2d 173 (2d Cir.1955) a control premium paid to a former controlling shareholder was held to be recoverable and payable to the nonselling shareholders pro rata on the theory that it was improper for the persons presently in control (who had paid the control premium to the defendants) to share in the recovery.

b. Such cases are a minority view. *Keenan v. Eshleman,* 2 A.2d 904 (Del.1938); *Norte & Co. v. Huffines,* 416 F.2d 1189 (2d Cir.1969). *Schachter v. Kulik,* 547 N.E.2d 71 (N.Y.1989) [recovery should go to the corporation even where there are only two shareholders].

c. A pro rata recovery to "innocent" shareholders often gives rise to serious logical, practical and conceptual problems.

Example: In the *Perlman* case, consider the situation if the persons presently in control of the corporation (who paid a control premium to Feldmann) themselves resell for another control premium. Can they argue that the noncontrol shareholders, having already been compensated for the absence of control by sharing in Feldmann's premium, cannot complain of the second sale?

Example: The controlling shares in *Perlman* that were sold for a premium constituted 35 per cent of the outstanding shares. The remaining 65 per cent of the shares were widely fragmented. If, however, the 65 per cent is combined or organized it may become the control block. Does it have any responsibility to return the "control premium" it previously received as noncontrolling shares?

3. OTHER RELIEF

In appropriate cases plaintiffs may obtain non-monetary relief, e. g. dissolution, *White v. Perkins*, 189 S.E.2d 315 (Va.1972), or the appointment of a receiver, *Robinson v. Thompson*, 466 S.W.2d 626 (Tex.Civ.App.1971).

I. RES JUDICATA

The res judicata effect of the termination of a derivative suit depends on the manner of or basis for the termination.

1. FINAL JUDGMENT ON THE MERITS

A final judgment on the merits is res judicata and binding on all other shareholders, including any who were original parties to the suit but thereafter withdrew.

Caveat: This assumes that the plaintiff shareholder was an adequate representative of the class of shareholders.

2. SETTLEMENTS

A court-approved settlement ordinarily has the same effect as a final judgment on the merits. *Berger v. Dyson*, 111 F.Supp. 533 (D.R.I.1953), though problems may arise as to whether shareholders are bound if they were not notified of the proposed settlement; *Manufacturers Mut. Fire Ins. Co. v. Hopson*, 25 N.Y.S.2d 502 (1940); *Shlensky v. Dorsey*, 574 F.2d 131 (3d Cir.1978); or if it is claimed that the settlement was based on culpable nondisclosure of relevant evidence or collusion between plaintiff's and defendant's counsel; *Alleghany Corp. v. Kirby*, 333 F.2d 327 (2d Cir.1964).

3. DISMISSAL OF SUIT

The res judicata effect of a dismissal of a derivative suit depends on the reason for the dismissal.

a. A voluntary dismissal, or a dismissal because the plaintiff shareholder does not qualify as a proper plaintiff is "without prejudice" and does not bind the class.

Example: A dismissal for failure to post security for expenses does not bind the class.

Example: A dismissal for failure to respond to interrogatories does not bind the class. *Papilsky v. Berndt*, 466 F.2d 251 (2d Cir.1972).

b. In some situations, the court may order that notice be given to all other shareholders before a derivative action is dismissed voluntarily. Such action may then be continued by intervening shareholders, or if none appear, the action may be dismissed "with prejudice."

c. A dismissal on the merits—that the complaint does not state a claim on which relief can be granted or that the decision of a litigation committee not to pursue the litigation is protected by the business judgment rule —binds all members of the class.

J. LITIGATION EXPENSES

If the plaintiff is successful, she is usually awarded her expenses, including attorney's fees. Such a recovery is justified in equity as encouraging meritorious shareholders' suits.

1. CREATION OF A FUND

Usually, the plaintiff's expenses are paid out of the funds obtained by the corporation as a result of the suit.

2. NON–FUND CASES

Expenses of the plaintiff may also be ordered to be reimbursed by the corporation even where the corporation receives no money as a result of the litigation so long as the result of the suit was of "some benefit" or "substantial benefit" to the corporation. *Bosch v. Meeker Co-op. Light & Power Ass'n*, 101 N.W.2d 423 (Minn. 1960); *Fletcher v. A. J. Industries, Inc.*, 72 Cal.Rptr. 146 (Cal.App.1968).

Caveat: MBCA (1984) § 7.46(1) adopts a "substantial benefit" standard. The Official Comment states that the purpose of the language is "to prevent the plaintiff from proposing inconsequential changes in order to justify the payment of counsel fees."

Example: Expenses may be awarded in a suit which results only in an injunction against the officers and directors of a corporation engaging in improper conduct.

Caveat: A payment of the plaintiff's expenses by the corporation does not compel the "losing party" to pay the other's expenses since both the corporation and the plaintiff are winning parties.

3. AMOUNT OF PLAINTIFFS' ATTORNEYS' FEES

The size of the attorney's fee to be awarded successful plaintiffs' counsel depends on a variety of factors: the nature and character of the litigation, the skill required, the amount of work actually performed, the size of the recovery, the nature of the harm prevented, and other factors.

a. The fee must be reasonable; its size is determined or approved by the court and is a question of fact on which evidence may be taken.

Example: A fee of $200,000 in a suit leading to a $1,025,000 settlement was upheld.

b. Where derivative litigation is settled, the plaintiffs' attorneys fees may be negotiated as part of the settlement. Such fees are subject to judicial review and approval.

1) As a practical matter, it may be difficult for a judge to effectively review the reasonableness of an agreed fee if all settling parties support the reasonableness of the negotiated fee.

2) If a case is settled in which no funds are received by the corporation, the corporation may pay the plaintiffs' attorneys out of its general assets.

4. DEFENDANTS' EXPENSES

In limited circumstances defendants may be entitled to have their fees and expenses paid by the plaintiffs or by the corporation.

a. If the plaintiff has posted security for expenses (see part XVIII C 4), the defendants' may have recourse to that security if authorized by the court.

b. If a court determines that the plaintiff has filed suit without reasonable cause or has interposed pleadings not in good faith, expenses incurred thereby may be recoverable from the plaintiff or her attorney if authorized by the court. (See part XVIII C 4) i.)

c. Defendants may be entitled to be indemnified by the corporation for their expenses. (See part XVI.)

d. Defendants may be entitled to require an insurance company that has written a directors and officers liability policy on behalf of the corporation to pay their expenses.

K. REVIEW QUESTIONS

XVIII–1. What is the difference between "direct" and "derivative" litigation?

XVIII–2. Is there a clear distinction between direct and derivative litigation?

XVIII–3. What is a "class" suit?

XVIII–4. Is a derivative suit a class suit?

XVIII–5. In a derivative suit, is the corporation named as a plaintiff or a defendant?

XVIII–6. A shareholder brings a derivative suit complaining that the board of directors approved the payment of a bonus of $20,000,000 to the chief executive officer of the corporation, who is also chairman of the board of directors and owner of 45 per cent of the voting stock of the corporation. The complaint alleges that payment of a bonus of this magnitude was unrelated to the value of the services provided by the chief executive officer and constituted waste. The complaint further alleges that no demand was made because it would be futile since all the directors "are personal friends of the chief executive officer and will not do anything that the chief executive officer opposes." The corporation moves that the complaint should be dismissed for failing to make a demand on directors. Should that motion be granted?

XVIII–7. In the preceding question, before filing the suit, the shareholder makes a demand on the board of directors that the bonus paid to the chief executive officer be rescinded on the ground that it is unrelated to the value of the services provided by the chief executive officer and constitutes waste. The board of directors appoints a litigation committee of two directors, neither of whom were on the board of directors at the time the bonus was approved, to consider the demand made by the shareholder. The two members of the litigation committee also have no direct connection with the corporation other than serving as outside directors. The litigation committee reviews the circumstances under which the bonus was paid and concludes in a written report that it is not in the best interests of the corporation to seek to rescind the bonus. The shareholder then files suit. The corporation moves that the suit be dismissed on the ground the decision of the litigation committee is final and conclusive. The plaintiff opposes this motion on the ground that he is entitled to a judicial decision on the merits of his claim. Should the corporation's motion be granted?

XVIII–8. To what extent are federal courts involved in derivative litigation?

XVIII–9. What is the "contemporaneous ownership" requirement and what is its justification in federal and state courts?

XVIII–10. What are the procedural prerequisites for maintaining a derivative suit?

XVIII–11. Why is derivative litigation often treated with mistrust?

XVIII–12. What are the policy considerations underlying a state legislative decision whether or not to eliminate the security-for-expenses statute?

XVIII–13. What are the consequences of a decision that a derivative plaintiff must comply with the security-for-expenses statute?

XVIII–14. Is the state security-for-expenses statute applicable in the federal courts?

XVIII–15. Is the security-for-expenses statute applicable to direct and class litigation?

XVIII–16. Is a final decision in a derivative suit *res judicata* and binding on all shareholders?

XVIII–17. Are any limitations placed on the power of a plaintiff to accept a settlement offer in a derivative suit?

XVIII–18. What is a "strike suit" and how are such suits handled under modern practice?

XVIII–19. May a plaintiff who is successful in a derivative suit recover attorneys fees and other expenses even if the corporation does not receive any money from the suit?

XVIII–20. Is there any situation in which a derivative suit recovery is paid directly to the shareholders?

XVIII–21. Ps are shareholders in X corporation which is incorporated in State A. They have brought a derivative action on behalf of X in the courts of State B against X's majority shareholder, a director of X, and another corporation also owned by X's majority shareholder. Ps claim that the majority shareholder has looted X by a series of transactions with the other corporation and that X is entitled to an accounting. Ps have obtained service of process on all defendants except X. The defendants have moved to dismiss Ps' petition on the ground that the court lacked jurisdiction of X, an essential party. Ps claim that if the suit may not be maintained in personam it may be brought as an action in rem in that the cause of action is property of X within the state. Are the defendants who were served entitled to dismissal?

XVIII–22. P brought an action against the directors of D corporation on D's behalf for breach of fiduciary duties. The court found the directors liable in an amount of $4,355,595, in that they had appropriated an opportunity of D to purchase shares in another corporation. The defendant directors contend the award of damages should be limited to those who were shareholders at the time of the share transaction. Are the defendants correct in their contention?

*

XIX

ORGANIC CHANGES

Organic or fundamental changes in corporations may be broadly classified by type: amendments to articles of incorporations, statutory mergers or consolidations, non-statutory amalgamations, sales of substantially all assets, and dissolution. The rules about how these changes are approved depend to some extent on the type of change involved and each is discussed below.

Analysis

- *C. Sales of Substantially All Assets*
    - *1. Sales in Ordinary Course of Business*
    - *2. Meaning of the Phrase "All or Substantially All"*
    - *3. Procedural Requirements*
- *D. Nonstatutory Amalgamations*
    - *1. Types of Transactions*
    - *2. Selection of Form of Transaction*
- *E. Recapitalizations*
    - *1. Economics of Transactions*
    - *2. Form of Transaction*
    - *3. Validity of Transactions*
- *F. "Going Private"*
    - *1. Economics of Transaction*
    - *2. Form of Going Private Transactions*
    - *3. Regulation of Going Private Transactions*
- *G. Leveraged Buyouts*
    - *1. Characteristics*
- *H. Right of Dissent and Appraisal*
    - *1. Scope of Right*
    - *2. Exclusiveness of Appraisal Right*
    - *3. Procedure for Appraisal*
    - *4. Evaluation of Appraisal Remedy*
- *I. Voluntary Dissolution*
    - *1. Dissolution Before Commencement of Business*
    - *2. Dissolution by Unanimous Consent of Shareholders*
    - *3. Regular Dissolution*
    - *4. Procedure Following Decision to Dissolve*
    - *5. Dissolution Procedures*
    - *6. Equitable Limitations on Dissolution*
- *J. Review Questions*

A. AMENDMENTS OF ARTICLES OF INCORPORATION

Under modern statutes, articles of incorporation may be freely amended. MBCA (1984) § 10.01.

1. SUBSTANTIVE OR CONSTITUTIONAL LIMITATIONS

MBCA (1984) § 10.01(b) states "A shareholder of the corporation does not have a vested property right resulting from any provision in the articles of incorporation, including provisions relating to management, control, capital structure, dividend entitlement, or purpose or duration of the corporation." Many state statutes contain similar provisions.

a. The argument that rights created by specific provisions in the articles of incorporation are "vested" or "property rights" is basically a constitutional argument. *Trustees of Dartmouth College v. Woodward*, 17 U.S. (4 Wheat.) 518 (1819) did impose restraints on the power of the state to adopt a statute that amended previously issued articles of incorporation.

   1) But the court also recognized that states might avoid this problem by enacting a "reservation" of power to amend statutes applicable to all corporations created thereafter.

   2) All states have reserved the power of amendment and hence the issues discussed in *Dartmouth College* are not constitutional issues for modern corporations. *Dentel v. Fidelity Sav. & Loan Ass'n*, 539 P.2d 649 (Or.1975).

   3) Constitutional arguments, however, continue to be made in cases, and in a few instances (mostly from the nineteenth century) courts have found a constitutional obstacle to specific amendments by construing the reservation power very narrowly.

b. Some cases have adopted a view of "vested rights" with respect to specific provisions of articles of incorporation that is not expressly based on constitutional right. These cases in effect require unanimous agreement by shareholders to amend the articles of incorporation; these cases probably have been overruled by statutes similar to MBCA (1984) § 10.01(b). *Cowan v. Salt Lake Hardware Co.*, 221 P.2d 625 (Utah 1950).

   1) The argument that certain rights are "vested" rights that cannot be eliminated over the objection of a single shareholder may continue to have limited vitality in a few states.

   2) One issue on which this theory was applied as late as the 1930s is whether arrearages of cumulative dividends on preferred stock may be eliminated by amendment to the articles of incorporation. *Keller v. Wilson & Co.*, 190 A. 115 (Del.1936).

3) The "vested rights" argument permits individual minority shareholders to act in an opportunistic manner by declining to agree to amendments unless they receive special consideration or payment.

4) In lieu of the vested rights theory some courts have evolved a broad equitable principle that majority shareholders and directors must act in a fair way toward the corporation and minority shareholders.

(i) This principle may provide entry into the courtroom for minority shareholders who claim that an amendment serves no purpose other than injuring minority shareholders. *Dentel v. Fidelity Sav. & Loan Ass'n*, 539 P.2d 649 (Or.1975).

(ii) The test may be phrased as "good faith" or "reasonableness" or "business purpose."

5) A transaction that runs afoul of the vested rights theory as an amendment to the articles may sometimes be valid if it is structured as a merger transaction. *Bove v. Community Hotel Corp. of Newport, R. I.*, 249 A.2d 89 (R.I.1969). Often an amendment may be indirectly effected by a merger of a corporation into its newly created and wholly owned subsidiary. (See part XIX B 3.)

2. STATUTORY LIMITATIONS

Amended articles of incorporation may contain any provision that may lawfully be placed in original articles of incorporation at the time of the amendment. MBCA (1984) § 10.01(a).

Caveat: Irrespective of the vested rights theory, amendments to the articles of incorporation may be invalid if the amendment is not authorized by the statute, if the procedural requirements set forth in the statute are not fully complied with, or if there is a failure to provide accurate and complete information about the effect of a proposed amendment.

3. PROCEDURAL REQUIREMENTS

State statutes relating to approval of amendments to articles of incorporation vary widely. In addition, most states permit amendments to be made in different ways.

a. Most states permit minor amendments to be made by the incorporators or initial directors before shares have been issued. MBCA (1984) § 10.05.

b. MBCA (1984) authorizes the board of directors, acting alone, to adopt certain minor types of amendments. MBCA (1984) § 10.02.

1) A few states have adopted similar provisions.

2) Amendments permitted under MBCA (1984) § 10.02 include extending the duration of the corporation if it was incorporated at a time when limited duration was required by law, to delete the names and addresses of the initial directors, to delete the name and address of the initial registered agent if the registered agent has since been changed, to change each issued share of the only outstanding class of shares into a greater number of whole shares of the same class, and to change the corporate name by substituting words of incorporation (e.g. "inc." "co.", "ltd.").

c. MBCA (1984) and the statutes of many states authorize amendments to articles of incorporation of corporations in bankruptcy or reorganization to be made by order of court without requiring approval of either shareholders or directors. MBCA (1984) § 10.08.

d. The most common pattern for amending the articles of incorporation involves action by the board of directors and approval by a specified percentage of the votes of shareholders. All important amendments must follow this procedure.

1) The board of directors must initiate a proposal to amend the articles of incorporation in most states.

Caveat: In Delaware and a few other states, shareholders may act by majority written consent without preliminary action by the board of directors. Presumably in these states, amendments to articles of incorporation may be proposed by shareholders when they seek majority consent to the action.

2) After action by the board of directors, the proposed amendments must be submitted to the shareholders for approval.

(i) Notice of the proposed amendment must be given to every shareholder, voting and nonvoting alike. The notice of the meeting must contain or be accompanied by a copy or summary of the amendment. MBCA (1984) § 10.03(d).

(ii) Some states require a ⅔ds vote of all outstanding shares, both voting and nonvoting to approve an amendment. Other states require either a majority of all outstanding shares, both voting and nonvoting, or a majority of the outstanding voting shares.

(iii) These are all supermajority provisions, requiring a higher percentage of shareholder approval than for ordinary actions.

(iv) There is a trend toward requiring only a majority vote of the outstanding voting shares to approve an amendment.

3) States require that certain types of amendments be approved by each class of shares voting separately. This is known as "class voting" in most statutes and "voting by voting groups in the MBCA (1984).

e. The MBCA (1984), adopts a different pattern for approval of amendments to articles of incorporation.

1) The board of directors, when it approves amendments to be presented to shareholders, may condition the submission on such terms as it desires, e. g., that the amendment be approved by each class of shares, voting as separate voting groups, even though not specifically required by statute.

2) The vote required for approval of an amendment depends on whether the amendment creates dissenters' rights (discussed in part XIX H).

(i) If the amendment does not give rise to dissenters' rights, it is approved by the vote required for approval of any ordinary matter at the shareholders' meeting: at a meeting at which a quorum is present, the votes in favor of the amendment must exceed the votes opposed to the amendment. MBCA (1984) § 10.03(e)(2).

Example: A corporation has 100 shares outstanding. At the meeting at which an amendment that does not give rise to dissenters' rights is considered, 60 shares are represented. The amendment is approved if the shares voted in favor of the amendment exceed those voted against the amendment at the meeting. If 28 shares are voted in favor of the amendment and 26 shares are voted against the amendment, 6 shares abstaining, the amendment is approved.

(ii) If the amendment does give rise to dissenters' rights, the vote required is a majority of the votes entitled to be cast on the amendment. MBCA (1984) § 10.03(e)(1).

Example: In the prior example, the amendment, if approved, would give rise to dissenters' rights. To be approved, the amendment must receive the favorable vote of holders of a majority of all outstanding shares—51 shares.

(iii) MBCA (1984) § 13.02(4) provides for dissenters' rights in connection with an amendment that:

A) alters or abolishes a preferential right of the shares;

B) creates, alters, or abolishes a right in respect of redemption, including a provision respecting a sinking fund for the redemption or repurchase, of the shares;

C) alters or abolishes a preemptive right of the holder of the shares to acquire shares or other securities;

D) excludes or limits the right of the shares to vote on any matter, or to cumulate votes, other than a limitation by dilution through issuance of shares or other securities with similar voting rights; or

E) reduces the number of shares owned by the shareholder to a fraction of a share if the fractional share so created is to be acquired for cash.

(iv) If the amendment makes a change in outstanding shares or rights of shareholders, or an exchange, reclassification or cancellation of shares or rights is to be made pursuant to the amendment, the amendment must specifically set forth the provisions necessary to effect the change, exchange, reclassification, or cancellation. Under the Model Business Corporation Act (1984) these implementing provisions may appear in the articles of amendment rather than in the amendments themselves. MBCA (1984) § 10.06(3).

f. After an amendment is approved, articles of amendment must be filed with the secretary of state.

g. A corporation that has filed several articles of amendments at various times may "restate" the articles of incorporation so as to create a single document for easy examination. MBCA (1984) § 10.07.

1) Restated articles of incorporation that do not make any substantive change may be approved by the board of directors acting alone.

2) Amendments to the articles of incorporation may be made while restating the articles of incorporation so long as notice is given of each amendment and the restated articles of incorporation are approved by the shareholders as though each amendment was submitted separately and not as part of a restatement.

Caveat: Restated articles of incorporation that change language of existing provisions should normally be submitted to the shareholders as an amendment to the articles of incorporation even though it is doubtful that a substantive change is being made. A common problem with restated articles of incorporation approved by the directors acting alone is concern that the restated articles of incorporation may differ substantively in some respect from the earlier articles of incorporation and articles of amendment.

4. PROCEDURAL PROTECTIONS AGAINST ABUSIVE AMENDMENTS

Since under modern statutes no shareholder has a vested right in any specific provision in articles of incorporation, the exercise of the broad power of amendment granted by modern business corporation acts may adversely affect the holders of one or more classes of securities to the advantage of holders of another class of securities. Important protections against such changes are procedural:

a. The principal protection against abuse, in most states, is the provision that requires an amendment that is burdensome to a single class of shares in a specified way be approved by a separate vote of that class of shares. In the Model Business Corporation Act (1984) the right to vote by classes is referred to as "voting by voting groups." See MBCA (1984) § 10.02, 10.03, 10.04, 7.25, 7.26, 1.40(26). In most statutes it is referred to as "class voting" or "voting by classes."

   1) MBCA (1984) § 10.04(a) lists nine types of amendments that give a class the right to vote as a separate voting group:

      (i) Amendments that increase or decrease the aggregate number of shares of that class;

      (ii) Amendments that effect an exchange or reclassification of shares of that class into shares of another class;

      (iii) Amendments that exchange or reclassify shares of another class into shares of that class;

      (iv) Amendments that change the designation, rights, preferences, or limitations of all or part of the shares of that class;

      (v) Amendments that change the shares of all or part of that class into a different number of shares of the same class;

      (vi) Amendments that create a new class with rights or preferences relating to distributions or dissolution that are superior to or equal with that class;

(vii) Amendments that increase the rights, preferences or number of shares of a class that have rights superior to or equal with the class;

(viii) Amendments that affect the preemptive rights of that class; and

(ix) Amendments that cancel or otherwise affect rights of that class to distributions that have accumulated but have not paid.

Caveat: The classes of amendments with respect to which the right to vote by voting groups is granted is similar to but not identical with the classes of amendments with respect to which a statutory right of dissent and appraisal exists.

2) The basic idea of voting by voting groups is that if a specified percentage of a class of shares adversely affected by an amendment is willing to accept that amendment, it should be approved.

3) Dissenting members of a voting group usually also have a statutory right of dissent and appraisal.

4) These statutes are generally construed to further the objective of requiring voting by voting groups on all amendments that are uniquely burdensome to the voting group as such. *Levin v. Mississippi River Fuel Corp.,* 386 U.S. 162, 87 S.Ct. 927 (1967).

5) Most statutes extend the right to vote by class only to classes of shares and not to series within a class.

(i) The theory is that the class of blank shares (out of which series are created) is itself a single class of shares.

(ii) This theory is unrealistic as a practical matter since differences between series may be as great as or greater than differences between classes.

(iii) MBCA (1984) §§ 10.04(b) and (c) in general terms extends the right to vote by voting groups to series that are affected in different ways but states that if an amendment affects two or more series in essentially the same way, the two series are to be combined as a single voting group on the amendment.

Caveat: Where separate classes (as contrasted with separate series) of shares are affected by an amendment in the same way, each of those classes is entitled to vote as a separate voting group and those classes may not be combined as a single voting group.

b. The second major protection provided by statute against abusive amendments is the right of dissent and appraisal. This right permits certain dissenting shareholders to have the value of their shares be ascertained by judicial proceeding and paid to them by the corporation. See part XIX H. The Model Business Corporation Act (1984) § 13.02(a)(4) grants the right of dissent and appraisal with respect to "an amendment of the articles of incorporation that materially and adversely affects rights in respect of a dissenter's shares because it:

"(1) alters or abolishes a preferential right of the shares;

"(2) creates, alters, or abolishes a right in respect of redemption, including a provision respecting a sinking fund for the redemption or repurchase, of the shares;

"(3) alters or abolishes a preemptive right of the holder of the shares to acquire shares or other securities;

"(4) excludes or limits the right of the shares to vote on any matter, or to cumulate votes, other than a limitation by dilution through issuance of shares or other securities with similar voting rights; or

"(5) reduces the number of shares owned by the shareholder to a fraction of a share if the fractional share so created is to be acquired for cash. . . ."

Caveat: The classes of amendments with respect to which the right of dissent and appraisal is granted is similar to but narrower than the classes of amendments with respect to which a right to vote by separate voting groups exist.

c. Examples of the interaction among the various provisions relating to amendments to articles of incorporation follow.

Example: A corporation has outstanding 200 shares of voting common stock and 100 shares of nonvoting preferred shares. The board of directors proposes amendments to the articles of incorporation to increase the size of the board of directors from 3 to 5 members, change the name of the corporation from ABC Corporation to Oomph Corporation, and grant all directors the right to be indemnified to the extent the corporation is lawfully permitted to do so. None of these amendments require voting by voting groups or create a statutory right of dissent and appraisal; under the MBCA (1984), each of these amendments may be approved by a simple vote at a meeting at which a quorum is present. If a quorum of common shares (more than 100 shares) is present at a meeting of common shareholders, the amendments are approved if the affirmative votes cast exceed the negative votes cast.

Example: In the previous example, if the preferred shares were also voting shares, the same principles would control. The preferred and common would vote together; the quorum required is 150 or more shares of the outstanding shares of both classes, and the amendments are approved if the affirmative votes cast exceed the negative votes cast.

Example: In the previous example, assume that the proposed amendment would reduce the preferential dividend right of the preferred shares from $5.00 per year to $4.90 per year. In this situation, the preferred is entitled to vote as a separate voting group whether or not it is entitled to vote generally under the articles of incorporation. Furthermore, the amendment creates dissenters' rights on the part of preferred shareholders if approved; to be approved by the preferred shares, the amendment must be approved by an absolute majority of the outstanding preferred shares: 51 votes. The common shares do not have dissenters' rights with respect to this amendment; as a result, the vote by common shareholders needed to approve the amendment is that the votes cast in favor of the amendment exceed the votes cast opposed to it at a meeting at which a quorum is present.

Example: If the proposal is to reduce the preferential dividend right of the preferred shareholders as in the previous example, and the preferred shares are entitled to vote generally under the articles of incorporation, the amendment would have to be approved by the same 51 votes of the preferred shares (voting as a separate voting group). The holders of the preferred shares have a statutory right of dissent and appraisal. At the meeting of voting shareholders, the combined common and preferred shares also vote; a quorum based on a total of 300 votes would have to be present, and the amendment is approved if the votes in favor of the amendment at that at a meeting exceed the votes against the amendment. In this situation the votes of the preferred shares are in effect counted in two different elections, first, in the separate voting group election of the preferred, and second, in the vote of the voting shares entitled to vote generally on the amendment by the articles of incorporation. The amendment is approved only if it is approved in both elections.

Example: The corporation has 200 shares of voting common stock outstanding and a single class of preferred shares that consists of three series, each with different preferential dividend rights. A proposed amendment would reduce the rate of dividend applicable to the Series A preferred and would change the dividend right of the Series B shares from cumulative to noncumulative. The Series C preferred's dividend right would not be affected. Since the Series A and Series B are affected in different ways, each would constitute a separate voting group and would have to approve the amendment separately. Each would also have the statutory right of dissent and appraisal. The Series C preferred is not entitled to vote as a separate voting group and does not have a right of dissent and appraisal; if nonvoting under the articles of incorporation, that series could not vote at all on the amendment. The voting of the common shares is not affected.

Example: In the previous example, if the proposed amendment would change the dividend right of both the Series B and Series C preferred from cumulative to noncumulative, the Series B and Series C would be affected in essentially the same way and would be entitled to vote only as a single voting group on the amendment. The Series A would continue to be entitled to vote as a separate voting group. If these series of shares were separate classes of shares (rather than series), the Class A, Class B and Class C would each be entitled to vote as separate voting groups. All three classes would have the statutory right of dissent and appraisal. Again the voting of the common shares is not affected.

Example: A corporation has outstanding a class of cumulative preferred shares as well as common shares. The board of directors proposes to amend the articles of incorporation to create a new class of preferred shares that would have cumulative preferential rights to dividends senior to those of the existing preferred shares. The class of existing preferred shares is entitled to vote as a separate voting group on the proposed amendment but individual holders of preferred shares do not have the statutory right of dissent and appraisal if the amendment is approved. Compare MBCA (1984) §§ 10.04(a)(6) and 13.02(a)(4).

B. STATUTORY MERGERS AND CONSOLIDATIONS

Business corporation statutes specifically refer to and authorize certain kinds of corporate amalgamations. Business corporation acts usually authorize the following type of transactions: (1) the "merger" of one domestic corporation into another domestic corporation; (2) the "consolidation" of two domestic corporations into a new domestic corporation; (3) the "merger" of a subsidiary of a domestic corporation into that corporation; (4) the "merger" or "consolidation" of a domestic corporation and a foreign corporation; and (5) in some states a compulsory "share exchange".

Caveat: Nonstatutory transactions may achieve the same economic result as statutorily authorized transactions. One may be able to vary the legal consequences of a transaction by choosing a nonstatutory form rather than a statutory form in which to cast the transaction.

1. BASIC DEFINITIONS

a. **Statutory Merger.** A "merger" of corporation A into corporation B means that the two corporations are combined and corporation B survives while corporation A disappears.

b. **Statutory Consolidation.** A "consolidation" of corporation A and corporation B means that the two corporations are combined but both corporation A and corporation B disappear and a new corporation C is created.

1) Statutory mergers and consolidations are often simply described as "statutory mergers" to distinguish them from nonstatutory asset-purchase and stock-purchase transactions described below.

2) The Model Business Corporation Act (1984) does not include the concept of a "consolidation". The Introductory Comment to Chapter 11 states that the concept of a consolidation is obsolete, since it is nearly always advantageous for one of the entities involved in the transaction to be the surviving corporation, and if not, a new entity may always be created and the other entities merged into it.

3) The Internal Revenue Code describes a statutory merger or consolidation as a class "A" reorganization.

4) In a merger between a domestic and a foreign corporation, the surviving corporation may be the foreign corporation if it complies with minimal statutory requirements. See MBCA (1984) § 11.07.

5) The combinations or amalgamations of assets and liabilities that occur in a statutory merger occur automatically upon the effective date of the transaction and are not deemed to be transfers of assets or liabilities. See MBCA (1984) § 11.06.

Caveat: This may be of importance when a corporation has assets that may not be transferred without the prior consent of a governmental agency or third person (e.g. a landlord).

c. **Statutory Share Exchange**. In a "share exchange" all shareholders of a class of shares are obligated to exchange their shares for the consideration specified in the plan of share exchange when that plan is approved by a majority of the shares of that class following essentially the same procedure that is applicable to the approval of a merger. The exchange is mandatory. A share exchange is similar in effect to a reverse triangular merger (described below).

2. BASIC PROCEDURES

Business corporation acts require statutory mergers to be approved by the board of directors and by a specific percentage of the shareholders of each corporation. The required procedure is as follows:

a. A plan of merger must be approved by the board of directors and recommended to the shareholders. MBCA (1984) § 11.03(a). The board of directors may condition the plan on such terms as it deems desirable, e. g. that the plan be approved by one or more classes of shares voting as separate voting groups or that no more than a specified number of shareholders elect the right of dissent and appraisal.

b. The vote required for approval of a merger under MBCA (1984) § 11.03(e) is a majority of all the outstanding voting shares. Voting by voting group is required if the plan of merger contains a provision that would require voting by voting group if it were contained in amendments to the articles of incorporation. MBCA (1984) § 11.03(f)(1).

   1) The older, more traditional statutory requirement for approval of a statutory merger requires the affirmative vote of two-thirds of all outstanding shares, both voting and nonvoting alike.

   2) Many states require a majority vote of all outstanding voting shares.

c. Shareholders have a right of dissent and appraisal if the plan of merger must be approved by the shareholders and the shareholder in question has the right to vote on the merger. MBCA (1984) § 13.02(a)(1).

d. Under § 11.02(g) of the MBCA (1984), the shareholders of the surviving corporation are not entitled to vote on a merger if the plan of merger does not amend the articles of incorporation, the shares owned by the shareholders of the surviving corporation are unaffected by the merger, and the number of new shares issued pursuant to the plan of merger does not increase the total number of outstanding shares by more than 20 per cent.

   Caveat: The shareholder vote by the surviving corporation may be avoided even if the number of shares is increased by more than 20 per cent by casting the transaction as a triangular merger rather than a direct merger.

Example: A corporation that is a party to a statutory merger has outstanding a class of nonvoting preferred shares that has unpaid cumulative dividends. The plan of merger provides that each preferred share is to receive one share of common stock in full payment of the unpaid dividends. The preferred shares are entitled to vote as a separate voting group on the merger. See MBCA 10.04(a). Further, holders of preferred shares who vote against the plan of merger have a right of dissent and appraisal pursuant to section 13.02(a)(1).

Caveat: In this example, it makes no difference whether the corporation with the class of preferred shares is to be the surviving corporation in the merger or is to disappear in the merger. In either event the right of the preferred shareholders to cumulative dividends may be eliminated pursuant to the merger subject to the procedural protections described above.

Example: A corporation is to be the surviving corporation in the merger. The plan of merger does not contain provisions affecting the non-voting preferred shares of that corporation in any of the ways described in MBCA (1984) §§ 10.04(a) and 13.02(a)(1). The preferred shares are not entitled to vote at all on the plan of merger and do not have a right of dissent and appraisal.

Caveat: The rules about voting and the right of dissent and appraisal are technical and vary significantly from state to state. The requirements may sometimes be avoided by casting the transaction in a non-statutory form. In some states with a two-thirds voting requirement, for example, a non-statutory transaction that has the same economic effect as a statutory merger may require only a majority vote at a meeting at which a quorum is present, and there may be no right of dissent and appraisal.

e. If the directors of the two corporations are not acting at arms length, e. g., in the case when one corporation owns enough shares of the other to name a majority or all of the board of directors of the other, the merger is a form of self-dealing and may be judicially reviewed for fairness. (*Weinberger v. UOP, Inc.*, 457 A.2d 701 (Del.1983); *Singer v. Magnavox Co.*, 380 A.2d 969 (Del.1977); *Sterling v. Mayflower Hotel Corp.*, 93 A.2d 107 (Del.1952); *Abelow v. Midstates Oil Corp.*, 189 A.2d 675 (Del.1963); *Smith v. Good Music Station, Inc.*, 129 A.2d 242 (Del.Ch.1957). The same standard is applicable to mergers of investment companies subject to the Federal Investment Company Act of 1940. *E. I. du Pont de Nemours & Co. v. Collins*, 432 U.S. 46, 97 S.Ct. 2229 (1977).

Caveat: Approval of merger transactions by disinterested directors of a party to a merger may avoid the full scale fairness review required of self dealing transactions.

f. If a merger transaction is completed when it has not been approved by the appropriate votes, e.g. if a class of shares is entitled to vote as a separate voting group but is not permitted to do so, the merger transaction is invalid. *Shidler v. All American Life & Financial Corp.*, 298 N.W.2d 318 (Iowa 1980).

3. TRIANGULAR MERGERS, CASH MERGERS, AND SUBSIDIARY-PARENT MERGERS

The word "merger" appears to contemplate that all shareholders in disappearing corporations receive shares in the surviving corporation in exchange for their shares in the disappearing corporation or corporations. Most merger transactions today do not involve the simple amalgamation of two businesses as the term appears to contemplate.

Caveat: Rejection of the layman's view of a merger as being an amalgamation of two independent businesses is critical for the understanding of modern merger law.

a. A "triangular merger" involves an acquisition of one corporation by another but does not involve a merger between the acquiring corporation and the acquired corporation. The acquiring corporation forms a wholly owned subsidiary with nominal assets into which the acquired corporation is merged with the shareholders of the acquired corporation receiving shares of the acquiring corporation rather than shares of the subsidiary into which the acquired corporation was merged.

   1) In order to validate triangular mergers, the merger statutes of virtually all states have been amended to provide expressly that the shares of some parties to a merger may be converted into "shares, obligations or other securities of the surviving *or any other corporation or into cash or other property in whole or in part".* MBCA (1984) § 11.01(b)(3).

   2) In such transactions the parent corporation is usually a publicly held corporation with a market for its shares while the subsidiary is created solely for the purpose of the particular transaction.

   3) In a triangular merger, the acquired corporation becomes a wholly owned subsidiary of the acquiring corporation.

   4) In a triangular merger the acquiring corporation does not become liable for the obligations and liabilities of the acquired corporation.

   5) Under modern statutes cash may be substituted for the shares of the acquiring corporation, creating a new type of merger transaction.

b. A "cash merger" is a merger in which some shareholders party to the merger are required to accept cash or property (other than shares) for their shares. A cash merger permits the statutory merger procedure to be used to squeeze out one or more shareholders. It is in effect a compulsory buy-out of the shares of certain shareholders.

Example: X, Y, and Z are the sole shareholders of a closely held corporation, XYZ Corporation. Z has a falling out with X and Y. In order to eliminate Z from participation in XYZ Corporation, X and Y form a new corporation, XY Corporation. X and Y propose to merge XYZ Corporation into XY Corporation with Z receiving cash for his shares and the remaining shares of XYZ Corporation being cancelled. The result of this transaction is that X and Y become the sole owners of the business and Z receives the amount of cash specified in the plan of merger. X and Y between them have a majority of the outstanding shares of XYZ Corporation, and they vote those shares in favor of the merger. Z votes his shares in opposition to the merger. Z's shares are not a separate voting group, and Z's vote is therefore insufficient to block the merger. Z does have a statutory right of dissent and appraisal. Z may also be able to attack the merger as a self dealing transaction, but the transaction is valid so far as the merger statute is concerned.

Example: A corporation merges into its own wholly owned subsidiary with the majority shareholders receiving shares in the subsidiary on a share-for-share basis while minority shareholders are compelled to accept a specified amount of cash for their shares. The same analysis set forth in the previous example is applicable.

Caveat: These transactions are expressly contemplated by modern corporation statutes, however unfair and counter-intuitive they appear to be.

c. A cash merger may be used as part of a two-step acquisition of all the outstanding shares of an unwilling target corporation. Such a merger is usually called a "back end" or "mop up merger"

1) A majority of the outstanding shares of the target are obtained by open market purchase or tender offer. Some shareholders of the target decline to sell or tender their shares for purchase.

2) The target is merged into the aggressor (or a subsidiary of the aggressor) through a cash merger in which the remaining shareholders of the target are compelled to accept cash. Typically the cash received in the merger is the same as originally paid in the tender offer.

3) The aggressor corporation thereby becomes the owner of all the outstanding shares of the target, and may thereafter require the target to assume the debts incurred to buy the shares. This is a leveraged buyout.

Caveat: In the takeover device known as a "front end loaded" tender offer, an offer is made for a majority of the stock at a favorable price. The offeror also announces that if the offer is successful it will acquire the balance of the shares in a back end merger at a price that is lower than the original cash offer and may be payable in debt securities rather than in cash. This device tends to cause shareholders to tender into the initial offer for fear of being "left behind."

Caveat: The front end loaded tender offer was widely used in the mid–1980s but fell into disuse as a result of effective defensive tactics and concern expressed by governmental agencies as to the fairness of the offer.

d. Many modern merger transactions involve mergers between parent and subsidiary corporations. The merger of a subsidiary into its parent is called an "up stream" merger. A merger of the parent into the subsidiary is a "down stream" merger.

1) A down stream merger may be used to change the state of incorporation of a publicly held corporation.

Example: Corporation Y, a publicly held corporation with six classes of nonvoting preferred shares and over 1,000,000 shares of common stock outstanding, decides to move its state of incorporation from Illinois to Delaware. It creates a wholly owned subsidiary in Delaware called "Y Corporation (Delaware)" with a capital structure that precisely mirrors the capital structure of Y corporation. It then proposes a down stream merger of Y corporation into Y Corporation (Delaware) with each share of Y Corporation being exchanged for the equivalent share of Y Corporation (Delaware). Upon approval by the board of directors and the shareholders of Y Corporation, the transaction is effected as a statutory merger. Y Corporation (Delaware) then changes its name to Y Corporation. Under the MBCA (1984), this transaction must be approved by a vote of the common shareholders of Y corporation but no vote by the preferred shareholders is required and no right of dissent and appraisal is available to any shareholder.

Caveat: In the previous example, Corporation Y may announce that certificates for its shares will be accepted as representing certificates of Corporation Y (Delaware) so that it is not necessary to exchange certificates.

2) MBCA (1984) § 11.04 permits a parent corporation that owns 90 percent or more of the outstanding shares of each class of a subsidiary corporation to merge the subsidiary into the parent without a shareholders' vote of either corporation. This procedure is usually called a "short form merger."

(i) MBCA (1984) § 11.04 is applicable only to up stream mergers.

(ii) The shareholders of the subsidiary may be required to accept a specified amount of cash for their shares; they also expressly have the statutory right to dissent and receive the appraised value of their shares. MBCA (1984) § 13.02(a)(1)(ii).

(iii) The theoretical basis for omitting the vote of the subsidiary's shareholders is that the minority shareholders of the subsidiary are unable to block the merger.

(iv) The theoretical basis for omitting the vote of the parent's shareholders is that the merger does not materially affect their rights which already include an indirect 90 percent interest in the subsidiary. The merger thus causes a relatively slight increase in the parent's interest in the subsidiary.

(v) The practical justification for short form merger statutes is that they avoid the cost of proxy solicitations and meetings of publicly held parent corporations.

(vi) The short form merger procedure creates no appraisal rights on the part of shareholders of the parent corporation since those shareholders are not entitled to vote on the transaction.

4. REVERSE TRIANGULAR MERGERS AND SHARE EXCHANGES

In some transactions, it is important that the continued existence of an acquired corporation be preserved. Such transactions may be achieved through reverse triangular mergers; in a few states mandatory share exchanges permit equivalent transactions in a simpler and more direct fashion.

a. Retention of the separate existence of the acquired corporation is important where that corporation is organized under a special statute under which incorporation is difficult (e. g., banks, insurance companies) or where the corporation has government or other contracts that do not permit assignment.

b. In a "reverse triangular merger" the acquiring or holding company creates a new subsidiary and "drops down" into that subsidiary the assets or its own shares to be used to acquire the shares of the target corporation. That subsidiary is then merged into the target corporation and the assets or shares of the acquiring corporation are exchanged for the shares of the corporation to be acquired. The shares of the new subsidiary owned by the acquiring company are exchanged for the shares of the acquired company owned by the subsidiary. The result is that the target corporation becomes a wholly owned subsidiary of the acquiring or holding company. The shareholders of the acquired corporation may receive either stock or cash for their shares.

c. A compulsory share exchange authorized by MBCA (1984) § 11.02 is a direct, simple, and straightforward procedure to accomplish the same end. This procedure permits the mandatory acquisition of all shares of a class of a corporation upon the affirmative vote of a majority of the shares of that class. The consideration for the shares being acquired may consist of cash, property, or shares in another corporation.

Caveat: The name "share exchange" is potentially misleading since it includes the "exchange" of shares for cash, a transaction that most persons would view as a compulsory sale.

1) A compulsory share exchange requires approval of the board of directors of the corporation whose shares are to be exchanged and submission of the proposed share exchange to the shareholders of the class of shares being exchanged.

2) If a majority of the shares being exchanged approve the transaction, it is binding on all holders of the class, majority and minority alike.

3) Shareholders of the class of shares being exchanged who object to the share exchange are entitled to the statutory right of dissent and appraisal. MBCA (1984) § 13.02(a)(2).

Example: An acquiring corporation seeks to obtain all the shares of a corporation engaged in radio broadcasting pursuant to a permit issued by the Federal Communications Commission. The corporation to be acquired has only common shares outstanding. It is important to preserve the existence of the acquired corporation to avoid FCC review. The shareholders of the acquired corporation by majority vote determine to exchange all common shares with the acquiring corporation for cash pursuant to the share exchange statute. Several shareholders of the acquired corporation object to the transaction. The sale is binding on all common shareholders of the acquired corporation and the acquiring corporation receives all outstanding shares; shareholders of the acquired corporation who object to the transaction have the statutory right of dissent and appraisal.

5. FAIRNESS STANDARDS IN CONNECTION WITH CASH MERGERS

The development of cash mergers, short form mergers, and related transactions raise the question whether such transactions should be accepted as valid so long as the formal statutory procedural requirements are complied with, or whether some kind of fairness standard should be applied when transactions are imposed on minority shareholders by controlling shareholders.

a. This issue is particularly acute where the plan of merger treats minority shareholders differently from majority shareholders: usually the minority are compelled to accept cash for their shares in an amount set by the majority shareholders.

b. Some early cases decided before the full development of nontraditional merger transactions described above took the position that courts should not judge motive or subjective fairness, and should be satisfied if the procedures and minority protection devices required by statute are made available. Reliance in these cases was placed on the right of dissent and appraisal which gave dissatisfied shareholders the right to receive cash for their shares.

c. Cases now agree, however, that the validity of such transactions should be generally based on a test of entire fairness and that compliance with statutory formalities alone is not sufficient. *Weinberger v. UOP, Inc.,* 457 A.2d 701 (Del. 1983). Courts, however, have struggled with the precise test to be applied to such transactions.

   1) *Singer v. Magnavox Co.,* 380 A.2d 969 (Del.1977), combined a "business purpose" test with the test of "entire fairness." Several cases accept this standard. *Gabhart v. Gabhart,* 370 N.E.2d 345 (Ind.1977); *Coggins v. New England Patriots Football Club,* 492 N.E.2d 1112 (Mass.1986); *Alpert v. 28 Williams St. Corp.,* 473 N.E.2d 19 (N.Y.1984).

   2) In *Tanzer v. International Gen. Indus., Inc.,* 379 A.2d 1121 (Del.1977), the court held that the business purpose requirement may be satisfied by considering the interests of the majority shareholder; a purpose of facilitating long term borrowing capacity of the majority shareholder also was a valid business purpose.

      Caveat: As so construed, the business purpose test has little force in preventing abusive transactions.

   3) In *Weinberger v. UOP, Inc.,* 457 A.2d 701 (Del.1983) the Delaware Supreme Court concluded that the business purpose test does not provide any additional meaningful protection, and substituted an increased emphasis on the "entire fairness" of the transaction.

Caveat: Despite the decision in *Weinberger,* other states may continue to require a business purpose test.

4) *Weinberger* states that "entire fairness" has two elements: fair dealing and fair price. Fair dealing includes full disclosure of all information relating to fairness.

5) *Weinberger* states that the statutory right of dissent and appraisal is normally the sole remedy for minority shareholders complaining about the price in freeze-out mergers. The court, however, significantly liberalized that remedy. (See part XIX H.)

6) The burden of proving "entire fairness" is on the corporation proposing the cash transaction. *Weinberger* suggests, however, that strong evidence of fairness of a transaction may be derived from (a) approval by independent directors unaffiliated with the controlling shareholder of the transaction after full disclosure, and (b) approval of the transaction by a majority of the minority shares being cashed out. If these steps are taken, the burden of proof shifts from the corporate defendant to the complaining shareholders.

Example: In a cash out transaction with a reasonable business purpose, a majority of the minority shareholders being cashed out approve a cash merger transaction after full disclosure. This approval is persuasive evidence of the fairness of the transaction. *Schulwolf v. Cerro Corp.*, 380 N.Y.S.2d 957 (1976).

Example: Corporation A owns 55 per cent of the outstanding shares of Corporation B. Recognizing that it may later wish to combine the two corporations, Corporation A places five outside, unaffiliated persons on the nine member board of directors of Corporation B. Corporation A later proposes a cash out merger by which it would become the 100 per cent owner of Corporation B. The outside directors of Corporation B take over all negotiation of the transaction, which approximates the negotiation that would occur between two unaffiliated corporations. This is strong evidence of the fairness of the cash out merger subsequently negotiated, and the burden of showing unfair dealing is on the minority shareholders attacking the transaction.

Example: In a cash out merger, the minority shareholders institute an appraisal proceeding complaining that the price is unfair. While in discovery, the plaintiffs discover evidence of wrongdoing in connection with the merger, including fraud, illegality and unfair dealing. The plaintiffs may then bring an independent suit to set aside the merger on these grounds; the appraisal proceeding is the exclusive remedy only for complaints that the price is unfair. *Cede & Co. v. Technicolor, Inc.,* 542 A.2d 1182 (Del.1988).

d. Similar principles apply to short form mergers of subsidiary corporations into parent corporations. *Roland Intern. Corp. v. Najjar,* 407 A.2d 1032 (Del.1979).

e. Federal law provides virtually no protection against unfair cash out merger transactions.

1) In *Santa Fe Indus., Inc. v. Green,* 430 U.S. 462, 97 S.Ct. 1292 (1977), the Supreme Court held that the essence of a rule 10b–5 violation was nondisclosure or misrepresentation of material facts and that unfair cash mergers and related transactions could not be attacked under federal law unless there was nondisclosure.

2) In *Virginia Bankshares, Inc. v. Sandberg,* __ U.S. ___, 111 S.Ct. 2749 (1991), the court held that a proxy statement issued in connection with a cash merger could not be made the basis of a federal claim under the S.E.C. proxy regulations if the votes being solicited by the proxy statement could not affect the outcome of the vote.

3) As a result of *Santa Fe* and *Virginia Bankshares,* control over the cash mergers and related transactions now appear to be solely a matter of state law. *Cole v. Shenley Indus., Inc.,* 563 F.2d 35 (2d Cir.1977).

Caveat: Cases prior to *Virginia Bankshares* have held that false statements or nondisclosure in connection with such transactions may continue to give rise to a rule 10b–5 claim despite *Santa Fe. Goldberg v. Meridor,* 567 F.2d 209 (2d Cir.1977) *cert. denied* 434 U.S. 1069, 98 S.Ct. 1249 (1978); *Healey v. Catalyst Recovery of Pennsylvania, Inc.,* 616 F.2d 641 (3d Cir.1980). The vitality of these holdings is now open to question.

C. SALES OF SUBSTANTIALLY ALL ASSETS

A sale, lease, exchange or other disposition of all, or substantially all, the property and assets of a corporation not in the usual and regular course of business must under the statutes of most states be submitted to and approved by the shareholders. See MBCA (1984) § 12.02.

1. SALES IN ORDINARY COURSE OF BUSINESS

A sale of all, or substantially all, the property and assets of a corporation in the ordinary course of business (which is not common), does not require shareholder approval. MBCA (1984) § 12.01(a)(1).

Example: A corporation is in the business of buying and selling improved real estate. It invests substantially all of its assets in an apartment house that it holds for speculation for eight months and then resells. The resale does not require shareholder approval.

a. Many state statutes provide that a pledge, mortgage, or deed of trust covering all the assets of the corporation to secure a debt is in the ordinary course of business. MBCA (1984) § 12.01(a)(2).

b. MBCA (1984) § 12.01(a)(3) provides that shareholder approval is not required where a corporation spins substantially all of its assets off to a wholly owned subsidiary.

   1) The purpose of this provision is to reverse the result reached in *Campbell v. Vose,* 515 F.2d 256 (10th Cir.1975), which invalidated such a transaction in the absence of shareholder approval.

   2) The Official Comment notes that MBCA (1984) § 12.01(a)(3) should not be permitted to be "used as a device to avoid a vote of shareholders by a multiple-step transaction."

2. MEANING OF THE PHRASE "ALL OR SUBSTANTIALLY ALL"

The scope of the phrase "all or substantially all" is a matter of dispute.

a. "All or substantially all" of the assets of a corporation are sold even if the corporation retains some small amount of property as a pretext. *Stiles v. Aluminum Products Co.,* 86 N.E.2d 887 (Ill.App.1949).

b. The official comment to MBCA (1984) § 12.01 sets forth one test. It states that the phrase "all or substantially all" should be read "to mean what it literally says. * * * The phrase 'substantially all' is synonymous with 'nearly all' and was added merely to make it clear that the statutory requirements could not be avoided by retention of some minimal or nominal residue of the original assets.

   Example: A sale of all the corporate assets other than cash or cash equivalents is the sale of "all or substantially all" of the corporation's property.

   Example: A sale of several distinct manufacturing lines while retaining one or more lines is normally not a sale of "all or substantially all" even though the lines being sold are substantial and include a significant fraction of the corporation's former business. If the lines are retained, however, only as a temporary operation or as a pretext to avoid the "all or substantially all" requirements, the statutory requirements of Chapter 12 must be complied with.

Example: A sale of a plant but retention of operating assets (e. g. machinery and equipment), accounts receivable, good will, and the like, which permits the operation of the same business at another location is not the sale of "all or substantially all" of the corporation's property.

c. Several decisions adopt a much broader view of the scope of the phrase "all or substantially all." These cases view the test as basically whether the change of business activity implicit in the sale is sufficiently important that it should be submitted to the shareholders for approval. *Gimbel v. Signal Companies, Inc.,* 316 A.2d 599 (Del.Ch.1974), aff'd per curiam 316 A.2d 619 (Del.1974); *but see Murphy v. Washington American League Base Ball Club, Inc.,* 293 F.2d 522 (D.C.Cir.1961).

Example: A corporation plans to sell a Canadian subsidiary that constitutes 51 per cent of the corporation's total assets and 44.9 per cent of the corporation's total revenues. *Katz v. Bregman,* 431 A.2d 1274 (Del.Ch.1981), holds that this is a sale of "all or substantially all" of a corporation's assets and requires shareholder approval.

3. PROCEDURAL REQUIREMENTS

Like other organic transactions, a sale of all or substantially all of a corporation's assets not in the ordinary course of business must be first approved by the board of directors and recommended to the shareholders for approval. The transaction must be approved by a majority of the shares entitled to vote on the transaction.

a. Voting by voting groups is not required.

b. Shareholders who vote against the proposed transaction have a right of dissent and appraisal. MBCA (1984) § 12.02.

Caveat: Some states do not grant the right of dissent and appraisal in connection with sales of asset transactions.

D. NONSTATUTORY AMALGAMATIONS

A statutory merger or share exchange is only one of several ways of effecting a corporate acquisition or combining or amalgamating two or more corporations into a single operation.

1. TYPES OF TRANSACTIONS

There are basically two types of nonstatutory amalgamations: a stock purchase transaction and an asset purchase transaction.

a. A stock purchase transaction is one in which one corporation purchases all or most of the outstanding shares of the other corporation in one or more voluntary transactions.

   1) As a result, the acquired corporation becomes a wholly owned subsidiary of the acquiring corporation. Thereafter, the parent may liquidate or merge the acquired corporation into itself, perhaps using the short form merger procedure discussed above.

   2) This transaction is referred to as a B type reorganization in the Internal Revenue Code.

   3) The purchase price for the shares may be paid in cash, debt, stock, other property, or in a combination of forms.

   4) The acquiring corporation may have to deal with a fairly large number of sellers, i. e., each shareholder of the acquired corporation.

   5) The acquired corporation remains liable for undisclosed or unknown liabilities, such as income tax deficiencies of prior years. If the business is liquidated or merged into the acquiring corporation, that corporation is responsible for the acquired corporation's liabilities.

b. An "asset purchase" or "asset acquisition" is a transaction in which one corporation purchases substantially all the assets of another corporation.

   1) The purchase may include all or virtually all of the assets of the acquired corporation, or it may include only the assets used in one line of business.

   2) This transaction is referred to as a class "C" reorganization (in the IRC terminology).

   3) The purchase price for the assets may be paid in cash, debt, stock, other property, or in a combination of forms.

   4) The liabilities assumed by the asset purchaser is a matter of negotiation, but typically includes only liabilities arising in the ordinary course of business and carefully enumerated additional liabilities.

      (i) Typically all claims and liabilities not specifically assumed are expressly excluded. The claims not assumed remain the responsibility of the selling corporation.

Example: Claims that an asset purchaser does not wish to assume include product liability claims arising from products sold before the sale, tax liabilities for earlier years, environmental responsibilities, and claims based on undisclosed contractual obligations or pending lawsuits.

(ii) The ability to avoid assuming certain types of liabilities is one of the most important advantages of an asset acquisition.

5) After the transaction is completed, the acquired corporation retains its separate existence as an independent corporation but its assets consist only of the proceeds of the sale, usually cash or stock, and whatever assets were not purchased.

(i) Such a corporation may continue in existence operating thereafter as a holding or investment corporation.

(ii) More commonly, however, such a corporation thereafter liquidates after making provision for liabilities not assumed by the purchaser, and distributes the remaining proceeds of the sale to its shareholders.

c. There is no right of dissent and appraisal in a nonstatutory transaction. A nonstatutory acquisition may be approved by the directors without shareholder approval even though shareholder approval would be required if the transaction were cast as a statutory merger.

Example: Corporation A plans to acquire Corporation B, a closely held corporation. Shareholders of Corporation B are to receive one share of Corporation A stock for each share of Corporation B stock they own. Corporation A has sufficient authorized shares to complete the transaction without amending its articles of incorporation. Since all shareholders of Corporation B approve the transaction, the board of directors of Corporation A simply authorizes the issuance of its shares in exchange for shares of B corporation. The transaction is not a statutory merger and none of the procedures for statutory mergers need to be followed by Corporation A.

2. SELECTION OF FORM OF TRANSACTION

These nonstatutory transactions have the same economic effect as a statutory merger or consolidation, (including, where appropriate, a triangular or reverse triangular merger, or a share exchange). The question as to which form a particular transaction should take is a complex one, involving a variety of tax and business considerations.

a. There is nothing inherently unlawful in structuring a transaction in one form rather than another in order to simplify the procedures to be followed or to avoid granting dissenting shareholders the right of dissent and appraisal. *Hariton v. Arco Electronics, Inc.*, 188 A.2d 123 (Del.1963).

b. The parties to a specific transaction may have different views on this question, one preferring an asset purchase, the other a stock purchase or statutory merger. Generally the controlling shareholders may shape the transaction in light of their own interests. *Grace v. Grace Nat. Bank of New York*, 465 F.2d 1068 (2d Cir.1972).

c. Because of the identical economic effect no matter which form is followed, there is a slight possibility that the selection of a particular form to achieve some goal may not succeed. A court may reject form, "look at substance," and recast the transaction into a different form. This is the "de facto merger" doctrine. *Applestein v. United Bd. & Carton Corp.*, 159 A.2d 146 (N.J.Super. Ch.Div.1960).

Example: In Pennsylvania, dissenting shareholders have appraisal rights in a statutory merger. A transaction is cast as an asset transaction where the "selling corporation" sells assets in exchange for shares of the "acquiring corporation" and thereafter dissolves and distributes those shares to its shareholders. The "selling corporation" is considerably larger than the "acquiring corporation" and, after the transaction is completed, the shareholders of the "selling corporation" own more than 50 per cent of the shares of the "acquiring corporation" and dominate the combined operation. In *Farris v. Glen Alden Corp.*, 143 A.2d 25 (Pa.1958) the court held that this transaction was the economic equivalent of a statutory merger and appraisal rights had to be granted to dissenting shareholders of the "acquiring corporation."

Caveat: Several cases are contra to *Farris* and academic writing is critical of the case. *Hariton v. Arco Electronics, Inc.*, 188 A.2d 123 (Del.1963); *Orzeck v. Englehart*, 195 A.2d 375 (Del.1963). The Pennsylvania statutes were later amended to reverse the result in Farris. See *Terry v. Penn Central Corp.*, 668 F.2d 188 (3d Cir.1981).

Example: Two corporations develop close working relationships so that one assumes most risks, responsibilities, and profits. However, there is no pooling of assets and liabilities. There is no de facto merger even though many of the economic attributes of a merger have been attained. *Good v. Lackawanna Leather Co.*, 233 A.2d 201 (N.J.Super.Ch.Div.1967).

Example: A closely held manufacturing corporation sells its assets to a large publicly held corporation for cash or stock, discharges its known liabilities, distributes the remaining proceeds to its shareholders, and dissolves. The acquiring corporation expressly does not assume liabilities of the manufacturing corporation (other than certain limited liabilities carefully spelled out in the agreement itself). The acquiring corporation continues the business of the acquired corporation using the same plant, same work force, and the same corporate or trade name. Four years later a product liability suit is filed for personal injuries caused by a defective product sold by the old manufacturing company. Despite the express disclaimer of the assumption of liabilities, several cases have held the publicly held corporation liable on the products liability claim on the basis of the de facto merger doctrine. *Knapp v. North American Rockwell Corp.*, 506 F.2d 361 (3d Cir.1974)

Example: In the prior example, a number of courts have reached the same result under a variety of theories: continuing enterprise," "product line," public policy, risk spreading, and perhaps simple sympathy for plaintiffs who apparently have no one to sue.

Caveat: A significant number of courts have also rejected the imposition of liability on the asset-purchaser in the circumstances of the prior example and applied traditional doctrine.

Caveat: In the prior example, the old manufacturing corporation may be liable for the injury caused by the defective product. However, under most state statutes, suit against a dissolved corporation must be brought within three years of dissolution. The MBCA addresses this problem by permitting such suits to be brought against the old manufacturing corporation if the suit is brought within five years of dissolution. MBCA (1984) §§ 14.06, 14.07. Provision is also made for the recovery of liquidating distributions from shareholders to satisfy the judgment.

E. RECAPITALIZATIONS

A recapitalization is simply a restructuring of the capital structure of the corporation to improve the ability to attract capital.

1. ECONOMICS OF TRANSACTIONS

The classic example of a corporation that benefits from a recapitalization is the corporation with many years of arrearages in cumulative preferred dividends.

a. Directors elected by common shareholders are unwilling to exhaust cash resources of the corporation by paying off the arrearages. As a result common shareholders do not receive dividends. Indeed, the board of directors usually declines to pay even current preferred dividends in order to pressure the preferred shareholders into accepting a recapitalization.

b. No one is willing to invest fresh capital in the form of new common stock so long as the arrearages remain as a restriction on future distributions.

c. In a recapitalization, most holders of the preferred with arrearages may be willing to exchange the preferred for common, giving up the arrearages, since they are currently not receiving dividends and the corporation is unlikely to pay them anything unless the recapitalization is approved.

2. FORM OF TRANSACTION

Recapitalizations usually take one of two forms:

a. An amendment to the articles of incorporation.

b. A merger into a wholly owned subsidiary or similar transaction that has the same economic effect.

3. VALIDITY OF TRANSACTIONS

These transactions are not subject to a frontal attack on the ground they impair vested rights. *McNulty v. W. & J. Sloane*, 54 N.Y.S.2d 253 (Sup.Ct.1945). However, established standards for evaluating such transactions have been created.

a. There may be different procedural rules applicable to these transactions depending on how they are structured and the precise language of the applicable state statute. In light of the objective need for a recapitalization in many cases, courts have usually allowed the transaction to be cast in a form in which it is likely to succeed. *Bove v. Community Hotel Corp. of Newport, R.I.*, 249 A.2d 89 (R.I.1969).

b. One protection to shareholders often applicable in such transactions is the right to vote by separate voting groups. (See part XIX A 4.)

c. A shareholder objecting to the recapitalization also may have the statutory right of dissent and appraisal under the statute.

d. Some courts have tested the validity of such transactions on a test of fraud, or "unfairness so great as to constitute fraud," *Porges v. Vadsco Sales Corp.*, 32 A.2d 148 (Del.Ch.1943); *Barrett v. Denver Tramway Corp.*, 53 F.Supp. 198 (D.Del.1943).

e. Some courts have construed narrowly the amendment and reservation of power sections of the business corporation act to invalidate transactions deemed by the court to be of questionable fairness. *Bowman v. Armour & Co.*, 160 N.E.2d 753 (Ill.1959). Most courts, however, have rejected arguments that in effect would restore the "vested rights" theory. *Langfelder v. Universal Laboratories, Inc.*, 163 F.2d 804 (3d Cir.1947).

F. "GOING PRIVATE"

The term "going private" refers to transactions by a publicly held corporation to force out its public shareholders. The transaction has the effect of permitting deregistration of the corporation under the Securities Exchange Act of 1934, thereby eliminating expensive reporting and disclosure requirements. A related type of transaction, the "leveraged buyout" is considered in the following section.

1. ECONOMICS OF TRANSACTION

Most corporations considering a traditional going private transaction "went public" by selling shares publicly at a time when market conditions were favorable. Typically only a minority interest was sold to the public. The going private transaction is likely to occur some years later when the stock prices are depressed.

Example: Power Mate sells shares publicly in 1968 at $5.00 per share. In 1975 the controlling shareholders propose a going private transaction at a time when the market price is under $2.00 per share and the price offered the public shareholders is $2.00 per share. This transaction may be enjoined as unfair to minority shareholders. *Berkowitz v. Power Mate Corp.*, 342 A.2d 566 (N.J.Super.Ch.Div.1975).

2. FORM OF GOING PRIVATE TRANSACTIONS

A going private transaction may be effected as a cash merger of the publicly held corporation into a corporation wholly owned by the control group or a cash tender offer followed by a mop up merger.

A going private transaction may also be effected by a "reverse" stock split.

a. The ratio between outstanding shares and post transaction shares is set at a level that makes the holdings of the largest public shareholder into a fractional share.

b. The corporation announces that all fractional shares will be purchased for cash at a specified price, as is permitted by modern corporation statutes. See MBCA (1984) § 6.04.

c. A reverse stock split is usually cast in the form of an amendment to the articles of incorporation.

3. REGULATION OF GOING PRIVATE TRANSACTIONS

Regulation of going private transactions may be under state law or the SEC regulations under the Williams Act.

a. The principles set forth by the Delaware Supreme Court in *Singer* or *Weinberger* (see part XIX B) of "entire fairness" apply to such transactions.

b. Some state statutes grant shareholders cashed out by a reverse stock split the right of dissent and appraisal. See MBCA (1984) § 13.02(a)(4)(v).

c. In 1979 the SEC adopted rules 13e–3 and 13e–4 to assure full disclosure of the transaction; disclosure must include a statement as to the belief of the issuer whether the transaction is fair or unfair to the public shareholders and a discussion "in reasonable detail" of the material factors upon which the belief is based.

d. As a result of *Santa Fe Industries v. Green*, going private transactions cannot be attacked under rule 10b–5 if there is full disclosure.

G. LEVERAGED BUYOUTS

A leveraged buyout (LBO) is a transaction by which an outside entity (that is not itself a publicly held corporation) acquires all the outstanding shares of a publicly held corporation. Initial purchase of a majority of the outstanding shares may be by tender offer followed by a mop-up merger of the balance. The outside entity includes investors, speculators, and incumbent management, though much of the financing may be from "junk bonds" or other borrowings. After the LBO is completed, the corporation is no longer publicly owned. Thereafter the acquired corporation assumes the obligation to repay the loans required to take the corporation private.

1. CHARACTERISTICS

The following characteristics are typical of modern LBOs:

a. A LBO differs from a going private transaction primarily in that outside investors rather than incumbent management acquire the predominant equity ownership of the company. However, incumbent management may participate in a LBO usually as a minority participant. Such a transaction may be referred to as an MBO (management buy out). The economic interest of management in the corporation is usually increased significantly as a result of the transaction.

b. As much of the purchase price for the publicly held shares as possible is borrowed. Following the LBO this debt is assumed by the acquired company, or portions of the acquired company are sold off to help pay down this debt.

An LBO in which sales of portions of the business are planned is sometimes called a "bust up" transaction.

c. The interest payable on the debt is tax deductible by the acquired company. Income tax liabilities may be reduced to zero by the LBO and cash flow formerly used to pay taxes may be used to pay interest.

d. The investors in the LBO and the managers, if included, may own virtually all of the common stock of the acquired company but that company is subject to the acquisition debt.

e. A number of LBO companies have been unable to meet the interest and debt obligations imposed on it by the LBO and have gone into bankruptcy.

f. Ultimately, the hope of the investors in the LBO is that the company will be able to reduce its LBO debt sufficiently so that it can again become a publicly owned company.

H. RIGHT OF DISSENT AND APPRAISAL

State statutes give shareholders the right to dissent from certain types of transactions and to obtain the appraised value of their shares through a judicial proceeding. See MBCA (1984) § 13.01 through 13.31.

1. SCOPE OF RIGHT

The appraisal right is a creature of statute and available only when the statute specifically so provides.

a. The statutory right may be lost if the statutory procedures are not precisely followed. *Gibson v. Strong, Inc.,* 708 S.W.2d 603 (Ark.1986). If the right is lost, the dissenting shareholder must go along with the objectionable transaction. See e. g. MBCA (1984) § 13.21(b), 13.23(c), 13.28(b).

b. The corporation has a duty to provide correct information as to the procedures to be followed. *Gibbons v. Schenley Indus., Inc.,* 339 A.2d 460 (Del.Ch.1975). See MBCA (1984) § 13.20(b), 13.22(a), 13.25(b).

c. The appraisal right extends only to transactions described in the statute. MBCA (1984) § 13.02 extends the right of the following types of transactions:

1) Plans of merger in which the shareholder has the right to vote on the plan, MBCA (1984) § 13.02(a)(1)(i);

2) Short form merger of subsidiary into parent (shareholders of subsidiary only), MBCA (1984) § 13.02(a)(1)(ii);

3) Plans of share exchange, if the shareholder owns shares in the corporation whose shares are being acquired and the shareholder is entitled to vote on the transaction, MBCA (1984) § 13.02(a)(2);

4) Sales of substantially all corporate assets if the shareholder is entitled to vote on the sale, MBCA (1984) § 13.02(a)(3);

5) Amendments of articles of incorporation "that materially and adversely affect" the rights of shareholders in any of the ways described earlier. See part XIX A 4 b.

6) Transactions on which the articles of incorporation, bylaws or a resolution of directors specify that dissenters' rights are to be provided, MBCA (1984) § 13.02(a)(5).

Caveat: Not all state statutes provide dissenters' rights in all the categories. Several states, for example, do not provide dissenters' rights in connection with amendments to the articles of incorporation. Some states also provide dissenters' rights in additional classes of cases.

d. Some states do not grant appraisal rights in connection with shares that are traded on a securities market (or held by a specified number of shareholders) on the theory that the existence of a liquid market on which the shares may be sold provides a reasonable alternative to the appraisal procedure. MBCA (1984) does not contain such an exception.

2. EXCLUSIVENESS OF APPRAISAL RIGHT

The statutes of a number of states provide that the statutory dissent and appraisal procedure is the exclusive remedy for dissenting shareholders.

a. MBCA (1984) § 13.02(b) provides the remedy is exclusive "unless the action is unlawful or fraudulent" with respect to the shareholders.

b. Several courts have allowed direct attacks on unfair transactions (or transactions without business purpose) that gave rise to an appraisal right under statutes similar to the MBCA (1984). *Alpert v. 28 Williams Street Corp.* holds that this language does not limit minority shareholders to their appraisal remedy where the price or other terms are unfair to the minority shareholders.

c. Other courts have accepted the statutory language at face value and limit a dissenting shareholder to his appraisal right, at least in the absence of fraud. *Matteson v. Ziebarth*, 242 P.2d 1025 (Wash.1952).

3. PROCEDURE FOR APPRAISAL

State statutes provide an elaborate procedure for establishing the right to an appraisal and fixing the price. See MBCA (1984) § 13.20 through 13.28.

a. A notice of meeting to shareholders at which the transaction is considered must state that dissenters' rights may arise from the transaction. MBCA (1984) § 13.20(a).

b. A written notice of intent to demand payment must be filed by each potentially dissenting shareholder before the vote of shareholders is taken on the proposed action. MBCA (1984) § 13.21(a).

c. Following approval of the transaction, each shareholder filing a notice of intent to demand payment must be sent a "dissenters' notice" by the corporation (MBCA (1984) § 13.22(a).

d. In order to perfect the right to dissent, each dissenting shareholder must then file a demand for payment. MBCA (1984) § 13.23.

   1) Because appraisal rights may constitute serious cash drains, it is not uncommon in merger and other agreements to provide an "out" for the parties if an excessive number of dissents are filed.

   2) Following the affirmative vote on the proposal, shareholders who file demands for payment have the status of creditor rather than shareholder. *Lichtman v. Recognition Equipment, Inc.,* 295 A.2d 771 (Del.Ch.1972).

   3) To reflect the creditor status of such shareholders, the statutes of many states require dissenting shareholders to submit their certificates together with the demand for payment. The corporation notes that the shares have been submitted for appraisal on the certificate and returns them to the shareholders. Under the Model Business Corporation Act (1984) the certificates are retained by the corporation in the expectation that payment will be made promptly.

e. Most statutes provide that the price is to be set through a two-stage process. No money is paid by the corporation until the judicial proceeding is finally concluded.

   1) The first stage involves negotiation between the shareholder and the corporation.

   2) If negotiation fails, a judicial proceeding to establish the appraised price follows.

f. In the procedure set forth in the Model Business Corporation Act (1984), the corporation must estimate the fair value of the shares and pay to each dissenter that amount immediately. If the dissenting shareholder is dissatisfied with this payment, he or she must submit an estimate of the fair value of his shares. If the shareholder and the corporation cannot agree as to an additional amount to be paid, the shareholder or the corporation may obtain a judicial appraisal of the value of the shares.

Caveat: Most states do not require that the corporation make immediate payment of the amount it estimates to be the fair value of the shares but all payments are deferred until after the completion of the judicial appraisal procedure. The result is that no payment at all may be received for several years after the transaction; this long delay is one of the unattractive features of the traditional appraisal procedure from the standpoint of shareholders contemplating dissent.

Caveat: The right to receive immediate payment under the Model Business Corporation Act (1984) opens up the possibility that a shareholder may be tempted to speculate on the availability of the dissenters' remedy. MBCA (1984) attempts to prevent such speculation by requiring (1) that a shareholder must dissent with respect to all the shares held (an exception is made for record owners where the beneficial ownership is held by more than one person), MBCA (1984) § 13.03, and (2) that a corporation may refuse to make immediate payment to a shareholder who acquires shares after the public announcement of the transaction, MBCA (1984) § 13.27. Such a shareholder is entitled to payment only upon the completion of the appraisal proceeding.

g. The "fair value" of shares is to be fixed as of a time immediately before the transaction in question occurs, but no account is to be taken of the impact of the transaction on the value of the shares. (MBCA (1984) § 13.01(3)). The MBCA (1984), however, allows consideration of the "appreciation or depreciation in anticipation of the corporate action" if that is equitable. MBCA (1984) § 13.01(3).

h. The traditional manner of establishing fair value is the "Delaware block" approach. In this manner of valuation, estimates of value are made on the basis of the value of assets, the market value of the company's securities, and the company's earnings potential. Weights are then assigned to each measure of value and the weighted price is determined.

Example: The calculations of value in *Gibbons v. Schenley Indus., Inc.*, 339 A.2d 460 (Del.Ch.1975) were as follows:

By the appraiser:

factor	*valuation*	*weight*	*assigned value*
market	$29.00	35%	$10.15
earnings	52.78	45%	23.75
asset	49.83	20%	9.97
			$43.87

By the Court:

factor	*valuation*	*weight*	*assigned value*
market	$29.00	55%	$15.95
earnings	39.79	45%	17.91
asset	49.83	0%	0.00
			$33.86

Explanation: The valuation is multiplied by the weight to obtain the "assigned value" [e.g., $29 x 35 = $10.15]. The "assigned values" are then added together to obtain the "fair value."

Example: In a case in which the market for the stock consisted of only a few transactions, market value was given a weight of 10 per cent, earnings value 40 per cent, and net asset value 50 per cent. *Piemonte v. New Boston Garden Corp.,* 387 N.E.2d 1145 (Mass.1979).

Example: In a close corporation there may be no market price for shares but a price may be "reconstructed" if there are a limited number of sales. *Brown v. Hedahl's–Q B & R, Inc.,* 185 N.W.2d 249 (N.D.1971); *Application of Delaware Racing Ass'n,* 213 A.2d 203 (Del.1965).

Example: Earnings value may be based on a capitalized value for average earnings over a recent prior period, such as five years. *Francis I. duPont & Co. v. Universal City Studios, Inc.,* 312 A.2d 344 (Del.Ch. 1973).

Caveat: There is no assurance under these tests that the court-determined price will be equal to or more than the price earlier offered voluntarily. In *Gibbons v. Schenley Indus., Inc.,* described above, for example, the dissenting shareholders had rejected an offer of $53.33 per share and exercised their right of dissent and appraisal.

i. In *Weinberger v. UOP, Inc.,* 457 A.2d 701 (Del.1983), the Delaware Supreme Court abandoned the "Delaware block" approach and adopted a more flexible approach that permits use of more modern valuation techniques that are acceptable in the financial community.

j. MBCA (1984) § 13.30 authorizes all appraisal proceedings to be resolved in a single proceeding in a single court. MBCA (1984) § 13.31 also authorizes the court to assess costs, including attorneys' fees, against either the corporation or the dissenting shareholders:

   1) Costs may be assessed against the corporation if it "did not substantially comply" with chapter 13;

   2) Costs may be assessed against the dissenting shareholders if they "acted arbitrarily, vexatiously, or not in good faith" with respect to the rights granted them by chapter 13.

4. EVALUATION OF APPRAISAL REMEDY

The appraisal remedy has a superficial appeal and plausibility. However, from the dissenting shareholder's point of view it is traditionally not an attractive remedy, and a considerable amount of litigation has been pursued by shareholders seeking to avoid that remedy.

a. From the shareholders' standpoint there are several disadvantages:

   1) The process involves potentially long delays while the price is established.

   2) Litigation over the value of shares is viewed as expensive and unrewarding.

   3) The corporation is an active participant in the judicial proceeding and seeks to establish the lowest possible valuation. The corporation has extensive knowledge about its own affairs and virtually unlimited resources to litigate the issue.

   4) In many states, no payment is made by the corporation until all litigation is completed, and there is no assurance that the final valuation will be in excess of the amount offered by the corporation originally.

b. The procedures established by the MBCA (1984) attempt to alleviate many of the traditional disadvantages of this remedy.

c. In Delaware, under *Weinberger* statutory appraisal is the shareholder's sole remedy when the only issue in the cash out merger is the fairness of the price. (See part XIX B 5.)

I. VOLUNTARY DISSOLUTION

Most state statutes have several dissolution provisions designed for different situations.

1. DISSOLUTION BEFORE COMMENCEMENT OF BUSINESS

Streamlined provisions permit dissolution before commencement of business by the incorporators or initial directors filing a simple notice of dissolution. MBCA (1984) § 14.01.

2. DISSOLUTION BY UNANIMOUS CONSENT OF SHAREHOLDERS

Dissolution is permitted in many states at any time with the unanimous consent of the shareholders if suitable provision is made for creditors. This provision is widely used by closely held corporations.

a. MBCA (1984) does not contain a special provision to this effect; even though shareholders may act by unanimous consent under the MBCA (1984), action by directors is also required for dissolution.

3. REGULAR DISSOLUTION

Where other dissolution provisions are not applicable, a corporation may dissolve only upon approval of the board of directors and vote of a majority (or some other specified percentage) of the shareholders. See MBCA (1984) § 14.02. In this regard, dissolution is similar to other organic changes by the corporation.

4. PROCEDURE FOLLOWING DECISION TO DISSOLVE

Some states require the filing of a notice of intent to dissolve, followed by a period in which the business and affairs of the corporation are wound up, followed by the filing of final articles of dissolution. The MBCA (1969) followed this multiple step procedure. In other states, only articles of dissolution are filed. See MBCA (1984) § 14.03.

a. Some states adopt a "file at the beginning of dissolution" procedure while others adopt a "file when dissolution is completed" procedure.

b. MBCA (1984) § 14.03 permits articles of dissolution to be filed at any time during the dissolution process.

5. DISSOLUTION PROCEDURES

Notice of the impending dissolution must be given to creditors. MBCA (1984) § 14.06, 14.07. Final dissolution occurs only after all franchise and other tax obligations have been fully satisfied.

Example: An Illinois corporation qualifies to transact business in New Jersey. It later dissolves under Illinois law but takes no steps to withdraw from New Jersey even though that state provides a procedure for withdrawal of dissolved corporations. The corporation remains liable to suit in New Jersey until it follows the required New Jersey procedure. *DR Hess & Clark, Inc. v. Metalsalts Corp.*, 119 F.Supp. 427 (D.N.J.1954).

a. State statutes usually provide that the existence of a corporation continues after dissolution for a stated period so that the corporation may be sued on pre-dissolution claims. MBCA (1984) § 14.07.

b. Doubt exists in many states as to the status of post-dissolution claims, e.g. claims arising from injuries after the corporation is dissolved but caused by products manufactured by the corporation before it was dissolved. (See the examples in part XIX D 2 c.)

c. For obvious reasons, there is no statutory right of appraisal in connection with a voluntary dissolution.

6. EQUITABLE LIMITATIONS ON DISSOLUTION

Equitable limitations on the power to dissolve have sometimes been imposed in situations where a voluntary dissolution is unfair to minority shareholders or is a "freeze out" of such shareholders. Standards, however, are elusive.

a. Where the business prognosis is bad and the corporation is losing money immediate dissolution is reasonable, since the majority should not be required to wait until the corporation is insolvent and their investment lost. However, dissolution in such circumstances may involve the sale of assets at grossly inadequate prices.

b. Cases have arisen where dissolution is part of a broader scheme to eliminate some shareholders from sharing in the future profits of a good business.

   1) The business may be turned over to a new corporation which is owned by some but not all of the original owners. *Lebold v. Inland Steel Co.*, 125 F.2d 369 (7th Cir.1941).

   2) In some early cases, dissolution and reincorporation was used to eject a minority from a successful venture. Today, such a transaction is normally cast as a cash out merger. The tests developed in the cash merger cases may have potential applicability in dissolutions that are designed to eliminate unwanted minority shareholders.

J. REVIEW QUESTIONS

XIX–1. An amendment to articles of incorporation may be freely made so long as it does not eliminate vested rights.

True _______ False _______

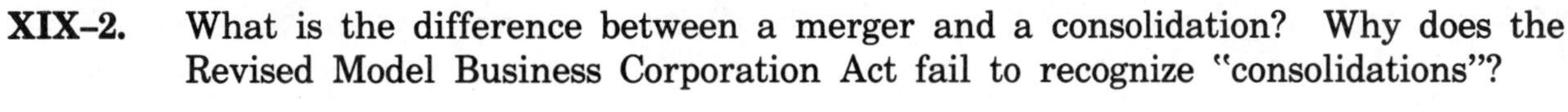

XIX–2. What is the difference between a merger and a consolidation? Why does the Revised Model Business Corporation Act fail to recognize "consolidations"?

XIX–3. How does a "cash merger" differ from an ordinary merger?

XIX–4. What is a "short form merger"?

XIX–5. What are the alphabetical references to reorganizations, "A", "B", "C", and so forth?

XIX–6. What is the relationship between statutory and non-statutory methods of combining two corporations?

XIX–7. What is a "de facto merger"?

XIX–8. What are "appraisal rights"?

XIX-9. May a corporation sell substantially all its assets without the approval of shareholders?

XIX-10. What are "going private" transactions and what legal requirements are applicable to them?

XIX-11. What is a "leveraged buyout"?

XIX-12. If a person has a right of dissent and appraisal he is fully protected and has no reason to complain about the treatment of his interest in the corporation.

True _______ False _______

XIX-13. Corporation A owns 93 per cent of the outstanding shares of Corporation B. The remaining 7 per cent of the shares are held by 50 individuals. Corporation A determines that it should eliminate the minority shareholders of Corporation B before entering into a transaction with Corporation B. It therefore creates a new wholly owned corporation, Corporation C, and merges Corporation B into Corporation C. The merger agreement provides that the minority shareholders of Corporation B are to receive $60 per share in cash, a fair price, and that the transaction is to be approved only if a majority of the minority shareholders approve it. If the required approval is obtained, is the transaction valid? What remedy, if any, do minority shareholders have who are dissatisfied with the $60 price?

XIX-14. D corporation has a provision in its articles of incorporation providing for cumulative voting for directors. The corporation law of D's state of incorporation does not require that shareholders be afforded cumulative voting. In addition the state statute gives the corporation the right to amend, alter or repeal any provisions in the articles of incorporation. D has sent a notice to its shareholders of a meeting at which a resolution to amend its articles of incorporation to eliminate the provision for cumulative voting will be considered. P is a minority shareholder who has enough shares to elect one director voting cumulatively but will be unable to do so if the cumulative voting provision is eliminated. P brings an action to restrain D from amending its article of incorporation by eliminating the cumulative voting provisions. Is P entitled to an injunction?

XIX–15. P is the owner of 40 of the stock in D corporation which operates the Grey Sox Baseball Team in Fun City, under a league franchise. D's directors have approved the removal of the franchise to another location. P brings an action to enjoin the club's move. He contends that D's directors have agreed to dispose of substantially all D's assets outside the ordinary course of business and that such a transaction is valid only if it complies with the state corporation act that requires the owners of ⅔rds of the common stock to consent to the transfer. Is P entitled to an injunction?

XIX–16. P is a preferred shareholder in D corporation, a corporation of State Y. There are accumulated unpaid dividends on P's stock of $1,800 per share. D has adopted a plan of merger wherein it plans to merge with its wholly-owned subsidiary DD. Under the plan of merger P's preferred stock would be converted into one share of new preferred and 5 shares of new common. Under the laws of State Y a shareholder who objects to a merger is entitled to dissent and appraisal, but this remedy is specifically not made exclusive. P brings an action to enjoin the merger on the ground that the merger is unfair to the preferred shareholders since they lose all their accumulated unpaid dividends. May P obtain an injunction?

*

FOREIGN CORPORATIONS

Analysis

Corporations that are formed under the laws of other states are referred to as foreign corporations. While corporations formed under the law of foreign countries are also referred to as foreign corporations, the discussion below is limited to corporations formed under the laws of other states within the United States.

A. RIGHT TO TRANSACT BUSINESS IN STATES OTHER THAN THE STATE OF INCORPORATION

States have the constitutional right to exclude foreign corporations from transacting local business within that state but may not exclude foreign corporations from entering into transactions with that state's citizens in interstate commerce. Every state permits foreign corporations to qualify to transact business in that state.

1. QUALIFICATION TO TRANSACT BUSINESS

A foreign corporation qualifies to transact business by obtaining a certificate of authority to transact business in the state.

a. An application for a certificate of authority must contain information required by statute. MBCA (1984) § 15.03(a). A certified copy of the foreign corporation's articles of incorporation must accompany the application. It must also be accompanied by the required filing fee.

b. The foreign corporation's name must meet the statutory standards for names. If the foreign corporation's name is in unavailable, the foreign corporation must designate a fictitious name under which it will transaction business in the state. MBCA (1984) § 15.06.

c. A foreign corporation qualifying to transact business in the state must designate a registered office and registered agent. MBCA (1984) § 15.07.

d. A qualified corporation may withdraw from a state by following mandated statutory procedures. MBCA (1984) § 15.20.

2. WHEN IS QUALIFICATION REQUIRED?

Qualification is required when the foreign corporation's local business activities are such that it is deemed transacting business in the foreign state; transactions involving interstate commerce are not considered in this determination.

a. This test is necessarily subjective and fact dependent.

b. Statutes contain a list of activities that do not constitute the transaction of business within the state. MBCA (1984) § 15.01(b). This list includes:

1) Maintaining, defending or settling litigation;

2) Holding meetings of the board of directors or shareholders of the corporation within the state, or carrying on other internal activities of the corporation within the state;

3) Maintaining bank accounts within the state;

4) Maintaining offices or agencies to transfer securities of the corporation;

5) Selling through independent contractors;

6) Soliciting orders by mail or through agents if the orders require acceptance outside the state;

7) Creating or acquiring indebtedness, mortgages, or securities interests within the state;

8) Securing or collecting debts or enforcing mortgages and security interests or property located within the state;

9) Owning, without more, real or personal property;

10) Conducting an isolated transaction that is completed within 30 days and is not one likely to reoccur or one that involves a course of repeated transactions of a like nature;

11) Transacting business in interstate commerce.

Example: A foreign corporation opens a local office to sell the products it manufactures in a state in which it is not qualified to transact business. It must thereafter qualify to transact business in that state.

Example: A foreign corporation solicits purchasers of its product by mail. It opens a warehouse in a state in which it is not qualified to transact business and fills orders from that warehouse in an eight state region, including the state in which the warehouse is located. The corporation must qualify to transact business in the state in which its warehouse is located.

c. Most large publicly held corporations qualify to transact business in all or virtually all states.

3. EFFECT OF QUALIFYING TO TRANSACT BUSINESS

A foreign corporation that qualifies to transact business in a state generally obtains the rights and privileges of domestic corporations formed within that state. MBCA (1984) § 15.05(b).

a. A qualified foreign corporation also becomes subject to suit in the state not only on transactions occurring within the state but on other transactions as well, subject to principles of forum non conveniens.

b. A qualified foreign corporation becomes subject to state taxes on the proportion of income earned from business within that state.

1) Allocation of income and expense is an important aspect of state taxation of multistate corporations. The United States Supreme Court has actively reviewed allocation provisions in state laws to assure that the taxation is not a burden on interstate commerce.

4. FAILURE TO QUALIFY WHEN REQUIRED TO DO SO

State statutes provide a variety of sanctions applicable to corporations that are required to qualify to transact business but fail to do so.

a. The corporation may be disqualified from suing in the courts of that state, or from interposing the statute of limitations in litigation brought against it within the state. MBCA (1984) § 15.02(a) (courts of state closed to proceedings brought by unqualified foreign corporations).

1) State statutes usually prohibit a successor to an unqualified foreign corporation, or an assignee, to maintain a suit that would be barred if brought directly by the predecessor or assignor. MBCA (1984) § 15.02(b).

2) The MBCA (1984) and the statutes of many states provide that qualification after suit is filed permits the suit to be maintained. In other words, the closure of the courts is designed to assure qualification rather than being a sanction for failing to qualify.

b. The statutes of some states make unenforceable contracts entered into by a nonqualified corporation that should have qualified to transact business. This is a true sanction for failing to qualify. The MBCA (1984) does not contain such a sanction.

c. Most states impose a monetary penalty on the corporation for each year that it should have qualified to transact business but did not. MBCA (1984) § 15.02(d). Some states also impose penalties on officers or directors who are within the state.

B. AMENABILITY OF NONQUALIFIED CORPORATION TO SUIT

A corporation that is not required to qualify to transact business in the state may nevertheless have sufficient contacts with that state to be subject to service of process within that state on suits arising out of those contacts. *International Shoe Co. v. Washington,* 326 U.S. 310, 66 S.Ct. 154 (1945); *Helicopteros Nacionales de Colombia, S.A. v. Hall,* 466 U.S. 408, 104 S.Ct. 1868 (1984).

C. LIABILITY OF NONQUALIFIED CORPORATION TO STATE TAXATION

A corporation that is not required to qualify to transact business in the state may also be subject to taxation in that state but the tax must be commensurate with the corporation's activities in that state. Requirements include a sufficient nexus with the taxing state, fair relationship of tax to benefits received, nondiscrimination against interstate commerce and fair apportionment. *Mobil Oil Corp. v. Commissioner* 445 U.S. 425, 100 S.Ct. 1223 (1980). A federal statute, the Federal Interstate Income Act of 1959, 15 U.S.C.A § 381, et seq., limits the application of state income tax laws to foreign corporations where the only contact with the state is solicitation of orders in interstate commerce.

D. INTERNAL AFFAIRS RULE

Litigation involving corporate issues may be filed in states other than the state of incorporation.

1. GENERAL RULE

The general conflicts of law rule is that the internal affairs of a corporation are governed by the laws of the state of incorporation. This rule is incorporated into statute in many states. MBCA (1984) § 15.05(c).

Example: A corporation planning a cash out merger is sued in a state other than its state of incorporation by shareholders resident in that state seeking to enjoin the merger, which is not permitted under the laws of the state in which suit is brought. The internal affairs rule requires the state court to apply the law of the state of incorporation in determining the validity of the cash out merger, the procedures that must be followed to approve it, and the rights of dissenting shareholders.

a. The internal affairs rule means that many issues of Delaware law are resolved in federal or state courts other than in Delaware.

2. SPECIAL RULES IN NEW YORK AND CALIFORNIA

New York and California have adopted statutes that require courts to apply domestic law principles to a limited number of issues to corporations that are incorporated in other states but have dominant economic contacts with New York of California.

a. New York requires corporations doing business in New York to be subject to New York statutory provisions imposing liability on directors for cash or property distributions to shareholders that is unlawful under New York law. N.Y. BCL §§ 1315–1319.

b. California requires corporations incorporated in other states that have their predominant business activities in California and more than half of their outstanding shares held by persons resident in California to provide procedural protections to shareholders, including cumulative voting, permitting removal of directors without cause, defining the directors' duty of care, and providing for dissenters' rights in specified situations. Corporations subject to these provisions are sometimes called "pseudo-foreign" corporations. Cal.G.C.L. § 2115.

c. The constitutionality of these statutes has never been definitively resolved. In recent decisions by the Supreme Court of the United States, the power of the state of incorporation to regulate the affairs of domestic corporations has been cast in near constitutional terms.

APPENDIX A

GLOSSARY

A

accredited investor is a defined term in Regulation D promulgated under the Securities Act of 1933. Accredited investors are basically sophisticated investors who do not need the protection of the Securities Act in making investment decisions; sales to accredited investors are not counted in applying exemptions in Regulation D that depend on the number of investors to whom sales are made.

accounts payable are amounts owed by a business on open account to creditors for goods and services. Analysts look at the relationship between accounts payable and total purchases as an indication of sound day-to-day financial management.

accounts receivable are amounts owing to a business for merchandise or services sold on open account. See liquidity.

accumulated earnings tax is a special penalty tax imposed on corporations that fail to pay dividends or distribute earnings and accumulate funds in excess of foreseeable needs in order to avoid the taxation of dividends.

adoption is a contract principle by which a person agrees to assume a contract previously made for his or her benefit. An adoption speaks only from the time such person agrees, in contrast to a "ratification" which relates back to the time the original contract was made. In corporation law, the concept is applied when a newly formed corporation accepts a preincorporation contract made for its benefit by a promoter.

affiliate is a corporation that is related to another corporation by shareholdings or other means of control. It includes not only a parent or a subsidiary but also corporations that are under common control.

aggressor corporation is a corporation that attempts to obtain control of a publicly held corporation, often by a cash tender offer to shareholders, but also possibly by way of merger, which requires agreement or assent of the target's board of directors.

air pocket is a market phenomena where shares fall sharply, usually in the wake of negative news such as unexpected poor earnings. Shareholders rush to sell and few buyers can be found: as a result, the price plunges dramatically, i. e., like an airplane hitting an air pocket.

all holders' rule is a rule adopted by the SEC that prohibits a public offer by the issuer of shares that is made to some but less than all the holders of a class of shares.

alternative constituencies or **non-stockholder constituencies** are groups other than shareholders that have an interest in the well being of corporations: employees, customers, communities, states, etc. Statutes in more than one-half of the states permit directors to consider the interests of alternative constituencies when making major policy decisions with respect to the corporation.

amortization is an accounting procedure that gradually reduces the cost or value of a limited life or intangible asset through periodic charges against income. For fixed assets amortization is called "depreciation," and for wasting assets (natural resources) it is "depletion." The periodic charges are usually treated as current expenses for purposes of determining income.

amotion is the common law procedure by which a director may be removed for cause by the shareholders.

antidilution provisions appear in convertible securities to guarantee that the conversion privilege is not affected by share reclassifications, share splits, share dividends, or similar transactions that may increase the number of outstanding shares without increasing the corporate capital.

appraisal. See **dissent and appraisal.**

arbitragers are market investors who take offsetting positions in the same or similar securities in order to profit from small price variations. An arbitrager, for example, may buy shares on the Pacific Coast Exchange and simultaneously sell the same shares on the New York Stock Exchange if any price discrepancy occurs between the quotations in the two markets. By taking advantage of momentary disparities in prices between markets, arbitragers perform the economic function of making those markets more efficient.

arbs is a slang term for arbitragers.

articles of incorporation is the name customarily given to the document that is filed in order to form a corporation. Under various state statutes, this document may be called the "certificate of incorporation," "charter," "articles of association," or other similar name.

authorized shares are the shares described in the articles of incorporation which a corporation may issue. Modern corporate practice recommends authorization of more shares than it is currently planned to issue.

B

bear is a slang term for a speculator who believes securities prices are going to decline. A pessimist is "bearish." Contrast: bull.

beneficial holders of securities are persons who have the equitable or legal title to shares but who have not registered the shares in their names on the records of the corporation. See also: record owner.

bid and asked are terms that deal with price quotations for securities or commodities. "Bid" is the highest price a prospective buyer is prepared to pay at a particular time for a trading unit; "asked" is the lowest price a prospective seller of the same unit is prepared to accept. Together, the two prices constitute a quotation by the market maker in the security; the difference between the two prices is the "spread." Although bid and asked prices are common to all securities trading, "bid and asked" usually refers to securities traded "over the counter" and to commodities and commodities futures trading. See also: spread; over the counter.

blank shares. See: series of preferred shares.

block is a large quantity of securities involved in a single trade. As a general guide, block trades involve 10,000 or more shares or bonds with a total face amount in excess of $200,000.

blockage is a price phenomenon: a large block of shares may be more difficult to market than a smaller block, particularly if the market is thin. The discount at which a large block sells below the price of a smaller block is blockage. Blockage is generally a phenomenon of shares which do not represent the controlling interest in a corporation. Compare: control premium.

blue chip shares are common shares of nationally known companies that have a long record of profit growth and dividend payment and reputations for quality management, products, and services. Blue chip shares typically are relatively high priced and low yielding, and are viewed as conservative investments.

blue sky laws are state statutes that regulate the sale of securities to the public within the state. Most blue sky laws require the registration of new issues of securities with a state agency that reviews selling documents for accuracy and completeness. Blue sky laws also may regulate securities brokers and salesmen.

bond discount. See: discount.

bonds are long term debt instruments secured by a lien on some or all the corporate property. Historically, a bond was payable to bearer and interest coupons representing annual or semiannual payments of interest were attached (to be "clipped" periodically and submitted for payment). Today, most bonds are issued in registered or book entry form. Bondholders in effect have an IOU from the issuer; they are creditors and not owners of the enterprise. The word bond is sometimes used more broadly to refer also to unsecured debt instruments, i. e., debentures. Income bonds are hybrid instruments that take the form of a bond, but the interest obligation is limited or tied to the corporate earnings for the year. Participating bonds take the form of a typical debt instrument but the interest obligation is not fixed so that holders are entitled to receive additional amounts from excess earnings or from excess distributions, depending on the terms of the participating bond.

bonus shares are par value shares issued without consideration, usually in connection with the issuance of preferred or senior securities, or debt instruments. Bonus shares are considered a species of watered shares and may impose a liability on the recipient equal to the amount of par value.

book entry describes the method of reflecting ownership of publicly traded securities in which customers of brokerage firms receive confirmations of transactions and monthly statements but not certificates. Brokerage firms also may reflect their customers' ownership of securities by book entry in the records of a central clearing corporation, principally Depository Trust Company (DTC). DTC reflects transactions between brokerage firms primarily by book entry in its records rather than by the physical movement of securities. Shares held by DTC are recorded in the name of its nominee, Cede and Company. See central clearing system.

book value is the value of shares determined on the basis of a calculation using the numbers appearing on the books of the corporation. Using the corporation's latest balance sheet, the liabilities are subtracted from assets, an appropriate amount is deducted to reflect the interest of senior securities (preferred shares), and what remains is divided by the number of outstanding shares to obtain the book value of a share. Book value is widely used as an estimate of value, particularly of closely held shares, but has certain limitations: it is based on accounting conventions, may not reflect unrealized appreciation or depreciation of assets, and does not take into account future prospects of the business.

broker in a securities transaction, means a person who acts as an agent for a buyer or seller, or an intermediary between a buyer and seller, usually charging a commission. A broker who specializes in shares, bonds, commodities, or options must be registered with the exchange where the specific securities are traded. A broker should be distinguished from a dealer who, unlike the broker, buys or sells for his own account. See: dealer; underwriting. Securities firms typically act as dealers and brokers, depending on the security involved.

bull is a slang term for a speculator who believes securities prices are going to increase. An optimist is "bullish." Contrast: bear.

bust up merger is a slang term for a leveraged buyout in which the acquiring corporation plans to sell off lines of business owned by the acquired corporation in order to pay down a part of the loans the proceeds of which were used to purchase the shares of the acquired corporation.

buyout is the purchase of a controlling percentage of a company's shares. A buyout often involves all of the company's outstanding shares. A buyout can be accomplished through negotiation, through a tender offer, or through a merger.

bylaws are the formal rules of internal governance adopted by a corporation. Bylaws define the rights and obligations of various officers, persons, or groups within the corporate structure and provide rules for routine matters such as calling meetings and the like. Most state corporation statutes contemplate that every corporation will adopt bylaws.

C

call for redemption. See: redemption.

calls are options to buy securities at a stated price for a stated period. Many calls (or call options) to purchase shares of companies listed on the New York Stock Exchange are themselves publicly traded. Calls also are written on a variety of indexes, foreign currencies, and other securities. The person who commits himself or herself to sell the security upon the request of the call holder is referred to as the call writer; the act of making the purchase of the securities pursuant to the call option is referred to as exercise of the option. The price at which the call is exercisable is the strike price. See also: puts; stock index future; index options.

capital stock is another phrase for common shares, often used when the corporation has only one class of shares outstanding.

capital surplus (in the old Model Business Corporation Act nomenclature) is an equity or capital account which reflects the capital contributed for shares not allocated to stated capital: the excess of issuance price over the par value of issued shares or the consideration paid for no par shares allocated specifically to capital surplus. Capital surplus may be distributed to shareholders under certain circumstances or used for purchase or redemption of shares more readily than stated capital.

capitalization is an imprecise term that usually refers to the amounts received by a corporation for the issuance of its shares. However, it may also be used to refer to the proceeds of loans to a corporation made by its shareholders (which may be in lieu of capital contributions) or even to capital raised by the issuance of long term bonds or debentures to third persons. Depending on the context, it may also refer to accumulated earnings not withdrawn from the corporation.

cash flow refers to an analysis of the movement of cash through a business as contrasted with the earnings of the business. For example, a mandatory debt repayment is taken into account in a cash flow analysis even though such a repayment does not reduce earnings. See: negative cash flow.

cash merger or **cash out merger**is a statutory merger transaction in which certain shareholders or interests in a corporation are required to accept cash for their shares while other shareholders receive shares in the continuing enterprise. Modern statutes generally authorize cash mergers, though courts test such mergers on the basis of fairness and, in some states, business purpose.

cash tender offer is a public offer to purchase for a specified fraction (usually a majority) of the target corporation's shares from persons who tender their shares. Cash tender offers are regulated by the Williams Act.

C corporation is a corporation that has not elected (or is disqualified from electing) S corporation tax status. The taxable income of a C corporation is subject to tax at the corporate level while dividends continue to be taxed at the shareholder level. Compare S corporation; double taxation.

Cede & Company is the nominee for Depository Trust Company, the principal central clearing corporation. See book entry.

central clearing system refers to the modern system of clearing securities transactions in which shares are held of record by a nominee for a central clearing corporation and most transactions are reflected solely by book entries on the books of brokerage firms and the central clearing corporation. See book entry.

CEO stands for "chief executive officer" of a publicly held corporation. *CEO* is a preferred and useful designation because official titles of such persons vary widely from corporation to corporation.

CERCLA is the Comprehensive Environmental Response, Compensation, and Liability Act, also known as Superfund. CERCLA provides for liability of owners and operators of waste disposal sites in which hazardous substances have been deposited.

certificate of incorporation in most states is the document issued by the Secretary of State that evidences the acceptance of articles of incorporation and the commencement of the corporate existence. In some states the certificate of incorporation is the name given to the document filed with the Secretary of State, i. e., the articles of incorporation. The Model Business Corporation Act (1984) has eliminated certificates of incorporation, requiring only a fee receipt.

charter may mean (i) the document filed with the Secretary of State, i. e., the articles of incorporation, or (ii) the grant by the State of the privilege of conducting business with limited liability. Charter may be used in a colloquial sense to refer to the basic constitutive documents of the corporation.

class A common shares. See participating preferred shares.

class voting. See: voting group.

class of shares. Classes of shares are shares with different voting and/or financial rights established in the articles of incorporation. Traditional classes of shares are common shares and preferred shares.

close corporation or **closely held corporation** is a corporation with relatively few shareholders and no regular market for its shares. There is no litmus test for when a corporation should be considered closely held and the definition may in part depend on the substantive context in which it arises. In addition to the small number of shareholders and lack of public market, close corporations usually have made no public offering of shares and the shares themselves are usually subject to restrictions on transfer. Close and closely held are synonymous in this context.

closely held. See: close corporation.

commercial paper is a generic term for short-term obligations usually with maturities ranging from 2 to 270 days, issued by banks, corporations, and other borrowers to investors. Such instruments are unsecured and usually sold at a discount from face value, although some are interest-bearing.

common shareholders are holders of common shares, the ultimate owners of the residual interest of a corporation. See: common shares.

common shares represent the residual ownership interests in the corporation. Holders of common shares select directors to manage the enterprise, are entitled to dividends out of the earnings of the enterprise declared by the directors, and are entitled to a per share distribution of whatever assets remain upon dissolution after satisfying or making provisions for creditors and holders of senior securities.

consolidation is an amalgamation of two corporations pursuant to statutory provision in which both of the corporations disappear and a new corporation is formed. The Model Business Corporation Act (1984) eliminates the consolidation as a distinct type of corporate amalgamation. Compare: merger.

control of a corporation by a person normally means that the person has power to vote a majority of the outstanding shares. However, control may be reflected in a significantly smaller block if the remaining shares are scattered in small, disorganized holdings.

control person in securities law is a person who is deemed to be in a control relationship with the issuer. Sales of securities by control persons are subject to many of the requirements applicable to the sale of securities directly by the issuer. In addition, controlling persons have a duty under federal law to prevent insider trading by persons under their control. See ITSFEA.

control premium refers to the pricing phenomenon by which shares that carry the power to control a corporation are more valuable per share than the shares that do not carry a power of control. The control premium is often computed not on a per share basis but on the aggregate increase in value of the "control block" over the going market or other price of shares which are not part of the "control block."

control share acquisition is the name of state antitakeover statutes that require a shareholder who acquires shares that causes his ownership to break through specified percentages (e.g. 20 per cent, 33 per cent, 50 per cent) to obtain shareholder approval of the acquisition if the acquired shares are to retain their voting right. The constitutionality of these statutes was upheld in *CTS Corporation v. Dynamics Corporation of America.*

conversion securities are the securities into which convertible securities may be converted. See: convertible securities.

convertible securities are securities that include the right of exchanging the convertible securities, usually preferred shares or debentures, for a designated number of shares of another class, usually common shares, called the conversion securities. The ratio between the convertible and conversion securities is fixed at the time the convertible securities are issued, and is usually protected against dilution.

co-promoters. See: promoters.

corporate opportunity is a fiduciary concept that limits the power of officers, directors, and employees to take personal advantage of opportunities that belong to the corporation.

corporation by estoppel is a doctrine that prevents a third person from holding an "officer," "director," or "shareholder" of a nonexistent corporation personally liable on an obligation entered into in the name of the nonexistent corporation on the theory that the third person relied on the existence of the corporation and is now "estopped" from denying that the corporation existed.

cumulative dividends on preferred shares carry over from one year to the next if a preference dividend is omitted. An omitted cumulative dividend must be made up in a later year before any dividend may be paid on the common shares in that later year. However, cumulative dividends are not debts of the corporation but merely a right to priority in future discretionary distributions.

cumulative to the extent earned dividends on preferred shares are cumulative dividends that are limited in any one year to the available earnings of the corporation in that year.

cumulative voting is a method of voting that allows substantial minority shareholders to obtain representation on the board of directors. When voting cumulatively, a shareholder may cast all of his or her available votes in an election in favor of a single candidate.

D

D & O insurance refers to directors' and officers' liability insurance. Such insurance, which is widely available commercially, insures such persons against claims based on negligence, failure to disclose, and to a limited extent, other defalcations. Such insurance provides coverage against expenses and to a limited extent fines, judgments, and amounts paid in settlement. D & O insurance also insures the corporation against its indemnification obligations to officers and directors.

deadlock in a closely held corporation arises when a control structure permits one or more factions of shareholders to block corporate action if they disagree with some aspect of corporate policy. A deadlock often arises with respect to the election of directors, e. g., by an equal division of shares between two factions, but may also arise at the level of the board of directors itself.

debentures are long term unsecured debt instruments. Historically, a debenture was payable to bearer and interest coupons representing annual or semiannual payments of interest are attached. Most debentures today are issued in registered or book entry form. See: bonds.

deep rock doctrine is a principle in bankruptcy law by which unfair or inequitable claims presented by controlling shareholders of bankrupt corporations may be subordinated to claims of general or trade creditors; this doctrine is now codified in the Bankruptcy Code. The doctrine receives its name from the corporate name of the subsidiary involved in the leading case articulating the doctrine.

de facto corporation at common law is a partially formed corporation that provides a shield against personal liability of shareholders for corporate obligations; such a corporation may be attacked only by the state.

de facto merger is a transaction that has the economic effect of a statutory merger but is cast in the form of an acquisition of assets or an acquisition of voting stock and is treated by a court as if it were a statutory merger. See: reorganization.

de jure corporation at common law is a corporation that is sufficiently formed to be recognized as a corporation for all purposes. A de jure corporation may exist even though some minor statutory requirements have not been fully complied with.

delectus personae is a Latin phrase used in partnership law to describe the power each partner possesses to accept or reject proposed new members of the firm.

Depository Trust Corporation is the principal central clearing agency for securities transactions on the public markets. See: book entry; central clearing system.

deregistration of an issuer occurs when the number of securities holders of an issuer registered under section 12 of the Securities Exchange Act of 1934 has declined to the point where registration is no longer required. See: registered corporation.

derivative suit is a suit brought by a shareholder in the name of a corporation to correct a wrong done to the corporation.

dilution of outstanding shares results from the issuance of additional shares. The dilution may be of voting power, if shares are not issued proportionately to the holdings of existing shareholders, or it may be financial, if shares are issued disproportionately and the price at which the new shares are issued is less than the market or book value of the outstanding shares prior to the issuance of the new shares. See also: antidilution provisions.

directory requirements are minor statutory requirements. At common law, a de jure corporation may be created despite the failure to comply with directory requirements relating to its formation. Important statutory requirements are called mandatory requirements.

discount shares are par value shares issued for cash less than par value. Discount shares are considered a species of watered shares and may impose a liability on the recipient equal to the difference between the par value and the cash for which such shares were issued.

dissension in a closely held corporation refers to personal quarrels or disputes between shareholders that may make business relations unpleasant and interfere with the successful operation of the business. Dissension, however, may occur without constitution oppression or causing a deadlock or adversely affecting the corporation's business.

dissent and appraisal is a limited statutory right granted to minority shareholders who object to specified fundamental transactions, e.g. mergers. In an appraisal proceeding a court determines the appraised value of their shares and the corporation pays such appraised value to the dissenting shareholder in cash. This right may be referred to as the "appraisal right" or "dissenters' rights." The Model Business Corporation Act (1984) uses the term "dissenters' rights to obtain payment for their shares" to describe this right. The right of dissent and appraisal exists only to the extent specifically provided by statute.

dissenters' rights. See: dissent and appraisal.

distribution is a payment to shareholders by a corporation. If out of current or past earnings (called "earned surplus" in the MBCA (1984)) it is a dividend. The word distribution is sometimes accompanied by a word describing the source or purpose of the payment, e. g., Distribution of Capital Surplus, or Liquidating Distribution.

dividend is a payment to shareholders from or out of current or past earnings (called "earned surplus" in the MBCA (1984)). The word dividend is sometimes used more broadly to refer to any payment to shareholders though a more appropriate term for payments out of capital is distribution.

double taxation refers to the structure of taxation under the Internal Revenue Code of 1954 which subjects income earned by a C corporation to an income tax at the corporate level and a second tax at the shareholder level if the previously taxed income is distributed to shareholders in the form of dividends.

down stream merger is the merger of a parent corporation into its subsidiary.

E

earnings per share equals a firm's net income divided by the number of shares held by shareholders. Earnings per share is a key statistic in evaluating a share's outlook.

efficient capital market hypothesis posits that securities markets are efficient so that securities prices accurately reflect all publicly available information about the security.

equity or **equity interest** are financial terms that refer in general to the extent of an ownership interest in a venture. In this context, equity refers not to a legal concept but to the financial or accounting definition that an owner's equity in a business is equal to the business's assets minus its liabilities.

equity financing is raising money by the sale of common shares or preferred shares. Equity financing is most popular when securities prices are high so that the most capital can be raised with the issuance of the smallest number of shares.

equity security is a security that represents an interest in the equity of a business. See: equity. Equity securities are usually considered to be common and preferred shares.

ESOP is an acronym for employee stock ownership plan. Such plans acquire shares of the employer for the benefit of employees usually through contributions of the employer to the plan. The purpose of such plans is to acquire ownership of shares of the employer corporation for the benefit of employees. This is usually accomplished through contributions of the employee to the plan. ESOPs are widely used as part of a defensive strategy against unwanted takeover attempts.

ex dividend refers to the date on which a purchaser of publicly traded shares is not entitled to receive a dividend that has been declared and the seller of such shares is entitled to retain the dividend. The ex dividend date is a matter of agreement or of convention to be established by the securities exchange. On the first day shares are traded without the right to receive a dividend, the price will decline by approximately the amount of the dividend; such shares are referred to as "trading ex dividend."

ex rights refers to the date on which a purchaser of publicly traded shares is not entitled to receive rights that have been declared on the shares. Compare: ex dividend.

F

face value is the value of a bond, note, mortgage, or other security, as given on the certificate or instrument, payable upon maturity of the instrument. The face value is also the amount on which interest or coupon payments are calculated. Thus, a 10 bond with a face value of $1000 pays bondholders $100 per year. Face value is also often referred to as the par value or nominal value of the instrument.

forced conversion refers to a conversion of a convertible security that follows a call for redemption at a time when the value of the conversion security is greater than the amount that will be received if the holder permits the security to be redeemed. Normally, a holder of a convertible redeemable security has a period of time after the call for redemption to determine whether or not to exercise the conversion privilege.

fraud on the market describes a principle accepted by the United States Supreme Court in *Basic, Inc. v. Levinson* that a plaintiff may presumptively establish reliance on a false statement in connection with the purchase or sale of securities by relying on the accuracy of the price of the security. This principle is based on to the efficient capital market hypothesis. The presumption may be negated by the defendant proving the plaintiff in fact relied on considerations other than the current market price of securities when deciding to enter into the securities transaction.

freeze-out refers to a process, usually in a closely held corporation, by which minority shareholders are prevented from receiving any direct or indirect financial return from the corporation in an effort to persuade them to liquidate their investment in the corporation on terms favorable to the controlling shareholders. See: squeeze out.

freeze-out merger. See: cash merger.

G

general partners are unlimitedly liable for the debts of the partnership. General partner is usually used in contrast with limited partner in a limited partnership, but general partner is also sometimes used to refer to any partner in a general partnership.

going private refers to a transaction in which public shareholders of a publicly held corporation are compelled to accept cash for their shares while the business is continued to be owned by officers, directors, or large shareholders. A going private transaction may involve a merger of the publicly held corporation into a subsidiary in a cash merger.

going public refers to the first public distribution of securities by an issuer pursuant to registration under the securities acts. If a corporation has been in business for several years, the initial registration by which the corporation goes public is apt to be difficult and expensive.

going short refers to selling a stock or commodity that the seller does not have. An investor who goes short borrows stock from his or her broker, planning to purchase replacement shares at a lower price. If successful, the investor keeps the difference as profit. See also: selling short.

golden parachute is a slang term for a lucrative contract given to a top executive of a company. The contract usually provides additional benefits in case the company is taken over and the executive is either forced to leave the target company or voluntarily leaves it. A golden parachute might include generous severance pay, stock options, or a bonus payable the executive's employment at the company ends.

greenmail is a slang term that refers to a purchase by the target to purchase at a premium over market shares that have been acquired by a potential aggressor. The acquirer in exchange agrees not to pursue its takeover bid.

H

holding company is a corporation that owns a majority of the shares of one or more other corporations. Usually a holding company is not engaged in any business other than the ownership of such majority shares. See: investment companies.

hybrid securities are securities that have some of the attributes of both debt securities and equity securities.

I

incorporators are the person or persons who execute the articles of incorporation. In modern statutes only a single incorporator is required, and the role of the incorporator is largely limited to the act of execution of the articles of incorporation. Restrictions on who may serve as incorporators have largely been eliminated.

indemnification refers to the practice by which corporations pay expenses of officers or directors who are named as defendants in litigation relating to corporate affairs. In some instances corporations may indemnify officers and directors for fines, judgments, or amounts paid in settlement as well as expenses. Broad indemnification rights may raise issues of public policy; on the other hand, it is usually difficult or impossible to persuade persons to serve as directors in the absence of indemnification.

indenture is the contract which defines the rights of holders of bonds or debentures as against the corporation. Typically, the contract is entered into between the corporation and an indenture trustee whose responsibility is to protect the bondholders. The indenture often constitutes a mortgage on specified corporate property to secure the bonds.

in pari delicto is a common law principle also known as the "unclean hands" doctrine. The principle limits a person intending to engage in wrongful conduct from suing another wrongdoer when things do not work out as expected.

inside directors are directors of a publicly held corporation who hold executive positions with management.

insider is a term of uncertain scope that refers to persons having some relationship to an issuer, and whose securities trading on the basis of nonpublic information may be a violation of law. Insider is broader than inside director. See: insider trading.

insider trading refers to transactions in shares of publicly held corporations by persons with inside or advance information on which the trading is based. Usually the trader is an insider with an employment or other relationship of trust and confidence with the corporation. See: tip.

insolvency may refer to either equity insolvency or insolvency in the bankruptcy sense. Equity insolvency means that the business is unable to pay its debts as they mature while bankruptcy insolvency means that the aggregate liabilities of the business exceeds its assets. Since it is not uncommon for a business to be unable to meet its debts as they mature yet have assets that exceed in value its liabilities, or vice versa, it is often important to specify in which sense the term insolvency is being used.

institutional investors are large investors, such as mutual funds, pension funds, insurance companies, and others who largely invest other people's money. Since World War II, institutional investors have accounted for an increasing portion of all public securities ownership.

integrated disclosure program describes the regulations of the Securities and Exchange Commission that permit corporations that have registered under section 12 of the Securities and Exchange Act of 1934 to incorporate by reference information in statements filed under that Act in registration statements under the Securities Act of 1933.

integration describes the regulations of the Securities and Exchange Commission that require all offerings of securities over a period of time to be viewed as a single offering for purposes of determining the availability of an exemption from registration.

interlocking directors are persons who serve simultaneously on the boards of directors of two or more corporations that have dealings with each other. Federal antitrust law prohibits interlocking directors of competing businesses; such directors may also create problems involving fiduciary duties.

intra vires means acts within the powers or stated purposes of a corporation. Intra vires is the opposite of ultra vires.

investment bankers are commercial organizations involved in the business of handling the distribution of new issues of securities. See: underwriters. An investment banker may also provide other investment and advisory services to corporations.

investment companies are corporations that are engaged in the business of investing in securities of other businesses. The most common kind of investment company is the mutual fund. An investment company differs from a holding company in that the latter seeks control of the ventures in which it invests while an investment company seeks the investment for its own sake and normally diversifies its investments. Investment companies are subdivided into "open end" and "closed end" companies. An "open end" company stands ready at all times to redeem its securities at net asset value and to issue new shares to investors on demand; such an investment company is usually known as a mutual fund. An investment company that has a fixed capitalization and neither issues new shares or redeems outstanding shares on request is called a "closed end" company.

issued shares are shares a corporation has actually issued and has not cancelled. Issued shares should be contrasted with authorized shares. Issued shares that have been reacquired by the corporation are called treasury shares. The Model Business Corporation Act (1984) and the statutes of several states have eliminated the concept of treasury shares.

ITSA is the acronym for the Insider Trading Sanctions Act of 1984.

ITSFEA is the acronym for the Insider Trading and Securities Fraud Enforcement Act of 1988.

J

joint venture is a limited purpose partnership largely governed by the rules applicable to partnerships. In an earlier day, many states permitted corporations to participate in joint ventures but treated as ultra vires an attempt by a corporation to become a partner in a general partnership.

junior securities are issues of debt or equity that are subordinate to other issues in terms of dividends, interest, principal, security, or payments upon dissolution. See: preferred share; senior security; subordinated.

L

leverage refers to the advantages that may accrue to a business through the use of debt obtained from third persons in lieu of contributed capital. Such debt improves the earnings allocable to contributed capital if the business earns more on each dollar invested than the interest cost of borrowing funds.

leveraged buyout (or "LBO") is a transaction by which an outside entity purchases all the shares of a public corporation primarily with borrowed funds. Ultimately the debt incurred to finance the takeover is assumed by the acquired business. If incumbent management has a financial and participatory interest in the outside entity, the transaction may be referred to as a management buyout or MBO. A number of leveraged buyouts have failed in the sense that the acquired corporation was unable to service the acquisition debt. See: bust up merger.

leveraged recapitalization is a transaction that involves the substitution of debt for equity in the capital structure of a corporation that fears it may be the subject of a leveraged buyout. A leveraged recapitalization may be undertaken by borrowing funds and distributing them as dividends to shareholders; by distributing evidences of indebtedness to shareholders; by a statutory merger with a subsidiary, and by other methods.

limited partner. See: limited partnership and general partner.

limited partnership is a partnership consisting of one or more limited partners (whose liability for partnership debts is limited to the amount originally invested) and one or more general partners (whose liability for partnership debts is unlimited). To create a limited partnership a certificate must be filed with a state official.

liquidating dividend is a distribution of assets in the form of a dividend from a corporation that is reducing capital or going out of business. Such a payment may arise, for example, when management decides to sell off certain company assets and distribute the proceeds to the shareholders. Such a distribution may not be from current or retained earnings.

liquidity refers to the market characteristic of a security or commodity with enough units outstanding and traded to allow large transactions to occur without a substantial variation in price. Most shares traded on the New York Stock Exchange have liquidity. Institutional investors usually prefer liquid investments since their trading activity have less influence on the market price than if they traded in less liquid securities.

listed security is a security that is publicly traded on a securities exchange or in the NASDAQ over-the-counter quotations. For a security to be listed on an exchange the issuing corporation must meet the requirements established by the exchange and, in most exchanges, sign a listing agreement with the exchange.

litigation committee is a committee of the board of directors created to consider what position the corporation should take with respect to demands made by shareholders that suits be brought on corporate claims or with respect to derivative litigation that has been filed by shareholders to pursue corporate claims. If the litigation committee is disinterested and makes a decision consistent with the business judgment rule that pursuit of that claim or litigation is not in the best interests of the corporation, the court may accept that conclusion and not review the merits of the claim. The precise effect given to a decision by a litigation committee depends on the nature of the litigation and may vary to some extent from state to state.

lockup is a slang term that refers to a transaction that is designed to defeat one party in a contested takeover. A lockup usually involves the setting aside of securities for purchase by friendly interests in order to defeat or make more difficult the competitive takeover.

M

management buyout (usually referred to as an MBO) is a leveraged buyout in which management is a participant. See leveraged buyout.

mandatory requirements are substantive statutory requirements that must be substantially complied with if a de jure corporation is to be formed.

maturity date is the date on which the principal amount of a note, debenture, bond, or other debt instrument becomes due and payable.

merger is an amalgamation of two corporations pursuant to statutory provision in which one of the corporations survives and the other disappears. Compare: consolidation.

misappropriation theory states that an employee violates the federal prohibitions against inside trading when he or she trades on the basis of information that is not publicly known if the trading is in violation of rules imposed by, or duties owed to, the employer. The information need not come directly or indirectly from the issuer of the securities in which the trading takes place.

money market fund is an open-end mutual fund that invests in commercial paper, banker's acceptances, repurchase agreements, government securities, and similar cash-equivalent short term securities. A money market fund pays money market rates of interest.

mutual fund is a publicly held open end investment company that usually invests only in readily marketable securities. See: investment company. An "open end" investment company stands ready at all times to redeem its shares at net asset value. A mutual fund thus provides the advantages of complete liquidity, diversification of investment, and skilled investment advice for the small investor.

N

NASDAQ is an acronym for "National Association of Securities Dealers Automated Quotations" and is the principal recording device for transactions on the over-the-counter market.

negative cash flow refers to a situation where the cash needs of a business exceed its cash intake. Short periods of negative cash flow create no problem for most businesses; longer periods of negative cash flow may require additional capital investment if the business is to avoid insolvency in the equity sense. See: insolvency.

net worth is the amount by which assets exceed liabilities.

new issue is a security being offered to the public for the first time. The distribution of new issues is subject to SEC and state blue sky rules. New issues may be initial public offerings by previously private companies or additional securities offered by public companies. See also: primary market; secondary market.

nimble dividends are dividends paid out of current earnings at a time when there is a deficit in earned surplus (or other financial account from which dividends may be paid). Some state statutes do not permit nimble dividends; these statutes require current earnings to be applied against prior deficits rather than being used to pay a current dividend.

NOBO refers to non-objecting beneficial owner. The Securities and Exchange Commission requires brokerage firms to provide issuers with the names of beneficial owners of securities held in book entry form who do not object to the disclosure of their names to the issuer. The issuer may thereafter communicate directly with the beneficial owner rather than through intermediaries.

nominee registration is a form of securities registration widely used by institutional investors and brokerage firms to avoid onerous requirements of establishing the right of registration by a fiduciary.

noncallable preferred shares or bonds are securities that cannot be redeemed at the option of the issuer. See: callable securities.

noncumulative voting or **straight voting** limits a shareholder to voting no more than the number of shares he owns for a single candidate. Compare: cumulative voting. In noncumulative voting, a majority shareholder will elect the entire board of directors.

nonvoting common shares are shares that expressly have no power to vote. Such shares may be created in most states; in some states, however, nonvoting shares may be entitled to vote as a separate voting group on certain proposed changes adversely affecting that class as such.

no par shares are shares issued under par value statutes that are stated to have no par value. Such shares are issued for the consideration designated by the board of directors; such consideration is allocated to stated capital unless the directors or shareholders determine to allocate a portion to capital surplus. As a result, in many respects no par shares do not differ significantly from par value shares.

novation is a contract principle by which a third person takes over the rights and duties of a party to a contract, such party thereby being released from obligations under the contract. In the law of corporations, the concept may be applied to the release of a promoter who is personally liable on a preincorporation contract when the corporation is formed and adopts the contract. A novation requires the consent of the other party to the contract, but that consent may be implied from the circumstances.

O

oppression in a close corporation involves conduct by the controlling shareholders that deprive a minority shareholder of his or her legitimate expectations concerning roles in the corporation, including participation in management and earnings.

organizational expenses are the costs of organizing a corporation, including filing fees, attorneys' fees, and related expenses. Organizational expenses may also include the cost of raising the initial capital through the distribution of securities.

outside directors are directors of publicly held corporations who do not hold executive positions with management. Outside directors, however, may include investment bankers, attorneys, or others who provide advice or services to incumbent management and thus have financial ties with management; the latter are sometimes referred to as "affiliated" outside directors.

over-the-counter refers to the broad securities market consisting of brokers who purchase or sell securities by computer hook-up or telephone rather than through the facilities of a securities exchange. At one time completely unorganized, the over-the-counter market is now relatively organized with computerized quotation and transaction reporting services.

P

par value or **stated value** of shares is an arbitrary or nominal value assigned to each class of shares issued under par value statutes. At one time par value represented the selling or issuance price of shares, but in modern corporate practice, par value has little significance and serves only a limited role. Shares issued for less than par value are usually referred to as watered shares. The Model Business Corporation Act (1984) and the statutes of many states have eliminated the concept of par value.

participating bonds. See: bonds.

participating preferred shares are preferred shares that, in addition to paying a stipulated dividend, give the holder the right to participate with the common shareholder in additional distributions of earnings, if declared, under specified conditions. Participating preferred shares may be called class A common shares or given a similar designation to reflect their open ended rights. See preferred shares.

pendent jurisdiction is a principle applied in federal courts that allows state created causes of action arising out of the same transaction to be joined with a federal cause of action even if diversity of citizenship is not present.

phantom stock plan is an employee benefit plan in which benefits are determined by reference to the performance of the corporation's common shares. For example, a person receiving benefits based on 1,000 "phantom shares" will have credited to her account each year an amount equal to the dividends declared on 1,000 shares; the number of "phantom shares" will be increased by share dividends or splits actually declared on real shares; on her death or retirement the person will receive a credit equal to the difference between the market price of the "phantom shares" in her account on the date of death or retirement (or a related date) and the market price of the "phantom shares" in her account on the date she was awarded the rights.

poison pill is an issue of shares by a corporation as a protection against an unwanted takeover. A poison pill creates rights existing shareholders to acquire debt or stock of the target (or of the aggressor upon a subsequent merger) upon the occurrence of specified events, such as the announcement of a cash tender offer or the acquisition by an outsider of a specified percentage of the shares of the target. A poison pill raises the potential cost of an acquisition, and either deters a takeover bid or compels the aggressor to negotiate with the target in order to persuade it to withdraw the pill.

pooling agreement is a contractual arrangement among shareholders relating to the voting of their shares. So long as such agreement is limited to voting as shareholders, it is enforceable.

porcupine provisions are defensive provisions in articles of incorporation or bylaws designed to make unwanted takeover attempts impossible or impractical without the consent of the target's board of directors.

preemptive rights give an existing shareholder the opportunity to purchase or subscribe for a proportionate part of a new issue of shares before the shares are offered to other persons. The purpose of preemptive rights is to protect shareholders from dilution of value and control when new shares are issued. In modern statutes, preemptive rights may be limited or denied.

preferred shares are shares that have preferential rights to dividends or to amounts distributable on liquidation, or to both, ahead of common shareholders. Preferred shares are usually entitled only to receive specified limited amounts as dividends or on liquidation. See: participating preferred shares.

preferred shareholders' contract refers to the provisions of the articles of incorporation, the bylaws, or the resolution of the board of directors, creating and defining the rights of holders of the preferred shares in question. Preferred shareholders have only very limited statutory or common law rights outside of the preferred shareholders' contract. However, even provisions creating and defining the rights of holders of preferred shares may usually be amended without the consent of each individual holder of preferred shares. The major protection provided by statute against onerous amendments is the right of preferred shareholders to vote as a separate voting group on such changes.

preincorporation subscription. See: subscription.

price-earnings ratio is the ratio of earnings per share to current stock price.

private placement of securities is the sale of securities to sophisticated investors without registration under federal or state securities acts under the private offering exemption or under Regulation D.

promoters are persons who develop or take the initiative in founding or organizing a business venture. Where more than one promoter is involved in a venture, they are usually described as co-promoters.

prospectus is a document furnished to a prospective purchaser of a security that describes the security being purchased, the issuer, and the investment or risk characteristics of the security. SEC regulations require a prospectus meeting specified requirements to be provided to each prospective purchaser of registered public offerings of securities.

provisional directors are directors appointed by courts pursuant to special close corporation statutes to serve on the board of directors of close corporations with deadlocked boards.

proxy is a person authorized to vote someone else's shares. Depending on the context, proxy may refer to the grant of authority itself, the document granting the authority, or the person granted the power to vote the shares.

proxy solicitation machinery is a phrase commonly used to describe the phenomenon that incumbent management of a publicly held corporation may usually produce large majorities of shareholder votes on any issue it desires. This power is based in part on the ability of incumbent management to use corporate funds to communicate at will with the shareholders and partially on the ability to represent their views as the views of "management."

proxy statement is the document that must accompany a solicitation of proxies under SEC regulations. The purpose of the proxy statement is to provide shareholders with the appropriate information to permit an intelligent decision.

public offering involves the sale of securities by an issuer or a person controlling the issuer to members of the public. Generally, any offering that is not exempt under Regulation D or the private offering exemption of the Securities Act of 1933 and/or similar exemptions under state blue sky laws is considered a public offering. Normally registration of a public offering under those statutes is required though in some instances other exemptions from registration may be available.

publicly held corporation is a corporation with shares held by numerous persons. Typically, a publicly held corporation has shares registered under section 12 of the Securities Exchange Act of 1934, though such registration is not an essential attribute of being publicly held. Shares of publicly held corporations are usually traded either on a securities exchange or over-the-counter.

PUPs or performance unit payments are bonus payments to corporate executives set on a predetermined formula for achieving long term corporate goals.

purchase fund is the provision in some preferred share contracts and bond indentures requiring the issuer to use its best efforts to purchase a specified number of the preferred shares or bonds annually at a price not exceeding par or face value. Unlike sinking fund provisions (which require that a certain number of bonds be retired annually) purchase funds require only that an offer to the purchaser be made at the specified price; if no securities are tendered, none are retired.

puts are options to sell securities at a stated price for a stated period. If the price declines, a holder of a put may purchase the shares at the lower market price and "put" the shares to the put writer at the contract price. Puts on some New York Stock Exchange securities are publicly traded but more securities have call options written than put options. See: calls.

Q

qualified stock option is an option to purchase shares awarded to an employee of the corporation under terms that qualify the option for special tax treatment under the Internal Revenue Code.

qualifying share is a share of common stock owned by a person in order to qualify as a director of the issuing corporation in a corporation that requires directors to be shareholders.

quo warranto is a common law writ designed to test whether a person exercising power is legally entitled to do so. In the law of corporations, quo warranto may be used to test whether a corporation was validly organized or whether it has power to engage in the business in which it is involved.

R

raider is a slang term for an aggressor in a takeover attempt—an individual or corporation who attempts to take control of a target corporation by buying a controlling interest in its stock.

recapitalization is a restructuring of the capital of the corporation through amendment of the articles of incorporation or a merger with a subsidiary or parent corporation. Recapitalizations usually involve the elimination of unpaid cumulated preferred dividends, but may also involve reduction or elimination of par value, the creation of new classes of senior securities, or similar transactions. See: leveraged recapitalization.

record date is the date on which the identity of shareholders entitled to vote, to receive dividends, or to receive notice is ascertained.

record owner of shares is the person in whose name shares are registered on the records of the corporation. A record owner is treated as the owner of the shares by the corporation whether or not the beneficial owner of the shares.

redemption means the reacquisition of a security by the issuer pursuant to a provision in the security that specifies the terms on which the reacquisition may take place. A security is called for redemption when the issuer notifies the holder that the redemption privilege has been exercised. Typically, a holder of a security that has been called for redemption will have a limited period thereafter to decide whether or not to exercise a conversion right, if one exists.

reduction surplus is a term used in a few states with par value statutes to refer to the surplus created by a reduction of stated capital. In many states, such surplus is treated simply as capital surplus.

registered corporation is a publicly held corporation which has registered under section 12 of the Securities Exchange Act of 1934. Section 12 may apply to issuers other than corporations. The registration of an issuer under this section of the 1934 Act should be contrasted with the registration of an issue under the Securities Act of 1933.

registration of an issue of securities under the Securities Act of 1933 permits the public sale of those securities in interstate commerce or with the use of the mails. That registration should be distinguished from the registration of corporations under the Securities Exchange Act of 1934.

registration statement is the document that must be filed to permit registration of an issue of securities under the Securities Act of 1933. A major component of the registration statement is the prospectus that is to be supplied prospective purchasers of the securities.

regulation A is a small offering exemption to the Securities Act of 1933 that entails the filing and distribution of an offering statement; it is more similar to a simplified registration process than to an exemption.

regulation D is the SEC's principal small offering exemption to the Securities Act of 1933. An offering that is exempt from registration under Regulation D of the Securities Act of 1933 may have to be registered under state blue sky laws.

reorganization is a general term describing corporate amalgamations or readjustments. The classification of the Internal Revenue Code is widely used in general corporate literature. A Class A reorganization is a statutory merger or consolidation (i. e., pursuant to the business corporation act of a specific state). A Class B reorganization is a transaction by which one corporation exchanges its voting shares for the voting shares of another corporation. A Class C reorganization is a transaction in which one corporation exchanges its voting shares for the property and assets of another corporation. A Class D reorganization is a "spin off" of assets by one corporation to a new corporation. A Class E reorganization is a recapitalization. A Class F reorganization is a "mere change of identity, form, or place of organization, however effected." A Class G reorganization is a "transfer by a corporation of all or part of its assets to another corporation in a title 11 or similar case."

retained earnings are net profits accumulated by a corporation after payment of dividends. Retained earnings are also called "undistributed profits" or "earned surplus."

reverse stock split is an amendment to the articles of incorporation that reduce the number of shares outstanding. The amendment must specify the basis on which existing shareholders will be adjusted to reflect the smaller number of shares outstanding. Reverse stock splits may create fractional shares and may be used as a device to go private by reducing the number of shares to the point that no public shareholder owns a full share of stock, and then providing that all fractional shares are to be redeemed for cash.

reverse triangular merger. See triangular merger.

rights are short term options to purchase shares from an issuer at a fixed price. Rights may be issued as a substitute for a dividend or as a "sweetener" in connection with the issuance of senior or debt securities. Rights are often publicly traded. Compare: warrants.

risk arbitrage is a strategy employed in takeover situations in which shares of a corporation that is about to be taken over are bought, while shares of the acquiring corporation that are to be exchanged are sold short or on a when-issued basis.

round lot is the standard trading unit of securities. On most securities exchanges a round lot is 100 shares.

S

s corporation is a corporation that has elected to be taxed under Subchapter S of the Internal Revenue Code. The taxable income of an S corporation is not subject to tax at the corporate level, but is allocated to the shareholders to be taxed at that level. S corporation taxation is similar but not identical to partnership taxation.

scrip is issued in lieu of fractional shares in connection with a stock dividend. Scrip represents the right to receive a portion of a share; scrip is readily transferable so that it is possible to acquire scrip from several sources and assemble the right to obtain the issuance of a full additional share.

secondary market consists of the securities exchanges and over-the-counter markets where securities are bought and sold after their original issue (which took place in the primary market). Proceeds of secondary market sales accrue to selling investors, not to the company that originally issued the securities. See also: primary market.

securities is a general term that covers not only traditional securities such as shares of stock, bonds, and debentures, but also a variety of interests that have the characteristics of securities, i. e., that involve an investment with the return primarily or exclusively dependent on the efforts of a person other than the investor.

securities exchanges are markets for the purchase and sale of traditional securities at which brokers for purchasers and sellers may effect transactions. The best known and largest securities exchange is the New York Stock Exchange.

security-for-expenses statutes require certain plaintiffs in a derivative suit to post a bond with sureties from which corporate or other defendants may be reimbursed for their expenses if they prevail. Designed as a protection against strike suits, security-for-expenses statutes have been widely criticized as being illogical and unnecessary. The Model Business Corporation Act (1984) does not impose a security-for-expenses requirement.

senior security is a debt security or preferred share that has a claim prior to that of junior obligations or common shares on a corporation's assets and earnings. See: junior security.

series of preferred shares is a subclass of preferred shares with differing dividend rates, redemption prices, rights on dissolution, conversion rights and the like. Typically, the terms of a series of preferred shares may be established by the board of directors so that a corporation periodically engaged in preferred shares financing may readily shape its preferred shares offering to market conditions through the use of series of preferred shares. Series may be created only if a special class of shares is created by the articles of incorporation and the board of directors is authorized to create one or more series within that class. Since none of the terms of this class of preferred shares are specified in the articles of incorporation, the class of shares is usually called "blank shares." Under the Model Business Corporation Act (1984), the board of directors may establish the terms of either a "class" or a "series."

share dividend is a proportional distribution of shares without payment of consideration to existing shareholders. A share dividend is often viewed as a substitute for a cash dividend, and shareholders may sell a share dividend without realizing that they are diluting their ownership interest in the corporation.

share repurchase plan is a program by which a corporation buys back its own shares in the open market. It is usually done when the corporation believes its shares are undervalued by the market.

share split is a proportional change in the number of shares owned by every shareholder. It differs from a stock dividend in degree; however, typically in a stock dividend no adjustment is made in the dividend rate per share while such an adjustment is usually made in a stock split. There are other technical differences in the handling of stock splits and stock dividends under the statutes of most states. Stock splits usually result in an increase in the number of outstanding shares; see: reverse stock split.

shareholders or **stockholders** are the persons who own shares of stock of the corporation. Such shares may be either common shares or preferred shares. The Model Business Corporation Act (1984) and modern usage generally tends to prefer "shareholder" to "stockholder" but the latter word is deeply ingrained in common usage.

shark repellent is a slang term that refers to measures undertaken by a corporation to discourage unwanted takeover attempts. At one time it also referred to state tender offer statutes.

short form merger is a merger of a largely or wholly owned subsidiary into a parent through a stream-lined procedure permitted under the Revised Model Business Corporation Act and statutes of many states.

short sale is a sale of a security or commodity futures contract not owned by the seller. The security to be sold is borrowed from a broker and the short seller anticipates replacing the borrowed security at a lower price at a later time. A short sale permits an investor: (1) to take advantage of an anticipated decline in the price, or (2) to protect a profit in a long position against an anticipated price decline.

short sale against the box is a short sale where the speculator owns enough shares of the security involved to cover the borrowed securities, if necessary. The "box" referred to is the hypothetical safe deposit box in which the certificates are kept. A short sale against the box is not as risky as a short sale.

sinking fund refers to an obligation sometimes imposed pursuant to the issuance of debt securities by which the issuer is required each year to devote or set aside a certain amount to the retirement of the securities when they mature. A sinking fund may be used each year to redeem a portion of the outstanding debt securities.

spin-off is a form of corporate divestiture that results in a subsidiary or division of a corporation becoming an independent company.

split is a proportional change in the number of shares owned by every shareholder. Other things being equal, a stock split does not affect the aggregate market value of the shares. Share splits differ from a share dividend in degree; typically in a share dividend no adjustment is made in the dividend rate per share while such an adjustment is usually made in a share split. There are other technical differences in the handling of share splits and share dividends under the statutes of most states. See also reverse stock split.

squeeze-outs are techniques by which a minority interest in a corporation is eliminated or reduced. Squeeze-outs may occur in a variety of contexts, e. g., in a "going private" transaction in which minority shareholders are compelled to accept cash for their shares, or the issuance of new shares to existing shareholders in which minority shareholders are given the unpleasant choice of having their proportionate interest in the corporation reduced significantly or of investing a large amount of additional or new capital over which they have no control and for which they receive little or no return. Many squeeze-outs involve the use of cash mergers. Squeeze-out is often used synonymously with freeze-out.

staggered board is a classified board of directors in which a fraction of the board is elected each year. In staggered boards, members serve two or three years, depending on whether the board is classified into two or three groups.

stated capital in the old Model Business Corporation Act nomenclature represents the basic capital of the corporation. Technically, it consists of the sum of the par values of all issued shares plus the consideration for no par shares to the extent not transferred to capital surplus plus other amounts that may be transferred from other accounts. Distributions generally may not be made from stated capital.

stated value. See: par value.

stock. See share.

stock appreciation rights (SARs) are bonus payments to corporate executives based on the growth in value of a predetermined number of hypothetical shares.

stockholders. See: shareholders.

straight voting. See: noncumulative voting.

street name refers to the common practice of registering publicly traded securities in the name of one or more brokerage firms with offices on Wall Street. Such certificates are endorsed in blank and are essentially bearer certificates transferred between brokerage firms. The use of street name shares has declined with the creation of a central clearing corporation and book entry registration of ownership.

strike suits is a slang term for derivative litigation instituted for its nuisance value or to obtain a favorable settlement.

subchapter S refers to the subchapter of the Internal Revenue Code of 1954 that regulations the S corporation election. See S corporation.

subordinated. See: junior security.

subscribers are persons who agree to invest in the corporation by purchasing shares of stock. Subscribers usually commit themselves to invest by entering into contracts defining the extent and terms of their commitment; at common law subscribers usually executed "subscriptions" or "subscription agreements." Modern contracts for the purchase of corporate shares from the issuer usually use the phrase "agree to purchase and subscribe for. . . ."

subscription is an offer to buy a specified number of theretofore unissued shares of a corporation. See: part III. If the corporation is not yet in existence, a subscription is known as a preincorporation subscription, which is enforceable by the corporation after it has been formed and is irrevocable despite the absence of consideration or the usual elements of a contract.

subsidiary is a corporation that is at least majority owned, and may be wholly owned, by another corporation.

surplus is a general term in corporate accounting that usually refers to either the excess of assets over liabilities or that amount further reduced by the stated capital represented by issued shares. Surplus has a more definite meaning when combined with a descriptive adjective from par value statutes, e. g., earned surplus, capital surplus, or reduction surplus.

T

tainted shares are shares owned by a person who is disqualified for some reason from serving as a plaintiff in a derivative action. The shares are "tainted" since for policy reasons a good faith transferee of such shares will also be disqualified from serving as a plaintiff.

takeover attempt or **takeover bid** are generic terms to describe an attempt by an outside corporation or group, usually called the aggressor or "insurgent" to wrest control away from incumbent management. A takeover attempt may involve purchase of shares, a tender offer, a sale of assets, or a proposal that the target merge voluntarily into the aggressor.

target corporation is a corporation the control of which is sought by an aggressor corporation.

temporary insider is a person or firm that receives nonpublic information from an issuer pursuant to duties owed by that person or firm to the issuer. A temporary insider is viewed as being subject to the same proscriptions against inside trading as an employee or director of the corporation and is not a "tippee."

tender offer is a public invitation by an aggressor that shareholders of a target corporation tender their shares for purchase by the aggressor at a stated price. Tender offers are regulated by the Williams Act. A creeping tender offer is a series of private acquisitions in the market place and may or may not be classed as a tender offer for regulatory purposes.

thin corporation is a corporation with an excessive amount of debt in its capitalization. A thin corporation is primarily a tax concept.

thin market refers to a market for publicly traded securities in which the number of transactions and/or the number of securities offered for sale or purchase at any one time are relatively few.

tip is information passed by one person (a "tipper") to another (a "tippee") as a basis for a decision to buy or sell a security. Such information is presumed to be of material value and not available to the general public. Trading by tippees in some circumstances violates federal law. See also: insider; insider trading.

transfer agent is an organization, usually a bank, that handles transfers of shares for a publicly held corporation. Generally, a transfer agent assures that certificates submitted for transfer are properly endorsed and that there is appropriate documentation of the right to transfer. The transfer agent issues new certificates and oversees the cancellation of the old ones. Transfer agents also usually maintain the record of shareholders for the corporation and mail dividend checks.

treasury shares are shares that were once issued and outstanding but which have been reacquired by the corporation and "held in its treasury." Treasury shares are economically indistinguishable from authorized but unissued shares but historically have been treated as having an intermediate status. Many of the complexities created by treasury shares revolve around accounting concepts. The Model Business Corporation Act (1984) and the statutes of several states have eliminated the concept of treasury shares, reacquired shares automatically having the status of authorized but unissued shares.

triangular merger is a method of amalgamation of two corporations by which the disappearing corporation is merged into a subsidiary of the surviving corporation and the shareholders of the disappearing corporation receive shares of the surviving corporation. In a reverse triangular merger the subsidiary is merged into the disappearing corporation so that it becomes a wholly owned subsidiary of the surviving corporation.

trust indenture. See: indenture.

U

ultra vires is the common law doctrine relating to the effect of corporate acts that exceed the powers or the stated purposes of a corporation. The modern view generally validates all corporate acts even though they may be ultra vires.

underwriters are persons who buy shares with a view toward their further distribution. Used almost exclusively in connection with the public distribution of securities, an underwriter may be either a commercial enterprise engaged in the distribution of securities (an investment banker), or a person who simply buys securities without an investment intent and with a "view" toward further distribution.

up stream merger is a merger of a subsidiary corporation into its parent.

V

voting group is a term defined in the Model Business Corporation Act (1984) to describe the right of shares of different classes or series to vote separately on fundamental corporate changes that adversely affect the rights or privileges of that class or series. The scope of the right to vote by voting groups is defined by statute. The right is of particular value to classes or series of shares with limited or no voting rights under the articles of incorporation. Most older state statutes use the terms "class voting" or "voting by class" to refer to essentially the same concept.

voting trust is a formal arrangement by which record title to shares is transferred to trustees who are entitled to exercise the power to vote the shares. Usually, all other incidents of ownership, such as the right to receive dividends, are retained by the beneficial owners of the shares. See: voting trust certificates.

voting trust certificates are certificates issued by voting trustees to the beneficial holders of shares held by the voting trust. Such certificates may be as readily transferable as the underlying shares, carrying with them all the incidents of ownership of the underlying shares except the power to vote.

W

warrants are a type of option to purchase shares issued by a corporation. Warrants are typically long period options, are freely transferable, and if the underlying shares are listed on a securities exchange, are also publicly traded. The price of warrants of publicly held corporations is a function of the market price of the shares and the option price specified in the warrants. See also: rights.

watered shares are par value shares issued for property which has been overvalued and is not worth the aggregate par value of the issued shares. Watered shares is also used as a generic term to describe all shares issued for less than par value—including discount and bonus shares. The issuance of watered shares may impose a liability on the recipient equal to the amount of the shortfall from par value.

white knight is a friendly suitor: a potential acquirer usually sought out by the target of an unfriendly takeover to rescue it from the unwanted bidder's takeover.

working capital is a measure of a corporation's liquidity and ability to discharge its liabilities as they arise. Working capital is the difference between current assets and current liabilities as shown on the corporation's balance sheet.

Z

zeroing out is a slang term that describes the common income tax strategy in C corporations of reducing taxable income to zero by paying out all earnings in the form of tax-deductible payments to the shareholders of the corporation.

*

APPENDIX B

ANSWERS TO QUESTIONS

PART I

I–1. ***False.*** While the corporate entity theory is useful and the assumption set forth in the question usually leads to the correct answer to questions, it is only a partial explanation of the concept of a corporation.

I–2. ***False.*** While a corporation almost always involves contractual elements, and the economic model of a corporation is basically contractual, there are also mandatory noncontractual aspects of corporation law. The economists' "nexus of contracts" approach is a useful analytic device but not a complete explanation of the modern corporation.

I–3. ***False.*** Rights and duties within corporations are largely defined by statute and by the governing corporate documents. Answers must be sought in these sources, at least initially.

I–4. ***Largely false.*** The law treats a wholly owned corporation as a separate entity for many purposes. For example, a wholly owned corporation is a separate taxable entity; it may enter into contracts with its shareholders, it may become insolvent even though its shareholder is still solvent, and so forth.

I–5. *False.* The state grant of corporate authority is itself subject to constitutional restrictions. Further, Supreme Court decisions have granted a corporation many (though not all) of the federal constitutional rights possessed by an individual.

I–6. *Largely true.* The articles of incorporation are generally viewed as the contract which defines the rights of the various classes of shareholders in the corporation. Most case law dealing with rights of preferred shareholders involve construction of specific provisions in articles of incorporation. Statutes, however, give some minimum rights to preferred shareholders independent of their "contract" and these rights may not be eliminated by provision in the articles of incorporation.

I–7. *False.* The law of the state of incorporation controls most of the internal relationships within the corporation, but both federal law and the laws of other states regulate corporate conduct generally. Federal law has also superseded state law in some areas of internal corporate governance in publicly held corporations.

I–8. See part I D. The number of shareholders is the most obvious difference. However, from an economic standpoint the most important difference is that a market exists for the shares of a publicly held corporation but no market exists for closely held shares, which may be unsalable except to other persons interested in the corporation.

I–9. States that do not maintain modern corporation statutes discover that more and more corporations that are transacting business in the state are incorporating in Delaware or other states. This results in a loss of revenue to the state and its citizens, and may lead to courts applying the law of the state of incorporation rather than the local law in matters relating to the internal affairs of the corporation.

I–10. Professor Cary's thesis had wide credence until it was subjected to careful empirical and theoretical economic analysis. It appears that the reasons for the success of Delaware in the incorporation race cannot be traced to the laxity of its statute or the biases of its judiciary.

PART II

II–1. *False.* Most local businesses should incorporate locally rather than in a distant state. While Delaware has advantages, particularly for large, publicly held corporations that do business in every state, a new business just starting out should usually incorporate in the state in which its principal business is to be conducted.

II–2. ***False.*** Under most state statutes incorporation is simple and inexpensive. Over the years most states have made the process even simpler and less expensive.

II–3. ***True.*** The role of incorporator today has no substantive significance.

II–4. ***False.*** Articles of incorporation may contain any provisions relating to the corporation's affairs or governance that the draftsman elects to include in the articles. The articles of incorporation generally may not contradict express provisions of the applicable corporation statute.

II–5. The most common reason is that articles of incorporation are more difficult to amend than bylaws. A second reason is the belief that important restrictions or limitations should be made a matter of public record.

II–6. ***False.*** In the absence of fraud or unfair competition a corporation may use an assumed name as freely as an individual. Compliance with "assumed name" statutes may be required.

II–7. See part II F 2, and 3.

II–8. ***Probably never.*** Even in a limited venture, perpetual duration creates no problem and may avoid later difficulties.

II–9. ***False.*** In most states a corporation may be formed for the purpose of "engaging in any lawful business." Such a corporation is not restricted by the articles of incorporation in the businesses in which it may engage. The RMBCA does not require any statement of purpose (unless a purpose narrower than "any lawful business" is desired).

II–10. ***False.*** While a broad clause minimizes the risk of ultra vires, participants in a corporation may sometimes wish to have their corporation restricted as to its activities. Also regulatory statutes may sometimes require narrower or qualified purposes clauses.

II–11. The purpose of these requirements is to make sure that the corporation has a place where it may be found for service of process, tax notices, and the like.

II–12. ***Generally no.*** The only exception is if the statutory list of powers in a particular state does not clearly cover some action that the corporation may wish to engage in.

II–13. Beyond the purposes or powers of a corporation.

II–14. The common law of ultra vires was erratic and sometimes led to injustice. The modern view is that a corporation should have essentially the same powers as an individual to engage in profit making conduct, and a person unaware of a restriction on a corporation should not be bound by the restriction.

II–15. The statutes limiting the scope of the doctrine, broad purposes clauses in articles of incorporation, and the broadening of the statutory list of powers of the corporation.

II–16. Adoption of bylaws, sale of stock and election of officers are the most important. Other steps include preparation of minutes, opening of a bank account, and so forth.

II–17. The most likely consequence is that participants will be held personally liable for corporate obligations on a piercing the corporate veil theory. However, many cases have not imposed liability in this situation.

II–18. The principal question is whether the two lawyers should form a professional corporation. A professional corporation to practice law (which may be formed under the laws of all jurisdictions) would offer more advantages than those enjoyed by the two lawyers under their present method of operation. The two lawyers might enjoy these corporate advantages: (1) continuity of life; (2) centralization of management; (3) limited liability; and (4) free transferability of interests.

Continuity of life means little in this situation, since the lawyers each have their own clientele, and when one leaves the firm, unless it adds more lawyers, those clients will probably retain other counsel, although the wills drafted by the estates lawyer might provide some basis for continuity.

In the corporate form, managerial responsibility can be conferred on one or the other lawyer, as spelled out in the articles of incorporation or more likely in the bylaws implemented by a shareholder agreement.

So far as limited liability is concerned, depending on the language of the statute, each might be able to achieve limited liability except for any negligent or wrongful act or conduct personally committed or committed by any person under that lawyer's direct supervision and control while rendering professional services on behalf of the corporation. Of course, the corporation would be liable vicariously for the tort of any employee of the corporation acting within the scope of employment.

In some states, a shareholder in a professional corporation may also be liable for malpractice by co-shareholders but not for liabilities, e. g. for rent, that are not related to the practice of a profession.

Free transferability, a normal corporate characteristic, means little in a professional corporation, since transfers of shares may be made only to eligible professional persons. The professional corporation statute itself imposes share transfer restrictions which can be implemented, within the statutory limitations, by first-option or buy-sell provisions.

The extra formalities and expenses in forming and operating as a corporation would be of little significance. The two lawyers themselves can attend to the legal matters involved.

Another advantage of incorporation would be to achieve the federal income tax advantages available to corporate employees, which the two attorneys would become. The major advantage today is the provision of tax-free benefits such as group hospitalization, group life insurance and similar employee benefits also with pre-tax dollars.

Family share ownership by nonprofessionals is not possible in a professional corporation. For the same reason, estate planning cannot be facilitated in a professional corporation.

Even in a corporation malpractice insurance to protect not only the professional and personal assets of the wrong-doing lawyer but also the firm assets in which both lawyers have an interest would be desirable.

In some jurisdictions, the corporate name would be subject to the limitations on partnership names of law firms and also would have to end with the abbreviation "Professional Corporation" or the abbreviation "P. C."

II–19. Some provisions are valid only if they appear in the articles of corporation. In addition, generally, it is desirable to place unusual provisions in the articles of incorporation where they have maximum legal effect (since articles of incorporation are approved by shareholders while bylaws may usually be amended by the board of directors acting alone.

II–20. ***False.*** Provisions appearing in the articles of incorporation alone are of course effective as a legal matter. However, officers and directors are more likely to be familiar with and consult the bylaws rather than the articles of incorporation. As a result, provisions relating to corporate governance should generally appear in the bylaws even if they also appear in the articles of incorporation.

PART III

III–1. ***False.*** An incorporator performs the symbolic role of signing articles of incorporation. A promoter is the organizer of a business.

III–2. ***Uncertain.*** Most such promoters have been held personally liable in the litigated cases but theories exist that would excuse him. See also question III–11.

III–3. ***Uncertain.*** While some courts might find a novation in these circumstances, many courts have refused to do so, holding both the corporation and the promoter liable on the obligations.

III–4. The de facto cases involve transactions entered into in the name of the corporation before it has been formed, and where one or both parties believe the corporation has been formed. Promoters' cases typically involve situations where both parties know, and the contract recites, that no corporation has been formed.

III–5. ***Uncertain.*** While earlier versions of the Model Act clearly attempted to eliminate the de facto doctrine, many courts continued to apply common law concepts despite the statute. As a result, the MBCA (1984) does not directly address the de facto corporation doctrine; it simply provides that persons who act as or on behalf of a putative corporation "knowing" that articles of incorporation have not been filed are liable on obligations so created.

III–6. The corporation by estoppel analysis accepts the argument that persons who deal with a "corporation" are thereafter estopped from claiming that the individuals are personally liable. The problem with this reasoning is that it completely reverses the traditional concept of estoppel; the person being estopped is not the one making the representation but the one relying on the representation. It also results in the possibility that one might obtain the benefit of limited liability without taking any steps to incorporate simply by consistently doing business in the corporate name.

III–7. ***False.*** A corporation assumes only the promoters' contracts it elects to assume.

III–8. ***True.*** Promoters have fiduciary duties to each other similar to those of partners in a partnership.

III–9. ***Uncertain.*** If the corporation represents subsequent investors who were unaware of the transactions, the answer is "true." If the investors knew of the transaction they cannot compel the corporation to sue since they presumably adjusted the purchase price to take into account the known transaction.

III–10. ***Usually False.*** While some courts have treated subscriptions as contracts between subscribers, the most common view is that they are mere offers since no corporation is in existence and therefore a bilateral contract cannot exist between the subscriber and the corporation.

III–11. ***Yes.*** Whether or not a promoter will be personally liable in acting for a proposed corporation depends on the proper construction of the contract. The promoter here may (1) take on behalf of the proposed corporation an offer from the other party, which being accepted by the corporation after incorporation becomes a contract; (2) enter into a contract initially binding the promoter with the clear understanding that if the corporation is formed it will be substituted and the promoter will be relieved of further responsibility (a "novation"); or (3) bind himself so that both he and the corporation are thereafter liable but seek indemnity from the corporation. Where, as here, the contract calls for some performance before the corporation is organized it is a strong indication that the promoter is intended to be personally liable on the contract. Nothing in the contract authorized D to substitute the corporation as the sole responsible party; therefore D, as well as the corporation, is personally liable on the contract. [See *O'Rorke v. Geary,* 207 Pa. 240, 56 A. 541 (1903).]

III–12. ***Yes.*** Although a corporation is not liable on a contract made by its promoter for its benefit unless it takes some affirmative act to adopt such contract, it is not necessary that the adoption be express. It may be inferred from the acts of the corporation after incorporation. Here the court can imply that XYZ adopted the contract by reason of the failure to object by shareholders and directors and the actions of the corporation after incorporation. [See *McArthur v. Times Printing Co.,* 48 Minn. 319, 51 N.W 216 (1892).]

PART IV

IV–1. The PCV cases all deal with correctly and fully formed corporations. The issue is, should the shield of limited liability be ignored under the circumstances despite the complete formation of the corporation? The other doctrines referred to in the question deal with formational defects.

IV–2. ***False.*** Motive, by itself, is not a ground for PCV.

IV–3. ***False.*** In contract cases, inadequate capital, by itself, should not be sufficient reason to PCV. There must be some additional abuse of the corporate form or misrepresentation of the capital actually invested in the corporation.

IV–4. ***Probably false.*** Most courts will impose *tort* liability on shareholders on PCV theory if the original capital was inadequate in light of expected business needs.

IV–5. ***Probably true.*** Failure to follow corporate formalities and intermingling of corporate assets are classic reasons for PCV. Usually, personal liability is imposed on the shareholder even though no harm resulted from the shareholder's conduct.

IV–6. ***False.*** So long as "hats" are properly labeled, a subsidiary and parent may share the same officers and directors without becoming liable for each other's debts.

IV–7. ***True.*** Relatively small amounts of intermingling of parent and subsidiary affairs will usually give rise to PCV. A few courts have rejected this result and have required a showing that the plaintiff was injured by the transactions in question.

IV–8. ***False.*** The use of corporations to defeat or further governmental policy in this way depends on an analysis of the goals of the governmental policy. Several cases have permitted persons to qualify for social security benefits in this fashion.

IV–9. ***No.*** A holding or parent company has a separate corporate existence and is treated separately from the subsidiary in the absence of circumstances justifying disregard of the corporate entity. The participation of A corporation in the affairs of S did not amount to a domination of the day-to-day business decisions of S even though A corporation had the opportunity to exercise control. Consequently, jurisdiction over A corporation cannot be established by reason of its stock ownership of S. [See *Quarles v. Fuqua Indus., Inc.,* 504 F.2d 1358 (10th Cir.1974).]

IV–10. ***Yes.*** This case is a good illustration of an unsuccessful attempt of the use of corporate process to avoid personal responsibility. The corporation never had any equity capital despite the dangerous nature of the business. There was confusion and intermingling of personal and corporate finances. Formalities were not followed. The case involves a tort not a contract. For all these reasons—but principally the lack of capital in a tort case—the court should hold the shareholder personally liable. [See *Dixie Coal Mining & Mfg. Co. v. Williams,* 221 Ala. 331, 128 So. 799 (1930).]

PART V

V–1. There are four major sources: the sale of shares, loans from shareholders, loans from third persons, and internally generated funds from operations.

V–2. Very little. Par value today provides a floor on the price of shares. Whether or not this is an advantage is questionable. It also establishes the amounts to be allocated to the capital accounts called stated capital and capital surplus (in the MBCA (1969) nomenclature) when authorized shares are issued. With the virtually universal use of nominal par value shares in modern corporate practice, it is fair to say that par value serves little purpose today. On the other hand, par value, and the complex rules with respect to capital accounts that it generates, may be affirmatively misleading since it appears to protect creditors against distributions to shareholders when in fact it provides little or no protection to creditors. See Question V–13.

V–3. Traditional no par shares do not solve all problems because they are tied in with the concept of par value. The artificial problems created by par value therefore also appear in a corporation that uses no par shares.

V–4. ***False.*** While watered stock liability may easily be avoided by proper planning, the issuance of shares with high par values today may well give rise to classic watered stock liability in many states.

V–5. The MBCA (1984) abolishes par value (except as a voluntary planning device as a matter of contract or when necessary to minimize tax liability in states that continue to compute taxes on the basis of par values).

V–6. Preferred stock has preferences over common stock in connection with either the payment of dividends or distributions on liquidation, or both. Preferred stock usually is nonparticipating, that is, it is entitled to a fixed distribution and no more.

V–7. A bond is a secured long term debt instrument while a debenture is an unsecured long term debt instrument. The word "bond" is often used as a generic term to describe both bonds and debentures.

V–8. ***False.*** Many corporations benefit from the leverage created by having a portion of the permanent capital be in the form of debt rather than equity. Further, in periods of inflation, debt financing may become even more attractive since money borrowed will be repaid in the future with inflated dollars. Of course, as inflation continues, interest rates tend to rise to offset this phenomenon. Most corporations today desire to maintain a significant amount of debt in their capital structures.

V–9. ***False.*** The Federal Securities Act exemption for private offerings is not controlled by the number of offers. Thus an offer to a relatively small number of offerees who need the protection of the Act may require registration under the Securities Act of 1933. In contrast, most state security statutes (blue sky laws) contain numerical exemptions for offers to a small number of persons but even these exemptions are usually lost if the plan of distribution involves a public offer or a public advertisement.

V–10. Preemptive rights are the rights of existing shareholders to purchase their proportionate share of new issues of securities by the corporation.

V–11. ***False.*** Even in the absence of preemptive rights, there is a fiduciary duty applicable to directors that prohibit the issuance of shares at prices that unreasonably dilute the interests of outstanding shareholders. The same fiduciary duty may prevent the issuance of shares at reasonable prices if issued for improper purposes, such as to influence control of the corporation.

V–12. When a corporation repurchases its own shares, it distributes assets equal to the purchase price to the shareholder from whom the shares are being purchased. However, the shares of a corporation are not an asset of the corporation in any real sense. One cannot own shares of oneself. Shares of a corporation that were formerly outstanding but have been reacquired by the corporation are no more an asset of a corporation than are authorized but unissued shares.

This can be seen graphically by the accounting treatment for treasury shares: the purchase price of the shares reduces the corporation's assets while an offsetting reduction is made in the "equity" portion of the right hand side of the balance sheet.

V–13. ***True.*** It is generally recognized that modern corporation statutes are so liberal that capital may be freely distributed by a corporation to its shareholders under the statutes. If a creditor wishes to assure that capital is not distributed to shareholders and that a cushion is available to make sure that its loan will be repaid, it must impose meaningful restrictions by agreement.

V–14. ***False.*** A share distribution is purely a paper transaction that does not reduce the real assets available to the corporation or increase the proportionate interest of any shareholder. In contrast, a cash dividend reduces the funds available to the corporation. If a shareholder receives a share dividend and sells the new shares (in order to obtain the cash) that shareholder's proportionate interest in the corporation is thereby reduced by a small fraction.

V–15. The legality of the dividend last year out of current profits of that year, at a time when there was an accumulated deficit in earned surplus, depends on whether or not the state of incorporation has a "nimble dividend" statute. A "nimble" dividend is one paid out of current earnings before those earnings are applied against the deficit in earned surplus from other years. If the state does have such a statute, the dividend was lawful because Commerce was not insolvent at the time of the dividend.

If the state of incorporation does not have a "nimble dividend" statute the dividend was unlawful unless the current earnings were large enough both to wipe out the earlier deficit in earned surplus and to cover the dividend.

If the dividend is unlawful, the directors are jointly and severally liable to the corporation for the benefit of its creditors or shareholders. Directors who fail to dissent from the action are also liable. The directors are entitled to contribution from other directors who concurred in the action. Moreover, shareholders who received the dividend with knowledge that it was unlawful are also liable for their pro rata share of the dividend.

In some states, Commerce, Inc. might be able to treat the distribution as a distribution of capital rather than a dividend.

If Commerce, Inc. were incorporated in a state that has adopted the MBCA (1984), the distribution would be lawful if the dividend was made at the time when Commerce was solvent in both an equity and a balance sheet sense. The MBCA (1984) completely eliminates the concept of earned surplus and, as a result, of nimble dividends as well.

V–16. ***Yes.*** The stock was par value stock and the property which was transferred to the corporation as consideration for the stock was worth only $100,000. It therefore cannot constitute full payment for the shares issued with a par value of $250,000. Thus, the shareholder remains liable at the suit of a creditor or creditors' representative. Two theories on which to base B's continued liability are (1) if there is no statute, expressly making B liable to pay at least the par value for newly issued shares, then B impliedly agreed to pay the par value of the shares upon their being issued to her; and (2) if there is a statute imposing such liability on B, then the provisions of the statute make B liable. This debt is a corporate asset which can be enforced by a creditor of the corporation.

If the valuation of $250,000 is made non-fraudulently by the board of directors (which seems implausible on the stated facts), B has an argument that that valuation is conclusive and cannot be attacked by R.

V–17. ***Yes.*** The shareholders may not use corporate assets to repurchase their shares and thus repay themselves their investment if to do so would leave the corporation without sufficient funds to pay its creditors. If, however, a corporation has sufficient assets to pay its creditors in full and also pay the purchase price of the stock it may enter into an agreement to purchase the shares. Instead of paying cash therefor, the corporation should be able to issue notes for all or part of the purchase price, in which case the stockholder becomes a creditor of the corporation rather than a shareholder. In any subsequent insolvency proceeding the former shareholder should be entitled to share proportionally with other creditors. Here, the purchase of shares was effected at a time when the corporation was solvent and subsequent insolvency does not affect the validity of the transaction.

[Several early cases agree with this rationale but several others do not so that it is possible that a court would subordinate the claim of P in the above situation. MBCA (1984) § 6.40 accepts the rationale set forth above and permits P to share in the assets on a parity with other creditors.]

V–18. ***Yes.*** Whether or not to declare a dividend is usually within the sound discretion and business judgment of the board of directors. The courts do not usually interfere with the exercise of such discretion, *except* when there is a clear case of abuse of discretion, bad faith or dishonesty. There is an implied obligation on the part of the board of directors and managers of the corporation to exercise good faith and reasonable business judgment in distributing profits to the shareholders. Of course, sound discretion dictates that there should be kept in reserve enough money with which to carry on the corporate business, make replacements of worn out machinery, pay taxes, pay insurance, and provide for unforeseen losses and expenses. But here there is a surplus built up over a period of 10 years which is four times the capital, a continued annual profit, a continuing prosperity, and not a single dividend during the entire 10 year period. With $2,000,000 cash on hand and the corporation in the condition disclosed by these facts, there seems to be a clear abuse of discretion on the part of the board in not declaring a dividend. *Dodge v. Ford Motor Co.,* 204 Mich. 459, 170 N.W. 668 (1919); *Gottfried v. Gottfried,* 73 N.Y.S.2d 692 (1947).]

PART VI

VI–1. These phrases refer to the statutory requirements that there be a board of directors and officers, that they be selected in a certain way, that they be invested with specific authority, and so forth. The statutory scheme is most realistic in corporations of a middle size and complexity.

VI–2. ***False.*** While the requirements of directors and officers make little sense when applied to such a closely held corporation, it is important to recognize that in the absence of statutory authorization, two shareholders who run a business as a partnership may well end up personally liable for the corporation's obligations. Also, control agreements that violate the statutory scheme may be unenforceable.

VI–3. Answers to questions such as this depend strongly on the statutes of the state in question. The traditional view, and one that is likely to prevail if there is no express statutory provisions dealing with close corporations or modifications of traditional roles of directors, is that C should lose on the theory that a corporation must have a board of directors and that neither the incorporators nor the shareholders of a corporation may render such board completely impotent, sterile or helpless, a board devoid of power. The quoted provision in the articles of incorporation arguably does just that. It provides that the board of directors shall have no power to bind the corporation without the unanimous consent of the shareholders. This arguably renders the board wholly impotent and without any power to act if a unanimous vote of the shareholders cannot be obtained. Therefore, the provision providing that the board of directors of X corporation has no power to act without the unanimous consent of the shareholders, may be wholly void, and the board of directors of X corporation may be able to act as though it did not exist.

Under modern statutes (and even under traditional statutes by innovative courts), many courts might enforce such a provision today. In the case of a traditional statute, a court might accept the argument that the requirement was accepted unanimously, does not hurt anyone, and is not a substantial impingement on the statutory norms. *Clark v. Dodge, Galler v. Galler.* Several states have adopted statutes that should expressly permit this kind of arrangement. Other states have close corporation statutes that, if elected, should permit this kind of arrangement. Even if the election is not made, a court might be persuaded to "reform" the articles of incorporation to permit the agreement to be enforced. *Zion v. Kurtz.* As a result of these various factors, the chances of enforcing this agreement are significantly higher than they were twenty or more years ago.

PART VII

VII–1. Under most statutes, a quorum must consist of a majority of the outstanding shares while a majority of the shares present at a meeting at which a quorum is present is necessary to adopt a resolution. As a result, in the absence of specific provision by the corporation, one half of one half, or approximately one quarter, of the outstanding shares, may adopt an ordinary resolution at a shareholder's meeting. The Model Business Act (1984) changes the rule as to approval of actions by requiring that the affirmative votes exceed the negative votes. This is designed to treat abstentions as neutral.

VII–2. The common law view was one vote per share but most state statutes today authorize a corporation to create a class of shares with multiple or fractional votes per share. Virtually all states also permit nonvoting common shares. However, the statutes of a specific state must be consulted before such a question can be answered definitively.

VII–3. Record ownership refers to the status of the ownership of shares as shown on the books and records of the corporation. Beneficial ownership refers to the person who actually owns the shares. That person may or may not be the record owner. The corporation generally treats the record owner as the sole owner of shares without any consideration of who the beneficial owner may be. A beneficial owner should have the shares transferred to his or her name as record owner if unhappy about the powers of the record owner.

VII–4. The corporation must set record dates for these actions in order to establish clearly, as between transferor and transferee of shares, who is entitled to vote or who is entitled to receive a dividend.

VII–5. ***True.*** The effect of cumulative voting is to permit a large minority bloc of shares to obtain representation on the board. The size of the minimum bloc necessary to obtain representation may be determined mathematically from a relatively simple formula.

VII–6. ***Sometimes true.*** However, such voting is more commonly known as straight voting.

VII–7. Since proxies are revocable, the latest one revokes earlier ones. In this situation, A's shares will be voted for the insurgents.

VII–8. ***False.*** A proxy appointment is irrevocable only if it is "coupled with an interest" in the underlying shares or in the corporation.

VII–9. A pooling agreement is a simple contract between shareholders to vote shares in a certain way while a voting trust involves a transfer of the shares to trustees so that the trustees have the legal right to vote.

VII–10. In a closely held corporation share transfer restrictions may: (1) assure each shareholder that she will have a voice in who else participates in the corporation, (2) provide a way for shareholders desiring to withdraw to liquidate their interests in the corporation in a systematic fashion, and (3) establish the value of the shares for estate tax purposes. While these advantages may not be assured in every case, they are the typical reasons for share transfer restrictions in closely held corporations.

VII–11. ***Yes.*** Share transfer restrictions are most commonly used in publicly held corporations to preserve the availability of securities act exemptions that are dependent on the shares not being reoffered or resold publicly.

VII–12. At issue are the validity of the removal of directors and of the merger.

The notice of the special meeting specified only consideration of a proposed merger. Therefore, the removal of the directors should not have been considered because specific reference to proposed removals of directors must appear in the notice of meeting. MBCA (1984) § 8.08(d) provides that only matters related to those specified in the notice of meeting ordinarily may be entertained at a special meeting.

Under 8.08 of the Model Business Corporation Act (1984), a director may be removed with or without cause by a vote of the holders of a majority of the shares then entitled to vote at an election of directors at a meeting called expressly for that purpose. When Gative and Servative were elected, their tenure as directors was subject to the statutory power of removal. However, because the meeting was not expressly called for removing directors, the purported removal is invalid and the two directors should be reinstated.

The effect of this invalid action on the status of the merger is not so easily resolvable. The substituted directors, Berl and Stamp, exercised their functions under at least color of office and arguably can be considered de facto directors, whose actions as directors are not subject to collateral attack. The action of the board during their tenure may thus be binding on the corporation. Also, an agreement of merger has been entered into with a presumably innocent party who has no notice of the infirmity of the action taken by the directors. It is likely that the merger could not be set aside.

The corporation may also argue that there was no causal relationship between the merger and the defective removal of directors if the votes of Berl and Stamp were not necessary for approval of the merger. This argument increases the likelihood that the merger could not be set aside.

VII–13. ***Yes.*** As to proposal 1, even though the shareholders do not have power to effect a change in the officers of a corporation such power being reserved to the board of directors, they may express their opinion to the board of directors on the matter. As to proposal 2, shareholders have the inherent power to remove directors for cause. See *Auer v. Dressel,* 306 N.Y. 427, 118 N.E.2d 590 (1954).

PART VIII

VIII–1. ***False.*** Unlike shareholders, directors may not vote by proxy. This rule is based broadly on the common law view that directors may only act at a meeting.

VIII–2. ***False.*** There are many statements in early cases to this effect. However, many cases recognize informal ratification or estoppel as binding the board of directors without a formal meeting. Statutes today also authorize directors to act by unanimous written consent without a meeting.

PART IX

IX–1. *No.* This lay view of the president does not reflect the traditional legal relationship, though the trend appears to be in the direction of recognizing broader inherent authority. In a corporation the directors, not the president, have the principal power of decision-making. However, many corporate presidents in fact exercise a great deal of power, either by virtue of their office, as a member of the board of directors, or as a shareholder.

IX–2. ***False.*** The period of the officer's employment contract and the term of the office are independent. If a board of directors grants an officer a contract for a period longer than the term of the office and a subsequent board refuses to elect the officer to that office, the corporation has breached the employment contract.

IX–3. *No.* Although in general there may be a presumption that the president of a corporation has authority to institute litigation and engage counsel, absent a provision in the bylaws to the contrary, any actual or implied authority which M had to do so was terminated when a majority of the board of directors refused to sanction it. The fact that the directors were deadlocked or that the directors who voted against the suit were interested in the transaction does not affect the result. Other remedies exist to resolve a deadlock—involuntary dissolution, receivership, or appointment of provisional directors, or a derivative suit by a shareholder of P corporation against P corporation's directors.

IX–4. *No.* The president of a corporation is an agent for the corporation. In any given situation whether the president acted within the scope of that agency is a question of fact for the jury. The president's authority may be derived from: (a) certain powers implied by virtue of the office which allow the president to perform the acts necessary for the convenient management of the day-to-day business of the corporation, (b) express grants of power found in statutes, the corporate charter and bylaws and resolutions of the board of directors, and (c) powers which arise by reason of a course of conduct of both the president and the corporation showing that the president had acted on similar matters in the past, and that the corporation had acquiesced in, approved and ratified such former actions. The charge to the jury that was held to be appropriate was: "If you find from the evidence that the president . . . was not acting within the usual scope of his office and that he had not in the past acted alone in the signing of contracts and that the defendant company had never recognized any acts of the president alone or had not held him out as qualified to transact singly and alone all business dealings for the company, then your verdict must be for the defendant, for I say to you it is only upon these principles, upon the proven facts of the case that the act of the president could bind the corporation. If, however, you find . . . that the president was acting within the usual scope of his employment or that he had on prior occasions entered into contracts and bound the corporation which recognized and approved such acts and held him out as authorized to deal with the company's affairs, then your verdict may be for the plaintiff. See *Joseph Greenspon's Sons Iron and Steel Co. v. Pecos Valley Gas Co.,* 34 Del. 567, 156 A. 350 (1931). [To avoid questions of this nature it is customary to require the President to supply a certified copy of an express resolution of the board of directors authorizing the execution of the transaction.]

PART X

X–1. ***Partially true.*** While not true as a matter of common law, as a result of decisions in the last ten or fifteen years, substantial fiduciary duties have been imposed on shareholders of closely held corporations. While these duties are usually imposed on majority shareholders who are also directors of the corporation, several decisions recognize that shareholders in a corporation have somewhat the same relationship to each other that partners have in a partnership. The leading decision in this regard is the Massachusetts case of *Donahue v. Rodd Electrotype Co.,* discussed in the text.

X–2. ***False.*** A deadlock situation may be created by high quorum or high voting requirements as well as by an even division of voting power.

X–3. While involuntary dissolution is the traditional remedy for the deadlocked corporation, that solution may destroy a valuable going business. Alternatively, if there is a single shareholder whose skills are essential to the success of the business, that shareholder may use dissolution in order to obtain the bulk of the going concern value of the corporation. It is true that dissolution at the option of any partner is the standard remedy in partnership law, but it may not always be a satisfactory solution for the reasons set forth in this answer.

X–4. It is by no means certain that dissolution is the best solution for partnership problems. But be that as it may, simpler and less damaging solutions to the problems of deadlock and oppression in the closely held corporation have been devised. By advance planning a buy-sell arrangement or arbitration may avoid a deadlock. Many state close corporation statutes also provide for provisional directors, custodians, or temporary receiverships designed to attempt to solve deadlock problems. Several state statutes also provide for a buyout at a judicially established price rather than involuntary dissolution, with the option of dissolution if that price is unacceptable. Even in states without such provisions, courts increasingly are willing to provide an equitable buyout remedy rather than the remedy of involuntary dissolution which is usually viewed as "harsh."

X–5. *False.* The evidence to date indicates that these statutes have not been widely used. In 1991, the drafters of the Model Business Corporation Act added two general provisions—one relating to shareholders' agreements and the other relating to a mandatory buyout arrangement available if a shareholder sues for involuntary dissolution. It is likely that these generalized provisions will ultimately be the accepted solutions for the "problem" the closely held corporation.

PART XI

XI–1. The "Wall Street Option" is a slang phrase to describe the option of a dissatisfied shareholder to sell his or her shares on the open market. This option is available in the publicly held corporation but of course is not generally available in closely held corporations. The extent to which this option is available to large holders of shares, such as institutional investors, depends, on the volume of the market in those securities.

XI–2. A question such as this should be answered carefully since it can be answered at different levels. Formally, the shareholders select the directors. However, in most publicly held corporations, the shareholders in fact ratify the decision made earlier as to who should be on the management slate of directors. In a real sense, the persons who put together the management slate determine who the directors of a publicly held corporation are to be. And this usually means either the incumbent management or a committee of the board of directors.

XI–3. *False.* All recent studies indicate that the professional management, not the board of directors, establishes the broad business policies of the corporation. The role of directors is more one of oversight than of direction.

XI–4. *Generally true.* The board of directors has the ultimate responsibility in this regard. Historically, the normal pattern was that the selection of a successor was largely the prerogative of the outgoing CEO. During the 1980s and 1990s, however, the role of the board of directors in selecting the CEO increased significantly, and an answer of "generally true" is probably most accurate today, whereas it would not have been ten years ago. Answers to broad questions like this must be qualified not only by the time frame under discussion but also by the possibility that a substantial block of shares owned by a single person may affect the locus of power within the corporation.

XI–5. "Book entry" refers to the predominant form of registration of publicly held securities today. Shares owned by investors or speculators are reflected only by monthly statements from the brokerage firm; the brokerage firm in turn has an account with Depository Trust Company or other central clearing corporation but all shares are owned of record by a nominee for the central clearing corporation. Transactions in shares are cleared by a simple netting process, first by the brokerage firm, and then by the central clearing corporation, with accounts of members being adjusted on a daily basis. More than 60 per cent of publicly held shares owned by individuals are today owned in book entry form.

XI–6. "Street name" refers to an older method of handling publicly traded shares to simplify back office bookkeeping by brokerage firms. Shares are registered in the name of brokerage firms with offices on Wall Street in New York City. Such certificates are endorsed in blank and transferred merely by delivery. Such "street name certificates" were the normal method by which the routine transfer of shares sold on the securities exchanges were effected before the book entry system developed. Most street name certificates were transferred directly between brokerage firms.

XI–7. Institutional investors include investment companies, mutual funds, pension funds, insurance companies, bank trust accounts, charitable foundations, university endowments and the like.

XI–8. Institutional investors have traditionally supported management on the theory that they simply are acting as investors. The late 1980s and early 1990s has seen a marked increase in activity by institutional investors in the corporate governance area, and it is likely that further interest will develop and the support given by institutional investors to incumbent management will decrease. In a few instances institutional investors have supported insurgent bids. There has also been increasing institutional investor opposition to "shark repellant" provisions adopted by management.

PART XII

XII–1. ***False.*** For a variety of reasons, including history, the law of proxy regulation in publicly held corporations arises under section 14 of the Securities Exchange Act of 1934, and, most importantly, the SEC regulations issued thereunder.

XII–2. Corporations (1) with a class of security that is traded on a national securities exchange, or (2) with $5,000,000) of assets and a class of shares owned by more than 500 shareholders of record, are subject to the federal proxy regulation. These are the requirements for registration under section 12 of the 1934 Act and SEC regulations.

XII–3. Corporations that are required to register under section 12 of the 1934 Act or that have made a registered public offering of shares under the 1933 Act are subject to the SEC periodic disclosure requirements.

XII–4. The constitutional bases of federal proxy regulation are the power to regulate interstate commerce and the mails. Proxy regulation has been in effect since 1934 and its constitutional validity is beyond question.

XII–5. The SEC proxy regulations require both proxy statements and annual reports to be distributed to shareholders by all registered companies even though they do not actually solicit proxies. In the absence of federal requirements, most states do not require the transmission of any information to shareholders.

XII–6. ***Yes.*** Rule 14a–9 forbids false and misleading statements in proxy statements. The early case of *J. I. Case v. Borak* held that a private cause of action is created for violations of this rule. Even though private causes of action have been largely restricted by the United States Supreme Court in recent years, it appears unlikely that *J. I. Case v. Borak* will be overruled.

XII–7. The requirement of materiality was emphasized by the United States Supreme Court in *TSC Industries v. Northway*, which defined "materiality" as a fact that *would* influence an investor in making a decision.

XII–8. ***Yes.*** Under *Mills v. Electric Auto–Lite Co.*

XII–9. ***No.*** *Virginia Bankshares, Inc. v. Sandberg* holds that a statement phrased as opinion is false and misleading if in fact the directors do not hold that opinion.

XII–10. ***No.*** The SEC proxy regulations require certain shareholder proposals to be included in proxy solicitation statements even though the corporation is opposed to them. A no-nuclear-energy proposal is one that must be included in the proxy statement.

XII–11. This regulation is a method of calling management's attention to shareholder concerns. Many corporate officers have stated that they pay considerable attention to shareholder proposals presented by individuals that receive a vote of five or ten per cent of the outstanding shares, even though management has the power as a practical matter to cause all such proposals to be defeated. Recent academic commentary has sought to cast doubt on this justification.

XII–12. ***Yes.*** A significant number have been approved in recent years as a result of the use of this device by institutional investors to compel changes in corporate governance. Unlike proposals submitted by individuals, proposals submitted by institutional investors receive significant support and in a number of instances have been approved. Of course, this is most likely in corporations in which institutional investors have large holdings.

XII–13. The SEC proxy rules do not apply to the solicitation of Hideaway's shareholders since it has no securities registered under section 12 of the 1934 Act. Therefore Case has no remedy under the principles discussed in Part XII. However, if the proxy statements are materially misleading, causes of action exist not only under state law (see part XIX B) but also under rule 10b–5 (see part XV B). The questions therefore presented are the lawfulness and fairness of the merger under state law and SEC rule 10b–5; claims against Expansion or the surviving corporation and against the former controlling shareholders and former management of Hideaway may all be pursued under these alternative principles. Also, a question is raised about Case's standing to attack the transaction since he is a dissenting shareholder of the merged corporation pursuing his appraisal remedy. (See part XIX H.)

Federal courts have exclusive jurisdiction over rule 10b–5 actions and can award full relief as to state law claims and corporate matters such as the unwinding of the merger. If the merger had not been consummated, the federal court could have issued an injunction restraining the merger pending a determination of Case's allegations.

The proxy statements seem to be clearly misleading in their failure to disclose the financial history of Expansion. This omission would appear to satisfy the conventional "deception" standard of "fraud" required by rule 10b–5 and the requirement of scienter of *Hochfelder*. (See part XV B.)

There would also appear to be a substantial prospect of attack under state law. (See part XIX.) Recent decisions of state courts, particularly in Delaware, have adopted the rule of "entire fairness" for merger transactions. The nondisclosure by Hideaway's management of the commitments it received might well be sufficient to invalidate a merger whose terms are unfair under state law.

While it is possible to unwind a merger, practical difficulties develop if any substantial period has elapsed since the transaction, primarily because of the existence of subsequent innocent shareholders of the surviving corporation. Thus, damages are a plausible remedy in these circumstances. The measure of damages might be difficult to determine here. The defendants would contend that the Hideaway shareholders received Expansion shares of equivalent value. Case would apparently argue against such valuation and that an independent appraisal would be necessary to determine the true value of the Expansion shares. If it can be demonstrated that the true value was below that represented in the merger discussions and proxy solicitations, then a basis for recovery could be established.

Case may bring an individual action to recover his damages or a class action seeking to recover the damages suffered by himself and those similarly situated, at least to the extent of any profits realized by Expansion and others who breached their duties to minority shareholders. Presumably the profits of the Expansion shareholders at the time of the merger are equivalent to the damages of the Hideaway shareholders but not all of the former were involved in the wrongdoing and a large proportion of the latter were wrongdoers—suggesting that any recovery of profits should be limited pro tanto to the damages suffered by innocent Hideaway shareholders.

Case may face a further defense directed to his standing to sue. Case is presently pursuing a statutory right of dissent and appraisal. (See part XIX H.) This is a remedy available to shareholders dissenting from extraordinary corporate changes and basically involves a proceeding to enable the dissenters to receive the fair value of their shares as if the change had not occurred. Some state appraisal statutes provide an exclusive remedy, precluding attack on the merger on the grounds of unfairness. Other states, either expressly or by court construction, permit a minority shareholder to sue in equity despite the availability of the legal appraisal remedy. MBCA (1984) § 13.02(b) makes the statutory remedy exclusive "unless the action is unlawful or fraudulent." The fact that Case has dissented and is pursuing an appraisal remedy raises unresolved questions under state law as to standing to sue. Arguably in the federal courts at least with respect to federal question issues Case's standing to sue under rule 10b–5 would not be precluded by the vagaries of the appraisal provision of the corporate statute of the state of incorporation of Hideaway, since the enforcement of federal law should be uniform throughout the United States.

Of course, to the extent that Case receives an award in the appraisal proceeding his claim in any action he brings should at least be reduced pro tanto.

XII–14. *No*. Under *Virginia Bankshares, Inc. v. Sandberg,* no claim may be asserted by Case and other minority shareholders of Hideaway under Rule 14–9 since the minority shareholders of Hideaway are unable to defeat the merger and therefore "causal necessity" is lacking. It is likely that the same argument will prevent a recovery under rule 10b–5; however, the Court in *Virginia Bankshares* clearly preserved possible remedies under state law to attack this transaction.

PART XIII

XIII–1. In a successful proxy fight in which the insurgents take control of the corporation it is likely that the corporation will end up paying both the management's unsuccessful defense costs plus the insurgent's costs. The outgoing management's costs will be paid before the management leaves office and the insurgents' costs will be paid after they take office. This result may be justified on the general view that the corporation may be asked legitimately to pay proxy contest expenses in policy disputes.

XIII–2. The argument basically is that proxy fights are a device for eliminating inefficient management and that making proxy fights easier will tend to keep management on its toes. The difficulty is that an unlimited right to reimbursement from the corporation would encourage proxy struggles in which there was little chance of success. Such fights could carry a high cost to the corporation.

XIII–3. Proxy contests are largely controlled by SEC regulations. These regulations impose a truth in campaigning requirement. There is virtually no state law of proxy contests.

XIII–4. A tender offer (or "cash tender offer," as it is often called) is a public offer by an aggressor to purchase shares of the target corporation. Usually the aggressor will seek working control of the corporation or all the publicly held shares of the corporation. In recent years most struggles for control have been in the form of cash tender offer rather than by proxy fight. They are partially regulated by the Williams Act, though aspects of them are also regulated by state law, particularly the validity of defensive tactics.

XIII–5. A merger is a consensual transaction which requires the approval of the board of directors of the target corporation. A cash tender offer is made directly to the shareholders of the target corporation, bypassing any need to obtain approval of the board of directors of the target corporation.

XIII–6. The Williams Act is a federal statute enacted in 1970 to regulate cash tender offers. Technically, the Williams Act is part of the Securities Exchange Act of 1934. The Williams Act is essentially neutral legislation, establishing ground rules and disclosure requirements for cash tender offers but not designed to make such attempts easier or more difficult.

XIII–7. State statutes relating to tender offers were enacted to make successful tender offers more difficult. Unlike the Williams Act, they are largely designed to protect local, incumbent management. The Supreme Court decision in *CTS Corporation v. Dynamics Corp. of America* largely validated state takeover statutes so long as they relate only to corporations formed under the laws of that state.

XIII–8. Arbitragers are speculators or investors who take offsetting positions in a single security selling at price differentials. In connection with cash tender offers, an arbitrager may purchase the shares of the target corporation on the open market at any price up to the cash tender offer price and submit their shares for tender to take advantage of the price differential. They may also sell short or on a "when issued" basis the aggressor's securities. In most takeovers, a very large percentage of the shares traded in the securities market after the announcement of a takeover attempt are purchased or sold by arbitragers. As a result of arbitrage transactions, virtually all target shares sold on the open market after the offer is announced are tendered into the offer (or into a competing offer at a higher price).

XIII–9. A leveraged buyout is a transaction in which the assets and earning power of the target corporation become the source of payment for the shares of the target corporation. A leveraged buyout involves borrowing very large sums of money to be repaid out of the earnings and assets of the target corporation.

XIII–10. "Porcupine provisions" is a slang term for defensive provisions in articles of incorporation adopted by potential target corporations to make takeovers more difficult. A typical porcupine provision requires a greater than majority vote for approval of mergers or other transactions that are opposed by the target's board of directors.

XIII–11. A poison pill is a new class or series of shares that provides valuable rights to shareholders upon the occurrence of a triggering event, such as when an aggressor purchases a specified percentage of shares. A number of varieties of poison pills have been developed but they all have in common the fact that they dilute significantly the interests of an aggressor if the poison pill is not redeemed.

XIII–12. ***Generally false.*** In a series of important decisions the Supreme Court of Delaware has created a set of rules as to when the business judgment rule may be relied upon by incumbent management in fighting an unwanted takeover. While there is a clear logic to these cases, the opinions are fact specific and some doubt exists as to the precise scope of some decisions.

XIII–13. The just say no defense claims that a corporation's board of directors may determine that the corporation is not for sale and refuse to redeem poison pills or otherwise negotiate or assist the aggressor, no matter how attractive the proposed transaction is to the target's shareholders.

XIII–14. ***Yes.*** There are equitable limitations to provisions governing the operation of a corporation. Here the management of X attempted to use the law to perpetuate itself in office and to obstruct the legitimate efforts of shareholders in their attempt to obtain new management. "Inequitable action does not become permissible simply because it is legally possible." [*Schnell v. Chris–Craft Indus., Inc.,* 285 A.2d 437 (Del.1971).]

PART XIV

XIV–1. The "duty of care" requires directors to exercise a minimum degree of skill and attention toward corporate affairs. While monetary damages for breach of this duty have been sharply limited by statute and judicial decision, this duty is nevertheless one of the fundamental duties owed by directors to corporations. Breaches of this duty may continue to give rise to monetary liability in cases involving knowing authorization of wrongful acts by directors or to a lesser extent in cases of a failure to pay any attention to corporate affairs. Directors who are elderly or infirm must meet a minimum standard of care applicable to everyone. A director with specialized knowledge, e. g., an attorney, must use care in light of that specialized knowledge.

XIV–2. The "business judgment rule" is a common law doctrine related to the duty of care that immunizes directors from liability for costly decisions if they act without conflict of interest, exercise good faith judgment in making the decision, and reasonably inform themselves of the facts relating to that decision. As a result, a decision entitled to protection under the business judgment rule that turns out unfavorably to the corporation may not be used as a basis for a claim against the directors making the decision. The business judgment rule has been applied in recent years to novel issues such as to authorize the dismissal of derivative suits brought against a corporation by disinterested directors and to validate self-dealing transactions. The "business judgment doctrine" makes the business decision itself (as contrasted with the liability of the directors) immune from judicial review.

XIV–3. Such a transaction is known as "self-dealing." The common law test for the validity of a self-dealing transaction is whether the transaction is fair and whether the director's interest has been fully disclosed. The burden of establishing fairness may be placed on the director, who should not participate in the corporate decision whether or not to enter into the transaction. Most states have enacted statutes relating to self-dealing transactions that uphold the transaction if it is approved by disinterested directors or shareholders in accordance with the business judgment rule or, if there has been no approval, if it is fair to the corporation.

XIV–4. Yes, by arranging for the transaction to be reviewed and approved by the disinterested directors after full disclosure of the fact of the conflict of interest and of the facts surrounding the transaction. Such action is preclusive under modern statutes in the absence of fraud or waste, and the common law rules would doubtless lead to the same result.

XIV–5. Such a transaction is an indirect self-dealing transaction and is also judged by the standards as self-dealing transactions. Many transactions of this nature are innocent in the sense that the common director did not participate in the approval of the transaction by either corporation, and indeed may have been unaware that such transactions were occurring.

XIV–6. The general view is that shareholders may not ratify a transaction which is fraudulent, oppressive, or overreaching. It is possible that a nonfraudulent transaction that may not upheld under the fairness test may be validated if it is approved by the disinterested vote of the shareholders. At the very least, such a vote will shift the burden of proof to those seeking to avoid the transaction, and under modern conflict of interest statutes may be given preclusive effect.

XIV–7. The test for executive compensation is that such compensation is valid unless it is so large as to constitute spoliation or waste. Such compensation is not generally viewed by the same standards as self-dealing transactions. As a practical matter, most corporations arrange to have compensation arrangements approved by outside, nonmanagement directors through the device of a compensation committee, and information about executive compensation levels is widely available, thereby providing a yardstick. If a problem exists with respect to the level of executive compensation it is unlikely that judicial intervention is the appropriate response.

XIV–8. Such arrangements may take the form of stock options or stock appreciation rights, stock bonuses, phantom stock plans, or stock purchase plans.

XIV–9. "Corporate opportunity" is a fiduciary duty that directors and officers owe to the corporation to give the corporation profitable business opportunities to which the corporation has a reasonable claim.

XIV–10. No single test has been generally accepted. The more traditional view is that an opportunity is a corporate opportunity only if it is something in which the corporation has an "interest or expectancy." Modern formulations of the corporate opportunity doctrine emphasize the fairness or unfairness of allowing an officer or director to take advantage of the opportunity and the degree to which the opportunity arises out of the corporation's line of business. Other factors may be relevant, such as whether the opportunity was addressed to the corporation when it was received by the director or officer.

XIV–11. ***Yes.*** If the corporation, for example, decides not to take advantage of the opportunity after full consideration, the director may do so. The burden, however, is in the director to establish the underlying premise.

XIV–12. Either standard may be applied depending on the nature of the transaction. If the transaction involves a contract or other arrangement between the parent and the subsidiary, the fairness test is applied. If the parent's action does not discriminate against the minority shareholders in the subsidiary, the business judgment rule is generally applicable. For example, a dividend paid by the subsidiary to all shareholders will be judged by the business judgment rule not the fairness standard. If the subsidiary's board of directors has outside, unaffiliated directors, it is likely that a judgment by them alone that meets the standards of the business judgment rule will be given preclusive effect as binding the subsidiary.

XIV–13. The transaction is a self dealing transaction since Corporation A is receiving something not received by all shareholders of Corporation B. Since the transaction is not intrinsically fair to the minority shareholders of Corporation B, it is voidable upon suit by them.

XIV–14. The directors may: (1) propose dissolution, subject to shareholder approval; or (2) first redeem the preferred shares, without the necessity of shareholder approval, in which case the preferred shareholders prior to the redemption date may convert each of their preferred shares into common shares. The corporation may then dissolve.

Since there are 1,000 outstanding shares of each class and all shares have equal voting rights, the directors are elected by the combined votes of the two classes. The facts do not indicate the respective shareholdings of the several directors.

The directors are under a fiduciary duty, not only to do what is in the best interests of the corporation, but also to be fair to the shareholders of both classes. Normally this would permit the redemption of the preferred before the dissolution of the corporation with full disclosure of the surplus.

There are two alternatives.

If the corporation were dissolved without redemption of the preferred, the preferred shareholders would receive their liquidation preferences of $200 per share or a total of $200,000 ($200 × 1,000 shares), leaving $10 for each common share ($10,000 × 1,000 shares). Voluntary dissolution generally would require approval by the holders of a majority or more of all the outstanding shares, depending on the applicable corporate statutory requirements.

If the preferred shares were redeemed (which would require only board of directors action), the preferred shareholders would receive the redemption price of $105 per share or a total of $105,000; there would then be available $105 for each common share ($105,000 × 1,000 shares). However, each preferred share is convertible into two common shares, which conversion privilege ordinarily would terminate on the redemption date set forth in the notice sent to the preferred shareholders of the intended dissolution. The economics should cause the preferred shareholders to convert if they are given accurate information, since, upon conversion, each would have two new common shares for each converted preferred share. If all convert, the former preferred shareholders would hold 2,000 or two-thirds of the then 3,000 outstanding common shares, and each former preferred shareholder would receive $70 for each new common share or $140 for each old preferred share or a total of $140,000 (⅔rds of $210,000). Each old common shareholder would also receive $70 for each of his shares or a total of $70,000 ($70 × 1,000 shares).

The latter course appears to be most appropriate for the directors under all the circumstances. This problem is patterned after *Zahn v. Transamerica Corp.*, 235 F.2d 369 (3d Cir.1956).

XIV–15. ***No.*** Directors of a corporation are not generally liable for losses suffered by the corporation by reason of its employees' violations of law. In managing the corporate affairs a director is required to use the amount of care which ordinary careful and prudent men would use in similar circumstances. Whether or not they have failed to exercise proper care depends upon the circumstances. Here the size of the enterprise and its wide geographical distribution made it necessary that directors confine their oversight to broad policy matters, and they should have no responsibility for employee misconduct until such time as something occurs to put them on notice that misconduct is occurring. Until that time they are entitled to rely on the honesty and integrity of their employees. Hence no liability is imposed. [*Graham v. Allis–Chalmers Mfg. Co.*, 41 Del.Ch. 78, 188 A.2d 125 (1963).]

XIV–16(a). ***No.*** Under common law principles, the contract should be cancelled. This contract was made between two corporations having an interlocking directorship, the directors, A, B and C, being common to the boards of both companies. In such case the two corporations may contract with each other and the contracts made are valid and enforceable if the contract is fair to both companies. If it is not fair to one corporation that one may avoid it. It is immaterial whether the common directors vote or refrain from voting on the approval of the contract. The fact that this contract provided that X corporation should pay M 10 per cent more for smelting ore than was the usual and customary price for such service, and the additional fact that the contract was to continue for 10 years without providing for any change in the price when the price of metals dropped made the contract unfair to X corporation and therefore gave it a right to cancel the contract. [*Globe Woolen Co. v. Utica Gas & Elec. Co.*, 224 N.Y. 483, 121 N.E. 378 (1918).]

XIV–16(b). ***Probably not.*** Under modern statutes, a transaction between corporations with common directors is an indirect conflict of interest. Since the transaction was brought before the board of directors, it is valid if the action of the board of directors of X corporation (excluding A, B, and C) meets the standards of the business judgment rule. The facts state that the directors approved the transaction because they thought that A, B, and C wanted the transaction approved. This is not a decision made in good faith in the reasonable belief that it is in the best interest of the corporation and therefore the decision is not entitled to the protection of the business judgment rule. Therefore the test again becomes one exclusively of fairness, and the analysis in part (a) presumably would control on this issue.

XIV–17. Possibly, if D can persuasively establish that X in fact lacked the ability to finance the purchase. The opportunity was probably a corporate opportunity since D learned of it through the corporation and the opportunity is in X's line of business. D, as the controlling stockholder in X corporation in complete control of the board of directors of X corporation, occupies a fiduciary relationship to X corporation similar to that of a director. Hence, when D learned of the value of B's properties and that it could be purchased at an advantageous price to the direct benefit of X corporation, D had a duty to give X corporation the first opportunity to buy that property for its own purposes. D violated his fiduciary duty in not letting X know of that opportunity. However, if it is assumed that such duty had been performed by D, it would have been futile because X was wholly incapable financially to take advantage of the opportunity. D's duty to X does not require him to lend money to X so that X can buy the property of B. And, D does not have to sit by and let the opportunity pass simply because X could not realize upon it. He may buy for himself for his own personal benefit. [See *Zeckendorf v. Steinfeld*, 12 Ariz. 245, 100 P. 784 (1909).]

Not all modern cases agree with this analysis; the ALI Corporate Governance Project also would not accept a defense of financial inability under these circumstances but would require the opportunity to be presented to X corporation since it is possible that the corporation might have been able to finance the purchase of B's property under the circumstances. In this case, the majority stockholder had a fiduciary duty by virtue of his complete control of the board of directors. In more typical cases of corporate opportunity, officers or directors are involved but the fiduciary duty is similar to that imposed on D in this case.

PART XV

XV–1. "Insider trading" refers to transactions by a corporate director, officer or employee in the shares of the corporation on the basis of information that is currently not publicly available. Insider trading may also refer to trading by other persons on the basis of nonpublic information obtained directly or indirectly from a director, officer, or employee. Insider trading is entirely a phenomenon of publicly held corporations.

XV–2. ***Both.*** The early principles were based on state law notions of fraud or deception, and later expanded to a "special facts" doctrine that required disclosure of special facts. Most modern principles of insider trading are based on rule 10b–5 promulgated under the Securities Exchange Act of 1934.

XV–3. ***Uncertain.*** Such an argument was accepted by the New York Court of Appeals in *Diamond v. Oreamuno* as a matter of state law. This view, however, has not been widely accepted. In *Chiarella* and *Dirks*, brought under rule 10b–5, the United States Supreme Court required that the disclosure of the information constitute a breach of duty if it is to be unlawful.

XV–4. ***False.*** Rule 10b–5 applies to transactions in "any security" involving the use of any facility of interstate commerce. It is applicable to closely held corporations as well as publicly held corporations. The insider trading aspect of rule 10b–5 is, as a practical matter, only applicable to publicly held corporations, but rule 10b–5 is also an important antifraud statute.

XV–5. ***False.*** If a single telephone call or other use of the facilities of interstate commerce or the mails is involved in connection with this fraudulent sale, the defrauded shareholder may sue under rule 10b–5 in Federal court.

XV–6. Rule 10b–5 is a broad antifraud statute triggered by any purchase or sale of a corporate security through the facilities of interstate commerce. Rule 10b–5 has been applied to insider trading, to fraudulent transactions between shareholders in a closely held corporation (see Question XV–5), to false press releases issued by corporations which influence the price of a security, to issuance of shares by a corporation at an inadequate price, to a sale of all the stock of a closely held corporation, and to other transactions as well.

XV–7. The U.S. Supreme Court has imposed three significant limitations on rule 10b–5. First, *Manor v. Blue Chip Stamps* holds that the plaintiff in a rule 10b–5 case must be herself a purchaser or seller of shares. Second, *Hochfelder* holds that a plaintiff must establish scienter (or possibly recklessness) in order to prove a 10b–5 claim. Third, *Santa Fe Industries v. Green* holds that rule 10b–5 only applies to misrepresentation, fraud or deceit, and not to transactions that are fully disclosed but unfair. The mere fact that a transaction is unfair does not create a rule 10b–5 liability so long as that unfairness is fully disclosed. These three cases do not significantly affect the "core case" applications of rule 10b–5 to insider trading, fraud in sales of shares, and so forth.

XV–8. Both of these principles deal with insider trading. However the application of the two is quite different, though to some extent overlapping. Section 16(b) deals only with offsetting transactions within a six-month period by an officer, director, or 10 per cent shareholder of a corporation that is registered under section 12 of the Securities and Exchange Act of 1934. Rule 10b–5 has none of these limitations. A second major difference is that liability under section 16(b) is automatic and not dependent on the actual profiting from the use of inside information in the transaction. Rule 10b–5 requires the proof of scienter and the establishment of the wrongful use of information.

XV–9. The theory under which profits are computed on "in-and-out" transactions under section 16(b) is to "squeeze out" all possible profit. To this end the highest sales price is matched against the lowest purchase price within each six-month period; the next highest purchase price is matched with the next lowest; all such transactions are sequentially matched until no profit remains. All losses in this comparison are ignored.

XV–10. ***True within limits.*** A shareholder may generally sell her shares for whatever price she can negotiate and if they carry a "control premium" she may keep it. However, the law recognizes that a controlling shareholder has certain duties by reason of her unique position with respect to the corporation. This duty is owed to minority shareholders, preferred shareholders, and creditors who are essentially defenseless. The duty is to take steps to avoid selling the shares to a person who may thereafter loot the corporation to the detriment of minority shareholders, preferred shareholders, and creditors. There is disagreement as to when the controlling shareholder must investigate a possible purchaser. In addition there may be situations where a sale of control breaches other fiduciary duties of a majority shareholder.

XV–11. The law has not adopted this view even though it has been contended for in several cases. This may be a legislative rather than a judicial issue. In addition, there is a fear that an "all or nothing" approach may prevent desirable transactions from occurring as argued by economists of the "Chicago School". The cost of such a rule may therefore exceed its benefits.

XV–12. The issues are the liability under state and federal law of Sider, an officer and director with insider information, for selling his shares and Taken's standing to assert such liability.

(a) *State law.* While the shares in question were registered under the Securities Exchange Act of 1934, the sale by Sider was over-the-counter or impersonal, and without any misrepresentation. Although there was a failure to disclose inside information, Taken was not a shareholder at the time of the nondisclosure. Because the transaction was anonymous and Taken was not a shareholder and thus was owed no fiduciary duty by Sider, the traditional common-law "special facts" and minority rules requiring disclosure by insiders of inside information in a person-to-person transaction to shareholders probably are not applicable.

However, *Diamond v. Oreamuno,* may have renewed the importance of state insider-trading law. In *Diamond,* the inside information was deemed to be a corporate asset. Any profit gained by corporate personnel through use of this asset was held to belong to the corporation. Therefore, under a *Diamond* approach, Sider would be liable to Dynamic, Inc. for the difference between what the shares were actually sold for and what they would have sold for had the information been public. This claim could be asserted directly by the corporation or derivatively by a shareholder or anyone else with standing to sue. Taken might not be able to maintain a derivative action because of the contemporaneous-share-ownership requirement of Federal Rule of Civil Procedure 23.1 since he was not a shareholder at the time of the transaction unless it can be shown that the wrong was a continuing one. This would be difficult since Taken bought his shares several days after Sider sold his shares.

(b) *Federal law.* The more likely basis of recovery is under rule 10b–5, creating a federal remedy for inside trading. Under rule 10b–5, the use of the mails or a facility of interstate commerce (such as the intrastate use of the telephone system) are the sole jurisdictional requirements; the shares do not have to be listed on an exchange or publicly traded (though the shares of Dynamic, Inc. were). Since Sider is an officer of Dynamic, Inc., his transactions constituted a violation of rule 10b–5 under the leading cases of *Texas Gulf Sulphur, Chiarella* and *Dirks.*

An implied private right of action exists under rule 10b–5. This right is now embodied in the recent statutes, ITSA and ITSFEA. Since Taken is a contemporaneous trader, he may bring suit against Sider, who has clearly failed to disclose material information, which, had it been made public, would certainly have dissuaded Taken to buy at the then market price. Moreover, Sider knowingly entered into the insider trading transaction, satisfying the scienter requirement of *Hochfelder.* While there is no privity between Sider and Taken, the statutory remedy does not require privity.

Sider should thus be liable to the extent of his profit or loss avoided. Presumably other new shareholders are in the same situation as Taken. However, Sider's maximum liability may not exceed the loss avoided by his insider trading violation, and this may be further reduced by any penalty paid to the SEC under these statutes.

XV-13. ***Yes.*** Maggie M. is guilty of insider trading in violation of rule 10b–5. The law firm of Jones and Smith is a temporary insider, so that the information obtained by Maggie M. is inside information. She may have breached a duty to the client in using the information to profit personally; even if not, she breached a duty to her employer, Jones and Smith, and this breach of a duty may be used to find a violation of rule 10b–5. The boyfriend is liable as a tippee if, as was the case, Maggie M.'s disclosure constituted the breach of a fiduciary duty.

XV-14. The only difference that the use of inside information about a takeover bid makes is that such use violates an explicit SEC rule, rule 14e–3, without regard to how the insider or tippee obtained the information.

XV-15. Under the *Dirks* case, trading by the "tippee" in a case such as this is unlawful only if Jones made an improper use of inside information when he divulged it to Smith. This in turn depends on whether Jones obtained a personal benefit from divulging the transaction; an intention to allow Smith to make a profit on the information seems to be the only motive for disclosing the information, and hence it is probable that both Jones and Smith violated rule 10b–5 in this transaction. Traders in derivative securities, such as puts and calls, are protected under ITSFEA to the same extent as holders of shares themselves.

XV-16. ***Yes.*** This case can be analyzed in a number of ways to reach the result that D breached his fiduciary obligation to the corporation. A controlling shareholder may usually sell a control block of shares for any price he or she can get; however, in disposing of control shares the shareholder owes a fiduciary duty to the corporation and to the minority shareholders not to injure them in so doing. It can be argued that: (a) D's sale of shares was an usurpation of the corporation's business opportunity to use the demand for steel to its advantage in attracting financing and new customers to its business, (b) the sale of the shares at a premium was really an usurpation by D of the grey market premium for steel which was an asset of the corporation, or (c) D's premium on the sale of his shares was actually the sale of control which is a corporate asset which belongs to all shareholders collectively. The best approach is probably (a) or (b) above. The shareholder has breached a duty to the corporation and is liable to account to it for the control premium received by him for the sale of shares. *Perlman v. Feldmann*, 219 F.2d 173 (2d Cir.1955).

Many commentators question the correctness of the result reached in *Perlman v. Feldmann*.

PART XVI

XVI–1. Indemnification permits the corporation to reimburse expenses incurred by officers or directors arising from litigation over their actions as officers or directors. In some instances it also permits reimbursements for payment of judgments, fines, or amounts paid in settlement of such litigation.

XVI–2. Indemnification is not against public policy if the defendant is absolved of liability or acted in good faith and without engaging knowingly in wrongful conduct. The underlying reason for permitting indemnification is the concern that persons might refuse to serve as directors if they always had to bear the cost of defending against groundless litigation out of their own pockets.

XVI–3. Certainly in most cases. Modern indemnification statutes, however, permit indemnification with court approval and in some cases, such as where the defendant settles or successfully prevails on a procedural defense, where it is possible that the defendant actually engaged in improper conduct. Indemnification in criminal cases is permitted where the defendant in good faith believed the conduct was lawful.

XVI–4. "D & O Insurance" refers to directors and officers liability insurance. It is commercially available insurance for some of the liabilities discussed above.

XVI–5. *No.* D & O insurance only covers insurable risks. Most if not all cases of wrongful conduct are not insurable and are expressly excluded from coverage by policy exclusions.

PART XVII

XVII–1. The basic test is that the shareholder's purpose must be a proper one.

XVII–2. It is relatively easy for a shareholder to allege a proper purpose. Additional restrictions are appropriate to prevent "fishing expeditions" and to prevent misuse of valuable corporate information. The problem is that a shareholder with an insignificant financial interest in the corporation may have a strong incentive to use corporate information to further private ends.

XVII–3. A director has a broader right to inspect than a shareholder since directors have management responsibilities. The right of a director is often stated to be absolute; in fact some courts have limited it if the possibility of misuse of the information is high. The Corporate Governance Project adopts a limited right of inspection for directors.

XVII–4. The traditional view is that virtually no information has to be disclosed. A number of state statutes, however, require some such disclosure, and the trend toward mandatory disclosure appears to be increasing. The MBCA (1984) requires financial and other disclosure. If a corporation is subject to the registration requirements of section 12, or has previously made a registered public offering of the Securities Exchange Act of 1934, it is subject to the significantly greater disclosure requirements imposed by federal regulation.

XVII–5. ***Yes.*** The bylaw is invalid. First, a requirement that three months notice must be given before an inspection of books is permitted is unreasonable. If the books would disclose mismanagement at the time of the notice, the three months thereafter might permit the management to "cook" the books to reflect a proper state of affairs or condition. Also, the two weeks notice given by P seems to be reasonable. Second, to permit the directors of the corporation to determine on a subjective basis whether or not a purpose of inspection by a shareholder is proper, would nullify the right of inspection in the very cases where inspection is most necessary, that is, when the books would disclose mismanagement on the part of the directors. Restrictions on the right to inspect the books may be valid if they are limited to time, place and proper purpose, and cannot in substance deny or significantly delay the right or make it exercisable only at the whim of the directors. [*State ex rel. Healy v. Superior Oil Corp.*, 40 Del. 460, 13 A.2d 453 (1940).]

PART XVIII

XVIII–1. "Direct" litigation is a claim brought by a shareholder for injury as a shareholder; a derivative claim is a claim brought by a shareholder on behalf of the corporation for injury to the corporation which indirectly injures all shareholders.

XVIII–2. ***No.*** Some claims may be phrased either as direct and derivative, and there is some judicial disagreement over whether certain types of claims, e. g., suits to compel a declaration of a dividend, should be classified as direct or derivative. To some extent this is a matter of pleading.

XVIII–3. A class suit is brought by a member of the class on behalf of the class as a whole. A typical class suit is a direct suit.

XVIII–4. A derivative suit is a class suit to the extent the plaintiff shareholder serves as a representative of the class of shareholders injured by the conduct in question.

XVIII–5. As a defendant, though in fact it is an involuntary plaintiff.

XVIII–6. ***Yes.*** Under both the Model Business Corporation Act (1984) and the Corporate Governance Project demand is required in substantially all cases. Under Delaware law, demand is futile only if the board of directors is interested in the transaction complained of or if the plaintiff establishes a reasonable doubt, based on particularized allegations, that the decision complained of was not protected by the business judgment rule. The allegations that the directors are friends of the CEO and will not do anything he opposes are not particularized and do not create a reasonable doubt that the directors are not independent or the decision was not made in accordance with the business judgment rule.

XVIII–7. ***Yes.*** Under both Delaware law and the Model Business Corporation Act, the motion should be granted unless the plaintiff can establish that the decision of the Committee was not a "good faith" exercise of business judgment or that the Committee was not disinterested. The allegations made by the plaintiff do not go to the valid exercise of business judgment by the committee or to its independence and therefore do not provide grounds for denial of the motion.

XVIII–8. The jurisdiction of the federal courts is not affected by the derivative-direct distinction. A suit brought under the Federal securities acts may be direct or derivative and in either event may or must be brought in Federal court. A direct or derivative claim based on state law may be brought in Federal court if there is diversity of citizenship or on the theory of pendent jurisdiction.

XVIII–9. The "contemporaneous ownership" requirement requires the plaintiff to be a shareholder at the time the cause of action arose. In the federal courts it is imposed to avoid the collusive creation of diversity jurisdiction. In the state courts it is justified in part because of dislike of derivative litigation and in part to avoid the purchase and sale of lawsuits. It is also believed that relatively few suits are barred from litigation on the ground there is no plaintiff who qualifies under the contemporaneous ownership requirement.

XVIII–10. In addition to the contemporaneous ownership requirement (see Question XVIII–7), the plaintiff must make a demand on the corporation and its directors, and (in some states) on its shareholders, or show why such demands should be dispensed with or are futile. In addition, a plaintiff may have to comply with the state security-for-expenses statute, which may require the posting of a bond. The MBCA requires a demand on directors in all cases but does not require a demand on shareholders or the posting of security-for-expenses.

XVIII–11. It is widely believed by members of the corporate bar that much derivative litigation is instituted without reasonable cause for the benefit of plaintiffs' attorneys, not for the corporation, or its shareholders.

XVIII–12. The purpose of security-for-expenses statutes is to prevent strike suits by plaintiffs with nominal interests in the litigation which itself may be without substantive merit. The security-for expenses statute makes it more difficult for small plaintiffs to maintain derivative suits without regard to whether the underlying suit has merit. These statutes are illogical in the sense that they tend to bar meritorious as well as groundless suits, and impose substantive requirements based on the size of the plaintiff's holdings rather than the merits of the law suit. Modern statutes such as the MBCA (1984) eliminate these statutes but substitute other devices in an effort to close off meritless litigation, e. g. by authorizing the court to impose litigation costs on the plaintiff if the suit is ultimately found to be without merit.

XVIII–13. In most states, the effect is two-fold: (1) the plaintiff is compelled to post a bond to secure the defendants' expenses, and (2) if the defendants are successful, the plaintiff may be required to pay their expenses. The proceeds of the bond may be used for this purpose.

XVIII–14. This statute is "substantive" under the *Erie* doctrine, and therefore is applicable in derivative litigation based on diversity of citizenship and pendent jurisdiction. It is not applicable to claims arising under the Federal securities acts.

XVIII–15. In most states, no.

XVIII–16. It depends on the basis of the decision. If it is on the merits it is *res judicata* and binding on all shareholders. A dismissal on the basis of a litigation commitee's decision that is entitled to business judgment rule protection is on the merits. If it is based on a defect in the plaintiff's standing to maintain the suit, such as failing to comply with the security-for-expenses statute, it is not *res judicata* and other shareholders may refile the same suit.

XVIII–17. In most states, a proposed settlement must be judicially approved before the suit may be dismissed. This is designed to prevent secret settlements.

XVIII–18. A "strike suit" is a slang term for suits brought solely for their settlement value. The major device now used to prevent such suits is the judicial review of proposed settlements. Increasingly suits that are believed to be strike suits are made the subject of litigation committee review.

XVIII–19. ***Usually, yes.*** The test for plaintiffs' expenses is whether the suit yields a "substantial benefit" to the corporation, not whether it recovers cash, or tangible property.

XVIII–20. There are a few such cases where members of the current management were found to be wrongdoers who should not have the use of the proceeds. A distribution directly to shareholders has some of the attributes of a partial or compelled dividend and as a result has not been widely required.

XVIII–21. ***Yes.*** In a shareholders' derivative suit any recovery runs in favor of the corporation because it is "in the right of", or on behalf of the corporation that shareholders sue. If the defendants are held liable it must be to the corporation and not to the shareholders. The decree also must protect the defendants against any further suit by the corporation. This cannot be done unless the corporation is a party to the action. Hence X is an indispensable party to the action and if it cannot be served with process the action must be dismissed. Since X has not been served with process, it is not within the jurisdiction of the court and the action must be dismissed. [*Dean v. Kellogg*, 294 Mich. 200, 292 N.W. 704 (1940).]

XVIII–22. ***No.*** In a shareholders' derivative action brought for the benefit of the corporation for damages caused by a breach of fiduciary duties to the corporation, the corporation is entitled to recover the entire amount of the damages suffered by it. The identity of the shareholders at the time is not a matter of proof in the action. It is the corporation as an entity which has been harmed and to whom the damages are to be rendered. [*Norte & Co. v. Huffines*, 416 F.2d 1189 (2d Cir.1969).]

A few courts have permitted the shareholders to recover individually in a derivative suit on the theory that the persons now in control of the corporation should not be permitted to control the proceeds of the recovery since they participated in the wrongful conduct. Certainly, however, the *defendants* should not be able to restrict their recovery on this theory.

PART XIX

XIX–1. ***False.*** Amendments are permitted without limitation since in most states there is no vested rights doctrine in modern corporation law. Shareholders are protected from adverse amendments by class voting (referred to as "voting by voting groups" in the RMBCA), and by the right of dissent and appraisal.

XIX–2. In a merger one of the two combining corporations survive, in a consolidation both combining corporations disappear into a third, new corporation.

The Revised Model Business Corporation Act eliminates the concept of consolidations because they are not used in practice. It is usually advantageous for tax or other reasons for one of the present entities to be the survivor; if not, it is customary to create a new entity and merge the other entities into it.

XIX–3. In an ordinary merger, the shareholders of the disappearing corporation receive shares in the continuing entity. In a cash merger, some shareholders receive cash or other property rather than shares of the surviving corporation.

XIX–4. A "short form merger" is a merger of a subsidiary into a parent corporation subject to special statutory procedural rules applicable to this type of amalgamation. See MBCA (1984) § 11.04.

XIX–5. The Internal Revenue Code uses the alphabetical designations for certain types of amalgamations. This terminology is so useful that it has spread beyond the tax area. The principal designations are:

a. Class A—statutory merger;

b. Class B—an acquisition of the stock of the acquired corporation;

c. Class C—an acquisition of the assets of the acquired corporation.

XIX–6. They are often functional equivalents that may have different legal and tax implications. Procedures and protections available in one type of transaction may not be available in other types of transactions even though they have the same economic effect.

XIX–7. A "de facto merger" is a nonstatutory amalgamation of two corporations that a court concludes is (a) the functional equivalent of a statutory merger and (b) participants should be accorded the rights they would have had in a statutory merger.

XIX–8. "Appraisal rights" (or "dissenters' rights," as they are called in the MBCA (1984)) or "the right of dissent and appraisal" allow a dissenting shareholder to obtain the value of his or her shares in a judicial proceeding rather than go along with the merger or other transaction that gave rise to the appraisal right.

XIX–9. In most states, shareholder approval is required if the sale is not in the ordinary course of business.

XIX–10. A "going private" transaction involves the elimination of the public shareholders of a corporation through a cash merger or similar transaction.

Such a transaction is widely believed to be susceptible of unfairness; the only special legal requirements are imposed by the SEC which requires a statement by management as to their opinion of the fairness of the transaction.

XIX–11. A "leveraged buyout" is a transaction by which an outside group acquires all the shares or assets of a public corporation. Incumbent management may participate in the outside group and thereafter continue to manage the business. Most of the purchase price is in the form of debt (often "junk bonds") which is assumed by the corporation that is acquired. The economic advantage of these transactions is a matter of controversy.

XIX–12. ***False.*** In most states the right of dissent and appraisal is hedged with procedural traps and subjects a dissenting shareholder to the risk that a court may significantly undervalue interests in the corporation. Because of the cost of a judicial proceeding, the long delays, and the formidable litigation power of large corporations intent on keeping the appraised value as low as possible, dissenters' rights are often viewed as an unattractive remedy.

XIV–13. This is a freeze-out merger, and must meet the intrinsic fairness tests of *Weinberger:* fair dealing and fair price. In some states, a business purpose requirement may also be imposed. Assuming there was full disclosure, the requirements of *Weinberger* appear to be met. Approval by a majority of the minority is also evidence of the fairness of the transaction. Thus, assuming that there was full disclosure the transaction is valid. Dissatisfied shareholders nevertheless have the right of statutory dissent and appraisal (Chapter 13 of the MBCA).

If the transaction is in a state with a business purpose requirement, that test would also have to be met if the transaction is to be upheld.

XIX–14. ***No.*** Since the state statute does not provide for mandatory cumulative voting, the shareholders may properly abandon the system without unanimous consent. Although the right to vote cumulatively is a valuable one, the corporation law that allows amendment of the articles is a part of P's contract with the corporation and he or she may not complain if the action is taken in the proper form with the requisite majority. [*Maddock v. Vorclone Corp.*, 17 Del.Ch. 39, 147 A. 255 (1929).]

XIX–15. ***No.*** The transfer of the franchise to another city is not a sale of all or substantially all the corporation's assets. The franchise remains an asset of the corporation with all of its rights and privileges intact. The corporation will continue to operate with substantially the same assets. [*Murphy v. Washington American League Base Ball Club, Inc.*, 293 F.2d 522 (D.C.Cir. 1961).]

XIX–16. *No.* A merger of a corporation with its wholly-owned subsidiary may eliminate preferred shareholders' rights to accumulated dividends if the terms of the merger agreement are fair and equitable in the circumstances. State law allows but does not require a shareholder objecting to the terms of a merger to obtain the value of his shares. Dissenting shareholders are thus not put to an election by the statute of State Y. While a merger is always subject to nullification for fraud, here P has alleged only that the allocation between the old preferred and common shareholders is so unfair that it amounts to fraud. P has alleged no misrepresentation, concealment or deception. "When fraud of this nature is charged, the unfairness must be of such character and must be so clearly demonstrated as to impel the conclusion that it emanates from acts of bad faith or a reckless indifference to the rights of others interested, rather than from an honest error of judgment." [*Porges v. Vadsco Sales Corp.*, 27 Del.Ch. 127, 32 A.2d 148 (1943); *Barrett v. Denver Tramway Corp.*, 53 F.Supp. 198 (D.Del.1943); *Bove v. Community Hotel Corp.*, 105 R.I. 36, 249 A.2d 89 (1969).]

*

APPENDIX C

TEXT CORRELATION CHART

CHAPTER	TITLE	W. CARY & M. EISENBERG CORPORATIONS, CASES & MATERIALS 6TH EDITION, UNABRIDGED	J. CHOPER, J. COFFEE & C. MORRIS, CASES & MATERIALS ON CORPORATIONS (3RD ED.)	HAMILTON ON CORPORATIONS, 4TH	L. SOLOMAN, D. SCHWARTZ & J. BAUMAN CORPS. LAW & POLICY (2D ED.)	R. CLARK CORPORATE LAW (1986)	R. HAMILTON LAW OF CORPORATIONS IN A NUTSHELL (3D ED.)	H. HENN & J. ALEXANDER LAWS OF CORPORATION (3D ED.)
I	In General	—	1–37	10–16, 160–189	1–32, 326–341	1–34	1–15	1–46, 127–138, 144–175
II	Formation of Corporations	91–130	123–129, 216–215	119–135, 190–216, 1213–1222	106–127, 128–134, 144–167	35–92	16–60	50–57, 176–201, 266–320, 466–486
III	Preincorporation Transactions	130–151	130–140, 165–193	216–252	134–144	706–7, 715–719	61–80	236–264, 327–344
IV	Piercing the Corporate Veil	151–191	140–165	253–295	238–269	37, 71–85	81–102	344–375
V	Financing the Corporation	1294–1398, 1399–1466, 1467–1601	336–337, 347–8, 903–1050	296–420	168–237, 447–501	593–638, 705–760	103–155, 385–409	377–445, 546–550, 786–813, 843–850, 869–950
VI	The Statutory Scheme of Management & Control	197–221, 378–402	195–6, 725–742	421–453	270–277, 301–302, 369–389	93–140	156–175	466–7, 490–492
VII	Shareholders' Meetings, Voting, & Control Arrangements	241–248	541–613	453–506	296–301, 308–319	93–105, 357–366	176–217	446–463, 486–490, 493–517, 528–536
VIII	Directors	221–228	263–268	506–513	289–296	105–113	218–232	550–585
IX	Officers	228–241	199–216	513–526	278–289	113–123	233–249	571–572, 586–610
X	Management of the Closely Held Corporation	329–470	683–784	527–557	342–446	499–518, 528–530, 761–800	250–267	694–783
XI	Corporate Governance and the Publicly Held Corporation	192–196, 256–270	333–458	160–189, 558–621, 1223–1237	326–341, 502–506, 1168–1177, 1313–1381	389–400, 675–703	268–282	785–866
XII	SEC Disclosure Requirements and Proxy Regulation	271–313	541–551, 579–588, 609–613, 626–682	622–673, 835–844	507–590	366–389	282–296	518–523, 527, 813–823
XIII	Proxy Fights, Tender Offers and Other Contests for Control	314–328, 1204–1268	561–567, 589–597, 1051–1055, 1068–1166	844–928	1031–1167	499–518, 531–592	296–302	523–526
XIV	Duties of Directors, Officers, and Shareholders	471–655	225–332	683–834	39–53, 591–808	123–140, 141–262, 478–498, 631–636	303–343	611–644, 651–656, 661–692
XV	Duties Relating to the Purchase or Sale of Shares	656–719, 720–927	459–539, 1055–1068	929–1113	996–1030, 1177–1312	263–356	344–367	644–650, 656–661, 823–843
XVI	Indemnification & Liability Insurance	1030–1047	887–901	1114–1134	905–925	664–674	367–374	1116–1146
XVII	Books and Records	249–256	613–626	673–682	319–326	96–105, 368–369	375–384	536–546, 578–581
XVIII	Shareholder Litigation	928–1030, 1047–1087	785–886	1135–1171, 734–768	809–939	639–664	319–321, 410–426	1019–1116
XIX	Organic Changes	1088–1203, 1268–1293	601–605, 1167–1281	1173–1191	301–308, 940–995	401–461, 463–478, 518–528	427–446	951–1018
XX	Foreign Corporations	—	129–130	—	—	—	—	201–235, 320–325

APPENDIX D

COMPREHENSIVE EXAMINATION

Comprehensive Examination: Total time 3 hours and 15 minutes

INSTRUCTIONS

1. This examination consists of *five* questions to be answered in *three hours and fifteen minutes.* The questions will be weighted in accordance with the times suggested for each questions.

2. You may bring into the examination only your copy of the Model Business Corporation Act (1984). Your notes in this statute must relate only to the provisions of that statute.

3. Unless otherwise specified, you are to assume that each corporation is a corporation incorporated under the Model Business Corporation Act (1984), and that all relevant action takes place within a state that has adopted the MBCA (1984) in its entirety.

4. Be sure to answer the specific questions that are asked.

5. If you feel additional facts are necessary to resolve an issue, please specify what additional facts you believe to be necessary and why they are significant.

6. Quality, not quantity, is desired. Think through your answer before you begin to write.

7. You may keep your copy of the exam questions.

8. Write legibly.

QUESTION I
(45 minutes)

Don Quie began a watch and clock repair business in downtown Austin, Texas, in 1980 as a sole proprietorship. By 1985, the business was moderately successful and Quie decided to incorporate the business so that he might raise additional capital and open additional stores. Quie hired an attorney who (1) filed articles of incorporation for a corporation called Quie, Inc., (2) prepared bylaws and minutes of initial meetings, (3) provided him with a minute book and stock certificates, and (4) arranged for a bank account to be opened in the name of Quie, Inc. The corporation was informally capitalized by treating the business assets of the proprietorship as the corporate assets; the assets had a value of about $60,000 but were subject to security interests to secure loans of $40,000. Thereafter, Quie kept meticulous records of receipts and payments but paid no attention to corporate formalities. Nothing was added to the minute book after the minutes of the initial meeting; no stock certificates were ever filled in; no meetings held; all decisions were made by Quie by himself, though in all communications with customers, landlords, suppliers, etc. he signed as "Quie, Inc., by Don Quie, President." The $40,000 of liabilities were eventually paid off by the corporation, but in the ordinary course of business substitute and additional liabilities were incurred.

By 1987, Quie's business was doing quite well; he was paying himself a salary of $50,000 per year and had also hired his live-in girl friend to work in the store as a receptionist and sales clerk; she was paid $25,000 per year, a generous salary considering the nature of her duties. Quie, Inc. elected S corporation treatment. At the end of each year Quie distributed to himself substantially all the earnings that remained after paying all salaries and other expenses. Quie maintained a personal checking account; there was no intermingling or cross-uses of funds between the corporate and Quie's individual accounts.

In 1986, Quie took the first steps toward expanding. On behalf of Quie, Inc. he signed a ten year lease for space in a new office building located on 15th street near the State Capital, and opened a new branch at that location. Unfortunately, his timing could not have been worse. The real estate market in Austin went into severe recession and the new store was a disaster since there were virtually no customers. The original store also began losing money as business dropped off. After struggling for two years, Quie decides to close down the second store; he asks, on behalf of Quie, Inc., to be released from the lease. The landlord refuses, and Quie decides to "walk."

He vacates the new premises and, when Quie, Inc., is sued, places that corporation in bankruptcy. The landlord then sues Quie individually.

A. (50%) Is Quie personally liable to the landlord on the lease?

B. (50%) Would the principles applicable to determine Quie's personal liability be different if a customer was claiming damages for personal injuries suffered in a fall in the downtown store, and the customer's claim significantly exceeds the available liability insurance?

QUESTION II
(30 minutes)

A. (50 %) *In this part of this question you are to assume the corporation is subject to a statute identical to the 1969 Model Business Corporation Act, the relevant provisions of which appear in the Statutory Supplement beginning at page 150.*

Bacchus Banquets Co. is a corporation that is involved in the catering business. Its authorized capital consists of one class of common stock with a par value of $5 per share; 3 million shares are authorized. At the time the initial capital was raised in 1971, 100,000 shares of stock were issued. At that time, the board of directors adopted the following resolution:

> Resolved, that in the future all common stock of this corporation shall be issued at a consideration of not less than $10 per share, this resolution to remain in force until modified or suspended by a subsequent resolution duly adopted by the board of directors.

Fifteen years later, this resolution has been completely forgotten. The corporation proposes to issue stock to three adult children of the founder on the following terms:

> Anna, 100,000 shares at $10 per share;
>
> Benny, 100,000 shares at $7 per share;
>
> Chris, 100,000 shares at $3 per share.

The different purchase prices are agreed to in order to equalize prior gifts made by the founder directly to his children. The corporation is clearly in need of $200,000 in additional capital. Are any problems created by this proposed transaction?

B. (50%) Assume that the Revised Model Business Corporation Act was adopted in the state in which Bacchus Banquets Co. is incorporated in 1985. Bacchus Banquets does not amend its articles of incorporation with respect to the description of its shares of common stock in any way after this new statute becomes effective. Would the enactment of this new statute affect the ability of Bacchus Banquets to validly issue the shares to Anna, Benny, and Chris on the terms described in part A?

QUESTION III
(30 minutes)

Philip M. Stern, a shareholder in the General Electric Company, a Delaware corporation, files a derivative suit against GE and sixteen of its eighteen directors, alleging that the directors had expended substantial sums from the treasury of the corporation to support the "Non–Partisan Political Support Committee for General Electric Employees" (GE–PAC). The complaint charges that GE–PAC funds had been used exclusively to support congressional incumbents without regard to their past position on business issues, and that this practice was harmful to the interests of GE's shareholders. It alleges that even though only relatively small amounts had been raised from contributions from GE employees, GE itself contributed between $5,000,000 and $50,000,000 each year, either directly, or indirectly by providing support services to GE–PAC. The complaint further alleges that the sixteen defendants were all aware of the manner in which GE–PAC was funded, that they had authorized the contributions from GE to it, and that on numerous occasions they had decided how much specific incumbents should receive. The complaint further alleges that GE had consistently misrepresented the manner in which GE–PAC was financed and operated in that it was represented that GE–PAC funds had been contributed exclusively by GE employees and that the decisions as to contributions were made by an independent panel of GE employees. In fact, the complaint alleges, all decisions were made by a vice president of General Motors subject to the specific direction of the board of directors.

The complaint further alleges that no demand was made on the Board of Directors of GE since any demand would have been futile, "in effect requiring the defendants to sue themselves."

After the complaint was filed, GE moves to dismiss on the ground that it is clear from the face of the complaint that the actions complained of were lawful and beneficial to the corporation. No litigation committee is formed. The District Court granted the motion to dismiss. On appeal, what result and why? See *Stern v. General Electric Company,* 924 F.2d 472 (2d Cir.1991).

In responding to this question you are to assume that no claim is made under the Federal Election Campaign Act of 1971, and that that statute does not preempt state law either as to the validity of corporate campaign contributions or affect the general responsibilities of directors.

QUESTION IV
(45 minutes)

Dunhall Pharmaceuticals is a small manufacturer of pharmaceuticals that was formed in 1960. In 1970, Monte Staha (Staha) and Jimmy Hatfield (Hatfield) entered into employment contracts with Dunhall, Staha as president and Hatfield as sales manager. These contracts provided for Staha's and Hatfield's compensation to be measured as a percentage of Dunhall's net sales—five percent in the case of Staha and four percent in the case of Hatfield. "Net sales" was defined in each contract. Each contract was for a term of one year but was to be automatically renewed each year unless Dunhall notifies the employee to the contrary at least 60 days before the close of the year. At the time these contracts were entered into, Staha and Hatfield were two of the four directors of Dunhall, but they did not vote on either contract. They were also substantial shareholders in Dunhall but their combined ownership was less than 50 per cent.

Dunhall's sales rose from $327,039 in 1970 to $16,221,941 in 1987, with the result that Staha's and Hatfield's compensation also increased markedly. During this period no dividends were declared by Dunhall. Dunhall's shares were owned by about 150 individuals, most of whom lived in Bentonville or Fayetteville, Arkansas. Shares were traded infrequently, and from time to time Staha and Hatfield purchased additional small blocks of shares from shareholders who contacted them and indicated a desire to sell their shares.

In 1986, Staha and Hatfield together owned 46 per cent of Dunhall's shares. Unexpectedly, Staha and Hatfield received offers from Jones Medical Industries, Inc. (JMI), addressed to them as individuals, to purchase their Dunhall shares at $12 per share. Before then, the highest price at which Dunhall shares had traded was $6 per share. Staha and Hatfield rejected the offer. A month later JMI made a second offer, this time addressed to Dunhall: it offered to purchase all or substantially all the outstanding Dunhall shares at $15 per share, and requested Dunhall to communicate this offer to each of its shareholders.

Staha and Hatfield discussed the desirability of the second JMI offer. Accurately perceiving that their employment contracts with Dunhall would be terminated or at least significantly revised if JMI obtained control of Dunhall, they resolved to block the JMI offer. They formed MED–MAX Associates Limited Partnership, in which they were the general partners, as a device to purchase Dunhall shares without revealing their personal involvement. MED–MAX was funded by informal loans from Dunhall. Offering $6 per share to three other Dunhall shareholders, MED–MAX quickly acquired over 5 per cent of Dunhall shares, which together with the 46 per cent they already owned, meant they controlled over 50 per cent of outstanding Dunhall shares. They then advised Dunhall shareholders of the JMI offer but announced that they recommended rejection of that offer and that they "believed" the offer would not be accepted.

A. (50 %) A shareholder of Dunhall, Billy Hall, brings a derivative suit against Staha and Hatfield based solely on state law, alleging excess compensation, improper use of corporate assets, breaches of fiduciary duty, conflict of interest, common law fraud, and violation of the voting trust statute. What result and why?

B. (50 %) Do the minority shareholders of Dunhall have a direct action against Staha and Hatfield? If so, please describe the basis or bases on which such a claim may be put forth, and what you feel to be the probability of success.

QUESTION V
(45 minutes)

Econometric Research Corporation (ERC) is a closely held corporation that offers professional services to businesses, educational institutions, trade associations, and similar entities. It was originally founded by three persons, but by 1989 its shares are owned by only two persons or entities: 354 shares are owned by the Mann–Paller Foundation, Inc., a not-for-profit educational corporation, while 636 shares are owned by Dr. Stephan Michelson, the only founding shareholder of ERC who is still alive.

In 1988, Dr. Michelson became the sole director of ERC, upon the death of another founding shareholder. Since then he has also served as president and secretary of ERC at a salary that began at $10,000 per month and by 1992 has risen to $25,000 per month. The earnings of ERC exceeded $1,000,000 per year during the period 1989–1991; the corporation has never paid a dividend. The phenomenal financial success of ERC is unquestionably due primarily to the skills and abilities of Dr. Michelson.

In 1992, Dr. Michelson asks ERC's outside auditor, Price Waterhouse, to recommend a compensation level for himself in the future, based on average compensation levels of senior executives in similar organizations. That study showed that Dr. Michelson was receiving less than the chief executive officers of five of six similar organizations, and that an additional payment of $347,000 would be necessary in 1992 if Dr. Michelson's compensation for the years 1989–1991 were to equal the average compensation as shown in that study, and that thereafter his compensation should be increased to $60,000 per month.

As sole director, Dr. Michelson approves the payment of $347,000 and the increase in compensation as recommended in the Price Waterhouse report. He also notifies the Mann–Paller Foundation, Inc. of this action, and states that a shareholders' meeting will be called in the near future to ratify the action of the board of directors.

Because of the nationwide recession in 1991–1992, Price Waterhouse projects that the earnings of ERC will drop during 1992 to the range of $700,000—$800,000. If the $347,000 payment and the increase in compensation from $25,000 per month to $60,000 per month is implemented, it is likely that ERC will show a loss for 1992, though the corporation has no shortage of cash.

You are consulted by Mann–Paller Foundation, Inc. Not surprisingly, the proposed increase in the compensation of Dr. Michelson is unacceptable to them. The Foundation officer advises you that she has discussed the matter with Dr. Michelson, and urged him to defer at least the increase in monthly compensation for a period of one year, and to institute a program of regular dividend payments, but that he rejected these suggestions and stated that he had already ordered the increase in compensation to be implemented.

Which of the following courses of action would you recommend?

A. File suit to compel payment of a dividend in a specific amount or in such amount as the court deems appropriate?

B. File suit to order the corporation dissolved by judicial decree?

C. File a derivative suit to compel Dr. Michelson to return a portion of his compensation to the corporation?

D. File suit to enjoin the payment of any additional compensation to Dr. Michelson?

Please state the probability of success of each of these options, and state which you would pursue and which you would not. See *Mann–Paller Foundation, Inc. v. Econometric Research, Inc.*, 644 F.Supp. 92 (D.D.C.1986).

END OF EXAMINATION

*

APPENDIX E

TABLE OF CASES

†